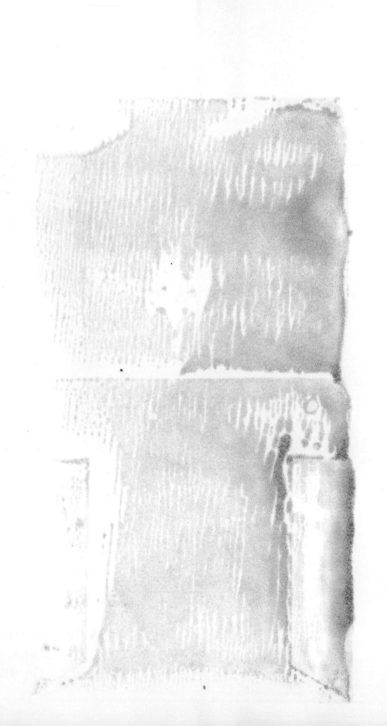

LIFE IN BRIGHTON

by the same author

REGENCY FURNITURE 1800–1830
ADAM AND HEPPLEWHITE AND OTHER NEO-CLASSICAL
FURNITURE

ROYAL PAVILION: AN EPISODE IN THE ROMANTIC
(*Leonard Hill*)

THE SUSSEX BOOK
(*Thames and Hudson*)

LIFE IN
BRIGHTON

from the earliest times
to the present
by
CLIFFORD MUSGRAVE

ARCHON BOOKS
Hamden, Connecticut

*First edition published
in the United States
1970*

To the memory of my parents
FRANCIS WILLIAM MUSGRAVE
and
FLORENCE MINNY MUSGRAVE
lovers of Brighton

Foreword

My primary purpose in writing this book has been to provide a reliable and comprehensive history of Brighton from the earliest times to the present day. The story of Brighton in early days and in the Regency period has been admirably told in a number of excellent works, but the present account deals fully also with the Victorian and Edwardian periods and the modern age. Furthermore, earlier books, because of the circumstances of their original publication, in newspapers and in serial form, have often been lacking in consecutive treatment, so that in several works on the town one is likely to find a chapter on the use of the Royal Pavilion as an Indian hospital during the 1914–18 War followed by one on the Saxon invaders: accordingly I have endeavoured to tell the story of Brighton as far as possible in consecutive form except where I have dealt with various distinctive features of the town such as churches, baths, hotels, piers, theatres, etc., where the information has been gathered more or less into single chapters. As well as being a comprehensive general history of this unique European pleasure resort, its architecture and its inhabitants, the work is at the same time a highly personal account of Brighton as I have known it over more than fifty years. I most gratefully acknowledge the help given me by many persons who have told me their recollections of life in Brighton, and my indebtedness to the authors of earlier works on the town, which are referred to in the text and bibliography, particularly to Miss Margaret Barton and the late Sir Osbert Sitwell, authors of *Brighton* (1935); to Mr. Antony Dale, for information from his admirable *Fashionable Brighton, 1820–1860* (1967); and to Professor E. W. Gilbert, author of *Brighton: Old Ocean's Bauble* (1954). I owe my thanks to Brighton Corporation for the use of photographs and information from the Public Library, Art Gallery and Royal Pavilion collections, and I most warmly acknowledge my debt to Alderman Miss Dorothy Stringer, O.B.E., Alderman Stanley Deason and Alderman Ronald Lucraft for the unfailing support and encouragement which they gave me during my service. I especially desire to record my gratitude to the Editors of the *Brighton and Hove Herald*, of the *Brighton and Hove Gazette* and of the *Brighton Evening Argus* for permission to use their photographs and for invaluable information obtained from their journals; to Mr. Douglas Gray for information from his remarkable collection of Brighton photographs; to Miss Margaret Jenner for the use of her photographs; to Mr. John Allan, Chief Librarian, Brighton Public Libraries, and Mr. Alan Ball, formerly Deputy Librarian; to Miss E. Baird, Librarian, Brighton Reference Library, and her colleague Miss B. Greenhill for their invaluable help in tracing information; to Mrs. Jean Garrett, Professor Marcus Cunliffe and Mrs. Mitzi Cunliffe, and Doctor Helmut Pappe; to Mr. John Morley, Director of Brighton Art Gallery and Museum and of the Royal Pavilion; and Mr. H. F. Brazenor, Deputy Director; to Mr. Derek L. Rogers, Assistant Curator, Miss Patricia Ranger and Mrs. Marie Rockell, to my son Stephen for photographs and for many sidelights upon life in Brighton, and above all to my wife Margaret for her unfailing encouragement and advice, for her help in obtaining information, and for her patience and forbearance during the many long hours of writing the work.

C.M.

Contents

CONTENTS

IV VICTORIAN MARVELS AND MYSTERIES
1840 to 1900

V BATTLE-SCENE AND TRANSFORMATION
1900 to 1969

Illustrations

PLATES

The Aquarium Entrance and Clock-tower as originally built in 1871, *c.*
1908
Brighton Public Library
The Church of the Holy Resurrection, Little Russell Street, in 1906
Brighton Public Library

'The Druid's Head', Brighton Place, *c.* 1950
Flint-cobble building of *c.* 1790, and slum-children of *c.* 1922, in the Carlton Hill area
Photograph by Miss Jenner

The Railway Viaduct at Lewes Road, being repaired after bombing in
1943
Drawing by Muirhead Bone
Brighton Art Gallery

between pages 384 and 385
Brighton in 1928, published by George Philip and Son

The Royal Pavilion, 1877: the Entrance Hall, with the statue of Lt.-Col.
Pechell, V.C.
Brighton Public Library
The Royal Pavilion: the North Drawing Room, *c.* 1930, before restoration
Brighton Public Library

The Royal Pavilion: the North Drawing Room, 1966, after restoration
Photograph by H. Barrow
The Royal Pavilion: Queen Victoria's Bedroom, after restoration, 1968
Photograph by C. Musgrave

St. Bartholomew's Church, 1872
Photograph by C. Musgrave
St. Bartholomew's Church, 1872: the interior
Photograph by C. Musgrave

St. George's Church, Kemp Town, 1824
Photograph by C. Musgrave
Brighton vernacular architecture: house in Grenville Place, built *c.* 1790,
demolished 1966
Photograph by C. Musgrave

Lewes Crescent, Kemp Town, designed by Charles Busby, 1824
Photograph by C. Musgrave
The Royal Crescent, built 1797–1806
Photograph by C. Musgrave

15

Brunswick Square, Hove: the East side
Photograph by C. Musgrave
The Sassoon Mausoleum, built *c.* 1880; now 'The Bombay Bar'

Brighton in 1939, published by John Bartholomew and Sons

between pages 448 and 449
The Royal Pavilion: the east front
Photograph by C. Musgrave

The Royal Pavilion: the Banqueting Room, 1966
Photograph by W. Dobinson

The Royal Pavilion: the Music Room, 1966
Photograph by W. Dobinson

The Royal Pavilion: the Saloon, with the Dolphin furniture
Photograph by 'My Home and Family'

Park Crescent, designed by A. H. Wilds, 1829
Photograph by J. F. Smith
Montpelier Villas, built *c.* 1845
Photograph by J. F. Smith

Old and new architecture: the portico of the Royal Newburgh Assembly Rooms, built 1826, and the Hotel Metropole conference block and 'Sussex Heights', 1968
Photograph by C. Musgrave
Trippers' fare on the lower promenade, 1960
Photograph by Stephen Musgrave

Brighton's new skyline, 1966
Photograph by Brighton Herald Ltd.

The *Skylark* setting out, 1890

I

FISHERMEN AND FARMERS

The beginnings to 1770

1 Early Brighton

There is little evidence that early man lived in what is now the central part of the town of Brighton. His settlements were on the outskirts of the town, on the high ground where the land was already fairly open and easily cultivated, and from whence an approaching invader could easily be seen.

If there were any dwellings of prehistoric man on the seashore, his remains are now far out to sea, for much of the shore has been lost in the last thousand years.

The earliest settlement in the Brighton area seems to have been at Whitehawk, on the Race Hill north-east of the town, a little to the south of the grandstand. The camp was excavated in 1933. It was one of the twelve causewayed camps of the neolithic Windmill Hill culture in Britain, and was for a fairly short time only, about 2700 B.C., the headquarters of a tribe of Continental immigrants. These people were among the first potters in Britain, and their pots, of dark grey earthenware, round-bottomed and of noble shape, may be seen in Brighton Museum, and show the decoration of scored lines in the clay which represented the thonging of the leather food-vessels made by their neolithic ancestors of a thousand years earlier. Such were the first glimmerings of art in a people whose life was probably otherwise brutish.

Remains of charred human bones among those of the ox and other animals in the ashes of their cooking fires suggest inescapably that these people were cannibals. Also at the Museum may be seen two skeletons that were found buried in the outer ditch of the camp. One grave, of a woman and her baby, was rudely formed with a circle of chalk blocks, and within it the mother had been placed in the primitive burial position, which is akin to the pre-natal position and the attitude of sleep, with her knees drawn up and her newly born baby in her arms. Two pieces of chalk bored through so that they might have been worn on a string lay by her neck, together with two fossilized sea-urchins, which for endless centuries have been used as charms. Not far away lay the remains of another woman, whose body had apparently been thrown into a hole without ceremony, for the limbs were flung about in disordered fashion. Both women belonged to the race of small people with long and relatively narrow heads which we associate with our neolithic period. They were about twenty to thirty years of age.[1]

[1] Numbered references in the text are listed on pages 471–81.

These pathetic remains are a moving memorial of the earliest inhabitants of Brighton some 5,000 years ago. By the later phases of the Bronze Age life had softened into a more gentle and civilized pattern, with agricultural communities living on scattered farms surrounded by their fields. Grazing for flocks was found on the comparatively bare tops of the downs, and the light scrub of gorse and bramble could be cleared fairly easily from the sides of the hills for their small-scale cultivation, and as well as more advanced forms of pottery man had developed skill in the casting of bronze and gold. Three bracelets, two of solid gold and one of bronze covered with gold, all of smooth and elegant form, were found in the remains of a settlement at Patcham, and three bronze armlets of a distinctive form, known as 'Brighton loops' were found at Falmer. All are now in the Brighton Museum. So also is the famous amber cup, carved from a single piece of translucent red amber, one of the most important of all Bronze Age relics in this country, which was found in 1856, together with the remains of a bronze dagger and other objects, in a round-barrow at what is now Palmeira Avenue in Hove. The singing-games that were played by the local children every Good Friday upon this burial-mound since time immemorial may have been a survival of the original burial ceremonies or other ancient observances, perpetuated through folk-memory. The person buried there must have been a person of some consequence, perhaps a chieftain of that rich Wessex culture which brought about the construction of Stonehenge about 1500 B.C., to have had articles of such richness buried with him.

Hollingbury Camp, on the hill above Brighton on the road to Ditchling Beacon, is one of the great Iron Age hill-forts of Sussex, and was built about 250 B.C. Although its grassy ramparts may now easily be climbed, at one time they consisted of a wall of timbers with a deep ditch in front, unscalable without ladders. The Romans occupied the district, but their settlements were isolated. The site of a Roman farmhouse at the corner of Preston Road and Springfield Road, showing signs of having been burned, perhaps in a Saxon raid soon after the departure of the Romans, was excavated in 1877 and has provided important finds on two occasions since.*

The name of Brighton could hardly have been improved upon for a gay, sophisticated pleasure resort, and indeed its smart glittering sound makes it seem almost as though it had been specially invented in modern times. Its derivation, however, is of venerable antiquity. Before the nineteenth century the town was most generally known as Brightelmstone. The modern form of the name first occurs as early as 1660, in the reign of King Charles I, but it did not come into general use until the last years of the eighteenth century. The official use of the name Brighton dates from 1810, when this

* Asterisks in the text refer to the Notes on pages 468–70.

form was adopted by the Town Commissioners, but the old name continued to be used by the older people and in various documents until the 1850s. As many as forty or fifty variations of the earlier name are known.[2] The most common versions of it are Brighthelmston, Brighthelmstead and Bright-Hampstead. In Domesday Book it is called Bristelmestune. The derivation of the name is uncertain enough to have given historians a wide field for speculation. Romantic conjecture has linked Brighthelmstone with a Bishop Brighthelm, who is said to have accompanied the Saxon army and died in battle in A.D. 693.[3] Even more poetic imaginings have suggested a derivation from the 'bright helm' of one of the invaders. A more generally accepted, and more prosaic supposition is that the derivation is from the name 'Beorthelm's Tun' or 'Brithelm's Tun'—Beorthelm or Brithelm's Farm.[4]

It would seem that the Anglo-Saxons were the first people to create an important settlement, several years after the landing of Aella and his three sons, Cymen, Wlencing and Cissa, near Selsey in A.D. 477.

The place had many advantages for the early Saxon settlers, with its easy communications along the coast and by the sea, and in being sheltered by the Downs to the north from the cold winds and mists of the Weald. On the western side were low hills near the sea providing a dry place for dwellings to be built, but the whole of the central valley must have been a swampy area, for a bourn or intermittent river ran from a spring at Patcham that overflowed every winter. This stream, known as the Wellsbourne, was joined at the flat grassy expanse now called the Level, north of St. Peter's Church, by another bourn that flowed from the Lewes Road, and together they ran down the valley of the Steine to the sea, entering it at 'the Poole',[5] which is now called Pool Valley.

It was undoubtedly because of the swampy nature of the land through the valley that the Level and the Steine were never built upon, and remained broad open spaces throughout the centuries, so that we now possess the mile-long chain of green gardens and lawns running from Park Crescent to the sea. In the time of the Prince of Wales he and the Duke of Marlborough caused a sewer to be laid down the Steine to take the Wellsbourne. Since the building of the railway and the waterworks at Patcham, the stream has overflowed very rarely, but in a very wet winter inundations still occur. The name Wellsbourne must be of ancient origin, for it was given to the Hundred—the subdivision of the county, having its own court of law—to which Brighthelmstone belonged.

The name of the Steine, the broad thoroughfare where the roads from London and Lewes join and run down to the sea, may be of Scandinavian origin, possibly Danish or Flemish, deriving from *staene*, meaning a place of stones.[6] A number of stones which have been formed into the base of the Steine fountain, erected in 1846, may be the stones which had lain there since ancient times, and were traditionally supposed to have been arranged in a 'Druids' circle'. These sarsen stones or 'greywethers', so called because of the resemblance of their smooth shape to the forms of sheep, are weatherworn blocks of grey sandstone brought there by the action of glaciers, and were discovered by workmen digging trenches to lay gas-pipes across the Steine in 1823.

In late Saxon times the first overlord of Brighton of whom there is any record is Wulnoth, who in 1008 commanded an English fleet which was sent to repel an invasion by the Danes. His son Godwin was created Earl of Kent, Surrey and Sussex for his services in fighting the Vandals in Denmark. At his death Brighton fell to Harold, who became King in 1065, but at the Norman conquest a year later the town, with other of his Sussex possessions, was granted by William of Normandy to William de Warenne, one of his generals, who afterwards married the Conqueror's daughter Gundrada. About 1070 the Earl and his Countess made a pilgrimage to Rome and on the way visited the famous Benedictine monastery of Clugny in Burgundy. On their return they set up outside the walls of Lewes the great Priory of St. Pancras which diffused education and the arts over the southern part of Sussex, fostering in particular the art of painting, of which survivals remain today in the churches of Clayton, near Brighton, and Hardham.

In the Domesday survey of 1086 Brighton and three manors are recorded in the entry for 'Bristelmestune'. These were known as Brighthelmston-Lewes, because it was in the Barony of Lewes; Brighthelmston-Michelham, because it belonged to the Augustinian Priory at Michelham; and Bright-elmston-Atlingworth. This last included the church of St. Nicholas and was the paramount manor. The name Atlingworth survives today as a street name. Domesday Book records that the number of inhabitants was ninety. Each of the manors was assessed at a value of £12, and the town paid an annual rent of 4,000 herrings. This was a comparatively small number and could have been found by a few fishermen in a few days. The Brighton industry in those days was therefore presumably much smaller than at other places in Sussex. Iford and Southease, now tiny villages on the river Ouse near Newhaven, sent far bigger tributes.

By the early years of the fourteenth century Brighton was prosperous enough to support a market, and this was granted by charter of Edward II in 1313,[7] together with a fair lasting three days at the feast of St. Bartholomew the Apostle.

A small chantry or free chapel and priory dedicated to the saint was built some time in the twelfth century, and was served by two or three monks from the mother Priory at Lewes.* The name of the chapel survives today in that of the street on the north side of the Town Hall. The Priory was partly burned down in the French raid of 1514, but the remains were rebuilt and it became the residence of the Vicar of Brighton after the Reformation, and probably even before. It was then known as the Prior's Lodge until it was demolished in 1790. At that time the earliest part of the building was judged by local antiquarians,[8] in view of the style of architecture and of the decayed state of the timbers used, to have been erected not later than the end of the thirteenth century. What was undoubtedly the cemetery of the chapel was disturbed when some building operations were being carried on during the Regency period. The workmen discovered ancient remains of a number of bodies and, being overcome with commendable awe and reverence for the dead, refused to continue digging. They were only induced to go on with their work when the Vicar of Brighton, Mr. Michell, was called in and assured them that there was no harm in disturbing the bones of these particular dead, for they were, he told the workmen, 'nothing but rank papists'!

A few yards away to the north, where the Regent Arcade has now been built, was the site of a field or small farm called Mockbeggars Croft. Throughout England, in the many places where the word 'Mockbeggars' occurs, it is always connected with a farm or field of the Franciscan friars. Although they were begging friars, they were under no compulsion to beg, and in due time became a wealthy order. There is no other trace of such an order in the town apart from the name, but it seems there is a possibility that there was once a small house of the begging friars where now the glittering windows of fashionable jewellers, costumiers, hairdressers and perfume-sellers once more make a mock of beggary.

2 A Town in Flames

The appearance of Brighton early in the sixteenth century is recorded with fair accuracy on a drawing which is preserved in the British Museum.[1] An engraving from the drawing is shown in the Brighton Museum. It is dated 1545, and purports to be a record of an attack made on Brighton in that year, but there has been much dispute on the subject, and it has been maintained that the drawing in fact depicts the raid made on Brighton in 1514, when the whole of the town was burned by the French.

The drawing is the earliest existing record of the layout and extent of Brighton in those days. The pattern of streets is so regular as to have given rise to the suggestion that the town was laid out on a chequer-board pattern like Winchelsea, Caernarvon and other towns planned in the time of Edward I.

The whole of the town, which is here called Brithampton, is contained within a square bounded on three sides by North Street, West Street and East Street. The Steine is the broad street running northwards at the east side of the town. Five rows of houses ran from north to south to the beach, where there was a double row of small houses, probably little more than hovels, that were the remains of South Street in the lower town on the beach where the fishermen lived. Most of them had been earlier swept away by incursions of the sea. Two 'wynd-mylles' stand on the north-eastern outskirts of the town.

The tiny village of Hove, with one street of houses and a church, is shown, and the coast west of the town is marked as 'lowe all dangerous and wout (without) cliffs'. Between two of the central rows of houses appears a long field. This was the Hempshares, where hemp was grown for the making of the ropes and cordage that were essential for the fishing trade. Outside the town stands the parish church of St. Nicholas on its little hill. It had been placed in this high position possibly for several reasons—as the most important building it was built on a dry site away from the marshy ground of the town valley, and could serve as a substantial refuge in the event of attack. Also being on a hill it would serve as a landmark for fishermen. Shown just outside the town to the east, near the bottom of the Steine, is the 'towne fyre-cage', or beacon, an open iron basket hanging by a chain from a yard-arm fixed to a post, in which the townspeople burned a highly inflammable substance, strongly impregnated

24

with sulphur, called 'strombolo', which they picked up on the seashore. It seems that the name was not given to this mysterious substance by English sailors who had, as Sir Osbert Sitwell suggests,[2] voyaged to the Mediterranean and seen the flaming peak of Stromboli and smelt its volcanic vapours borne to them on the wind, but that it is of Flemish origin, deriving from 'Stromballen', meaning stream or tide-balls, from the fact that pieces of the substance are found floating on the water, having no doubt been washed out of deposits of sea-coal coming to the surface at the shore, and that the name was brought to England by Flemings, who according to the chronicler Holinshed, migrated to this country in A.D. 1107, in the time of Queen Matilda, who was herself a Fleming, after an inundation of their own country by the sea.

The presence of Flemings at Brighton is also supposed to have been confirmed by the Flemish character of the names of several old Brighton families, and by some technical terms connected with fishing, but it seems to have been established that any words of this sort of early origin are of Saxon derivation, or if of a later date, then brought to this country by Protestant immigrants from the Netherlands after the Reformation.

From the days of the prehistoric invaders of Britain, the immigrants from the Rhine and the Marne; from the time of the Romans, the Saxons and the Danes and up to the days of Napoleon and Hitler, Brighton has never been free of the fear of attack from the sea.

For some four hundred years after their subjugation by William the Conqueror and his Norman lords the people of Brighton enjoyed peace from raiders, but in the fourteenth century, when the hold of Britain upon her French possessions was weakening, raids were carried out on the English coast by the French in retaliation for the despoiling of their own countryside and towns by adventurers like Sir Edward Dalyngrigge, who with the treasure he had accumulated on the Continent returned to Sussex and built Bodiam Castle to protect the low-lying eastern part of the country from reprisals by the enemy. In 1377 the French raided, burnt and plundered most of the towns along the coast from Portsmouth to Hastings. They landed near Brighton at Rottingdean, and despite the bold stand made by the local 'Watch and Ward' forces, ravaged the countryside round about, and carried off as prisoner the Prior of Lewes himself, who like many another prelate in those days was accustomed to handling the mace as well as the crozier, and had placed himself at the head of the local armed forces.

When Henry VIII was pursuing his quarrels against Louis XII of France the ships of either side fought in the Channel and raids were carried out at night on either coast. The town of Brighton suffered the most grievous disaster in the whole of its history in one of these raids when one night in June 1514 the French landed on the coast and burnt the entire town, except for the church. This raid was first described by Edward Hall in his Chronicle of 1542.[3] He tells how the attack was made by the French Admiral Pregent de Bideaux, a Knight of Rhodes, who was known in this country as Prior Jehane, or more familiarly to the English as 'Prior Jhon'.*

It was this 'great capitayne of the French navy who', Hall wrote, 'with his galeys and foysts charged with Grete basylyskes and other greate artilery, came on the border of Sussex and came a-land in the night at a poore village in Sussex called Bright-Helmstone'. The galleys and foysts were small vessels, the latter usually with sixteen oars a side, each pulled by two men, but it would seem that there must have been larger ships also for the 'grete basylyskes and other greate artilery'. The account continues: 'and or the watche could him escry, he sett fyre on the towne and toke such poore goodys as he founde. Then the watche fyred the bekyns, and people began to gather; which seyenge; Prior Jhon sowned his trompett to call his men aborde; and by that time it was day. Then VI archers which kept watche folowed Prior Jhon to the sea and shott so fast that they bett the galeymen from the shore; and Prior Jhon himselfe waded to his foyst, and th' Englishmen went into the water after; but they were put back with pickes, or else they had entered the foyst; but they shott so fast that they wounded many in the foyst; and Prior Jhon was shott in the face with an arrow and was like to have dyed. And therefore he offered his image of wax before Our Lady of Bolleyn [Boulogne] with the English arrow in the face for a myracle.' The chronicler Holinshed, writing much later, describes the same incident, with the additional detail that Prior Jhon lost one of his eyes.[4] Brighton was almost completely destroyed, except for the church on the hill. Most of the houses must have been of wood, many of them probably tarred, and they would therefore have burnt down rapidly. The ancient Priory of St. Bartholomew almost completely disappeared, leaving little more than a name behind. Thus nothing survives of medieval Brighton, except the pattern of its streets, which is preserved in the layout of the narrow alleys of the Lanes.

The date of 1514 for the burning of Brighton is confirmed by one of the State Papers, dated from Calais 5th June 1514, which speaks of arrangements for a raid to be carried out in France 'in revenge for the burning of Brighthelmstone'. This punitive expedition was led by Sir John Wallop of Hampshire, a soldier and diplomatist who had accompanied Sir Edward Howard on the gallant but unsuccessful attempt which he made to destroy the French naval base of Brest. Holinshed[5] wrote of Wallop's expedition: 'The lord admerall offended with this proud part of theFrenchmen, in making such attempt on the English coasts, sent Sir John Wallop to the sea with divers ships, which sailing to the coast of Normandie, landed there, and burnt one and twenty villages and townes. . . .'

There is evidence that another raid or an attempt at one was made by

26

the French in 1545. In that year the French carried out a heavy attack on the Isle of Wight and Portsmouth, in the course of which the great English ship the *Mary Rose* capsized and sank.

It is this raid of 1545 that purports to be the subject of the drawing of a French attack on Brighton which is preserved at the British Museum, and in which the town is shown as being burned by the French. The drawing is dated by an inscription, '1545 Julye 37. Hen. VIII', and much confusion has been caused thereby as to the exact year in which the burning of Brighton took place. Holinshed described this later attack also, but it does not seem conceivable that his account was connected with any raid so disastrously successful and complete that the whole of the town was then burned to the ground. He wrote 'In 37 Hen. 8th, 1545, July the 18th, the admiral of France, Mons. Donebatte, hoisted up sails, and with his whole navy (which consisted of 200 ships and 26 gallies) came forth onto the seas, and arrived on the coast of Sussex, before Bright Hampstead, and set certain of his soldiers on land to burn and spoil the country, but the beacons were fired and the inhabitants thereabouts came down so thick, that the Frenchmen were driven to their ships with loss of divers of their numbers, so that they did little hurt there.'

In some respects, especially with regard to the firing of the beacons, and the townspeople forcing the French back to their ships, Holinshed's account of the 1545 raid resembles his own story and Hall's description of the attack of 1514, except for the fact of the burning of the town, but the Admiral on this occasion is not Pregent, but 'Donebatte' or Donnebault.

In the drawing an inscription written near the foot of the Steyne states 'Here landed the Galeyes.' Near by is 'The towne fyre-cage' which has given warning of the attack to the beacon at the north-west of the town. Out at sea are twelve large men of war, and the inscription states 'Thesse grete Shippes rydeng hard abord shore by shoting into the hille valleys out the towne sore oppresse the towne that the Country dare not adventure to rescue it.'* This last statement would again seem to suggest that it refers to the attack of 1514, when the French were not prevented from investing the town and firing all the houses.

It was suggested by Dr. James Gairdner[6] that in fact the drawing does not represent the attack of 1545 but the raid of 1514, since it shows the burning of the town, and he was moreover of the opinion that the date 1545 had been put in at a later time by someone believing that the drawing represented the later attack and that the burning took place at that time.* Doctor Gairdner even went so far as to question whether the attack of 1545 ever took place at all, and later historians have repeated this assertion. It does not seem likely, however, that Holinshed would have described a second attack, with the positive assertion that the French 'did little hurt', unless there was sound evidence of the fact.

The important question arises as to the reason for the making of this drawing, and for its preservation in official records. It would seem most probable that it was made to illustrate and support a petition from the people of Brighthelmstone to be given the means of defending their town from foreign attack, and that it was some such petition as this that resulted eventually in the building of the battery with cannon at Brighton.

When the town was rebuilt after the burning by the French, the new houses were in many places re-erected on the site of the old, and it is indeed possible that some of the ancient flint and pebble walls of buildings in the Lanes, in parts of great thickness, and some large ancient fireplaces, may date back to medieval times, but most of the houses date from the eighteenth and early nineteenth centuries.

Because of the attacks on Brighton made by the French it was decided to provide some defences for the town, and in 1559 the Lord of the Manor made over to the inhabitants a piece of land[7] on the shore for the building of a blockhouse or small fort. It was erected on the cliff near the southern end of Middle Street and consisted of a circular building, 50 feet in diameter, 18 feet high, with walls 7 or 8 feet thick, in which there were arched recesses for keeping powder and shot. In front was the 'gun-garden', somewhat poetically named for a place of such stern purpose. In it were four pieces of 'great iron ordnance' sent from the Tower of London, besides ten qualivers or small cannon which were provided by the inhabitants.

Near by to the east stood the Town house, with a dungeon beneath it for the imprisonment of malefactors, and above it a turret containing the town clock. At the same time as the blockhouse a massive wall with embrasures for guns was built, extending as far as East Street in one direction and beyond West Street in another. There were four gates in the wall: the East Gate; Portall Gate; Middle Gate, or the Gate of All Nations; and the West Gate.[8] These were obviously intended to control the various gaps or clefts in the cliffs down which the houses on the beach were reached by sloping ways descending westwards, and which would have given easy access to the upper town for an invader. One is tempted to wonder why the Middle Gate should sometimes have been known by the romantic name of the Gate of All Nations. Was it through this gate that persons landing on the shore from countries across the water were required to enter, passing perhaps before some sort of port warden or customs officer? There is no explanation in any of the chronicles of Brighton.

In the year 1587, when it was known that the Spaniards were fitting out a fleet to attack England, the two Deputy Lieutenants of Sussex made a survey of the fortifications and stores of ammunition, but the Armada did not appear in the Channel until the following year. Because of neglect, the fortifications were gradually undermined by the sea, especially by the great storms of 1703 and 1705, which finally swept away the part of the town beneath the cliff, until the gun-garden in front of the blockhouse and the defensive wall with its gates were completely destroyed.

By 1726 it had become necessary to guard the edge of the cliff with a paling. The fort itself endured a little longer, but in 1761 half of it had fallen below the cliff, and eventually the whole of the ruins were removed.

The East Gate remained until the year 1777, and was then taken down to make room for a battery of guns at the bottom of East Street. It was this battery that was to distinguish itself some years later in firing salutes of welcome to various Royal visitors to the town, but unhappily with disastrous results to the artillerymen.

3 Fishermen and Townsmen

The blockhouse had been erected 'in warlike manner by the fishermen with the profites of the quarter-share' from fishing, but in 1579 the fishermen petitioned the Privy Council for relief from what they considered was a burdensome proportion of the cost of defence, in which they held the landsmen should share. Accordingly the Privy Council in 1580 appointed two Commissioners, Lord Buckhurst and Richard Shelley, under the Earl of Arundel to investigate the complaints of the fishermen, who were ordered to meet and 'sette down in writynge their aunccient customs and orders'. By this time the fishing industry in Brighton had reached its highest level and it was then estimated that the town possessed eighty fishing-boats, 400 mariners and 10,000 nets. Since late medieval times the town of Great Yarmouth had come to be of increasing importance as the centre of the herring fishery because of its nearness to the fishing-grounds of the North Sea. Since before the Conquest the herring had been one of the staple articles of English diet and the extent to which it dominated our economy is almost comparable to the importance of sheep-farming in later times. Boats sailed to Yarmouth from the Cinque Ports and from all along the South Coast, from France and from the Netherlands. It is not to be wondered at that disputes frequently broke out between the Yarmouth men and the visitors, who were regarded as robbing the natives of the harvest of their own sea. Boats were destroyed and lives were lost in these quarrels, but at length the Yarmouth folk passed a number of by-laws forbidding the sale of herrings by any people but her own inhabitants within a radius of fourteen miles. The Brighton fishermen strove for a time to circumvent these orders, but at length they were compelled to sell their fish only as hirelings of the Yarmouth men. By 1609 their prosperity had begun sadly to decline, and a petition was sent by the Brighton men complaining of the way in which they, together with the fishermen of other counties, had been oppressed and were likely to be ruined. By the early years of the eighteenth century, however, the Brighton fishery had revived considerably.

When the Brighton fishermen came to draw up their 'Auncient Customs' in 1580 they described how the fishing industry was based on a number of seasonal voyages in search of fish called Fares (after the Dutch fahr), each of which was named in accordance with the fishing-grounds to be visited or the type of boat used.[1]

The value of a catch was divided into a number of places, ranging from about thirty down to about ten, varying always according to the number of men employed and the number of hooks used. From one-half to three and a half shares went to the maintenance of the boat, the men usually took one share each, and almost invariably a share each went to the Vicar, to the town and the master of the boat. The disputes had arisen chiefly over the payment of a quarter-share after every voyage to the churchwarden of Brighton to be used in the building of forts and walls for the defence of the town, for shot and powder, for the entertainment of soldiers in time of war, and 'other public service of the prince', and maintenance of the parish church. This practice was confirmed by the Commissioners and provision was made for contributions of money from the farming folk and artisans also for the benefit of the town. These rates ranged from 4d to 3s 4d a year. A new body was also set up for the future government of the town, particularly for the keeping of order, and for the licensing of lodging and 'tipling' houses. This body was known as 'The Twelve', as it was composed of 'the ancientist, gravest and wisest inhabitants, eight fishermen and fower landsmen for assistants to the Constable in every public cause'. All these ordinances were inscribed in black letter on parchment in *The Book of All the Auncient Customs*, dated 23rd July in the 22nd year of Elizabeth. The signatures of the Commissioners were followed by those of the principal inhabitants. Many of them could not write, but they appended their own personal marks. Some of these represented the trades of the various signatories; for example, a ships' carpenter's sign was a hatchet; that of a wheelwright a wheel, and that of a millwright a windmill. Most of the others seem quite arbitrary, but inasmuch as some of the signs resemble Icelandic runes, there would seem to be fresh material for conjecture by some scholarly historian regarding the Scandinavian origin of many of the Brighton residents.

In the year 1618 the landsmen and fishermen met and agreed upon a revision of the Auncient Customs. The share of the landsmen towards the charges of the town was now settled at one-half of the sum raised by the fishermen's quarter-share, and the two parties agreed upon the various charges to be made for the maintenance of the church, the lights on the fire-cage and the setting-forth of the soldiers and sailors for warlike operations. No one was allowed to apply to the Justices of the Peace for an ale-house licence without the consent of The Twelve.

By the end of the seventeenth century there were more than fifty mackerel boats operating from Brighton, but during the next thirty years the number was reduced by half. Brighton had its own characteristic type of fishing-boat, the Hog-boat or 'Hoggie', which was developed in a form that was especially suited to the particular conditions existing on our coast. They had a great deal of beam in proportion to their length, and so were not easily capsized, and could manoeuvre and turn quickly when dealing with nets. At the same time they drew very little water and were thus able to be beached easily. Because of their shallow draught they were easily blown to windward when sailing, and to prevent this they were fitted with lee-boards, a device of Dutch origin, consisting of triangular boards hung on to the sides of the boat, which could be let down into the water to provide resistance to sideways motion. The last of the 'Hoggies' was burnt at a 5th November bonfire, rather curiously, because it is usually believed by seamen that it is unlucky to burn a boat. A fine old model of a Hog-boat is preserved by the Brighton Museum in its branch collection at The Grange, Rottingdean.

For several centuries bitter feuds existed between the fishermen and the landsmen, the latter consisting mostly of farming people and artisans. At one time the fisherfolk lived almost entirely below the cliffs, but as the foreshore disappeared in the encroachments of the sea they were compelled to move on to the higher land. It is believed that the fisher people built the houses of East Street and West Street, while the landsmen built the streets in between and North Street, which bordered on the farming lands beyond the town.

The layout of the arable fields had an important effect on the development of the town after the early nineteenth century. Up to that time they were still being farmed. They were divided into five great fields known to the inhabitants as 'tenantry laines'. (They are not to be confused with the narrow alleys called the Lanes in the centre of Brighton.) These five fields were called West Laine, North Laine, Hilly Laine, Little Laine and East Laine. In 1738 they covered an extent of 921 acres and were held by twenty-five persons. The Laines were divided into furlongs separated from each other by narrow tracks called leakways, running from east to west, and these were connected by other tracks called paul-pieces, running from north to south. As builders bought up the land furlong by furlong, the leakways became main streets and the paul-pieces side-roads. St. James's Street, Gloucester Road and North Street are examples of the former, while Upper Gardner Street and High Street are instances of the latter. The pattern of streets thus imposed on the modern town, with the principal streets running either due north and south or directly east and west, has become less of a disadvantage in modern traffic conditions than if the streets of Brighton had been laid out for the greatest convenience to foot and horse-drawn traffic, following the contours of the hills in easy gradients but by a winding course. Straight roads, even though they may be fairly steep, are more satisfactory for modern transport.

4 The Royal Escape

appy are the people who have no history' we are told in an ancient proverb, and after the nightmare horror of the burning of Brighton the townspeople seem to have enjoyed a comparatively uneventful existence, to judge from the unsensational character of the few records that exist, until the coming of the Civil War, when Brighton cannot have been exempt from the agonies of that struggle in which father was estranged from son, brother from brother. Arundel Castle in the west of Sussex changed hands several times in the course of the war, the last time after a bombardment that made it a ruin for centuries, followed by the destruction of the Earl of Arundel's wonderful collection of art treasures, and Bodiam Castle in the east suffered 'slighting' by the Roundheads after a short display of resistance. With no great houses of any consequence in their midst, the humble fisherfolk and landsmen of Brighton seem to have favoured the Parliamentarian cause more than that of the King, but he had some loyal supporters amongst the local landowners and the more substantial traders. For a few hours in the year 1651 the stage of history was lit as by the fitful light of torches to reveal Brighton as the scene of an episode of no little import for the course of the English monarchy, when King Charles II escaped to France from Brighton after his defeat by Cromwell at the Battle of Worcester. The story of the King's escape is gathered from several narratives, but chiefly from the account of Colonel Gounter, a Sussex gentleman who led the King's party during the last stages of the adventure, and from the book called *Miraculum Basilikon*, or the Royal Miracle, which was compiled principally from the King's own story.

For six weeks after the lost battle Charles Stuart had eluded his pursuers, only narrowly escaping recognition and arrest on many occasions. One attempt to cross to France by boat from Charmouth in Dorset had failed, through the seamen taking fright at the last moment. The King was accompanied in his wanderings by Lord Wilmot, who was the only one of his followers whom he had not dismissed after the lost battle. Wilmot, who was travelling under the name of 'Mr. Barlow', sought the help of Colonel Gounter of Racton near Chichester, a loyal landowner who it was supposed might know where a boat could be hired. The Colonel approached a merchant of his acquaintance, Francis Mansel, who because of his trading contacts with France seemed most likely to be able to help. He was told the passage was required for two friends who had to fly the country because of a duel, and £50 was offered as the price for the passage. Gounter was introduced by Mansel to Nicholas Tettersell of Brighthelmstone, the owner of a little coal-brig called the *Surprise*, then lying off Shoreham half laden, and it was eventually agreed that for £60 the Colonel's friends should be set on the coast of France. The ship was to be ready to sail with very little warning, and for the sake of secrecy it was moved away from Shoreham into the mouth of the river Adur. During these negotiations the King had been in hiding near Salisbury, and he now began his journey towards Brighton, wherever possible riding along the trackways of the Downs through Hampshire and western Sussex in order to avoid encountering danger. While passing by Arundel Castle they ran full tilt into Captain Morley, the Parliamentarian Governor, but they dismounted and hid their faces against their horses and were not recognized. On entering Bramber they found the town full of soldiers, but the Colonel advised on riding boldly through them, and again they were not suspected. Gounter then decided to press on to Brighton alone to make sure that the town was safe, and promised to send word to Charles when this was so. The King was to find a quiet place near by at which to stay in the meantime. Gounter found Brighton empty of soldiers and took the best rooms at The George Inn. It has been much disputed as to where this inn stood. For many years it was believed that the 'King's Head' in West Street was the inn, and that its name was changed at the Restoration. Fanny Burney, writing in her diary in 1778 from Brighthelmstone, says 'Mrs. Thrale's house is at the court end of the town, exactly opposite to the King's Head, where Charles II stayed just before his escape to France.* I fail not to look at it with loyal satisfaction,' she continues, 'and his black-wigged majesty has from the time of its restoration been its sign.' It was discovered, however, that this inn was known as 'The George' as late as 1745, so its name was not changed at the Restoration but long after, and furthermore, in town records of the time of the King's escape, the house was not mentioned as being an inn at all.

There was an inn called 'The George' recorded as being in Middle Street in 1656, and for long it was believed that this was where the King must have stayed.[1] In 1926, however, a handsomely engrossed Brighton document, which had been known of for many years but which had been lost to sight for some time, once more came to light and was deposited in the Library of the Sussex Archaeological Society at Lewes.[2] This document known as the Rentall of Brighthelmstone Manor, drawn up by Charles Goodwin, one of the stewards of the manor, in 1665, has an entry which revealed that in that year an inn called the 'Ould George' stood on the site of the 'King's Head' in West Street. Presumably it ceased to be an inn some time later when the new 'George Inn' was opened in Middle Street. It is even possible that the innkeeper of the 'Ould George' gave up the inn soon after the escape for fear of being held to blame for assisting the King. Thus the traditional site of the inn where Charles II stayed in Brighton as being in West Street was re-established.

Soon after Colonel Gounter arrived at the inn he was joined by the King, together with Lord Wilmot, who had not found a suitable place to rest outside Brighton, and had decided to follow on without delay. A little later they were joined by Francis Mansel and Captain Tettersell. Throughout the evening the King alone seemed cheerful and unperturbed, although Gounter felt that majesty was so natural to the King 'that even when he said nothing, did nothing, his very lookes (if a man observed) were enough to betray him'. And indeed that striking appearance seemed to defy all disguise, the extremely tall figure, the dark hair, heavy features, sallow complexion, and above all the drooping mouth with protuberant lower lip framed between two deeply etched lines from the nostrils, making up a likeness that must have been stamped upon the mind of almost everyone in England. Indeed, the King had earlier noticed that Tettersell was observing him very closely, and after a while the Captain complained to Mansel that he had not been fairly dealt with, for although the merchant had given him a fair price for the passage, he had not been frank enough to tell him the identity of his passenger. 'For he is the King, and I very well know him to be so,' and added, 'for he took my ship, with other fishing-vessels from Brighthelmstone in the year 1648.' He had reason to be in the King's debt, for after being commandeered his ship had been let go again, although he omitted to mention this. He also reminded Mansel that a reward of £1,000 was offered to anyone assisting in the discovery of the King, but protested his loyalty, saying, 'Be not troubled at it, for I think I do God and my country good service in preserving the King, and by the grace of God I will venture my life and all for him, set him safely on shore, if I can, in France.' The King's friends, although made uneasy by this outburst, felt they must trust the man, but were rapidly becoming more and more anxious, and both Gounter and the King asked Tettersell when he could be ready. The Captain replied that his ship was aground and would have to wait for the tide, also that the wind was contrary, but the King opened the window and pointed out that it had changed in their favour. Gounter now offered Tettersell another £10 if he would leave that night, but the Captain maintained it was impossible, although he offered to get his crew aboard in readiness for departure.

Tettersell's strongly professed loyalty did not prevent his now raising one difficulty after another. He demanded that his boat must be insured for £200, to which Gounter impatiently agreed, but the sailor insisted that a bond should be drawn up to this effect. Gounter now threatened to find a boat elsewhere, but the King interposed, reminding Tettersell that a gentleman's word was as good as a bond, especially, he added somewhat cynically, when given before witnesses. Eventually, as Gounter wrote later, 'the man's stomach came down' and he maintained that 'carrie them he would, whatever became of it, and before he would be taken he would run his boat under the water'. Tettersell now insisted on going home to collect some necessities, although the King's friends were loath to let the sailor out of their sight. The attempted flight from Charmouth had been frustrated because the boatman had returned home, and had been shut up in his room by his wife, who feared the consequences of helping the King. Tettersell was eventually allowed to leave in order to gather together his crew, who consisted of four men and a boy. He also returned home for a bottle of spirits to nerve him for the dangerous enterprise ahead, and for a clean shirt, which was apparently his one contribution to the historical solemnity of the occasion. Taking this was the signal to his wife of a most unusual and unquestionably exalted circumstance, and she immediately concluded that the passenger whom her husband was to convey could be no less a person than the King. However, the lady proved to be no less loyal than her husband and charged him to deliver the King to safety, declaring that she would not care afterwards if she and her children had to beg their living.

At The George Inn the King and Lord Wilmot were lying down in their clothes to snatch a rest, until two o'clock, when Colonel Gounter aroused them. Horses waiting at the back of the inn took them to the beach, and to Shoreham, where the *Surprise* lay aground. The King and Lord Wilmot then took their leave of Colonel Gounter and Francis Mansel and climbed aboard, where they rested in the little cabin of the ship until the tide rose and they were afloat. By seven o'clock the ship was making for the open sea. Her usual port was Poole, and so as not to arouse suspicion on the part of any possible watchers, Tettersell kept at first a course in that direction. Colonel Gounter followed along the coast on horseback, keeping them in sight all day, every moment fearing that some mishap might occur, when suddenly late in the afternoon the *Surprise* altered course, her sails vanished over the horizon and Gounter turned his horse's head for home. The King must now be safe, but the faithful Colonel had not finished his reckoning with Tettersell. Upon the *Surprise* the King sat on deck, dressed in his disguise as a Puritan, and when the captain rebuked one of the crew for staring at their passenger the man retired muttering, 'Surely a cat may look at a king.' As we shall see later, it is probable that at least one member of the crew had a very shrewd idea of the identity of their mysterious passenger.

The wind held steadily until the following morning, when about ten o'clock the ship reached Fécamp on the coast of Normandy, and the King was put ashore in a little boat. Almost immediately a squall arose so suddenly that the Captain was compelled to cut his cable and lose his anchor in order to get away from that dangerous coast to the safety of the open sea. A day or two later Tettersell was at Chichester, where he sought out Colonel Gounter and made him pay £8 in compensation for the loss of his anchor and cable. Gounter heard later that two hours after he had left Brighton a party of soldiers had arrived searching for 'a tall, black man six feet and two inches high', and before many more days had passed almost every person in England had heard of the town of Brighthelmstone.

Tettersell bided his time and upon the return of Charles to England in 1660 sailed his ship up the Thames and moored it opposite the King's palace at Whitehall, decorated from stem to stern with bunting and with the ship's name altered to *The Royal Escape* in fresh bright lettering, so as to attract as much attention as possible and to leave no doubt in anyone's mind as to the part the vessel had played in the drama of the King's preservation. The ship under its new name was taken into the English fleet as an unarmed 'smack', and Tettersell was given an appointment as Captain in charge of *The Royal Escape* and later of a larger ship called *The Monk*, which carried out various escort duties, including on one occasion attending a convoy to Lisbon.[3] It appears from various State Papers that Tettersell was on one occasion reprimanded for losing some small boats, and was eventually dismissed the service in 1667 for his behaviour during a naval engagement, the details of which have not come down to us.

In 1663 Tettersell had been given a pension of £100 a year, which was to be continued for his son and daughter if they lived after him. Colonel Gounter died before the Restoration, and by 1662 his widow was in some financial straits. After two petitions to the Crown she was granted a pension of £200 a year for twenty-one years and the King himself wrote to the headmaster of Winchester School asking that the Colonel's son should be admitted as a scholar.[4] Francis Mansel was appointed 'Customer Inward' at the Port of Southampton for £60 a year, but in 1661, after petitioning the King that this small salary did not cover his expenses, he was granted a pension of £200 a year, by which it appeared that his services had been valued above those of Tettersell, but possibly through the action of officials rather than of Charles himself the pension was not paid after the first year, and Mansel petitioned the Crown again, pointing out that after the King's flight he had been outlawed and unable to pursue his business, whereupon the pension was restored.[5] Mansel lived at one time, if not at the time of the King's escape then after the Restoration, at The Grange, Ovingdean, an ancient and picturesque village in the Downs near Brighton. In Harrison Ainsworth's highly romantic novel called *Ovingdean Grange* the King is described as spending the night before his escape at that house, but, as we have seen, it was in Brighton at The George Inn that Charles stayed.

The Royal Escape was eventually released from the Navy and continued for some years to be moored in the Thames and to be visited as an object of curiosity, but as public discontent with the King's manner of life increased, and popular interest in the legend of his flight declined, the ship was moved downriver, till it ended up in the naval shipyard at Deptford, where at last in the year 1791 it was broken up for firewood.

Upon his dismissal from the Navy, Tettersell retired to Brighton, where for the rest of his life he strove to repair the damage caused to his self-conceit through his disgrace by the most odious behaviour to all with whom he came in contact. In 1670 he became High Constable of Brighton, a position in which he was able to exercise the full force of his malevolent nature, especially in his persecution of Quakers and other nonconformists. On one occasion, being annoyed by the smallness of a fine imposed by the magistrates on some Quakers who had been convicted on false evidence of his own, he broke into a warehouse belonging to one of the Quakers, took away sixty bags of salt and sold them for his own benefit. Although the modest rank and small honours he had attained had been of little consequence in the metropolis, and had of late been discredited, they still enabled him to cut something of a figure in Brighton. One person whom he is said to have persecuted with special malevolence was Anthony Smith, who had been landlord of 'The George' where Charles had stayed before his escape. He seems to have given up the inn after the flight of the King, desiring perhaps not to call attention to himself for fear of punishment, and it may be for this reason that the identification of the inn in later times became so difficult. Smith continued in business instead as the principal maker of ropes and cordage to the Brighton fishermen.

Tettersell seems to have been actuated by the bitterest malice against Smith, fearing that he might be compelled to share with him the glory of having helped the King, whereas, in fact, Smith had been content to recognize his sovereign and to proclaim his loyalty in the humblest fashion, without ever presuming afterwards to claim any reward.

In 1670[6] Tettersell acquired a property 'containing by estimation one road the Old Shipp & in the Hempshares'. This was undoubtedly the Old Ship Hotel, which is the oldest hostelry in Brighton. The earliest record of it, dated 1559, is the first for any inn in Brighton, and its beginnings may go back to early Tudor times. The origin of its name is uncertain, but it most probably derives from the inn having been constructed, at least in part, from the timbers of an old vessel. A piece of carved timber which appears to have been part of a ship's stern for many years formed part of the entrance to the stables. It has, in fact, been supposed that this carved beam came from *The Royal Escape* when that vessel was broken up, but as this event did not take place until 1791, more than a century after the death of Tettersell, it seems hardly likely that anyone at that date would have had sufficient interest in the matter to have gone to the very great trouble of obtaining the beam from the shipbreaker's and bringing it by the long and difficult journey to Brighton. Whatever its origin may be, the beam was eventually given to the Brighton Museum, where it may still be seen hanging on one of the walls. It is probably from a vessel of earlier date than *The Royal Escape*, one perhaps that may have been wrecked upon the shore at Brighton. Tettersell died in 1674, and was buried in the church-yard of St. Nicholas, where the tombstone of himself and his wife may be seen bearing a fulsome and grandiloquent inscription apparently written by his son, who is also buried there. The lettering on the stone is now damaged and difficult to decipher, but as far as it is possible to tell, reads as follows:

> *Within this marble Monument doth lie*
> *Approved faith, honour, and loyalty;*
> *In this cold clay he hath now ta'en up his station,*
> *Who once preserved the church, the crowne, and nation!*
> *When Charles the Greate was nothing but a breath,*
> *This valiant soul stept 'tween him and death:*
> *Usurper's threats, nor tyrant rebels' frowne,*
> *Could not affright his duty to the crowne;*
> *Which glorious act of his, for church and state,*
> *Eight Princes, on one day, did gratulate—*
> *Professing all to him in debt to bee,*
> *As all the world are to his memory;*
> *Since earth could not reward the worth him given,*
> *He now receives it from the King of Heaven.*
> *In the same chest one jewel more you have,*
> *The partner of his virtues, bed, and grave.*

5 Faith and Fanaticism

Aremarkable sequel to the escape of Charles II from Brighton was the intervention of the mate of Tettersell's ship to bring about the release from prison of the author of *The Pilgrim's Progress* together with some other dissenters. Thomas Carver, mate of the *Surprise*, who was a Quaker, had recognized the King during the crossing, and assured him of his loyalty. When they reached France it was Carver who rowed him in a small boat near the shore and carried him on his back through the waves to the land. On returning from a voyage to the West Indies many years later Carver found that several hundred of his fellow Quakers had been imprisoned for their religious beliefs. Knowing of Carver's encounter with the King, two leaders of the Society of Friends, Whitehead and Moore, entreated him to seek an interview with the King to plead their cause. Charles immediately recognized Carver and asked why he had not been to claim his reward before. Carver replied that his satisfaction had been in relieving a man in distress and now he desired nothing but that the King should set his friends at liberty. He showed Charles a list of over a hundred people who had been in prison for six years. The King complained that there were so many troublesome dissenters and that the country gentlemen pestered him about the activities of the Quakers. Even if he released them they would be back in prison within six months. However, the King said he was willing to release any six whom Carver cared to name, whereupon the sailor exploded with the retort: 'What! Six poor Quakers for a King's ransom?' This blunt answer delighted the King so much that he promised to examine the matter and asked Carver to see him again. A second interview resulted in a pardon being granted for no less than 471 Quakers and twenty other dissenters by a Royal Proclamation which is still preserved at the headquarters of the Society of Friends in London. Amongst those who were freed at this time was John Bunyan, who had written his immortal work while imprisoned in Bedford Jail. It might be thought somewhat strange, none the less, that Carver should have been loyal to the King, and did not betray him to the Roundheads before the escape, because during the Commonwealth the Quakers had been relieved of persecution by General Monk, in an order instructing his soldiers 'to forbear to disturb the peaceable meetings of the Quakers, they doing nothing prejudicial to the Parliament of England'.

Quite possibly Carver had little regard for the political quarrel between the Royalists and the Puritans, and his sympathy for a human being in distress, who was about to achieve his liberty at the end of a long pursuit, triumphed over any narrow sectarian loyalties that might have stood in his way. Such tolerance and compassion was by no means general amongst the religious folk of those times. It seems possible that Richard Carver was a descendant of Derek Carver, who a hundred years or so earlier had been the first person to suffer martyrdom for the Protestant cause during the persecutions of Queen Mary. Derek Carver was a Fleming by birth who had come to this country to find refuge from the Catholic persecutions in the Netherlands. He had become the owner of the Black Lion Brewery, named after the Black Lion of Flanders, which gave its name to Black Lion Street, where the building stands. The early part of it is probably the oldest building in Brighton and its preservation is now assured, although threatened for a time by new building projects. A wind-vane in the form of the Black Lion, of eighteenth-century date, still stands above the building, having been restored recently.

Derek Carver must have been one of the most substantial citizens of the town, for he was the only one who undersigned the document of the 'Auncient Customs' prefixing his signature with 'Mr.' One night at the end of October 1554, Carver was at prayer in his house with some friends who shared his Protestant views when they were arrested by the county magistrate, Edward Gage of Firle Place, near Lewes, and sent to Newgate. After lying in prison for over seven months, they were examined as to their religious doctrines and sentenced to be burnt. Carver was brought to Lewes for the execution and ascended the pyre with great courage by himself. Then he spoke to the people, saying he had forsaken all to follow Christ, and as the fire was lit he flung his Bible into the crowd.*

Stephen Gratwicke of Brighton was put to death at Southwark in 1557 and was not even allowed the consolation of a Bible during several years' imprisonment, the Bishop of Winchester forbidding it, saying 'because you will damme your soule with the Word, therefore you shall not have it!' There must have been many people in those days who were revolted by the religious persecutions of both sides, and who felt that nothing could be further from the teachings of Christ or less pleasing to God than the burnings and tortures that went on, but remembering this we can understand the difficulties of humane people in Nazi Germany, who dared not speak out against the persecution of the Jews and the horrors of the concentration camps for fear of punishment by the authorities. In 1658 John Pullot, a Quaker of Brighton, was whipped and given six months' imprisonment for raising his voice against the priest in the 'Steeple-house', as a church was called in those days.[1] Devout Christians coming from church one Sunday in Brighton carrying their prayer-books burst in at the house of William Gold, where a Protestant meeting was being held, and flung filth upon the people there and beat them. Marjery Causton and her daughter when coming from a Quaker meeting were attacked and the girl 'cruelly stoned and wounded in the face . . .' and her blood spilt to such a degree that her persecutors boasted that they had killed a Quaker. When Richard Pratt complained to the Lewes justices that he and his friends had been stoned at Brighton and asked their protection for innocent people he was whipped and sent to the House of Correction for hard labour.

Persecutions of this kind continued until General Monk, the Parliamentarian leader, issued the order permitting 'peaceable meetings of the Quakers', which has already been mentioned, and ever since then Brighton has been an important stronghold of the Society of Friends, who eventually received support from King George IV, and whose meeting house today is an important centre of the religious and cultural life of the town.

6 Terrors and Joys of the Sea

There are many records of the existence of a Port of Brighton, and it has been suggested[1] that when the foreshore extended farther seawards there was a spit of land which ran into the sea, and that a creek was thus formed extending into Pool Valley and the Steine, forming a safe anchorage. But if this ever existed at all it must have been changed by the incursions of the sea early in the sixteenth century, for the drawing of the attack on Brighthelmstone in 1514 shows no sign of a creek or harbour.

At times in the past Pool Valley has been deep in water from the sea or from the Wellsbourne, and it is recorded that in November 1723 'a pretty large Vessel was by ye violence of the wind and tide carried into the Pool'. In later times, and probably earlier, most landings at Brighton from large craft were made in small boats. Moreover, since early in the thirteenth century and even as late as the early nineteenth, Shoreham with its long harbour inlet was regarded as coming within the limits of Brighton, and from a maritime point of view the two places were often regarded as one. It is possible that in Saxon times, under Wulnoth, the inhabitants were called upon to provide ships to repel the Danish invaders, and from 1301 onwards there are records of men and ships being summoned from Shoreham, Hove and Brighton for the King's service. It was not until Tudor times that a regular Royal Navy was established. In 1558 and 1565, Brighthelmstone is named in the official list of seaports of England where measures were to be taken for the suppression of piracy. Early in the days of Charles I the Brighton fishermen were sending petitions to Parliament complaining of the ravages committed on their vessels by the pirates of Dunkirk. One petition stated that twenty-eight or thirty vessels, fishing in the North Sea, were seized by the Dunkirkers, and the crews put on shore to shift for themselves. In the year 1628 a French man-of-war captured 'five barks of Brighthelmstone' laden with wheat. Two Brighton vessels were therefore granted letters of marque to capture pirates. Two years later the men of Brighton were revenged. One Sunday in February 1630 a warship of Dunkirk of 160 tons, with seventy-eight men and ten guns, was chased by English ships and driven on shore at Brighton. The inhabitants stormed the ship, broke it to pieces and mounted the ten guns in the blockhouse. Nothing is told of the fate of the seventy-eight men, but it seems probable that the townspeople, with the burning of Brighton still smouldering in their memory were little inclined to mercy. In 1570 Brighton had the largest vessel in Sussex, *The Bartholomew* of 60 tons, probably so named in memory of the chapel and Priory that had been burned by the French.

It is a remarkable circumstance that the appearance of Brighton, as it were the physiognomy of its sea-front of cliffs and shore, formed throughout countless aeons of time, should have been changed considerably in the comparatively short span of three or four centuries only. Between the thirteenth century and the early part of the eighteenth the shape of Brighton was profoundly altered by the incursions of the sea. Up to the seventeenth century, as we have seen, an important part of the town, mostly inhabited by the fisherfolk, lay below the cliffs on a foreshore that must have extended far beyond its present tidemarks. Two streets of houses, including South Street, lay below the cliffs. It is clear from the established state of these dwellings that they cannot have been disturbed by the sea since human settlers first built there. Between 1260 and 1340 more than forty acres of the land became submerged, and the sea continued to make inroads upon the lower town. At some time before 1665 twenty-two tenements below the cliffs belonging to the Manor of Brighthelmston-Lewes were swept away.[2] Among them were twelve shops, with four capstan-places attached to them, and three cottages. At that time there still remained 113 tenements below the cliff, but most of these can have been little better than hovels, as only twenty-four of them were listed in the returns for the Hearth Tax of 1665, but these were all to be destroyed in the great storms of the next forty years.

The storm of November 1703 which swept over the greater part of Britain was believed to have been the worst in the whole history of these islands. So prodigious did it appear that Daniel Defoe was inspired to write a long treatise on storms in general—on the 'exhalation, dilation and extension of winds'—and upon this appalling tempest in particular. Accounts from Brighton told how the storm began at midnight and raged without intermission for over eight hours. 'Brighthelmston being an old built and poor, tho' populous town, was miserably torn to pieces, and made the very picture of desolation, that it lookt as if an enemy had sack't it.' Many of the houses were entirely demolished and others lost their roofs. Sheets of lead were torn from the roof of the church and two windmills belonging to the town were destroyed. Several of the town's fishing-vessels were lost at sea with many members of their crews. Walter Street of the *Happy Entrance* was rescued after clinging to a mast off Yarmouth for three days.

In August 1705 a hardly less dreadful storm completed the destruction of all the buildings in the lower town which had escaped the fury of earlier inundations. Every house under the cliff was demolished and concealed under mounds of pebbles fifteen feet deep. Again the church suffered, the lead roof being completely torn off. At the restoration of the church in 1853 a tablet of sheet lead commemorating the disaster was found in the roof, inscribed with the date 1705, together with the names of three churchwardens and representations of cherubs, scrollwork and figures of children and two angels sounding trumpets. It now hangs in the bell-tower.[3]

The early town of Brighton had been built upon an ancient beach from which the sea had retreated countless centuries before, and now some unknown cataclysm had caused the ocean almost at one stroke to regain its old territory. A few years later the sea began to undermine the low cliffs themselves, so that even the houses of the upper town began to be threatened, and it became necessary to build wooden groynes or break-waters to cause a protective mass of shingle to accumulate on the beach. After their recent calamities the people of Brighton could not pay for these works themselves, and in 1713 they were given permission to organize collections in churches and chapels throughout the county to raise the sum of £8,000 that it was believed would be needed, and £1,700 was, in fact, raised in this way. By 1757 the groynes were in a ruinous state and other appeals were made for money to build new defences. The decline of the fishing industry and the destruction of so many houses had reduced the inhabitants of Brighton to a wretched plight, the rates for the relief of the poor amounting to nearly 6s in the pound. Gradually the sea undermined the cliffs until the gun-garden, and the sea-wall with its gates, fell on to the beach, and in 1749 part of the blockhouse was swept away.[4] By 1761 it was completely in ruins, and it was later removed to permit the building of a wall to support the sea-front road at the foot of Ship Street. The new sea defences were paid for out of a duty of 6d a chaldron levied by a Town Act of 1772 on all the coal brought into the town by sea.[5] There was a measure of justice in this, since the cliffs had been weakened by the many gaps made by the colliers to bring their cargoes from the beach into the town.

The fear of foreign attack was still far from being absent and the anxie-ties of the townspeople were allayed by the erection in 1761 of new defences in the shape of a battery of eight guns at the bottom of East Street, where the East Gate of earlier times had stood.[6] But as so often happens, the building of the battery was little more than a gesture, for the eight guns were old ones, four of them known to be honeycombed with rust, and not to be relied upon for anything more than a ceremonial salute nor to be fired to any distance with safety, so that when in 1779 a French privateer appeared off Brighton and captured a coal-boat it was able to keep out of reach of the guns, and would have got away with its prize had not a British cutter intercepted it. The defence of the coast was delegated rather to a couple of horse-soldiers, in long scarlet cloaks, who patrolled up and down the shore 'making their utility understood by no one'.[7]

Some fourteen years later these poor defences were improved by the building of two new batteries, one on the West Cliff with eight 36-pounder guns, and the other on the East Cliff, with four of the same calibre. The guns were from French ships, captured by Lord Howe in his victory of 1st June 1794. The former battery stood near the site of the Grand Hotel and is commemorated by the name of Artillery Street near by. The other was on Marine Parade, but after about ten years the vibration caused by the firing of the guns and the encroachments of the sea made the walls dangerous and it was dismantled.

For centuries most of the centre of the town, at least between West Street and Black Lion Street, consisted of open fields, for these were the Hempshares, open plots or holdings where hemp was grown for the making of ropes and cordage.

As the population grew, and the encroachments of the sea reduced the number of houses, two new streets were built on the Hempshares. These two streets took their names from the two inns that stood in them, and became Black Lion Street and Ship Street. The Black Lion Inn, which had taken its own name from Derek Carver's Brewery, became a private house early in the nineteenth century and vanished many years ago. The ground to the west of the town, where Brunswick Square and its twin terraces now stand, was devoted to the growing of flax for the making of linen thread and cloth. No one living in Brighton early in the eighteenth century could have dreamed that in no more than a hundred years the sea-front of the town would present one of the most magnificent façades in Europe, consisting of a panorama nearly three miles long of stately classical buildings in crescents, squares and terraces, with fronts of white stucco or iridescent black tiles; pediments and porticoes, columns and pilasters.

In those early years of the eighteenth century Brighton was in a wretchedly insignificant state. Humbled by the burning of their town by the French and by the devastations of the sea, the inhabitants seemed hardly to dare to raise the roofs of their houses above the level of the ground and indeed it was said[8] that the place had escaped destruction by the French at several times only because it was built so low that the cannon-balls of the enemy flew over the town. By 1740, when the population reached its lowest point, there cannot have been more than about 1,000[9] inhabitants, and it was thought that in a few years it would be utterly depopulated. Yet even in those days, when the people of Brighton seemed depressed beyond the hope of recovery, there were some who were aware of those beauties that have attracted visitors to the place ever since—the glittering sea, the brilliant sunshine, the intoxicating air, and at that time what can no longer be seen from the town itself, the encircling ring of green downs. In the 1730s and 1740s, we are told,[10] there were 'visitors of distinction' who made the journey to Brighton as soon as the deep narrow lanes through the clay-lands of the Sussex Weald became passable. In winter Brighton was then almost as completely cut off from the rest of England as she had been in early times, except by sea, and the inland roads were so bad that one lady mentioned by Defoe could only get to church by having her coach dragged through the clay by a team of six oxen. The townsfolk had hardly yet learned to provide for the needs of visitors. That peculiar institution, the seaside lodging house, had not yet come into being, the only accommodation was provided by a few inns and rooms in private houses.

Not long after the death of Tettersell the Old Ship Inn passed in 1714 into the possession of Richard Rogers, but by 1733 William Hicks was proprietor, and during his lifetime the ancient building was rebuilt and enlarged. By this time the Old Ship was the principal hostelry and the chief posting and coach house of the town. In earlier days it had sometimes taken as long as a week to reach Brighton from London, but in 1745 a coach aptly (for those days) named *The Flying Machine* left the Old Ship at 5.30 in the morning and arrived in Southwark some twelve hours later. The impressions of one of the visitors to Brighton in those days have been recorded for posterity in a letter written to a friend in July 1736. He was the Rev. William Clarke, known as 'mild William Clarke, rector of Buxted and an antiquary.' He wrote:

'We are now sunning ourselves upon the beach at Brighthelmston, and observing what a tempting figure this Island made formerly in the eyes of those gentlemen who were pleased to civilize and subdue it. Such a tract of sea; such regions of corn; and such an extent of fine carpet, that gives your eye the command of it all. But the mischief is, that we have little conversation besides the *clamor nauticus*, which is a sort of treble to the plashing of the waves against the cliffs. My morning business is bathing in the sea, and then buying fish; the evening is riding out for air, viewing the remains of old Saxon camps, and counting the ships in the road, and the boats that are trawling. Sometimes we give the imagination leave to expiate a little—fancy that you are coming down, and that we intend next week to dine one day in Dieppe in Normandy . . .' (a weekly sailing packet-boat service had just been established between Brighton and Dieppe.) 'But though we build these castles in the air, I assure you that we live here *almost underground*. I fancy that the architects here usually take the altitude of the inhabitants, and lose not an inch between the head and the ceiling, and then dropping a step or two below the surface, the second storey is finished in something under 12 feet. I suppose this was a necessary precaution against storms, that a man should not be blown out of his bed into New England, Barbary or God knows where. But as the lodgings are *low* they are cheap; we have *two parlours, two bed chambers, pantry, &c,* for 5s per week; and if you will really come down you need not fear a bed of the proper dimensions. And then the coast is safe; the cannons are all covered with rust and grass; the ships moored, and no enemy apprehended. Come and see. . . . How you would surprise all your Friends in Fleet Street, to tell them you were just come from France, with a vivacity that everybody would believe to be just imported from thence!'

Already there was an appreciation of the heightening of one's spirits that resulted from a visit to Brighton!

So we see that Mr. Clarke was bathing in the sea at Brighton in 1736, and writing of it as a matter of course, years before Dr. Russell came from Lewes and made sea-bathing part of a fashionable medical treatment. Indeed, the sea-water cure itself was apparently being practised in Brighton at least as early as 1641, according to an entry in the Brighton Parish Register for 12th November, which records the burial of 'Mary Askall, a woman who came for cure'. It is hardly likely that the town in those days could have offered any other remedy but that of the sea.

The practice may be said to have become an organized pursuit with the invention of the bathing-machine. The earliest record of these devices seems to be a print of 1735 showing a bathing-machine on the beach at Scarborough.[11] They were undoubtedly in use at Brighton by 1750, probably even earlier. The virtually complete disappearance of them from our coasts since the last war makes it necessary to explain to modern readers that these machines were like small sheds or sentry-boxes on wheels, or, as A. W. Lower describes them in 1865,[12] like 'little Noah's arks on wheels', and were used as dressing-rooms by bathers who entered them on the beach and were then drawn in them out into the required depth of water by horses.

In 1796 a writer remarked that the Brighton female bathers were 'all severely inspected by the aid of telescopes, not only as they confusedly ascend from the sea, but as they kick and sprawl and flounder about its muddy margins, like so many mad Naiads in flannel smocks'.[13]

Bathing-costumes were not worn by men until about 1863. Women wore long flannel gowns, but there were instances, certainly at Scarborough[14] and probably elsewhere, of women also bathing naked. To obviate the scandal of naked figures being seen from the beach, bonnet-shaped canvas screens or 'modesty-hoods' fitted over the steps of bathing-machines, which are believed to have been the invention of a Quaker named Benjamin Beale, were introduced at Margate and adopted later at Weymouth and Scarborough. The air of permissiveness which has always prevailed at Brighton was apparent in this connection, for the canvas hoods seem never to have come into use here on the central beaches of the town, but only at the more genteel district of Kemp Town in the late Georgian period.

The business of sea-bathing was a highly practical matter into which the fisherfolk plunged with enthusiasm. It was concerned with an unpredictable and sometimes dangerous element in dealing with which they were the acknowledged experts, and it gave employment not only to themselves, when not engaged in fishing, but also to their womenfolk, in acting as attendants to the bathers, their function being principally to ensure that their charges were very thoroughly immersed. The attendants for men were called 'bathers', the brawny and muscular hand-maidens of lady bathers being known as 'dippers', the term possibly deriving from the women attendants known as 'dippers' who officiated at mineral water spas. The former were led by 'Smoaker' Miles, the latter by the redoubtable Martha Gunn. It would seem that they were first established about 1750 and for at least thirty years their rule remained unchallenged, until an advertisement appearing in the *Lewes Journal* in March 1780 indicated the rise of an opposition in the form of 'five strong women, all used to the sea' who had 'fitted up a set of NEW MACHINES, with a careful man and horse to conduct them in and out of the water'. By this time the increased number of visitors called for additional bathing-attendants.

7 Dr. Russell and the Sea-water Cure

In 1753 Dr. Richard Russell, a physician of Lewes who for three years had been sending sick people to Brighton to undertake the sea-water cure, found his patients so numerous and the treatment so remarkably successful that he decided to move his residence to the coast, and Brighton was at the dawn of its golden age. For £40 the doctor bought some land at the southern end of the Steyne where the Royal Albion Hotel now stands, and there built a house which he called Russell House, and which was conveniently near the beach for those patients whom the doctor had to stay with him. It must have been one of the most substantial houses in the town at that time, built of red brick and white stone, with round-headed windows in angular bays and an impressive pedimented doorway on the north side. In 1771, some years after the doctor's death, and for several following seasons, the house was rented by the Duke of Cumberland, and at those times became the centre of the fashionable Brighton society led by the Duke and his Duchess.

Dr. Russell was far from being the first to proclaim the virtues of the sea-water cure, for nearly a hundred years earlier, in 1660, a Dr. Wittie of Scarborough had published a book recommending the use of sea-water both internally and externally, and by this means widened the attractions of Scarborough.

By the end of the century the sea-water treatment was well established, and in 1702 two London practitioners, Sir John Floyer and Edward Baynard, published praises of the cure in a volume in which asthma, cancer, consumption, deafness, ruptures, rheumatism and madness were shown to be among the diseases it could banish. Carried away with enthusiasm, the distinguished authors burst into verse:

> *Cold bathing has this good alone:*
> *It makes old John to hug old Joan!*
> *And does fresh kindnesses entail*
> *On a wife tasteless, old and stale.*

From the days of sea-bathing to those of royal jelly and wheat-germ oil the prospect of renewed sexual vitality has always been the surest guarantee of a cure's success.

Dr. Richard Russell was a native of Lewes, and had made a runaway marriage with the only daughter of William Kemp of Malling Deanery at

South Malling near Lewes. He had become reconciled with his father-in-law and went to study medicine at Leyden University, where he took his degree as a doctor in 1724. His professor was the famous Herman Boerhaave, a physician and botanist of European repute. In fact, a medicine known as 'Dr. Boerhaave's Elixir' was frequently advertised in the *Sussex Weekly Advertiser* in the latter years of the eighteenth century. Returning to England, he practised as a doctor at Lewes, living at Malling Deanery after the death of his father-in-law. In 1750 he published the work by which he hoped to establish his simple treatment as a major contribution towards the science of medicine: *DeTabe Glandulari; sui De Usu Aquae Marinae in Morbis Glandularum Dissertatio*. An unauthorized English translation 'by an eminent physician' was published in 1752, with the title *Dissertation on the Use of Sea Water in Diseases of the Glands*. This pirated edition was published also in Dublin in 1753, but an authorized translation was published at Oxford in the same year.

In its various editions the work was so successful, though not always with direct benefit to the author, that other editions were produced in 1755, 1760 and 1769. Both the original work and the official translation were published under the imprimatur of the Vice-Chancellor of Oxford University by the University Press, and the title-page bore a representation of the Radcliffe Camera at Oxford. When the question of establishing a university at Brighton was being discussed a few years ago many persons were of the opinion that Brighton, as a town dedicated to pleasures not invariably of the most high-minded order, was hardly the obvious place in which to set up a great seat of learning. It is an intriguing thought, therefore, that as suggested by Professor Gilbert,[1] it was the ancient University of Oxford that in a sense sponsored the foundation of Brighton as a modern resort.

The popularity of Dr. Russell's work must have continued for many years for in 1780 Fanny Burney mentioned in one of her letters[2] that Mrs. Thrale overheard a Brighton visitor in Bowen's circulating library asking for 'Russell on Sea-water'.

The popularity of the work with the public is in one sense difficult to understand, for the book does not make pleasant reading. Among the instances of diseases which Dr. Russell claimed to have cured—he refers to them with professional relish as 'ellegant cases'—are examples of maladies often too revolting to describe. Most of them were in the nature of tumours, eruptions, 'fluxions of redundant tumours', and 'imposthumes' or purulent swellings and abscesses. But no doubt a morbid curiosity over the details of human ailments, as well as hope and anxiety over the possibility of one's own particular malady being found to be curable, was as in all ages a powerful incentive to buying the book. The remedies suggested were often as revolting as the diseases themselves; in fact, it might have been believed by many that, by some process of sympathetic magic, it was appropriate they should be so. It would never have done for the treatment to consist simply of sea-bathing or a drink of ordinary sea-water. Were this so there would have been no need for the medical profession at all. The doctor obviously believed that desperate diseases required desperate remedies, and so he experimented with sea-water taken in conjunction with concoctions of crab's eyes, coral, burnt sponge, viper's flesh, cuttle-fish bones, snails, tar and 'prepared wood lice'. Doses of these were taken at night in a pill or bolus followed in the morning by a draught of a pint or half a pint of sea-water. 'A pint', observed Dr. Russell with professional enthusiasm, would be 'commonly sufficient, in grown Persons, to give 3 or 4 sharp stools'. One hardly feels inclined to question the truth of this. In addition to these rigours the patient was usually compelled to undergo a severe course of blood-letting, the amount taken at one time varying from six to as much as fifty ounces.

Dr. Russell's work opens with a solemn prelude in which he speaks of 'That vast collection of waters . . . which we call the Sea, and which the omniscient Creator of all Things seems to have designed to be a Kind of common Defence against the Corruption and Putrefaction of Bodies'. Like other writers on the sea-water cure, Dr. Russell invoked the names of ancient physicians and naturalists such as Pliny, Hippocrates, Celsus and many others, in giving his work an air of venerable authority, and thus preventing his treatment from being regarded as a quack remedy, or at best as based on a mass of popular superstitions. 'I might claim', he wrote, 'the Credit of having brought a medicine of the ancient Physicians again into Practice that had been too little regarded.' He acknowledges nevertheless that in 1730 he had read a work entitled *The Domestic Companion* in which the use of sea-water was commended as a purge, especially useful to sailors, and that he had observed that the inhabitants of the sea-coast often made use of sea-water in healing diseases. Even the simple practice of sea-bathing was to be invested with a proper air of solemnity, if the utmost benefit was to be obtained from its use. 'A perfect repose of the Body, and Calmness of the Mind, is to be observed before the Use of the Cold Bath', he wrote, 'and all the Exercise of the parts effected must be forborn, that the Fibres by these means, when they contract themselves may have the greater Force to overcome any Obstruction.'

Here we find the doctor anticipating, with what intuitive common sense, the modern technique of relaxation, now so universally commended. He advised further: 'The greatest care is to be taken, to know whether the Bowels are sound or not before the Use of the Bath. . . . A little Draught of the Sea-Water is convenient immediately upon coming up out of the Sea; because by purging the Body, it prevents the Blood from flying into the Head.' 'Many persons', he also warned his followers, 'are apt to hurry into a course of bathing before the body is altered and sufficiently prepared by drinking sea-water, or by a previous course of other remedies; which hurry is always detrimental to the patient, by protracting his cure.'

Many genuine and even startling cures seem to have been effected, possibly in spite of the wood lice and viper's flesh, no doubt by the sea-water acting as a mild disinfectant and cleanser when used externally, and as a strong purge when drunk, when in those days the habit of frequent washing had by no means become general, and when many people indulged in spectacular overeating and drinking, or at best lived on hopelessly unsuitable diets. Another important factor in curing diseases of the glands, such as goitre, a swelling of the thyroid gland in the throat, often known as 'Derbyshire Neck', from which people suffered in those days more commonly than now, was the fact that by merely living at the sea, and even more by drinking sea-water and bathing, they absorbed great quantities of iodine, the lack of which is one of the chief causes of the complaint. Indeed, the Prince of Wales himself seems to have suffered from this malady, as was apparent from his rather protuberant eyes. It is also supposed that he wore his customary high cravat, which immediately became fashionable, so as to hide the swelling of his throat, and it has been stated by several writers that he first came to Brighton in order to cure his affected glands by means of the sea-water treatment.*

Dr. Russell again brought a modern note into his writings, when he spoke of sea-water as having a detergent action, which must have been invaluable in those many cases of illness that were due to sheer dirt. An especially beneficial practice which he recommended was to give affected parts, especially in cases of tumours and eruptions, a 'mild friction' several times daily, with *Quercus Marina*, a kind of seaweed called sea-wrack, freshly taken from the water. Russell again spoke of its saponiferous and detergent action. Despite the doctor's fondness for medieval remedies like wood lice and viper's flesh, some of his ideas were so advanced that they were not generally accepted until modern times, especially where the treatment of delicate children was concerned. He advocated giving them fresh air and removing the heavy clothing in which they were often muffled up. 'I have had children sent to me,' he wrote, 'weak, pale, loaded with hair, their necks and throats wrapt up in flannel, and in short the whole texture of the body relaxed, by too hot clothing, and night sweats; whom I have returned to their parents, bare necked, their heads shaved, the tumours of the neck cured, and their whole countenance healthy, after having strengthened them by bathing in the sea.' Relieved of their stifling clothes, and after bathing in the sea, and running about on the beach in the sunshine, they soon became as healthy and vigorous as the children of the fisherfolk.

Dr. Russell had observed that fisherwomen have 'generally white teeth and firm gums', and he believed the reason for this lay in the fact 'that the surrounding atmosphere is loaded with saline particles which rise from the surface of the sea, or rather are forced off by the dashing of the waves'. Consequently he was led to conclude that 'sea-water is an excellent dentifrice', and the doctor was most probably correct in this particular. All over the world, from Brighton to Tristan da Cunha, fisherfolk have been noted for the remarkable quality of their teeth, but this is more certainly due to the ample fresh vitamins and natural mineral salts they derived from the fish that formed their staple food, and in this respect they were probably more fortunate than poor townspeople, especially those inland, who lived on a more limited diet. The author was told by a Brighton woman of remarkable health and physique, with wonderful teeth, who came from an exceedingly poor family, that when she was a child in the 1930s she and other poor children would go to the fishmarket on the beach early every morning and assuage their perpetual hunger by eating the offal removed by the fishermen when cleaning the fish they had caught. This offal, especially the fish-roes and livers, was undoubtedly extremely rich in fresh natural vitamins, mineral salts and protein, which must have compensated very largely for the poverty and scantiness of other food.

The fisherfolk of Brighton had welcomed the advent of Dr. Russell with enthusiasm, for he encouraged people to require their services for the hire of bathing-machines and dipping the bathers. Their joy can have known no bounds when they realized that as well as all this sea-water could actually be *sold* to people living at a distance who wished to drink the magical 'oceanic fluid', as one contemporary writer rather excruciatingly described it. And so we find an advertisement appearing in a London journal in 1756 announcing that 'Sea-water, from Brighthelmstone, in Sussex, took of the main Ocean by T. Swaine' could be bought at the Talbot Inn in Southwark, and before long sea-water was being sold at Tunbridge Wells and other inland towns. Although the doctor elaborated at length on the sea-water treatment, he was far too astute to neglect those invalids who were convinced that they derived the greatest benefit from drinking the waters of a mineral spring. Indeed, taking the water was one of the most agreeable and sociable diversions to be enjoyed at any health resort, and the existence of a small spa on the outskirts of Brighton was probably one of the factors which had attracted a number of visitors to Brighton in search of health, and which caused the doctor to come to the town. The spa was a chalybeate spring known as St. Anne's Well, at the Wick, half a mile west of St. Nicholas's Church, and now in Hove. Dr. Russell is said to have made this primitive little spa more impressive and convenient by having the spring 'enclosed within a bason'. Later a furnished Pump Room was built in the form of a low classical building with an Ionic portico, but this delightful little spa was quite needlessly

54

destroyed by Hove Corporation in 1935. The success of Dr. Russell's sea-water cure made a great impression on the medical faculty throughout the country. He corresponded with several of the most noted physicians of his day, and was elected a Fellow of the Royal Society in 1752. In 1754 Dr. Russell published another work, *The Oeconomy of Nature in Acute and Chronical Diseases of the Glands*, in which he dealt with the treatment of tubercular glands by means of sea-water.

Professor Gilbert tells[3] us that the Doctor retained many contacts with Oxford, visiting and corresponding with his friends Dr. Frewin and Dr. Lewis there, and that Russell's books were being read on the Continent as well as in England far into the nineteenth century. In his poem 'La Mer' (1861) Michelet called him 'l'inventeur de la mer'.

While visiting a friend in London, Dr. Russell died there on 19th December 1759, and he was buried on Christmas Day at South Malling Church, where there is a tablet to his memory in the chancel. It bears upon it the same line in Greek from the *Iphigenia in Tauris* of Euripides that is quoted on the frontispiece of his book—'The sea washes away all the ills of mankind.' Another memorial tablet was placed in modern times on the outside of the Royal Albion Hotel recording his having resided at that site. Borrowing the words of Sir Christopher Wren's epitaph in St. Paul's Cathedral, the tablet reads: 'If you seek his monument, look around'. While no one can deny the magnificence of his memorial, in the splendid terraces and crescents of Brighton sea-front, a more original Latin epigram about the doctor was written by one of his friends, Dr. Simon Manningham, Rector of Jevington:

> *Clara, per omne aevum,*
> *Russelli fama manebit,*
> *Dum retinet vires unda*
> *marina suas.*

A contemporary translation reads more euphoniously than the original:

> *Admiring ages Russell's*
> *fame shall know,*
> *Till Ocean's healing*
> *waters cease to flow.*

An imposing portrait of Dr. Russell by Benjamin Wilson hung in the Assembly Rooms of the Old Ship Hotel for many years, and it was believed that it had been commissioned by William Hicks, the proprietor of the hotel, in recognition of the benefit to his own prosperity which had resulted from the doctor's activities. Benjamin Wilson, one of the most fashionable portrait painters of his day, had also acquired a considerable reputation as a man of learning for his interests in chemistry and electricity, and was elected a Fellow of the Royal Society in 1756. He must have met Dr. Russell at many of the Society's functions. It is said that having first been hung in the Coffee-room of the hotel the portrait was removed to 'the noble Card Room' when that room was completed about 1768 as being 'the most honourable place which could be assigned to it, the room being constantly resorted to by the rank and fashion visiting the town'. It hung there until 1887, when it was presented to the town by Mr. Robert Bacon and Alderman Samuel Ridley, who were then joint proprietors of the Hotel. The portrait, in which the doctor is depicted wearing a full-bottomed wig and an expression of pompous complacency, now hangs in the principal hall of the Brighton Art Gallery.*

Dr. Russell's properties and estate were bequeathed by him to his wife, Mary Russell, and after to his son William, who became a barrister and took his mother's maiden name of Kempe. Serjeant Kempe gained a great reputation as a wit, and was the author of some well-known but rather excruciating lines in which possibly for the first time Brighton is commemorated as a place favoured by the appropriately sea-born goddess Aphrodite as well as by the nymph Hygeia:

> *Brighthelmstone was confess'd by all*
> *T' abound with females fair,*
> *But more so since fam'd Russell has*
> *Preferred the waters there.*

> *Then fly that dangerous town ye swains,*
> *For fear ye shall endure*
> *A pain from some bright sparkling eye*
> *Which Russell's skill can't cure.*

The venerable doctor himself might have been astonished to learn that it was his own son who attributed to him the responsibility for establishing Brighton's reputation as a town dedicated to amorous pursuits.

There must have been many physicians who were envious of the fame and also possibly of the wealth that was undoubtedly acquired by Dr. Russell in his practice, and possibly there were a number of doctors who pursued a similar treatment with their patients. Consequently we find not a little competition after the doctor's death amongst those wishing to succeed to his lucrative practice. In March 1760 the *Sussex Weekly Advertiser* announced that a Dr. Poole 'Will attend at Brighthelmstone during the ensuing season', and in July a Dr. Schomberg made no secret of his ambitions when in the same paper it was stated that he was 'settled at Brighthelmstone to succeed the late Dr. Russell there'. The great man's mantle, however, descended more truly upon the shoulders of Dr. Anthony Relhan. Relhan was an Irishman who had antagonized the College of

Physicians in Dublin by advising the use by his patients of a proprietary medicine called Dr. James's Fever-powder, the formula for which was kept secret and which was believed to be highly dangerous.

On Dr. James's own advice, which Relhan sought, he settled in London. He married the widow of a London banker, Sir William Hart, and she had a house built in East Street, Brighton, for their summer residence. Dr. Relhan took over the greater part of Dr. Russell's practice, coming down to Brighton for several months every year until his death in 1766.

The work in which he embodied his observations upon Brighton was not as elaborate a medical treatise as Dr. Russell's; it took instead the form of *A Short History of Brighthelmston, with Remarks on its Air and Analysis of its Waters*, published in London in 1761. It was, in fact, the first guide to Brighton, and he attracted many wealthy and fashionable visitors to the town with his enthusiastic descriptions of the place, which he compared more than favourably with the ancient resort of Baiae in Campania, where wealthy Romans retired for bathing and pleasure. He gave Brighton the preference not least because of the fortunate fact of its being removed from 'the dangerous vicinity of Mount Vesuvius'. Dr. Relhan broke fresh ground in expounding the virtues of Brighton's soil and climate. 'Chalky ground', he observed, 'has no perspiration, and therefore must be extremely healthy.' He noted also that the absence of a river was one of Brighton's especial advantages: 'As the nearest river to the town is really distant six miles, and as this is a circumstance peculiar to itself, no other maritime town being equally remote from one, I may venture to affirm that the soil here is extremely dry, and that the air of this place must be proportionately pure.'

If Dr. Russell 'invented' the sea, then it was Dr. Relhan who invented the Brighton air. He observed how the town was refreshed in summer by a 'tempering breeze', and how in winter frost and snow are quickly banished by a warm sea wind, and he commented upon that most distinctive aspect of Brighton's summer climate, the prevalence of breezes which are at their freshest and coolest on the hottest days. In short, being free, as Relhan maintained, from the 'insalutary vapour of stagnant water' and the 'noxious steam of perspiring trees', Brighton's climate in his opinion could only be compared to that of the Elysium of the poets, a belief he supported by appropriate quotations from Homer.

Relhan continued Dr. Russell's policy in advising the drinking of sea-water, and remarked that the proportion of salt in the sea at Brighton was probably greater than at any other seaside place in England, because of its distance from any rivers. He also wrote a long account of the water of the chalybeate spring at St. Anne's Well, after analysing it in various ways, and concluded that, while it should be used with caution, in suitable cases the drinking of the water was likely to be followed by 'an increase of appetite and spirits, and in habits of a lax and feeble nature an additional power of exercising without lassitude'. Furthermore he offered the comforting information that 'bodies labouring under the consequences of irregular living and illicit pleasures were by the water greatly relieved'. The waters of the well had some reputation for promoting fruitfulness, local shepherds having observed the remarkable fecundity of the sheep that drank from it, but Dr. Relhan was somewhat sceptical about its having a similar effect with human beings. Another Brighton physician, Dr. Richard Henderson, remarked that its taste was 'not unpleasant, something like that upon a Knife after it has been used in cutting lemons', which bears out the notion that the water was rich in iron. This belief was later confirmed by an analysis made by Dr. Marcet, which showed that the water contained more than one grain of oxide of iron to the pint.[4]

St. Anne's Well continued to enjoy a gradually diminishing popularity as a spa until after the middle of the nineteenth century, but the Pump Room and the surrounding grounds remained a fashionable resort for recreation for many years after that time. In the long succession of Brighton doctors the third most famous figure after Russell and Relhan was John Awsiter, who in 1768 published in London a pamphlet entitled *Thoughts on Brighthelmston concerning sea-bathing and drinking sea-water with some directions for their use.*

These three personages in Brighton's early development stand out like priestly wizards or Magi, who offered to the town the gifts of their discoveries, Russell and Relhan bringing the knowledge of sea-water bathing and drinking and of the air of Brighton. The gift of the third was indoor sea-bathing, a cult which persisted in Brighton for over a century, but for which unhappily no proper provision has been made since the 1930s in Brighton itself. In this regard Hove has been more enterprising.

In his pamphlet Dr. Awsiter stated that he had 'not been at Brighthelmston above three days' when he came to the conclusion that 'a further discussion' of sea-bathing and sea-water drinking was necessary. He had quickly realized that the sometimes all-too-bracing winds of Brighton and the wave-battered, pebbly beach were often too fiercely uncomfortable and terrifying, especially to feeble invalids and timid ladies, and proposed that hot and cold sea-water baths should be provided 'for those who are so unhappy as to be invalids'. By this means, he went on, 'bathing would become more universal, be unattended with terror, and no cure protracted and the stay of the company prolonged. Moreover invalids would have the advantage of this bathing remedy all the year round, whereas, on account of the variableness of our climate, it is denied them at present, except in the summer months and then only in calm weather.' The doctor especially advocated the use of hot sea-water baths, which would cause the pores of the skin to open and allow the 'poisonous humours' to be released.

Although, as Dr. Awsiter wrote, 'The town of Brighthelmston has been

58

much favoured by the countenance of many noble and genteel families
. . .', the town authorities were not yet alive to the desirability of providing attractions for visitors, nor could any private speculator be found
who would embark on the building of baths, and so the doctor eventually
felt constrained to undertake their erection himself. He employed as
architect Robert Golden 'of London', who probably came to the doctor's
notice by his being engaged also to design the new Assembly Rooms at the
Old Ship Hotel at the same time. The foundation-stone was laid in 1769.

Dr. Awsiter's Baths took the form of a small single-storey classical
building with a pediment and dentil cornice and round-headed windows.
The façade bore the grandiloquent dedication 'Hygea Devota' and the
more practical designation also, 'Hot and Cold Baths'. The building was
on the western side of Pool Valley, near the beach, from whence sea-
water was pumped to the baths by an 'engine' presumably driven by
steam. The pipes from the sea were laid in a groyne that was built for the
purpose extending a hundred feet into the sea.[5] On top of the groyne was
a pump-house that was a familiar landmark on Brighton beach until it was
demolished in 1826.

Dr. Awsiter by no means neglected the drinking of sea-water, of the
virtue of which so many visitors were by now deeply convinced, but he
recognized that 'there are many constitutions too delicate, and stomachs
too weak to bear the nausea and sickness it produces, and even where this
inconvenience is overcome by struggles, it makes the party very thirsty for
the remainder of the day'. The idea of making the sea-water more palatable
by mixing it with milk was a brilliant inspiration, especially as the latter
itself was often regarded in those days as more of a medicine than a food,
and so, he wrote, 'they became a noble medicine, they are correctors to
each other, and neither the milk or sea-water, so combined, will disagree
with the stomach that could not bear either of them separately'. The doctor
placed especial reliance upon the following prescription: 'Take of sea-
water and milk each four ounces; put them over the fire; and when they
begin to boil, add a sufficiency of Cremor [Cream of] Tartar to turn into
whey, strain it from the curd, and when cool drink it.' It was with something of a note of triumph that he also announced that sea-salt was a
'present cure for the bite of a mad dog', and followed Dr. Russell in
recommending that for such cases the salt should be dissolved in human
urine and applied to the wound, when it would act 'in destroying the
acrimony and poisonous quality of sores and wounds, and as such dis-
posing them to heal'. Any patient who might have been reluctant to
pursue such a remedy was probably encouraged by the doctor's advice
that in such cases he should not 'live low, but moderately indulge himself
with wine'.

Finally Awsiter cited the particular virtue of sea-water in cases of barrenness, when he looked upon it 'to stand before all other remedies. There is a remarkable fecundity in sea-water', he wrote, 'beyond even the much-famed mud of the River Nile.' With such a variety of intriguing remedies recommended with pontifical authority by three physicians of such impressive standing as Russell, Relhan and Awsiter, as well as by a host of minor followers, the success of Brighton as a health resort was assured.

8 Fashionable Visitors

lthough the fisherfolk had been quick to adapt themselves to the needs of the visitors, it was more than twenty-five years after the publication of Dr. Russell's book before there was any substantial change in the buildings of the town. A visitor in the 1750s describes the Brighton houses as consisting of only one or two storeys, with doorways so low that one must stoop to enter, and then probably stumble down one or two steps into the sitting-room. For more than a century after the burning of Brighton by the French in 1514 the houses were most probably built of timber and weatherboarding, many of them, especially those nearer the sea, tarred to give some protection against the weather. Possibly the only exceptions were the church of St. Nicholas and the Vicarage in the Bartholomews, which incorporated in its fabric part of the ruins of the ancient priory, which also had been burnt in the fire. It was probably early in the seventeenth century that a greater number of buildings were erected with the flint-cobble walls and red brickwork at the angles and round the apertures of doors and windows that are mentioned by Dr. Relhan in 1761,[1] and by other writers since. Nevertheless Dr. Relhan, who had a vested interest in the success of Brighton, spoke enthusiastically about the progress made in the town. 'It improves daily,' he wrote in 1761, 'as the inhabitants encouraged by the late resort of company, seem disposed to expend the whole of what they acquire in the erection of new buildings, or making the old ones convenient.' Yet at that time the population numbered only four hundred families, who were for the most part too poor to spend any money on building improvements, 'their not being any person of fortune in the Town', as John Warburton wrote,[2] 'but one Masters, a gentleman of good birth'.

The town still consisted of only six principal streets, with no houses extending beyond North Street, West Street and the Steyne on the east, except for Thomas's Circulating Library on its far side. As one stood on the outskirts of the half-mile square of buildings and looked around there was nothing beyond but a wide half-circle of green downland and cornfields. Many visitors found the place quite unattractive. 'Gilly' Williams, a well-known wit and friend of Horace Walpole who went to Brighton in 1763 for the sea-bathing, found that 'the regimen agrees with me so perfectly well, that as long as the weather will give us leave, I propose to follow it', but tried to dissuade his friend George Selwyn from coming down. 'As to the lodgings in this place,' he wrote, 'the best are most execrable, and what you would find now, I believe, not habitable.'[3] Even as late as 1787 a Mrs. Hill[4] was complaining of 'doors opening direct into the sitting-rooms', which caused her the inconvenience of not being able to be 'out' to unwanted visitors. Even the newer houses were often built in this fashion, with only one principal room on each of three or four storeys. The traditional method of vernacular building with flint and brick was popular when a great deal of new buildings took place in East Street and other old streets of the town in the 1770s, and continued into the 1790s, when the tall terraces of houses were built on the Steyne fronting the recently erected Marine Pavilion of the Prince of Wales. In the houses of this period the window bays rose through two or three storeys, but stopped short below the roof parapet, and were finished off with a light dentil cornice. A few of these attractive houses now survive in Charles Street and elsewhere, but are rapidly disappearing.

The tall houses with strongly curved bow-windows crowned with a deep frieze and boldly projecting cornice-moulding belong to the late Georgian period of the 1820s. The bow-windows which we now look upon as such charming and distinctive features of Regency architecture, especially at the seaside, seem to have had their earliest general development at Brighton, after being introduced into domestic architecture by Robert Adam in the 1760s. Peregrine Phillips, the author of a rare work known as *Bew's Diary*,[5] wrote in 1778: 'This town is built in spots, in patches, and for want of regularity does not appear to advantage: every man, as to building, seems to have done what appeared right in his eyes.' The following year he writes: 'Am viewing my worthy friend, Mr. Bull's house, or rather box, upon the Clift, between Ship Street and Black Lion Street. He beckons me in, and shews it throughout. It is one pretty room to the height of three storeys, with a semi-circular window comprising most of the front, and on each floor overlooking the sea all ways, which makes the situation most delightful.' Peregrine Phillips was a 'whimsical writer, fraught with variety and some pleasantry', who seems to have aroused some agitation at Brighton by his outspoken comments on such matters as the stupidity of the local parsons as expressed in their sermons and the churlishness of the waiters in the taverns, to such as extent that the seats along the Cliff became miraculously empty as he approached, so greatly did their occupants fear being 'taken off' in some subsequent instalment of the *Diary*. A favourite haunt where he could be sure as a rule of overhearing some intriguing gossip was the little covered wooden seat with an arched and pointed roof called The Alcove which stood facing eastwards in front of Dr. Russell's old house, and which is shown in a delightful drawing in the Royal Pavilion collection.

One particular visitor to Brighton in the 1770s found nothing in the town itself to arouse his interest. This was the Rev. William Gilpin, the celebrated water-colour painter and one of the principal exponents of the cult of the 'Picturesque', for whom scenic beauty was compounded of stock effects found in the ideal landscapes of the classical painters like Claude and Salvator Rosa, and composed according to strict philosophical ideas on the nature of beauty. To him the whole of the South Coast was too 'tame'; a truly beautiful coastline should consist, Gilpin considered, not of stark chalk cliffs and bare stretches of pebbly shore, but of 'winding bays—promontories—rocks of every kind and form—estuaries—mouths of rivers—islands—shooting peninsulas—extensive sandbanks; and all the furniture of navigation', just as in one of the great seascapes of Claude Lorrain. In the summer of 1774 Mr. Gilpin had been making a tour of Hampshire, Sussex and Kent in search of subjects for one of the series of illustrated books he was producing on the picturesque scenery of Britain, but he found little to please him in the harsh coastline of Brighton, and in the straight streets of little houses huddled into a square and surrounded by bare fields and downland, unrelieved by a single tree—'a disagreeable place', he called it. 'There is scarcely an object in it or near it of nature or of art, that strikes the eye with any degree of beauty', but then one day as Mr. Gilpin watched the commonplace scene on the beach there occurred one of those magical transformations of light that occur so often at Brighton, and touch everything with beauty. As though at a signal there was a quickening of activity among the fishing-boats riding offshore and a sudden bustle amongst the figures of fishermen on the beach, and in a flash the whole scene with 'all the furniture of navigation' seemed in a moment to have become like one of Claude's great marine compositions, depicting perhaps 'The Departure of Aeneas from Carthage', and suffused with the unearthly golden light of that master's paintings. 'One of the most picturesque sights we met with at Brighthelmstone', he afterwards wrote, 'was the sailing of a fleet of mackerel-boats to take their evening station for fishing, which they commonly continue through the night. The sun was just setting when they all appeared to be alive. Every boat began to weight anchor and unmoor. It was amusing to see them under so many different forms. Some in a still calm with flagging sails were obliged to assist their motion with oars; others were just getting into the breeze, which rippled the water around them, and began gently to swell their sails; while the fleet, the water and the whole horizon, glowed with one rich harmonious tint from the setting sun.'

One of the most important houses in Brighton about the middle of the eighteenth century was the old Manor House, a small red-brick building facing north at the south end of the Steine. From 1771 to 1792 it was occupied by Richard Scrase, one of the joint lords of the Manor of Brighthelmston. After his death it was enlarged and continued to exist until 1817, when it was demolished to make room for the Royal York

63

Hotel, now Royal York Buildings. Adjoining it on the east side was Russell House. Next to these two in importance was Marlborough House, facing eastwards from the west side of the Steine. This was built in 1769 by Samuel Shergold, the enterprising and far-seeing proprietor of the Castle Inn, for the better accommodation of fashionable visitors, and was probably the first house to be erected with this object in mind. When first built, of red brick and looking rather stilted, with its three storeys of height and steeply pitched tiled roof with dormer windows, it must have appeared already rather old-fashioned for its date, but it probably created quite an impression at the time amidst the low earlier houses round about, and no doubt it looked quite impressive with its white-painted dentil cornice giving a sparkle of light from the sun, and its small pedimented classical doorway. In 1771 it was sold to the Duke of Marlborough, who lived there during his visits to Brighton in a state of great opulence with a staff of forty servants.[6] The *Lewes Journal* commented: "'Tis incredible to think what a deal of money His Grace expends there, and the help he is to the poor. We are well assured that he buys half a bullock at a time, a whole calf, and his mutton by the carcase, so that, by the over-abundance of his tables the poor have joints given them hardly touch'd, which is a prodigious relief to numbers who at this dear time cannot afford to purchase butcher's meat; a worthy example and worthy of imitation.' During his absences, the Duke let off the rooms of the house separately to visitors, as many as fifty being accommodated there at one time.[7]

The Duke retained the house until 1786, when it was sold to William Gerald Hamilton, M.P. Fanny Burney said of him:[8] 'This Mr. Hamilton is extremely tall and handsome; has an air of haughty and fashionable superiority; is intelligent, dry, sarcastic and clever. I should have received much pleasure from his conversational powers had I not previously been prejudiced against him, by hearing that he is infinitely artful, double, and crafty.' He was known as 'Single-speech Hamilton' from the fact that early in the course of his long career in Parliament he made only one speech, when he spoke against the Government with such devastating effect that he was rendered silent for ever after by means of 'some douceur'.[9]

His keen taste and sensibility is shown by the fact of his employing Robert Adam, who for more than twenty-five years had been the most fashionable architect in Britain. In 1787 the house assumed its present form, which justifies its being regarded as the most distinguished individual building still standing in the town. Now the offices of the Education Department, it is remarkable in being one of the few surviving examples of a small domestic house designed by Robert Adam, embodying in a limited compass all the principles of elegance and refinement, and of charm and variety in the form and decoration of the rooms which had caused the Adam style to effect, in the words of Sir John Soane, an

KING GEORGE IV
by Sir Thomas Lawrence, 1822

PERSPECTIVE VIEW OF THE STEINE, 1778
by J. Donowell after Peter Mazell

BRIGHTON RACES, 1789
Water-colour by Thomas Rowlandson

DR. AWSITER'S BATHS, 1803
Engraved by S. Rawle after I. Nixon

BRIGHTON BEACH, *c.* 1795
Water-colour by Richard Earlom

THE CASTLE HOTEL BALLROOM, 1783

THE PRINCE REGENT ENTERING A BATHING-MACHINE AT BRIGHTON,
1818
Sepia drawing

THE MARINE PAVILION, 1801
Engraved by J. C. Newton

THE STEINE
showing Marlborough House (left) and Mrs. Fitzherbert's House (centre)

MRS. FITZHERBERT, 1785
Stipple engraving by John Condé after Richard
Cosway

GEORGE, PRINCE OF WALES, 1786
Engraved by Rafael Smith after T. Gainsborough

SAKE DEEN MAHOMED, SHAMPOOING SURGEON
TO H.M. KING GEORGE IV
Drawn and engraved by T. M. Baynes

THE PRINCESS CHARLOTTE, 1819
Engraving after A. E. Chalon

BRIGHTHELMSTON IN 1779
surveyed by T. Yeakell and W. Gardner and published by Richard Thomas

'electric revolution' in the field of domestic architecture and decoration. In particular the exquisite small octagonal Dining-room displays the same genius for creating a room of beautiful shape and proportion that is to be found on a larger scale at Syon House in Middlesex and Newby Hall in Yorkshire, and the Drawing-room (now a Committee-room) retains its original fireplace of Sicilian marble, with a finely carved centre plaque of Venus in a chariot drawn by Cupids. Robert Adam's original plans for the houses are preserved today at Sir John Soane's Museum in Lincoln's Inn Fields, London.

There were, contrary to general belief, several Royal visitors to Brighton before the Prince of Wales came to shed upon the town the lustre that henceforth marked it as a resort especially privileged among the towns of this country. The first was the Duke of Gloucester, who came on Thursday, 11th July 1765. He visited the Castle Tavern Assembly Rooms in the evening, and the next day breakfasted at Stanmer, the seat of Thomas Pelham, later to become first Earl of Chichester, who gave his guest an extremely lavish reception. Stanmer House, built between 1722 and 1727, was designed on true Palladian principles by Nicholas Dubois, an architect who, as the translator of the principal English edition of Palladio's works on architecture, exercised much influence in establishing in this country that harmonious phase of classical architecture which is named after the sixteenth-century Italian architect. The Pelhams had served the administration of this country for many years with a greater sense of integrity than of the possible opportunities for the founding of a large fortune, and consequently Stanmer was a rather more modest mansion than some of the great Palladian palaces that were being built about the same time for the leaders of the Whig oligarchy. Nevertheless Mr. Pelham spared no pains to make his Royal visitor's stay at Stanmer a pleasant one. It is recorded[10] that 'Whilst His Royal Highness was walking in the Groves of that delightful place he was most agreeably surprised with the Harmony of an excellent Band of Music, artfully stationed, who, unseen, saluted the Prince at each avenue.' This must indeed have provided in ample measure that element of 'the unexpected', which 'Mr. Gall', an exponent of the Picturesque, in Thomas Peacock's novel *Headlong Hall*, assured his friends was an essential ingredient in the creation of the perfect landscape garden.

The Stanmer Estate is now the property of the Brighton townspeople, by a purchase in 1947 which ranks with that of the Royal Pavilion in far-sightedness, and nowadays it is the cries of children and of cricketers or footballers rather than the sound of a 'Band of Music' that greet the ear of the visitor to the Park. Laid out soon after the middle of the eighteenth century by some pupil or rival of 'Capability' Brown, perhaps even by the master himself, the Park still retains much of its original character, with its lawns and slopes, its wooded hillsides and clumps of trees, and the impertinent pointed spire of the little church appearing at the focal point of the vista, all precisely disposed according to the artifices of English 'natural' picturesque landscape gardening. It is to be hoped, however, that there will be no further encroachments of municipal formality and over-neatness in the Park, where already some incongruous features have been admitted, such as a belt of flowering cherry trees round the skirt of a wooded hillside.

The exterior of Stanmer was plain and reticent in the best tradition of even the greatest Palladian houses, but the interior at the time of the Duke's visit, although consisting of only a few important rooms, was of fairly considerable splendour. It did not reach its finest state until some forty years later. However, the Entrance Hall with its great stone fireplace bearing the Pelham arms and the niches for busts and statues had been completed some years earlier, as also had the broad oak staircase with turned balusters carved as Corinthian columns, made by a Lewes carpenter, and the handsome Dining-room, the serving end of which is separated by a Corinthian screen, the columns made with beautifully detailed capitals. The cornice has a frieze of swags of fruit and foliage, and the Pelham badge of a buckle, modelled in the robust and vigorous baroque fashion of the early eighteenth century, but the ceiling itself is designed in the more delicate fashion that was being introduced under the influence of the early French rococo taste from about 1735 onwards.

We have no knowledge of the original appearance of the Drawing-room, since it must have been altered—assuming that it was originally completed in early Georgian style—at some time round about the 1770s, in the newly fashionable neo-classical manner of Robert Adam. A more precise dating for the redecoration of this room may be suggested by the fact that some beautiful gilt chairs with cartouche-shaped backs and curved rococo legs, in the elegant French taste as interpreted by the followers of Chippendale and Hepplewhite, were bought in 1777, according to the evidence of two of the chairs being marked with this date. They remain in the possession of the present Earl of Chichester, and for many years were exhibited in the Royal Pavilion. These chairs seem always to have been used in the Drawing-room, for which they were eminently suitable, until the family vacated the house in 1940. The freshly decorated room with its handsome new furniture would thus have been complete by 1782, when the Princess Amelia, sister of King George III, stayed at the house, an event celebrated by the Pelhams with the acquisition of the Princess's portrait by Van Loo, showing her attired in a blue silk dress.

Every season the number of visitors mounted, the place becoming more and more the favoured resort of the aristocratic and fashionable world, especially following the coming in 1771 of the Duke of Marlborough with his purchase of the house on the Steine, and the visit in the same year of the Duke of Cumberland, whose arrival was greeted with the ringing of church bells and the firing of a salute from the Battery, which was answered by a discharge of guns from the packet-boats that lay off the town. In the evening some of the principal houses displayed illuminations. In return the Duke gave a public breakfast and a ball. Gradually the visitors became aware of the beauty and charm that Brighton possessed in the spring and autumn, and from now on the season lengthened itself beyond the three summer months for which it had lasted hitherto. From 1777 until the coming of the Prince of Wales some six years later successive seasons surpassed themselves in brilliance.

From Brighton's early days until modern times the bracing air of the place and its easy access to the source of advanced ideas on the Continent seem to have encouraged a sense of intellectual excitement that led to the growth in the town of liberal and radical thought. One of the very first progressive politicians who favoured the place was John Wilkes, whose stormy political career had involved his having fought two duels, being committed to the Tower, and being outlawed from this country upon his conviction for publishing his notorious *Essay on Woman*. Wilkes had always been a popular hero because of his rebellious defiance of authority, and his electioneering slogan 'Wilkes and Liberty' became immortalized upon hundreds of articles of pottery, some examples of which are to be seen in the Brighton Museum.

When Wilkes first came to Brighton, in 1770, the tide of official opinion was beginning to turn in his favour, and a year later he was elected Sheriff of London and Middlesex. He came again in 1773, in 1774, when he had become Lord Mayor of London, and again in 1782, a culminating year of triumph, when all the resolutions invalidating his previous elections to Parliament were formally wiped out.

A no less intransigent thinker, but of a more secluded mode of life, was Edward Gibbon, who came to Brighton in 1781. He had just published the third volume of his *Decline and Fall of the Roman Empire*, the greatest historical masterpiece in the English language, which was arousing intense bitterness in religious circles at the time because of the famous attack on Christianity in the fifteenth and sixteenth chapters. Gibbon wrote to his stepmother in July: 'My house, which is not much bigger than yours, has a full prospect of the sea, and enjoys a temperate climate in the most sultry days. The air gives health, spirits and a ravenous appetite. I walk sufficiently morning and evening, lounge in the middle of the day on the Steyne, booksellers' shops, etc., and by the help of a pair of horses can make more distant excursions. The society is good and easy, and though I have a large provision of books for my amusement, I shall not undertake any deep studies or laborious compositions this summer.' He

67

enjoyed the sea-bathing, too, which he indulged in with all the solemnity prescribed by Dr. Russell and his followers.

Of all those who surveyed from the windows of their houses the brilliant company promenading the Steine, none did so with a more penetrating eye than Fanny Burney, while she was staying with Mr. and Mrs. Thrale, who as she wrote 'lived on the Steine where they indulged the pleasure of viewing, all day long, who walked with who'.[11]

The Thrales had been visiting Brighton at least since 1765, and possibly even earlier, staying at the house on the Steine belonging to Richard Scrase, Lord of the Manor, which stood on the site of the present Royal York Buildings. Mr. Scrase 'was an old gouty solicitor, retired from business', Mrs. Thrale wrote, and as a friend of her husband's father it was to him that she turned in 1772 upon the failure of a fruitless speculation to do with making beer without either malt or hops, in which Mr. Thrale who was himself a London brewer had engaged. The family were threatened with bankruptcy and ruin, when, as Mrs. Thrale told, 'first we made free of our mother's money, her little savings, about £3,000—'twas all she had; big as I was with child I drove down to Brighthelmstone to beg of Mr. Scrase £6,000 more—he gave it to us—'

It seems almost certain that it was at his house that the Thrales and Fanny Burney stayed during their early visits to Brighton, where they came each year after their usual season at Bath or Tunbridge Wells. In 1779 Fanny was staying with the Thrales at the house they had by then built for themselves near the bottom of West Street, opposite the 'King's Head' tavern,* which, as she wrote, was 'the court end of the town, here as well as in London'.

In that summer of 1779 Fanny Burney was pointed out everywhere as the author of the sensational best-selling novel, *Evelina*, in which she had portrayed the emotions of a girl of seventeen so faithfully that everyone was convinced its author had been only that age when she wrote it. From her window in Mrs. Thrale's house, or from her seat at the Assembly Rooms, Fanny cast a keen eye upon Brighton society, recording her observations for posterity in her *Diary*, which gained far greater fame than her novels. Lord Mordant, she remarked, was a 'pretty, languid, townish young man'; Dr. Delap, the Rector of Lewes and also a playwright of some account, was 'smug and reserved'; the Bishop of Peterborough 'gaily sociable'; Sir Philip Clarke a 'wit and libertine'; Mr. Gerald Hamilton, who had bought the Duke of Marlborough's house, was, as we have heard, 'intelligent, dry, sarcastic and clever'. She had a kindly glance for Richard Cumberland, the dramatist, with his wife and daughters, at whom, she wrote, 'everybody laughs for their airs, affectations and townish graces and impertiness.' She noted, too, the presence of Lady Pembroke and Lady Diana Beauclerk, 'both of whom have still very pleasing remains of beauty', and of pretty Mrs. Musters, 'the reigning toast of the season'. The lively charm and freshness of the early portions of her *Diary* gave place in its later pages to a Johnsonese pomposity and ponderousness, but there is a touch of magic in the passage describing an excursion which she made down to the beach very early one morning in 1782. 'Mrs. and the three Miss Thrales and myself', she wrote, 'all arose at six oclock in the morning, and "by the pale blink of the moon" we went to the sea-side, where we had bespoke the bathing-women to be ready for us, and into the ocean we plunged. It was cold but pleasant. I have bathed so often as to lose my dread of the operation, which now gives me nothing but animation and vigour. We then returned home and dressed by candle-light, and as soon as we could get Dr. Johnson ready, we set out upon our journey in a coach and chaise, and arrived in Argyle Street at dinner-time.'

Dr. Samuel Johnson, third of the eighteenth-century literary giants to visit Brighton after Defoe and Gibbon, was virtually a member of the Thrales' household at Streatham for some sixteen years. They brought him to Brighton in 1765, when the doctor was fifty-four, and a year later we hear of the bather 'Smoaker' Miles being so impressed by his prowess as a swimmer that he paid him the dubious compliment of remarking, 'Why, sir, you must have been a stout-hearted gentleman forty years ago.' Few of the fashionable amusements of Brighton seem to have appealed to him, however. 'You hunt in the morning', he wrote, 'and crowd to the rooms at night, and call it *diversion*, when your heart knows it is perishing from poverty of pleasures and your wits get blunted for want of some other mind to sharpen them upon.' And truly there must have been few amongst even the most intellectual souls in Brighton who would have cared to match their wits against the bludgeon-like arguments of the doctor. The only person, at least in Brighton, who was able to challenge Johnson in a 'good solid knock-down argument' was Dr. Michell, the Rector of St. Nicholas, who met Johnson one evening at the Old Ship Assembly Rooms. While the company were enjoying a dance the two men stood by the fireplace, talking amicably at first, until Dr. Johnson's indignation was aroused by a remark of the Vicar's, and he raised his powerful voice to quell his opponent. Not to be outdone by sheer noise, Michell thumped the fender with the poker to emphasize his point, whereupon Dr. Johnson seized the tongs, and the pair were soon making such a din that the dancers stopped in alarm and the Master of Ceremonies tactfully intervened and quietened the two disputants. It was only because Johnson could not bear to be away from his friends the Thrales that he ever tolerated Brighton, for, as he told Mrs. Thrale, he found the place 'so truly desolate, that if one had a mind to hang oneself for desperation at being obliged to live there, it would be difficult to find a tree on which to fasten the rope'.

Mrs. Thrale possessed an intellectual and commanding presence, but she was also vivacious, witty, frank and charming, and was herself a voluminous and accomplished writer whose own talents have been somewhat overshadowed by those of her friends Fanny Burney and Dr. Johnson. It was at Brighton that Mrs. Thrale encountered for the second time in her life the engaging and talented Italian musician Signor Piozzi, to whom she was eventually married after the death of her first husband. She had been introduced to Piozzi by Fanny Burney's father, but their second and more significant encounter took place in the summer of 1780, at the door of one of the libraries on the Steine when she and her seventeen-year-old daughter Queenie were setting out for a walk after their morning bathe. Mrs. Thrale received a letter from Fanny Burney saying that her father's friend, Mr. Piozzi, would be staying in Brighton, and not only that she hoped they would meet, but also, bearing in mind, no doubt, Mr. Thrale's frequent neglect of his wife and his infidelity to her, as well as his mismanagement of their financial affairs, that Mrs. Thrale would find him so delightful a companion as 'to lighten the burden of life for her', and that he was 'just a man to her natural taste'. The acquaintance soon ripened into a friendship so close that Johnson felt himself excluded and slighted. His attachment for Mrs. Thrale went far beyond the fact that he found her kind, appreciative, sympathetic and possessing an acute literary sense; in their relationship he had found satisfaction for some of his deepest and strangest psychological cravings, but now, deprived of this, he felt himself emotionally forsaken, and withdrew for ever from Mrs. Thrale's circle.

In 1781 Mr. Thrale died and Mrs. Thrale came to Brighton alone that summer to recover from the shock of her husband's death. Three years later, in the face of public criticism, and only when her elder daughters had relented of their opposition, she married Piozzi and travelled with him in Europe for three years, living happily with him until his death in 1809.

II

PRINCES AND PALACES

1770 to 1820

1 Balls and Assemblies

Some indication of the importance of Brighton as a pleasure resort, even before the coming of the Prince of Wales, is given by the fact that like few other towns in the country Brighton possessed two sets of Assembly Rooms, established at the two principal inns of the town, the Castle and the Old Ship.

The Castle Inn stood on the site of the present Electricity Showrooms at the north-east corner of Castle Square, and was opened in 1755. In 1766 the Assembly Rooms were erected, designed by the architect John Crunden. He was born in Sussex in 1740, and is believed to have worked for the well-known builder, Henry Holland the elder, father of the architect of the Prince of Wales's first classical Pavilion at Brighton. Crunden was a follower of Robert Adam's style, and built Boodle's Club in St. James's Street, one of the most charming buildings of the Adam movement, and one that was for long believed to have been the work of the master himself.

Externally the Castle Ballroom was a tall building of red brick with arched windows, but the interior expressed all the grace and elegance which Crunden had absorbed from Robert Adam and from Henry Holland. There were four rooms, the principal ones being a Ballroom and a Card-room. The Ballroom was a double-cube in its proportions, 80 feet long and 40 feet high and wide, with recesses at the ends and one side framed by columns of a charming form similar to some that Adam himself had frequently used, with capitals like a plain inverted bell having a single row of acanthus leaves, like those of the Tower of the Winds at Athens. The walls were decorated with plaster reliefs in panels and medallions, like Wedgwood cameos, and with delicate plaster Adamesque mouldings and scroll ornament. Above the frieze at the ends were paintings of Dawn and Night. The ceiling was in the form of a shallow arched vault similar to that of the Subscription-Room at Brooks's Club, which Holland had built opposite Boodle's a year after the erection of the latter building. In 1824 the Ballroom was purchased by George IV and converted into a Royal Chapel, but when the Royal Pavilion Estate was bought by the townspeople in 1850 the authorities of the Church of England claimed the building as a consecrated edifice, demolished it carefully and re-erected it as St. Stephen's Church in Montpelier Place, where it still stands. It ceased to be a church in 1939, and is now an institute for the deaf and dumb, but it has been sympathetically preserved, and the original neo-classical interior with much of its charming original ornament may still be seen.

In order to compete with the attractions of the new Ballroom at the Castle Inn, in 1775 the landlord of the Old Ship Hotel commissioned Robert Golden, the London architect who was a little later to build Dr. Awsiter's baths, to undertake some splendid new Assembly Rooms at the rear of the hotel. These consisted of a large Ballroom and a Card-room or Supper-room adjoining. Both were designed in Adamesque style similar to the Castle Ballroom. The Ballroom has a flat coved ceiling, a curved musicians' gallery with a delicate ironwork railing on one side, and a balcony for spectators at one end, though these last two features are probably of a later date than the building itself. The Card-room was designed with a shallow vaulted ceiling, decorated with plasterwork garlands, reeded mouldings and plaques of classical figures in relief. The Ballroom of the Castle Inn was looked upon as 'more elegant' than that of the Old Ship, while the latter was regarded as 'more neat and commodious', and for splendour 'not to be excelled, perhaps, by any in England that of York excepted'.[1]

From 1767 onwards the public assemblies, balls and promenades that were such a delightful feature of Brighton life were shared between the two sets of rooms. They were part of a new era of social life that came into being in the latter part of the eighteenth century, and that found tangible expression in the building of many delightful ballrooms all over the country of which those at Bury St. Edmunds and Shrewsbury are other famous examples. The new movement of delicacy and elegance in architecture and decoration which Robert Adam had introduced, and which he intended to serve what he called 'the parade of life', coincided with a new phase of refinement in social intercourse at this time. It contrasted strongly with the pompous ponderousness and overbearing grandeur of the earlier classical architecture with its heavy mouldings and tabernacle frames which Adam so detested; the new code of social behaviour was in contrast, too, with the coarse manners of early Georgian times which Hogarth had satirized and which Beau Nash, as Master of Ceremonies at Bath, succeeded eventually in abolishing there during his reign. The delicate neo-classical beauties of Thomas Baldwin's Banqueting Hall at the Guildhall in Bath, built in 1775, were an expression in that town of the new movement.

The somewhat lumpishly provincial character of social events in Brighton before the building of the Assembly Rooms is suggested by the account of a ball held at the Old Ship in January 1751. Twenty-one couples were present, and the proceedings were opened by the High Sheriff of the County, Robert Ball of Chichester, dancing a *contre-danse* to the fashionable tune of 'The Sow in the Sack' with the not inappropriately named Miss Treadwell of Lewes, 'an heiress of £5,000', as the *Gentleman's Magazine* recorded after the couple's subsequent marriage.

The existence of two such enterprising and energetic hosts as Samuel Shergold of the Castle Inn and John Hicks of the Old Ship, each strenuously encouraging the patronage of his own establishment, made it necessary eventually for them to arrive at an amicable *modus vivendi*. It was the appointment of a Master of Ceremonies sharing his duties between both ballrooms that was discovered to be the solution to this problem, and the individual appointed to fill this position consequently became a person of great influence in the town. He not only regulated the days and times of the principal balls and assemblies, which by mutual arrangement were held alternately at the two rooms, but was the sole arbiter of public conduct in both places.

'The Master of Ceremonies', wrote the Brighton historian Bishop,[2] 'became Dictator, he promulgated laws, and all willingly yielded obedience. Hence the first duty of visitors to Brighton was to pay their respects to him. Mothers with marriageable daughters were anxious to stand in his good places; the unprotected maiden of uncertain age, the lone dowager, reluctant to relinquish her waning opportunities of shining in society, each sheltered herself under his aegis; portionless sons, or it may be needy adventurers, seeking prizes in the matrimonial market, assiduously sought his favour; the proprietors of the respective assembly rooms were content to do him homage; and as for the town authorities, such as they were at this period, they neither interfered, nor sought to interfere, in the domains over which the sway of the "M.C." extended.'

The first record of the office occurs in 1767, when with the building of the Castle Inn Ballroom that hostelry was able to challenge for the first time the supremacy of the Old Ship. The name of the holder of the post was mentioned for the first time in 1770, in an announcement stating that tickets were 'to be obtained of Capt. Wade, at his house in Black Lion Street'. Wade was to become almost as celebrated in Brighton as the great 'Beau' Nash had been in Bath some years earlier. Indeed, Captain Wade is said to have assisted Nash at Bath at one period, and to have followed his successor there, Mr. Derrick, as M.C. The seasons in the two towns did not coincide, Bath being chiefly popular as a winter resort, and so Wade was able to officiate in both towns for a time. Unhappily the Captain (who dropped his title before long) made himself unpopular in Bath by openly ridiculing some love-letters which had been addressed to him by an admirer, and he was accordingly compelled to leave that town for good in 1770, and to make his home henceforth in Brighton. That amusing though somewhat acidulated commentator on the manners of his day, John Williams, under the pseudonym of 'Anthony Pasquin,' described the alternating assemblies in his customary sour fashion in his *New Brighton Guide* of 1796:

'There are two taverns, the Castle and the Old Ship, where the richer visitors resort, and at each of these houses a weekly assembly is held, where a master of ceremonies attends, to arrange the parties, not according to the scale of morality, but that of aristocracy. There is a ball every Monday at the Castle, and on Thursdays at the Old Ship: every subscriber pays three shillings and sixpence, and every non-subscriber five shillings, for which they are entitled to a beverage which they call *tea* and *coffee*.—The masters of the respective inns receive the profits, except on those nights appointed for the benefit of the master of ceremonies; to whom all, who wish to be arranged as people of distinction, subscribe one guinea—and who would not purchase distinction at so cheap a rate? Independently of this vain *douceur*, they must pay most liberally for their tickets! The card assemblies are on Wednesdays and Fridays.'

These card assemblies took place four times a week, when from two to three hundred people sat down to play each time. Card-playing was one of the favourite social pastimes, and it was especially popular with the Royal Family and the nobility. Sunday evenings were enlivened by a Promenade and Public Tea at the Assembly Rooms. This function gave friends the opportunity to meet and converse, and at the ringing of a bell they formed themselves into parties and sat down for tea. It was an innocent and civilized way of passing the time, but it is impossible to imagine people of today taking part in such a stilted and uneventful form of pleasure. The visitors obtained introductions to the social life of the town by putting their names down in the visitors' books, which were kept at the bookshops, or circulating libraries. The Master of Ceremonies then called upon the visitors at their lodgings, provided them with invitations to the various assemblies, and if anyone was without a partner effected suitable introductions. As the town became more and more popular, and the throngs of visitors swelled, so the number of events at the Assembly Rooms of the Castle and of the Old Ship increased, and the duties of the Master of the Ceremonies must have become more and more bewildering and perplexing. It was no longer so easy for him to keep control of all that passed, and during the closing years of Mr. Wade's reign there was a noticeable diminution in his power and authority. With the increasing informality of social intercourse that was becoming apparent at the end of the eighteenth century, people were less disposed to accept his pompous and consequential ministrations; his introductions no longer had the supreme importance that once attached to them, and his services were less and less called upon.

Wade died in 1808, but his successor, William Forth, did not enjoy anything approaching the status and authority of the office in its early days. Mr. Hicks of the Old Ship would have nothing to do with the newcomer, who was compelled to concern himself almost entirely with functions at the Castle. Social life in the day-time revolved around the circulating libraries. These were not merely bookshops, where one could read, buy or borrow the latest novels, plays and poems, or buy materials for elegant amusements like painting and sketching. They were to a much greater extent public clubs, where both men and women could meet and gossip, write letters, look through portfolios of the latest scandalous caricatures, try over a new piece of music, take a ticket for a raffle, or make up a party for cards or some other game. The first establishment of this kind to be set up in Brighton was built on the eastern side of the Steine by Mr. Baker, a bookseller of Tunbridge Wells, in 1760. It was a one-storey building of white-painted timber weather-boarding with a delightful arched veranda in front where the lady visitors used to sit to read and gossip, and which they found an excellent place for picking up titbits of scandal, according to the *New Brighthelmston Directory* of 1769:

> *For whilst you discourse,*
> *to each word that is said,*
> *Attentive they listen, and*
> seem *but to read.*

The ladies were eager frequenters of the billiards-room, too, in a way that would have been frowned on a century later. 'Oh! How I did stare', wrote the author of the *New Directory*. 'They handled the sticks with a grace! and an air!'

The library was open only until October, when most of the fashionable visitors disappeared. A year or two later Mr. Baker added the Rotunda, an octagonal wooden building, where a small band performed on fine afternoons. The somewhat unusual and ill-assorted combination of instruments, one trombone and two French horns, while no doubt sounding rather monotonous to those seated near, had at least a penetrating resonance capable of being heard across the expanses of the Steine and attracting people across from the town side by what might have seemed to be sounds of revelry and festivity. In May 1774, after the death of Mr. Baker, the place was taken over by a Mr. Thomas, who kept the place open regularly winter and summer, and continued to run it for many years. Later the proprietors of Thomas's Library were Dubot and Gregory, but it became most famous in its later years as Donaldson's Library.

Another library was opened on the south side of the Steine by a Mr. Woodgate about 1767 and eventually carried on by a Miss Widgett, whom Fanny Burney referred to as 'the milliner and library-woman'. Further competition arose some five years later when a new library was opened a few yards away from Thomas's Library by a 'Mr. Bowen from London'. After a while a number of smaller shops sprang up on the Steine around the libraries. These were said to be chiefly the resort of 'fops, women and children'. They were stocked with toys, china, lace and millinery, ribbons and muslin, chintz and 'cambricks' and tea, and skilfully playing upon human weakness and the hope that the goods were to be bought at much less than their real value, the proprietors carefully conveyed the notion they were smuggled articles, a suggestion that was indeed in many cases only too true. Smuggling was so prevalent a fashion at the time that people felt they were losing some of the best opportunities that life had to offer if they did not acquire some smuggled goods. It is hard to imagine people risking fines and imprisonment for such articles as lace, but this material was still in such demand for the dress of both ladies and gentlemen, until fashions became drastically simplified after the French Revolution, that to be able to buy it cheaply was a powerful inducement. One day in 1776 a chaise was brought to Brighton from Dieppe, and the preventive officers, made suspicious by the firmness of cushions inside, found that they were stuffed with lace worth £1,000.[3] The craze for gambling was exploited by the proprietors of the fancy-goods shops, for the rather tawdry and gimcrack articles on show were not usually to be obtained by ordinary purchase, but by a group of people staking small sums of money against the fall of dice, and the perpetual rattle of dice in the 'rattle-traps' of the Steine became notorious. Even the libraries had their 'rattle-traps', although on a lesser scale. In these establishments a more reputable form of gambling was preferred. This was the game of 'Pam' or 'Loo', a simple form of sweepstake, played for by cards, the public taking their chances under fictitious names such as 'The Enchantress', 'Poor Peter', 'Prudence', and so on, which gave opportunities for trivial banter and mild flirtation. Eventually the game, which as 'Loo' gave its name to a distinctive type of circular or octagonal table in Regency days, was declared illegal.

Of all the enjoyments that offered at Brighton, nothing so pleased the visitors as promenading upon the Steine, where the inhabitants had walked on summer evenings and Sundays from time immemorial. Here there was some shelter from the winds of the cliff-top, and away from the narrow streets of the town one gained a sense of release upon this broad grassy expanse, with the luminous overarching sky above. A wide view of the sea opened to the south, and to the north the green Downs rose up steeply towards the distant ramparts of Hollingbury Camp. The Steine was almost entirely covered with grass except for tracks at the side, and from ancient times the fishermen had been accustomed to sit there making and mending their nets and spreading them to dry. Although dependent on the visitors for a great deal of their income from the bathing industry and the hire of boats, the fishermen often resented the intrusion of the fashionable people on their own preserve, and as late as 1799 G. S. Carey, author of a little book on baths and bathing in England called *The Bagnio*, complained that the 'fishing-nets are daily spread from one end of the Stayne to the other, so that the company, while walking, are frequently tripped up by entangling their feet; and if any of the barbarians to whom the nets belong should be standing by, you are sure to be reprobated and insulted for what you cannot avoid'. This nuisance was disposed of about 1776, when wooden railings were placed around the Steine, despite the protests of the fishermen, who lost their ancient rights by this enclosure.

By 1787 the Master of Ceremonies was asserting his jurisdiction over the Steine, as well as in the Assembly Rooms and libraries, for in that year Captain Wade issued a notice threatening prosecution for anyone who should 'run any Foot, or other Race, on this Place, or *Fight*, play at Cricket, Trap or Ball, or any other Game or Games thereon' and he announced with great complacency that 'The Steine is now enclosed, there is a FINE TURF, which is kept constantly mowed and swept every day, where Ladies and Gentlemen and their Children may walk with the greatest Safety and Pleasure; and care is taken to keep off all Beggars and Disorderly Persons.' The place that the Steine held in the minds of the visitors was summed up in the words of a ballad of the time:

> *Though in pleasing excursions you spend the long day,*
> *And to Lewes or Shoreham, or Rottingdean stray;*
> *Or to drink tea at Preston, to vary the scene,*
> *At eve with new raptures you'll fly to the Steine.*

Much as we regret nowadays the passing of so many delightful features of Brighton—the broad grassy Steine unravaged by traffic; the delightful early houses with their cobbled walls and bow-windows, the green slopes of the Downs rising so closely at hand from the edge of the town—there were certain aspects of Brighton life the passing of which we cannot deplore. We should, for example, hardly wish to see again a stag turned out on the Steine, as was done for the Duke of Cumberland in October 1780 before 'an immense concourse of spectators, and sportsmen innumerable', and to follow the wretched creature while it was pursued to Rottingdean, where rather than be torn to pieces by the hounds, it leaped from the cliffs and was killed on the rocks below. After this keen disappointment to the huntsmen, the Duke had a deer turned out a few days later away from the cliffs inland at Withdean. The 'timid creature' was pursued far beyond Lewes, and eluded her pursuers for a long time by doubling and twisting, but was eventually found lying down in a thicket unable to run any further, her feet being 'entirely worn out'. Even the Duke of Cumberland and his friends felt that this anticlimax left something to be desired, and no more deer were turned out on the Steine.

The ancient sport of cock-fighting seems to have been in existence in Brighton at least from 1746, when the first surviving advertisement for it appeared.[4] The last public announcement appeared in 1811, but the practice may have continued for some years after that date. The even more revolting practice of bull-baiting was apparently never practised at Brighton, although it took place at Rottingdean and at Preston in the 1750s. There was a bull-ring at Hove where baiting went on until about 1810, when it was brought to an end after fighting between the promoters and members of the public who objected to the barbarous pastime.

The firm turf and the long stretches of the Downs, which make them incomparable for riding, caused them to be used for horse-racing from early times. Eastbourne, Steyning and Shoreham had their meetings of one or two days' duration. The inhabitants and visitors of Brighton, however, resorted to Lewes Races, which were held from about 1760 onwards. A 'Brighthelmston Plate of £50' was given at Lewes every year until 1783, when the first races at Brighton were organized by a group of noblemen and gentlemen including the Duke of Cumberland, the Duke of Queensberry, Lord Egremont of Petworth, Lord George Cavendish, Sir Charles Banbury, and Sir Harry Featherstonehaugh of Uppark. Whitehawk Down, a mile or two north-east of Brighton, offered a magnificent site for a course, and a number of private races had been run there before, as in 1770, when the horse of Mr. Shergold of the Old Ship Hotel was matched for ten guineas against the horse of Dr. Kipping, a remarkable person, who was an expert swordsman as well as a physician and who once fought an impromptu duel in West Street with an army officer who had insulted him. In the encounter the doctor secured his opponent's sword, and did not return it to him until after a week, greatly to the officer's humiliation.

The first Brighton Races took place on Tuesday and Wednesday, 26th and 27th August 1783. The principal races were a plate of fifty pounds for four-year-old colts, a sweepstake of five guineas each with a purse of thirty guineas for ponies, and a plate of fifty pounds for any horses. The intimate connection between Brighton Races and the town authorities, which has lasted nearly two centuries, began with the presentation of the purse of thirty guineas 'by the Town of Brighthelmston'. From this modest and extremely leisurely beginning, with only three races in two days, developed the meetings on the scale of the present day, with eighteen races in three days, and prizes amounting to over £13,000.

The Prince of Wales, who came to Brighton for the first time in September 1783, missed these first races by ten days, but he attended the course when races were held the following year, and ever after took the most enthusiastic interest in the meetings. In 1785 the number of races and of horses running, and of the visitors attending, had increased to such an extent that it became necessary to introduce a number of regulations governing the entry of the horses and the erection of booths and stalls for the sale of beer and other refreshments. There was no stand for the use of spectators until 1788, when a small structure was erected by subscription. It was said that 'For convenience and elegance, the new Stand challenges any in the Kingdom.' To judge, however, from an amusing engraving that was made after a drawing by Rowlandson during his visit to Brighton in 1791, the stand was a small and very ordinary erection, holding about twenty-four people, in six open-fronted boxes. This drawing, which is to be seen in the Brighton Art Gallery, and the engraving in the Royal Pavilion, show the Brighton race-course at the time, with the sea in the distance. The course was about two miles long, and ran in a hair-pin shape along the top of the hill. Apparently there were no railings at first. As well as the spectators in the stand, there were people watching from carriages and carts. In the foreground a 'thimble-rigger' is plying his deceptive trade, and a fashionable lady is lashing with her whip at a man who seems to be picking her pocket.

2 The Coming of the Prince of Wales

Since 1779, when he first came to Brighton and rented the house which Dr. Russell had built on the Steine, the Duke of Cumberland had been the leader of the hunting, racing and gambling set in the town. Henry Frederick, Duke of Cumberland (born 1744, died 1790), was by no means the favourite brother of the King. In 1770 Lord Grosvenor had obtained £10,000 damages from him on a charge of having seduced Lady Grosvenor, and in 1771 he married Lady Anne Luttrell, a widow who was much older than himself. She was not only blasphemous and indecent in her conversation, but the marriage was felt by the King to be likely to increase the influence of the Irish families with whom the Duke's bride was connected, and who were antagonistic to the King, through this new connection with the Royal Family. In consequence the King caused to be passed in 1772 the Royal Marriage Act, by which none of the descendants of George II, unless of foreign birth, can marry under the age of twenty-five without the consent of the monarch. It was this Act that was to be one of the causes of a great deal of misery to the Prince of Wales before many years had passed.

For a long time the Cumberlands were forbidden to attend the most important functions of the Court, and in return the Duke and Duchess did all they could to annoy his brother. They cultivated the society of the leading members of the Whig party, who were then in Opposition, and openly encouraged the rebellious attitude towards his parents of the Prince of Wales, who was then chafing under his father's domination in the final years of his minority.

From the early days the King appears to have disliked his eldest son, lavishing more fatherly affection upon his next son, Frederick, Duke of York, and later on his youngest daughter Amelia, who was an invalid for the whole of her brief life of twenty-seven years. The Prince himself stated that his father had hated him 'from seven years old'. The Prince's education was by the conventional standards of the time an excellent one, no less than eight hours a day being given to languages and the classics alone. He learned to speak French, German and Italian fluently. In addition the polite accomplishments were imparted to him by the best masters of the day. He was instructed in fencing by the celebrated Angelo, and in elocution by the actor Bartley. Sir William Parsons, Master of the King's band, taught him singing and Crosdill the cello. The Prince had a great fondness for music, including that of C. P. E. Bach, Handel, Haydn, Mozart, and especially of the lesser-known eighteenth-century Italian composers like Cimarosa, Paisiello, Corelli and Albinoni. He had been taught drawing and painting by Alexander Cozens, one of the greatest of the English water-colour painters of the time, and even though achieving no success as an artist, acquired a knowledge and appreciation of painting which was of service to him later on in building up those Royal art collections, especially of Dutch and English pictures, that are now among the wonders of Europe.

As a result the Prince grew up into a young man of remarkable abilities and accomplishments; indeed, as Byron was to write many years later to Sir Walter Scott, 'certainly superior to any living *gentleman*'. The poet was a person of profound common sense, and would not have stooped to senseless flattery, despite his ironical hint concerning the abysmally low intellectual level of most members of fashionable society.

Perhaps because of the King's jealousy of his son's intellectual abilities, the Prince's education was interfered with by arbitrary changes in his principal tutors. The master under whom he made the greatest progress, in artistic taste and personal graces as well as in learning, Dr. William Markham, Bishop of Chester, was compelled for political reasons to give way to Dr. Hurd, Bishop of Lichfield and Coventry, who instituted a much less liberal and imaginative scheme of studies than his predecessor had pursued, but who was none the less unable to keep pace with his pupil's own development.

The Prince complained more than once that his tutors had taught him all they knew, and pleaded for masters of greater knowledge and ability. Had these been granted the Prince, there is little doubt that his mental powers would have been developed to a very high degree indeed. Unquestionably the Prince's character suffered through an excessively strict and insistent moral training. The King had professed that he rated a devotion to the truth above all other virtues, but the result of the Prince's upbringing was that, as he himself confessed, he 'learned to equivocate'. To such a person as the Duke of Cumberland, the spectacle of his nephew spending the early years of his manhood at Windsor under the harsh and pious domination of his father, and smothered by the cloying possessiveness of his numerous sisters, in a household without gaiety or merriment, must have been genuinely distressing, and for several years the Duke had done all he could to rescue his nephew from his depressing surroundings, and to persuade him to enjoy with him the lively pleasures of Brighton, but this was not possible while the Prince was not yet his own master. Horace Walpole tells us that in 1780, when the Prince was eighteen years old, he told his uncle 'I cannot come to see you now without the King's leave, but in three years I shall be of age, and then I may act for myself. I will declare I will visit you'.

Amongst many people the character of a young Prince of Wales in the time approaching the attainment of his majority is always the subject of the liveliest conjecture. They are especially prone to excuse any wildness in a young man, if only because they believe such behaviour may be condoned in one who is eventually to undertake the heavy burdens and responsibilities of the monarchy. In the case of the son of George III, his disreputable behaviour is often excused as a natural rebellion against the strict domination of his severe and pious parent. But, as Mr. Roger Fulford has asked,[1] would the Prince of Wales's character and behaviour have been any different had he been brought up in the 'elegant licentiousness' and 'glittering fatuity' of a Court like that of Louis XV of France, which is always looked upon by the shallow-minded as embodying to the utmost the brilliance, the elegance and refinement of the eighteenth century? The first intimations of the Prince's becoming involved in a tangible love-affair came in November 1779 with the rumours of his infatuation for Mary Hamilton, one of the ladies attached to the Court. She was a jolly, sensible, attractive girl seven years older than the Prince, who was then not quite seventeen. Her *Diary* records his pursuit of her with a passion that increased as she strove to discourage his advances. 'My God,' she wrote, 'what will become of you if you suffer yourself to be led away with such impetuosity?' Mary Hamilton's resolution not to give way to the Prince's appeals, although she was unquestionably flattered by his attentions, was never finally put to the test, for in a very few weeks the attraction of a girl encountered for brief moments only in the bustle of life about the Court gave way to the promise of more substantial delights that offered with the more easily accessible person of Mary Robinson, the pretty actress whom he had met at the theatre while she was playing the part of Perdita in *The Winter's Tale*. With his final letter to Mary Hamilton, we realize that his passionate outpourings were not so much expressions of love addressed to another living being, but rather colloquies with himself on the idea of being in love with love, for in his last missive telling her that he had fallen in love with another person he ends somewhat surprisingly with the words '*Adieu, adieu, adieu,* TOUJOURS CHÈRE, oh! Mrs. Robinson!'

This lady was a highly accomplished and successful actress, no less so away from the stage than upon it, for she was pursued by most of the professional seducers of the day and gallants of society, including the Duke of Cumberland and the Duke of Rutland, who is said to have offered her six hundred a year to become his mistress. She had been married at sixteen, either to cover up the birth of an illegitimate child, or being forced into it by her mother for financial reasons, to a lecherous and contemptible clerk named Robinson. Soon after he had served a term in prison for debt she embarked upon her stage career with the help of Garrick, and also of

Sheridan, who before long became her lover. She was a very beautiful woman, with a figure that was said to make her especially attractive in 'a breeches part'.[2] It may have been the Duke of Cumberland himself who called the Prince's attention to her. At their first encounter the Prince bowed to her and she afterwards said, 'I felt the compliment and blushed my gratitude.' The Prince sent her his miniature together with one of those French mottoes with which the fabric of his amorous life was to become so plentifully adorned—'Je ne change qu'en mourant.' Through the whole of 1780 he was besieging her with passionate love-letters, addressing her as Perdita and signing himself Florizel, in exactly the same romantic way in which he had seen himself and Mary Hamilton a few weeks earlier. Perdita deserted the stage when the Prince set her up in a house in Cork Street, but their attachment came to an end after she had made the unforgivable mistake of insulting in public one of the Prince's dearest friends, the Duchess of Devonshire. Unfortunately the Prince's letters contained matters far more serious than the romantic imaginings of a fairy-tale. In them he had promised that he would pay Mrs. Robinson £20,000 as soon as he became of age, and made more than veiled promises of marriage. Eventually the King was compelled to pay Mrs. Robinson £5,000 to recover the letters. To this episode, the first great affair in the long series of the Prince's amorous adventures, we owe the picture of him that is given us in the words written by Mrs. Robinson many years later. 'The graces of his person, the irresistible sweetness of his smile, the tenderness of his melodious yet manly voice, will be remembered by me till every vision of this changing scene shall be forgotten.'

Mrs. Robinson at first declined the King's offer of £5,000 in place of the £20,000 his son had promised her, and when the Prince's friend, Charles James Fox, was sent to plead with her to accept this sum, in the form of an annuity of £500, he succeeded in his mission, chiefly by taking Perdita as his own mistress.

For a while the Prince became the lover of Mrs. Armistead, an extremely witty and intelligent woman who was one of the most beautiful and sought-after courtesans of the day. Later, when the Prince turned from her to other loves, Fox took her into his keeping just as he had relieved his friend of the embarrassment of Perdita. Mrs. Armistead and Fox eventually married happily and remained steadfast to each other until death parted them.

It was only a few weeks after the Prince's twenty-first birthday that he came to Brighton for the first time, early in the evening of 7th September 1783. With this visit of the heir to the throne, everyone was conscious that Brighton was embarking upon a new era of brilliance and importance, and the whole town thrilled with excitement.

As Sir Osbert Sitwell wrote,[3] 'Brighton's great day had dawned, and, as if to herald it, as if in imitation of more primitive days, when the tribe would assuredly have made some sacrifice to the God of Fortune, now arrived in the guise of the Young Prince, the life of a man was offered up.' 'At half after six', the *Sussex Weekly Advertiser* reported, 'His Royal Highness's arrival was announced by the ringing of bells and a royal salute from the guns at the battery, when unhappily, through some indiscretion in reloading one of the pieces, it went off and wounded the under-gunner mortally, and he died in a very short time afterwards.' Ironically enough, a similar although not so total sacrifice had been exacted twelve months earlier, on the arrival of the Princess Amelia, the aunt of King George III, when one of the guards lost his hand in a premature explosion. After the second accident the practice of giving Royal salutes was discontinued.

Later the newspaper account continues, 'The Heir Apparent and his royal uncle the Duke of Cumberland appeared on the Steine, where their Highnesses walked about half an hour and then went to the rooms. It being Sunday evening, the Steine was thronged with *company*, who flocked in motley groups to see the Royal Guest. The town and Steine were illuminated, and the brilliancy of the evening concluded by a grand display of fireworks before the Duke of Cumberland's house.'

The Duke was now living on the Steine at Grove House, so named from the nearby Promenade Grove, a sort of miniature Vauxhall, which was eventually taken into the Pavilion grounds. Grove House was a large red-brick house, having a fine bow-window rising through two storeys on the east front. It stood on the site of the present music room of the Royal Pavilion, and was demolished when John Nash carried out his final transformation of the building for King George IV. At that time Grove House belonged to Lord Egremont's brother, George Wyndham, who had rented it to the Duke of Cumberland. In 1786 the Duke of Marlborough bought Grove House on selling his house in the Steine to Mr. Gerald Hamilton, and named his new residence Marlborough House in turn.

The Prince stayed at Grove House for eleven days. The morning after his arrival he and his uncle rode out with the stag-hounds, and in the evening the royal party attended a ball at the Castle Inn Assembly Rooms, which was said to 'be the most splendid ever known at that place'.

On Wednesday the 10th of September the Prince set out for London, having expressed to everyone he met his delighted approval of Brighton. The first intimation of a second visit was the announcement in the *Sussex Weekly Advertiser* of 19th July 1784 that Mr. Weltje, Clerk of the Prince of Wales's Kitchen, had been to Brighton earlier that month 'to engage a house there for His Royal Highness, who has been advised by his physicians to sea-bathing, as necessary to perfect the re-establishment of his health'. Again the Prince was to stay at Grove House. The Prince arrived at an early hour between three and four o'clock in the morning on 23rd

July, and a few days later performed a remarkable feat of endurance, leaving Brighton on horseback at five o'clock on the morning of the 26th and returning from London in the same day, having taken $4\frac{1}{2}$ hours going and $5\frac{1}{2}$ returning.[4]

The newspaper account adds the not altogether astonishing news that the Prince 'immediately on his return very prudently retired to his rest', although by so doing he disappointed the company at the Castle Ballroom, who had assembled in the expectation of seeing him.

After his adventures with Perdita Robinson and Mrs. Armistead, the Prince seems to have formed an attachment for a while with Lady Melbourne, mother of Queen Victoria's Prime Minister, but although he engaged in a number of fleeting affairs, and frequented the theatres and the most exclusive houses of pleasure that London had to offer, it appears that at the time of the Prince's second visit to Brighton he was by some strange mischance not in the throes of a love-affair. This deplorable state of affairs was remedied, however, when an incident took place which the Prince's biographer Robert Huish asserts was the chief cause of the Prince's becoming attached to Brighton. According to this extremely scurrilous writer, 'It was neither the marine views, the benefit of the change of air, nor the salubrity of the place, which possessed in the eyes of His Royal Highness at any time any great attractions, but that he was drawn thither by the angelic figure of a sea-nymph whom he one day encountered reclining on one of the groins on the beach.' It is undoubtedly this encounter that Rex Whistler has commemorated in his famous allegorical mural painting 'H.R.H. The Prince Regent awakening the Spirit of Brighton' which is preserved at the Royal Pavilion.

This entrancing being was a girl named Charlotte Fortescue, who although, as Huish goes on to tell, was 'of the first order of fine forms . . . was one of the most illiterate and ignorant of human beings'. However, Charlotte's charms, together with her air of simplicity and innocence, effectively concealed the lack of any more dependable qualities, and soon the Prince had become her abject slave. Making a pretence of virtue and timidity, she skilfully led the Prince on, carefully avoiding any risk of giving way to his desires, until his passion was almost uncontrollable. However, when he discovered that she was carrying on an intrigue at the same time with his friend George Hanger the girl found herself deserted by both, and thus completely failed to achieve that transition from a dull and obscure provincial existence to a life of sophisticated gaiety, which as the Spirit of Brighton in Rex Whistler's painting she eternally symbolizes.

This incident was probably only one of a number of escapades in which the Prince was concerned during this visit, which lasted ten weeks, and there had been much criticism of the disreputable companions with whom he had filled Grove House. When the Prince next came to Brighton, in

June 1785, the *Morning Post* commented: 'The visit of a certain gay, illustrious character at Brighton, has frightened away a number of old maids, who used constantly to frequent that place. The history of the gallantries of the last season, which is constantly in circulation, has something in it so voluminous, and tremendous to boot, that the old tabbies shake in their shoes whenever his R—— H—— is mentioned.'

But all the amorous escapades in which the Prince had so far engaged were to be completely eclipsed by an affair that was to become one of the famous love-stories of history. This was his passion for Mrs. Fitzherbert. The lady was Maria Anne Fitzherbert, daughter of Walter Smythe of Brambridge in Hampshire. Her family was an ancient Roman Catholic one, but impoverished, and having no dowry she felt compelled to please her parents by marrying at the age of eighteen the wealthy Edmund Weld of Lulworth Castle. He was a childless widower of forty-four, who died within a year of their wedding from the effects of a fall from his horse. Her second husband, Thomas Fitzherbert of Swynnerton, Staffordshire, succumbed about three years after their wedding to a chill he caught while trying to restrain a violent mob in the Anti-Popery riots led by Lord George Gordon. In 1784 this fascinating widow, who now possessed a modest fortune of her own, was creating quite a sensation in Society with her beauty and her charm. The *Morning Herald* of 27th July commented: 'A new *constellation* has lately made an appearance in the *fashionable hemisphere*, that engages the attention of those whose hearts are susceptible to the power of beauty. The widow of the Mr. F—h—t has in her train half our young Nobility: as the lady has not, as yet, discovered a partiality for any of her admirers, they are all animated with hopes of success.'

As we see her in the most familiar portrait of her at this period, the coloured engraving by Richard Cosway, a copy of which is to be seen in the Royal Pavilion, Mrs. Fitzherbert appears in the full-skirted panniered eighteenth-century dress that is so soon to be supplanted by the straight simple classical costume of the Revolutionary period. Her pale clear complexion gave her face a delicacy that was emphasized by her dark hazel eyes, by her deep-golden coloured hair which she brushed into an aureole around her head, disdaining the use of powder, and by the fairness of an ample and beautifully shaped bosom which the frank fashion of the day revealed to the admiration of men and the envy of women. Something of that charm and sweetness that all who knew her remarked upon is seen in this portrait, and so also is a little of that strength of character which stood her in good stead during many crises of her life, expressed in the fine line of that imperious aristocratic aquiline nose.

It is believed that the Prince first met Mrs. Fitzherbert in Lady Sefton's box at the Opera. He immediately fell deeply in love and was distracted with passion as never before, while she received his devotions with amused attention, and indeed was possibly not a little flattered and gratified to find herself pursued by one of the most exalted, charming and romantic young men in Society. But she was a woman of unimpeachable moral character and deep religious feelings and would not for a moment have countenanced an attachment to any man except with the sanction of marriage. This could not be thought of where the Prince was concerned because of the Royal Marriage Act of 1772, and the marriage of a Catholic to the heir to the throne would never have received the consent of the King. The Prince was hysterical with passion, until at last late one night he sent two of his friends and his surgeon, Mr. Keate, to fetch Mrs. Fitzherbert to Carlton House, where they explained that the Prince lay in danger of death, having stabbed himself. Suspecting a trap, and fearing the scandalous consequences of being left alone at night in a bachelor's bedroom, she wisely took with her the Duchess of Devonshire. They found the Prince prostrate on a sofa and covered with blood, and crying that nothing would persuade him to live unless she promised to marry him. Almost fainting with horror, Mrs. Fitzherbert consented, and the trifling wound was bound up, but the following day she wrote to Lord Southampton denouncing the incident as a trick, and repudiating any obligation to fulfil a promise given in such circumstances. A few days later she fled to France. There the Prince pursued her with impassioned letters, sent with the aid of his friend the Duc de Chartres, which kept couriers riding through the roads of France with such speed and frequency that a political plot was suspected, and some of the messengers were arrested. However, it was quickly discovered that the matter was only an affair of the heart, in which the French with their natural intelligence immediately realized they could exercise supreme tolerance and delicacy. The Prince was beside himself with frustrated passion, and wrote to Mrs. Fitzherbert offering to renounce the throne and live with her in Holland, or to fly with her to America.

Possibly while abroad she consulted with authorities of her church to inquire about the validity of a marriage to one of another faith, and may have received some assurance, for early in December 1785 she returned to England and a few days later, about six o'clock on the evening of 15th December, the Prince and Maria were united at a ceremony conducted in her house in Park Street, London, by the Rev. Robert Burt, a young curate of the Church of England, who was induced to officiate after two other clergymen had declined, in return for the sum of £500 and promises of future advancement. The witnesses were her uncle Henry Errington and her brother Jack Smythe. Their names were afterwards cut out of the marriage certificate by Mrs. Fitzherbert herself, in order to save them from a possible charge of treason. This document, together with a letter from the Prince of Wales in which he refers to the witnesses, and a letter from the officiating clergyman, are still preserved at Coutts's Bank, sealed up in a cover under the seals of the Duke of Wellington, Sir William Knighton, the Earl of Albermarle and Lord Stourton.

Some days before the ceremony took place the fact that a wedding had been arranged was commented upon in several newspapers, which variously announced that the sum of £8,000 and £6,000 a year had been settled on Mrs. Fitzherbert, and that the lady was to be made a Duchess as soon as 'a certain illustrious character' had the power. The marriage did not escape the venomous attentions of the caricaturists, who published several savage lampoons of the incident. The best of them is a fine etching by James Gilray called 'Wife and no Wife; or, a trip to the Continent'. (It was believed by many that the ceremony had been performed in France.) The artist's sympathy with the Prince and Mrs. Fitzherbert is revealed by the fact of their portraits being beautifully drawn, the Prince handsome and dignified, Mrs. Fitzherbert shown as a gracious lovely and reserved figure. On the other hand, Fox, coarse and unshaven, who is giving away the bride; Sheridan, who is standing by with two bottles of liquor in his coat pockets; Burke, who is represented as the officiating Jesuit priest; and Lord North, a bloated coachman asleep on a bench, are all shown as repulsive creatures.

Other caricatures were even more scurrilous, to such an extent that Fores the publishers were prosecuted for issuing 'infamous libels'. One might be tempted to wonder how a woman of such high moral character and firmness of mind as Mrs. Fitzherbert could have imagined that the heir to the throne would consider himself indissolubly bound by a marriage that was illegal by the laws of the Church of England and of the realm. But no doubt Mrs. Fitzherbert was deeply in love with the Prince, and seized eagerly upon a means of becoming united to him that at least satisfied her religious feelings. Perhaps she felt it was not unreasonable to hope that she might be allowed to experience the happiness enjoyed by countless women throughout Europe who had become united to their Royal lovers by a morganatic marriage. Almost immediately after the wedding an avalanche of debts descended upon the Prince. Despite his income of £70,000 a year, he found himself owing some £300,000. Of this sum about £54,000 had been spent by the Prince on jewellery for Mrs. Fitzherbert and silver and furniture for her establishment in London. Again one is tempted to wonder that a woman some six years older than the Prince should have permitted him to lavish presents on her to such an amount, but presumably she never dared to inquire into his financial affairs.

The King was so infuriated that he refused to sanction an increase of his son's income, until the Prince promised to set aside £40,000 a year towards the payment of his debts, whereupon his allowance was increased by £10,000 a year. In fairness to the Prince it must be remembered that although £12,000 of his annual allowance came from the Duchy of Cornwall, the revenues from this source which had accumulated during the Prince's lifetime before the attainment of his majority were never paid over to him. These funds, admitted by Pitt in Parliament to amount to £234,000, and stated by Fox to be as much as half a million, had been applied by the King towards the payment of his own debts, mostly incurred over new buildings and other improvements at Kew Palace. In the face of this parental example it can hardly be wondered at that the Prince had so little sense of responsibility over incurring debts and indulging in expensive building programmes, for which he has so often been criticized.

Full of pious resolutions for economy, the Prince suspended work on the rebuilding of his London establishment, Carlton House, and sold his valuable stud of racehorses, although this only raised the small sum of £7,000, a fact that provided the caricaturists with fresh derisory material. The Prince travelled down to Brighton for the summer on 11th July, it was said by some in a hired chaise with hack horses, but the *Morning Post*[5] stated authoritatively that 'His Royal Highness was an *outside passenger* on the *Brighton Dilly*'. He was followed two weeks later by Mrs. Fitzherbert, the delay being caused by her desire to avoid scandal through living under the same roof as her husband. The Prince was probably then staying at Thomas Kemp's house on the Steine, which when later enlarged was eventually to become the Royal Pavilion. However, a house was soon found for Mrs. Fitzherbert near by. Its exact location is unknown, but it was said[6] to have stood near the present North Gate, and to have been later demolished to make room for improvements at the Pavilion. If this is correct, it was probably one of the early or mid-Georgian houses of Marlborough Row, of which only No. 1, the present North Gate House, remains. Some nine years later Mrs. Fitzherbert was to move to the house on the Steine which is more familiarly known as hers, and which was for many years in recent times in the hands of the Y.M.C.A.

As soon as they were comfortably installed at Brighton the couple no doubt felt the bleak prospect of leading a life of extreme economy would be made more entrancing for them by the consciousness that they were at least following that engaging but unpractical cult of idyllic simplicity which was advocated by certain eighteenth-century philosophers. The *Sussex Weekly Advertiser*[7] observed sententiously at this time that 'the resolution adopted by the Prince for a retrenchment in his expences . . . affords an illustrious example for the imitation of many, very many, who live in lower spheres'.

There are in the collections of Sir John Soane's Museum in Lincoln's Inn Fields some drawings by Robert Adam for the enlargement of Mrs.

Fitzherbert's house, but there is no record of the rebuilding ever having been carried out by him. The plans mention the Steine, and there is a possibility that this first house actually stood on the site of the present one.

The Prince and Mrs. Fitzherbert spent the summer of 1786 very quietly together at Brighton, too happy in their own company to need many friends about them, though no doubt they amused themselves with visits to the theatre, driving in their carriage, riding upon the Downs, and attending the races. Everyone at Brighton must have known of the wedding that had taken place, and Mrs. Fitzherbert's charming ways endeared her to everyone she met. It was confidently believed by many that here was the future Queen of England. A writer quoted by the Brighton historian Bishop[8] wrote: 'The most beautiful object in the world seemed to me to be Mrs. Fitzherbert. Had I seen the lady sitting or standing I should doubtless have thought her beautiful; but her fine and graceful person was in motion—her countenance, at all times singularly expressive, was unusually animated by the fineness of the weather, and as she suddenly came upon me, with all her personal attractions heightened by some adventitious setting-off, I saw her more than usually beautiful . . . She needed nothing but a diadem to make her a queen.'

At last that lovely honeymoon summer was over and by the end of October the Prince and Mrs. Fitzherbert had left for London. A few days later the local newspaper[9] announced that the Prince had taken a lease of the house on the Steine belonging to Mr. Thomas Read Kemp, father of the founder of Kemp Town. In fact, the house had been leased for three years from 17th October to Louis Weltje, Clerk of the Prince's Kitchen, at a rent of £150 a year, with a clause allowing the house to be purchased for £3,000. After the lease was settled Weltje sublet the property to the Prince, on condition that the former should rebuild the house and charge a rent according to the cost.

No picture survives of this house, but it is marked on a map of Brighton published by the bookseller Richard Thomas in 1797, on which it appears that the house had two bow-windows on the Steine side, with a semicircular plot of land in front.

Sydney Smith, who had dined at the house some years earlier, spoke of the building as a respectable farmhouse, and the Prince's biographer Croly, writing after his death, remarked that 'it was a singularly pretty picturesque cottage in a small piece of ground where a few shrubs and roses shut out the road and the eye looked undisturbed over the ocean . . . the happiest hours of the Prince's life were spent in this cottage'.

3 The Marine Pavilion

As on several occasions later in his life, the Prince seems to have decided that the best way to distract his mind from the worry of his tiresome debts was to embark on some intriguing new building programme. It was obviously never intended that his house at Brighton should remain in its existing condition, for rebuilding began almost immediately, in 1787. The architect chosen was Henry Holland, who since 1783 had been rebuilding Carlton House, the Prince's London residence, that 'chaste palace', as Horace Walpole called it,[1] which in its 'august simplicity' marked the reaction that was then setting in against the high elaborate decorative style of Robert Adam which had hitherto been fashionable. Holland had been a partner of 'Capability' Brown, the landscape gardener, and through him had in 1776 been commissioned to design the stronghold of the Whigs, Brooks's Club in St. James's, London. He was later to carry out important commissions for leading members of the Whig aristocracy, such as Woburn Abbey for the Duke of Bedford, Althorp for Lord Spencer, Broadlands for Lord Palmerston, and Southill for Samuel Whitbread, among many other outstanding works. It was presumably Fox, the leader of the Whigs, who had brought Holland to the Prince's notice, and caused him to be appointed to rebuild Carlton House and to enlarge the house on the Steine which the Prince had rented from Mr. Kemp.

We may perhaps imagine that it was not merely in the fact of their political opposition to his father that the Prince found a congenial atmosphere amongst the Whigs, but that he discovered also that in contrast to the more crusted Tories of those days, whose interests were mostly confined to agriculture and sport, the Whigs were more deeply concerned with the world of art, literature and ideas and with the civilization and aspirations of the European countries, above all of France. The Prince was thus able to discover in that society an intellectual and imaginative atmosphere in which he found emotional release.

The Marine Pavilion, as it was soon to be called, came into being in about three months during the early summer of 1787. Work began in April and the Prince took possession on 6th July, arriving from London at eleven o'clock that night. To get the house finished in time over a hundred and fifty workmen were engaged on the building, but the excitement of completion was marred by a tragic accident during the finishing of 'the great Dome', in which a man was killed.

The Pavilion then showed no sign of the fantastic changes that were eventually to come over it. It was built in the form of a small classical villa on the Palladian model of a central domed saloon or rotunda with flanking wings, in the graceful and elegant fashion characteristic of what James Elmes later called Holland's 'Graeco-Roman' style. The house was timber-framed, and faced with the cream-coloured geometrical tiles of which Holland was particularly fond, and which he used on his own house in Sloane Place and at Althorp and Woburn also.* On the entrance front, facing west, was a small portico of four columns with a pediment, in the centre of a courtyard between two projecting wings at the sides. The courtyard was closed in front with iron railings and lamp-posts. On the Steine side the central rotunda, surmounted by a shallow cupola (the 'Great Dome') on a rather deep rim, was encircled by six Ionic columns carrying classical statues, probably made of Coade's patent artificial stone. An especially charming feature of the Steine front were the bow-windows, two to each wing, rising from the ground through both storeys to the narrow cornice of the roof. In each of these curved window-bays the windows reached the floor to ceiling in the manner that was to become one of the most distinctive fashions in house-building throughout the Regency and even into early Victorian days.

The coming of the Prince of Wales and the creation of the Marine Pavilion gave an enormous fillip to house-building in Brighton, and in the years following the completion of the Prince's residence the combined features of curved bays, long windows and iron railings became charmingly characteristic not only of the hundreds of houses that were built during the next few years in the town, but in those of many other seaside resorts such as Hastings, Ramsgate, Margate, Weymouth, and eventually in towns all over the British Isles.

Holland's early interior decorative style was in a simplified form of the Adam style, such as we may still see, for example, in the beautiful rooms which he designed at Berrington Hall in Shropshire. His later works, however, especially Southill in Bedfordshire, were infused with a French spirit that he had absorbed from his study of the works of French architects. He visited Paris himself in 1785,[2] and at Carlton House he surrounded himself with French draughtsmen, decorators and craftsmen and purveyors of furniture and ornamental metalwork. Something of this French influence was to manifest itself in the Prince's new Pavilion. On the ground floor of the north wing the Library was 'fitted up in the French style' with a paper of brilliant yellow. The 'Eating Room' adjoining was painted in yellow and maroon with a ceiling of sky-blue, and in it were four columns of 'scagliola'—imitation marble. The corridors were painted 'French blue'. The walls of the staircase were bright green, and the ceiling grey and white. The impression is given of a colour scheme more positive than the delicate colours of the fashionable Adam interiors of a few years earlier. In fact, the colours might have been of a depth that became characteristic of Regency decoration some twenty years later. In adopting such a brilliant decorative scheme the Prince was probably aiming deliberately at a liveliness that would be suited to a gay seaside holiday pavilion.

An intriguing aquatint after a drawing by Rowlandson shows the first interior of the Saloon with what appears to be an Aubusson carpet, a domed ceiling with plasterwork leaf ornaments, and a branched chandelier. The liveliness of this decoration probably owes more to the exuberance of the artist's vigorous line than to anything which Holland designed. The print appears in a book of views which Rowlandson and his friend Henry Wigstead produced describing a tour they made of the south of England in 1789, in which they said of the building:

'The Marine Pavilion of His Royal Highness, the Prince of Wales, on the west side of the Stein, is a striking Object, and is admirably calculated for the Summer Residence of the Royal Personage for whom it was built; and whose Munificence and Affability endear him to all who are not biassed by Party, blinded by Prejudice or hostile to dignified Merit. This Pavilion, correctly designed and elegantly executed was begun and compleated in five months. The Furniture is adapted with great taste to the Stile of the Building. The grand Saloon is beautifully decorated with Paintings by Rebecca, executed in his best manner. The *tout ensemble* of the Building is, in short, perfect Harmony.'

The Prince's bedroom on the upper floor of the south wing was said to have been 'divided into three compartments; the centre enclosing, by sliding partitions, the bed, which was fitted up as a tent; around this were reflecting glasses, which enabled His Royal Highness, while reclining on his pillow, to see the Promenade or the Steine very distinctly.'

We are also told that there was ample provision for the gambling to which at least Fox and other of the Prince's friends were addicted, even though he himself confessed he was 'not a gaming man'. The billiards-room was extensive, and included 'Hazard, billiards and money tables'.

This first Marine Pavilion must have been exquisitely elegant and charming, yet that jaundiced and venomous commentator 'Anthony Pasquin' succeeded in finding inspiration in it for one of his customary sour outbursts. In his *New Brighton Guide* of 1796 he wrote:

'The Pavilion is built principally of wood; it is a nondescript monster in building, and appears like a mad house, or a house run mad, as it has neither beginning, middle nor end. . . . The room in which the Prince usually dines may be compared to a sort of oven; when the fire is lighted the Inmates are nearly baked or incrusted.'

One evening at dinner Sheridan, the dramatist, and chief orator of the Whig party, asked George Hanger if he did not feel hot. 'Hot, hot, hot as hell,' exclaimed Hanger. Sheridan replied with wry complacency: 'It is well that we should be prepared in this world for that which we know will be our lot in another!'

During the summer of 1787 the Prince stayed for three months at his new house, leading in Mrs. Fitzherbert's company a comparatively quiet and circumspect life, although Brighton was filled with a gay and fashionable company who had come to the place in the wake of the Prince. The visitors were double the number of any previous year, and the assemblies, balls, libraries, theatres and concerts were crowded to overflowing. The Prince and Mrs. Fitzherbert attended the races followed by a dazzling throng of fashionables. As well as the Duke and Duchess of Cumberland and many members of the nobility, there were the Princesse Couronne and the beautiful Princesse de Lamballe, who courageously returned to Paris after the Revolution two years later in order to give comfort and help to the Queen and was savagely murdered and torn to pieces by the mob.

During the following winter Weltje arranged for the purchase of Mr. Kemp's house with its grounds and buildings for £5,850, and began to charge the Prince a rent for the reconstructed property of £1,000 for twenty-one years. By 1799 the rent had increased to £1,155, but Weltje was compelled to write pathetic pleas for payment before he got his money. Weltje had also paid all the costs of the rebuilding, including Holland's expenses. Altogether his expenditure amounted to £22,338 10s 11d, including some of the furniture. It appears that the Prince purchased the property for £22,000, probably about September 1793, when the question of the price to be paid was submitted for settlement by arbitration. The Pavilion must have belonged to the Prince by 1796, when an annuity of £3,000 a year, later increased to £4,000, began to be paid to Mrs. Fitzherbert, for this annuity was raised by means of a mortgage on the Pavilion.

At no time since the Prince's marriage were rumours silent concerning his relations with Mrs. Fitzherbert. Everyone who knew her concluded that as she was continuing to attend Mass and to go to Confession she could not possibly be involved in a shameful liaison. When the question of the Prince's debts was being debated in Parliament in April 1757, Fox deemed it expedient to declare that any suggestion of the Prince's marriage was 'miserable calumny and a low, malicious falsehood'. It is conceivable that Fox had been deliberately kept ignorant of the fact of the marriage. Indeed, he had written to the Prince in December 1785 advising him against such a step and been assured that there was no truth in the reports which had been 'so malevolently circulated'. Only ten days later the ceremony took place.

The Prince himself was completely taken aback by Fox's categorical denial of the marriage, and hurried to Mrs. Fitzherbert's house where, according to the Hon. Charles Langdale,[3] 'He went up to her and taking hold of both her hands and caressing her, said "Only conceive, Maria, what Fox did yesterday! He went down to the house and denied that you and I were man and wife! Did you ever hear of such a thing?"'

Mrs. Fitzherbert almost fainted from the shock, but when she had recovered said that Fox had 'rolled her in the kennel like a street-walker; he knew every word he said was a lie'. She felt that she had been betrayed not only by Fox but by the Prince himself and gave him to understand that their association must come to an end. Uneasily conscious no doubt of the justification he had given Fox for believing he was not married, the Prince did not have the courage to challenge his friend directly over the statement he had made in the Commons, but complained about him to Lord Selby and Sheridan, with the result that the latter made several vague and contradictory speeches in the House which only served to confirm everyone's convictions that a marriage had taken place. However, Parliament was by now tired of the matter and agreed to the settlement of the Prince's debts, while the King himself added another £10,000 a year to his son's income. After a while life at Brighton resumed its normal course for the Prince and his wife.

4 Early Theatres

For over two centuries Brighton has been famous as a home of the drama. The town's first acting company were literally 'barn-stormers', the 'Chichester Company of Comedians', who in 1764 performed some plays in a barn in Castle Square, which when not in use for storing corn was often used as 'a Repository of the Fine Arts, learned pig exhibitions, etc.' In July 1770 another company came from Chichester, to what was no doubt the same barn, 'near the Stein', and probably on the site of the southern part of the Royal Pavilion. The manager was a Mr. Johnson, who had turned a malthouse into a theatre at Chichester in 1764, and was the proprietor of theatres at Southampton and Portsmouth also. Johnson's devotion to the drama must have been intense, for knowing that he must vacate the building in a few short weeks when the harvest was brought in from the cornfields, he went to the lengths of covering the walls with painted canvas and digging out the floor literally to form a 'Pit' to accommodate a hundred people. He was under the further disadvantage of being compelled to hold most of their performances in the afternoon, so as 'not to intrude upon the regular Assembly nights'. On race days the plays were given as early as eleven o'clock in the morning.

It was four years before another theatre opened in Brighton, but now it was of a more permanent character, in a building in North Street. Peregrine Phillips, the author of *Ben's Diary*, remarked 'it is a pretty building, something larger than that at Richmond'. The manager was Roger Johnstone, who had been a property man at Drury Lane. He produced a series of good plays, with actors from Drury Lane and Covent Garden. Not long afterwards, in 1777, the theatre was let for fifteen years at a rent of sixty guineas a year, to a Mr. Fox of Covent Garden, and the building was redecorated and equipped with new machinery. A fine series of plays was given after an opening concert with the celebrated *prima donna* Signorina Storace. The Wards, the Farrens, Dighton and Creswick, and the celebrated Mrs. Baddeley were among the famous performers who came to the theatre, and Mrs. Robinson appeared in 1779 in *The Winter's Tale* in the role of Perdita,[1] a short while before at the age of twenty-one she met and became the mistress of the nineteen-year-old Prince of Wales. The Prince did not come to Brighton himself until four years later.

The best plays were produced with many of the great actors of the day, and the presentation was elaborate in the extreme. Dryden and Davenant's version of *The Tempest* was staged 'with Music, Machinery, Decorations and other Incidents proper to the Play, with the representation of a Ship in Distress, and afterwards Wrecked'. The theatre in Brighton in those days reached fairly great heights for the provinces, but despite the patronage of the Prince of Wales, Mrs. Fitzherbert and several of the Royal princes, it was not a success. Perhaps the antagonism of the M.C.s caused the visitors to keep away, or the unpleasantness of having to make their way back to their lodgings at night through the then outlying and ill-lit neighbourhood of North Street.

When the Prince of Wales made his first visit to Brighton, in September 1783, he attended the North Street Theatre, where, it is said, 'the captivating dames of Cytherea—one a self-styled Duchess—vied with each other to attract the eye of the Royal youth', and on this occasion the theatre was crowded. From this time onwards the Prince was a frequent visitor while staying in Brighton, and in September 1788, with Mrs. Fitzherbert and the Duke of Gloucester 'and all the rank and fashion in Brighton', he was present three times in one week. One of the Prince's circle of friends, Earl Barrymore, known as 'Hellgate' because that was undoubtedly his ultimate destination, fancied himself as an actor, and although putting up a very poor performance (he pleaded rather unconvincingly of 'being under the influence of timidity') his notoriety was such that the theatre was always crowded for his appearances.

In spite of Royal patronage and occasional successes, the theatre did not pay its way, however, and in 1789, without warning, it was closed. Nevertheless the manager was determined not to give up the struggle for a theatre in Brighton, and opened a new one in Duke Street, a more central part of the town, two years later.

The new theatre was built in a very short time and opened in July 1790. It was a plain building, with a windowless front of timber painted to resemble stone, and relieved only by a little pedimented portico with columns. The interior, however, was said to have been 'little inferior to the Haymarket' in its elegance. Much of the interior fabric of the building, including a staircase, still survives, and is in use today as part of a furniture warehouse.

The Prince of Wales and Mrs. Fitzherbert were frequent visitors to the theatre, and on one occasion that lady gave her patronage to a performance of a tragedy entitled *The Orphan* which was performed with such excruciating effect by a company of amateurs that the audience were in bursts of laughter throughout the evening, and it was said that the Prince 'would have cracked his sides'. By 1793 the theatre was less well patronized, because of the establishment of Brighton Camp on the Downs near by, which formed a powerful counter-attraction. The great sensation of that year, however, was the appearance of the celebrated fencer the transvestite

99

'Chevalier' D'Éon, who passed as a woman for the greater part of his life, and gave his name to this particular form of psychological aberration. The theatre was crowded, the pit was entirely laid out as boxes at a specially high price, and Duke Street was thronged with people unable to gain admittance. The audience paid little attention to the preliminary play, nor indeed to the excellent fencing displayed by D'Éon and a Guards officer from a regiment then in Brighton. The sole concern of the public was to detect the true sex of the 'Chevalier', who appeared looking like a caricature of Britannia, clad in the extraordinary costume of 'a blue satin shape, a white satin petticoat, and a large helmet, decorated with a plume of white feathers, which gave her, or him, a formidable, but somewhat droll aspect'. It is reported, however, that the curious went home unsatisfied. It was on 4th September 1798 that Mrs. Sarah Siddons appeared in Brighton for the first of her many performances in the town. She took the part of Calista in *The Fair Penitent*, but the theatre was not full, possibly because the prices had been increased for the occasion.

All the earlier efforts of the management in staging spectacular representations of historical events were surpassed after Nelson's victory of the Nile in 1798, when an entertainment was produced entitled *The Glorious First of August, or, British Tars Triumphant*. As well as showing views of Alexandria, 'an Arabian camp', and the French Fleet in Aboukir Bay, the performance showed how 'after an obstinate contest the French Admiral's ship is blown up, one ship is sunk, and two only out of the whole effect an escape'. 'The Battle over, a grand Transparency of the Noble Admiral descends gradually; Britannia enters in a triumphant car, drawn by seahorses, bearing in one hand a wreath or laurel, with which she graces the brow of the British Conqueror.'

Most of the famous actors and actresses of the day appeared at the theatre. One of them was Harriet Mellon, who later married Thomas Coutts, the banker, when he was in his eighty-sixth year. The marriage proved perfectly happy and successful. After his death she was said to be the richest woman in Europe. She eventually married the Duke of St. Albans, and was the figure round whom for season after season the world of gaiety and fashion in Brighton revolved. She was no less celebrated for her boundless gifts to charity. The third in the trio of actresses appearing in Brighton who were famous because of their association with royalty was Mrs. Jordan, who after being the Duke of Clarence's mistress for many years, and bearing him several children, was deserted by him when the prospects of his succession to the throne made him decide to marry. Described by Hazlitt as 'all gaiety, success and good nature', her distressed predicament and eventual death in poverty aroused the greatest public sympathy. Mrs. Jordan, whose real name was Dorothy Bland, performed in Brighton for a short season in 1800.

5 Fashion, Fugitives and the Brighton Camp

The years from 1788 until 1794 were something of a golden age in the history of Brighton. Members of the wealthy and fashionable classes flocked down to the place in the wake of the Prince of Wales in their hundreds and were willing to pay fantastic prices for the accommodation which was far short of what was needed to satisfy everyone.

The building of new houses now went on at a great rate, and by 1794 the number of houses in the town had increased from the 600 that existed in 1783, the year of the Prince's first visit, to over 1,200. Two rows of houses on the east side of the Steine, the North and South Parades, were erected in 1786.

Four houses built in 1790 facing south at right angles to North Parade, were painted in the Whig colours of blue and buff by followers of the Prince and James Fox, and were ever after known as the 'Blue and Buffs'. Of these four houses, only nos. 3 and 4 remain, the former with its original façade almost unaltered, built in vernacular style with cobble walls set off by painted brick window-surrounds and groins. North of the 'Blue and Buffs' came Pavilion Parade, built about 1800, with two houses at its north end still in their original state with fronts of tarred cobbles relieved with white-painted brickwork. The 1790s saw also the building of houses eastwards along the Marine Parade and in streets running north from the sea— Manchester Street, Charles Street, Broad Street, Margaret Street and Rock Gardens.

One of Brighton's most famous surviving early buildings, Cowley's Bun Shop, on the west side of Pool Valley, was built in 1794, its tall front with three angular bays faced with the attractive black-glazed iridescent mathematical tiles that are still to be found in various older parts of the town. The building retained its original shop-windows complete with small panes of glass, and it was until recently used for its traditional trade as a pastrycook's by the family by whom it was first established. After being closed for a time, and in danger of demolition, a new tenant has been found and the building is thus for a time reprieved. Another ancient shop by which visitors are intrigued, and dating from the same period, is the double bow-windowed shop in Bartholomews, facing the east side of the Town Hall. At present a tailor's shop, for many years up to the Second World War it was a picturesque, untidy establishment where a fisherman named

Andrew sold fishermen's gear. Later it became a private dwelling and was called Andrew's Cottage after its previous owner. The shop originally possessed a pedimented doorway, and the right-hand bow-window is certainly ancient, but that on the left replaces an earlier angular bay that existed in the 1850s, when the shop was Colliers, the left-hand portion then being a stationery business and the right carrying on the trade of 'Furnishing Ironmonger and Wholesale Hardware Man'.

North Street became a more important thoroughfare in the 1790s, with sixty-two new houses; Bond Street and King Street were formed, and thirty-four houses were built in Church Street, which was then called 'Spring Walk'. Russell Street, begun in 1778, now, in 1794, had seventy-eight houses, and similar activity was going on all around. The population, which in 1788 had been only 3,600, now numbered 5,669, but in the summer when the visitors came there were said to be 10,000 people in the town. The crowds of visitors brought hitherto unknown prosperity to the inhabitants, whose livelihood had been precarious until now, and a bank, Mitchell, Mills and Co., was opened in Brighton for the first time. Until then the people had done their banking in Lewes. All the gratitude of the townspeople for their new prosperity was centred upon the Prince, who had created it by choosing Brighton for his visits. Despite any failings he may have had, here he was regarded with unlimited indulgence and affection. The Prince added to his popularity by his endless generosity. He subscribed large sums to charity, and responded to every hint of private need with boundless liberality, as when he sent the contents of his pocket-book by a page to a tradesman whom he was told had attempted to commit suicide because of financial distress. 'Bid him make use of these', said the Prince. 'I may perhaps owe him something, and under the circumstances the routine of payment must appear odious.' The utterance was a superb combination of sympathy and dignity, concealing perhaps more than a little sense of misgiving that he himself might possibly have been to some extent responsible for the man's misery. The money was found to amount to over £700 in bank-notes.

The Prince's birthdays, which he celebrated every August for many years in Brighton, were occasions when the whole town joined in the festivities, which usually, as in 1789, according to 'an eyewitness',[1] took the form of the ringing of church bells, and the appearance of the Prince, together with Mrs. Fitzherbert, the Royal dukes, Mr. Fox and their friends, on a field just outside the town where sports were held. There was 'Jack-ass racing', foot-races by girls for the prize of a gown, sack-races for men and other diversions which were said to have caused much amusement because of 'the many ludicrous situations in which the several competitors were placed'. A whole ox was roasted on the green and the people pushed and jostled to get pieces of meat that were often burning hot cut off the carcass with a broadsword, while hogsheads of beer were set about from which people helped themselves. There were sailing matches in the afternoon and a ball at night, when the town was illuminated. The Prince and Mrs. Fitzherbert and their friends, as well as many of the nobility, joined the general throng of visitors on the Steine almost every day. Although the fashionable promenade, it had not invariably been the most delightful place for walking, especially in winter. In its early years the ground was rough and often muddy or encumbered by the nets spread around to dry by the fishermen, the grass was uneven, and a stagnant pool of dirty water was almost perpetually in front of the Pavilion. In wet weather the water of the Wellsbourne flowed into it and ran down the Steine into the sea at Pool Valley.

This nuisance was remedied in 1792–3, when an arched brick sewer was provided at the cost of the Prince of Wales and the Duke of Marlborough, who then owned Grove House to the north of the Pavilion, and in return for this public service the Lords of the Manor gave the Prince and the Duke permission to enclose a portion of the Steine in front of their houses, but never to build upon it nor to allow any encumbrance that would obstruct the view or in any way be a nuisance on the Steine. It was during the first eight years of the Pavilion's history that the building and its inhabitants acquired that reputation for riotous pleasures that has clung to them ever since, not always with justification, and very often to the exclusion of any other claim to interest. Certainly in those early days the Prince's circle included a number of thoroughly disreputable characters such as Sir John Lade, who had charge of the Prince's stables, and the hard-riding Lady Lade, whose coarseness of speech became a byword. There was also Major George Hanger, who had been sent from Eton to the university at Göttingen, where he acquired an astonishing vocabulary of German oaths, an unlimited capacity for drinking beer and some skill in duelling with the sabre. His uncouth manner gave some amusement to the Prince and his friends, but he seems to have been a generous, warm-hearted person, and gained the title of Honest George Hanger when he refused, on the death of his brother, Lord Coleraine, to assume the title, which he felt would be an embarrassment in the low company he preferred to keep. The notorious Barrymore family also were no doubt witty and amusing company, although the victims of their incredibly crude and heartless practical jokes would have thought otherwise. They were all members of the notorious Hellfire Club, and their nicknames gave some indication of their various proclivities. The eldest, Earl Barrymore, was called Hellgate; the second, the Hon. and Rev. Augustus Barry, was Newgate, and the Hon. Henry Barry, who was club-footed, was Cripplegate. Their sister was called Billingsgate because of the remarkably picturesque quality of her speech. Some of the Prince's other friends did him greater credit. There was Edmund Burke, a leading spokesman of the Whig party, one of the greatest of all English political thinkers and orators, and author of the remarkable essays on *The Sublime and Beautiful* and on *The French Revolution*. An even closer friend up to the time of his death in 1806 was Charles James Fox, leader of the Whigs; a hard drinker and gambler, but one of the most humane and generous of men, an opponent of slavery, and called by Burke 'the greatest debater the world ever saw'. Richard Brinsley Sheridan, owner of Covent Garden Theatre and author of *The School for Scandal* and *The Critic*, was under Burke the most brilliant orator of the Whig party and the especial mouthpiece and defender of the Prince of Wales. In later years the Prince's intellectual gifts and many good qualities were to earn for him the respect of men of no less perception than Byron, Sir Walter Scott and the Duke of Wellington.

Public entertainment in those days being so much less lavishly provided than now, the aristocracy seem to have taken upon themselves the responsibility for diverting the inhabitants, as well as themselves, by means of the spectacular bets and wagers upon which they sometimes exercised an ingenuity that would have taken them far in some more reputable sphere, but which more often astonished by their fatuity. An example of the former kind is the wager made by Lord Queensberry, or 'Old Q' as he was called, when he undertook to send a letter by hand a distance of fifty miles in an hour. This was accomplished by enclosing the letter in a cricket-ball, which was then thrown from hand to hand by a team of expert cricketers, so that the feat was performed within the hour. The writer 'Nimrod' tells us[2] that twenty-four cricketers were employed, which has led one writer to lament the lack of men today capable of throwing a cricket-ball a distance of over two miles, or of catching it from the same distance. The key to the riddle, however, is not that there were giants in those days, but that the cricketers stood in a circle and that the ball made a circuit of them many times in the hour. On one occasion the Duke was challenged by Sir John Lade to produce a man who could eat more at one sitting than a protégé of his own. The Duke did not witness the contest, which must have been a revolting spectacle, but received a note at the end 'to inform your grace that your man beat his antagonist by a pig and an apple pie'.

Almost any extraordinary behaviour that might be observed was no doubt to be accounted for as being for a bet, as when Honest George Hanger, ridden by a jockey wearing boots and spurs, was seen one day racing a fat bullock across the Steine. One of the hangers-on of Lord Barrymore was an enormously fat man, appropriately named Bullock, who was at one and the same time a brewer, a moneylender, the owner of a gaming establishment, and a racehorse owner and dealer. He offered to race Lord Barrymore over a hundred yards on foot, with the proviso that he could have thirty-five yards' start and choose his own time and place, and backed himself to win for a large sum of money. Lord Barrymore was confident that he could easily win despite the handicap, against a man so grossly fat that he could hardly walk, let alone run, and cheerfully accepted the wager. When the time came Barrymore and the Prince were taken to the narrow 'twitten' which still exists between Black Lion Street and Ship Street, and with his free start Mr. Bullock pounded along, filling up the narrow passage with his huge bulk and rolling from side to side so that Barrymore found it quite impossible to pass him.

Another friend of the Prince who visited him again at Brighton during the summer of 1790 was the Duc d'Orléans, originally the Duc de Chartres, who had assumed his new title in 1785. He had made the acquaintance of the Prince of Wales at the time of his first visit to England in 1783, and in September of the following year the Duke was amongst a number of foreign personages who entered horses for the races at Lewes. While the races were on the Prince invited to dinner several of these visitors, who included, as well as the Duc d'Orléans, the Duc de Lauzun (who later became the Duc de Biron) and the Marquis de Conflans. These newcomers were among a large number of fashionable Frenchmen to whom Brighton was something of a mecca for those who found their pleasure in horse-racing, hunting and coaching. The road between London and Brighton was one of the best in the country, and the Downs with their springy turf provided a paradise for horse-lovers. In June 1790 the Duc d'Orléans was in Brighton again, and had taken Marlborough House for the season. He had come to England not long before, apparently intending to make a long stay, for he took out a large annuity on a London bank and built a house in Park Lane.

Now aged forty-three, the Duke did not present an attractive appearance. His life of dissipation was causing his hair to fall out and his face to be discoloured and pitted by carbuncles. Yet he possessed such great charm and intelligence as made him seem to almost everyone, including even the censorious King George III, a witty and entertaining companion. According to Mme Campan, the Duc de Chartres was the originator of the *Anglomanie* which had been sweeping through French society for a number of years, causing young aristocrats to abandon the artificial life of the Parisian *salons* and the society dress of silk coats and breeches, powdered wigs, red-heeled shoes and lace ruffles, for the life of the stable and race-course, and for the smart young Englishman's practical dress of leather breeches, hunting-coat and riding-boots, so that it came to be said that Paris resembled a vast racing-stables, filled with English horses and grooms and London-built carriages. The Duke and his friends also bought from England the plain reticent furniture of Chippendale and Hepplewhite design, which they preferred to the elaborate French marquetry furniture lavishly ornamented with ormolu.

One of the kindest, most generous and sympathetic of men, he held progressive and liberal opinions which led him to dream of the overthrow of the existing regime in France. Long before anyone thought of a republic, he himself aspired to replace Louis XVI as a constitutional monarch, or at least as regent, as his great-grandfather had been before him during the minority of Louis XV, and believed he could bring social justice to France by means of humane and intelligently planned reforms. He was widely loved for his profuse charity, and he lavished a large part of his fortune on disseminating propaganda by liberal writers which paved the way for the revolution in France. Only a short while before the taking of the Bastille in 1789 the Duke had been banished to his country château by Louis XVI with the words 'You desire my head—You are a second Cromwell', and it was asserted that he later fled to England because of allegations that he had encouraged the Parisian mob that marched on Versailles. Suddenly he cut short his stay in England and returned to France. When titles were abolished in 1792 he took the name of Philippe Egalité, and became one of the Deputies of Paris to the Convention. In January 1793 he was among those who voted for the death of the King, and forfeited then the friendship and respect of the Prince of Wales and all his other English aquaintances, but when his son Louis Philippe joined the Austrians, who were giving their support to the Royalists, the Duke was thrown into prison and executed a few months after. With the irony of fate his ambitions of kingship were at length realized by his son, who had been the cause of his death.

Even before the Revolution Brighton had begun to acquire its air of elegance and gaiety that gave it so much of the atmosphere of a Continental city, and which attracted such Anglophile French visitors as those we have already met. The town possessed a particular quality of liveliness which not even the gayest of other European cities possessed. The place was free of the most grossly debased poverty that was to be seen in some Continental towns, and there was an absence not only of the muttered threats of revolt as in Paris, but of the oppressive and stifling hand of the secret police that was felt in Berlin, Vienna, Venice and Rome. When in the autumn of 1789 the early idealistic ardour of the Revolution swelled into frenzy and menace, thousands of the greatest landowners in France sold their houses and estates, their pictures, porcelain and furniture, and crossed to these shores to settle in England. In one fortnight alone, we are told,[3] as many as 6,000 passports were issued to fleeing French aristocrats. Dieppe was the nearest French port to Paris, and Brighton the closest point on these shores, so it was to this place that many of these refugees came, if only on their way to London, or to Dover, to re-embark there for Belgium, where in Brussels a large French colony was being formed.

Amongst these early fugitives arriving in Brighton were the Marquise d'Osmond and her husband, with their little girl Adèle and her English nurse. The Marquise was an Englishwoman, Eleonore Dillon, whom the Marquis had met and courted in romantic circumstances and married against strong opposition. Only a week before their arrival in Brighton they had been at their home in Versailles when the Paris mob, crazed with hunger and hatred, marched there at night and invaded the palace, seeking to murder the Royal Family. The Marquis himself had left his wife and child in order to help the Royal Family to escape, but the centuries-old apparatus of etiquette completely frustrated even the simplest actions that were out of the ordinary or of urgency; not even clothes or a carriage could be brought without involving the whole ancient machinery of formal procedure. Because of the consequent delays, all attempts at flight failed. By dawn the mob had broken into the palace, the Royal Family were taken by them to be imprisoned at the Tuileries, and the Marquis d'Osmond fled to England with his wife and child. They were welcomed at Brighton by Mrs. Fitzherbert, who had gone down to the shore to watch the arrival of the cross-Channel boat. She had become an intimate friend of the Marquise during her stay in Paris a few years earlier when she had been in flight from the Prince of Wales. They were invited to stay for a time at Mrs. Fitzherbert's house, and to visit the Prince of Wales at the Pavilion, where Mrs. Fitzherbert astonished the little girl by showing her a dressing-table covered with innumerable shoe-buckles, and a cupboard containing enough shoes for him to wear a different pair on every day of the year.

After a while the d'Osmond family settled in Rome. After the restoration of the French monarchy the Marquis was appointed Ambassador in London, and while in this country returned with his wife many times to Brighton at the Prince Regent's invitation. Their daughter Adèle, who had become the Comtesse de Boigne, often accompanied them on their visits to the Pavilion, and it is from her lively *Memoirs* that we learn much that we know, not only of the Court life of France from 1781 to 1830 but of day-to-day affairs at the Pavilion in Regency days.

With the September massacres of 1792 the stream of French refugees arriving at Brighton swelled to a flood. They no longer came by the Dieppe packet with some wealth obtained by the sale of their possessions, but more often now by fishing-boats they had hired in haste and secrecy, and often possessing little more than the clothes they wore. Most of them made their way onwards to London, by coach if they had money, but when destitute on foot.

In October the cross-Channel packet landed at Shoreham a party of thirty-seven nuns who had been driven from their convent at Lille, with only £30 between them. On hearing of their plight the people of Brighton sent their carriages to bring them here, where they were put up at the New Ship Inn, although the landlord was hard put to it to accommodate them, as, despite all their terrible experiences, they refused to sleep more than one to a bed. The Prince of Wales paid them a lengthy visit at the hotel and afterwards opened a subscription for their relief. Eventually the nuns departed for Dover and Brussels.

After a while the fleeing aristocrats were no longer permitted to leave France with the ease of a year or two earlier. The ports were now closely watched for refugees, and those who escaped did so only by cunning. It was said that the Marquise de Beaule escaped by dressing as a sailor, helping the crew during the whole of the crossing. Her maid, who came with her, was carried on board in a trunk in which some holes had been bored to give her air. On the same boat was the Comtesse de Noailles, who also dressed in man's clothes and escaped detection by hiding in a large coil of rope for fourteen hours. Many of these refugees were acquaintances of the Prince and Mrs. Fitzherbert, and were received at the Pavilion and given help by them when they were in need. The news of these romantic escapes quickly ran round Brighton. Mrs. Fitzherbert took Madame de Noailles to her house and gave her woman's clothes, so that a day or two later she was able to go with the Prince and his wife to a cricket match and to dine in a marquee to the strains of a military band. In the evening the heroine of the adventure displayed herself to an admiring crowd on the Steine in the company of Mrs. Fitzherbert and Lady Clermont. She was then only about twenty-one, and her figure and deportment were said to be 'very interesting'.[4]

In February 1793 England declared war against France, and defences were set up and put into order all along the South Coast. At Brighton the East and West Batteries were overhauled and a large encampment was established in August 1793 with its left flank in Belle Vue field, on the site of the present Regency Square, and extending westwards along the coast. The Army, which numbered 7,000 men, afterwards increased to 10,000, including regular soldiers, militia and volunteers, had marched from Ashdown Forest, and they were accompanied by heavy artillery and a large corps of artificers. The Army arrived on the Prince's birthday, 5th August, and were met by him at Preston. His own regiment headed the column. An elaborate tent was set up for the Prince near the remains of the old church in the village of Hove. The Royal tent was far from being a spartan affair intended for the rigours of campaigning. It consisted of three large compartments, a dining section, a sleeping portion, and a 'very spacious kitchen' to provide for the needs of the Prince and his personal staff, and altogether it was regarded as 'one of the most elegant things of the kind ever made use of in this country'.

The Prince was sufficiently conscious of his responsibilities as Colonel-in-Chief of 'The Prince of Wales's Own' Regiment to take command of the picket-guard on 2nd September, remaining on duty all night, it is reported, fortified for the ordeal no doubt by the congenial company of some fellow officers and by adequate provision for keeping out the cold of the night. On another occasion when he had detailed himself to remain on duty all night a severe storm arose and several of the tents were blown down. The officers of the guard went to ensure the safety of the Prince, but they discovered he had long before left the camp for the safety and comfort of his own bed at the Pavilion. With the onset of winter the camp broke up and by early November the last of the soldiers had left. The following summer a second camp was set up, about a mile and a half west of the town, again with 7,000 men, later increased to 15,000 when the harvest had been gathered and the farm labourers were freed for militia service.

During the weeks when the camps were in being the streets of the town when crowded with soldiers off duty and in their gay uniforms must have presented a brilliant and exhilarating sight, and the continual parades, marching, playing of bands, manoeuvres and reviews on the Downs must have provided fresh excitements for the inhabitants and the visitors.

Suddenly, in May 1795, a shock-wave of horror shuddered through the town when the news went round that thirteen soldiers of the Oxford Militia were on trial for their lives for mutiny. Some troops stationed at East Blatchington, near Newhaven, had rebelled in protest at the small quantity and bad quality of the food issued to them. They had broken into a flour-mill, and emptied the cargo of a vessel laden with corn into the river at Newhaven. Brighton was the military headquarters for the district, and the court martial was held at the Castle Tavern, which stood on the site of the present Electricity Showrooms. After the eight days of the trial two men, Edward Cooke and Henry Parish, were sentenced to be shot, and six others to the even more terrible punishment, amounting to being flogged to death, of receiving 1,000 lashes. Another man who was sentenced to death was afterwards reprieved 'on condition of being transported to Botany Bay for ten years'. The townspeople, some of whom had taken food to the men every day during the trial, were overcome with horror at these savage sentences, although these were not unusual in the Army in those days, and vigorously expressed their indignation to the military authorities. Several of the more important residents twice submitted petitions for mercy to be shown, but with little result. The sentences were carried out at Goldstone Bottom at Hove. Three of the men sentenced to be flogged were given 300 lashes each, the surgeon intervening to say they could stand no more. A fourth was reprieved after the dreadful experience of being tied to the flogging-post, and cut down after a while, and the other two were also reprieved. A number of loaded cannon were trained on the spot where the executions were to take place, to prevent any attempt to interfere with the sentences, but, not surprisingly, 'no smallest symptom of opposition, resistance or revenge appeared'!

Cooke and Parish were shot after they had been compelled, again with a refinement of sadistic horror, to kneel upon their coffins. The clergyman who attended them, the Rev. M. Dring, Chaplain to the Regiment, fainted at the sound of the firing and afterwards never wholly recovered his mind. A farewell letter that Cooke wrote to his brother is preserved in the Brighton Museum. In it he expressed astonishing peace of mind and fortitude in the face of his execution, but confessed to no guilt other than in 'Drinking and Breaking the Sabbath'.

By next season the horror of these events had faded, and the presence of the military was welcomed again when the camp was opened. For some ten years to come, parades, grand reviews, field days and sham fights on the Downs were part of the season's delights. It was not invariably possible for them to be conducted with the strictest military discipline and decorum. The townspeople came to regard them as entertainments got up expressly for their benefit, rather than for the serious purpose of military training, and turned out for these occasions in every sort of conveyance—barouches, landaus, landaulets, sociables, curricles, tandems, and even fish-carts all crammed with spectators and with provisions for a merry day's outing on the Downs. On one occasion the spectators seemed to disregard entirely the attempts of the opposing forces to manoeuvre, and cheerfully mingled with the columns of men and guns on both sides, until the confusion was complete, with ladies fainting, horses rearing and plunging, and carriages becoming entangled with each other, so that at last both forces were compelled to retreat.

Before long Brighton Camp was by far the most famous along the South Coast. It gave its name to one of the gayest and liveliest military marches ever written—'Brighton Camp, or the girl I left behind me'. A famous song and a long-popular country dance were arranged to the tune, and the same title was given to a pair of engravings after paintings by Francis Wheatley, published in 1796, one of them entitled 'The Encampment at Brighton', showing two mounted troopers with a group of country folk who are offering chickens and eggs, with a view of the Downs in the distance and the lines of tents and baggage-wagons, while the second represents 'The Departure from Brighton', with a soldier bidding a tender farewell to some local girls.

Soon Brighton had become the Mecca of every young lady who dreamed of being escorted by a smart young officer in a dazzling uniform. 'In Lydia's imagination', Jane Austen wrote in *Pride and Prejudice*, 'a visit to Brighton comprized every possibility of earthly happiness. She saw with the creative eye of fancy, the streets of that gay bathing-place covered with officers. She saw herself the object of attention to tens and scores of them at present unknown. She saw all the glories of the camp—its tents stretched forth in beauteous uniformity of lines, crowded with the young and gay, and dazzling with scarlet; and to complete the view, she saw herself seated beneath a tent, tenderly flirting with at least six officers at once.' At the time Miss Austen was writing, in 1796, *The Times* also noted that the Prince's own regiment was the most popular in the Army among fashionable young men. Almost every one of the officers was a personal friend of the Prince. 'They associate with no one but their own corps. Most of them keep their own blood horses, their curricles and their girls.' Their military duties were by no means exacting. 'At one o'clock', wrote the same commentator, 'they appear on parade to hear the word of command given to the subaltern guard; afterwards they toss off their *goes* of brandy, dine about five, and come about eight to the theatre. *Vivent, l'Amour et Bacchus.*' The local paper revealed that 'The Cyprian corps stationed in this town is now estimated to amount to over 300, exclusive of those at Brighton Camp.' The fact that those 'good-natured but unfortunate creatures could be supported by the wages of prostitution cast a melancholy reflection on the increasing depravity of the age'.[5]

The season must have been about to come to an end, however, for a week later the same journal reported that 'The Paphian Temples at Brighton are now quite deserted, the presiding goddesses having taken their flight to dispense their favours in the more polluted brothels of the Metropolis.'[6]

One of the Prince's closest friends at this time was George Brummell, usually known as 'Beau Brummell', with whom he shared a taste for sartorial perfection, for personal cleanliness and for Boulle furniture. It was at one of these military parades that Brummell, who had been made a subaltern in the Prince's own regiment, disgraced himself by falling off his horse in front of the whole parade, and broke his nose. A somewhat similar disaster befell Sir Osbert Sitwell, as he himself confessed, at a presentation ceremony held at the Royal Pavilion in 1945, when as a young man serving in the Hussars he fell off his horse at the feet of the colonel of his regiment, though happily without the painful consequences suffered by Beau Brummell.

But the brilliant life of military parades and reviews at Brighton was not merely a gay charade for the Prince. He seems to have borne out in himself Dr. Johnson's dictum that 'a man thinks badly of himself who has never been a soldier', and despite his honorary colonelcy, he felt it acutely that he was not allowed to go on active service abroad as several of his brothers had done. In August 1803 he wrote from Brighton to his father, the King. 'I asked to be allowed to display the best energies of my character, to shed the last drop of my blood in support of your Majesty's person, crown and dignity, for this is not a war for empire, glory or dominion, but for existence. In this contest the lowest, the humblest of your Majesty's subjects have been called in; it would therefore, little become me, who am the first and who stand at the very footstool of the throne, to remain a tame, an idle, and a lifeless spectator of the mischiefs which threaten us, unconscious of the dangers which surround us and indifferent to the consequences which may follow.' In this and in several similar letters the Prince seems to have unusual seriousness of intention, for it is clear from the style of the letters that he had not trusted to his own abilities, but had enlisted the help of a more eloquent and practised writer to attempt to move the King in this matter. His pleas failed to achieve their object. It was not so much the Prince's disappointment over being denied active service that wounded him as the utter contempt for his desires that the King displayed by his refusal.

The sea offered spectacles no less exciting than did the Downs and fields around Brighton. Indeed, nowadays, apart from a few oil-tankers and coal-boats moving in and out of Shoreham Harbour, a few sailing-dinghies at week-ends, one or two fishing-boats and an occasional yacht passing along the coast, the sea offers very little of interest by comparison with the days when the Brighton fishing-fleet numbered more than a hundred vessels, and its departure and return were a stirring sight; when a frigate or other small man-of-war was more or less permanently stationed off the town, revenue cutters patrolled up and down the coast, and the sea was dotted with a host of sailing vessels of all kinds. Sham sea-battles were fought for the exercise of the ships' crews and for the amusement of the Prince of Wales, and from time to time the sight of a fleet of ships passing up-Channel, their white square sails on tall masts shining in the sun, would bring hundreds of people flocking to the beach and cliff-top, as once in July 1794, when 'the homeward bound Jamaica fleet consisting of between 70 and 80 sail under convoy of the "Powerful" of 74 guns afforded a most pleasing spectacle to the company and inhabitants of Brighton'.[7]

As Napoleon's flat-bottomed boats gathered in ever-increasing numbers on the French coast to carry his troops across the Channel the fear of an invasion grew, until, as in the summer of 1940, an enemy landing was expected at any moment and the local commanders were in a state of perpetual apprehension. At last, in February 1794, a message was received at the cavalry barracks that the dreaded moment had come, and the troops hurried down to the beach, where their sudden appearance caused them to be mistaken for the French by the fishermen and the bathing-women, who defended themselves valiantly against the attackers with mops, broomsticks and other primitive weapons. But the alarm was soon discovered to be just one more practical joke of the Prince of Wales and his friends, and a day or two later a lively caricature was published, entitled 'Attack of the French, or Brighton in a Bustle'. It shows the fisherfolk fiercely engaged in combat with the military, and Martha Gunn wielding a mop with great effect, while Fox and Sheridan watch the fun from the safety of some bathing-machines. In August of the same year the English frigate *Aurora* and two cutters were seen cruising off Brighton on the look-out for some French raiders which had been reported.

The local smugglers were quite undeterred by the frequent appearance of French privateers and raiders off the Sussex coast. One day in April 1794 the two revenue cutters, the *Swan* and the *Swallow*, captured at sea off Brighton a smuggling lugger laden with 266 casks of contraband spirits, thirty-one bags of snuff and two bags of tobacco. The next day the same cutters intercepted a smuggling cutter carrying 400 casks of foreign spirits and a quantity of tea.[8] Early one morning in October of the same year some officers of the Prince's 10th Light Dragoons were returning to camp at Brighton when they observed a gang of smugglers unloading a cargo of contraband spirits on to the beach. With the aid of some soldiers from the camp they attacked and arrested the smugglers and secured the cargo, which consisted of four or five hundred tubs of 'geneva' or gin. While helping to carry the casks to the customs warehouse at Shoreham, two of the soldiers managed to take 'such inordinate draughts of the baleful spirit' that they were incapable of moving from the place and were both found dead drunk early the next morning.[9]

There were occasionally some fierce encounters between smugglers and revenue men. In January 1795, when the customs officer in a ten-oared galley drew alongside a smugglers' cutter to inspect its cargo, the smugglers called to the revenue men to keep off, and without waiting for an answer fired on them, wounding one of them so that he died soon after.[10] About the same time customs officers from Rottingdean found thirty-eight casks of contraband spirit concealed in a cave in the cliff at Ovingdean.[11]

From now on the enemy's activities off the coast increased alarmingly. In February 1795 a French cutter privateer—a sort of licensed pirate, authorized to attack our shipping by letters of Marque—appeared at Brighton and captured a large sloop and a brig, and made off with them to the French coast. A few weeks later a notorious French privateer named the *Eagle* appeared off the coast and captured a sloop which had become separated from her convoy. The *Eagle* had originally been an English boat, belonging to some Sussex smugglers; her success in capturing small English vessels was thought to be partly due to the fact of her being sheathed with copper, and a very fast sailer, but most of all because her crew consisted not of Frenchmen, but of renegade English and Irish sailors[12] whose native dash and courage were, of course, not regarded as being affected by their treachery.

The English frigate *Diamond* was often on the Brighton Station, and for some months there were comparatively few alarms of any consequence, but in April Sir Sydney Smith's squadron of warships was seen heading up-Channel, led by the *Diamond*. A few days later the frigate landed back at Brighton with the depressing news that the Admiral with his ship had been captured by the French.[13] He escaped some two years later. A few weeks after his capture the town was in an uproar when the master of the telegraph observed a French frigate of thirty-two to thirty-four guns approaching Brighton. The alarm was given, the Royal Artillery and the Sea Fencibles turned out on to the beach and prepared to resist the expected attack, but the French frigate turned about and escaped before the English guns could be brought to bear upon it.[14]

By now our coastal trade was being seriously affected by the activities of French privateers. Nevertheless, English seamen on the South Coast had a remarkable record of success against the enemy. Captain Amos of the revenue cutter *Swallow*, stationed at Shoreham, captured three French privateers, one of them called *Le Petit Diable*, within fifteen days. In all he captured seven or eight enemy raiders at this time, but the gallant Captain complained that his prize money was almost entirely swallowed up by his expenses.[15]

Another local seaman, a Mr. Roberts, had an even more astonishing success. The owner of a small pleasure boat came into Shoreham to give information that he had sighted a Spanish ship off Brighton. Mr. Roberts put out in a row-boat and took possession of the Spanish ship single-handed. It was found to be laden with pitch and lime, and was the first Spanish prize taken in English waters after the breakdown of relations between the English Government and the Spanish Court.[16]

Towards the end of 1796 French prisoners taken from enemy vessels along the Sussex coast tried, with a singular lack of success, to intimidate their captors by telling of the enormous numbers of flat-bottomed troop transports and heavily armed gunboats that were being assembled on the French coast in readiness to invade England.[17]

Although far from being demoralized by these accounts, the defenders of Brighton were a little on edge, and prone to imagine that the slightest untoward happening was the prelude to the long-awaited attack. One afternoon a British sloop-of-war, the *Fly*, which was for obvious reasons not showing any distinguishing colours, fired some shots at a smuggling cutter to which she was giving chase, and several of the cannon balls fell on the shore near the West Battery. It was at once concluded that the sloop was an enemy vessel and some shots were fired at her from the Battery, whereupon the *Fly* displayed her colours. She afterwards pursued the cutter and captured her, but the smugglers had taken advantage of the confusion to transfer their illegal cargo to another vessel which made for the shore and escaped.[18]

The smugglers benefited very greatly from the war, because the heavily increased duties that were imposed on spirits, tea and coffee made their operations more profitable than ever.[19] After a while the threat of invasion receded when Napoleon's thoughts turned to other theatres of war, and the revenue-cheating gentry were given a clear field.

6 The Luckless Marriage

wo matters in which the Prince was involved were pursued by him with a singular lack of enthusiasm after the initial period of excitement. One was the campaign of economy upon which he had so piously embarked when he came down to Brighton with Mrs. Fitzherbert in the summer of 1786. The other was the fidelity to his bride that he had sworn at their secret wedding. After the first few years of their marriage the Prince departed with increasing frequency from the path of virtue, while Mrs. Fitzherbert greeted these amours successively with indignant protestations and weeping, and at length with philosophic resignation; at least so long as none of them reached the stage of a grand affair. Furthermore she had been made to realize that although she was the Prince's wife, and not his mistress, were their marriage to be properly proclaimed at any time, it could only be declared as illegal. This had already occurred in the case of the unauthorized marriage in Hanover of Prince Augustus, a younger brother of the Prince of Wales, to Lady Augusta Murray, daughter of the Earl of Dunmore, which had been set aside under the Royal Marriage Act.

Mrs. Fitzherbert realized she was fortunate to have kept the Prince's love for so long. She admitted that, as Sheridan expressed it, 'the Prince was too much every lady's man to be the man of any lady', and excused his behaviour by thinking of the many temptations by which he was surrounded, in the form of the numerous charming and complaisant women in society who were eager to profit by an affair with the Prince, and even willing to create doubts in his mind as to the genuineness of Mrs. Fitzherbert's own attitude to him, such as that 'it was the rank of his Royal Highness that she loved, more than his person', although she proved the contrary by every action of her life. The Prince regarded her tears and reproaches as outbursts of unreasonable jealousy and was filled with a sense of injury, and quarrels between them became more and more frequent. The Prince now fell under the spell of Lady Jersey, a bewitching but vicious and vixenish grandmother of forty. Once more he had succumbed, as he would again later more than once, to the appeal of an older woman. Mrs. Fitzherbert was not prepared to tolerate an intrigue of this magnitude, and for the summer of 1794 rented the exquisite little Palladian mansion of Marble Hill at Twickenham, built and decorated about 1723 by Roger Morris for Henrietta, Countess of Suffolk, mistress of

George II. Here she stayed in a state if not of separation from the Prince then as it were of dignified independence, until one evening in June while she was dining with the Duke and Duchess of Clarence, where they had expected the Prince might join them, a note was brought to her in which he stated with the heartless brutality that he was to display to her again on a later occasion, that he intended never to see her again. Only a few hours earlier she had received a note from him that was presumably intended to explain his absence from the dinner-party at the Clarences', telling her he had been suddenly asked to dine with his sister at Windsor, and that afterwards he would go back to Brighton. The explanation was probably false, covering a meeting with Lady Jersey, but in the note the Prince had addressed Mrs. Fitzherbert with great affection as 'My dearest love', and ended 'ever thine'. On reading the letter of dismissal, Mrs. Fitzherbert left the Clarences' table almost fainting with shock and returned to Marble Hill heart-broken and disillusioned. On re-reading the Prince's earlier note she now probably realized the subterfuge it concealed, and appended to it a note saying: 'This letter I received the morning of the day the Prince sent me word he would never enter my house (Lady Jersey's influence).' For some time the Prince had been threatened by a new avalanche of debts, now amounting to nearly £640,000. In fairness to the Prince it must be said that this sum had not been squandered fruitlessly. Little of it had been thrown away at the gaming-tables, for unlike his brother the Duke of York the Prince was 'not a gaming man'; neither had it been lost on the turf, for the Prince had given up frequenting the races since his own jockey had been accused in 1791 of 'pulling' his horse Escape in a race one day when it could have won easily, so as to improve the odds for a victory in the next race. The Prince obviously had not the slightest conception of the value of money. For years he had allowed unscrupulous tradesmen to send in enormously exaggerated bills, so that a single farrier could claim to be owed £40,000. And although his casual love-affairs were often short and were ended by the Prince without a pang he was generous to excess in consoling his discarded mistresses financially. He had given Mrs. Crouch, the beautiful opera singer who was his mistress for hardly more than a few days, his bond for £10,000 and about £5,000 worth of jewels and trinkets, and settled on her an annuity of £1,000 a year, although this was repudiated and ceased to be paid when the debts were settled. Most of the Prince's money had been spent on the rebuilding and decoration of Carlton House, and in laying the foundations of his great collections of furniture, pictures, silver, porcelain and other treasures which are a tribute to his taste as the greatest Royal patron of the arts since King Charles I, and which are part of our national heritage. None the less, the gigantic debts had to be paid.

For some years it had been taken for granted in Royal circles that the Prince of Wales must at some time make an acceptable marriage in order to provide an heir to the throne, and it was generally assumed that the match would be with one of the princesses of Brunswick. Until he married, as Burke pointed out years earlier, the Prince would be 'liable to every suspicion and daily insult. He will not be considered as one of the corps of Princes, non-aggregated to that body which people here, even more than in other countries are made to look at with respect. No Prince appears settled unless he puts himself into the situation of the father of a family.'

The Prince of Wales, possibly inspired by Lady Jersey, now conceived that the only means by which the King could be persuaded to ask Parliament to settle the debts was to offer to contract an acceptable state alliance. In order to justify this course to himself he was compelled to construct a vast tissue of imagined misunderstandings, annoyances and shortcomings of every conceivable kind existing between himself and Mrs. Fitzherbert, and even conjectures regarding her possible infidelity to him.

A letter from the Prince to Isabella Pigot, Mrs. Fitzherbert's companion, which is preserved in the Royal Pavilion collection, is a tortured effusion, fourteen pages long, in which he writes agonizingly concerning rumours of Mrs. Fitzherbert's being suspected of having flirted with the Comte de Noailles, husband of the lady who had escaped to Brighton from France, dressed as a boy, in 1792. The letter is undated, but refers apparently to the spring of 1794. Although he had been unable 'to substantiate criminal intercourse', the Prince was beside himself with anguish, despite the innumerable infidelities of which he himself had been guilty. 'Gracious God of Heaven, Bell, what were my sufferings' he wrote, 'what are they, and what must they now ever be to the latest moments of my existence . . .'

On the 29th August 1794 he wrote to his brother, the Duke of York, describing the 'commerage, chit-chat, tracasseries which the various disagreements and misunderstandings' between Mrs. Fitzherbert and himself naturally occasioned and telling him that 'In short we are *finally parted, but parted amicably*. . . . However tout est fini entre nous, and I have obtain'd the King's consent to my marrying my own cousin Princess Caroline, the Duke of Brunswick's daughter.'[1]

Soon after the King was able to inform the Prime Minister, William Pitt: 'I have this a.m. seen the Prince of Wales who has acquainted me with his having broken off all connexion with Mrs. Fitzherbert and desire of entering into a more creditable line of life by marrying, expressing at the same time his wishes that a niece of the Prince of Brunswick is the person.'

The only other eligible person was the Queen's niece, the Princess Louise of Mecklenburg, a pleasant, attractive, cultivated girl, but the Prince resisted his mother's suggestions that he should take her as his choice, again possibly through the influence of Lady Jersey, who might well have feared that her position might not be so secure with the Prince married to such a charming bride.

Although Princess Caroline was a merry, warm-hearted and affectionate girl, and quite attractive with her great vitality, splendid bosom and beautiful fair hair, she was coarse in her manners and speech, and unfastidious in her personal habits. At his first meeting with Caroline, the Prince was aghast at her vulgarity and uncleanliness of person and stepped aside calling for brandy. The Princess on her part was as much disconcerted by his brusqueness and lack of affection as by his unexpected plumpness. Then, at the age of thirty-three, the Prince weighed seventeen stone. Within a month the Prince was regretting his dismissal of Maria and through a friend, Admiral Payne, was once more besieging her with pleas for forgiveness. Although no unwilling to consider a reconciliation, Mrs. Fitzherbert wisely maintained a dignified reserve and refused to write him any letters, fearing lest they should fall into the hands of Lady Jersey. A few days later she sailed for the Continent.

The wedding took place on 8th April 1795. The day before the Prince had been seen riding furiously alone up and down past Mrs. Fitzherbert's house at Twickenham in a frenzy of misery and despair. Years later the Duke of Clarence, who had been given the task of escorting his brother throughout the wedding proceedings, remarked that as they passed through the garden of Carlton House before the ceremony the Prince said to him: 'William, tell Mrs. Fitzherbert she is the only woman I shall ever love.' When Pitt announced in Parliament that the Prince's income would be increased to £125,000 a year, not counting his revenues from the Duchy of Cornwall, but that his debts must be paid for out of income, the payments to be spread over nine years, the Prince felt he had been betrayed. The Duke of Clarence believed he was supporting his brother by voicing his indignation at this arrangement in the House of Lords in the course of one of his all-too-frequent well-intentioned but foolish and ill-advised speeches. He declared that 'it was a matter of public notoriety, that, when the Prince of Wales's marriage was agreed upon, there was a stipulation that he should in the event of that union be exonerated from the debts'. He accomplished nothing, however, by this indiscreet outburst, beyond making it plain to everyone in England, and above all to Mrs. Fitzherbert and the Princess Caroline, that the Prince had deserted the woman he loved and married one he did not solely in order to pay his debts.

About two months after the wedding the Prince brought his bride to Brighton, arriving between one and two o'clock in the morning. They stayed at Mr. Gerald Hamilton's elegant house on the Steine, which they had taken for three weeks, as the Pavilion was still in the hands of the decorators. The town was brilliantly illuminated, and, despite the heavy rain which had set in, the Prince 'perambulated the town in his great coat to view the devices'. A brilliant round of festivities was planned for the Royal couple. They visited the theatre, walked upon the Steine and were present at the opening service of the Chapel Royal in Prince's Place, on 2nd August, when 'a charity sermon' was preached. For the Prince's birthday on 12th August, as well as the usual illuminations and other festivities, a fête was held at the Promenade Grove, the pleasure gardens immediately to the west of the Pavilion, which were now at the height of their popularity. The firework display given then was the most elaborate ever held in the town, with 'Horizontal Wheels in Brilliant Fire, adorned with Roman Candles and Pot de Brins; transparencies, scintillating with Rayonnant Fire and Maroons; Gillickes in Brilliant Fire'; the evening concluding with 'discharges of Pot de Grades and Illuminated Bomb-shells'.

The Princess attended with her husband a number of army reviews and field-days that were held at the camp on the Downs that year, at Goldstone Bottom. At one of these reviews the Prince of Wales's Regiment, then newly named the 10th Hussars, appeared dressed in entirely new uniforms of unparalleled splendour, designed by their Colonel-in-Chief himself.

The Princess had been accompanied from the first moment of her arrival in this country by Lady Jersey, who had been appointed her lady-in-waiting by the Queen, a diabolical arrangement tolerated by the Prince with unbelievable heartlessness and supine acceptance. All through the honeymoon Lady Jersey had spared no pains to make the life of the Princess miserable, by means of continual cruel practical jokes and humiliations. Even on the wedding night Lady Jersey caused Epsom salts to be put into the pastry served to her for supper, arranged for her to be given almost unmanageable horses to ride at military parades, and caused spirits to be added to the wine she drank so as to make her usually free conversation even more indiscreet and outrageous. When the pearl bracelets which the Prince had given Caroline disappeared, the Princess saw them again on the arms of her rival. The letters she had written home to her mother were intercepted by Lady Jersey, and the uncomplimentary remarks she had made about 'de old Begum', as she called her mother-in-law, were assiduously conveyed to the Queen.

The shameful way in which the Princess had been treated after coming to England, and her courageous reaction to these circumstances, had caused a great deal of sympathy for her to be aroused amongst the public, and when this last episode was reported in the newspapers the strength of public feeling on her behalf enabled her to triumph at last over Lady Jersey, who eventually was forced by the King to resign from the Princess's household. In September 1795 a grand ball was arranged by Mr. Wade in honour of the Royal couple at the Castle Hotel Assembly Rooms, but only the Prince was present. The Princess, who was pregnant, was becoming less and less inclined for joyous festivities, but instead pursued more peaceful distractions. Most fashionable carriage drives and excursions were made at that time in the direction of Preston Village, on the London

Road, or eastwards along the cliffs towards Rottingdean. The Princess accordingly decided to make her drives away from the fashionable stream into the country west of Brighton, towards Shoreham, attended only by a couple of ladies and a gentleman of her suite. Here she spent the days 'in all the simplicity of rural life', as a writer said at the time, seated beneath a clump of elm trees or under a hedge, gazing for hours at the prospect of Downs and sea, reflecting perhaps on the sad disappointments and miseries she had suffered after coming to this country full of such eager hopes of happiness.

Curiously enough, Lady Jersey herself was also pregnant at this time, and in October gave birth to a son 'at the house of Lord Jersey next to George's Library on the Steine'.[2]

In November the Princess returned to London, where at Carlton House a daughter, the ill-fated Princess Charlotte, was born on 17th January 1796. There were great hopes in Brighton that the Princess would visit the town again with her child next summer, but at the last moment the visit was cancelled because, it was said, of the indisposition of the Infant Princess, for whom 'an elegant nursery had been constructed at the Pavilion'. The Princess's failure to visit Brighton again may have been due less to any illness of the child than the fact that the Prince had written to Princess Caroline announcing his intention of separating from her, in another of those brusque and callous notes with which at crucial moments in his dealings with the women who were close to him he demonstrated his utter inability to behave towards them with any semblance of human feeling. He wrote, on 30th April 1796: 'Our inclinations are not in our power, nor should either of us be held answerable to the other, because nature has not made us suitable to each other.' He went on to express the hope 'that the rest of our lives will be spent in uninterrupted tranquility'. He devoted more thought and many sheets of paper to writing a will, which now lies in the Windsor archives, by which he left all he possessed to Mrs. Fitzherbert. Writing with unbelievable pomposity, self-satisfaction and nauseating piety, in it he speaks of Mrs. Fitzherbert as 'my Wife in the eyes of God, and who is, and ever will be, such in mine . . .'

He bequeathed to her the whole of the furniture of Carlton House: 'all the Bronze ornamental chimney-pieces, all the Hangings, chairs, Tables, ornamental and inlaid Tables, bronzed Tables, Cabinets and Consoles, girandoles, Clocks whether of Bronze or other material . . .' Here the Prince seems to have rambled on in a reverie over the splendour of the treasures with which he had filled the place, until he bethought himself of the 'immense Sum of money due to me from the Crown and the Nation on the arrears of the Duchy of Cornwall', which 'just tribute' he also bequeathed to Maria. After repeatedly referring to Mrs. Fitzherbert as 'my only true and real Wife', and with many appeals to Heaven, he goes on to speak of 'the falsehood and treachery' towards himself of 'the Mother of the Child, called the Princess of Wales', and of 'the convincing and repeated proofs of her entire want of judgement and feeling', which caused him to deny the Princess Caroline the custody of his daughter or any hand in her management. He showed more human kindliness for Mrs. Fitzherbert's companion, Isabella Pigot, to whom he left £500, and for his other servants, for whom he made provision with great consideration, and who seem to have worshipped him. The will concluded with directions that he should be buried at his death with the miniature of 'my beloved Wife . . . right upon my Heart', and if possible that the coffins of Mrs. Fitzherbert and himself should ultimately be buried together, 'and if she has no objection, that the two inward sides of the two Coffins should be taken out and the two Coffins soldered together'.

In this soul-searching document, however, there is no mention of Lady Jersey. Although he had not yet broken with the lady, her fascination for him was weakening. As Lady Jerningham mentions in her letters,[3] she had by July 1796 handed in her resignation, long delayed at the Prince's own suggestion, as she said, because 'he represented that such a step could only be regarded as confirmation of every absurd and abominable falsehood'.

Lady Jersey had taken a house at Brighton for that summer, but the Prince soon found that recent events had caused his popularity there to suffer so much that it was quite impossible to go on staying there with her. So they decided to spend the autumn together at Bognor. They eventually parted in 1798, when the Prince sent word to her through a friend of his 'difference or diminution of regard'.

After several despairing efforts to recapture his affections which only caused him much annoyance, Lady Jersey abandoned the struggle and sought other consolations. During the next year or two the Prince was at Brighton during the summer, amusing himself chiefly by attending the military parades and sham fights on the Downs. He probably felt that his beloved Pavilion was the only still centre in a tumultuous world, and his behaviour was now so circumspect that in 1798 a local newspaper was able to remark that 'the change of Society and manners which has taken place at the Pavilion, gives most heartfelt satisfaction to every lover of his country; it is, now, every way worthy of the Heir Apparent of the British Empire'.

7 Oriental Experiments

E ver since that fateful day in June 1794 when he had sent Mrs.
Fitzherbert his brusque note of dismissal there had hardly been
a moment when he did not think of his wife, despite the distractions of life with Lady Jersey, and after the final break with her
he began once again to bombard Mrs. Fitzherbert with letters, messages
and appeals, exactly as he had done fifteen years earlier. Miss Pigot,
Admiral Payne and the Prince's brothers were all compelled to carry his
notes to her at every hour of the day and night. When his efforts to persuade
her to a reconciliation achieved nothing he resorted to the threat to publish
the details of their marriage, and Mrs. Fitzherbert was in an agony of fear
that her brother and uncle, the witnesses to the illegal ceremony, might be
put in danger. At last the Prince pretended to be ill and, as years before,
protested that his life would be threatened if Mrs. Fitzherbert did not
return to him. She was under pressure not only from the Prince and his
brothers, but from the Queen herself, who had always had a respect for
Mrs. Fitzherbert's great integrity and good influence on the Prince, and
who now wrote imploring her to consider a reconciliation. To show the
genuineness of his feelings the Prince sent Mrs. Fitzherbert a copy of the
will he had made in her favour, together with a painting of his right eye in
a gold locket engraved with the words 'Rejoindre ou mourir', another of
those French mottoes which seemed to the Prince to have a magical
compulsive power akin to the virtue of the sacred sentences worn as charms
by Tibetan monks. Beside herself with apprehension for her family and
for the Prince's health, overcome with affection for her husband himself,
despite his failings, and anxiety for her own dignity and moral position,
she decided to seek the advice of the Pope regarding the validity of her
marriage. If he ruled against her she would leave the country for ever. Her
chaplain, Father Nassau, journeyed to Rome and, after an interview in
Latin with the Pope, presented the case in writing for his decision. The
Church of Rome had always held that marriages are not made by a priest
or clergyman, or by a civil official, but with the administration of the
sacrament of marriage by the two persons concerned to each other and the
exchange of solemn vows, and that the office of a priest is only to witness
and bless. Accordingly the ruling of the Pope, conveyed in a Papal brief,
was that Mrs. Fitzherbert could regard herself as the only true wife of the
Prince of Wales.*

The Prince, naturally, was delighted, and somewhat patronizingly remarked that Catholicism was 'the only religion for a gentleman'. The couple were reunited at the turn of the century, early in 1800, and were before long seen together again at the opera. At first even some of Mrs. Fitzherbert's friends were puzzled. 'The affair of the Fitzherbert and the Prince of Wales becomes very uncomprehensible', wrote Lady Jerningham, a fellow Catholic. 'I had thought Mrs. Fitzherbert a woman of principle.' However, to signalize the event Mrs. Fitzherbert gave a formal although long-delayed wedding-breakfast in the form of an afternoon reception with dancing at her London house. Although Mrs. Fitzherbert had not informed her friends of the Papal brief, almost everyone in Society now realized that a woman of her high moral character and deep religious convictions would not have taken this new step and proclaimed it so openly without being completely at peace with her conscience and her Faith. Presumably both Mrs. Fitzherbert and the Prince, in view of the secret and illegal religious ceremony in which they had taken part many years earlier, regarded the State wedding by which the Prince had been joined to the Princess Caroline, and the solemn vows which he had sworn on that occasion, as completely meaningless and invalid. However, Mrs. Fitzherbert's reputation was such that before long almost all criticism had been stilled. Soon after the reconciliation the couple were resuming their visits to Brighton.

Mrs. Fitzherbert could not help reflecting, as she drove around Brighton once again with the Prince and promenaded with him on the Steine and on the cliffs, how vastly the town had grown since she had come to Brighton with her husband for the first time after their marriage. The place now consisted of eighteen streets with 1,500 houses, and the population numbered more than 7,000. By comparison with fourteen years earlier, the houses and population had more than doubled. But although Edward Cobby, compiler of the *Brighton Directory* for 1800, called Brighton 'the most frequented', and 'without exception one of the most fashionable towns in the Kingdom', much of its great appeal in those days was that with the gaiety and elegance of a town it still possessed much of the charm and prettiness of a country village. Beyond Artillery Place to the west extended an open tract of gently undulating country towards Shoreham, and hardly any buildings yet extended beyond North Street. The trend of fashionable building was all towards the east. Beyond York Street and Margaret Street, running north from the Marine Parade, there now rose the houses of New Steine with its gardens, and farther still Rock Buildings, of which the first to be erected was Rock House. These were all so called because of a group of large and curiously shaped rocks that were to be seen above the sand at low water. They became covered over not many years after as a result of more efficient groynes being built, which caused the beach to pile up around them. The builder of these houses, Mr. John

Smith, was looked upon as mad for having built so far out of the town, but building was now going on again at Royal Crescent, which poor Mr. J. B. Otto, the West Indian speculator, had begun in 1798. Getting into financial difficulties, he had 'bolted, leaving his creditors in the lurch' for a time, as a local chronicler tells us,[1] when he had built only three houses at each end of the Crescent. This group of houses was the first ever planned in Brighton as a single architectural composition, and was an audacious conception for its time, as well as being today one of the most attractive features of the sea-front, the houses having charming classical doorways, ironwork balconies and bonnet-like canopies, and being faced with the black, iridescent, glazed 'mathematical' tiles that create such delightful effects in the changing lights of the sky. These tiles were especially favoured for use at the seaside because they resisted wind-driven rain and sea-spray better than ordinary bricks. It appears that the window-bays, now angular with one exception, were originally all curved, for the author of Attree's *Topography of Brighton* wrote critically of the design of the Crescent in 1815, when he declared that '*bow-windows in a crescent destroy*, in a great measure, the elegance of the *curve*', while another writer remarked upon 'the unfortunate effect caused by curved window-bays in a curved terrace'. The Crescent was completed by 1807, and Mr. Otto, who had by then no doubt satisfied his creditors, erected in the centre of the grass enclosure before the houses a buff-coloured statute of the Prince of Wales designed by that somewhat mediocre sculptor Rossi. Standing 7 feet high on a pedestal 10 feet high, it showed the Prince in the uniform of a Colonel of the 10th Hussars, and making a grandiloquent military gesture. Mr. Otto's hopes that the erection of the statue would be recognized by the Prince's issuing to him an invitation to the Pavilion was not realized however, for the plaster-like Coade's Artificial Stone of which the statue had been made was not capable of withstanding the scarifying gales and rain-squalls of the Brighton sea-front, and before long one of the arms broke off, with the result that the statue was frequently mistaken for a figure of Lord Nelson. Mutilated and decayed, the eyesore remained in front of the Crescent for several years, to the intense indignation of the Prince of Wales, until it was at last removed in 1819.

With the reconciliation of the Prince and Mrs. Fitzherbert a new brilliant era of gaiety and excitement began at the Pavilion, and the Prince was in the mood to celebrate this gay new phase in their life together by some startling new adventures in building. The chief of these was to be a stupendous new building to serve as Royal stables on the northern side of the grounds, but before this could take shape some additional land had to be acquired. In the meantime old and new friends were flocking round the Prince and Mrs. Fitzherbert as never before, and it became clear that the Pavilion itself would have to be enlarged.

When Holland was asked to prepare some designs the Prince seems to have impressed him with his desire to infuse some spirit of gaiety and fantasy into the place. Amongst the sketches in the Royal Archives, dated July 1801, is one for the rebuilding of the exterior of the classical Marine Pavilion in Chinese style, very much in the manner of the delightful little Chinese dairy (still standing) which Holland had built at Woburn Abbey some fifteen years earlier, but much more elaborate. If the Prince had any memories of happy hours in his early childhood spent amongst the fantastic little oriental pavilions and pagodas which Sir William Chambers had built in the gardens of his father's palace at Kew, the Prince would have been delighted with this design, which, in fact, represents the earliest manifestation of the oriental taste in the Prince's buildings at Brighton. We do not know for what reason he did not proceed with this project— perhaps it was on account of the extra cost that would have been involved. Instead a simpler scheme was adopted for retaining the Pavilion's original classical character, and enlarging it by means of two new wings projecting at angles from the eastern façade, the northern one to form a dining-room, and the southern one a conservatory or drawing-room.

The alterations were carried out, not by Holland himself, who was then absent in Cornwall, but by his nephew and assistant, P. F. Robinson. This young architect was later to become famous as a designer of picturesque cottages and village buildings, and as the creator of the Egyptian Hall in Piccadilly and the 'Swiss Cottage' in St. John's Wood. Carrying out Holland's design, he introduced some picturesque elements which his master had not shown in his drawings by adding to the bow-windows of the Pavilion some of those shell or pagoda-like green-painted canopies or hoods of the kind which eventually became so delightfully distinctive of Regency houses. At the same time he removed the statues from around the base of the cupola. Their classical serenity may have appeared, in those early days of the Romantic movement, as a highly distasteful formal stiffness.

With the canopies at the windows and the long trellised verandas before the lower windows, the once classically severe Pavilion now took on something of the cosy, almost rustic appearance of a picturesque *cottage orné* of the kind that was becoming increasingly fashionable. Whatever his reasons for not proceeding with a Chinese exterior, the Prince eventually was not to be deprived of his longed-for setting of oriental fantasy, for he suddenly transformed the whole of the interior by having the rooms completely decorated and furnished in Chinese style. The Victorian topographical writer Brayley tells us how the change came about:

'In 1802 several pieces of a very beautiful Chinese paper were presented to the Prince, who for a time was undecided in what way to make use of them. As the Eating Room and the Library, which were between the

Saloon and the new northern wing, were no longer required for their original purposes, Mr. Robinson, on being consulted, advised the Prince to have the partition removed and the interior formed into a Chinese Gallery. This was immediately agreed to; the walls were hung with the paper described and the other parts of the Gallery were painted and decorated in a corresponding style. About the same time, the passage room between what was then called the Small Drawing-Room and the new conservatory, or Music Room, at the south end of the Pavilion, was constructed in a singular manner. A space was enclosed within it, measuring twelve feet by eight, the sides and upper part of which were entirely formed of stained glass, of an oriental character, and exhibiting the peculiar insects, fruit, flowers, etc. of China. It was illuminated from without; and through it, as through an immense Chinese lantern, the communication was carried on; its effect is stated to have been extremely beautiful.'[2]

The Prince can hardly have needed any persuasion over adopting the new scheme, for some ten years earlier a Chinese Room which had been created for him at Carlton House had become famous through two engravings of it being included in one of the most popular furniture-design books of the period, *The Cabinet-Maker's and Upholsterer's Drawing Book*, which Thomas Sheraton published between 1791 and 1794.

It was some forty years since, in the days of 'Chinese Chippendale' furniture, the vogue for *chinoiserie* in this country had been at its peak, although Chinese porcelain, painted wallpapers and lacquer furniture had been sought after almost continuously since the days of Charles II. After the failure of Lord MacCartney's trading embassy to China in 1794, Chinese furnishings and decorations had not been so popular, but the Prince was henceforth to carry this gay and colourful fashion to hitherto undreamed-of heights of magnificence. The Chinese Room in London was dismantled, and its most important articles of furniture were brought to Brighton to enhance the oriental atmosphere.

There were two splendid pier-tables, or open cabinets in ebony veneer, one having supports in the form of terminal figures of Chinamen, made in bronze and painted. The tables had delicate filigree ormolu mounts of Chinese character. They are believed to have been made by the great French craftsman Adam Weisweiler, and had probably been among the Prince's early purchases of French furniture.[3] They were most probably supplied through Holland by Dominique Daquerre, a French furniture purveyor who had set up a business in Sloane Street, London, and supplied several of the great English houses, including Carlton House, Althorp and South-hill.

Through the Prince's decorators, the firm of Crace and Sons, the Prince also bought immense quantities of Chinese porcelain, chairs, stools, and 'very handsome Sophas' of bamboo, and cabinets of 'Japan lacquer'. There were as well Chinese decorations and curiosities of all kinds, Chinese costumes, weapons, and even 'a miraculous jug', all from cargoes brought from China by Dr. James Garrett, who also supplied china and lacquer furniture for Carlton House. With painted wallpapers representing groves of bamboos, peonies and flowering shrubs of many kinds, with brightly coloured birds and butterflies flitting through the branches; with figures of fishermen standing in the niches of the Corridor, dressed in real Chinese robes and with lanterns instead of fish dangling from their rods; with delicately fretted models of junks and pagodas in ivory standing on lacquer cabinets; with Chinese lanterns hanging from the ceilings, the Prince strove to re-create that legendary land of Cathay sought by travellers for hundreds of years, but found only by poets and painters, described by Hugh Honour as 'that lotus land of everlasting afternoon . . . a land of poetry and graciousness—a spacious garden of azaleas, peonies and chrys-anthemums, where the most serious business in life is to drink tea in a latticed pavilion, beside a silent lake, beneath a weeping willow, to listen to the sound of piping and tinkling instruments; and to dance, to dance for ever, among the porcelain pagodas'.[4]

After the new Chinese interior had been completed, there were no interior alterations to the Pavilion of any consequence for another twelve or thirteen years. Most of the Prince's visitors were enchanted by the new decorations. In a letter to Lord Granville Leveson Gower from the Pavilion in 1805 Lady Bessborough wrote:

'His way of living is pleasant enough, especially if one might chuse one's society. In the Morning he gives you horses, Carriages etc., to go where you please with you; he comes and sits rather too long, but only on a visit. Everybody meets at dinner, which, par parenthèse, is excellent, with the addition of a few invitations in the evening. Three large rooms, very comfortable, are lit up; whist, backgammon, Chess, trace Madame—every sort of game you can think of in two of them, and Musick in the third. His band is beautiful. He has Viotti and a Lady who sings and plays very well. A few people have the entrée and a few more are invited. Mrs. Fitzherbert is ill at present and confined to her bed, so he makes me do the honours.'

In a following letter she wrote again:

'To-day I have been going all over the Pavilion, which is really beauti-ful in its way. I did not think the strange Chinese shapes and columns could have look'd so well. It is like Concetti in Poetry, in *outré* and false taste, but for the kind of thing as perfect as it can be, and the Prince says he had it so because at the time there was such a cry against the French things, etc., that he was afraid of his furniture being accus'd of Jacobinism.'

These years of Mrs. Fitzherbert's second reign were, as she confided to

THE ROYAL STABLES, 1805
From John Nash's *Views of the Royal Pavilion*, 1826

THE CHINESE CORRIDOR AT THE MARINE PAVILION, 1815
From John Nash's *Views of the Royal Pavilion*, 1826

'2, 3, 5 & 8, OR A SUMMER'S EVENING AT THE ROYAL MARINE
LIBRARY, BRIGHTON', 1826
Water-colour by C. W. Wing

THE THEATRE ROYAL, *c.* 1818
Water-colour by T. Wakeman

BRILL'S BATHS, *c.* 1824
Water-colour by C. W. Wing

MAHOMED'S BATHS, 1822

FISHING BOATS AT BRIGHTON, 1824
Sepia drawing by John Constable

THE CHAIN PIER, 1825
Engraved by W. Cooke after a water-colour by J. M. W. Turner

BRIGHTELMSTONE
from an actual Survey made by J. Marchant, Parish Vestry Master, Brighton Place.

BRIGHTELMSTON IN 1803,
surveyed and published by J. Marchant

THE ROYAL PAVILION, EAST FRONT, 1818

'MORNING PROMENADE UPON THE CLIFF, BRIGHTON, 1826'
Engraved from a drawing by J. Morse

THE ROYAL GERMAN SPA, QUEEN'S PARK, 1826
Drawn and engraved by M. V. Sears

THE 'AGE' COACH, *c.* 1826
Lithograph by M. Gauci after C. C. Henderson

Lord Stourton in her old age, 'the happiest of her connection with the Prince', and both she and her husband seem to have recaptured something of their first idyllic companionship. Mrs. Fitzherbert seems even to have tried to revive their first illusions of romantic poverty, for she declared that although 'they were extremely poor, they were as merry as crickets'.

This heightened romantic atmosphere was not immediately discernible to their friends, who perceived rather that the couple were now becoming, although very affectionate, somewhat elderly, staid and comfortably stout. 'My neighbours here,' Sir Harry Englefield observed, 'go on most lovingly. Their affection seems to grow with their growth and fatten with their fat.' The riotous parties of the Prince's early days in Brighton were by now a thing of the past. Under the renewed influence of Mrs. Fitzherbert social life at the Pavilion was now conducted with dignity and propriety. A letter written in 1802 by a visitor to the Pavilion, the Rev. G. H. Glasse, to his father gives a delightful impression of an evening's entertainment there, and incidentally an amusing glimpse of the Prince observing some warlike experiments. Mr. Glasse was a celebrated scholar and divine of the period, and had been a domestic chaplain to the Duke of Cambridge. At the time of his visit to Brighton he may have been acting as an intermediary between the Prince and Princess Caroline, possibly in negotiations over her establishment or in connection with their child, the Princess Charlotte. He wrote:

To the Rev. S. Glasse.

East Bourne.
Monday Morning
Oct. 4, 1802.

I went to the race-ground on Friday at about 12 o'clock. The Prince was making some experiments in firing bomb-shells at a target, upon some newly-invented principle. He came immediately to me, and literally received me with open arms, in the most gracious and flattering manner possible, coram omnibus. He said that he had not time then even to cast an eye over his brother's (the Duke of Cambridge's) letter—but that I must not fail to dine with him at the Pavilion and to come to him, for some private conversation, an hour before dinner. . . . By five I was at the Pavilion. . . . I delivered all my difficult, delicate confidential messages; and I hope I shall never forget the manner in which I was heard. Few human beings were ever in a more critical position, or had so nice a course to steer, but I trust I came off tolerably well.

The dinner was—what I had no idea of—what I could have no idea of. The like I never saw; and the like I probably shall not see again. I was called on to say grace, by His Royal Highness, in the best way that ever such an injunction was given, and though certainly a more cheerful meeting never passed, there was as much decorum as if we had been dining at the table of the most correct among our Bishops. Such music, such brilliant conversation, such a profusion of luxuries—the Master of the feast so condescending and gracious! At my humble request, sanctioned by his brother's name, he was pleased to favour his party with three songs, which he executed in the style of a most distinguished amateur. He has promised to take the Chair for the Duke of Cambridge on St. Patrick's day.

At a little after eleven he rose from table. 'Well, Gentlemen, I think I never spent a happier day in my life.' To me—'Now remember that my coming to see you rests not with me, but with you. I am at your service, whenever you call upon me.'

Adieu, Adieu,

Ever yours,

G. H. GLASSE.

A note on the letter records that the Prince fulfilled his promise by visiting Mr. Glasse's rectory for dinner in May 1803.

The fear of invasion reached such a pitch in that year that few people in search of pleasure or health were willing to risk travelling to the South Coast, and for the first time since Dr. Russell set up his practice in the town Brighton was almost deserted. But when Napoleon withdrew his armies from the French coast the popularity of the town revived.

Although the Prince had given up going to Newmarket after the Escape affair of 1791, he continued to patronize Brighton Races. In 1804 he bought the horse Orville from Christopher Wilson of Wetherby, Yorkshire, who has been called 'the Father of the Turf' for having abolished many of the objectionable practices which had prevailed in horse-racing up till then. The Prince was so pleased with his purchase that he invited Wilson to visit him at the Pavilion whenever he wished, promising to have 'the largest and handsomest Glass in His Majesty's Dominions for your Ale'. He also sent a present of a china tea-service to Mrs. Wilson.[5] For the July Meeting of Brighton Races in the following year the Prince presented a cup of silver-gilt called the Brighton Cup, and entered Orville in the race. The horse was only an outsider, and was behind the other runners over most of the course, but on the finishing stretch Orville shot out beyond the rest and won the race. The Prince could hardly award the cup to himself, so he presented it to Christopher Wilson. The cup was designed by John Emes for Rundell, Bridge and Rundell, the Prince's silversmiths, and is in the form of a classical vase of beautifully restrained shape. It bears emblems of the Prince of Wales's feathers, and a modelled plaque of the Pavilion and of a classical horse-race, and is preserved at the Royal Pavilion together with some surviving articles from Mrs. Wilson's china tea-service. That year of 1805 was one of the most brilliant and eventful the town had known up till then. The Royal Stables with its immense glass dome was now taking shape, and Mr. Humphrey Repton, the celebrated landscape gardener, had been seen wandering about in the grounds with his sketching apparatus, pausing from time to time to perch himself on his ingenious combined folding-seat walking-stick while he drew the buildings from various angles. In August the great French general Dumouriez came, and attracted much attention as he promenaded on the Steine. He was entertained by the Prince at the Pavilion, and was present also at a grand review of troops on Newmarket Hill near Brighton. During the Revolution he had accompanied Louise Philippe, son of the Duc d'Orléans, when he escaped from France to join the Austrians.

Also visiting Brighton that summer was Warren Hastings, the some-time Governor-General of British India, now aged, who had been living in retirement since his trial in the House of Lords years earlier on charges of 'high crimes' in connection with his administration. Hastings had been indicted as the scapegoat for the crimes of many lesser men in India, which was a political move of the Whigs to discredit the Tories, and the administrator's chief opponent had been the party's orator Sheridan, who had spoken against him with venomous brilliance in a speech four hours long. Hasting's reply had lasted over two nights, and had been given to almost empty benches. It had been seven years before a verdict was given in Hasting's favour, but the case had ruined him financially. With remarkable generosity and insight the Prince invited Hastings to the Pavilion and arranged for him to be greeted by Sheridan, who now came forward and explained with all the wit and charm that he commanded that his part at the trial had been dictated only by political expediency, and that no one had a greater respect for Hastings than himself. For once in his career Sheridan was discomfited by Hastings's dignified rejoinder 'that it would be a great consolation to him in his declining days if Mr. Sheridan would make that sentence more public' and 'Sheridan was obliged to mutter and get out of such an engagement as well as he could'.[6]

In receiving Hastings the Prince seems to have wished to atone to him for the great injustice done by the party he had supported, in prosecuting one who had not only extended the bounds of the British Empire in India but had made great contributions to learning through the investigations he had set up while in India into the language, literature and arts of that country. Instances of criminal stupidity of this kind on the part of the Whigs such as their persecution of Hastings, were among the many reasons that caused the Prince, on assuming the Regency, to withdraw his support from them. Warren Hastings may have been drawn to Brighton by rumours he had heard in London that the great new Stables that the Prince was building in Brighton were designed in the style of the Mughal buildings of India, and may have wished to see these results of a movement he had himself inspired.

The gay, crowded season ended with a sense of triumph shadowed with disaster, when a messenger from London brought to the Prince at the Pavilion the glorious yet tragic news of the Battle of Trafalgar that had been fought on 21st October 1805, and of the death of Nelson.

One of Mrs. Fitzherbert's closest friends was Mrs. Creevey, wife of the famous diarist who was a member of the intimate circle of the Prince's Whig supporters. In a letter of 6th November Mrs. Creevey wrote to her husband:

'When I got to the Pavilion last night . . . the Prince sat down beside me directly, and I told him my headache had made me late, and he was very affectionate. . . . Harry Gray has just come in with the news of a great victory at sea and poor Nelson being killed. It has come by the express to the Prince and it is said 20 sail are taken or destroyed.'

A few days after the news was received the town was illuminated, and a 'Victory Ball' was held at the Castle Assembly Rooms, which the Prince attended. He gave a great ball at the Rooms himself for 150 of the principal inhabitants, and it was followed by another for the benefit of the dependants of those who fell in the battle.

In 1806 and the following years the brilliance of the seasons at Brighton far surpassed anything known before. The year was commemorated by the publication of a large and very fine coloured engraving after a drawing by the artist Cracklow. This engraving shows the fashionable company of residents and visitors promenading on the east side of the Steine in front of Donaldson's Royal Circulating Library. In the background across the Steine are the Castle Inn, with the great bulk of its Assembly Rooms behind, and to the right is the Marine Pavilion with its verandas and canopies to the balconies that were added four years earlier. Behind it rises the immense dome of the Royal Stables. In the right foreground the Prince of Wales himself is seen seated on a black horse. Beside him to his right are standing Mrs. Fitzherbert and her adopted daughter, Minny Seymour. On a white horse at his right is Colonel Bloomfield, then the Prince's Gentleman-in-waiting, but later to become Equerry and eventually Private Secretary, and at the extreme left is seen the bulky figure of Martha Gunn, the bathing-woman.

The music on the Steine had been greatly improved since the early days of the trio of wheezy brass instruments which had played on the Rotunda of the Library. The Steine was now said to be 'enlivened every evening by bands of Savoyards with hand organs, tambourines, etc.'

In July a meeting of the inhabitants was convened by the Town Commissioners to consider a suggestion from the Prince of Wales that the town should become incorporated as a borough, but this very advanced and far-sighted proposal was not agreed to on the grounds of the expense that would be involved.

The Commissioners, 'ever assidious to please', engaged Mr. Richer the famous performer on the tightrope, to amuse the crowd on the Steine for a few evenings, and a number of gentlemen created diversions by running races and by laying wagers on leaping over the handrails surrounding the grass. One of the Prince's frinds, a Mr. Crampton, excelled all others at the jumping, although it was said to be nothing compared to his great feat at Harrogate, some time before, when he jumped from a dancefloor into 'a very high orchestra'. Alas the following day he hurt his ankle in leaping over Lord Barrymore's horse and finishing up with a somersault. However, two nights later he was dancing at the Castle Ballroom as lively as ever. Such diversions as these strike us today as inconceivably simple and innocent. Whenever Mrs. Fitzherbert appeared on the Steine, usually with Minny Seymour, she was rapturously greeted by everyone. Four o'clock in the afternoon was the moment when the parade of the nobility and gentry reached its zenith of brilliance. In the August of 1806 the favourite dress for ladies consisted of pink, lilac or white mantles, a gipsy hat, brown parasols trimmed with white lace, and dove-coloured stockings and shoes.

Amongst the younger and more frivolous members of fashionable Society, the only hope of achieving any distinction seemed to be by adopting some harmless eccentricity, usually of dress or in one's carriage turnout. Mr. Mellish not only had chosen white for the colour of his carriage, his horses, and his servants' liveries, but even dressed entirely in this colour himself. The Hon. Tommy Onslow, whose chief claim to fame was that some years before he had driven a phaeton and four through the gates of the Steine twenty-five times without touching the posts, distinguished himself by adopting black. One individual, however, who was seen frequently on the Steine at this time attracted attention to himself by more extreme measures. 'He was generally known', says the *Annual Register* for 1806, 'as the GREEN MAN. He dressed in green pantaloons, green waistcoat, green frock[-coat], green cravat; and though his ears, whiskers, eyebrows and chin were powdered, his countenance, no doubt from the reflection of his clothes, was also green. He ate nothing but greens, fruits and vegetables, had his rooms painted green, and furnished with green sofa, green chairs, green tables, green bed and green curtains. His gig, his livery, his portmanteau, his gloves and his wigs were all green. With a green silk handkerchief in his hand, and a large watch-chain with green seals, fastened to the green buttons of his green waistcoat, he paraded every day on the Steine.' 'His whiskers', wrote another writer, who saw him in the August of that year, 'met under his chin, his hair very highly powdered, and a round hat fixed on the side of his head.' 'Sometimes', commented another, 'he wore a huge cocked hat with gold tassels. He was surrounded with company, who expressed their surprise at the size of his hat: when he answered that he was then performing a different character from that of the previous day. He is the gaze of Brighton.' A fourth commentator remarked: 'He appears about thirty years of age, his name is said to be Cope, and with all his eccentricity of appearance, looks like a gentleman; he is always alone; walks slow; and stops and looks at every lady as he passes. We cannot call him the courteous stranger as he never honours us even with a smile. If notoriety be his object he has fully succeeded, as the windows are filled with ladies whenever he passes. Even Mr. Townsend [the Bow-street runner] does not know what to make of him.'

A doggerel jingle about him even appeared in the Press. Alas, after he had diverted the Brighton public for some three months with his 'innocent absurdities', it became clear that his eccentricities went deeper than the usual fashionable extravagances of behaviour. One day in October he sprang out of the window of his house and leaped over the cliff. It seems he had imagined from some cries he had heard that there was a riot, and that his presence was required to quell the disturbance. Although badly bruised and shaken, he suffered no serious hurt, and friends in London arranged for him to be cared for. In the 1950s a young man in Brighton who habitually wore a suit of bright yellow satin and a gilt paper crown excited much less remark, while in the late 1960s every conceivable aberration of dress seemed acceptable.

Also in October 1806 amongst the names of the fashionable company in Brighton appears for the first time that of Lady Conyngham. It has hitherto been imagined that the Prince did not meet the last in the succession of his lady companions until about 1819, but it is hard to imagine that she was not received by him at the Pavilion amongst most other members of the nobility at the time of that first visit. Indeed, it is very probable that they met as early as 1802, for in that year the name of Lady Conyngham as a stall-holder at Drury Lane Theatre appeared on a fan, which was no doubt intended to be sold at the Theatre, and which was printed with the seating plan of the stalls and the names of all the seat-holders for that season. Lady Conyngham's seat was then almost immediately behind those of the Prince and Mrs. Fitzherbert.

The Princess Charlotte was twelve years old when she came to Brighton for the first time. Early in her life she had been removed from the care of her mother, the Princess Caroline, and taken into the charge of the Royal Family. One Sunday evening in July 1807 she was driven past the Pavilion in her carriage on her way to stay at Worthing. The crowds of people who lined the route were delighted by her lively ways and charming appearance with her slender figure, blonde hair, and penetrating blue eyes, and they commented upon her resemblance to her father. Although she did not stop at the Pavilion this time, a few days later she drove over from Worthing to attend the grand Review on the Downs and the sham naval battle that were now indispensable and riotous features of the Prince's birthday festivities every year. At the Pavilion she was warmly greeted by her father the Prince and her uncles the five Royal Dukes, who showed her the fantastic wonders of the Chinese rooms, which she passed through entranced with amazement, and which must have far exceeded the most astonishing scenes in any of her books of fairy-tales. After watching the Review on the Race Hill, the party returned to the Pavilion, where the Prince's band was playing and refreshments awaited them. Later the Princess was seen dancing on the lawn with the Duke of Cambridge, and at six o'clock she drove away in her carriage for Worthing.

The Prince's birthday celebrations were even more magnificent the following year. Among the guests at the Pavilion the young Lord Byron was present. Then only twenty and in his second year at Cambridge, he was spending the summer week-ends in Brighton accompanied by 'Gentleman Jack' the champion boxer, and by a girl of very great charm and beauty who dressed in a boy's jacket and trousers, but who deceived no one by this stratagem, especially when she was heard to speak in a penetrating cockney voice and to call Byron her 'bruvver'. He was staying at a house on the Marine Parade where the Albemarle Hotel stood in later years, and spent his time with his friends swimming, boating and riding on the Downs, at night playing hazard until four o'clock in the morning.[7] The Prince was probably intrigued to meet the young man around whom so many romantic rumours had already been woven, especially of fantastic parties and of drinking from skulls at Newstead Abbey. Byron did not record his impressions of the Prince on this visit, but in 1812 he met him again at a ball at Carlton House, and after a long conversation with him wrote to Sir Walter Scott, as we have already noted, that the Prince's language had given him 'a very high idea of his abilities and accomplishments, which I had hitherto considered confined to manners, certainly superior to those of any living *gentleman*'.

In the pages of *Don Juan* he was to write, not long before his death in 1823:

> Shut up—no, not *the King, but the Pavilion,*
> Or else t'will cost us all another million.

The news which came to the Pavilion in July 1809, of another great victory of the Napoleonic wars, was, in fact, the first announcement of the event made in this country, when dispatches from Sir Arthur Wellesley arrived for the Prince at Brighton while his guests were seated at dinner, informing him of the victory of Talavera in the Spanish peninsula, when nearly 50,000 French troops were defeated by an English force of hardly half that number. In those days a great deal of important news of the Napoleonic wars came first to Brighton, the only communication with France being through Dieppe. Intelligence was often brought secretly by smugglers, some of whom were ancestors of some of the most thriving and respected families now living in Brighton. An agent of the Comte de Provence, later Louis XVIII of France, the Duc de Castries, lived in Brighton expressly for the purpose of managing the correspondence between the exiled King and his supporters in France. The tidings of the victories of Talavera and Vittoria, and of Napoleon's rallying call to his army on escaping from Elba in 1815, were among many items of news that were first received at Brighton and then transmitted to London, chiefly through the agency of the *Brighton and Hove Herald*.

The Prince had not entirely given up the notion of having a Chinese exterior built for the Pavilion, and Holland in 1802 made some drawings for garden and stable buildings in the Chinese style, but he was now ageing, and in 1803 William Porden was chosen as the Prince's architect. He was a pupil of James Wyatt, and was responsible for some important work in London. The designs for a Chinese pavilion that Porden produced were exhibited at the Royal Academy in 1805, and are now preserved at the Royal Pavilion, but they were never put into affect. It may be that the Prince realized even then that the Chinese style was, as Humphrey Repton was to say a few years later, 'too light and trivial' for exteriors. What is certain is that he became carried away by a tremendous scheme for the building of vast new Royal Stables and a Riding House on the northern side of the Pavilion grounds, and Porden also became engaged in designing a new house for Mrs. Fitzherbert on the western side of the Steine, adjoining Marlborough House. This was the house which in more recent years was in the occupation of the Y.M.C.A. The plans for it were exhibited at the Academy at the same time as those for the new Stables. Mrs. Fitzherbert complained bitterly at the expense she became involved in over the house, which she said the Prince had persuaded her into having built. It has often been supposed that an underground passage existed between the Pavilion and Mrs. Fitzherbert's house, which would have explained why the Prince was frequently seen having breakfast in summer on the veranda with Mrs. Fitzherbert, when he had been known to retire to rest the night before at the Pavilion. The existence of extensive cellars and rambling passages, now bricked up, beneath the house have led to this intriguing idea, which would not have been impracticable, for the distance from the Pavilion to the house in a straight line was barely a hundred yards.

Before the Prince's architect could go ahead with building the new Royal Stables, more land was needed, and between 1802 and 1804 he acquired most of the land that makes up the grounds on the western side of the Pavilion. In 1802 the Prince bought 'the Brighthelmston Promenade Grove', the famous pleasure garden that existed in a narrow strip of land in the centre of what is now the Western Lawn. This pleasure garden had come into existence as a sort of miniature Vauxhall in the hope that it would be patronized by the Prince and fashionable visitors. It was opened by a public breakfast in 1793 and during the season there was a continuous round of concerts, fireworks, illuminations, donkey-racing, stage performances, 'rural fêtes' and dancing, which the Prince and his friends often attended. When he bought the grounds in 1802 he allowed festivities to be carried on for another season on condition that the usual rent should be given to the poor. This last season was the most brilliant in the whole career of the gardens, and culminated in a final gala performance in September 1802, when a firework display illustrated 'The Grand Spectacle of Mount Vesuvius at the time of the greatest eruption'.

The Prince also bought some remaining land of the original farm, the Dairy Field; some small properties at the bottom of Church Street and in Marlborough Row which ran southwards from there; and a long narrow strip known as Quakers' Croft, and used by them as a burial-ground. It lay beyond Promenade Grove, where the present avenue of elms exists on the far western side of the grounds. The Quakers' Meeting House was then near by in North Street, beyond the Chapel Royal. Now that the Prince owned so much land opposite the Pavilion on the west side the existence of a public road at the northern end of East Street and passing close to the entrance front of the building was more tiresome than ever before. The Prince accordingly arranged with the Town Commissioners for the closing of this road and for the making of an alternative road farther west. This was completed a few years later and called New Road, not because it was new, but apparently because it displaced an old thoroughfare almost on the site called New Street. The construction of the road was carried out by soldiers under William Porden. The old theatre in Duke Street had for a long time been too small for the increasing number of visitors, and a new site for it was bought in New Road. The construction of the present Theatre Royal began in 1806, and the first performance was held in June the following year.

The Prince of Wales's grounds now formed a small enclosed park of about eight acres in extent, and, according to Mrs Calvert,[8] it was laid out as a picturesque landscape garden by two pupils of 'Capability' Brown, named Lapidge and Hooper.

The building of the new Stables and Riding House began in 1803. A great deal of the supervision and even some of the actual designs may have been in the hands of Joseph Kay (1775–1847). He was Porden's architectural assistant, and married his daughter in 1807. He had been a pupil of C. R. Cockerell, and later built the east side of Mecklenburgh Square, one of the early great terraces of London, and also Pelham Crescent, Hastings, with the astonishing semicircular Church of St. Mary-in-the-Castle in the centre. The erection of the buildings dragged on with painful slowness, and it was more than five years, in 1808, before they were finished. Napoleon's blockade of the Baltic ports was making it difficult to obtain the specially long lengths of timber that were needed for the roof of the Riding House, and delays in the payment of contractors brought some of them to despair and ruin. The Stables at least, however, were in use by August 1806, and substantially complete externally, for in April of the following year Mrs. Calvert was writing: 'They are a most superb edifice, indeed quite unnecessarily so.' The conception of the building was a stupendous one, and the Prince of Wales's Royal Stables must rank as one of his greatest architectural achievements. Indeed, it is one of the most impressive architectural compositions in Britain, with its immense dome of glass crowning the central angular bay, the flanking wings topped with pinnacles, and the whole structure possessing long dignified lines giving a sense of stability and serenity. Even in the Brighton of today the building strikes one as being of monumental proportions. In the undeveloped town of 1806, surrounded by tiny dwellings, it must have appeared of gigantic scale. The structure was modelled on the Halle au Blé (Corn Market) in Paris, which had been built in 1782. The central cupola, 85 feet across and 65 feet high, which gave the building its later name of the Dome, was framed of timber with immense leaf-shaped panels of glass, and was crowned with a ventilating lantern like a coronet of gilded leaves. For that time it was an audacious engineering achievement. Within, the horses were accommodated in forty-four stables ranged round a great circle, while in the balcony were harness-rooms and living-quarters for the ostlers and grooms. In the centre of the floor was an octagonal pool and fountain for watering the horses. It was also said to have a 'cooling influence' that counteracted the heat from the glass roof. The original interior with its pointed saracenic arches no longer exists. It gave place to one designed in Moorish style in 1867, and in 1935 it was made into the present fine concert and conference hall.

The Riding House, in the western wing of the building, was reached through a high archway. It was 178 feet long, 58 feet wide and 34 feet high. On the east side of it was a Royal box that was removed in 1934 when alterations were made, but the general appearance of this impressive interior remains much the same as when first built. The roof of this building was again remarkable because of the great open span unsupported from below. The eastern wing was intended for an indoor tennis court, but this was left as an open court with only a screen wall at the end until the time of King William IV, when stables and coach-houses were built over it. It now forms the principal hall of the Art Gallery and Museum of

Brighton. The total cost of these buildings was over £55,000 up to 1808, but it was years before the accounts were finally settled. But long before the Royal Stables were completed the buildings had begun to arouse the most intense astonishment among the inhabitants and visitors because of the fantastically outlandish manner in which they were designed. It was style which a few knowledgeable people recognized from engravings that were being published at the time as being inspired by the Mughal mosques and palaces of India.

Since the beginning of the seventeenth century, when Sir Thomas Roe visited the Court of the Mughal Emperor Jehangir as Ambassador from King James I, a sense of wonder at the marvels of the great mysterious subcontinent of India had been aroused amongst those who read of them in works like Roe's *Journal* or later in the *Voyages* of the French traveller Bernier, published in 1670. This writer gave one of the earliest descriptions, in lively and enchanting fashion, of the beauties of 'The Kingdom of Kachemir', that was soon to become known by Europeans as well as by orientals as the 'Terrestrial Paradise of the Indies'. During the eighteenth century the fascination existing amongst poets and thinkers for the rationalistic, precisely ordered civilization of the Chinese and for the urbane thought and formal arts of China gradually gave place to a growing enthusiasm for the strange philosophies and romantic beauty of India.

Towards the end of the century Warren Hastings, on beginning to build up a system of government in Bengal, set on foot a great movement of inquiry into Indian art, philosophy and literature, encouraging the East India Company's officers to learn Sanskrit and Persian and to study the ancient writings of the Hindus. They made collections of Indian sculpture, or like Hastings himself of Indian paintings. The revelation of Indian thought, art and culture swept over Europe with a force that has been compared to that of the Renaissance. The influence spread to the English romantic poets, Southey, Byron, Shelley and Keats, and later to Browning and Emerson. Indian muslins and silks, printed cottons and Kashmir shawls became popular in England, and before long English artists travelled to India and revealed in their works 'all those wonders and glories of the most lovely country under the sun'. Reviewing the engravings in a volume of *Views of India* by the artist William Hodges, the *Gentleman's Magazine* wrote with nostalgia of 'These palaces of the Princes of the Empire . . . having courts within courts, showing, in their present desolated state what riches must have been possessed by their owners, and the luxury of their lives, remains of fountains and baths curiously inlaid with different coloured marbles, representing ornaments and flowers, in a beautiful style.'

The artist Thomas Daniell, R.A., went to India in 1784, taking with him his fourteen-year-old nephew William, whom he was teaching to draw and to make aquatint engravings. Around the turn of the century the Daniells published their aquatints in several series of volumes, the most important and popular of which was in six large folio volumes, at a price of £210 a set, entitled *Views of Oriental Scenery*. This famous work enthralled the English imagination with the beauty of the Indian country and with 'the splendour of the minarets and pagodas that shone out from the depths of its woods'. The engravings of Indian buildings seem even to have stirred a number of English artists and architects almost as much as many had been roused half a century earlier by the revelation of ancient Greek architecture in Nicholas Stuart and James Revett's *Antiquities of Athens*, and one contemporary writer was confident that in the mosques and palaces of Hindustan might be found 'the inspiration for a new poetic architecture'. It was a moment of which Humphrey Repton was later to write 'we were on the eve of some great change in Landscape Gardening and Architecture, in consequence of our having become better acquainted with Scenery and Buildings in the interior provinces of India', and he went on to say that artists and architects had 'discovered a new source of richness and variety . . . new sources of grace and beauty', in 'the accurate designs of Mr. Thomas Daniell'. The Indian movement in architecture in this country had its nerve centre at a house near Moreton-in-the-March in Gloucestershire called Sezincote, which in 1805 was being rebuilt in the Indian manner for a retired nabob, Sir Charles Cockerell. All the prophets of the new enthusiasm were gathered here. Thomas Daniell was designing the beautiful garden features—a Temple, the Indian Pool and an Indian Bridge, all of which survive today. Humphrey Repton was laying out the gardens, which have not been substantially altered since, and the architect was Sir Charles's own brother, Samuel Pepys Cockerell (a connection of the great diarist), Surveyor to the East India Company. But the building of the Prince of Wales's Indian Stables at Brighton was begun two or even three years before Sezincote took on its new Indian appearance, and it was thus the first, as well as the most stupendous, building to be erected in this country in the Indian style.

William Porden, the Prince's architect, had been a pupil of S. P. Cockerell, and was thus closely in touch with the Indian movement, and he may have obtained his Indian architectural detail from Daniell's engravings or directly from the artist himself. But Porden's interest in the Indian movement went back at least to 1797, when he exhibited at the Royal Academy a 'Design for a place of Public Entertainment in the style of the Mahometan architecture of Hindostan'. We are never likely to know for certain if the Prince's oriental enthusiasms originated in his own childhood memories of the Chinese Pagodas and the Indian Temple at Kew, and whether it was perhaps this early design for an Indian building that suggested Porden to him—the Prince was a regular visitor to the Royal

Academy exhibitions—or whether it was the architect himself who inspired his master with a taste for oriental romanticism. The fact remains that the Prince's desire for an oriental Pavilion was one that persisted over a period of more than thirty years and during the time of four different architects.

If ever the Prince had indulged in nostalgic dreams of the legendary regal splendour of the Mughal courts, which would have been especially entrancing in those days when the very principles of monarchy were being assailed all over Europe, he had to some extent realized these fantasies now that the great dome of the Royal Stables could be seen rising against the deep blue skies of summer, the lotus-shaped leaves of glass shining in the sun, and at night gleaming spectrally in the opaline moonlight, the soaring pinnacles silhouetted against the silver clouds.

Nothing could content him now more than to have an Indian Pavilion. While staying at Ragley with Lord and Lady Hertford he had visited Sezincote at least once, his first visit being signalized by the failure of the Serpent Fountain to work, but in spite of this aggravating disappointment, he must have been deeply intrigued by the Indian villa which had just been built of honey-coloured Cotswold stone in the heart of the green Gloucestershire countryside, for he summoned Humphrey Repton from Sezincote to Brighton, as the landscape architect later wrote, 'to deliver his opinion concerning what style of Architecture would be most suitable for the Pavillion', although the Prince had obviously already made up his own mind on that subject. Repton had been consulted by the owner of Sezincote with regard to introducing there 'the Gardening and Architecture which he had seen in India', and wrote further: 'Immediately after I had reconciled my mind to the adoption of this style in Sezincote I received the Prince's command to visit Brighton, and there saw in some degree realized the new forms which I had admired in drawings.' Clearly the Gloucester villa had not then begun to blossom out into its scalloped arches, minarets and domes. Repton presented to the Prince a folio volume of water-colour drawings showing by means of folding flaps the appearance of the grounds as he found them and as they would appear if the projected improvements were carried out. These were accompanied by a text in manuscript explaining his proposals, much on the lines of the celebrated little 'red-books' that he usually provided for his clients, but in this case much larger and more elaborate. Realizing that the Prince's heart was set on an Indian Pavilion, Repton diplomatically declared that he 'could not hesitate in agreeing that neither the Grecian nor the Gothic style could be made to assimilate with what had so much the character of an Eastern building'.

Quite apart from the element of Indian architecture, one of the most important aspects of Repton's proposals was the entirely fresh treatment he proposed for the gardens. 'The gardens', he wrote, 'should not be affected by any variations of season or soil or weather or situation; and thus form a perpetual garden, enriched with the production of every climate', for, as he remarked with profound truth, 'in the winter our open gardens are bleak inhospitable unsheltered dreary fields'. Accordingly he planned to surround the grounds with a 'flower corridor' or continuous conservatory, linking the house itself with greenhouses and hothouses that would supply a profusion of flowers and plants for all seasons. At intervals along the length of the corridor were to be such features as an aviary, an orangery and a pheasantry. Some of these structures would be covered with glass in winter which could be removed in summer leaving open rafters over which roses and creeping plants could be allowed to climb. In summer the glass frames of the orangery would be replaced by striped awnings, when it would become a 'chiosk'. In front of the Stables was to be one of those rectangular pools or tanks that are to be seen before mosques and palaces in India, reflecting their domes and minarets in the water. At the side was to be a place for an orchestra, flanked by two little Indian temples. This part of the scheme resembled very closely the contemporary engravings of the lakeside gardens of Kashmir. The new design for the Pavilion itself bore a striking resemblance to Sezincote, although on a much larger scale. There was the same square central block, crowned by a single large bulbous dome, and with small domes surmounting little lantern-towers on minarets at the angles. Both Sezincote and Repton's projected Pavilion seem to resemble very closely an Indian building in a painting by a Colonel R. Skelly, who exhibited at the Royal Academy between 1792 and 1794,[9] and both Repton and the designer of Sezincote, to say nothing of the Prince himself, may have seen it at the Royal Academy a few years earlier.

The Prince appeared to be enchanted by Repton's designs. He wrote: 'Mr. Repton, I consider the whole of this work as perfect, and will have every part of it carried into immediate execution; not a tittle shall be altered—even you yourself shall not attempt any improvement.'[10]

Repton was paid £713 15s 6d during 1806-7 for supplying the 'Drawings of a new Palace at Brighton',[11] and they were published in 1808 as a handsome folio volume with aquatint engravings from his original watercolour drawings and with the descriptive matter complete. Nothing was done, however, to put the designs into effect. The cold reality of a fresh avalanche of debts again blotted out the Prince's romantic visions. In fact, after his first enthusiasm the Prince must have forgotten completely about Repton's designs. Seven years after their publication, in 1815, after John Nash had superseded Repton as architect of the new Pavilion and had actually begun his work on it, Repton discovered that the original drawings and text had remained unclaimed at the engraver's establishment where they had been sent for printing. In a pathetic letter now preserved with the volume at Windsor, Repton expresses his apologies to the Prince's librarian for not having returned them before. It must have been with the acutest misery that Repton realized that in all those years the Prince had not shown enough interest in the drawings to have discovered their absence from his possession.

8 The Regency

For the first eight years of her life the Princess Charlotte remained in the keeping of her mother, who lived mostly at Montague House, Blackheath, after being compelled to leave Carlton House in 1797. After 1804 the young Princess passed into the care of her father, and lived partly at Carlton House and partly at Windsor. Her mother remained on good terms with the Royal Family, especially the King, and was allowed to visit her child once a week, until her husband's animosity caused even this consolation to be withdrawn from her, and as a result she decided in 1814 to live abroad henceforth.

During the time of her separation from the Prince Mrs. Fitzherbert became distracted from her own anxieties by the plight of one of her dearest friends, Lady Horatia Seymour, who was ill with consumption and wished to join her husband, Lord Hugh Seymour, who was stationed with the Fleet at Madeira, in the hope of recovering her health. Lady Seymour was in great distress at having to leave five of her seven children, and Mrs. Fitzherbert immediately offered to take charge of the youngest, a year-old baby girl named Mary, or Minny, as she came to be called. The mother was overjoyed, and wrote to her 'dear Mrs. Fitz' to say she had told Lady George Seymour that '*little Mary is to be your child*'. Mrs. Fitzherbert was passionately fond of children and hoped to adopt the little girl. If there is any truth in the suggestion that has often been made, that Mrs. Fitzherbert had several children of her own by the Prince, as Minny Seymour herself hinted in later life, and even if Minny was not actually her own child, as is often supposed, it may have been that by taking the child as her own she was satisfying at last her passionate love of children that must have been agonizingly frustrated when she parted from her own babies, as it is imagined she must have done, soon after they were born. Minny was taken into Mrs. Fitzherbert's household, and when the Prince became reunited to his true wife, he was delighted to discover that their marriage was to be enlivened and made cosily domestic by the presence of a fascinating little girl.

Although the Prince could find little affection for his own child, mothered by Princess Caroline whom he hated, he developed the greatest fondness for the child fostered by the woman he loved. Every day Prinny and Minny, as they called each other, played together, and she would sit herself on his knee without the slightest hesitation.

Before long both of Minny's parents had died, and her uncles, Lord Hertford and Lord Euston, who had been appointed guardians of the child, began to be concerned over the advisability of her being brought up by a Roman Catholic. They refused to allow Mrs. Fitzherbert to adopt the child legally, or even to permit Minny to stay with her for longer than a limited time. When Minny heard that she might be taken away she flung herself into the Prince's arms and cried: 'Prinny, won't you fight for me? You won't let them take me away from you.' The Prince now saw himself in the role of one who had been engaged to fulfil a parent's duty by the dying wish of the mother, and resisted all attempts to take the child out of his care, offering to add £10,000 to the funds already in trust for Minny and to undertake that she should be brought up under the spiritual care of a Church of England bishop. The trustees were alarmed at the offered gift, for they feared that it would be taken as indicating that an intimate relationship had existed between the Prince and Lady Horatia Seymour. Indeed, when the matter came into the law courts after three years of fruitless negotiations, to the consternation of the Seymour family the Prince himself succeeded in obtaining the support of eighty or ninety members of the House of Lords, having allowed it to be understood that Minny was, in fact, his own child. An impression was then created that has never been dispelled to this day. The Prince had never before pursued any single course of action with such determination over so long a time. At length he called upon the head of the Seymour family, Lord Hertford, who was shocked and embarrassed when he realized the lengths to which the Prince was prepared to go, in making fresh scandalous allegations in order to ensure that Mrs Fitzherbert would be allowed to retain the custody of the child. As a result in 1806 Lord Hertford cut across all other proceedings by claiming jointly with his wife the guardianship of the child, and when this was granted by the Court of Chancery, they appointed Mrs. Fitzherbert to act as their deputy. As soon as the affair was settled, Mrs. Fitzherbert brought the child down to Brighton. 'On Sunday last', wrote her friend Lady Jerningham, on 10th August 1806, 'arrived Mrs. Fitzherbert and little Miss Seymour, a pretty child not quite eight years old. Mrs. Fitzherbert was very pleasing and conversible, said she attributed her late ill health to the uneasiness she had undergone over this little girl, that she was particularly fond of children and should have liked to have a dozen of her own.'

Although by the Hertfords' intervention over the guardianship of Minny Seymour Mrs. Fitzherbert had secured for herself one of the greatest joys in her life, she had by the same means opened the way for the loss of even greater happiness, for the close contact that developed with Lady Hertford was to lead to the final separation of Mrs. Fitzherbert from her own husband. Narrowly Tory and Protestant in her views, Lady

Hertford had perceived the political advantage to be gained by acquiring influence over the Prince, and from 1807 she encouraged more and more his visits to Hertford House. There he was able to indulge his love of pictures, French furniture, silver and works of art of all kinds among the magnificent collections gathered by Lord Hertford and his son Lord Yarmouth, which eventually became the Wallace Collection, one of the nation's richest assemblages of works of art, which is still housed in its original home in Manchester Square. It was with the encouragement of these fellow connoisseurs that the Prince bought at this time many of the superb articles of French furniture, clocks and other treasures which then came on the market with the break-up of great houses in France, and which now enrich the Royal collections.

It was not long before the strange compulsive influence that Lady Hertford exercised had its effect on the Prince. The maternal image which he sought in all the women under whose spell he came was certainly embodied in Lady Hertford's ample, though handsome and dignified form. Several years older than the Prince, frigid and puritanical, that image was in her manifest in an aspect of dominating severity rather than with the tender sweetness in which it appeared in Mrs. Fitzherbert. Although he may never have been permitted any amorous consolation by Lady Hertford, before long he was her abject slave, indulging in fits of weeping and becoming pale and ill under the influence of his obsession. 'I think the Prince looks dismally', wrote Mrs. Calvert of him. 'He has quite lost his affable ways.' Of Lady Hertford she wrote: 'She is near fifty, has been and indeed still is beautiful, but on a very large scale. I think her, without exception the most forbidding, haughty, unpleasant-looking woman I ever saw.'

Exploiting the obligation that Mrs. Fitzherbert owed her, and assuming more and more the role of guardian and chaperon of Minny Seymour, she penetrated deeply into the intimate life of Mrs. Fitzherbert and her husband, until she almost ruled at the Prince's table. With incredible callousness he insisted on Mrs. Fitzherbert's being present at all the parties he gave for Lady Hertford, in order to avert scandal, and indeed that person had enough regard for her own dignity not to give the impression that their friendship was other than platonic. The Prince's manner with Mrs. Fitzherbert became more and more remote, and as her friend Lord Stourton wrote: 'She was frequently on the point of separation, but was prevented by the influence of the Royal family from carrying her resolution into effect.'

The whole matter was brought to a climax with the declaration of the Regency in February 1811, when the King was pronounced incapable of playing any further part in the government of the country. It is now realized that the malady from which the King was suffering was not insanity, as was believed for nearly a hundred and fifty years, but the metabolic disturbance known as Porphyria.[1]

The final break with Mrs. Fitzherbert came when in June 1811 the Prince held a magnificent banquet to celebrate the Regency. As this could not be openly stated as the object, because of the slight that would be offered to the King, the banquet was officially given in honour of the future King Louis XVIII of France, who was then in exile in this country. At all the Prince's banquets hitherto, the strict precedence of guests had not been observed, so that Mrs. Fitzherbert could always sit at the Prince's right hand. The guests were now to be seated strictly according to rank. Lord Stourton tells us that 'When assured of this novel arrangement, she asked the Prince, who had invited her with the rest of the company, where she was to sit. He said, "Madam, you have no place." "None, Sir," she admitted "but such as you choose to give me." Upon this she informed the Royal family that she would not go. The Duke of York and others endeavoured to alter the preconcerted arrangement, but the Prince was inflexible, and aware of the peculiar circumstances of her case, and the distressing nature of her general situation, they no longer hesitated to agree with her that no advantage was to be obtained by further postponement of her own anxious desire to close her connection with the Prince and to retire once more into private life. She told me she often looked back with wonder that she had not sunk under the trials of those last two years. . . . Thus terminated this fatal, ill-starred connection.'

Mrs. Fitzherbert left Brighton and retired to Sherwood Lodge, Battersea, which she had taken a little while earlier. Whatever complex psychological motives might have reinforced the Prince's determination to break with his wife, there seems no doubt that the overriding reason was the fear now that he had become Regent lest any acknowledgement of the marriage, whether formally or by their continuing to associate with each other, might prove an obstacle to his eventual succession to the Throne.

Whatever his reasons may have been, nothing can excuse the brusque and heartless way in which he brought about the end of their life together. Nevertheless the Prince's fondness for Minny Seymour never abated. A letter from her thanking him for a birthday present which he sent to her in 1812 is preserved at the Royal Pavilion:

My dear Prinny,

How kind you were to remember my birthday, and send me such a beautiful present; I have placed it in a very conspicuous situation, and it is very much admired, pray accept my grateful thanks for it. I must not omit thanking you, for the piece of paper, I found inclosed in Colonel McMahon's letter, it was very acceptable, as sometimes I am rather an extravagant personage. I ride almost every day, and Adonis is as great a favourite as ever, dear little Sancho, is rather neglected, for I fancy myself almost to big to ride on him. I hope my dear Prinny that you enjoy good health, and that you will ever believe me to remain,

Your most grateful,
and affectionate,
MINNY.

Brighton
November the 25th 1812.

Although in the Prince's early association with the Whig party he had almost certainly decided to dismiss the Tory Government when he came to power, he had latterly become more and more aware of the ineptitude and ineffectiveness of Whig policy, and some years earlier, in 1806, when he wrote to their leader on the death of Fox, he stated he 'must no longer be regarded as a partyman'. After some preliminary consultations with the Whigs the Prince ultimately decided to keep the Tories in power.

With the coming of the Regency, the Prince became acutely aware not only of the political responsibilities but of the dignities and pomp that would be involved in his new office. The mounting British victories were bringing the wars against Napoleon to a triumphant finish. Britain, which once had stood alone against Bonaparte, was now the leader of some fourteen allied kingdoms, and already the great scheme of rebuilding in the West End of London that was to become known as the Metropolitan Improvements was being planned, with the object of making London worthy of its new status as the capital of Europe.

The little Marine Pavilion would now be far too small and unimpressive for the entertaining of foreign ambassadors and visiting princes; a new palace at Brighton was obviously a necessity, and the question of the architect to be employed became important. William Porden was very heavily occupied at Eaton Hall in Cheshire, where he was installing romantic Gothic tracery in cast iron. The Surveyor-General was now James Wyatt, architect of the Pantheon in Oxford Street and of William Beckford's immense fantastic pseudo-medieval Fonthill Abbey in Wiltshire. Wyatt was already executing some fairly considerable alterations at the Pavilion and Marlborough House, and when he was asked to estimate for building an entirely new palace at Brighton his figure of £200,000 did not seem at all outrageous. After all, the new palace at Kew that Wyatt had designed for King George III had cost over half a million. Wyatt was a notoriously offhand and dilatory artist, so it is unlikely that he ever produced any designs, but we may imagine that if he ever did so they would have been not for an oriental dream palace of the kind that eventually arose at Brighton, but for a vast neo-Gothic building like a medieval abbey with crocketed pinnacles, octagonal towers and cloisters, equalling Fonthill in romanticism. However, Wyatt's death in a carriage accident in 1813 put an end to these possibilities, and the Prince Regent was 'very much affected', as the diarist Farington tells us, 'even to shedding tears' and saying 'he had just found a man to his mind and was thus unhappily deprived of him'.

When a new appointment to Wyatt's post was made the title was modified to that of *Deputy* Surveyor-General, with the object of curbing the powers of the office which Wyatt had exercised in arbitrary and overbearing fashion. Some astonishment was caused when the coveted post was offered to John Nash, over the heads of Sir John Soane and Sir Robert Smirke, both of whom were regarded as more highly qualified, but after a short while these two were brought in to share the post with Nash as 'attached architects'. Nash had won the competition for the development of Regent's Park and was already working on this great scheme and on the grand project that resulted in the creation of Regent Street, the Carlton House Terraces and the building of Buckingham Palace. The fact that Nash was already an intimate member of the Prince's Carlton House circle, and in 1806 had taken part in the abortive 'Delicate Investigation' into the conduct of the Princess Caroline, may have been one of the reasons why he had been chosen. He must have been known to the Prince at least since 1798, when he exhibited at the Royal Academy a design for a 'Conservatory for His Royal Highness the Prince of Wales'. Nash's meteoric rise to fame and wealth had created something of a sensation. Soon after arriving in London from Wales, where he had developed a successful practice as a designer of country houses and cottages, he made a wealthy marriage and blossomed into Society as a close friend of the Prince. In fact it was widely believed that Mrs. Nash had been a mistress of the Prince, and that Nash had incurred his master's gratitude in taking her off his hands. Even after the wedding Mrs. Nash and the Prince were depicted in caricatures as disporting themselves together on the Royal yacht. In 1812 he converted Cumberland Lodge at Windsor Park as a *cottage orné* that became the Royal Lodge. In 1814 he designed the pagoda, bridge and other buildings in St. James's Park to celebrate the Treaty of Paris, and the Temple of Concord in the following year for the fête in honour of the Duke of Wellington. The first hint of any new schemes being contemplated at the Pavilion was given when the Prince Regent's Private Secretary, Sir Benjamin Bloomfield, was seen with John Nash in the grounds of the building in January 1815. Something of the future state of the Pavilion must have been decided by them, for work began of the rebuilding in the March of that year. The first alterations were to the interior. The Corridor was enlarged, and provided at each end with the present new staircases of delicate openwork cast-iron construction, the railings simulating bamboo. Cast iron was used also in the new Kitchen, in the exotic palm-tree columns that support the roof, creating a reconciliation of two ideas characteristic of the Regency age—fantasy and functionalism.

When Queen Charlotte made her second visit to the Pavilion, for Christmas 1815, the transformation of the Pavilion had hardly progressed beyond these improvements. With the Queen came also the Duke of Kent, the Princesses Augusta and May, and the Princess Charlotte, whose twentieth birthday was celebrated on 7th January 1816. Among the guests was the Prince's architect, John Nash, who in a letter[2] to a friend reveals once again the decorous character of the entertainment at the Pavilion in those days. He wrote:

'I returned from Brighton on Saturday where I was most flatteringly honoured by the Prince and before some of his Ministers—I stayed a whole week—the Society very pleasant, nothing so regular and decorous— the Ladies withdrawing at 8 and the Gentlemen at $\frac{1}{4}$ of an hour after— Coffee in an adjoining room and the delightful Concert beginning at $\frac{1}{2}$ past 8—and the Pavilion cleared at 12—I believe there are no grounds for the report of the Princess Charlotte and one of the Archdukes neither have we seen her and how such a report got into circulation I am at a loss to conceive.'

The rumours among the guests had without doubt arisen over the approaching engagement of the Princess, not to an archduke, but to Prince Leopold of Saxe-Coburg-Saalfeld, and two Councils were held at the Pavilion in January and March 1816, which concluded with the Royal Assent being given to the match, and the signing of the marriage treaty.[3]

These events marked the end of the long quarrel between the Princess and her father over the choice of a husband for her. Her first suitor, Prince Frederick of Prussia, had sworn eternal fidelity to her, only to return home to marry another princess. The Princess had broken off her engagement to the next prospective bridegroom, Prince William of Orange, when she discovered that she would not be allowed to continue living in England. The Regent was infuriated by his daughter's defiance of his wishes, but he was genuinely fearful that his daughter's capriciousness, and worse still what he regarded as the corrupting influence of her mother, might already have reduced her chances of a suitable marriage. Not long before Princess Caroline had, possibly in order to injure the Regent, tried to involve her daughter in an affair with a certain Captain Hesse, but despite the compromising circumstances an inquiry revealed her complete innocence— 'the hand of Providence alone, I am sure, has, and could alone have preserved you, my child,' the Prince wrote to his daughter sententiously, a mental cloud conveniently blotting out the memory of the innumerable amorous indiscretions he had indulged in at a much earlier age.

When the young Prince Leopold sought to pay his advances, the Regent found his suave ingratiating manners almost as distasteful as his slender means—he possessed only £200 a year—and continued to write pompous letters to his daughter urging her to renew the engagement to Prince William of Orange. But Charlotte found her new suitor's dark handsome features attractive, and was touched by his charm and tenderness. Though she was not willing to admit she could ever give her heart again, she confessed to her friend Miss Mercer Elphinstone: 'As I care for no man in the world now . . . I don't see what there is against my connecting myself with the most calm and perfect indifference to a man who, I know, has the highest and best character possible in every way, and is extremely prepossessing in his figure and appearance, and who *certainly did like me*. . . . I should, if left me to choose, still pick him out.' During those bright dry exhilarating winter days of the New Year at Brighton the Princess fell completely under the spell of Prince Leopold's charming ways, and by February 1816 she had completely made up her mind. She confided to her friend: 'As *far* as he is concerned I have not one anxious wish left, as I am thoroughly persuaded and can see that he will do all and everything he can to please and make me happy. The Prince Regent I find vastly better than I expected, in high spirits and good humour. He wheels himself perfectly in a merlin chair and in that sits the whole e[venin]g with his legs down. He is grown thinner and his legs considerably reduced . . . there is not a soul that is not in extacies at my fate and choice.'

The gout from which the Regent had been suffering had without doubt aggravated his exasperation over his daughter's wilfulness, but as soon as he realized that her determination was fixed and that the question of her future was now happily settled he was full of cheerfulness and benevolence, and in granting his assent to the marriage, most generously gave the couple Claremont House, near Esher, the Princess's favourite house, to be their home, and persuaded Parliament to settle £50,000 on them. The merlin chair which the Princess mentioned was a type of wheeled invalid chair which is still in use today, and was invented by the 'ingenious and well-known Merlin', a Belgian instrument-maker, who also introduced roller-skating into this country and designed the 'Merlin Swings' that were used in Ireland's pleasure gardens at Brighton and elsewhere in the country. It was said of the chair that it could 'usefully be adapted for military purposes by using it to mount a small portable cannon'. The Regent's merlin chair still remained in the passage behind his bedroom at the Pavilion in 1846, when the building was being dismantled, as the inventory of the contents that was compiled at that time somewhat pathetically reveals. The Regent was determined also not to let the gout interfere with his outdoor exercise, and arranged for a complicated apparatus to be made to enable him to be lifted on to his horse. *The Times* newspaper described the process with its customary solemn exactitude:

'It is true that the Prince has been on horseback, and has rode for some time about the Pavilion lawn. An inclined plane was constructed, rising about the height of two feet and a half, at the upper end of which was a platform. His Royal Highness was placed in a chair on rollers, and so moved up the ascent, and placed on the platform, which was then raised by screws, high enough to pass the horse under; and finally, his Royal Highness was let gently down into the saddle. By these means the Regent was undoubtedly enabled to enjoy in some degree the benefit of air and exercise; but the exercise implied little of spontaneous muscular power, and cannot, certainly, be considered as a criterion of renovated strength.'

Despite the sober comment of *The Times*, and its lack of confidence in such passive exercise, the affair was probably a tremendous joke to the Prince himself. The incident was a heaven-sent opportunity for the irrepressible caricaturists, who depicted the Prince with immensely bandaged legs and feet, being pushed up a slope in his wheel-chair by several attendants in Chinese dress with the Royal Pavilion in the background.

For a few months life at the Pavilion reached heights of excitement and delight seldom attained there in its earlier history. The Princess's gay and lively personality endeared her to everyone, and she revelled in the fantastic Chinese surroundings that were made more convincingly exotic than ever by the tropical heat of the Regent's patent stoves. Lady Ilchester, one of the Princess's ladies-in-waiting, wrote to a friend in February 1816:

'The fortnight at Brighton has had a very happy effect on Princess Charlotte's spirits and she has an air of cheerful interest that would please you. . . . Everyone seemed delighted to have her under her father's roof. It certainly was a great gratification to the Prince to find it really gave so much pleasure to the Princess, for he had been led to suspect that she did not like to come, which was a complete mistake, and of which he is now convinced.

'The Chinese scene is gay beyond description, and I am sure you would admire it, as well as the manner of living at the Pavilion, though the extreme warmth of it might, perhaps, be too much for you. Everyone was free in the morning of all Court restraint, and only met at six o'clock punctually for dinner to the number of between thirty and forty, and in the evening about as many more were generally invited; a delightful band of music played till half-past eleven, when the Royal Family took their leave, and the rest of the company also, after partaking of sandwiches. The evenings were not in the least formal. As soon as the Queen sat down to cards everybody moved about as they pleased, and made their own backgammon, chess or card party, but the walking up and down the gallery was the favourite lounge. All the rooms open into this beautiful gallery, which is terminated at each end by the lightest and prettiest Chinese staircases you can imagine, made of cast-iron and bamboo, with glass doors beneath, which reflect the gay lanterns, etc., at each end.

'There are mandarins and pagodas in abundance, plenty of sofas, Japan and China. The centre of the gallery has a skylight, but each staircase communicates to a large room into which, at one end, the Queen's apartments opened; at the other the Princess's (Charlotte) and mine. The effect of this centrical common room is very good. There was in it an excellent fire and books and newspapers, and from one set of rooms to the other is a private communication round the sky light, so that you need not go down at one end to get up by the other to the Queen's apartments from ours.'

The gaiety of those months was not even hindered by the distasteful news which had to be conveyed to the Regent that a period of financial stringency made it advisable for him to placate public feeling by putting a stop to the alterations for a time.

In a little while Prince Leopold joined the company again and stayed for two months. Then in May 1816 the young couple were married at Carlton House. Queen Charlotte, the Princess and her husband, and various other members of the Royal Family came again to the Pavilion for Christmas in that year, and the festivities that were held in honour of their visit filled Brighton with fashionable visitors. Princess Charlotte's twenty-first birthday was celebrated at the Pavilion in January 1817 with a dinnerparty 'sumptuous in the extreme'—and a grand ball given by the Regent. Lord Clive, who had once lived at Claremont, was one of the guests. This function was one of the last to be held in Marlborough House, which was before long to be demolished, though at that time it was still connected with the Pavilion. Later in the month a round of splendid entertainments and festivities was held to celebrate the visit of the Grand Duke Nicholas of Russia. Minny Seymour was present at a great ball given in the Pavilion to 350 guests, and herself danced with the Grand Duke. The Regent's relations with Minny were quite unaffected by the breach between himself and Mrs. Fitzherbert, and the little girl was a frequent guest at the Pavilion, although her adoptive mother never again entered the building in the lifetime of her husband.

Soon the whole nation was delighted with the news of the expected birth of a child to Princess Charlotte, and Prince Leopold began to negotiate for the purchase of Marlborough House on the Steine, so that his wife could recuperate by the sea after the birth of their child. There is almost unbearable pathos in the lines in which the Princess confided to Miss Mercer the hopes of ordinary human happiness that seemed at last within her reach, after a lifetime of uncertainty and of being buffeted between the contending hatreds of her parents, both of whom she loved:

'I am certainly a most fortunate creature and have to bless God', she wrote. 'A P(rince)ss never, I believe, set out in life, or married; with such prospects of happiness, real domestic ones like other people.'

But these hopeful dreams vanished in November 1817, when the

153

Princess's child was born dead after a long-drawn-out labour, and she herself died soon afterwards from exhaustion. They were both victims of the orthodox medical system of the time, by which the prospective mother's 'excessive animal spirits' were reduced by a starvation diet and bleeding so that she was drained of all the vitality she needed for her ordeal. Furthermore the Princess was denied the physical help she should have been given, because of the inability of her surgeon, Sir Richard Croft, to overcome his fear of touching the body of a Royal personage. Soon after the tragedy Croft shot himself.*

The whole nation was stunned with shock at the loss of one of the most popular Royal figures in English history. The Prince Regent was heart-broken and was copiously bled in the course of the day. After the funeral he retired into seclusion at Brighton, all those who attended upon him shocked by his sorrow-ravaged face. Queen Charlotte wrote of her son's behaviour towards the Princess: 'He granted and accomplished her Wish to marry the man She chose herself, and gave Her the place to reside at she was always partial to . . . God be praised that the Prince can have nothing to reproach himself with, but can say with truth "I made her happy."'[4]

The alterations at the Pavilion had now been resumed, and may have afforded the Prince some distraction, as possibly did also the arrival in the spring of rooks in the grounds for the first time since 1802. The local newspaper reported:[5] 'The black gentry, yclept rooks, are now busily employed, about the towering trees of the Pavilion Grounds, framing their nests for the pleasure of incubations, and the multiplying their sooty species'—surely one of the earliest examples of the 'plashy' school of nature-writing!

By December 1817 the Regent had so far recovered his customary high spirits that he gave a supper to the servants in the new Kitchen of the Pavilion. 'A scarlet cloth was thrown over the pavement: a splendid repast was provided, and the good-humoured Prince sat down, with a select party of his friends and spent a joyous hour. The whole of the servants, particularly the female portion, are delighted at this mark of Royal con-descension.' But as with many other innocent and well-intentioned inci-dents of the Prince's life, the occurrence was made the subject of yet another of those innumerable attacks aimed to discredit him politically, on this occasion in the form of a caricature by Cruikshank entitled 'High Life Below Stairs', in which the Prince is shown drunkenly carousing with his cronies, and watched by contemptuous servants. The rather stiff formalities of Court life at the Pavilion in those years are more reliably described by John Wilson Croker in his *Journal* for 1818. In December he wrote:

'The etiquette is, that before dinner when he comes in, he *finds* all the

154

men standing, and the women rise; he speaks to everybody, shakes hands with new comers or particular friends, then desires the ladies to be seated. When dinner is announced, he leads out a lady of the highest rank or when the ranks are nearly equal, or when the nominal rank interferes a little with the real rank, as yesterday, with Lady Liddell and Mrs. Pelham, he took one on each arm. After dinner the new dining-room was lighted and he took the ladies to see it. It is really beautiful, and I liked it better than the other, if I can venture to say that I prefer either. Everybody was comparing them, and the praise of one was always, as is usual in such cases, expressed by its superiority over the other. I ventured to say that this was not a fair way of judging them; that though different they were, perhaps, both equally beautiful in their respective kinds, like a "handsome man and handsome woman". This poor little phrase had great success. The ceilings of both rooms are spherical and yet there is no echo. Nash says he has avoided it by some new theory of sound, which he endeavoured to explain, and which I did not understand, nor I believe he neither. The rooms are as full of lamps as Hancock's shop.

'After dinner there was music as usual. . . . The supper is only a tray with sandwiches and wines and water handed about. The Prince played a hand or two at Patience, and I was rather amused to hear him exclaim loudly when one of the Kings had turned up vexatiously, "Damn the King!"'

When the Pavilion was in the last stages of its completion the Regent stayed during his visits in 1819 and 1820 in one or other of the houses in Marlborough Row, which ran southwards from Church Street in the northern part of the Pavilion grounds. Only one of these houses remains today, known as North Gate House. Colonel Bloomfield, the Prince of Wales's Secretary, had lived there at one time, and after 1820 it became the residence of Lady Conyngham, Lady Steward of the Royal Household. Today it houses the Administrative Offices of the Art Gallery and Museum and the Royal Pavilion.

Long after the closing of the Castle Hotel the brilliant tradition of the great balls was continued at the Old Ship Hotel. They were organized by a committee of lady patronesses, with Mrs. Fitzherbert at their head. All the fashionable residents and visitors thronged to these private subscription dances, which were said to be arranged 'on the model of the London Almack's', an allusion to the dances held at the famous assembly rooms of that name in St. James's. Here Lady Jersey, Lady Castlereagh, the Princess Esterhazy and the Princess Lieven were among the lady patronesses who wielded despotic power in granting admission to what Captain Gronow described in 1814 as 'the seventh heaven of the fashionable world. Of the three hundred officers of the Foot Guards not more than half-a-dozen were honoured with vouchers of admission to this exclusive temple of the *beau monde.*'

In his *Letters on England* Prince Pückler-Muskau describes[6] how he 'was to execute myself in the evening at a great subscription ball', at the 'Brighton Almack's, for so these very fashionable balls are called'. As at the London Almack's, 'five or six of the most intensely fashionable ladies who are called Patronesses, distribute the tickets. It is an immense favour to obtain one, and, for people who do not belong to the very highest, or most modish world, very difficult. Intrigues are set on foot months beforehand, and the Lady Patronesses flattered in the meanest and most servile manner, to secure so important an advantage; for those who have never been seen at Almack's, are regarded as utterly unfashionable—I might almost say disreputable. . . . In Brighton we find the copy of London in little.'

After the decline in the popularity of grand balls and assemblies, the renown of the Old Ship centred rather upon the concerts that were held in the Assembly Rooms, although dances continued to be held on a smaller and more intimate scale.

9 The Pavilion Transformed

When Queen Charlotte came to Brighton in February 1817, to join her son, the Princess Charlotte and Prince Leopold, she was so delighted with the new appearance of the Pavilion that she 'most graciously and liberally contributed to the promotion of the splendid improvements of the Palace by a grant of fifty thousand pounds from her private purse'.[1]

A little later it was stated that 'the contract for the improvements now going on at the Pavilion was drawn in the Queen's name'. By the following October Marlborough House had been demolished, and for a few months the Pavilion presented a grotesque aspect with two large square additions jammed on the ends of Holland's little classical villa. Each of the additions had pointed oriental windows and concave pagoda-like roofs rising up from circles of pointed battlements. Fortunately this phase lasted only a short while, and it was not long before the existing shallow classical dome had been replaced by the new spherical Indian dome, built on a framework of cast iron weighing over 60 tons. This was flanked by two smaller pairs of Indian domes; screens of Indian columns were built before the new end blocks, and the Pavilion began to assume a more unified appearance. The Pavilion had attained something of its final exterior design by September 1818, although the alterations continued for another four years. A few years after the building was completed John Nash arranged in 1826 for the publication of a volume of engraved *Views of the Royal Pavilion*, to serve as souvenirs of the building for the King to present to his guests. In an unpublished preface to this work, a draft of which is preserved in the Royal Archives,[2] Nash explained the reasons for the adoption of an Indian style, and complained bitterly about the great difficulties attending the architect who attempts to graft the state rooms of a palace on to the domestic apartments of a villa. Indeed, in the early stages of the rebuilding there was little promise of the brilliant success with which Nash caused the building to appear as though created in a single flash of inspiration.

Nash revealed his great genius in the way he endowed the whole composition of the east front with a sense of unity, emphasizing the long reposeful lines by means of the continuous cornice of Indian battlements, by the broad shadowing eaves—the Indian *chujahs*—of the new blocks, and with the Indian columns forming loggias before the windows of the central

Saloon and the new rooms. These colonnades he made into especially beautiful features by linking the columns with gracefully arched Indian *jalis* of pierced stone latticework that cause delightful patterns of sunlight and shadow to be cast on the stucco walls behind.

As a whole the west front does not possess the breath-taking loveliness of the eastern façade, but if anything it is more picturesquely irregular in outline and with the informal landscape garden before it is no less romantic in character. The balconies and Indian colonnade of the north front and of the Private Apartments have a pleasing restrained dignity, and one of the most brilliantly devised features of the whole scheme is the charming free-standing *porte-cochère* on the entrance front, with triple clusters of columns at the angles and its own delightful dome. This is obviously modelled on the engraving of a little Indian temple on the Ganges which was published as a title-page vignette in a book of Indian travels by a Colonel Forrest. Although the book was not published until 1824, we may imagine that Nash would have sought out recent travellers to India, and seen Forrest's drawings before they were engraved. We also know, from records in the Lord Chamberlain's Office, that in November 1815 Nash borrowed from the King's own library at Carlton House '4 volumes of Daniell's Views of India to make drawings for the Brighton Pavilion'.

The last portions to be completed, in 1821, were a new north front, intended to accommodate visitors, and the King's new Private Apartments. The latter were facing westwards at the northern end, under a broad stone balcony supported on Indian columns with bracketed capitals. The rooms opening on to the balcony correspond to the King's Apartments below, and are believed to have been used by Lady Conyngham during the lifetime of King George IV. During the reign of King William IV they became the Private Apartments of Queen Adelaide.

While the Pavilion was assuming its final appearance, in 1818, Humphrey Repton died. His last days had been filled not only with disappointment at the failure of his designs to be acted upon by the Prince Regent, but with bitterness at being superseded by Nash, who had been his partner and had been brought to the Prince's notice through Repton's influence, 'that very friend, who, in earlier life, had participated in his bright visions of future fame'.[3]

It has frequently been suggested that Nash copied Repton's unexecuted scheme, but there seems to be no feature in which the two designs correspond, other than in the general Indian conception, and as we have seen, Nash derived his inspiration more directly from Indian sources. The abandonment of Repton's proposals, and the appointment of Nash to re-build the Pavilion were not, as Repton might have supposed, the result of political intrigue or influence in the Prince's intimate circle.

The Prince himself, although expressing extravagant praise of Repton's designs, may have sensed their somewhat hard and unsympathetic character. Although closely following Indian models, they seem to have nothing of that breath of poetic beauty which distinguishes Nash's designs, and which makes the Pavilion such a unique memorial of those romantic notions of the East that were brought to Europe by English scholars and artists and infused the work of the poets, philosophers, architects and designers of the Regency age.

Although a great many changes were to be made in the decorations over the next three years, by 1818 the principal new features of the interior had been installed—domes, dragons and chandeliers, as Croker mentions in his *Journal* for this period: 'in the place of the two rooms which stood at angles of 45° with the rest of the building—one of which I remember, a dining-room and which was also a kind of music-room, and the other, next the Castle Inn, a Chinese drawing-room, which was hardly ever opened—have been erected two immense rooms, sixty feet by forty; one for a music-room and the other for a dining-room. They both have domes; an immense dragon suspends the lustre of one of them. The music-room is most splendid, but I think the other handsomer. They are both too handsome for Brighton. . . .' After a short absence in London Croker returned to Brighton, but disliked the idea of a formal dinner with the Prince. But his absence had not gone unnoticed. 'After breakfast Bloomfield called to scold us for not going to the Pavilion at once, and to command us on the part of His Royal Highness to come there. We went there and walked through the rooms again and visited the offices. The Kitchens and larders are admirable—such contrivances for roasting, boiling, baking, stewing, frying, steaming and heating; hot-plates, hot closets, hot air and hot hearths, with all manner of cocks for hot water and cold water, and warm water and steam, and twenty saucepans all ticketed and labelled placed up to their necks in a vapour bath.'

The interior was now, by 1818, substantially complete, but in the course of his incessant search for perfection the Prince Regent had the decorations changed over and over again. The decoration in the southern wing was changed no less than four times between July and December in 1815 before he was satisfied, at least for the time being, Mr. Crace the decorator attending with from six to ten assistants at a time, putting up sample panels and patterns of different decorations.

The first barbarically colourful and realistically Chinese interior— 'the *chinoiserie* of the tea-merchant'—had remained almost entirely unchanged since its introduction in 1802. Between 1815 and 1818 a greater sophistication became apparent. The new Corridor was now decorated with a wallpaper of bamboos, peonies, rocks and birds painted in cerulean blue on a background of deep pink. The smaller rooms, including the original Corridor with its painted glass 'like an immense

Chinese lantern', were at the same time opened up to form a single large Drawing-room in each of the original wings flanking the Saloon, the Blue and Yellow Drawing-rooms.

In these rooms, in the Corridor and everywhere there were chairs, sofas and tables of bamboo imported from China, English cabinets and chairs carved and painted to simulate bamboo, cabinets of Chinese and Japanese lacquer, enormous quantities of Chinese porcelain vases, bowls and dishes, Chinese banners and standards, and models of pagodas and junks carved in delicately fretted ivory standing on tables under glass shades.

These fresh splendours, completed by 1818, reflected to some extent the Prince's consciousness of his new status as Regent. Before very long he was to find them inadequate to support his even higher elevation. King George III died in 1820, and the new monarch was for a time preoccupied with the details of his coronation, which was to demand the exercise of all his talents as a decorator and designer in planning a pageant of revived medieval splendour that must have far surpassed any event of the kind known to have taken place in the Middle Ages.

When this was past the King was able to devote his attention to new improvements at the Pavilion that would truly express his conception of the 'splendour of the Crown'. This was a notion the necessity of maintaining which he solemnly recalled to the Treasury in his letters whenever they felt disposed to question his lavish expenditure.[4] A new spirit of dignified magnificence appeared in the Corridor with the sweeping away of the barbaric Chinese banners and trophies. Bookshelves now took the place of the figures of Chinese fishermen in the niches. The ivory models of pagodas and junks were removed to the upper rooms of the building, together with most of the light bamboo furniture, their place being taken by more elaborate and conventional sofa-tables of mahogany, and some chairs and settees made of engraved ivory veneer on sandalwood in Chippendale style by craftsmen in Madras.

Although only completed two years before, by 1821 the Blue and Yellow Drawing-rooms with their riotous colour were out of harmony with the new mood. Now their brightly coloured walls gave place to a restrained decoration of a Chinese trellis in gold leaf, on an ivory ground in the southern wing and on pale lilac-grey in the north room. In each of them functionalism combined with fantasy in the stylized palm-tree columns of carved, painted and gilt wood that clothed the cast-iron supports to the ceiling above.

The brilliant oriental gaiety of the Saloon was now superseded by a more rarefied and stately grandeur, with gilt mouldings, pilasters of palm-like stems entwined with serpents, and a carpet woven with serpents and dragons. In place of the Chinese wallpapers of three years earlier were now hung panels of pleated silk of crimson and gold, to match the heavy crimson and gold window draperies. The curtain-pelmets and the crestings of wall-panels and mirror-frames were shaped in a lotus-design with leaf ornament in a spirit approaching the Indian more closely than the Chinese.

With the magnificence of the two great new State Apartments added by Nash the building achieved its transformation from a gay little holiday pavilion to the palace of a king. Under the hands of a new decorative genius, Crace's collaborator Robert Jones, the Banqueting-room became a universe as fantastic as the Indian cosmology. The great dome of the room became a sky, painted with the fronds of an immense plantain tree, with four of its leaves gigantically modelled in copper, amidst them crouching a huge carved dragon covered with silver scales, holding in its claws a great chandelier like a cascade of brilliants, out of which rise six smaller gilt dragons, each supporting its own lotus-flower of light. In the corners of the roof lurk strange fabulous birds, the legendary *Fum* of China holding four smaller chandeliers shaped like waterlilies. At the sides of the room were eight tall pedestals of blue porcelain carrying lotus-shaped lamps, and the walls were hung with painted groups of Chinese figures which were said to have been copied from models wearing dresses used a little while before in performances of an oriental opera at the Paris Opera House.

The Music-room achieves a solemn grandeur that is far removed from the brittle gay *chinoiserie* of the first Pavilion. In creating it the designer, Frederick Crace, seems to have sought inspiration in the description of the Palace of the Great Khan at Shandu written by Marco Polo in his *Travels* early in the fourteenth century. 'The sides of the great halls and apartments are ornamented in dragons of carved work and gilt, figures of warriors, of birds and of beasts. . . . The inside of the roof is contrived in such a manner that nothing besides gilding and painting presents itself to the eye.' Here the great dome is covered with innumerable scallop-shells carved of wood and gilded, set in ascending circles and diminishing in size, so that the perspective is exaggerated and an illusion of stupendous height is created. From an immense stylized flower ornament in the centre of the dome hangs the central chandelier in the form of a waterlily, its petals formed of panels of painted glass. Around it hang eight smaller similar lamps. The borders of the walls are filled by paintings of Chinese columns entwined by immense serpents, strangely fulfilling Marco Polo's description: '. . . a royal pavilion, supported upon a colonnade of handsome pillars, gilt and varnished. Round each pillar a dragon, likewise gilt, entwines its tail . . . the roof is of bamboo cane . . .', and these very roofs are here, in the curved ceilings of simulated bamboo at either end of the room. But it is with the wall-paintings themselves that the artist achieved the supreme vision of the East in the Royal Pavilion. These landscapes, of an idealized, legendary China, with palm-trees, immense drooping willows, bamboos, pagodas, temples, junks, sampans, fishermen and mythical birds, are painted as though to resemble the lacquer panels of a gigantic oriental cabinet, in scarlet, yellow and gold, giving them a strangely remote unearthly beauty. Yet all the details of the paintings, the temples and pagodas, the boats and figures, were copied accurately from drawings made in China by William Alexander, the artist who had accompanied Lord Macartney's luckless trading embassy to China nearly fifty years before.

It was Robert Jones, too, who devised the new Private Apartments on the ground floor of the Pavilion, overlooking the western part of the grounds with their thickets of picturesquely arranged shrubs and young trees. By this time the King was ageing, and suffering so grievously from gout and corpulence it was a blessing not having to climb the stairs, however graceful and elegant, to the bedroom in the south wing of the old building that he had used for thirty-five years. It was a restful, softly toned colour scheme that was provided for the three new rooms, the anteroom, library and bedroom, in a design of phoenixes, dragons, serpents, stars and waves in white outline on a green ground. Samples with a yellow ground as well as of green were shown to the King for him to choose from. The yellow was not chosen, but the green decoration did not survive fifty years of municipal use after the building had been bought by the townspeople. However, when the King's Apartments were being restored in 1948 the yellow samples were found in the cellars, still brilliantly fresh, and served as the pattern for reproducing the design.

On 29th January 1820 King George III died, and George, Prince of Wales, who had ruled as Prince Regent for nearly nine years, succeeded him as King George IV. He was then in his fifty-ninth year. The new King came to Brighton a month after his proclamation, and was again compelled to stay at Marlborough Row. For several weeks he was seriously ill, and it was said that on one occasion he had eighty ounces of blood taken from him. The Princess Lieven, the vivacious, witty and attractive but unscrupulously malicious wife of the Russian Ambassador, was attending the Court at Brighton at this time and wrote to her friend Prince Metternich:

'In the middle of all this, the King occupies a little house (houses would be more exact) two hundred yards from his palace, or Pavilion, or Kremlin, or mosque—for it bears all these names and deserves them—quite alone, without means of receiving anybody, since his lodging is no bigger than a parrot's cage.'

Princess Lieven was greatly amused by the attentions that the Duke of York was now showering upon her, and one day in September 1820 paid a visit to the Pavilion with him:

'I went with him again to see the work going on at the Kremlin. We were shown a chandelier which cost eleven thousand pounds sterling—I write it out in full because it is really incredible. The chandelier is in the form of a tulip held by a dragon. I send you a bad, but faithful, engraving of the King's Palace here. How can one describe such a piece of architecture? The style is a mixture of Moorish, Tartar, Gothic and Chinese, and all in stone and iron. It is a whim which has already cost £700,000, and it is still not fit to live in.'

On 19th July 1821 George IV was crowned King at Westminster in the course of one of the most glorious spectacles ever staged in this country, and which cost nearly a quarter of a million pounds. Early in the proceedings the Princess Caroline, who now regarded herself as Queen of England, demanded admission at the doors of the Abbey for her crowning, but was refused entry.

A few weeks later the King visited his subjects in Ireland, and while the Royal yacht waited for bad weather to abate before making the crossing, news was brought to him of the Princess's death. The humiliation of being refused entry to the Abbey, so soon after the long-drawn-out ordeal of her trial in the House of Lords, despite the eventual abandonment of the charges brought against her, undoubtedly hastened her end.

In Brighton preparations for the Coronation were beginning to be discussed in June, and a meeting was convened by the magistrates at the Old Ship Hotel, of which it was reported: '. . . . the spirit of the resolutions passed involved the roasting of three oxen whole, for distribution among the populace, with a suitable quantity of bread and strong beer; bonfires and a grand display of fireworks, instead of illuminating the houses in the evening; and a variety of rural sports and diversions, to give a merry complexion to the day.' The proposal to illuminate the houses was vetoed, as on the last occasion when this was done several houses were burned down. A clergyman at the meeting protested against the unpleasant and barbarous custom of roasting oxen, but a butcher, Mr. Myrtle, declared in reply that the carcass of a fine fat bullock whether 'on or off the spit' was a 'noble and gratifying object', and the proposal was carried. The whole day was carefully planned: 'At one oclock therefore the busy task of carving and serving out will commence, to be announced by signal-cannon on the Downs, the sound of bugles, and the combined bands to the strain of "The Roast Beef of Old England"', recorded the *Brighton Herald*, concluding with some truth that it 'would require the genius of a Hogarth to depict all the scenes that would ensue on the great day'. 'The sound of cannon and the ringing of bells ushered in the morn', as the paper afterwards described, 'and Colours, in all directions, were flying . . .'

In the morning a Musical Festival was held at the Chapel in St. James's Street, where among the singers 'the sweet tones of Mrs. Turnstall trilled upon the listening ear, and found a grateful and free admission to the heart'.

The 'charity children' were marshalled upon the Steine and plum cakes and sweet cakes distributed to them. In addition, 'fifteen hundred medals were presented to the juveniles, apparently of gold, but of inferior metal, by the Rev. Mr. Everard, with the King's head embossed on one side. . . .'

In the valley leading from the Steine northwards there were innumerable awnings, marquees, booths, 'drinking-boxes', stalls, benches and tables, and on the Level a large ring for the sports. 'A population of nearly five and twenty thousand souls, joined by nearly as many from surrounding near and distant parts, all assembled with one accord, as one and the same family, breathing the same social spirit, uttering the same sentiments, actuated by the same impulse. . . .' All, that is, we regret to say, but a somewhat furtive little band of men who assembled in the stable-yard of the Old Ship. The Hotel was at this hour deserted, for everyone had gone to swell the crowds at the Level. The excisemen were here, too, determined not to be absent from all the demonstrations of loyalty to their King. But at the Ship Hotel a signal was suddenly given, and a band of smugglers brought up from a hiding-place on the beach a consignment of about thirty kegs of Hollands Gin, on which duty had never been paid, slung them on to the backs of waiting horses and drove them swiftly away before anyone could realize what was happening. At noon a salute of twenty-one guns was fired from the battery, and answered by two armed cutters in the roadstead, by firing from the packet-boats, collier-brigs and other craft, and from a sort of private battery of four guns that had been set up by a Mr. Izard at the bottom of Middle Street.

The carving of the three oxen, which had been roasting for ten hours, then began, and it was remarked that even 'the most delicate and beautiful females of fashion suffered themselves to be squeezed most indelicately in the throng of people waiting to be served'.

During the afternoon 'the potent libations of ale had gained such influence that order became lost in unspeakable rapture, and a harmless though uncontrollable confusion prevailed'. The sports and dancing were a complete fiasco and several people were injured, yet 'the loyal character of the assembly was never for an instant lost'. While the celebrations were at their height, an aged lady was brought to the scene in a carriage, accompanied by the Vicar of Brighton. She was Phoebe Hessell, the famous woman soldier, who against the advice of her doctor, and in spite of her 107 years, had insisted on being present. As she declared, 'The voice of the King himself, her best and dearest friend, seemed to call her, she would be there if she crawled to the ground upon hands and knees.' This ancient crone was one of the most famous of all Brighton's remarkable characters. Since 1808 she had been receiving a pension from the Prince of Wales and for many years she had been a familiar sight as she sat at the corner of the Old Steine and Marine Parade selling gingerbread and apples, pincushions and toys from a little basket. She presented a quaint appearance as she sat there swathed in a voluminous brown serge dress, spotlessly clean white apron, and huge black cloak with a hood, her pugnaciously prominent nose and pointed, determined chin protruding out of her weatherbeaten face under an old black straw bonnet that she wore over a 'comfortable-looking' mob-cap. She wore long mittens on her arms. A great many people patronized her for the sake of hearing her talk of how she had served for many years as a soldier without her sex being discovered, and sometimes she would be persuaded to show the scar of the bayonet wound she had received upon her arm. When she was only fifteen years old, in 1728, her sweetheart Samuel Golding was sent with his regiment, 'Kirke's Lambs', to the West Indies. She was a strongly built girl with a deep voice, and succeeded in enlisting as a boy in another infantry regiment that was being sent out to the colony. Later she served in various parts of Europe, and in 1745 fought in the battle of Fontenoy, where she was wounded. She confided her story to the colonel's wife, who obtained her discharge and had her sent to England. Her lover had been invalided home and she was allowed to nurse him in Plymouth Hospital. When Golding was discharged on pension from the Army, the couple married and lived happily together for twenty years. After Golding's death she married a man named Hessell. Phoebe had nine children, but none of them reached adult age except one who became a sailor and was never heard of again. After Hessell's death she bought a donkey and cart and travelled round Brighton and the neighbouring villages selling fish. When a great festival was held at Brighton on the Level to celebrate Napoleon's imprisonment at Elba, Phoebe sat at the Vicar's right hand, and the crowd contributed a large sum in gold and silver to present to her. After her death in 1821, at the age of 107, Phoebe was buried in the churchyard of St. Nicholas, where her gravestone records that her life extended from the days of Queen Anne to those of George IV.

In the October of Coronation year the famous aeronaut Charles Green announced that he would make an ascent in his 'Coronation Balloon' at the Black Rock Gas Works. When the appointed day came large crowds assembled, but the weather was stormy with a strong wind off the land, and Green perceived that were he to take the flight he would be carried out to sea. However, determined not to disappoint the public, he decided to ascend and reached a considerable height, until he realized that he was about two miles off the coast. He then released the gas and descended upon the water near some ships, in the hope that his balloon would be picked up, but when he was eventually rescued in an exhausted condition the balloon was torn to ribbons and all his 'philosophical instruments' were lost or destroyed. Soon after a meeting was announced at the Old Ship 'to consider of a proper subscription to be raised for the benefit of the above intrepid aeronaut as a remuneration for the danger and loss he has sustained, to gratify the public'.

By the time of his accession to the throne the King had broken off his friendship with Lady Hertford. For over fifteen years she had been the King's principal confidante and adviser. Lady Hertford herself maintained their association had never been other than platonic, and the political influence she wielded through this attachment was undoubtedly sweeter to her than any other delights the King was able to offer. The King was now completely under the spell of the Marchioness of Conyngham, continually fondling and kissing her hand, and gazing upon her even in public with abject adoration. Lady Conyngham possessed the ample proportions that the King seemed so often to require in all his intimate companions, but unlike the frigid Lady Hertford and the vixenish Lady Jersey, she had a warm-hearted, relaxed temperament that the King found soothing and restful. The post of Lady Steward was created for her, while other appointments in the Royal Household were given to her husband and two of her sons, and the end house in Marlborough Row (now North Gate House) was set aside for her use. The King's willingness to leave all his domestic affairs in her hands, and his generous presents to her, naturally caused intense animosity to be aroused amongst her acquaintances. 'All the members of her family are continually there,' wrote Greville in May, 'and are supplied with horses, carriages, etc, from the King's stables. She rides out with her daughter, but never with the King, who always rides with one of his gentlemen. They never appear in public together. She dines there every day. Before the King comes into the room she and Lady Elizabeth [Conyngham] join him in another room and he always walks in with one on each arm. She comports herself entirely as mistress of the house, but never suffers her daughter to leave her. She has received magnificent presents and Lady Elizabeth the same; particularly the mother has strings of pearls of enormous value. . . . The other night Lady Bath was coming to the Pavilion. After dinner Lady Conyngham called to Sir William Keppel and said "Sir William, do desire them to light up the saloon as Lady Bath is coming this evening." The King seized her arm and said with the greatest tenderness: "Thank you, thank you, my dear; you always do what is right, you cannot please me so much as by doing everything you please, everything to show you are mistress here." ' Those who have 'the Royal ear' are not infrequently envied, feared and even hated, but Lady Conyngham seems to have been ridiculed and vilified to a far greater extent than almost any other person associated with the King, and this campaign of slander has continued even into our own day. Creevey wrote in his diary in December 1822: 'Brougham says *many of the best informed* people in London, such as Dog Dent and others, are perfectly convinced of the truth of the report that dear Prinny is really to marry Ly. Elizabeth

Conyngham; on which event the Earl here humorously observes that the least the King can do for the Queen's family is to make Denison "Great Infant of England".' A footnote in Sir Herbert Maxwell's edition of the Creevey papers (1903) mentions that Lord Albert Denison Conyngham, third son of Elizabeth Denison, first Marchioness of Conyngham, was born in 1805 'and was supposed to be the son of the Prince of Wales (George IV)'. This belief, widely held at the time, was quite conceivably not incorrect. It has already been shown that the King and Lady Conyngham could have known each other as early as 1802. Also, in 1805 she was among the fashionable visitors to Brighton and it seems most improbable that the Prince did not meet her then.*

Lady Conyngham was accused of being 'avaricious and insatiable in her lust after anything of the least value she could seize', persuading the King to lavish upon her jewellery of enormous value, including even some articles of the Crown jewels which the King had been compelled to recover from Prince Leopold after the death of Princess Charlotte. It can quite convincingly be argued that the wealthiest people are often the meanest, especially in small matters, but the accusation of avariciousness seems very much out of place in connection with the Conynghams, who were one of the richest families in England. She herself was the daughter and heiress of a wealthy London banker, Joseph Denison, and the sister of a multi-millionaire. Sir Thomas Lawrence's dramatic portrait of her, painted in 1802, shows a handsome woman of queenly build, and a portrait in enamel by Charles Muss,[5] while throwing a cast of beauty over her ample form, conveys an impression of a woman of great shrewdness as well as charm of character. The greatest tribute to her ability was made by the Duke of Wellington, who confessed that he invariably consulted her and asked her advice in public matters, and stated that no decision of importance in affairs of state during the years of her ascendancy was made without her opinion being sought. The picture of a selfish, grasping woman, using her influence with the King solely for her own personal ends, changes when one considers the tradition in the Londesborough family to the effect that she prevailed upon the King to abolish the flogging of women prisoners. The author was informed of this tradition by the late Dame Edith Sitwell, a descendant of Lady Conyngham's on her mother's side. 'What an atmosphere the King lives in!' wrote Lady Anne Becket to the monarch's biographer Croker. 'He never, since he has been at Brighton, has left his own room, except to walk *across* at half-past three or four to Lady C's house, and at six to walk back, he then dresses and comes down to dinner, and that is the whole of his air and exercise. Bye the bye, all the world, if they chose, might see this daily visit; for the King goes out at the south* gate of the inclosure and has a few yards of the common street to walk to reach the steps of Lady C's house.' This house, now North Gate House, has since

1935 been the administrative offices of the Royal Pavilion, Museums and Libraries, and the room where the King and Lady Conyngham sat conversing and drinking tea every afternoon was for nearly thirty years the present writer's office.

Dinner would be served at the Pavilion at six-thirty. The King sat on one side of the table, with Lady Conyngham on his right, and her daughter, Lady Elizabeth, on his left. At one end of the table sat Lord Conyngham, with his son Lord Francis Conyngham at the other. Opposite the King was his Private Secretary, Sir Francis Bloomfield. On one occasion reported by Croker the party retired after dinner to the Music-room, where the King sang some Italian trios with the two pretty Miss Liddells, daughters of Lord Ravensworth, who Lady Conyngham suspected were trying to insinuate themselves into the King's favour. He also sang *Life's a Bumper* and *A Friar of Orders Gray*. After a minor uproar over the King's snuff box, which had become mislaid, but which was eventually found reposing safely in his pocket, at eleven-thirty the King retired to bed. The next night after dinner he sang again, this time with two young choristers from the Chapel Royal. There were some glees, *Glorious Apollo*, and *Lord Mornington's Waterfall*—so popular was the latter that he had to repeat the performance—and *Non Nobis Domine*. 'His voice, a bass', remarked Croker, 'is not good, and he does not sing so much from the notes as from recollection. He is, therefore, as a musician merely, far from good, but he gave, I think, the force, gaiety and spirit of the glee in a superior style to the professional men.' Croker also noted that 'Lady Conyngham and Lady Elizabeth did not conceal their dissatisfaction to all this music, and particularly at the Liddells'.' The King had never enjoyed music so much as in this new Music-room he had devised, and he told Lady Granville that he cried for joy whenever he reflected on the delights of the Pavilion.

During his first visit to England, Rossini was invited to the Royal Pavilion on 29th December 1823. A grand concert was held in the Music-room at which the overture to *La Gazza Ladra* and a selection from *Il Barbiere* were played by the King's band, and the composer himself sang two songs from his own operas. When the Coronation anthem was played the *maestro* had not the slightest hesitation in taking a seat, uninvited, by the King's side, an act of familiarity that greatly displeased Lady Granville and other guests, although the King willingly overlooked it in an artist for whom he himself had so much respect.

The glories and extravagances of the Pavilion excited the Princess Lieven's customary shrewish disapproval, accompanied by her usual inaccurate estimate of the cost of things. 'I do not believe that, since the days of Heliogabalus, there has been such magnificence and such luxury. There is something effeminate in it which is disgusting. One spends the evening half-lying on cushions; the lights are dazzling; there are perfumes, music, liqueurs. . . . Here is one single detail about the establishment. To light the three rooms, used when the family is alone, costs 150 guineas an evening; when the apartment is fully opened up, it is double that.'

The King's Band now numbered seventy performers, and was costing him between £6,000 and £7,000 a year. Even so the musicians complained bitterly about the inadequacy of their pay, and it was worked out that the least a man with a wife and three children could live on was £2 9s 6½d a week, the cost of lodging, furniture, the schooling of children and clothing not being included. Most of them got no more than about £2 6s od, and as a result the wages were increased by about 7s a week for each man. Their difficulties were further alleviated by allowing some of their musically inclined sons also to be 'put on the strength and allowed to draw wages'.[6]

It was about this time that the King made the munificent gift to the nation of the great library which had been formed by his father, and which included many important manuscripts and early printed books. The gift was conveyed to the Prime Minister in a letter written from the Pavilion by the King while in the midst of great pain during a severe illness.[7] £40,000 was voted by Parliament for the building of a new wing at the British Museum, and it is there that the King's Library is housed to this day. It has been said that the Emperor of Russia had offered £100,000 for the collection, and that King George IV was compensated for the loss of this sum by a grant of the amount from the Admiralty Prize Fund.*

George IV was genuinely interested in literature. He was an avid reader of the works of Sir Walter Scott, who became a close friend and whose baronetcy was the first conferred by the King upon his accession. He was an admirer, too, of the novels of Jane Austen, and when at his suggestion she dedicated *Mansfield Park* to him he invited her to visit Carlton House in order to inspect his own library there. His admiration and respect for writers is shown by the subscriptions of 1,000 guineas a year which he made to the Literary Fund of the Royal Society of Literature, by means of which pensions were paid to ten men-of-letters. He also subscribed heavily towards the cost of a new headquarters for the Society. One of the pensions was paid to the poet Coleridge, whose poem *Xanadu* had seemed to speak of the Pavilion—'In Xanadu did Kubla Khan A stately pleasure-dome decree'. Now in his old age, afflicted by sickness and fits of insanity, Coleridge had been kept from misery since 1825 by the King's generosity, but after the death of George IV the new King declined to continue the pensions, on the advice of the Whig Ministers Grey and Brougham.

The generosity and sympathy of King George IV were no less powerful when they were exercised on behalf of the very humblest people, even if the fact was not likely to become known. The King's Ministers were accustomed to his frequent exercise of the Royal prerogative of mercy—'a word more consoling to the King's mind than words can express'[8]—and his clemency was a redeeming light in that age of harsh and brutal punishments. He was incapable of realizing the appalling conditions in which many thousands of his subjects existed, although these horrors were possibly not at their greatest until the Industrial Revolution reached its zenith in a later reign, but his compassion was quickly and strongly aroused by individual instances of need. Croly has described how the King would keep his Ministers for hours at a time going through the lists of condemned criminals 'who had no other advocate', considering minutely in every individual case whether there were circumstances that would justify a remission of sentence. He was especially horrified by the multiple executions that were common at the time, and often caused the Home Secretary, Sir Robert Peel, great annoyance by compelling him to reduce the number of those who were to suffer in this way.

It has sometimes been suggested that George IV lost interest in his Pavilion once he had completed it, but this is certainly not true. The day-books at the Lord Chamberlain's office (Jutsham's Day-books) which record the movements of furniture and other property between the Royal palaces during the years from 1821 to 1827 when the King was visiting Brighton give an account of a fascinating series of objects sent down to the Royal Pavilion. Apart from large quantities of furniture required especially for one visit or another, some of the articles sent reveal intriguing aspects of the King's character, including a continued interest in oriental notions. They included two ivory dice-boxes; carpets and pocket books from the Bey of Algiers; embroidered purses from China; a toilet-case containing the astonishing quantity of '30 quart bottles of perfume'; and a large model of an 'Indian Temple or Mansion'.

The year 1826 was remarkable not only for the vast number of fashionable visitors, but also on account of the curiosities of fashion which then reached unprecedented heights of absurdity. These were caricatured in the famous colour print drawn by 'A. Crowquill Esq.' and etched by George Cruikshank. Entitled 'Beauties of Brighton', it depicts a number of Society notables on parade in the Steine, whose extravagance of dress completely eclipses the fantastic outlines of the Pavilion itself in the background. Three dandies in tight pantaloons are the artist Alfred Forrester himself and his brothers. Near them are the Duke of York and the Duke of Gloucester. A portly man in black is Nathaniel Rothschild the banker, with his wife in a large flowered hat. A fat person in black is talking to Colonel d'Este, a much-whiskered officer in a grotesque Polish 'chapska', with his sister on one arm and Mrs. Coutts, the banker's wife, on the other. Muffled up in a thick coat and huge neck-cloth and wearing heavy top-boots is Talleyrand, then serving as French Ambassador in London.

There was another side of life in Brighton, however, more akin to Thomas Hardy's Wessex than to Britain's most sophisticated resort. In May 1826 a woman was put up for auction at Brighton Market with a halter round her neck, and was bought by a man for a sovereign and four half-crowns. Her husband kept her elder child but 'threw in a younger child as a make-weight'. The sale was duly entered in the market register, and the purchaser paid a shilling to the auctioneer for his trouble, and another shilling for the halter. The *Herald* declared that the woman seemed perfectly happy to be sold and went off with her child arm in arm with her new husband.[9]

The last visit of the King was for six weeks early in 1828. It had been hoped that he would arrive in time for Christmas, but a crisis in Portugal necessitated his presence in London. On 30th December the *Brighton Herald* showed that a close watch had been kept on premonitory comings and goings at the Pavilion and reported the astonishing fact that 'four carriages, each containing a piano-forte, arrived at the Pavilion, from London, and, for several days, Sake Deen Mahomed, the proprietor of the Indian Baths here, and who, for years past, has had the superintendence of the Royal Baths at the Palace, has been seen to enter the Pavilion'. The nature of the musical works for which four pianofortes were required is a subject for interesting conjecture, and the vision of the Indian 'Shampooing Surgeon' busying himself in the King's bathroom, with its two marble baths, among the '30 quart bottles of perfume', is also an intriguing one. At last the King arrived on 23rd January accompanied by the Lord Steward.

During the King's visit a Privy Council was held at the Pavilion, and he left for London again on 7th March. In September it was again believed that the King intended to come, and lodgings were engaged for the band and other servants who did not live at the Pavilion. From then onwards it was daily expected that the King would be arriving at Brighton, until in November 1829 a messenger arrived from Windsor with orders that all preparations should be suspended. On 26th June 1830 the King died at Windsor Castle.

What is probably the fairest summing-up of the King's character was made by the Duke of Wellington, who had been one of his closest friends in his later years, to Robert Raikes, the reformer, whom the King had also known, and had helped in his work for the first Sunday schools. The Duke remarked:

'He was indeed the most extraordinary compound of talent, wit, buffoonery, obstinacy and good feeling,—in short, a medley of the most opposite qualities with a great preponderance of good that I ever saw in any character in my life.'[10] The King's own sister, the Princess Elizabeth commented 'He was all heart . . .'.

III

LATE GEORGIAN

1820 to 1840

1 Buildings of the 1820s

I t is an ironic fact that although Brighton has always been regarded as a Regency town very few buildings of this period survive here, other than the Royal Pavilion. That is if we interpret the word Regency strictly in the sense of the period between 1811 and 1820, when the Prince of Wales ruled this country as Regent. It was the period between 1820 and 1830 when George IV was King that saw the creation not only of the two great architectural groups of Kemp Town and Brunswick Town, but also the building of most of the other squares both large and small, and the crescents, terraces, streets and individual buildings that, together with the Royal Pavilion, today give the combined towns of Brighton and Hove their remarkable distinction. In those boom years of building between 1820 and 1830 the number of houses almost doubled in number, increasing from about 4,000 to nearly 8,000, and according to a census taken at the beginning of 1826 by the Brighton architect Charles Busby, no less than 500 houses were in course of erection at that time.

The great building boom of the 1820s brought about a remarkable change in the appearance of the town, not only in its extent, but also in the scale of the buildings, as the need arose to accommodate a larger population and as the value of land increased. There was at the same time a distinct alteration in the character of the houses. In many of those built before 1820 the curved window-bays were shallow and extended across only part of the front of the house. Often the bays did not extend to the whole height of the façade, and the cornices were delicate, with narrow mouldings and small dentils. These are to be found at No. 7 Pavilion Parade, in Charles Street and Broad Street, west of the Steine, and at No. 23 New Road, but houses of this early character are rapidly disappearing in Brighton.

The new manner of the 1820s, with which Busby and the Wilds are predominantly associated, was based on the style of grand houses built a few years before, such as Mersham-le-Hatch in Kent, designed by Robert Adam in 1762, and Heaton Hall, Manchester, built by James Wyatt ten years later. Both possessed the distinctive features of bold, semicircular bays and deep, strongly projecting cornices. In many respects the new houses were influenced also by the great mansions being built in Regent's Park by John Nash and Decimus Burton in the early 1820s. The architect Charles Busby was one of the three men who, sometimes working together, sometimes independently, were between them chiefly responsible for the

175

massive architectural development in Brighton during this period. The others were the firm of Amon Wilds and his son Amon Henry Wilds, who for years conducted an important architectural and building practice in Brighton.

Charles Augustus Busby was born in 1788, the son of a musician and author. He attended the Royal Academy School of Drawing and at the age of twenty won the Academy's Gold Medal. In his early years he published two books of architectural designs, one for *Villas and Country Houses*, the other for *Verandas, Chimney Pieces and other embellishments*. It is highly probable that Euston Square, Bloomsbury, which was built in 1808, was erected to his designs, when he was only twenty years old. He also designed the Commercial Coffee Rooms in Corn Street, Bristol, with its fine cupola supported by twelve caryatids, but he was chiefly interested in designing houses. He poured scorn on the style of the Adam brothers, which he regarded as an 'example of the decay of genius and the depravity of taste'. His preference was for the elegant simplicity of form found in Greek architecture, and he devoted special attention to interior planning for what he called 'the Comforts and Elegancies of Modern Life'. In this he allied himself with the beginnings of the modern movement in domestic architecture, even going so far as to remark, in his book of house-designs: '... the true impressions of cheerfulness, elegance and refinement, are so well understood and so happily united in our modern domestic dwellings, that I hesitate not to say we are rapidly advancing to a state of perfection.'[1]

After spending some years in America, where he seems to have interested himself in dreary problems concerning the design of penitentiaries, and also in the propulsion of paddleboats, he returned to England in 1821 and settled at Brighton. A year after his return from America Busby established himself in partnership with Amon Wilds, an older man, who was carrying on business as a builder in the Lewes Road, Brighton, with his son Amon Henry Wilds. The father was a Lewes man, born in 1762, who had moved to Brighton in 1815, and the two were working in both towns until 1820, when they devoted themselves exclusively to building in Brighton.

Busby seems never to have lost his interest in paddleboats, and as late as 1832 caused great diversion amongst spectators upon the sea-front by means of a small steam paddleboat which he had constructed embodying his own improvements. This he navigated from Brunswick Square to beyond Kemp Town, 'taking a circuit round several sailing boats in this way and outstripping every other vessel'.

Busby lived at 11 Waterloo Place for some years, and later at Stanhope Place, Hove, where he died in 1834 at the early age of forty-six. It seems that he never married.

Some fairly considerable building activity had been going on in the western part of Brighton from 1807 onwards with the building of Bedford Square, which consisted chiefly of lodging houses, but the most interesting development towards the end of the Regency was the building of Regency Square during a period of ten years from 1818 onwards, it is believed by the firm of the Wilds. This charming square was laid out as a speculative enterprise by the landowner, Joshua Flesher Hanson, in what had been known as Belle Vue Field, possibly so named after Belle Vue House, which had belonged to the Count de St. Antonio. Before 1807 Belle Vue Field was a favourite site for fairs, shows and military reviews, but after that date fairs and fêtes were usually held on the Level. It is supposed that the two Wilds were responsible for the building of the Square, as they were the most important building firm in Brighton at the time, and also because the houses lack those pronounced features and details of architectural design that one associates with Busby's work. The houses, apart from the last ones to be completed, were designed in the longstanding tradition of the town terrace house, which had been exemplified, if not established, during the last ten years of the previous century by Henry Holland, architect of the early classical Marine Pavilion, in the terrace houses of his own speculative enterprises in Hans Town and Sloane Street, London. Like them, the houses of Regency Square had only the ground floor portion of their façades stuccoed, the rest being in yellow brick, with ironwork railings at the balconies, and neat classical porches.

The houses on the northern side have the strongly curved window-bays of the 1820s, some of them with the bulbous canopies of this later period, but the houses at the western end of that side are of much later date.

Responsibility for the design of the individual buildings erected in Brighton by the Wilds was chiefly in the hands of the father, who was usually referred to as 'Builder' or 'Surveyor', until about 1822. One of their first important commissions was for the chapel in Ship Street which they built about 1818 for Thomas Read Kemp as the meeting house of his newly founded religious sect. This building, which was absorbed into the Church of England in 1825 as Holy Trinity Church, and which was later rebuilt in its present Gothic style, was originally designed with a four-column Doric portico, and a square pylon-like tower.

Kemp was born in 1782 of a wealthy and influential Lewes family. His father, M.P. for Lewes, was the owner of the house on the Steine which Louis Weltje bought for the Prince of Wales, and which was demolished for the building of the first Marine Pavilion. After coming down from Cambridge, Thomas Read Kemp married one of the daughters of the great banker Sir Francis Baring, and her large marriage portion was added to the large fortune and property that her husband inherited on the death of his father in 1811, the year of the proclamation of the Regency. Kemp also succeeded to his father's seat in Parliament. During the next few years he enjoyed to the full the life of pleasure and sport that was the lot of a fashionable young man in the gay days of the Regent. He was a lavish host and an enthusiastic horseman and excelled in yachting and archery. But within five years the life of gaiety and pleasure he was leading seems to have palled, and possibly under the influence of his wife's sister, who was an ardent Evangelical, Kemp gave up his seat in Parliament and became the minister of a dissenting religious sect that he founded, for which he built a chapel in Lewes and the Trinity Chapel in Ship Street, Brighton. A year or so after the building of this chapel, in 1819, Mr. Kemp gave up his home at Herstmonceux Place for a house built for him in Montpelier Road which was called 'The Temple', as it was supposedly built to the measurements of Solomon's temple. To the local residents it was known as 'Kemp's Folly'. Kemp's sister, Mrs. Ann Sober, had already employed the Wilds to build a house called Western Lodge for her not far away in Western Road, and it is assumed that the Temple was also built by the Wilds, probably to the father's design. Western Lodge no longer exists. Kemp's new house is now occupied by the Brighton and Hove High School for Girls. It was an extraordinary house in its day, built in the form of a large square block surmounted by a flattened dome and with a tall chimney at each corner. Inside, a central hall extended the whole height of the building, and the only means of access to the upper rooms was by a peculiar winding staircase enclosed within a tall cylindrical chamber, possibly with the idea of preventing draughts. In the advertisement of its sale by auction in 1842 it was described as 'entirely adapted to the purposes of a Nobleman. It is full of comfort and constructed especially to give effect to those who would live in the busy world of fashion.'[2] The dome, the four chimneys and the tubular staircase have in recent years been swept away, and the central hall has been altered, and today the only interesting features that remain are the strange Egyptian-like pilasters of the exterior, tapering towards their bases, and the original encircling wall and gateway.

Amon Henry Wilds is believed to have been the designer of the Unitarian Chapel in New Road, in 1820, in the form of a Greek temple with an imposingly severe Doric portico, but the father is supposed to have been the designer in 1825 of the Congregational Chapel in Union Street, now the Elim Tabernacle of the Church of the Four Square Gospel.[3] This was a rebuilding of Brighton's first nonconformist chapel, first erected in 1683, as a stone set into the front wall still proclaims. The new chapel was designed in Grecian style, without a portico, but with a fine pediment and a pair of impressive pylon doorways.

In the centre of the town A. H. Wilds built, or more probably refronted, several houses in the Old Steine to Busby's designs. Of these Nos. 23 and 26 are the most striking, both of them with Doric porches and with bow-fronts extending the full width of the façade. The latter has a fine shell ornament over each of the first-floor windows, and imposing fluted pilasters surmounted by 'Ammonite' capitals in the form of those geological fossil ammonites consisting of voluted shells which derive their name from their resemblance to the legendary horn of Jupiter Amon. The device was originally invented by the architect George Dance, who used it on the façade of Boydell's Gallery in Pall Mall in 1789. The firm of Wilds had used it on the house in Lewes of Gideon Mantell, the famous doctor and geologist, for whom they no doubt considered it especially appropriate, and they adopted it for several other houses they built in Brighton, no doubt being also attracted to its use because of the punning allusion to their own unusual Christian name.

Many of the older houses of Brighton, such as those of the North and South Parades of the Steine, were rebuilt or re-fronted in the new manner of the 1820s, with deeply curved, often semicircular window-bays, with bold, strongly projecting cornices and deep parapets or balustrades. Often the fronts are divided vertically into three by broad pilasters, and are with arched recesses for the windows as at No. 30 Old Steine, which also has a Doric porch. A. H. Wilds also built No. 1 Castle Square, on the corner of the Old Steine, and the Royal Pavilion Hotel a few doors away on the south side of the Square.

North of the Steine in the Lewes Road are Richmond Terrace and Waterloo Place, both of them with fine houses built in 1818 as a speculation by the younger Wilds. The father himself took No. 9 Richmond Terrace, and Busby lived at No. 11 Waterloo Place for many years. The houses in Richmond Terrace now known as Nos. 4 to 6 have iron lamps bearing crowns flanking the front steps. This building was occupied in the time of King George IV by the Lord Chancellor, who in 1826 was Lord Cumbermere. It is said also to have been occupied at other times by members of the Royal Family.

A fascinating group of buildings at the corner of New Road and Church Street form as it were a specimen collection of Regency architecture, ranging from the black cobbled-fronted Brighton vernacular building of Crabb's wine-shop, originally the Regent Hotel, and the adjoining bow-fronted shop with its fine balcony, to the neo-Greek Unitarian Church built by A. H. Wilds in 1820 and the Regency Gothic Central National School, built in 1829 by Stroud and Mew and later enlarged byCheeseman.

Kemp's dissenting phase did not last long. He returned to the Church of England and once more in 1823 took a seat in Parliament, this time as M.P. for the Borough of Arundel. It was then, too, that he conceived the magnificent enterprise of building the great estate in Brighton which is called by his name. It has been suggested that he undertook this great scheme in order to improve his finances, which were by now considerably reduced by his youthful extravagances and his various building operations, but Kemp was also something of an idealist and a visionary, and may have been as much inspired by the grandeur of John Nash's great terraces around Regent's Park, and with the idea of creating a similar grand project on the cliffs to the east of Brighton, as by the financial possibilities of such an immense speculative enterprise. In the making of plans for carrying out this great project the Busby and Wilds partnership bore its first fruits in 1823.

John Nash's prodigious Regent's Park development, carried out as part of the 'Metropolitan Improvements' by which the West End of London was transformed in the reign of King George IV, was one of the greatest early town-planning schemes in this country, and was imitated soon after on a smaller scale in several other towns, such as Cheltenham, Buxton, Bristol, Edinburgh and elsewhere. The character of the Kemp Town buildings closely followed the model of the Regent's Park terraces, and like that enterprise the scheme was planned to provide within its own limits not only housing but also places of worship, entertainment and education for every section of the community, the aristocracy living in the grand palatial mansions of the great terraces, the professional classes occupying neighbouring groups of smaller houses, and the artisans and servants to the great houses being accommodated in terraces of small houses standing behind the main groups, but none the less designed in harmonious though modest fashion.

The design of Kemp Town surpassed even the Regent's Park terraces in originality of layout. It consisted of Sussex Square with houses on three sides opening on the south side into the vast Lewes Crescent, which terminated in two gigantic flanking terraces facing the sea, Chichester Terrace on the western side, Arundel Terrace on the east. A fine engraving by J. Bruce published in 1825 shows the full extent of the scheme as originally conceived. In designing the houses, Busby and Wilds did not rely for their effects upon rich and elaborate architectural treatment. The houses were originally three storeys high with an attic, and the façades were quite plain except for Corinthian pilasters on one house only in every three. The whole composition derives its impressiveness from its vast scale and noble proportions, the span of Lewes Crescent being 840 feet, 200 feet wider than that of the Royal Crescent at Bath. It was originally intended that the estate should consist of more than double the number of houses that were actually built. There were to have been two other squares of more modest houses inland from the terraces, and a number of streets of smaller houses and mews in between, but this part of the scheme was never carried out. Thomas Read Kemp paid the penalty which is often exacted for enterprise of this kind, for such a gigantic and far-seeing scheme as this could only reach fruition in the distant future, and his money was exhausted before the completion of even the principal houses, so that many of them remained merely empty shells for years. In order to give untrammelled expression to the magnificent design, which makes Kemp Town a remarkable example of early nineteenth-century town planning, Kemp had chosen for the site the large expanse of vacant land east of the town, but here again he was creating for posterity, and suffered from the lack of resources that would enable him to survive a preliminary period of stagnation, for one of the reasons for the slow rate at which the houses were sold was their isolation from the rest of the town, while transport was still far too inadequate to enable people to come down from London to live in the houses, even if only at week-ends and in the summer season. Unlike London, or the big industrial towns, Brighton then had no vast population anxiously in need of more and better housing. The first portion of the estate to be completed was Arundel Terrace, and this was the only part to be designed and built as a whole. The design is more elaborate than in other parts of the estate, the houses having a free-standing Corinthian portico of four columns in the centre of the Terrace, and porticoes of engaged columns at the ends and in between. The house at the east end of the Terrace, now called Arundel House, was originally the Bush Hotel, and was occupied by June 1826. All the façades in the Crescent and Square were finished by 1827, but most of the houses were mere skeletons. They were not completed until they were let or sold for occupation, and interiors were then designed according to the wishes of the various occupants, and constructed by different builders. The first recorded occupation was in February 1826, when No. 25 Sussex Square was taken by T. R. Kemp's brother-in-law, Philip Laycock Storey. Kemp himself moved from the Temple to No. 22 Sussex Square in October 1827, and a plaque placed on the house by the Regency Society records that he lived there for ten years. For many years Chichester Terrace consisted only of Chichester House at the west end and three houses at the other end. The space between was not filled until the unsold part of the estate was taken up about 1850 by the great London builder Thomas Cubitt. When filling the intervening gap of eleven houses he abandoned Busby and Wilds's original design for the façades, and thus the Terrace lacks the Corinthian pilasters of the rest of the scheme, except the original houses at the end. Cubitt had introduced in his great building schemes in London new standards of good materials and fine craftsmanship which were welcomed and proved a sound investment after the jerry-building of many of the Regency developments. Consequently the houses in Kemp Town that were finished by Cubitt can be recognized by the high quality of construction embodied in them, the staircases being of stone instead of wood as in the earlier houses.

By 1828 only eleven out of the total of 105 houses were occupied, and the number had risen to only thirty-six by 1834. After that date the houses were taken up more rapidly, and the estate could begin to be regarded as a success. As the most palatial group of houses in Brighton, Kemp Town attracted a number of distinguished people to live there for varying periods. One of the first proprietors was the sixth, or 'Bachelor', Duke of Devonshire, who from 1820 to 1854 occupied No. 1 Lewes Crescent and No. 14 Chichester Terrace. These are adjoining houses at the western corner of the Crescent, and a large room was presumably formed extending through both of them, for during the winter of 1848–9 he gave a series of grand dinners and balls there for 150 guests. Among the guests on several of these occasions the Princess Metternich, her daughter Princess Melanie and stepson Prince Richard Metternich were present. The Princess was the third wife of Prince Metternich, the great Austrian Chancellor, now aged seventy-five, who was then staying in Brighton. In 1896 the two houses were taken by the Duke of Fife. The Duchess, daughter of King Edward VII, became Princess Royal in 1901. The houses were occupied by the Duke and Duchess until the death of the former in 1912, and again by the widowed Princess in 1924. King Edward VII spent a week there in February 1908, and in 1914 Queen Alexandra stayed there for three days. From 1831 to 1839 Nos. 19 and 20 Sussex Square were the property of the first Marquess of Bristol. In April 1850 he lent the house to King Louis-Philippe, who was then in exile from France. They stayed a fortnight with members of their family, and walked almost every day on the Chain Pier. Cubitt himself took one of the houses, No. 13 Lewes Crescent, and made use of it from 1846 to 1855. As already mentioned, it was originally planned that the estate should be completely self-sufficient, providing, as Regent's Park intended, all the desirable amenities of life within itself. Apart from the Bush Hotel, the only adjunct to life here that materialized was St. George's Church, which was built as a chapel-of-ease for the estate in 1824–5.

Kemp not only paid for the building of St. George's Church out of his own pocket, but he gave to the town the large expanse of open land known as the Level, north of St. Peter's Church on the Lewes Road, in 1822. Despite his enormous wealth, his fortune was entirely absorbed by his various building operations. He was compelled to raise loans and mortgages of the most extortionate kind, and fell into the hands of sharks and usurers. In 1837 he left England for good to escape his creditors, 'taking refuge in that asylum for broken men, Boulogne, and other places on the Continent',[4] where he lived for the rest of his life.

On 10th January 1844 a proclamation of outlawry against Kemp was nailed to the door of St. Peter's Church, Brighton, while a service was in progress. Four months later he died in Paris, in his sixty-first year, and is buried in the cemetery of Père-La-Chaise.

Work had hardly begun on Kemp Town in 1823 when a similar development was put in hand at the western end of the town, just beyond the boundary of Brighton, in the parish of Hove, for the freeholder of the land, the Reverend Thomas Scutt. The site was a dreary expanse used as a brickyard, covered with heaps of ashes, rotten rubbish, and ruinous sheds, and the 'mephitic vapours' given off by the brick-kiln gave great annoyance to people living near by. The estate was quite clearly a building speculation inspired by Kemp Town, and its conception was probably due to the architect Charles Busby himself. Mr. Scutt was an extremely retiring and diffident person who hardly ever appeared in public. The fact that Busby countersigned the plans of the various builders to give them his approval suggests that a leading part in the foundation of the estate was played by him. In those days there were no Town Commissioners for the little parish of Hove as there were for the flourishing town of Brighton. The only official body were the Overseers of the Poor-rate. To remedy this deficiency a private Act of Parliament was obtained in 1830, known as the Brunswick Square Act, by which a body of twenty-one Commissioners was set up for the regulation of the affairs of Brunswick Town. Their powers were much the same as those given to the Brighton Town Commissioners by their Act of 1825, and in 1875 the Brunswick Town body became the Hove Commissioners and in 1898 Hove Corporation.[5] The title of Brunswick Town was given to the whole estate, there being no suitable local name which seemed appropriate. Together with his design for Kemp Town, Busby's drawing of Brunswick Town was exhibited at the Royal Academy, in 1825, and the companion engraving to that of Kemp Town was published by J. Bruce. The layout of the estate was simpler than that of Kemp Town, consisting only of a square flanked by terraces. The architectural features, however, were much more elaborate. The two terraces were identical. Each had a central portico with engaged Corinthian columns, as did the end-blocks, or pavilions of each terrace, and the façades of all the intervening houses were fronted with pilasters of the same order. The inspiration of the Regent's Park terraces was again obvious. The sides of Brunswick Square were given treatment of a completely different character. The house fronts are strongly bowed, and crowned with the deep friezes and boldly projecting cornices that are typical of the Regency style after 1820, and these are supported by engaged Ionic columns. Especially in the strong clear light of a sunny day, when strong shadows are cast on the sunlit stucco by the bold cornices and columns, and with the repeated rhythm of the successive bow-fronts up the Square, the effect is dramatic and stately. There are some curious differences, however, at two points on each side of the Square, where some houses, narrower than the rest, have been introduced. These could be explained away by citing them as examples of the idea of 'variety in the midst of unity', which was so dear to the mind of Regency designers, but the prosaic fact is that they were squeezed in to

183

fill gaps that were originally left in the sides of the Square to provide passages to the backs of the houses. The afterthought was a great improvement in filling the unsightly gaps, although the architectural character of these houses is somewhat clumsy and discordant and has been emphasized by later modifications.

Work on the Terraces began in 1824, and on the Square in 1825. The easternmost sections of the Terrace were finished by 1828, the western section between 1827 and 1830. The houses with columnar fronts were finished by 1828, but those in the upper portion of the eastern side, together with the two short northern sides, were completed later. The architectural treatment at the upper end on the eastern side was different from the earlier houses. Although bow-fronts are used, they rise to five storeys in height instead of four, have only a thin cornice moulding, with no columns, and are crowned instead with a stone balustrade of the Italianate type popular after about 1830. The somewhat plain surfaces of the façades are relieved by rather slight pediment mouldings above the first-floor windows. Brunswick Town differed from its model, Kemp Town, in that from the beginning the Terraces were intended to be let as furnished houses to different tenants each season, while the Square was taken up to a greater extent by permanent residents. Again like Kemp Town it was intended to be self-contained, and went further in this direction than the eastern estate. As well as the church of St. Andrew in Waterloo Street, which was rebuilt by Sir Charles Barry in 1827-8 to serve the residents, a market-hall which appears in Bruce's engraving behind the eastern range of Brunswick Terrace was actually built, between Upper and Lower Market Street, and opened in 1828. As shops began to grow up around Brunswick Town the market became less necessary, and by 1839 it was being used as a school. Later it was famous over many years as Dupont's Riding School. The building still survives as the warehouse of a wholesale grocery firm.

The creation of Kemp Town stimulated a great deal of building activity on the land outside the boundaries of the estate, immediately to the west of Kemp Town. By 1825 Busby and the Wilds were laying out Marine Square as a speculation for Mr. Thomas Attree, the well-known Brighton solicitor, who later lived in the Italian Villa at Queen's Park. Bloomsbury Place and Portland Place followed, the latter built on land belonging to a Major Russell. The noble width of Portland Place was to some extent determined by the desire to leave unobstructed the whole length of the façade of Portland House, which commanded the view down the street to the sea, and which was built for Major Russell's own occupation. A fairly well-known engraving of the house published in 1825 shows it as a great mansion with an impressive portico of six Corinthian columns and a grand flight of steps. On the eve of its completion, the house was burned down.

It was replaced in mid-Victorian times by three houses designed as a single unit, and known as West House, Portland House and Portland Lodge. Before 1847 two of the houses were occupied by the Earl of Abergavenny, and in January of that year Brighton College began its existence in No. 13 Portland House, the centre house of the three, and remained there until its removal to the new school buildings in Eastern Road, designed by Sir George Gilbert Scott in Victorian Tudor style, which were ready some two years later. Nos. 12 and 13 are now in use as part of St. Dunstan's Institute for the Blind, and are known as Pearson House, after Sir Arthur Pearson, the founder of the famous institution for war-blinded men. An especially fine house standing on the south-west corner of Portland Place has a classical portico, large rooms and a good staircase.

Although many of the houses in Marine Parade have been altered or rebuilt in Victorian times and later, several houses built by Busby and Wilds have had their original character in the bold robust style of the 1820s preserved more or less intact. Among them are the Marine Hotel,* with its fully curved corner bay and another deeply curved bay adjoining. Nos. 41-4 have strongly bowed fronts, each with triple-arched window recesses and Doric porches. The delicate ironwork balcony railings are of an early pattern originally designed most probably by James Adam, for they appear at the Adelphi building in John Street, London, where he had his own apartment. The design was reproduced in L. N. Cottingham's *Ornamental Metal Worker's Directory* of 1824, and was used not only in many houses of Brighton and other seaside towns but all over London and as far afield as Newcastle and Edinburgh. The early pagoda-like canopies of balconies now gave place to more ponderous hoods of bulbous, bonnet-like shape, such as those of the later houses on the northern side of Regency Square. These changes in boldness of scale and pronounced character of design are especially associated with the buildings designed by Busby. In fact, the architectural details and features of this architect's work are distinguishable by their bold theatrical quality rather than by delicate sensitivity. In this he was truly a follower of John Nash, whose genius inclined to spectacular dramatic effects rather than to scholarly perfection of detail. The elder Wilds was reticent in his use of architectural detail, relying on simple traditionalism in his work, as in the early part of Regency Square, but the younger Wilds and Busby made much use of classical details like the various orders of columns, shell ornaments and other pronounced features, most of which were drawn from such well-known architectural works of the day as Robert Wood's *Ruins of Palmyra* and the *Ruins of Balbec*, and *The Antiquities of Athens* by James Stuart and Nicholas Revett, all of which had had a sensational effect on British and indeed also on Continental designers in revealing to them the wonders of ancient architecture.

Beyond Portland Place is Eastern Terrace, a fine L-shaped group of buildings erected about 1828. The front of the corner house, No. 1, is so strongly curved that the rooms within are almost circular. The house was occupied from 1876 to 1896 by Sir Albert Sassoon, the first member of that family to live in England. He owned a large strip of land behind the house, and during his lifetime built a mausoleum for himself at the corner of Paston Place. Designed in an oriental style obviously inspired by the Royal Pavilion, it has often been thought to be an outlying appendage to the Prince Regent's palace. Sir Albert was buried there in 1896 and his son, Sir Edward Sassoon, in 1912, but their remains were removed by Sir Albert's grandson, Sir Philip Sassoon, when the latter sold the property in 1933. In recent years it has become part of the Hanbury Arms public house, and is called the Bombay Bar. On the opposite corner of St. George's Road the family had a riding school, which was later rebuilt as the Odeon Cinema. This has now become a bingo hall.

The years 1826 and 1827 saw the building by the younger Wilds of Hanover Crescent, at the north-eastern corner of the Level. Here again there are Ammonite capitals, but some of the houses have been disfigured by the addition of ugly attic storeys. The Crescent is terminated by two charming and minute Doric lodges.

An especially well-preserved house of about 1825, very probably designed by Busby and built by the Wilds, is No. 87 London Road, better known as St. Bartholomew's Vicarage. This elegant little house is a particularly charming example of a small Regency villa, with its broad eaves, fluted pilasters with voluted capitals, and recessed arches in which the ground-floor windows are set.

In the western part of Brighton one of the most fascinating houses built by the Busby-Wilds partnership must have been Gothic House in Western Road, later known as the Priory, or Priory Lodge, which was built in 1825 in the style of the early Gothic revival. Something of the pointed Gothic windows, crocketed pinnacles and tracery of the house may be seen above the modern shop-windows of Plummer Roddis's department store. To the side of Plummer's is Western Terrace, a small cul-de-sac with several delightful stuccoed houses designed by A. H. Wilds, some of them with Ammonite capitals. Here also is the Western Pavilion, which has often been supposed to be a kind of extra-mural *pavillon d'amour* of the Prince Regent, but which was, in fact, built by A. H. Wilds himself in 1833 as his own residence.

It was a great disappointment to Busby and Wilds, as the principal architectural and building firm in Brighton, not to be given the commission for the erection of two of the town's most important new buildings. It was all the more galling that both of these commissions were given to the same man, Charles Barry, later to be the designer of the new Houses of Parliament, and to be knighted. The first of these two works was the building of

St. Peter's Church, or Chapel as it was at first called. Busby and Wilds submitted plans for a classical building in the competition that was held for designs in 1823, but the partners only reached second place and received a premium of £30, the commission being given to Charles Barry for his design for the present Gothic church.

The second prize that was wrested from their grasp by Barry was the commission for the building of the original portions of the Sussex County Hospital. It seems possible that despite the partners' virtual monopoly of building in Brighton there were persons in the town who disliked their bold, robust style, or who wished to favour a promising new architect, then only about thirty years of age. It is no doubt fortunate for us that Barry's inspired design for St. Peter's Church was accepted, but it is hard to imagine that Busby could have produced anything more pedestrian than Barry's stolid and unimaginative hospital building.

From 1822 onwards A. H. Wilds worked a great deal independently both of his father and of Busby. He was almost invariably referred to as 'Architect' and achieved a superior social position to that of his father, his name frequently appearing in the 'Fashionable Chronicles' of the period. When in 1822 Thomas Read Kemp gave the Level to the town, the younger Wilds was commissioned to supervise the planting and laying-out of the land in conjunction with Henry Phillips, a well-known local botanist and landscape gardener, who laid out the gardens of Sussex Square and Lewes Crescent.

It seems almost inevitable that Phillips should have been assailed by dreams of oriental splendour, with the insidious example of the Pavilion perpetually before his eyes, for in 1825 he conceived the idea of creating an Oriental Garden in the western part of Brighton, beyond Cavendish Place. Again he obtained the co-operation of A. H. Wilds in designing the project, which was to consist of a new street of fine houses, called Oriental Place, leading up from the sea to a large garden in the centre of which was to be built the Athenaeum, a large domed conservatory of oriental design heated by steam, and tall enough to contain palm trees and other tropical trees. The project was illustrated by an engraving published at the time showing a Pavilion-like building with oriental onion-domes. As the name Athenaeum suggested, the place was not intended merely as a centre of relaxation and amusement, but also to minister to the higher aspirations of mankind by means of a library, reading-room and museum, and a school for the sciences and the liberal arts, in which Henry Phillips and his friends would give lectures.

Alas, the project was only one of many elaborate gardening and landscaping schemes conceived by Henry Phillips which came to nothing, and the Athenaeum and Oriental Garden proposal came to grief through the lack of financial support. A later scheme of his, for a vast domed conservatory called the Antheum to be built at Hove, failed through the collapse of the great iron-framed dome immediately upon its completion. Only a few of the houses of Oriental Place and part of Oriental Terrace on the seafront had been built. The land intended for the Oriental Garden and Athenaeum was bought in 1827 by Sir David Scott, magistrate, a local magnate and a director of the East India Company, who employed A. H. Wilds to build a house for his own use on the site. It was called Sillwood House after Sir David Scott's country estate in Berkshire, Sillwood Park. In fairly recent times the house became the Sillwood Hall Hotel, but it is now part of Plummer Roddis's premises. Wilds now completed for Scott the building of Oriental Place, where his favourite device of Ammonite capitals is once more to be seen. In recent years an occupant of one of the houses seems to have made some attempt to maintain Phillips's original ideas of an Eastern atmosphere, by advertising on a card in her front window 'Oriental Massage'. The three houses which had been built in Oriental Terrace, on the sea-front, were by 1864 converted into a private hotel called the King's Hotel, which is in existence today. It was not named after any monarch, but after its first owner, a Mr. T. H. King.

Wilds also continued the building of houses farther north on the Athenaeum site towards Sillwood House, forming Sillwood Place, once a charming little close with gardens instead of a roadway between the two rows of houses. Two of them facing each other at the northern end are especially interesting, for they were built in 1833 in oriental style closely resembling the exterior of North Gate House, on the Royal Pavilion Estate, which was orientalized by William IV a year earlier to match the newly built North Gate to the Pavilion grounds. One of the houses, No. 9, was occupied until 1856 by Mrs. Cecilia Margaretta Mostyn, youngest daughter of the Thrales, and her husband Bertie Mostyn, with whom she had made a runaway marriage years before. The other house, No. 21, belonged to Eliza and Rosalind, the maiden daughters of the poet and novelist Horace Smith, and it was here that they continued the literary parties formerly held by their father and entertained many of the literary or artistic personalities of the day. Alas, the houses of Sillwood Place, including those on the western side which fronted on to Montpelier Road, are in a state of sad disrepair and dereliction, and are not likely to survive.

In the same boom year of 1825 the younger Wilds built the Royal Newburgh Assembly Rooms at the corner of Cannon Place and St. Margaret's Place. This building was for many years the social centre for the west end of Brighton, and now, although the interior has in modern times been converted into flats, the beautiful classical portico with its bold columns and charming leaf capitals survives, and has been restored and repainted, together with other buildings in the street, by the promoters of the Metropole development near by. Russell Square, a delightful long narrow square of smaller houses with yellow brick façades, stuccoed lower storeys and charming balconies, was also completed at this time.

When Kemp Town was first being built, a somewhat rough road from Rottingdean ran along the cliff-top, which was here of a considerable height. In Bruce's engraving of the original scheme a magnificent esplanade was shown in front of the houses, and it was realized that a sea-wall with promenades was not only a structural requirement to protect the foundations of the houses but also an aesthetic necessity, to provide a visually satisfying base to the immense architectural group of Kemp Town. Invitations for designs were advertised and a reward of £50 offered for the best. The winner was the architect Henry Edward Kendall, junior, a resident of the estate, who was at the time building 19 and 20 Sussex Square for the Marquess of Bristol, and 24 Belgrave Square, London, for Thomas Read Kemp.[6] The design consisted of a main sea-front road at the top of the cliff with a sloping sea-wall and flights of steps leading down to two lower esplanades. In the wall of the upper esplanade was an arched entry to a tunnel leading to the private gardens of Lewes Crescent above. This entrance was flanked by two gardeners' cottages built into the cliff face. Also built into the sloping cliff wall were alcoves with tables and seats, and in summer until fairly recent times processions of servants in long black dresses with white caps and fluttering aprons could be observed carrying trays of tea-things to be laid out in the alcoves for the residents who had been spending the afternoon on the beach or esplanades.

In the wall of the lower esplanade was built a reading-room for the residents that was also occasionally used for committee meetings. When the Madeira Drive from Brighton to Black Rock along the lower part of the sea-front was made in 1872 the slopes between it and the lower esplanade were planted with tamarisk and other shrubs, but the 'Slopes' remained as private property of the Kemp Town Estate until 1948, when they were conveyed to the Corporation by a private parliamentary bill. Mr. H. S. Goodhart-Rendel, the distinguished architect and authority on nineteenth-century buildings who had been the freeholder of the estate for forty-six years, spoke of the Slopes as a remarkable example of Regency urban engineering, and exerted valuable influence in assisting the scheme through Parliament.

The flower-beds, grass slopes and shrubs have been well maintained by the Corporation, but the original walling, tunnel entrances and other architectural features have for long been in a dreary and neglected condition. Their repair and improvement would be less costly than the total reconstruction that might otherwise become necessary, and it is to be hoped that this handsome and dignified feature of Brighton's sea-front will long be preserved.

The beginnings of the modern age in Brighton may be set earlier than the coming of the railway in 1840, or even at the building of the Chain Pier in 1823. The first portent of the coming industrial age in the town was surely the singularly unromantic circumstance of the building of the town's first gasworks. This was established in 1818–19 at Black Rock, in the Parish of Rottingdean, just outside the boundary of Brighton, so as to avoid the payment of the dues of 6d a ton that were levied on all coal brought into the town. The coal for the gasworks was landed from ships on to the beach, and taken to the gasworks either by hauling to the top of the cliff or by carting through a tunnel from the shore. The Pavilion grounds were the first part of the town to be lit with the new illuminant. The new chandeliers in the Banqueting-room and Music-room were fitted for gas, and in September 1818 the Prince Regent and his architect Nash came down to Brighton to see them lit for the first time. By no means all the inhabitants were in favour of the new illuminant, which was regarded by some as dangerous and unhealthy. However, on a vote being taken at a public meeting held in May 1818, 400 persons were found to be in favour and only 150 against. Gas was installed in the Theatre Royal in July 1819, and it was remarked that 'the new and superb Hydraulic Gas Chandelier continues to receive ample and unequivocal testimonials of approbation, and it is very satisfactory to assure the frequenters and admirers of the Theatre Royal that the House is much cooler and better ventilated by this method of lighting. . . .'[7] Gas lighting was installed in the Old Steine about the time of the improvement of this part of the town in 1824, when the roads were laid out afresh and the grass enclosed by high iron railings.

The enormous growth of Brighton in the 1820s necessitated important improvements in the layout of the main streets and roads of the town. Above all it became essential for a continuous road to be provided along the sea-front, where for most of the way only a rough track had existed hitherto. Carriages travelling westward had to turn up Middle Street, proceed along Middle Street Lane, into South Street, and then down West Street.

A public subscription was opened in 1821 to which the King himself contributed £200, for the construction of a carriage-road between West Street and East Street. This was opened by King George IV in January 1822, on the anniversary of his accession, and named the King's Road. It was still necessary, however, for carriages to pass through the narrow streets of Pool Valley in order to reach the East Cliff, and between 1825 and 1827 a sea-wall was built from the bottom of Ship Street to the foot of East Street. Groynes were erected and the sea-wall extended eastwards in front of the Royal York and Royal Albion Hotels, until in 1829 the Grand Junction Road was opened with a carriage-procession of the inhabitants, forming an uninterrupted carriage-way along the whole of the sea-front from west to east. Another outlet from west to east had been created in 1825, when Castle Square, which up till then had nothing more than a narrow alley way leading into the Steine, was opened up with a broad roadway for vehicles. An esplanade from the West Battery (now the Grand Hotel) to the eastern end of Brunswick Terrace, was formed in 1834 under the supervision of the architect Amon Henry Wilds.

At the time that the Chain Pier was built, about 1823, a sea-wall was erected eastwards from the Steine and the Marine Parade itself was widened.

2 Georgian Churches

So insatiable were the fevers of fashion in Brighton that its votaries invaded even the fanes of faith. Indeed, the sophistication of life in the seaside metropolis was so extreme that many of the Brighton churches had their very origin in the conception of church-going as an episode in the social round. The remarkable expansion of Brighton during the lifetime of George IV would naturally have called for a corresponding increase in the activities of the Church, but this was not forthcoming with the rapidity that might have been expected. Nowadays it is difficult to realize the spiritual apathy and the extreme poverty of the Church traditions which existed in the early days of Brighton's development. It was general throughout the country, but was emphasized by the worldly appeal of Brighton as a gay social resort. Eventually the success of the Wesleyans and other dissenters provoked an apprehensive Government into passing the 'Million Pound Act' for the building of new churches, and the Tractarian movement of the 1830s was to bring about a rebirth of devotion amongst members of the Church of England. But when the first Marine Pavilion was built for the young Prince of Wales in 1787 the only church in Brighton was that of St. Nicholas. This tiny building soon ceased to suffice for the spiritual needs of the town, and the fishermen and their families, who regarded the church as their own especial shrine, found themselves crowded more and more into the galleries by the increasing number of wealthy residents and visitors who rented the old-fashioned 'cattle-pen' box-pews. The Vicar of St. Nicholas, the Rev. Thomas Hudson, had set his mind on attracting the young Prince of Wales to his church, but it seemed impossible to persuade the Royal visitor to make the journey up the steep hill half a mile out of the town. Mr. Hudson realized that to have the leader of fashion, not only of Brighton, or of London, but the First Gentleman of Europe among his congregation would make the reputation of any church. Accordingly the Vicar seems to have decided that as he 'could not bring the Prince to the church, he would bring the church to the Prince', so he raised money at interest to buy some land near the Pavilion, and promoted the necessary Act of Parliament to establish the church as a chapel-of-ease to St. Nicholas, 'not only for the accommodation of the company, but also *for the use of such of the inhabitants as are disposed to become purchasers of pews'*. The chapel was designed by the architect Thomas Saunders of Golden Square, London, and the founda-

THE ROYAL SUSPENSION CHAIN PIER, *c.* 1838
Engraved by Charles Hunt after a water-colour by G. B. Campion

LEWES CRESCENT, *c.* 1838
Water-colour by G. B. Campion

THE WEST BATTERY, c. 1828
Water colour by W. H. Fern.

'BEAUTIES OF BRIGHTON', 1826
Etched by G. Cruikshank after, A Crowquill, Esq'

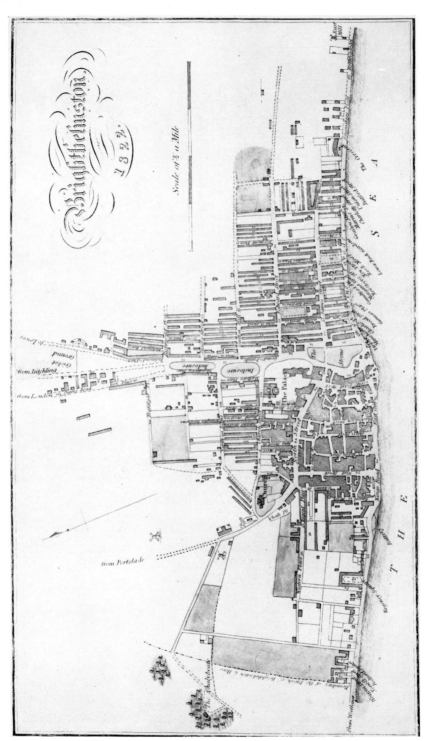

BRIGHTHELMSTON IN 1822,
engraved by W. Belch

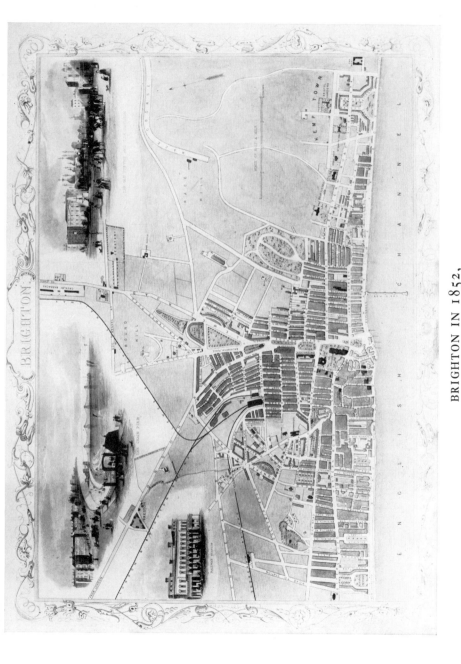

BRIGHTON IN 1852,
drawn and engraved by J. Rapkin

THE OPENING OF THE SHOREHAM BRANCH OF THE LONDON AND
BRIGHTON RAILWAY, 1840
Engraving by Charles Hunt

THE RAILWAY VIADUCT AT PRESTON, 1845
Water-colour by George Smith

'A PROPOSED HARBOUR AT BRIGHTON ON THE RECOIL PRINCIPLE'
Lithograph, 1842

THE RACE COURSE, 1852
Lithograph by E. Walker after S. Alken

THE NORTH GATE, 1832

tion stone was laid by the Prince of Wales in 1793. The building was named the Chapel Royal after its illustrious patron, who rented a pew there for many years at a charge of thirteen guineas a year. He attended occasionally, though not as frequently as the incumbent would have wished, until Mr. Hudson based a highly critical sermon on the text 'Thou art the man . . .', which the Prince took as a personal affront, and he never attended again.

The opening of the Chapel Royal did little to remedy the spiritual emptiness of Brighton, although the fashionable *élite* found its situation in the centre of the town much more agreeable. The scurrilous 'Anthony Pasquin' wrote: 'There is a Parish Church where the *canaille* go to pray, but as that is on a hill, and the *gentry* found their Sabbath visit to the Almighty very troublesome, the amiable and accommodating *master* priest has consigned the care of his common *parish mutton* to his journeyman, the curate, and has kindly raised a Chapel Royal for the *lambs of fashion*, where a certain sum is paid for every seat; and this, it must be admitted, is as it should be; as a well-bred Deity will assuredly be more attentive to a reclining Duchess, parrying the assaults of the devil behind her fan, than the vulgar piety of a plebeian on his knees. There were books open in the circulating libraries, where you would be requested to contribute your mite of charity to the support of the rector, as his income is somewhat less than seven hundred pounds a year; the last incumbent died worth thirty thousand pounds.'[1]

The Chapel Royal was, in fact, the first of the many 'proprietary chapels' that were established in Brighton under the pernicious system that encouraged their exploitation as financial speculations. They reserved their ministrations almost exclusively for the fashionable and wealthy folk, and the Chapel Royal was open only to those who purchased or rented pews or paid a shilling for a seat.

The present Chapel Royal in Prince's Place, North Street, is the result of rebuilding by Sir Arthur Blomfield from 1874 to 1891, in red brick, flint and terracotta in what was stated at the time to be 'Renaissance' style.*

Following the Chapel Royal, St. James's Chapel in St. James's Street was built in 1810 by subscribers on land given by Mr. N. Kemp, uncle of Mr. Thomas Read Kemp. In this case the body of the church, consisting of about nine hundred sittings, was entirely free for the poor, and pews in the galleries only were rented to provide an income for the maintenance of the church. No doubt some of of the founders, such as Mr. Hudson or Mr. Thomas Read Kemp, were actuated by genuine piety in establishing their chapels, but in other cases they became profitable financial undertakings, and the proprietary system was the only means available in those days for carrying out such a purpose, other than by private gift, or by Government assistance, as was given in London by the 'Million Pound Act'. A popular preacher who could acquire or become appointed to a proprietary church and attract a smart and wealthy congregation was assured of financial success. The rents from a certain number of pews constituted the stipend of the curate. All other pew rents went as interest to the persons who owned the chapel. Even the liveried servants of the wealthy patrons were often expressly excluded, and if in some cases the poor were admitted at all, it was only to benches in the gallery.

The connection of the proprietary chapels with the Establishment was very exiguous. Some were ancillary to existing churches, but St. James's, like others later, was independent, and much controversy raged over the appointment to it of a clergyman by the Trust Governors without the approval of the Vicar of Brighton. St. James's was eventually rebuilt in 1874 as a Gothic church by Edmund Scott, the architect of St. Bartholomew's. In later years the congregation fell away and it was demolished in September 1950.

Trinity Chapel in Ship Street was built in 1817 in classical style for Mr. Thomas Read Kemp, M.P., as an independent chapel. Together with his brother-in-law George Baring, Kemp had founded a dissenting religious sect that was remarkable more for the rank and wealth of its adherents than for any particular appeal in the novelty of its doctrines. The two leaders had already set up chapels in Taunton and Lewes, and Kemp himself undertook the office of minister at Trinity Chapel, but after some six years, realizing that he was by no means a compelling speaker, and that the duties were burdensome, he handed the post over to another dissenting layman, his friend and solicitor George Faithful, who was later to become one of Brighton's first Members in the Reformed Parliament of 1833-4. Eventually Kemp passed through his dissenting phase, rejoined the Establishment, and in 1825 sold the freehold of Trinity Chapel to the Rev. Robert Anderson, who raised the money among the congregation, and it then became absorbed into the Church of England. By 1850 the original Doric portico of the Trinity Chapel had been removed, no doubt to permit of road-widening, but it retained the remainder of its classical façade and tower until, in 1855, the church was rebuilt of flint and stone in Gothic style with an octagonal tower inspired apparently by the towers of Ely Cathedral. As the Church of the Holy Trinity, the Trinity Chapel became famous throughout the country for a few years between 1847 and 1853 as the seat of the ministry of that remarkable preacher, the Rev. F. W. Robertson.

George Faithful, once minister of the original Trinity Chapel, remained a dissenter when his patron Kemp joined the Church of England, and left to found another chapel in Church Street, which became the Trinity Independent Presbyterian Church, later the Pavilion Baptist Chapel. It was a handsome classical building with a portico of Ionic columns. It stood opposite the present Art Gallery and Museum building. By 1897 it had ceased to be used as a chapel, and became an emporium of fancy goods called the Oriental Gallery. In 1900 it was in use as a warehouse, and about 1925 it was rebuilt to form new showrooms of the Brighton Gas Company (later the South-Eastern Gas Board). In 1964 the building was taken over by the Brighton Public Library as a reading-room, music-library and lecture-theatre.

Kemp's religious sect fell into dissolution when its members were won back one after the other into the fold of orthodoxy. Their return may have been hastened by the 'awful extremes of error' into which some of their leaders were regarded as having fallen. Kemp signalized his own return to the Church of England by obtaining an Act of Parliament for the building of St. George's Chapel, Kemp Town, in order to serve the inhabitants of the new and fashionable Kemp Town Estate.

The architect of this severely classical but pleasant little church with its recessed Ionic portico, round-headed windows and charming Grecian tower was Charles Busby. Like most of Brighton's early churches, and being intended for a fashionable community, it was built as a proprietary chapel at a cost of £11,000 by T. R. Kemp, who hoped to recoup the cost of it from the pew-rents, but he was actuated more by piety than by the hope of financial gain. During the reign of William IV his consort, Queen Adelaide, used it as her Chapel Royal on Sunday afternoons while staying at Brighton, and the silver vessels and ornaments which she presented to it are used to this day. Before long the congregation grew so that a gallery had to be built. This was erected in a single week by the firm of Cubitt, and it became known as the 'Sky Parlour' by the children who were usually relegated to it. Eventually Kemp sold the church to Sir Laurence Peel, younger son of the famous Sir Robert. It was later bought by a committee of the congregation and friends from its owner, Mr. Charles Lennox Peel, for £4,000, and in 1890 it became vested in the Church Patronage Society, as it still is.

Eventually such proprietory rights in privately established chapels and churches generally were similarly bought out. In the case of St. George's the purchase was prompted by the desire of the congregation to preserve the evangelical form of worship that had been established there, but its financial independence as well as the early simplicity of doctrine was so well secured that as lately as 1962 the church trustees were able to defy attempts made to have it closed, despite the falling-away of the congregation to a mere handful of worshippers. Their efforts were so successful that the dwindling congregation grew appreciably once more, and money was found to carry out repairs to the church and to repaint its charming exterior, so that the building now stands as one of the most successful instances in the town of the rehabilitation and restoration of an almost derelict Regency

195

building. With its white-painted steeple and pedimented portico and columns it is one of the most attractive ornaments of Kemp Town.

The preponderance of faith over financial advantage was not so evident in the establishment of St. Margaret's, which was built in 1824 to provide for the religious needs of the new district of Regency Square, Russell Square and Cannon Street. It was founded purely as a speculation by a many-sided but unpleasant individual named Barnard Gregory, who at one time or another was a banker's clerk, dentist, wine-merchant, chemist and druggist, actor and newspaper proprietor. He was the editor of the *Brighton Gazette*, and proprietor of a scurrilous London newspaper called *The Satirist*. Because of a libel on the Duke of Brunswick which he published in this paper he was imprisoned for a year in Newgate. St. Margaret's was one of the most important and delightful Regency churches of Brighton. It was designed by 'Mr. Clarke of London' with a neo-Greek columnar portico and a little tower based on the tower of the Temple of the Winds at Athens. By the 1850s it had become so fashionable that it was difficult to obtain admission, unless one rented a pew annually. There were hardly any free seats, and it was not until the days of a devoted minister, the Rev. Edward Clay, between 1855 and 1872, long after the proprietary rights had been bought out, that the gallery was enlarged to accommodate a larger number of fishermen and other poor people. Clay conducted an evangelical mission in one of the sea-front arches and was known as 'the Apostle of the Brighton fishermen'. By the 1950s the congregation, which had filled the 1,500 seats of the church every Sunday for many years, had become so small that the church was closed. Suggestions were made that it should be converted as a museum of costume and children's toys.[2] The prospect of the body of the church displaying the fashions that were worn during the century when it had been one of the haunts of fashion was an attractive one, but the cost of repairing and restoring the building, estimated at £43,000, was thought by the Council to be too great; the project was abandoned and the church was demolished in June 1959.[3]

The deep religious ardour of dissenters of several different kinds inspired the building of some of Brighton's earliest places of worship. Indeed, one of the oldest churches in the town apart from the parish church of St. Nicholas was the chapel built in 1761 by Selina, Countess of Huntingdon, in the grounds of her private house in North Street. She had come to Brighton in 1755 hoping that the sea and air of the place would be beneficial to the health of her ailing youngest son, but in 1757 both her sons died of smallpox. The daughter of Earl Ferrers, and married to the 9th Earl of Huntingdon, she had been converted to Methodism by her sister-in-law, Lady Margaret Hastings, and finding herself surrounded by a number of poor women who were eager to hear all she had to say on religious matters, she invited the Rev. George Whitefield, her chaplain and a famous preacher, to speak in Brighton, and in 1760 he addressed a large crowd in a field behind the White Lion Inn at the top of North Street. Soon after she opened her chapel to the public it became too small for the crowds that flocked to hear the new faith preached there, and in 1767, by selling some of her jewels for £700, the Countess was able to enlarge the chapel. The building was, in fact, the first of a number of churches of 'Lady Huntingdon's Connexion' that were built throughout the country, and especially in such a centre of fashion and frivolity as Brighton the sect she founded became one of the most important branches of Methodism and the chief means of bringing the 'new faith' to the aristocratic world. Several times after its founding the Countess of Huntingdon's Church was enlarged, and in 1871 it was finally rebuilt as an attractive Gothic church in stone and flint with a graceful spire, on its original site in North Street, facing the end of New Road. With its white marble pulpit and two excellent stained-glass windows the interior was quite distinguished, but as the old residential area of the town gave place to business premises, the congregations dwindled, although the week-day lunch-time services were always well attended, and it became impossible to raise the funds to keep the church in repair. The church was sold and demolished in 1968, and the proceeds devoted to the upkeep of other churches of 'Lady Huntingdon's Connexion'.

Another early nonconformist church, still happily surviving, is the Queen's Road Presbyterian Church. It was built in classical style in 1824 as the Hanover Chapel, and with its pleasant proportions, twin porches, round-arched windows and shallow pediments, it is one of Brighton's most attractive late Georgian buildings. Its burial-ground, now laid out as a garden, is a haven of quiet from the hurrying traffic and crowds of Queen's Road. The interior is remarkably pleasant, slightly reminiscent of American churches of the colonial period. Although with the migration of the residential population to the suburbs its congregation has shrunk, the continuity of its existence may be ensured by combining its work with that of the Union Congregational Church in Queen Square, a later and less attractive building that will give place to a modern centre for Christian work with young and old people, thus providing an admirable example of unity of purpose and effort between the Free Churches.

One of the most striking of the late Georgian buildings of Brighton is the Unitarian Church in New Road, north of the Theatre Royal. Built by Amon Wilds in 1820, it has a very fine neo-Grecian Doric façade, of four great columns and a pediment modelled upon that of the Temple of Theseus at Athens.

Brighton's earliest surviving nonconformist church was the Union Chapel, Union Street, at the corner of Meeting House Lane. It is now occupied as the Elim Four Square Gospel Tabernacle. Originally built in

1683, the building bears this date on a stone incorporated in the east end of the south wall. This wall, of cobble-flint and red brick, with a fine round-headed window, may belong to the original building, but the church was mainly rebuilt in 1825 by Amon Wilds, with impressive Grecian canted pylon doorways. The interior is in the form of a semicircle, and the gallery is upheld by slender cast-iron columns with pleasant foliated capitals.

The community of Quakers in Brighton has existed from the seventeenth century, and their first meeting house was built in 1700 in North Street almost opposite the Countess of Huntingdon's Church. In 1800 the building was demolished and a new meeting house erected in Ship Street. This was altered and enlarged to form the present building in 1876, and as well as being still a flourishing place of worship, has been established since the last war as a highly successful adult education centre where concerts, lectures, language courses and many other activities for young and old people are organized by a dedicated warden and her colleagues.

3 The Baths

B y the beginning of the nineteenth century the practice of sea-bathing was fully established in Brighton, and the dynasty of the dippers was still at the height of its power. The *Morning Herald* remarked from time to time on the flourishing state of their occupation:

'July 15th, 1805.—The venerable Priestess of the Bath, Martha Gunn was busily employed this morning.'

'August 4th, 1806.—The bathing-machines were in active use this morning, and Neptune's *pickling tub* exhibited many beauties in brine.'

'August 28th.—The Beach this morning was thronged with ladies, all anxious to make interest for a dip. The machines, of course, were in very great request, though none could be run into the ocean in consequence of the heavy swell, but remained stationary at the water's edge, from which Martha Gunn and her robust female assistants took their fair charges, closely enveloped in their partly coloured dresses, and gently held them to the breakers, which not quite so gently passed over them. The greatest novelty, however, that this part of the coast exhibited this morning, was in a Gentleman undressing himself on the Beach, for the purpose of a duck-ing, in front of the town, attended by his lady, who *sans diffidence*, supplied him with napkins, and even assisted him in wiping the humid effects of his exercise from his brawny limbs, as he returned from the water to dress.'

In the following season the practice of bathing from the beach had become so common that a Parish Vestry meeting was held at the Old Ship for the purpose of preventing 'the indecent practice of indiscriminate bathing in front of the town'.[1] Lord Bathurst and William Wilberforce felt so strongly about the matter that each subscribed five guineas towards the cost of prosecuting any offenders, but there was strong public feeling that 'the sea was free', and that there was an immemorial right for people to bathe from the beach. However, in 1809 a Brighton tailor, John Crunden, was fined for 'having daily exposed himself naked on the beach'. Neverthe-less for many years men continued to bathe naked, even though using bathing-machines.

'The gentlemen', wrote Granville in 1841, '. . . . lacking courage after they have stripped to the skin, will stand on the outer steps of the machine, shivering and hesitating, their persons in the meantime wholly exposed owing to the want of hood that ought to project over the steps, as in the case of all decent sea-bathing places. No attempt has as yet been made by the authorities to set this right, and the practice remains as a stain on the *gentility* of the Brighthelmstonians.'[2] The idea of Victorian prudery which is so often taken for granted was by no means as pervasive in fact as is generally supposed. It was not until as late as 1863 that men bathers at Brighton at length took gradually to wearing long bathing-drawers, called *calençons*, which were so much approved that the town was said to be 'hence crowded with ladies of refinement'. Margate had prided itself years before upon its use of Dr. Beale's modesty-hoods on the bathing-machines, but gentlemen there at this time still lagged behind their fellows at Brighton in the matter of 'refinement', and were still continuing to bathe naked. Although not generally used in Brighton itself, modesty-hoods were fitted to the bathing-machines on the beach below the Kemp Town slopes, as may be seen in a fine oil-painting of about 1850 in the Royal Pavilion collection.

This beach was kept almost exclusively for the Kemp Town residents, and a standard of refinement may have been maintained here far higher than obtained on the central beaches of the town. The Prince Consort bathed twice from a bathing-machine from the Kemp Town beach at seven o'clock in the morning during the visit to Brighton of the Queen and himself in 1843, when they also walked in the private gardens. It is hardly likely that Prince Albert would have bathed on the more public beaches where laxer customs prevailed. An interesting light is cast upon the popular notion of Victorian feminine prudery and squeamishness by the story of a French visitor's experience at Brighton about the middle of the century.[3] He relates how returning to the beach from a long swim he found the sea had retreated, and that his bathing-machine, which he had left 'with the water lapping the hubs of the wheels', was now fifteen paces up the shore. Between him and his machine, on the very edge of the water, three ladies, a mother and her two daughters, each holding a prayer-book, were sitting on three camp-stools. He was wearing no bathing-dress of any kind, and though he looked frantically all around, could not find so much as a drifting bunch of seaweed to cover his nakedness. In his embarrassment he dropped on all fours, and began to crawl cautiously forward, raising himself by degrees 'as much as decency permitted', in the hope that the ladies would take the hint and remove themselves. But they continued to sit on their three stools 'in supreme unconcern', ostentatiously clasping their prayer-books. Hoping they would eventually go away, he turned back to the sea and resumed his swimming, but, as he summed up the situation, 'one cannot swim for ever, while one can sit without fatigue for hours.' At length he decided to face the matter out boldly. 'I rose slowly like Venus from the waves. Striving to adopt a bearing both modest and unconcerned, reminiscent of the lost traditions of innocence of a younger world, I stepped briskly past the three ladies, who made no pretence of looking away.' The poor gentleman later discovered that the three ladies were 'quite puritanical' and had deliberately adopted this extraordinary method of punishing him, not for bathing naked, but for bathing on the Sabbath day! The story is often repeated as showing how three hypocritical Victorian ladies could combine their disapproval of a man's bathing on a Sunday with deliberately setting out to enjoy the fascination of gazing upon the naked male form. But it is difficult to believe that a puritanical Victorian lady would have allowed her daughters to witness such a sight unless in fact at that time, while the breaking of the Sabbath was a horrifying thing, the spectacle of a naked man was not invariably regarded as objectionable. None the less, one cannot help wondering why the modest Frenchman did not leave the water farther along the beach and avoid the censorious ladies by taking a wide circuit around them to his machine. Naked bathing was still being permitted as late as 1871 'to the great disgrace of the authorities'.[4]

The final disappearance of the women dippers and the men bathers was heralded by the ceremonial attendance of a party of them, about 120 strong, at the Great Exhibition of 1851 in Hyde Park under the escort of Mr. Lewis Slight, Clerk to the Town Commissioners, and two other officials. The women were dressed in new dark-blue dresses and bonnets, while the men wore blue guernseys and straw hats. Many of them had never set foot out of Brighton before, nor had travelled in a railway carriage. On arriving at the station the party was mustered and marched off in a column of twos to the Exhibition, where they aroused much curiosity amongst the other visitors.

During the first half-century of Brighton's career as a health resort the emphasis had been on sea-bathing (and drinking), so that by 1800 there was only one set of baths in the town, which had been opened by Dr. Awsiter in 1769. Later these baths changed ownership and became 'Wood's Original Hot and Cold Sea-water Baths', and another storey was added to the quaint little classical building. They were supplied with water from the Old Pump House.[5] Later on they became known as Creak's Baths, and survived until as late as 1861, when they were demolished to make room for extensions to Brill's Baths.

With the coming of the new century more and more indoor baths were established. The first were Williams's Royal Hot and Cold Baths, opened in 1803 at the south-west corner of the Steine, and they became very popular among the fashionable visitors. The *Morning Herald* reported on 17th August 1807 that 'Numberless *elegantes* were in hot water there this morning.' Sicklemore described them in 1813 as 'scarcely to be equalled in Europe' and remarked that they were equipped with 'a douche upon a principle exactly similar to that of the Prince Regent's at Carlton House'.

On Mr. Williams's death the baths were carried on by Mr. Bannister, who gave place in turn to his son-in-law William Knight, but eventually the baths dwindled in favour and after remaining in a state of great dilapidation for some years were demolished to make room for the Lion Mansion building (now the Albion Rooms). The Artillery Baths in Artillery Place, near the West Battery House, were established by Nathan Smith in 1813 and achieved their early fame because of the method introduced by Smith of treating gout by means of an air-pump, which extracted the air from a kind of bell placed over the affected part and by doing so may have stimulated the circulation of the blood. The baths became Hobden's Royal Artillery Baths in 1824. They stood on the western side of the site of the Grand Hotel, in a position now occupied by the hotel ballroom. When the Grand Hotel was erected the baths were rebuilt in palatial style, with tiles adorning the vestibule and corridors, and with an entrance direct from the hotel as well as from the street.

Lamprell's Baths were built in 1823 on the site of the old East Battery, which had been washed away in 1776, at the foot of East Street. The building, which was circular, 53 feet across and crowned by a dome, was for many years one of the most distinctive buildings on the Brighton front. It was given the name of the 'bunion' because it jutted out across the road within a few feet of the edge of the sea-wall, and in rough weather the spectacle of ladies in crinolines and people on horseback running the gauntlet through the narrow passage between one large wave and the next was a familiar sight described in an account in the *Illustrated London News* of 1st January 1859, together with a lively drawing. Lamprell's Baths became known as Brill's Baths when Charles Brill, Lamprell's nephew, succeeded to the ownership. For years Brill's Baths was one of the most famous and popular institutions of the town. Charles Brill introduced a remarkable innovation in 1862 when he extended the establishment by opening new swimming-baths for ladies on the site of Awsiter's old baths (later Wood's and Creak's Baths) on the western side of Pool Valley, facing north. These baths were opened by the Duchess of Cambridge and Princess May, and were described as 'the only sea-water swimming baths for ladies in the Kingdom and in Europe'. Female instructors were in attendance, and the subscription book was said to display 'a long list of names, comprising many ladies of rank and station'. Princess Mary of Teck, later Queen Mary, is said to have taken her first lessons in swimming there, and to have become 'quite proficient'[6] in the art. As a result, no doubt, of the success of the new baths, Brill's put forward a great scheme in 1865 for an even grander building, in red-brick Venetian Gothic style, the architect being no less a personage than Sir Giles Gilbert Scott. It was to have been three storeys high, with a short Gothic tower breaking the skyline. With some modification of the original design the new buildings were erected between 1865 and 1870 at 76 to 79 East Street, and extending round into Pool Valley. At the same time Lamprell's original circular bath, which had obstructed the Junction Road on the sea-front for many years, was at last removed.[7] The new Gentlemen's Swimming Bath was said to be the largest circular bath in Europe. Sixty-five feet in diameter, it was 12 feet larger than Lamprell's original circular bath. There was a balcony seating 400 spectators and round the walls ran a Latin inscription announcing that the water was as fresh as the sea, but safer. There were also first and second class men's and ladies' swimming baths, medical douche and vapour baths, reading- and billiards-rooms, and a barber's shop. The cost of the new baths, which were said at the time to rival in elegance the Thermae of the Ancient Romans,[8] was over £90,000, and three public houses, the Duke of Wellington, the Rising Sun and the White Horse, were swept away to make room for them. The proprietors went to great trouble to obtain a pure supply of sea-water, which was obtained as far away as Cliftonville, Hove, in order to avoid the contaminated sea-water close to the centre of the town. In the depressed state of Brighton in the early years of the twentieth century the buildings became more and more dreary, the baths became more and more out of date and unattractive, and the exterior was disfigured by ugly advertising boards. Eventually the whole block was demolished in 1929 to make room for the Savoy Cinema.

It was probably at Brill's Baths that Clayton Glyn, husband of the romantic Edwardian novelist Elinor Glyn, author of the once-sensational novel *Three Weeks*, hired a swimming-bath for several days during their honeymoon so as to give his bride the opportunity of displaying her charms to him in private. Entranced, he watched her as she swam naked up and down the pool, her long red hair trailing in the water. Later in her life Elinor Glyn lived for several years before and during the Second World War at No. 17a Curzon House, Saltdean, near Brighton, and was very scornful of some people who panicked in the hall of an hotel at Rottingdean when an air-raid alarm sounded.[9]

The most remarkable bathing establishment of all in Brighton was the one opened in 1786 as a vapour and shampooing bath by an Indian named Sake Deen Mahomed. (Sake was a form of the title Sheikh.) Mahomed's Baths, which stood on the site of the present Queen's Hotel, facing west, did not provide the usual hot and cold sea-water baths, but were more of the nature of a Turkish Bath, with a medicated steam- or vapour-bath and facilities for massage, then called 'shampooing', the word not having then acquired its modern meaning of washing the hair. After spending a time in the great heat of a vapour-bath, and while perspiring freely, the patient was placed inside a kind of flannel tent with sleeves protruding inwards for the arms of the operator, who proceeded to massage his patient vigorously while the latter enjoyed a state not only of complete privacy but also of freedom from chill. Mahomed was born at Patna in 1749 and received some training as a surgeon while serving in the East India Company. After coming to England he visited Cork and ran away with a pretty Irish girl. The pair came to Brighton in 1786 and set up the vapour-bath, but met with little success at first, until a few cures which he brought about aroused interest in his novel treatment. The fashionable invalids were eager for some fresh means of whiling away their time, and the highly scented steam-baths were found by many to be far more agreeable than sea-water baths, whether cold or hot, and to sufferers from rheumatism and kindred ailments the massage was soothing and relaxing. There was, moreover, the intriguing sensation that one was enjoying something of the voluptuous indulgences of the East. Before long Mahomed's Baths was one of the most popular establishments in Brighton. He was the author of several publications, his *Travels* were published at Cork in 1794, and a pamphlet issued at Brighton in 1820 gives a long list of cases he claims to have cured. His most important work, published in 1822, was entitled *Shampooing, or benefits resulting from the use of the Indian vapour-bath*. In it he described instances of the cure of asthma, paralysis, rheumatism, sciatica, lumbago and even loss of voice by his method, and also included a number of poems by various writers inspired by his success. In one of these, entitled 'Ode to Mahomed, the Brighton Shampooing Surgeon', the author attributed the recent growth of the town to the Indian's reputation:

> *While thus beneath thy flannel shades*
> *Fat dowagers and wrinkled maids*
> *Re-blown in adolescence,*
> *I marvel not that friends tell friends,*
> *And Brighton every day extends*
> *Its circuses and crescents.*

Mahomed had a strong instinct for publicity, and attracted attention to the cures he claimed to have effected by exhibiting in the vestibule of his baths a huge collection of what he called his 'testimonials', consisting of the 'crutches, spine-stretchers, leg-irons, head-strainers, bump-dressers and club-foot reformers'[10] which he hung on the walls so that the place looked like the grotto of some miracle-working shrine. Unfortunately he was not unduly scrupulous over using the names of illustrious persons who had attended his establishment and occasionally various people who had never suffered a day's real illness in their lives learned with astonishment that they had been cured of appalling diseases by Sake Deen. Nevertheless the success of his work was generally recognized and he was appointed 'Shampooing Surgeon to His Majesty King George IV', with the particular task of superintending arrangements of the King's bathroom at the Pavilion, where there was a large marble plunge-bath, with pulleys attached to the ceiling by means of which the Royal person could be lowered into the water in a chair. The appointment was continued by King William IV. Mahomed's visitors' book containing the names of many eminent people is preserved in the Public Reference Library, and his ceremonial dress, consisting of a handsomely embroidered green and gold silk jacket, cream silk robe, scarlet trousers and turban, is in the collections of the Royal Pavilion, where a portrait of him dressed in this costume is also to be seen. He was himself the most outstanding example of the success of his vapour-bath, which he must have partaken of while administering it, for he survived to the remarkable age of 102, and is buried in the churchyard of St. Nicholas, where a simple stone records the fact of his having lived for over a century. Mahomed's son, Arthur Akhbar Mahomed, continued his father's practice as a 'Professional and Medical Rubber' into the 1870s, and the building was eventually demolished to make way for the new Queen's Hotel.

The medical profession was not unimpressed by Mahomed's methods. Dr. John Gibney, an Edinburgh graduate who became Senior Physician to the Royal Sussex County Hospital and the General Sea-Bathing Infirmary at Brighton, sent patients to Mahomed and wrote two short books on bathing.[11] The first, which appeared in 1813, was entitled *Practical Observations on the Use and Abuse of Cold and Warm Sea-Bathing in various diseases: particularly in Scrofulous and Gouty cases*. In it he foreshadows the modern use of shock treatment in cases of mental disturbance when he writes 'in some cases of insanity considerable advantage may be derived from sudden and unexpected immersion in cold water'. He also observed that shrimp-gatherers, who 'for the space of four hours continue exposed to the cold of the sea-water . . . while thus employed have their pulse diminished in frequency from the natural standard, thirty beats in a minute'. His second book, *A Treatise on the Properties and Medical Application of the Vapour Bath*, published in 1825, obviously owed much to his knowledge of the work of Mahomed, and included not only a description of the vapour-baths at Brighton, but an account of shampooing as practised in India. A further testimonial to Mahomed's success was the setting up in 1825 of a rival establishment known as Molineux's Shampooing Baths a short distance away from those of Mahomed, and the increasing popularity of this kind of treatment led to the building in 1868 by the Turkish-Bath Company of the Brighton 'Hammam' or Turkish Bath on the east side of West Street at a cost of £14,000. The exterior, 'rising like some Moorish Temple, resplendent with crimson and gilt, encaustic and terracotta', was said to be in striking contrast to the 'Saxon gables and bow-windows' around it.[12] The interior, with its gaily coloured tiled walls and scalloped arches, seems to have been modelled on the lines of the Alhambra. A smaller and less pretentious Turkish Bath had been opened some little while before in Western Road, Hove, by a Dr. Toulmin. Numerous lesser bathing establishments were set up in Brighton from time to time, and enjoyed varying degrees of success.

Granville,[13] who visited all the baths, noted that the charge at almost every one was a guinea for eight hot baths, while a course of lectures on swimming at Brill's Baths cost five guineas. The old practice of supplying sea-water 'freshly drawn off the ocean' was continuing in 1857, when H. Buggins's Brunswick Baths, at 2 Western Street, between the Norfolk Hotel and Brunswick Terrace, advertised that the proprietors were able to supply families 'with either hot or cold sea-water in any part of the town', at a charge of 4d a bucket if hot, and 3d if cold. The sea-water was pumped to Buggins's Baths by means of a steam engine.[14]

The idea of making sea-water artificially from sea-salt was by no means new, and as late as 1857 the sale of sea-salt for baths was being advertised by Brew and Schweitzer, Chemists, of East Street.[15] The firm announced that their marine salts would unfailingly produce what would nowadays be called 'instant sea-water', which would be of great advantage in scrofulous and similar cases. Mrs. Merrifield stated that the salts 'on being dissolved in soft water in the proportions directed, will produce sea-water as it exists in its natural state in the English Channel'. In 1876 the Brighton Corporation purchased the West Brighton Waterworks Company and continued to supply salt water from the sea as well as fresh water, as the old company had done. In 1904 about 100 houses were still receiving salt water, and the service was continued to a few houses even up to the outbreak of the Second World War in 1939.

4 Coaching Days

Great improvements in the organization of commercial coaching in Brighton, as all over England, were stimulated by the establishment in 1784 of the revolutionary system of Royal Mail coaches, for the purpose of procuring a speedy and reliable means of transport for the mails. Up till then these had been carried by post-boys, who might be of any age between sixteen and sixty, who rode alone, and who often dawdled drinking at inns on the way, were held up by bad weather, or were attacked and robbed by highwaymen. John Palmer, the son of the owner of the theatres in Bath and Bristol, who needed to have prompt replies to letters and contracts regarding theatrical performances, conceived the idea of carrying the mails in fast coaches protected by a guard armed with a blunderbuss, and with four passengers on board whose fares would pay the cost.

As soon as William Pitt came to power in 1784 he overruled the objections which the Postmaster-General had made to the scheme and put Palmer in charge. He and his successor Thomas Hasker organized the mail-coach system with such painstaking efficiency that it became accepted not only as the safest, speediest and most reliable way of carrying the mails, but of travelling about the country. The mail-coaches were lighter and more elegant than the stage-coaches, and were painted lemon and black with scarlet wheels, and the doors were decorated with the Royal Arms. Higher speeds were made possible by arranging for the horses to be changed every ten miles instead of twenty; the horse-keepers at the changing points were required to have the fresh horses already waiting in the road when the coach arrived, even in the middle of the night, so that the coach could be got away again within a few minutes,[1] and an end was quickly put to the practice of stopping frequently for drinks and lengthy meals at inns.

The two essays that were written by Thomas De Quincey, entitled *The English Mail-Coach* and *Going Down with Victory*, at once summed up the excited response of the public to the new form of transport and immortalized the mail-coach as one of the most romantic and successful of English inventions. By the time that Hasker retired in 1817 the mail-coach system had established its supremacy over every other kind of transport on the roads of Britain.

In Brighton the mails had been carried for years by private coaches, but the Royal Mail coaches began running between Brighton and London in 1810, at night starting at ten o'clock, going by 'the new cut to Croydon', and doing the journey in eight hours, 'no pretences being permitted to cause a delay in the journey'.

Coaching at Brighton had begun by 1800 to be put on a more dependable and expeditious basis than it had been a few years earlier, by the establishment of several firms devoting themselves entirely to the business. Among them Crossweller's of East Street was the most famous. In addition to the usual post-coaches, a night coach started at 10 p.m. every other day in the high season. Coaches also ran three times a week through Chichester and Portsmouth to Bath and Bristol. A number of local carriers ran carts to Lewes, Shoreham and Eastbourne. For the poorer passengers there were wagons that took two days and a night over the journey to London. The fast coaches now did the journey to London in nine hours, instead of the eleven of 1790, but passengers still had to walk up the worst hills.

An account written in 1801[2] describes a more leisurely journey by pair-horse coach from London to Brighton, in the course of which every possible opportunity was taken to benefit the proprietors of roadside hostelries by making frequent stops for refreshment. The coach left at seven o'clock, and the passengers breakfasted at Sutton at nine o'clock. The next stop was at Banstead for a glass of Miss Jeal's famous elderberry wine, brought 'smoking hot' from her cottage, and very welcome on a cold morning. George IV was said frequently to have stopped to sup a glass in his carriage. Lunch was at Reigate, where time was allowed for passengers to visit the Baron's Cave. At Handcross the landlord of the inn was already waiting with 'strong liquors' ready. A 'grand halt' was made for dinner at Staplefield Common, famous for its black-cherry trees, under which in the season the coaches drew up and the passengers were allowed to pick the fruit. The favourite dish here was a rabbit pudding, and what with 'Grogs, pipes and ale', the meal usually dragged on for two hours. The coach then went on to Clayton Hill, and as the passengers had to walk up, a cup of tea was found necessary at Patcham, after which Brighton was reached about seven o'clock.

In the next few years coaches became much faster, chiefly as a result of better roads and by choosing routes avoiding hills, and the coaching trade prospered enormously, one firm paying $7\frac{1}{2}$ per cent on the capital employed.

In 1823 as many as forty-eight coaches were running between London and Brighton every day, and twenty-six on the other roads out of the town, besides many other vehicles which conveyed passengers. Luggage was now brought from London by vans in less time than the coaches had performed the journey twenty-five years earlier.[3]

All the principal coach offices, including 'The Blue', 'The Red', 'The

Spread Eagle', 'The Age', 'Snow's' and 'The Globe', were in Castle Square, where most of the important departures and arrivals took place. At these times Castle Square was a centre of intense bustle, activity and excitement. Cads, touters, porters and hangers-on were about all the time amongst the groups of travellers on the look-out for a chance to earn a shilling, and there was often a crowd of people waiting for the news that would be brought from London by the coaches, especially in times of national excitement, as during later victorious stages of the Napoleonic wars, at the time of the trial of Queen Caroline and during the various stages of the Reform Bill. Outside the different coach offices stood the brightly coloured coaches, the splendid horses covered with richly braided and gold or silver-mounted horse-cloths; the coachmen, celebrated characters, some of them 'swell' amateur coachmen, perhaps a nobleman or baronet like Sir St. Vincent Cotton, who often drove the 'Age' coach, conscious of being watched by their admirers. As the hour struck from the clock in the water-tower next to the south gate of the Pavilion the horse-cloths were snatched away by the ostlers, the guard would sound a tune on his trumpet and the horses would plunge into action. By 1830 the 'Red Rover' Coach was doing the journey between London and Brighton in only four-and-a-half hours,[4] but the pleasures of a more leisurely journey through the countryside were still not to be ignored, and in the same year the 'Item' Coach was making the journey to London in six hours 'by a pleasantly diversified route'.[5] One hundred and twenty-seven years later the 'Red Rover' Coach, preserved by coaching enthusiasts for all this time, and now freed from the spur of competition, took ten and a half hours over the trip to Brighton.[6]

5 Georgian Inns and Hotels

From the earliest times Brighton has been well provided with inns, drinking houses and beer-shops. In 1800 there were no less than forty-one inns and public houses, a number that works out at about one to every thirty of the private dwellings that made up the town. Before the 'Auncient Customs' were drawn up, and regulations made to govern 'the great disorder of the tipling houses', beer and spirits were sold from a great many private houses, without licence or control of any kind. In 1749 'Mary Saunders', Widow, at the Block House, Brighthelmston', advertised in the *Lewes Journal* that she sold 'fine genuine French Brandy, at nine shillings a gallon'.

Amongst the earliest inns still surviving in some form was the Gun Tavern, now Harrison's Hotel, on the sea-front at the bottom of Market Street. It was much used for parish meetings, and at the end of the eighteenth century Wessen's coaches and 'Tucker's Diligence' used to set out from the inn. In early days the building was a low one, with a forecourt enclosed by a dwarf wall much used by the fishermen and longshoremen for resting upon in their less active moments. The Star and Garter Inn opposite also dates back to before 1785, when 'Two Gigantic Twin Brothers—very near Eight Feet High' were exhibited there. Right in front of the inn was a large capstan used for hauling up the boats, and when the new Grand Junction was being built in 1827, which made the road along the sea-front continuous, the removal of this capstan provoked the last of the many fights between fishermen and landsmen, in which the latter were victorious. One of the most picturesque of Brighton's surviving inns, with its flint walls and bow-windows, is The Cricketer's in Black Lion Street. It was originally known as The Last and Fish-cart, but it was usually called The Last (a measure of 10,000 fish). Under the sign, immediately over the door were painted these lines:

> *Long time I've looked for good beer,*
> *And at 'The Last' have found it here.*

The name was altered to The Cricketer's in 1790 by a Mr. Jutten, one of the leading devotees of the game who used the inn as their headquarters. It is a favourite resort nowadays of literary, artistic and theatrical people.

The Seven Stars in Ship Street is nowadays chiefly esteemed by connoisseurs of public houses for its Victorian character, its fantastic architecture and engraved glass windows making it a superb example of the type. Yet it is one of the oldest inns in Brighton. The sign now inscribed upon it, 'Established 1535', cannot be substantiated, but there was a house on the site which may have been a tavern in 1692, and the present name of the inn is mentioned in a deed of 1785.[1]

The Sea House Hotel at the bottom of Middle Street began as 'a small miserable looking building' called The Ship in Distress, which was the favourite haunt of the West Street fishing community. Over its porch was a picture of a wrecked ship and the words

> *By danger we'er encompassed round*
> *Pray lend a hand, our ship's aground.*

There was at this point a deep break in the cliff-top which was bridged by a wooden causeway, but in 1822 King George IV opened the new carriage way, the King's Road, which had been built along the sea-front. All the property here now increased enormously in value, and about 1825 The Ship in Distress was rebuilt and its name changed to The Sea House. It was here that in 1830 Nelson's widow, the Viscountess Brontë, stayed for a time, and during her stay King William IV called upon her one afternoon, after which the landlord called his house The Royal Sea House Hotel. The place was rebuilt towards the end of the nineteenth century.

The principal public house in West Street itself was The George, much frequented by the tradesmen. This inn was the third of that name, for The King's Head close by had originally been called the 'George', and was the inn where, as already described, King Charles II stayed the night before his escape to France. Its name was changed to The King's Head about 1745. The second 'George' was in Middle Street, and has in the past erroneously been thought to have been the inn where the King stayed.

Outside the central square of Brighthelmstone beyond Church Street, in North Row (now Marlborough Place), The King and Queen provided for the agricultural community just to the north of the town. It had originally been a farmhouse itself, but had become an inn by 1779.[2] Apart from the farming folk who used the inn, until the town expanded around it, it would have been in some demand from time to time when cricket matches and other sports and celebrations were held on the grassy expanses north of the Steine which were enclosed in 1817 and became known as the North Steine Enclosure, now the Victoria Gardens. There was also a considerable though unofficial clientele of another kind, for The King and Queen backed on to the barracks north of Church Street, and for years there was a hole in the back wall through which liquor was passed to the soldiery. The Brighton Corn Market was held at the inn until 1868, when it was transferred to the Corn Exchange, which was originally the Riding House of King George IV. The 'King and Queen' of the inn's name were most probably King George III and Queen Charlotte, but in the 1930s the Regency period structure of the inn was demolished and reconstructed as a building in the 'Tudor' style that was popular in the 1930s before the discovery of Regency, with herringbone brickwork, oak beams, a portcullis gate to the inn-yard and other 'olde' features. The King and Queen now became Henry VIII and Anne Boleyn, whose painted representation now appears at the entrance.

The origins of the Old Ship Hotel, the most ancient of all in Brighton, have already been described. The first to make his mark in a notable series of enterprising proprietors was William Hicks, who had built the beautiful Adamesque ballroom and card-room. After his death in 1765 he was succeeded by his son, who extended the building upon the sea-front in 1794. For years it shared the honours of the fashionable balls, assemblies, parties and concerts with the Castle Inn, and 'though the rays of Royalty seldom irradiated the premises, the first families of the Nobility resorted thither'. From early times nearly all the important town meetings, property sales and business meetings were held there. After the creation of the Town Commissioners in 1810 their deliberations were held there, and almost every important project in the development of the town was decided upon at a meeting in the Old Ship—almost invariably with the accompaniment of a banquet of a splendour appropriate to the occasion. One of the most treasured associations of the Old Ship in the 1830s is that with Paganini the violinist, who stayed at the Old Ship from time to time over several years. It is a link commemorated by an inscription upon the walls of the Assembly Rooms, where this artist, the greatest instrumentalist of his day, performed on 9th December 1831. The era of magnificent balls came to an end towards the end of the century, when in 1872 the brilliance of the Brighton assemblies flared up for a dazzling moment before sinking into the diminished light of a more utilitarian age, with a grand *Bal Costumé* given by one Mr. Morrell Dorington Longden, who seems to have been inspired by the magnificence of the ancient Assyrian court at Nineveh, which had recently been revealed by the archaeologist Layard. Longden obviously conceived himself as embodying in his own person all the grandeur of Sardanapalus, for it was in this character that the host enthroned himself to receive his guests.

As the *Brighton Herald* wrote: 'Having travelled abroad a great deal and contracted a taste for Continental decorative art, Mr. Longden gave his fancy full play. . . . At the north end (of the Telemachus Room) was a scarlet dais and golden throne alluded to in Layard's *Nineveh* as used by the Assyrian Kings. The drapery of it was embroidered with gold, being thrown carelessly over the back; and the whole was surmounted by a light azure-coloured canopy fringed with gold. On each side of the throne was a scarlet banneret bearing the "winged bull"; and the dais was flanked on each side by a magnificent display of flowers. The Company began to arrive shortly after ten o'clock, and were received by Mr. Longden enthroned in the character of Sardanapalus. He wore a gorgeous costume, richly embroidered with gold and jewels and emblazoned with Egyptian characters. This dress of the voluptuous Assyrian was complete in every detail.'

In following years the renown of the Old Ship Assembly Rooms centred more upon the concerts for which they had always been famous than upon grand balls, although these continued, but in a more intimate form.

Not only music but musicians found a home at the Old Ship. Madame Schumann, the wife of the composer, stayed there in 1870, when she came to perform at the Dome. A frequent visitor was Simms Reeves, the tenor, who married a Brighton lady, a Miss Larcombe, whose father was the proprietor of the famous circulating library on the Steine. Other musicians who stayed at the Old Ship in this period were Lablache, Ginglini, Mme Alboni, Mme Grisi, Sir Julius Benedict, the conductor and composer of the 'Lily of Killarney', and Sir Charles Santley, the famous baritone. From its very early days the Old Ship has had a reputation also as a place especially favoured by actors and actresses visiting the town to perform at its theatres.

In later Victorian days Sir Henry Irving and Beerbohm Tree were visitors, but of all theatrical people who knew the Old Ship none was more loved than that great comedian of the Victorian era, J. L. Toole, who was unexcelled in his day for character parts. Toole was occasionally invited to Windsor to entertain a week-end party, and the late Ralph Straus used to tell how on one occasion after dinner he was sent for by the Queen, who taxed him with having imitated her. Toole was aghast with horror, and begged the Queen not to believe 'such a malicious rumour'. But Her Majesty had the report on very good authority, and commanded him: 'Now, Mr. Toole, imitate me!' Toole's only hope was to make the act as brilliant as possible and so to the smallest but most exacting audience he had ever known he gave the most magnificent performance of his career. When it was finished the Queen was for a little while silent and serious, but then began to laugh, gently at first, and then more and more heartily. At last Her Majesty said: 'Mr. Toole, that was very very clever, and very very funny, and you must promise me you will never, never do it again!'

Thackeray stayed at the hotel while writing his novel *Vanity Fair*, and made Brighton the place where two of his chief characters, George and Amelia, 'would pass the first few days after their marriage, and having engaged apartments at the Ship Inn, enjoyed themselves in great comfort and quietude. . . .'

In his novel *Old Court*, Harrison Ainsworth mentioned not only the Old Ship but its proprietor Mr. Bacon, whom he portrayed as serving with affection the fine wine for which the hotel was noted. Bacon had taken over the hotel in 1852, and paid a rent of £100 a year for it until the tenancy expired in 1878, when he bought the property for £8,300, a very considerable sum in those days. Bacon began to modernize the Ship Street frontage of the hotel in 1895, and it was then it became necessary to demolish the original façade of the Assembly Rooms entrance, with its delightful projecting bow-window on the first floor, which had become much decayed.

The New Ship Hotel, almost opposite the Old Ship in Ship Street, was only new by comparison with its ancient rival, for it was known to be in existence at least as early as 1741, when coaches began their journeys from it. It was here in 1764 that passages in the cross-Channel packet-boat the *Prince of Wales* were to be booked.

It was at the New Ship that in October 1789 the Prince of Wales and Mrs. Fitzherbert paid a visit to the thirty-seven refugee nuns who had been brought from France in the *Prince of Wales* packet. In later times the hotel became highly favoured amongst the tradesmen of the town.

For nearly a hundred and fifty years the Castle Hotel has ceased to exist, except in the name it gave to Castle Square. The hotel occupied the site of the present Electricity Board showrooms, and had an important frontage on to the Steine. It was originally a private house, and was opened up as an inn in 1755 by Mr. Samuel Shergold, who realized the needs of the growing numbers of visitors who were coming to the town under the influence of Dr. Russell. There was already a small inn near by called the Fountain, but this was incorporated into the Castle when the latter was rebuilt and enlarged in 1766. It was at this time also that the handsome ballroom was built to John Crunden's design. Although it lacked the antiquity of the Old Ship the Castle captured the patronage of most of the titled, wealthy and fashionable visitors, at least until the Old Ship built its own Assembly Rooms in 1767, after which the two hotels shared the honours of the fashionable balls and assemblies between them.

Being so near at hand to the Pavilion, the Castle was resorted to by the Prince of Wales and the Royal Family more often than was the Old Ship, and for many years it was believed that it hardly yielded to any tavern in the kingdom. In 1814 the hotel came under new proprietorship, but in spite of a number of improvements in the building and the erection of a fine organ in the ballroom, the place seemed to have lost its attraction, for at the reopening ball the number of subscribers was only twenty. Possibly the new owner had failed to enlist the support of that all-powerful being, the M.C., for when a ball was held a little later for that functionary's benefit there were over 500 guests.

The owners strove to keep up the attractions of the place by means of promenade concerts and other events, but the hotel's prosperity continued to diminish, possibly because of changing patterns in social life, and also because the Old Ship now commanded the chief loyalty of the M.C.s. At length the fate of the Castle was determined by King George IV, who bought the whole property at the time of the final transformation of the Pavilion in order to enlarge the grounds, and to convert the splendid ball-rooms into a private chapel, which was opened as such on 1 January 1822. The other parts of the hotel building were demolished in 1828, and by this means the width of Castle Square and also of the Steine roadway at that point was greatly increased.

When the Castle Hotel was bought by King George IV one enterprising property-owner on the Steine realized the opportunity that now presented itself to cater for the illustrious and fashionable visitors who had been accustomed in the past to stay at the Castle, especially members of the Royal Family and others visiting the Pavilion. This was Dr. Hall, who in 1801 had acquired from Mr. Richard Scrase Steine House at the southern end of the Steine, facing north. It was the old Manor House of Bright-helmstone and had been bought by Mr. Scrase in 1771. Mr. Hall built three houses on the site of the stables adjoining Steine House and the row of houses became known as Steine Place. In 1819 Mr. Hall converted the houses into a hotel which with the sanction of Frederick, Duke of York, he named the Royal York Hotel. The hotel immediately became the most fashionable hotel in Brighton, and numbered amongst its visitors such distinguished persons as the Dukes of Clarence, York and Cambridge, the Duke of Wellington, Disraeli, Thackeray and many eminent foreign visitors, including the Prince Polignac, the Marquis de Custin, the Russian ambassador Count de Lieven and his wife the Princess Lieven, Prince William of Austria and many others. The hotel owed its popularity to more than its nearness to the Pavilion. Its principal windows commanded a complete view of the Steine, which was still the most fashionable centre of social life in the town, and from the upper windows of the hotel the eye took in the whole prospect of the valley between the Downs leading north-wards as well as an unbroken view of land and sea, and of the white cliffs stretching into the distance eastwards. In 1827 the hotel was enlarged by taking in some adjoining houses, forming the building as it stands today.

One of the grandest occasions in the history of the hotel was on 15th October 1829, when the Duke and Duchess of Clarence (later King William IV and Queen Adelaide) stayed there on their return from a visit to France. The Royal party landed at the Chain Pier from the Admiralty yacht while a salute was fired by the guns of the frigate *Hyperion*. Afterwards the party were received at the hotel by Mrs. Fitzherbert and the Dowager Mar-chioness of Devonshire, Lady Mary Hill, and they were compelled to make an appearance on the balcony in answer to the repeated cheers of the crowd outside. The fortunes of the hotel waned in later years, and by 1898 it had become almost derelict, but it was acquired in 1901 by Mr. (later Sir) Harry Preston, who quickly restored its former brilliance, and its history during his ownership is like that of all the great hotels of Brighton, closely bound up with the history of the town itself.

After Sir Harry Preston's retirement in 1929 the Royal York Hotel was bought by Brighton Corporation and is now used as the offices of several municipal departments. The original façade, with its fine bow-windows, survives at the eastern end of the building, while the angular bays of the western part belong to a later enlargement.

With the continued boom expansion of Brighton in the 1820s even the Royal York Hotel with its hundred rooms was not enough to accommodate the crowds of visitors. In 1826 a magnificent new hotel, the Royal Albion, was built at the south end of the Steine on the site of Russell House. After the death of Dr. Russell in 1759 it had been occupied by a succession of distinguished visitors to the town, including the Duke of Cumberland, who lived there during the season of 1786 and in the two or three following years. Later it came to be looked upon more and more as unfashionably out of date, and declined in favour as a family mansion. For some five years after 1807 it continued as a boarding house, but later on it came to be used for popular amusements such as a toy repository, and for a 'mechanical theatre' with 'animated objects' which had been removed from the Grand Parade, where they 'had been complained of as a nuisance'. A *camera obscura* was set up in one of the rooms, and 'the art and practice' of copper-plate printing was carried on in another part. In 1822 an Indian juggler held his performances in the principal room. By then the house was becoming ruinous, and before long it was demolished.

With the removal of the house a magnificent opening to the sea was presented at the foot of the Steine, and the suggestion was made that the space should be bought by the town and kept open for ever. The Town Commissioners agreed on a price of £6,000, but delays arose and the deal was never concluded. The original portion of the hotel, consisting of the main cube-shaped block at the eastern end of the building, was planned by the architect A. H. Wilds in 1822[3] and completed in 1826. The shell ornaments in the arched upper windows are similar to those used by Wilds in Oriental Place, and are a distinguishing mark of his work.

Apart from the distinction of its visitors in early years, who rivalled in importance those of the Royal York, the Royal Albion Hotel played a part of some significance in Brighton's history as the place where the foundations of the principal cultural institutions of the town were laid, for it was in a large room on the ground floor at the western end of the hotel that the Albion Rooms Literary and Scientific Institution was established in 1841. Their first activity was a lecture in September of that year upon phreno-logy, a subject that was of continuous fascination for the Victorians. In time the Institution collected a fine library of some thousands of books, together with many pictures and objects of historical and artistic interest. During the years they acquired also a heavy burden of debt, and at last the members decided to shake off the burden by raising a subscription to clear off the debts and presenting the Library and Museum to the town. This gift eventually resulted in the establishment by the Corporation of the Public Library, Art Gallery and Museum of the town on the Royal Pavilion Estate.

In more recent times the Royal Albion Hotel became famous as the resort of many of the most distinguished figures in the world of literature, art, the theatre and sport, especially during the years when that most genial of hosts, the late Sir Harry Preston, was proprietor.

The Royal Pavilion Hotel was established in Castle Square about 1820 as a family and commercial hotel, no doubt to cater for the middle-class customers who would at one time have stayed at the Castle. In 1826 it was rebuilt by the Brighton architects Charles Busby and A. H. Wilds and given its still surviving Regency bow-front with the charming portico and ironwork balcony bearing emblems of the crown and a dolphin from the borough arms, which represent the two foundations of the town's success, King George IV and the sea.

One of the oldest hotels in Brighton, and one that has retained its early appearance more closely than any other, is the Clarence Hotel in North Street. Originally called the New Inn, it was built about 1785 to provide accommodation for visitors, and for those who came by the usual route from London by coach through Steyning it was the first place of rest that was offered. When the coach route was altered, about 1807–8, to come by Pyecombe, 'avoiding all hills', it was equally well placed near the end of the New Road which had been made two years before. The owner then was William Henwood, the leading partner of a famous London firm of coach proprietors, Henwood, Crosweller, Cuddington, Pockney Harding and Co., and the hotel had accommodation in its large stables and two yards for fifty horses and six coaches. But after 1808 the hotel's popularity as a coaching inn declined. During the nineteenth century and after it gradually increased in favour as a family hotel and as an inn for commercial travellers. Today it preserves almost unaltered the rather severely plain appearance it possessed in 1818, with its flat façade, dentil cornice and square classical portico with iron railings above. The name was changed from the New Inn to the Clarence Hotel in 1831, in compliment to the Duke of Clarence, who had succeeded to the throne as King William IV a little earlier.

After the building of Brunswick Town, fashionable attention was focused more and more upon the western end of the town, and when the Bedford Hotel at the bottom of Cavendish Place was built in 1820 it rapidly challenged the Royal Albion and Royal York Hotels as the most important hotel in Brighton. It was designed by Thomas Cooper, who was the architect also of the Brighton Town Hall, and the son of a Brighton builder who was killed by a fall from one of the houses upon which he was working in Brunswick Square. It was of massive scale, but relieved by the two elegant recessed Ionic porticoes and the receding attic storeys on the front and west side, and by the Corinthian pilasters of the west wing. In recent years, painted in grey and white, it was obviously the most distinguished late Georgian building in Brighton after the Royal Pavilion, and its interior was no less splendid, with its central 'Grecian Hall' rising through four storeys to the roof, each floor having a gallery carried on elegant Ionic columns, and with iron railings of palm-leaf design.

After the closing of the Pavilion in 1845, any members of the Royal Family who came to Brighton preferred to stay at the Bedford, and it became the almost invariable choice of foreign royalty and notabilities visiting Brighton, as well as being favoured by hundreds of eminent English visitors.

The Duchess of Gloucester, the Duke and Duchess of Cambridge and their children, Princess Mary, Duchess of Teck, and the second Duke of Cambridge, the Duc de Bordeaux (Comte de Chambord), King Louis-Philippe of France and his family, Louis Napoleon, the Prince of Parma, Lord Aberdeen, Palmerston, Macaulay, the singer Jenny Lind were among the many celebrities who stayed at the Bedford. Princess Lieven, Prince Metternich, who had been her lover in earlier years, and Guzot, the French historian and politician who was her lover in later years, were all guests at the hotel. Charles Dickens stayed there while writing *Dombey and Son*, and made the elder Mr. Dombey a guest there in the novel. One of the characters in Cuthbert Bede's novel of Brighton, *Mattins and Muttons*,[4] Mrs. Melladew, asked her son if the Bedford was a respectable hotel for ladies. He 'smiled at her innocence and replied that two live ladies and a countess, with a liberal sprinkling of honourable mistresses and misses were sheltered beneath its roof the last time he was within its palatial walls'. He went on to say that the landlord 'was a highly cultivated man,—a student and a book-worm—a good classic—a poet, with a knowledge of poets—a judge as well as a collector of pictures—a connoisseur in various branches of the fine arts, and with an original theory as to the author of Junius'.

A remarkable feature of the hotel was a large building on the east side which was used as an indoor tennis-court from 1853 or even earlier up to as late as 1939. Originally it had been a private riding house, attached to a house belonging to the Count de St. Antonio. Later on the riding house was taken over by the Duke and Duchess of St. Albans. After the last war it was used for a time as a dining-room and was later on demolished to make room for a garage. By the tragic fire of April 1964, in which the Bedford Hotel was destroyed and three people lost their lives, one of Brighton's most distinguished and beautiful landmarks was lost. By the irony of fate, the question of a preservation order on the building was being considered by the government department concerned only the day before the fire.

6 The Windmills

Windmills are now regarded as familiar and immemorial features of the Downs around Brighton, yet at one time there were none to be seen in these particular places. Instead there were altogether at different times in the past some twenty mills in or close to Brighton itself.

In 1514, at the time of the French attack on Brighton, there were two post-mills on the hill near St. Nicholas's Church, but by 1580, when the grievances of the fishermen were being investigated, it was reported that one of these was 'now utterly decayed'.[1] In 1638 there was a 'town-mill', for which the town paid the rates, on the Steine, and during the next hundred years there were three mills on the eastern side of the town, near the present Marine Parade. These, which were all post-mills with canvas sails, are seen in James Lambert's 'Perspective View of Brighthelmstone' of 1765.

A mill on the cliff near West Street which is shown in Rowlandson's lively drawing of bathing-machines on the beach at Brighton did not exist there when that artist visited the town in 1791, for it had been moved to Black Rock in 1759. Rowlandson had drawn the background of his sketch from an old print. No doubt he also found that the windmill greatly improved the composition and interest of his picture. As the town expanded eastwards the mills on this side of Brighton disappeared, and by 1813 the only mill there was one erected in 1793 near the present Sudeley Place in Kemp Town. Lambert's engraving showed as well as the three East Cliff mills a mill to the west. This was probably the West Mill, a black post-mill, which was in existence in 1744, in Belle Vue Gardens, now Regency Square. As houses came to be built west of the town the residents complained about the mill and asked for its removal, and this was accomplished in sensational fashion, in 1792, by having it placed on a sledge-like framework and dragged by about thirty-six yoke of oxen to a new site outside the town near the top of Miller's Road, off the Dyke Road. The name of this mill was changed successively from West Mill to Streeter's Mill, Preston Mill, Dyke Road Mill, Black Mill (i.e. black tarred) and Trusler's Mill. The oxen were lent by a number of gentleman farmers of Brighton who seemed to have entered into the spirit of this notable enterprise, for a famous engraving was made of the transportation of the mill, and shows it being dragged up the steep slope of the Downs from Brighton by the seventy-two oxen in six long ranks.

After this stupendous operation no one hesitated over moving a windmill when it became necessary, which usually occurred because the sweeping tide of houses was driving the mills away from the centre of the town. The large post-mill in Clifton Gardens, near St. Nicholas's, was transported in 1831 to Queen's Park, to replace an older mill. The Windmill public house in Upper North Street at the corner of Clifton Place probably took its name from this mill. Another mill near by, Vine's Mill, built in 1806 and demolished in 1848–9, is commemorated by the name of Vine Place where it stood. The East End Mill at Sudeley Place was moved in 1835 to Sussex Street, also near Queen's Park, and it was moved again in 1862 to the Race Hill, where it survived until it collapsed in 1913. The same travelling carriage, made of iron and with ten or twelve wheels, that had been used to move the Regency Square mill some sixty years before was brought out again for this removal. While being placed on the carriage the mill suddenly toppled over, killing one of the workmen and also a little boy who was looking on. The mill was damaged, and was not shifted for another nine months, and then the journey, in which twenty horses and thirty cattle were used, took three weeks. The same carriage was again used to move a white weatherboarded post-mill called Lashmar's New Mill, built in 1780, from Dyke Road to its present position on the top of Clayton Hill, where it now keeps company with a tower-mill a short distance away. The two mills are called 'Jack and Jill'. The fine mill still standing at the top of Mill Road, Patcham, near the Dyke Road, was built in 1885. There were two earlier mills at Patcham, one existing from 1724 to 1791, another built in 1791 and demolished in 1902. A mill built on the East Hill at Rottingdean in 1700 was pulled down in 1817, but the black-tarred smock-mill on Beacon Hill, Rottingdean, was in existence before 1800, and is still standing. Originally the mill stood much farther inland near the cricket-ground, but it was moved to its present position on Beacon Hill by a team of oxen in 1802. This mill is probably the most famous of all windmills, being known all over the world as the trade-mark of the publishing firm of William Heinemann and Sons, and was drawn by the artist William Nicholson in 1897, when he was living near by at The Grange, Rottingdean. The mill was leased by the landowner, the Earl of Abergavenny, in 1923 to a trust formed to restore and preserve it, and it was repaired by the Brighton Corporation in 1935, when they became the landlords. Heinemann's and the Rottingdean Preservation Society are now the tenants of the mill and carried out repairs in 1966 by means of a grant from the Corporation and from private subscribers.

7 Pleasure Gardens and the German Spa

After the closing of the Promenade Grove in 1802, when the Prince of Wales bought the land in order to extend the grounds of the Royal Pavilion, Brighton people keenly felt the lack of the miniature Vauxhall Pleasure Gardens which the Grove had provided. Various festivities of a more formal kind were held on the Level, the flat expanse of grass immediately north of the junction of the London Road and the Lewes Road, and also on the Prince's Cricket Ground which formed the northern part of the Level.

The Prince's birthdays and other momentous events were often celebrated by the roasting of oxen and the holding of sports here, as on the occasion of the celebration of the overthrow of Napoleon and his imprisonment at Elba, in August 1814, when roast beef and plum puddings were served to over 7,000 persons, at seventy-five double rows of tables, each row being attended by a president and six stewards, all wearing white sashes bearing the inscription 'Brighton Festival'. After many toasts and the playing of various stirring airs and marches by the band of the 3rd Buffs, the rest of the day was devoted to dancing, blind-man's-buff, 'jingling matches', foot-racing, stoolball, kiss-in-the-ring and 'jumping in sacks', the throng of merry-makers ending by joining hands and forming long chains of people and 'threading the tailor's needle' to Castle Square, where after singing 'God Save the King' they dispersed to their homes.[1]

For a while after the closing of Promenade Grove its place as a resort for small parties was taken by some tea-gardens on the Marine Parade near the part now occupied by Eaton Place. They were especially popular in summer as a retreat for a cup of tea during an afternoon stroll, or for a glass of hot elderberry wine in winter.

Upon coming to the Throne the Prince Regent retired from cricket and gave up his ground on the Level, whereupon the Lord of the Manor, Mr. Thomas Read Kemp, made a grant of the land to the town for the recreation of the inhabitants, and a road was formed across its northern end. Not long after, in 1822, a Mr. James Ireland purchased ten acres of land north of the road, where Park Crescent and its gardens now stand, and in the following year opened Ireland's Gardens and Cricket Ground.

Ireland was a woollen-draper and undertaker who in 1806 had purchased the drapery business belonging to Mr. Daniel Constable and his brother

William, which eventually became the celebrated establishment of Hannington and Son in North Street.

Between the Pleasure Gardens and the Cricket Ground stood a 'noble and conspicuous building' with reading-, refreshment- and dressing-rooms on the lower floor, and an 'elegant promenade room' 80 feet by 30 feet over them. Inside the entrance to the Gardens was a ladies' bowling-green surrounded by lawns and tea-arbours, with an aviary and an ornamental grotto near by. At the north end of the central avenue of the Gardens was a bridge spanning a small lake, which led to a Gothic tower and gateway that formed the entrance to a Maze, in the centre of which was a 'Merlin swing', another product of the fertile brain of the inventor of the Prince Regent's famous invalid chair.

William Constable, whose drapery business had been bought by Ireland, was ardently devoted to scientific novelties, and one day publicly announced by the town crier that he would fly from the top of the Assembly Room to the extreme end of the grounds. A scaffolding was erected on the roof of the building, and from it a wire stretched to the bridge by the Maze. A large crowd assembled to watch the promised feat, and after a long wait Constable appeared attired in 'light-fleshings' with Zephyr-like wings and ascended the scaffold. After the firing of guns from a near-by mimic fort, Constable glided gracefully down the sloping wire hanging from a pulley to which he was attached, waving a flag in each hand. A great many people who had paid to see the performance, already exasperated by the long wait, felt that it had fallen short of what was advertised, and closed in threateningly upon the performer, but he was quickly unfastened from the machinery and took his flight through the Maze, the intricate turnings of which were no doubt familiar to him. Constable's apparatus was eventually developed into a device for rescuing people from burning buildings and wrecked vessels, and after a period spent in America with his brother Daniel promoting various scientific devices, he returned to Brighton in 1841 and introduced the new art of photography to the town in the form of the daguerreotype at his studio known as the Blue Room on Marine Parade near Atlingworth Street.

Despite such sensational attractions as the demonstration of 'flying', the Cricket Ground was by far the most successful part of the enterprise, and its fame is perpetuated by Mason's well-known large engraving representing a match between the famous players of Sussex and Kent. The print was engraved from individual portraits of various players and supporters, but it was not completed to coincide with any particular match, and the artist went on adding portraits for several years.

The Pleasure Gardens were never patronized to the extent that the proprietor hoped, despite all his efforts, which included arranging for a balloon ascent in October 1824. The Gardens soon fell into neglect and

decay. The flower-beds became a wilderness of weeds, the buildings became dilapidated and unsafe, and the grounds reverted to a jungle inhabited by foxes and rabbits, parts occasionally given over to travelling
shows and fairs of the lowest description. Eventually the land was taken
over for the building of Park Crescent in 1829.

A most regrettable caprice on the part of Providence had been its
failure to provide a natural supply of mineral waters in any but a few
favoured cities in Europe. As the fashionable cult of drinking the waters
developed, whether attended by any discernible benefits to health or not,
this deprivation was keenly felt by the less fortunate cities, but Nature's
deplorable omissions in this regard were remedied by a certain Dr. F. A.
Struve, M.D., of Dresden, who conceived the ingenious idea of imitating
by chemical means the waters of famous resorts such as those of Carlsbad,
Marienbad, Spa, Kesselbrunnen, Ems, Pyrmont, Kissingen and Seltzer,
and setting up centres for dispensing them in places where mineral waters
were lacking. After starting artificial spas at Dresden in 1821 and Leipzig
in 1823, Dr. Struve turned his attention to England, and concluded that
Brighton, a delightful holiday resort, with its Continental atmosphere and
its ready-made fashionable clientele, but lacking its own natural spring,
was an ideal place for establishing a spa for his manufactured waters.
Although there were the chalybeate waters of St. Anne's Well at Hove,
where a pleasant little classical building erected about 1800 had replaced
the wooden structure provided earlier by Dr. Russell, this was somewhat
distant from the Steine, the ballrooms, the libraries, the theatre and the
other centres of fashionable life of Brighton. Dr. Struve opened his
'German Spa' in June 1825 at the southern end of a little park called
Brighton Park, about half a mile east of the Steine and a similar distance
inland. The building was erected 'by the firm of Cooper and Lyon for
Mr. Loraine', who was presumably the architect, between July 1824 and
September 1825, at a total cost of £2,506.

Dr. Struve's Pump Room was a small building with a low portico of six
fluted Ionic columns extending across the front, surmounted by the Royal
arms, and with round-headed windows to the main room behind. Within
the Pump Room was a counter and behind it a number of round-arched
apertures in the wall, each framed with a Greek key-pattern moulding, and
containing a tap labelled with the name of the foreign spa whose imitated
waters were dispensed from it. Behind the scenes these waters were compounded by adding mineral salts of various kinds and in different proportions to ordinary water, drawn from an artesian well which had been
driven deep into the chalk in order to obtain a pure supply.

Dr. Struve, who described himself as a Knight of the Saxon Order of
Civil Merit and Fidelity, and a member of several learned societies,

obtained the patronage of King George IV and called his establishment the Royal German Spa. He announced in a prospectus that he possessed recommendations from a large number of well-known medical personages, including the King's own advisers, and described the effects of the various 'Factitious Mineral Waters and Gas Baths prepared at the Pump Room, Brighton'. The doctor was commendably cautious in his claims. 'Many persons are restored to health in a gradual and almost imperceptible manner: whilst with others whose disorders are more severe, the inconveniences incident to their respective complaints not unfrequently appear to be increased, or at least do not lessen at commencement. Such patients after drinking the waters for a week or a fortnight experience a sensation of lassitude, together with fever and irritability, from the immediate action of the water on the suffering organs.' Eventually, however, the doctor promised, 'this state of excitation gradually gives way to health and vigour'. The waters were dispensed from May till November, every morning as early as six o'clock until eleven. The weekly subscription was a guinea, and the course of taking the waters usually lasted for four to five weeks.

The cold waters were also sold in bottles, not only at the Spa but in Brighton, London and from agents in several provincial towns. Even in recent years one London public house still possessed an engraved glass panel dating from Victorian times and advertising 'Genuine Brighton Seltzer'.

It was during the 1830s, when Queen's Park had become fully developed, that the Spa enjoyed its greatest fashionable popularity. King William IV and Queen Adelaide, the Duchess of Kent and other members of the Royal Family who visited Brighton frequently attended at the Pump Room. The medical profession were genuinely impressed by the value of the 'factitious' Brighton waters. Soon after the opening of the Spa Dr. William King somewhat fulsomely asserted that 'Dr. Struve has introduced among us one of the greatest blessings which this country has known', while some years later, in 1841, Dr. Granville expressed his conviction that the German Spa was the only 'reason for sending real patients to Brighton',[2] a comment that shed a somewhat dubious light on the idea of Dr. Russell's early sea-water treatment as having any medical value at all.

Perhaps it was the growing veneration for the wonders of science that was already developing in early Victorian times, and here evident in the artificial production of medicinal waters, that caused the German Spa to be so successful, despite the rather spartan appointments of the Pump Room. Dr. Granville complained that 'The pump or promenade room in rainy weather is soon filled, for it is small, and has none of those gay and showy appliances which are so attractive at the German Kursaals.'[3] There was nothing approaching the splendours of Bath, or Cheltenham or of Leamington Spa: no gracious ballroom, no glittering chandeliers, no attractive statues of females representing the goddess Hygeia. 'Unlike what takes place at the German springs,' Granville went on, 'the water-bibber here drinks in faith; for the water does not bubble up from the earth, but flows from a silver or glass spout, on the turning of a stop by the fair hand of the smart lass who is always ready with a beaker of the respective water required.'

The most popular time to make a visit was between eight and eleven in the morning, and although the Pump Room itself was not roomy enough for a large company, in fine weather at least the visitors could stroll in the park, or practise archery at the targets that were set up on the lawns outside the Spa.

The Spa was still being advertised in *Brighton* in 1860, but by 1886 it had ceased to function in its original fashion, for in *D. B. Friend's Brighton Almanack* for that year it is stated that 'years ago, visitors of all ranks and grades among the Upper Ten, drove in their carriages daily to the Royal German Spa, to partake of Dr. Struve's Mineral Waters; indeed the number of vehicles standing along one side of the street, leading from the Spa in the direction of the sea, often ran largely into three figures. At the present day such a sight is not to be witnessed; the once fashionable method of drinking waters by persons going in carriages to the Royal German Spa is a thing of the past, never probably to be revived.'

The Spa continued as a manufactory for table waters, and continued so until as late as 1960, under the firm of Hooper Struve, Ltd., some of whose members were descendants of the founder. Until the closing of the business the original artesian well continued to serve as the main water supply for the firm's products. After lying derelict for some years, the little classical building of the Spa came into the hands of Brighton Corporation, who it is hoped will find some means of preserving this link with Brighton's early fashionable society. As I write, there still remain in the ruined Pump Room the original apertures that once contained the taps labelled with the names of their 'factitious' waters—Carlsbad, Ems, Marienbad, Kissingen, Pyrmont and Spa—but alas, the fashionable visitors of the past and the 'smart lass' who was always ready with 'a beaker of the respective water required' have long since vanished.

8 The Chain Pier

King George IV had spent the Christmas of 1824 at Brighton, and stayed until 12th February 1825, when he departed for Windsor. It is said that as the King was leaving Brighton on this occasion he made a farewell drive along the sea-front of the town which under his influence had grown into one of the great seaside resorts of the world. As the carriage was passing along the Marine Parade he signalled for it to stop, to allow him to survey a remarkable new structure which had been built two years before. This was the Royal Suspension Chain Pier, which stretched out into the sea like a delicate bridge hung on chains suspended in graceful curves from four tapering towers shaped as Egyptian pylon gateways. It was one of the first of the great suspension bridges of the early nineteenth century such as the one built across the Menai Straits by the engineer Thomas Telford, or Brunel's Clifton Bridge at Bristol, and it was in works like these that a new spirit of beauty was now emerging from the complex moods of the Regency age —not the romanticism of Greek, Roman, Gothic or oriental nostalgia, but the beauty of functionalism that was to mark so many of the great engineering achievements of the early nineteenth century. The design of the structure must have been completely alien to the King's own romantic imaginings, at least as they were embodied in his visions of the East at the Pavilion. He gave no hint of his thoughts upon this portent that had appeared at Brighton, but we can imagine that it was to him a symbol of an incomprehensive new world. After contemplating it for a time, the King gave the word for the carriage to begin the journey towards the romantic parkland glades and medieval towers of Windsor.

To the inhabitants of Brighton and many of the visitors the Chain Pier opened up a new era of development for the town, enabling it to maintain and improve its place as an important seaport by providing better landing and embarkation facilities for the ever-increasing passenger and goods traffic which had been growing up between England and France. For countless years passengers had been carried to and from the packet-boats and other vessels by means of large rowing-boats called 'punts', which also did duty as tugs for pulling the rafts on which goods, luggage, horses and carriages were conveyed to and from the boats.[1] Even then, the passengers had often to be carried the last few yards to shore through the waves on the backs of fishermen and bathing-attendants.

Now the cross-Channel traffic had grown to such a size, with over a dozen sailing-packets regularly serving on the Brighton station, that a pier or jetty was an inescapable necessity. Furthermore, all the coal and almost all the merchandise that came to Brighton in those days before the railway was brought by sea and unladen on the beach, and in bad weather delays in unloading sent up the price of coals and provisions enormously. A new pier would be an immeasurable boon to traders. The company formed to build the Pier were well advised in their choice of an engineer. He was Captain Samuel Brown, who had retired after a brilliant career in the Navy, although he was not then rewarded with commensurate rank. He was a specialist in naval architecture and marine engineering, and introduced a number of improvements in the making of chain cables which resulted in their adoption by the Navy, and in the design of suspension chains for bridges, which enabled structures of this kind to be built on a far larger scale than ever before. Brown had built the Union Bridge across the Tweed at Berwick, a pier at Newhaven, near Edinburgh, and designed the iron-work for Hammersmith Suspension Bridge. While working on designs for the Menai Straits Bridge, the great engineer Thomas Telford heard of Brown's experiments. The two men met and pooled their knowledge, and Brown's innovations were incorporated in Telford's new bridge.[2] Brown's work in designing and erecting the Chain Pier was recognized by his being created a Knight of the Hanoverian Guelph Order by King William IV, and with the award of a knighthood by Queen Victoria in 1838. He died in 1852.

The Brighton Suspension Chain Pier was an extremely advanced and audacious engineering achievement for its day. It was erected in 1823, in less than twelve months, and survived for nearly three-quarters of a century. The Pier struck out into the sea from the foot of the East Cliff near the New Steine for a distance of some 350 yards. The roadway or platform was suspended on iron rods hanging from chains strung in graceful curves from the tops of four tapering towers of cast iron built on clumps of wooden piles driven into the rocky sea-bed. The fourth clump of piles carried a T-shaped platform 80 feet wide which was the actual landing-stage for ships. The beautiful tapering towers were inspired by the pylon gateways at Karnak, but it was not solely in the spirit of Egyptian romanticism that they were built in this form, which was also adopted for the towers of Brunel's Clifton Bridge at Bristol years later, but because the form that had sustained the colossal gateways and temples of Ancient Egypt was found to be ideal for the immense strains of the new engineering structures, including the great railway viaducts of some twenty years later. Thus the fanciful Egyptian taste that Napoleon and Nelson brought home from Egypt found serious fulfilment in England. At the shore end of the Pier the suspension chains were carried 54 feet into the cliff, and fastened into huge steel plates weighing 3 tons set into the cliff with cement. The Pier was reached along a new esplanade a quarter of a mile long that was built at the top of the beach, with its entrance at a toll-house near the bottom of the Steine. After the official opening on 25th November 1823 there was a grand fireworks display in the evening, and 'to give further *éclat* to the memorable day' Captain Brown gave a grand ball and supper to a hundred of his friends at his own house, where the guests were astonished to find a representation of the Chain Pier beautifully drawn in chalk on the ballroom floor by the Brighton artist Edward Fox. 'The *coup d'oeil* when the company . . . including some of the loveliest women in creation, were seated, was enchanting . . .', wrote J. G. Bishop.[3]

Today a small brass plate attached to the railings of the Madeira Drive indicates where once the Chain Pier joined the cliff, but its position is shown more exactly by the black, jagged stumps of the broken piles of the first and second towers, which at very low tides can still be seen protruding above the surface of the shingle.

In 1825 the first steam-vessels began to operate at Brighton. The *Rapid* began in May and sailed from the Pier three times weekly. The *Union* steam-packet was on the station by July. Before long a steamboat began to make daily trips to the Isle of Wight and back. The journey to or from Dieppe took nine or ten hours each way according to the weather. Soon the old sailing-vessels were completely superseded, the last of them being the *Nautilus*. With the new steam-packets the Continental traffic to and from Brighton increased enormously. On one occasion sixty passengers, with five carriages, disembarked from the *Rapid*. Whenever this crack vessel of the Brighton station arrived a cannon was fired and a large crowd never failed to gather to witness the landing.

The Chain Pier was to be destroyed in a storm in 1896, and almost exactly a year after it was opened it was subjected to a violent storm which is depicted in a well-known coloured print, but the Pier withstood the ordeal with only trivial damage, although the toll-house at the end of the Esplanade was swept away. One evening in October 1833 during a severe storm the Pier suffered disastrously when a terrible flash of lightning was seen to strike the Pier and to run along the roadway to the centre, where it developed into an immense fire. The second bridge was ruined, the roadway hanging down into the water, while for about 40 feet of the third bridge the whole of the roadway, the woodwork, railings and suspension rods had almost entirely disappeared. The third tower was forced out of the vertical, and the fourth bridge hung down several feet towards the sea. The sad spectacle of the ruined Pier was distressing to hundreds of people who had come to love the beautiful structure, and a subscription of about £1,300 was raised by means of which the Pier was rebuilt and strengthened. Little more than three years later the Pier underwent another catastrophe during a hurricane in November 1836. About midday, because of the intense force of the wind, the roadway of the centre bridge began to swing up and down, till at last one of the towers began to rock, and the supporting piles to twist, and finally the roadway platform of the third bridge was lifted up several feet, the suspension rods broke and the platform collapsed into the seas below. Again it was repaired, but attempts to raise a public subscription failed, for Brighton was then passing through a period of depression. The stimulus which had been given to the life of the town by King George IV and the lively society that surrounded him was spent.

The town was suffering from the overbuilding of a few years earlier, and in those days, just before the coming of the railway, communications between Brighton and London and other towns were insufficient to maintain its economy or to attract people to come to the town. Kemp Town was isolated, there was no public transport, and many of the houses were still untenanted. Towards the west a tangle of iron girders of the ill-fated Antheum, a great domed glass building intended as a winter garden, lay rusting in the grass where the top of Palmeira Square now is. In Adelaide Crescent only a few of the ten houses designed by Decimus Burton had been built, and the skeletons of many more unfinished houses presented a dreary sight. With the death of George IV it seemed that one glorious age had come to an end, and although a decade had passed, a new era had not yet begun.

9 King William IV

The Duke of Clarence, who succeeded to the throne in 1830 as King William IV, was as fond of Brighton as his brother had been. On receiving soon after his accession a loyal address from the High Constable on behalf of the town he replied: 'Tell the inhabitants of Brighton that I shall soon be with them.'

In August the King arrived, though not as it was hoped with the Queen. Early the following morning he appeared in the grounds of the Pavilion with John Nash, the architect, who was seen drawing in the gravel of the drive with the point of his cane, thus indicating, the observers no doubt conjectured, not without considerable misgiving, that the programme of continuous alterations at the Pavilion was not to be interrupted by the death of the late King. A fortnight later the new King made his first ceremonial visit to the town, accompanied by the Queen. They were welcomed at the gates of the Pavilion with a great triumphal arch, 50 feet high, formed of laurel, bay and flowers, where were seated 500 children of the Charity Schools 'in holiday attire', while seventy-five seamen from H.M.S. *Hyperion*, dressed in their blue jackets and white trousers, manned the top of the structure, 'in compliment to His Majesty's membership of the Naval profession'. Soon after his arrival the King sent several messages inviting Mrs. Fitzherbert to the Pavilion. Now seventy-four years old, she had been living in Brighton for a considerable time. She replied to the King explaining her inability to visit the Pavilion and describing 'the peculiar difficulties of her situation', and without hesitation the King decided to visit the old lady at her own house on the Steine. Alone with him in her drawing-room, she resolved, as she afterwards told Lord Stourton, to 'tell him everything', and place before him the marriage certificate which proved her to have been the wife of the late King, and the will he sent to her after his marriage to Princess Caroline. The King was moved to tears by Mrs. Fitzherbert's recital of her long sufferings and forbearance, and was astonished when he considered what use could have been made of the documents in her possession by a less scrupulous person at various critical stages of the late King's career. In his anxiety to make reparation the King offered to give her the title of Duchess, but this honour she declined, remembering how often such a title had been borne by a King's mistress. However, she consented to go into Royal mourning and to dress her servants henceforth in the Royal livery. A few days later Mrs. Fitzherbert accepted the Royal Family's invitation to dine at the Pavilion, and on her arrival the King hurried to the entrance to welcome her and himself helped her out of her carriage.

'I was overwhelmed with Kisses from male and female,' she wrote to her adopted daughter Minny Seymour, now Mrs. Dawson-Damer. 'The Princess Augusta was particularly gracious. I felt very nervous, never having been in the Pavilion since I was drove away by Lady Hertford. I cannot tell you my astonishment at the magnificence and the total change in that house since my first acquaintance with it. They lead a very quiet life —his family the only inhabitants. I think I counted eight FitzClarences.'

Mrs. Fitzherbert was a frequent visitor to the Pavilion from now on, and the friendliness of the Royal Family undoubtedly added to her happiness in her last years, although she was much embarrassed by the incessant quarrelling of the FitzClarences over their money and titles. 'I feel very uncomfortable with respect to the royalties,' she wrote; 'they are all very kind to me, and I feel very grateful, but you know *what it generally is* . . . the whole family are in a sad state of confusion and quarrel.'

Mrs. Fitzherbert survived until the age of eighty-one, dying in the year of the death of her protector William IV and of the accession of Queen Victoria, at the threshold of a new age with which she could have had little affinity. A contemporary newspaper account described how her coffin was slung out of her first-floor bedroom window before being carried to the hearse. She was buried near the altar in the Roman Catholic church of St. John the Baptist in Kemp Town, where a marble monument shows her as a veiled figure in a kneeling, penitential pose, wearing the wedding-rings of her three marriages upon her left hand.

Sir Shane Leslie used to describe how in her old age she came to St. John the Baptist's Church to make her confession every Saturday evening, but so that she would not have to wait kneeling in a pew with the other penitents, she was allowed to come after the church had closed, the char-woman being instructed by the Irish priest-in-charge to let her in and out. 'And when ye see her out, ye'll bob her a curtsy, for maybe she's the rightful Queen of England—and maybe she's not!'

During his first State visit to Brighton, King William IV gave an audience to Mr. Lewis Slight, Clerk to the Town Commissioners, a person whose influence in connection with the Pavilion was eventually to prove as fateful as that of its creator. Slight's purpose on this occasion was to discuss the removal of an 'eyesore' in the shape of one of the houses and a black-smith's shop adjoining it in Marlborough Row. The Commissioners had purchased the property intending to present it to the late King in order to complete his ownership of the whole property between Church Street and Castle Square, but it was now presented to King William IV. It was near this spot that the King intended to erect the North Lodge which George IV had proposed building in 1816. Although Nash had been consulted by

William IV on first coming to Brighton, he never reappeared at the Pavilion, and all the new works were carried out by Joseph H. Good, Clerk of the Works to the Board of Ordnance, who had been appointed Architect to the Royal Pavilion in 1822, after Nash had left in disgrace over the excessive cost of the building.

King William IV seems to have anticipated Queen Victoria in the insistence upon the complete separation of the monarch's State existence and private family life. All he and the Queen ever wished for in a home, he insisted repeatedly, was *to be comfortable*; a house should be *plain*, and above all should have no touch of gilding, which he told everyone he disliked extremely. It was the domestic comfort of the Pavilion and the intimate scale of the rooms, apart from the two great State Apartments, that appealed to him and his consort. At the same time he appreciated the value and importance of the Pavilion's grandeur for Royal entertaining, and the State functions held there in his reign were often much more splendid affairs and with many more official guests than had been usual in the last decade of his brother's life there. In her *Journal*, in February 1831, Mary Frampton wrote:

'The magnificence of the parties given by the King and Queen at the Pavilion at Brighton are spoken of as realizing the ideas of the entertainments spoken of in the "Arabian Nights", the dinners consisting daily of about forty persons. The King is very temperate. He consults Mrs. Fitzherbert much as an old friend in matters relating to the fetes, etc.'

Another writer commented on the King's frugality. 'The new King is most abstemious,' it was stated, 'never drinking above a pint of sherry at dinner'.[1]

The first new works to be carried out were the erection of a range of buildings at the southern entrance of the grounds opposite the Pavilion which were intended for visitors, and became known as the 'Dormitories'. Some vestiges of these buildings, of flint and yellow brick, still remain at the rear of the offices of the *Brighton and Hove Herald*. At the same time a new South Lodge was built with a scalloped Indian arch to the gateway. The historian Brayley was sorely affronted by the mean and forbidding appearance of this erection, and considered that it had 'more resemblance to a gate-house prison than to any object of architectural beauty'. A little later the Royal Stables were extended by the building of extra standings for horses, together with coach houses, a kitchen and farriers' shop, with lofts and living-quarters over them, in the open space on the eastern side of the Stables which had been intended for an indoor Tennis Court. Up till then only a screen wall at the southern end had been built. This wing was rebuilt in 1877 and became the Art Gallery and Museum.

The fulfilment of the King's recognition of the grandeur of the Royal Pavilion came with the building of the new North Lodge in 1832. Although

233

the work was carried out by Good, the inspiration may have survived in a 'model prepared by the late Mr. Nash' from which Good is said to have taken his design. Brayley recorded that it was the desire of the King that the new North Lodge should be 'a striking public ornament' and also be 'commemorative of the Palace having been provided by His Late Majesty King George IV', but it would appear from the original drawings for the North Lodge, which were discovered in 1950, that the King had in mind an even more momentous purpose, for in the original drawings appears the following inscription to be carved over the north front of the Gateway: 'The Royal Pavilion became a Royal Palace MDCCCXXX', while inscriptions at the side would announce that 'This Gateway and Lodge was erected MDCCCXXXII.' However, a less grandiloquent inscription was eventually decided upon, and above the arches on both fronts now appear simply the cipher of the King and the date of erection:

WRIIII   AD   MDCCCXXXII

The somewhat consequential inscription first suggested may not have been due to any feelings of undue grandeur on the part of the King, but to the excessive devotion of his architect.

At the same time No. 5 Marlborough Row (now North Gate House), where Lady Conyngham had lived for a while in the days of King George IV, was re-faced in oriental style to bring it into keeping with the Indian design of the North Gate. In 1830 King William IV had presented the house to his sister the Princess Augusta to serve as her residence during her visits to Brighton.[2]

Despite the great splendour of the new King's State banquets, Sailor William was no gastronome, and those of his guests who remembered the late King's *cuisine* noticed a sad falling-off in the menus and in the serving of the various dishes. 'What a change to be sure,' remarked Lord Dudley, recalling past gastronomic glories, 'cold *pâtés* and hot champagne!' The King and his consort were only too pleased after these elaborate and tiring official occasions to relax in the seclusion of the Queen's private apartments on the first floor, directly above the King's Apartments. These rooms overlooked the Western Lawn and the Royal Stables, and because of the broad balcony upon which the windows opened the rooms seemed, although in the centre of the life of the Pavilion and of Brighton, to be curiously withdrawn from it. Hardly any sound from the outside world seemed to penetrate into the rooms with their vaulted ceilings and walls covered with a Chinese wallpaper of flowering trees and shrubs on a green ground. Here the Royal couple, surrounded by young FitzClarences, were able to enjoy the simple domestic life they loved, the King dozing by the fire with the Queen busily knitting opposite.

The late King, especially in his earlier days, and many members of the

Royal Family had been accustomed to joining in the fashionable throng that promenaded upon the Steine or rode in carriages upon Marine Parade, and King William IV, who for years had pottered about the streets of Brighton by himself, made little change in his habits after his accession to the throne. While his consort, Queen Adelaide, drove out every day in her carriage to drink the waters at the Chalybeate Spa at the Wick, in St. Anne's Well Gardens at Hove, the King took his exercise walking along the cliffs, or more often on the Chain Pier, which delighted him especially because it reminded him, as he said, 'of the most beautiful place in the world—the deck of a ship'.

Only a year before his accession, as Duke of Clarence he had landed at the Chain Pier with his Duchess on returning from Dieppe. A Royal salute was fired by the guns of the frigate *Hyperion* and the Pier was illuminated, and when he came to the Throne the Pier had been the centre of a wonderful sight in the evening of his arrival in Brighton, when the Pier and the houses on the shore were illuminated and the two steam-packets and the *Hyperion*'s tender, also illuminated, sailed about discharging fireworks and Bengal lights. As King William walked up and down the Pier, he would give a bluff, boisterous greeting to everyone he passed, regardless of whether he knew them or not, and to those who fled overcome with terror at the prospect of speaking to a Royal personage he would call out, 'Don't go, don't mind me, pray don't mind me, ma'am,' and often some very ordinary person would be able to speak afterwards of having had a long informal talk with the King.

At that time there was nowhere else, except the German Spa a little way inland at Queen's Park, which was so favoured as a place of agreeable outdoor recreation as the Chain Pier. The Steine had now ceased to be the fashionable promenade it was in earlier years, because of the enormous increase in the thronging crowds of people, and the continual traffic not only of sedately trotting carriages, but the pounding horses of the fast coaches, of which about fifty a day now travelled to and from Brighton. The Pier was regarded as being kept more or less exclusively for 'select Society', by the fact that 2d was charged for admission. A number of little kiosks and shops were set up in the towers and round about for selling newspapers, sweets, toys and souvenirs, and to provide some shade in hot weather a large canvas awning was stretched over the decking. Room was even found on the large round platform at the Pier-head for a dozen shower-baths for ladies and gentlemen, 'fitted up with every convenience'. The band of the local regiment played on the pier once a week, there were displays of fireworks, and the dizzy round of entertainment was further enlivened from time to time by exhibitions such as one of the latest types of life-saving belts.

A *camera obscura* which had for years been stood near Russell House was now placed on the Pier-head. Later it was moved to the Marine Parade, just above the cliff end of the Pier. At the shore end under the cliff a saloon lounge and reading-room was established, for which a subscription of a guinea a year was charged, and concerts were held there from time to time. An excellent library was provided, with several telescopes for studying shipping and the bathers on the shore, and 'meteorological prognostications' were posted for inspection. A couple of Tyrolean musicians played 'German guitars' for the delectation of the visitors, and altogether the Saloon, or 'Bazaar', as it came to be called, was regarded as one of the most delightful places in Brighton.

A foreign resident in Brighton in those days was Count Guiseppi Pecchio, an Italian writer, administrator and liberal politician of Milan who had fled from the Austrian domination in 1821 and came to England. He married a rich heiress, Philippa Brooksbank, in 1828, and came to Brighton in that year, where he lived at Mills Terrace, Hove, until his death in 1835. A friend of the Italian economist Sismondi and of another refugee, Pannizi, Librarian of the British Museum, he wrote a number of works on finance, administration and on English poetry while in Brighton.* He wrote to his friend Baron Ugoni:

Brighton, 10 December 1828
. . . Here we are still for the next three months in a most comfortable little house close to the sea. Every morning I enjoy the Papal pleasure of having my feet washed by the Ocean. House, food, horses, everything is here even more expensive than in London. But the sky is free from fog and fumes; from October to January, Brighton is inhabited only by Dukes and Peers. Here you can see, daily and gratis, a princess of the royal blood, four duchesses, etc. taking their walk . . . *Ca vaut bien votre Girafe*. Nor is there so much etiquette as in London. The princess of Madagascar (Lady Holland) was pleased to invite me for luncheon, and to grant me admission to her evening receptions whenever I like to go. I have met there, apart from Mr. Rose, many courteous people, amongst them Mr. Hallam, whose History of the English Constitution is talked of in England with the greatest praise. In case you ever come our way, remember that there are three spare rooms in my house . . .

and again

Brighton, 6 May 1831
. . . The King whom the poets are going to treat as an *Agis* [this refers to the impending Reform laws of 1832] is a rough sailor, sans façons, loath of all refinements and foreign sillinesses, honest, frank, sincere, and nothing but firm and obstinate . . . He is the very contrast to his defunct brother. I frequently see his daughter, Mrs. Fox, who is his favourite daughter; she

has the good qualities of her father with a little more education and elegance . . . after a stay in Paris and Switzerland in August and September we'll be back in Brighton. The longer I live in this valiant island, the more do I prefer living here, and the more do I prefer it to any other place. How many courtesies I receive here every day . . .

His Italian biographer said of Brighton that it was 'a country town favoured by the English because of its seafront, its air free from fog and fume, its charming surroundings, and its healthy climate'; he mentions 'the sweet leisure of life at Brighton . . . full of attractions and satisfactions'.

King William IV was no less capable than his brother George IV of acts of personal generosity. This is revealed by a letter recently added to the Pavilion Collection* which had been sent to the King by Benjamin Kitchen, 'a poor boy 15 years old', of Radstock, Somersetshire, who wrote saying he had 'great love and a great desire to learn music, as my father is so poor and he works at a coalpit, that he cannot afford to by an instrument. If you have such a thing an old piano or any old instrument . . . if you would be so kind as to faver me with . . . when i can play well enough i will come up and play to you and I hope you will have a long and happy reinge'. A note added to the letter records that 'The King desired Lord James O'Bryen to buy him one.'

After a comparatively uneventful reign, King William IV died at Windsor on 20th June 1837.

IV

VICTORIAN MARVELS AND MYSTERIES

1840 to 1900

1 Queen Victoria

Queen Victoria never visited Brighton before her accession to the Throne, probably because of the antipathy that existed between King William IV and her mother the Duchess of Kent. At one time a house in Kemp Town had been taken for them, at 31 Sussex Square, but the proposed visit was cancelled. However, the new Queen came to Brighton only four months after her accession, on 4th October 1837. On this occasion the decorations of the northern entrance to the Pavilion were even more elaborate than they had been for the visit of William and Adelaide, the whole North Gate being turned into a Triumphal Arch covered with flowers. In the evening the dome of the Music Room, that once had resounded to the baritone voice of King George IV singing 'Glorious Apollo' and 'Mighty Conqueror', now rang to the pure clear voice of the young Queen as she sang an aria from an opera by da Costa. During this first visit, which lasted five weeks, the Queen sat to Sir David Wilkie for a State portrait, and to the sculptor Pistrucci for the new coinage.

The Queen was a little bewildered at first by the exotic strangeness of her uncle's seaside pleasure palace. 'The Pavilion is a strange, odd, Chinese-looking thing, both inside and outside, most rooms low', she wrote in her *Journal*. 'I only see a little morsel of the sea from one of my sitting-room windows.' But the following day the charm of the place had asserted itself and the sitting-room had become 'pretty and cheerful' with 'a nice little peep of the sea'.[1]

The celebrations in the town of the Queen's Coronation in June 1838 were on a scale of lavishness approaching that of the festivities for King George IV, though they were much more orderly. The chief event was an enormous repast of roast beef and plum pudding provided for 2,000 children of the town, including the 'charity children'. From the records of the quantity of meat supplied it appears that each child would have received about half a pound of beef. Furthermore each of the children was served with a glass of wine, an indulgence that would today send a spasm of horror through every child-welfare organization in the country! The Queen returned at the end of 1838, but did not come again until 1842, when she stayed for a month, accompanied by the Prince Consort and her two eldest children, the Princess Royal and the Prince of Wales. In August 1843 the three Royal children who had by then been born, the two eldest and the

Princess Alice, were left at the Pavilion while the Queen visited Louis-Philippe, the Emperor of the French. The Queen's return to Brighton in the Royal yacht, landing at the Chain Pier, was a brilliant event in the town's history, commemorated by a fine large painting of the scene by the Brighton marine painter R. H. Nibbs, in the Art Gallery's collection. A few days after her return from France the Queen embarked again from the Pier to visit her uncle, King Leopold of the Belgians, who had been the husband of Princess Charlotte. After her death he had married again, and accepted the throne of Belgium in 1830, when that country broke away from Holland.

A plan of the Pavilion which is preserved in the Library at Windsor shows the allocation of rooms in the building at the time of another Royal visit in 1845. The Queen and Prince Albert shared a bedroom on the first floor over the Entrance Hall, and this room has now been refurnished as a Royal bedroom, with a bed draped in the fashionable Louis-Philippe manner, Victorian *chinoiserie* furniture and some relics of the Queen. The two dressing-rooms of the Queen and her husband were near by, between the bedroom and the south wing, and their sitting-rooms, again side by side, were above the present South Drawing-room, overlooking the Steine.

The Queen seems to have shown far greater concern for her mother's comfort than for that of herself and her husband, for the Duchess of Kent was given the far more spacious self-contained suite of rooms which had been Queen Adelaide's private apartments, over the King's Library and Bedroom. The Royal children's rooms were above the present North Drawing-room, and their nursery dining-room and kitchen were in the projecting wing immediately north of the Entrance Portico. The original cast-iron kitchen range is still in position, and there are still bars at the window of the Dining-room. In the south wing, near the present South Gate, were Baroness Lehzen on the first floor, with Mr. Anson, Baron Stockmar, and Dr. Pretorius on the ground floor. During this visit, which was to be their last, the Queen, Prince Albert and their friends went out daily, riding on horseback or in carriages, or promenading on the Chain Pier and sea-front, but the Queen quickly found that the lack of privacy at the Pavilion, which probably more than any other cause drove the ageing King George IV in his last years to seek the seclusion of Windsor, made the place quite unsuitable for a couple who demanded the complete separation of their private family life from their State existence. Buildings of different kinds were now overlooking the Pavilion on all sides, and from the tops of coaches and farm carts passing by on the Steine all that went on on the lawns of the Pavilion could be seen. It only needed the rudeness of a section of the Brighton populace to make the Queen, 'who disliked being run after', decide to leave Brighton. Writing to her aunt, the Duchess of Gloucester, from the Pavilion in February 1845, the Queen complained 'the people are very indiscreet and troublesome here really, which makes this place quite a prison', and at the same time *Punch* published an account entitled 'The New Royal Hunt', which protested fiercely against the fact 'that a set of unmannerly curs should poke their noses under the bonnet of a Queen' and that 'Her Majesty and her Royal Consort cannot walk abroad, like other people, without having a pack of ill-bred dogs at their heels, hunting them to the very gates of the Pavilion'. In February the Royal party left Brighton for the last time, accompanied to the railway station by a troop of Dragoons. Twenty years went by before the Queen visited the town again.

2 Early Victorian Buildings: 1830 to 1850

After the death of George IV in 1830 the erection of houses in Brighton continued if not with the intensity of the previous ten years, yet still on a considerable scale, and the buildings now began to exhibit the characteristics and features of new styles that were being developed.

A link between Brighton's buildings of the late Georgian age and those of the era of William IV and Queen Victoria is provided by the architect A. H. Wilds, who, as we have seen, was working from 1822 and earlier and continued until about 1846. Park Crescent, designed by him in 1829, was his most ambitious scheme. Built on the site of Ireland's Pleasure gardens, north of the Level, and designed as a crescent enclosing private gardens, its conception was a fine one, and although the external street façade is unremarkable, it has a pleasing reticence. The proportions are good and emphasize the sweeping curve of the Crescent. The interior façade, however, facing the private gardens which the Crescent encloses, is less harmonious, the line of houses being broken by small detached attic storeys with prominent gables, which were intended to convey the picturesque character that was being sought after at the time, but which achieved instead a fussy and trivial effect. With their broad overhanging eaves and widely spaced brackets beneath, and their square tower-like attics, the houses express the Italian spirit that was being more and more favoured from about 1830 onwards. The garden is enclosed on the south side by a wall and a gateway which has a fine pair of piers surmounted by figures of a lion and a lioness.

Two or three years later Wilds was engaged on the supervision of the early stages of the erection of the ill-fated Antheum in Hove, on the site of Palmeira Square. This was another ambitious scheme for the building of a gigantic conservatory, conceived by the botanist Henry Phillips, who was apparently not at all deterred by the failure of his Oriental Garden and Athenaeum project of 1825. The Antheum (from the Greek, *anthos*— flower), for which the plans were begun in 1832, was intended to be an immense domed conservatory constructed entirely of cast iron and glass, and was expected to be the largest structure of its kind in the world, 164 feet in diameter and 64 feet high. The interior of the building was to be large enough to be laid out with gravel walks, arbours and recesses, and to be planted not only with shrubs and flowers of all kinds, but also with large tropical, oriental and European trees, in which birds would be encouraged. There was to be even a lake and a small hill of rocks, as well as seating for 800 persons.[1]

The dome itself was to be formed of cast-iron ribs carried to a depth of 10 feet into the earth and fixed to iron plates on a foundation of solid brick and masonry. It was originally intended that these ribs should be supported by the capital of a central iron pillar with bracings. Round the top of the pillar there was to be a gallery 27 feet across with an observatory in the centre. Later it was proposed to do away with the centre pillar entirely, but Wilds protested, and when overruled resigned his appointment, or according to one report was dismissed. Later the engineer in charge, C. Hillis, also departed, and building went on towards its completion under the sole direction of the contractor. Henry Phillips himself had strong misgivings about the building and desired to consult the engineer, Sir John Rennie, as to the soundness of the design, but before he could be called in the contractor removed the temporary supports without waiting for instructions, and the whole structure collapsed, less than an hour after the workmen had left the site, on 30th August 1833. The head gardener, who was attending to some of the plants inside the dome at the time, was warned of danger by the cracking of girders above him, and escaped just as the mass of glass and iron came crashing to the ground. Henry Phillips was so deeply shocked by the news of the ruin of his second great scheme that he became blind ten days later.[2] The fault in the design of the structure which led to its collapse was due, apart from the absence of the central support, to the curve of the dome being flattened, and not designed as part of the curve of a true sphere, which would have given greater strength. The tangled wreckage of twisted and broken ironwork lay untouched on the spot where it had fallen, with grass and brambles growing up through the debris. The site was then isolated, in the middle of open fields, and in certain evening lights the fantastic mass of black claw-like iron girders was silhouetted against the crimson of the western sky. Twenty years went by before the ruins were removed for the building of Palmeira Square. In 1850 Sir Joseph Paxton (then Mr. Paxton) visited Brighton with the express purpose of inspecting the remains with the object of seeing if he could find some information that might be useful to him in the designing of the immense new glass building of the Great Exhibition, which was later to be re-erected as the Crystal Palace, but it seems unlikely that he learned anything of any practical value. Wilds's next important work was the building of Montpelier Crescent, on the high part of the town near the Seven Dials, north of Montpelier Road. Here the houses are on the grandest scale in all Wilds's work, being designed as a series of large mansions, each containing two residences, the façades ornamented with pediments and pilasters, some of the latter of Ammonite form.

Nos. 1–6 and 34–38 in the Crescent are of different design and probably of later date.

Some little distance below Montpelier Crescent is Montpelier Road, where several of the houses, particularly Nos. 53–56, are by A. H. Wilds, and have Ammonite capitals. Near by is Montpelier Villas, a delightful street of small stuccoed houses built about 1845, with charming bow-windows with ironwork railings and deep canopies on the lower storey, and overhanging eaves with widely spaced brackets or consoles in the newly fashionable Italian manner. It is said that the houses were built on the site of a bluebell wood, a belief that seems to be substantiated by the large numbers of bluebells that still appear in the gardens every spring.

In 1843 Wilds took out a patent for a new method of cleaning horizontal chimney flues that he had invented, which would have done away with the need to use climbing boys, and about the same time he proposed to apply for a parliamentary Bill for the erection of a fixed breakwater at Brighton. He served as a Town Commissioner from 1845 to 1848, but was not prominent in local affairs.

In 1846 Wilds was given the commission to design the delightful Victoria Fountain in the Steine gardens, which had been laid out in 1824. The fountain was bought by public subscription and constructed in cast iron, in the form of two shallow basins, the lower one supported on three dolphins. This was his last important work in the town. Wilds lived between 1827 and 1850 at various houses in Western Terrace, including No. 8, the Western Pavilion, and at Priory Lodge, the Gothic villa, but after the latter date he seems to have retired from Brighton to Old Shoreham, for it is recorded that he died there in his seventy-third year in July 1857.[3]

The Town Hall was built in 1830, to the design of Thomas Cooper, architect of the Bedford Hotel. The building was originally designed on the plan of a cross instead of a T as completed, but the southern projection was never built. Though not as elegant a building as the hotel, it is nevertheless a very successful and scholarly exercise in classical design. The interior is severely criticized nowadays because of the enormous amount of space devoted to halls, staircases, corridors and landings, instead of offices, but Cooper's re-creation of a classical interior court, rising through three stories, gives great dignity to the interior. Constructed upon a high basement, the main portion of the building was intended to rise clear above the surrounding mass of small buildings, and as fortunately it now seems likely that the Town Hall will remain in use for many years to come, it will continue to create an impressive effect, and to stand as a noble symbol of Brighton's civic life even though high modern buildings should arise around it.

Ever since John Nash, in 1802, designed two small country houses, Cronkhill in Shropshire and Sandridge Park in South Devon, in the style of the traditional houses of the Roman Campagna, the Italian influence in house design had been growing more and more strongly in England, and there was eventually to be a fairly considerable revival of Renaissance and Palladian ideas from about 1830, so that the Italian style of house became as characteristic of the early Victorian period as the red-brick 'Christopher Wren' type of house had been of the days of William and Mary and Queen Anne. Sir Charles Barry achieved general acceptance of the Italian style in 1829 with his Traveller's Club building in Pall Mall, and in Brighton about the same time he provided what is probably his earliest important example of what was referred to as the 'non-Palladian Italian house',[4] in the shape of the Italian Villa in Queen's Park which he built for Thomas Attree.

Attree's father William had set up in No. 8 Ship Street an attorney's practice that eventually enjoyed almost a monopoly of the town's important legal business. William Attree became Clerk to the Town Commissioners and also Vestry Clerk, as well as carrying out for the Prince of Wales negotiations for the purchase of portions of land intended for the grounds of the Royal Pavilion. In later years he worked in a similar capacity for William IV. In 1825 a new Act of Parliament put the government of Brighton on a different basis, and deprived Attree of all his town appointments except that of Vestry Clerk, but although no longer regarded, as he had been, as 'The King of Brighton', he nevertheless retained enormous influence. He was Lord of the Manor of Atlingworth, Distributor of Stamps for Sussex and Surrey, and jointly with the Rev. Edward Everard was Honorary Secretary of the Sussex County Hospital.

Thomas Attree bought the whole of Brighton Park, where Dr. Struve's Royal Spa stood, and with the permission of King William IV renamed it Queen's Park in compliment to Queen Adelaide. Attree planned an ambitious scheme to build a number of detached villas in their own grounds surrounding the Park, but this project came to nothing, and the Italian Villa which Attree had built for himself by Charles Barry was the only one erected.[5] A house that achieved a dignified effect without the use of the classical orders—without the usual columns, pilasters, pediments and capitals—was a refreshing innovation. Its appeal depended more upon its simple satisfying square form, the shallow roof with its broad eaves and plain walls relieved by a loggia of three round-headed glass doors in the Italian fashion, and by light mouldings over the windows. The house is surrounded by a terrace and stone balustrades, and at the angle of the wall of the lower lawn is a little square open Ionic pavilion. The amusing dome-topped tower which stands at the north-west corner of Queen's Park and is now known as the 'Pepper-pot' was originally built as a water-tower, though later called an observatory. For many years the Villa was used as a college by the Xaverian order and was for a time afterwards derelict, but it is hoped that under new owners this beautiful example of an important phase in the domestic architecture of this country will long be preserved.

Two of the finest terraces upon the sea-front, immediately west of Chichester Terrace, are Clarendon Terrace and Percival Terrace. They were erected between 1845 and 1850 as a speculation, on land which had been sold in 1828 by T. R. Kemp to Thomas Cubitt, the London builder, in return for ten thousand pounds' worth of building work in Kemp Town and London. Later the land was bought from Cubitt by William Percival Boxall, a wealthy Brighton resident.[6]

Boxall was prominently associated with charitable work in Brighton, and had much to do with the foundation of the Children's Hospital. His son, who bore the same Christian names, achieved fame as a distinguished K.C., and as Recorder of Brighton for some seventeen years. He was one of the most humane of judges and was often known as William 'Merciful' Boxall.[7] He was deeply interested in the arts, and often lent pictures from his own collection for exhibitions in the Art Gallery.

Herbert Spencer, the philosopher, lived at No. 5 Percival Terrace from 1898 until his death in 1903. He wrote: 'I think I shall get on with my writing very well here, and hope to benefit in all respects.' Also in 1903 until his death in 1908 the adjoining houses, Nos. 3 and 4, were taken by Sir James Knowles, founder of the Metaphysical Society and of the *Nineteenth Century* magazine.[8] Trained as an architect, he designed the Thatched House Club in St. James's Street, London, and laid out Leicester Square, as well as being the designer of the Prince's Hotel in Kingsway, Hove, and several other buildings in the avenues near by. He may very well have been the architect of the Clarendon and Percival terraces, for in their reticent classical design they have much in common with the restrained Palladian outlines of the Prince's Hotel. Otherwise the architect of the terraces is unknown.

The terraces are impressively dignified in their grand scale and fine proportions. The houses have bowed fronts, but of a restrained shallow curve, unlike the exuberant curves of the late Georgian age, and instead of the deep heavy cornices of the 1820s the cornice moulding is delicate, with small dentils. There are elegant ironwork balconies to the first floors, but no canopies. The terraces are especially pleasing, not only because of their admirable design, but because they have survived in a state of good preservation. Unlike most of Brighton's great squares and terraces, the façades have not been disfigured by the later addition of extra attics, sun-roofs, porches, glazed-in balconies and other ugly accretions.

It is on a sunny hill-top overlooking Brighton, a little way above St. Nicholas's Church, that we find early Victorian charm and vigour united with Regency gaiety and exuberance, in the smart little white-stuccoed houses of Clifton Terrace, built about 1850. These were the last houses in

Brighton to be built with bonnet-like canopies above the bay-windows which are angular in the early Victorian fashion. Behind Clifton Terrace lies Powis Square, another group of charming, small Victorian houses built also about 1850, but having the bowed fronts of late Georgian inspiration rising to the full height of three storeys, but without balconies, the windows marked with the small pediments of the early Victorian Palladian revival.

Among the most imaginative developments ever carried out by the Brighton Council was the building of the Marine wall from the bottom of Middle Street to Kemp Town, a distance of a mile and a half. This gigantic work, which replaced the irregular line of crumbling cliffs which then formed the sea-front, was begun in 1827 and went on until 1838. When finished it provided a magnificent sea-front road and promenade—Marine Drive—at the upper level, and another fine sea-road—Madeira Drive—below the wall. The two roads were linked by ramps at Black Rock and Duke's Mound, a little west of Lewes Crescent.

Dr. Granville wrote:[9]

'The corporate body of Brighton may indeed claim the merit of having in a most spirited manner caused to be executed, at an expense that would have appalled even the Government, one of the finest, indeed the finest marine promenade in the world. One hundred and fifty thousand pounds applied to the erection of a lofty and solid sea-wall, in many parts sixty feet in height . . . such results, I say, and at such an expenditure of money may well be considered as a Roman work.'

The crowning feature of the whole development was the creation some sixty years later of the Madeira Terrace and arches, stretching three-quarters of a mile from the Aquarium to Duke's Mound. The work was begun in 1895, an extension which included the provision of a shelter hall and the hydraulic lift was carried out in 1896, and the whole scheme was completed by May 1898. The Terrace, which formed a broad promenade half-way up the sea-wall, was carried on columns of cast iron linked by scalloped arches of cast-iron latticework, obviously inspired by the pierced stonework arches of the Indian screen on the east front of the Royal Pavilion. Thus a covered promenade was formed the whole length of the Terrace. Above, on the Marine Drive, a magnificent range of tall cast-iron lamp-posts was erected, each carrying a pair of spiky lanterns, inspired by the Chinese lanterns of the Pavilion. The whole project of terraces, arches and lamp-posts form a remarkable example of Victorian architectural design, which it is difficult to imagine could ever be surpassed in modern terms for the sense of perfect functional fitness for purpose which they convey and the delightful sense of grace and elegance and of playful allusion to the palace of King George IV which crystallizes the atmosphere of pleasure to which the town is dedicated.

From 1901 onwards, when the Madeira Drive was given a tarmac surface for the first motor-races to be held in Brighton, the Marine Drive promenade and the Madeira Terrace below have formed an unrivalled grandstand for watching the innumerable motor-races, speed-trials, *concours d'élégance*, and the finishes of road events of every imaginable kind that have taken place ever since on the Madeira Drive below.

The two batteries of guns at Brighton survived until past the middle of the century. The West Battery, on the sea-front before the site of the present Grand Hotel, was fairly up to date with 42-pounder cannon and pyramids of cannon-balls piled alongside. On the hotel site stood the Battery House, the residence of the naval lieutenant in charge, while behind in Artillery Street were the ammunition store and powder magazine. The West Battery was removed in 1858[10] and the East Battery, at the foot of East Street, was demolished about the same time.[11]

3 Purchase of the Royal Pavilion

When Queen Victoria left the Royal Pavilion for the last time it was generally expected that the building would be demolished, and between 1847 and 1848 as many as 143 van-loads of furniture, decorations, porcelain, clocks, carpets, and other works of art were removed to Buckingham Palace and Windsor Castle. The dislike which the Queen had developed for Brighton clearly did not extend to the contents of the Pavilion, for together with King George IV's palatial furniture which had been removed from Carlton House, demolished in 1826, it formed an important part of the surroundings in which Queen Victoria spent her life. A sale of the contents of some of the smaller rooms and garden equipment of the Pavilion was held in 1847, and it was then that various articles of the furnishings which are now in private hands were purchased.

The townspeople of Brighton had by now developed a deep affection for the fantastic building that had arisen in their midst, and made numerous requests to the Government that the building should be preserved, but the Commissioners of Wood and Forests went ahead with a Bill in the Commons to 'sell or otherwise dispose of or to pull down' the Pavilion. After several town meetings and a deputation to Parliament it was agreed by the Government that the Royal Pavilion Estate should be offered to the town for the sum of £53,000. Opposition to the proposal now arose, chiefly out of personal animosity against the Clerk to the Town Commissioners, Mr. Lewis Slight, to whose intelligence, imagination and energy the entire scheme for the purchase of the Pavilion was due. Slight's response to threats of resignation from several of the Commissioners was to remove the names of all the Commissioners from the draft contract and, with sublime assurance, to substitute his own alone. The Draft Bill to purchase the Pavilion was now submitted to a Vestry meeting, and after seven and a half hours of acrimonious debate the Bill was about to be thrown out when Slight dumbfounded the Opposition by bluntly announcing that he had signed the contract himself the day before. A poll of the inhabitants was held in December 1849, with 1,343 persons voting for the Bill and 1,307 voting against. Thus by the narrow margin of thirty-six votes was the momentous decision to buy the Royal Pavilion upheld.[1]

The Royal Chapel, once the Castle Hotel Ballroom, was not included in the Estate, because the Bishop of Chichester objected that a building once consecrated could not be used for other than religious purposes. As described elsewhere, it was demolished and re-erected in Montpelier Place as St. Stephen's Church. A sum of £3,000 was allowed in compensation, so the townspeople of Brighton paid £50,000 for the buildings and grounds which must have cost nearly ten times that sum. The great building firm of Cubitt's had, in fact, offered £100,000 for the Estate and they had already prepared plans for laying out the grounds for building houses.

The Pavilion had already been denuded of its furniture. The remaining fixtures and decorations were now removed by the Board of Woods and Forests with a ruthlessness that shocked Brightonians deeply. As a writer in the *New Monthly Magazine* of 1851 recorded, 'To get at the copper bell-wire, which was afterwards sold at the nearest marine store for threepence a pound, these devastators tore off the skirting-boards in every apartment in the palace; to take down the glasses, they broke away large masses of brickwork sufficient to build another small Pavilion: to remove the hearths, they tore up the flooring with pickaxes, crowbars, jemmies, and every housebreaking instrument on which they could lay their hands; they shivered the household gods—the Chinese idols—wherever they were to be met with, either sculptured on pedestals or painted on the walls; the rare and curious paper, with all its emblems of the Celestial Empire, was torn into shreds; in short, if a pack of Kozács from the Don, a band of Red Republicans from Paris, or a host of Californian gold-seekers had been turned loose into the Pavilion, with instructions, as the Americans say, to do their——worst, they could not have committed a tithe of the ravages effected by the delegates of the "Woods and Forests", in simply *removing the fixtures!*'

New decorations, looking-glasses and chandeliers had to be provided before the building could be used, and the redecorations and refurnishing carried out between 1850 and 1851 were conceived with remarkable taste. In 1863, in response to appeals made by the Custodian of the Pavilion, Mr. P. E. De Val, Queen Victoria returned to the building the larger chandeliers and wall-paintings, which she had been unable to use, and the rooms began to reassume something of their original appearance.

For another hundred years the Royal Pavilion served as the public assembly rooms of the town, where civic and private entertaining was carried on, and balls, banquets, concerts, lectures and meetings were held. Only too often, however, the functions held in the building were sadly out of accord with its character as a past Royal residence, and were of a kind more suited to a village hall.

4 Early Victorian Writers and Artists

Of all the epithets that have ever been bestowed upon Brighton, the most famous is undoubtedly the name which Thackeray gave the place—'Dr. Brighton'. 'It is the fashion to run down George IV,' he wrote, 'but what myriads of Londoners ought to thank him for inventing Brighton! One of the best physicians our city has ever known is kind, cheerful, merry Dr. Brighton! Hail, thou purveyor of shrimps and honest prescriber of Southdown Mutton! There is no mutton so good as Brighton mutton; no flies so pleasant as Brighton flies; nor any cliff so pleasant to ride on; no shops so beautiful to look at as the Brighton gim-crack shops, and the fruit-shop and the market.' The novelist often stayed in Brighton during the 1840s, usually at No. 62 East Street, but also at Pegg's Hotel, the Bedford Hotel, and at Mutton's Hotel. In 1846 he lived at No. 54 Grand Parade. One year he took a house for himself and his family at the corner of Marine Square.[1] Amongst his many contributions to *Punch* were four articles on Brighton. In one of them he made a sly but penetrating attack on certain lodging-house keepers who charged as much as a guinea a day for a room, or nearly £100 a month for 'three rooms, and a bedstead disguised as a chest of drawers in the drawing-room'. Thackeray confessed to having received afterwards over fifteen score of letters in protest from lodging-house keepers, who complained that his article had 'passed like a whirlwind over the lodging-houses of Brighton and prematurely closed their season', but he was unrepentant, and commented upon various letters he had received from 'Mrs. Skrew', 'Mr. Squeezer' and 'Mr. Skiver'. Readers of *Vanity Fair* will remember that George and his bride spent their honeymoon at the Old Ship Hotel at Brighton, where the promenade afforded the prospect of bow-windows on the one side and blue sea on the other. 'Brighton, a clean Naples with genteel lazzaroni,' Thackeray described it, 'Brighton, that always looks gay and gaudy, like a harlequin's jacket; Brighton which used to be seven hours distant, but is now only a hundred minutes off. . . .' Lord Steyne, the elderly rake in *Vanity Fair*, is believed to have been modelled upon the Prince Regent's friend Lord Hertford, and the figure of Lady Southdown, the devout nonconformist with her pamphlets about salvation, to have been drawn from the mother-in-law of Lady Huntingdon, founder of the famous dissenting 'Connexion' which had a church in North Street.

Thackeray was a frequent visitor to the literary parties held at No. 21

253

Sillwood Place by Eliza and Rosalind Smith, the two unmarried daughters of Horace Smith the novelist, continuing the salon formerly held there by their father. Other personalities who attended these brilliant gatherings were Dr. Gideon Mantell the geologist; Charles Dickens, Harrison Ainsworth, Charles Young the actor, Thomas Hood, Samuel Rogers, the Rev. Sydney Smith, Charles Kean, Copley Fielding the landscape painter and Henry Buckle the historian.

In January 1851, Thackeray gave at the Town Hall his lectures on *The Four Georges*, originally intended for republican Hanoverian-hating American audiences and in which Thackeray vented his spleen upon the memory of George IV—'But this George, what was he? I look through all his life and recognize but a bow and a grin. I try and take him to pieces, and find silk stockings, padding, stays, a coat with frogs and a fur collar, a star and blue ribbon, a pocket-handkerchief prodigiously scented, one of Truefitts' best nuttey-brown wigs reeking with oil, a set of teeth and a huge black stock, underwaistcoats, more underwaistcoats and then nothing.' When asked by Henry Martin, the Brighton historian, why he did not give his lecture on George IV in the Pavilion he had created, Thackeray replied that he 'did not like to abuse a man in his own house'.[2]

Charles Dickens stayed at Brighton at many different times from 1837 until 1868, on the first occasion at the Old Ship, and once at the Junction House Hotel, but later mostly at the Bedford Hotel. It was there that he wrote much of *Bleak House*, and also of *Dombey and Son*. Readers of the latter novel will remember that it was at the Bedford Hotel that Captain Cuttle called to negotiate a loan for the unfortunate Solomon Gills, and that little Paul Dombey was placed under the care of Mrs. Pipchin to begin his schooling in that 'infantine boarding-house of a very select description in a steep by-street of this town, where the soil was more than usually chalky, flinty and sterile, and where the front gardens grew nothing but marigolds and—snails!' From then the child passed to Dr. Blimber's Academy, which Harrison Ainsworth asserted was located at 1 Chichester Terrace.

Dickens was an even more popular speaker than Thackeray, and in giving readings from his works at Brighton, also at the Town Hall, used his fine voice and great histrionic talent to the full in exploiting the rich dramatic quality of his material, so that his audience were convulsed with laughter in the comic passages and overcome with weeping in the sadder episodes, especially when Dickens read of the death of Mrs. Dombey, telling how her spirit 'drifted out into the dark and unknown sea that rolls round the world . . .' Dickens used to have audiences of 1,000 persons in the upper room at the Town Hall, and he told a friend that everywhere he had 'found that peculiar personal relation between my audience and myself on which I counted most when I entered on this enterprise'.

For some thirty years after the visit of Thomas Rowlandson and his friend Henry Wigstead to Brighton in 1789 topographical artists and water-colour painters of greater or lesser fame had been coming to the town in ever increasing numbers in search of picturesque subjects, and especially to make drawings from which engravings could be made to sell to visitors.

During a number of weeks in the summer of 1824 the fishermen on the beach became accustomed to seeing the figure of a man perched on a fol-ding stool drawing the scene with a paintbox on his knees, and his paper or a piece of millboard resting on the lid, or else walking about on the beach making quick drawings in his sketchbook of boats, capstans, anchors and fishermen's huts. It was the landscape painter John Constable, to whom the clear, sparkling air and sunshine of Brighton seemed especially attrac-tive in those days when London was overhung with dense acrid smoke from a multitude of chimneys, and the Thames was one great sewer. Constable said, 'There is not a healthy man in London, such is the state of the atmosphere and the mode of life,' and the painter was glad to bring his wife and children to spend the summer at Brighton nearly every year from 1824 to 1830. If ever he had to return to London, he left his family at the seaside.

Although his name was never mentioned in the 'Fashionable Chronicle' of new arrivals in the local newspapers, nor indeed even remarked upon by any of Brighton's later historians, John Constable was to bring a degree of fame to Brighton hardly less than did Dr. Russell and King George IV. 'I am looking for a month's quiet here,' he wrote to his friend Archdeacon Fisher of Salisbury in July 1824, 'and I have brought with me several works to complete.' Constable, one of the greatest of all English land-scape painters, was then engaged in preparing seven pictures for exhibi-tion at the Louvre in Paris that year. 'My purchasers say they are much looked for at Paris', he wrote. 'The Director of the Academy at Antwerp, Mr. Vanbree, has been here; he says they will make an impression on the Continent.' Indeed, Constable's landscape pictures at that time, painted with the poetic realism that was so different from the stilted formulae practised up till then, were rather less well appreciated in this country than in France, where they were to awaken artists to an awareness of the nature of light and colour that was eventually to lead to the great achievements of Impressionism.

As Constable sat on the beach his all-seeing artist's eye took in far more than his immediate subjects. What he saw around him was not altogether to his taste, but his pen dashed off impressions as graphic as those of his pencil.

'I am busy here, but I dislike the place, and miss any letter from you', he wrote to his friend Archdeacon Fisher on 29th May.[3] 'I am however getting on with my French affairs; one of the largest is quite complete, and is my best in sparkle with repose, which is my struggle just now. Brighton is the receptacle of the fashion and the off-scouring of London. The magnificence of the sea, and its, to use your own beautiful expression, 'everlasting voice', is drowned in the din and tumult of stage-coaches, gigs, flips, &, and the beach is only Piccadilly or worse by the seaside. Ladies dressed or undressed; gentlemen in morning-gowns and slippers, or without them or anything else, about knee-deep in the breakers; footmen, children, nursery-maids, dogs, boys, fishermen; and Preventive Servicemen with hangers [cutlasses] and pistols; rotten fish, and those hideous amphibious animals, the old bathing-women, whose language, both in oaths and voice, resembles men, all mixed together in endless and indecent confusion. The genteeler part, on Marine Parade, is still more unnatural, with its trimmed and neat appearance, and the dandy jetty or Chain Pier, with its long and elegant strides into the sea a full quarter mile [here he drew a sketch]. In short there is nothing here for a painter but the sea and sky, which have been lovely indeed, and always varying.'

The great painting of which Constable wrote was exhibited at the Royal Academy in 1827. Six feet long and four feet wide, it now dominates the room where it hangs at the Tate Gallery. In it he has brought together many of the separate glimpses rendered in his small sketches and united them in one grand composition. In the foreground is the beach rising up to the left, with boats, an anchor, and pieces of timber in front, and a brilliant patch of sunshine lighting the waves to the right. The figures of people strolling by the edge of the sea lead the eye towards the Chain Pier in the distance, and to the parade of smart new stucco-fronted houses on the East Cliff. The sky is filled with dramatically lit stormy-looking clouds. Like many of Constable's grand works, it was of necessity created in the studio, and possesses a rather solemn grandeur that is lacking in his smaller sketches with their vivid immediacy, but is the greatest commemoration of Brighton ever achieved in the world of art.

The sense of excitement that is the essence of the spirit of Brighton is conveyed with greater intensity and within the space of a few inches only in his small oil-sketches, several of which are to be seen at the Victoria and Albert Museum. In 'Brighton Beach with Colliers' there is the deep blue of the summer sea, the intense luminosity and lighter blue of the sky, the burning gold of the sun-drenched beach, and the black smudges of the coal-boat hulls. Another sketch, of a 'Windmill near Brighton', evokes the deep gold of ripening corn in a field on the Downs, the shimmering heat, and the sky full of windy hurrying clouds. Two small pen and ink sketches in the Brighton Art Gallery are of fishing-boats on the beach, one of them so expressively drawn that one seems almost to feel on one's cheek the wind that is tearing at the corner of a sail, and to hear the slap of ropes against a mast. There is in Constable's sketches of this time a liberated

BRIGHTON BEACH, 1864
Water-colour by 'Cuthbert Bede' (Edward Bradley)

THE LAST JOURNEY OF KING GEORGE IV

The removal of Chantrey's statue from the Steine to the North Gate, 1922

THE 'BRIGHTON BELLE'

by horse-brake to the Devil's Dyke, *c.* 1908

FLYING AT BRIGHTON, 1912

OPENING OF VOLK'S ELECTRIC RAILWAY, 1883

'DADDY-LONG-LEGS':
Volk's Brighton to Rottingdean Seashore Electric Railway, 1896

THE EMANCIPATION MOTOR-CAR RUN, 14TH NOVEMBER, 1896:
at the Hotel Metropole

VOLK'S ELECTRIC RAILWAY, *c.* 1908

THE FISH MARKET, *c.* 1908

'THE BEACH HOTEL'

'SKETCHING FROM NATURE'

'DON'T BE FRIGHTENED, DEAR!
IT'S ONLY A LITTLE SWELL
FROM THE PIER!'

Lithographed by G. J. Basebi after drawings by 'Alfred Crowquill', 1848

THE GOTHIC HOUSE, WESTERN TERRACE, 1880
Built by Amon Henry Wilds, 1828

THE WESTERN PAVILION,
residence of Amon Henry Wilds, architect, 1828

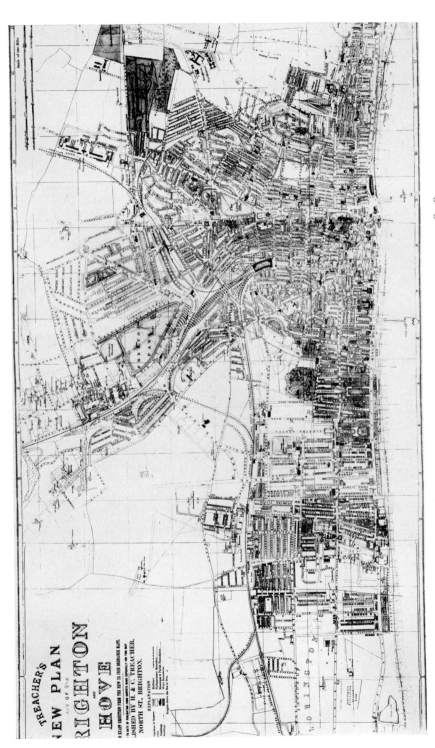

TREACHER'S NEW PLAN OF BRIGHTON AND HOVE, 1898

quality which suggests that the atmosphere of the place and the happiness of his wife and children there brought him a degree of relaxation and happiness he was hardly ever to enjoy again.

Another giant of the English romantic movement in painting, James William Mallord Turner, must have visited Brighton on several occasions, no doubt while staying at Petworth House with his patron and friend Lord Egremont. No written record of his visit to Brighton survives, other than some short notes in his 'Brighton and Arundel' Sketch Books of 1830, preserved at the British Museum, in which there appear in Turner's handwriting the following notes under the heading 'A View Looking Out to Sea with a Sailing Boat':

'Beautiful effect of—' 'Green Top' (i.e. the waves), 'foam grey in shade', 'reflections of the Boat . . . in water', 'Reflection of the B[u]oy on the Sail', 'The warmth of the Tan Sail', etc.

Perhaps it was from these notes that he painted the large sketch in oils of 'The Old Chain Pier, Brighton', which is now in the Tate Gallery's collection, and also composed the finished version of the same subject which can be seen today at Petworth. In these luminous and peaceful works the sun, which is shining in a golden haze, is lighting to a warm glow the deep red of a fishing-boat's sail, while the reflections of the boat and sail, as well as of the long, filigree lines of the Chain Pier itself, are seen reflected in the calm, pearly-grey sea. Another picture at Petworth, 'A Ship Aground', which appears to be a pendant to the Chain Pier painting, is in the same mood of peaceful luminosity, despite the slight swell and the movement of the small craft around the disabled ship. Some five years earlier Turner had painted in water-colour a 'View of Brighton from the Sea', this time in more stormy conditions, with small boats and the Chain Pier in the foreground, and the town and beach in the distance, with the old church on the skyline, the Steine and Royal Pavilion to the left, and the grand houses of the East Cliff extending to the right. This water-colour was published as an engraving by George Cook in 1825 in the topographical work *Harbours of England*, which was one of several popular volumes for which Turner provided the illustrations.

5 The Railway, 1820 to 1860

The use of steam-engines of a primitive sort in the mines and factories of the north had been growing during the later years of the eighteenth century, and it had even been suggested that an invalid chair like the Regent's 'Merlin' chair might be propelled by a small portable steam-engine, but generally the 'miraculous power of steam' was regarded as something to stimulate the fertile imaginations of George Cruikshank and other caricaturists, which ran riot with fantasies of carriages and even airships driven by this means. Before long reports were reaching Brighton of experiments in the new form of locomotion, in which a steam-engine was used instead of horses to draw trucks on the iron railroads of the north, and in 1813 there came the news of 'Puffing Billy', the first successful steam-locomotive to run on smooth rails.

The first suggestion to build a railway between Brighton and London was made as early as 1823,[1] two years before the first public railway in the world had opened between Stockton and Darlington. This was put forward in a pamphlet by William James illustrating 'the advantages of direct inland communications through Kent, Surrey, Sussex and Hants, to connect the metropolis with the ports of Shoreham (Brighton), Rochester (Chatham) and Portsmouth by a line of engine rail-road . . .'. Two years later a company was formed with the object of constructing a line in accordance with James's proposals.

William James (1771–1837) was a solicitor, land agent and colliery-owner, and a far-sighted enthusiast for canal undertakings and early railroads, a number of which he surveyed and constructed. In 1824 he became bankrupt, chiefly because of the gigantic expense of his fruitless search for coal in Sussex, and he never recovered financially. His south country railway scheme shows that he clearly conceived the capabilities of a railroad worked by steam-engines, but nothing came of his proposal. Two years after the formation of James's company the great engineer Sir John Rennie proposed building a railway from London to Bristol *via* Brighton, Southampton, Salisbury and Bath for the Surrey, Sussex, Hants, Wilts and Somerset Railway; also in 1825 a town meeting at the Old Ship decided in favour of building an iron railway from Brighton to Shoreham. The railway was to bring coal from Shoreham, and thus dispose of the nuisance of collier-boats landing coal on the beach. All these early proposals were chiefly with the object of transporting goods and merchandise rather than passengers, and it was, in fact, the need to provide for this kind of heavy traffic, for coal and iron-ore especially, that had brought the 'iron-railway' into being, and in which it had proved its practicability. None of these early schemes were acted upon, however.

During the 1830s several steam-driven coaches were operating over short distances in various parts of the country. Walter Hancock was one of the chief pioneers of this form of travel and in 1828 proposed a service of his 'land-steamers' between London and Brighton, but he did not actually appear on this road until November 1832, when he made a trial trip at the wheel of his steam-carriage the 'Infant'. The contrivance made the journey down to Brighton without the slightest difficulty in six hours, a slower time than that of the best coaches on account of the frequent stops for water and 'the heavy and unfavourable state of the roads'. The return journey on the following day, although successfully accomplished, was delayed by a mechanical breakdown in starting.

In October 1833 a fourteen-seater coach of Hancock's bearing the ominous name 'Autopsy', which had been running successfully as an omnibus between Paddington and Stratford, drove to Brighton from the works at Stratford in eight and a half hours, of which three hours were taken up by a halt on the road. In the same year Sir Charles Dance's steam-carriage set out for Brighton from Wellington Street, Strand. It consisted of a large van holding fifteen passengers, which a contemporary writer declared 'compared unfavourably for beauty with a prison-van'. This was towed by a four-wheeled road-locomotive, one of Gurney's steam-carriages, which was rather like a large horse-coach with a wide, stumpy conical chimney on top. It drove the fifty-two miles down to Brighton in five and a quarter hours and returned in a slightly shorter time. Although the steam-coaches met with some success, their chief appeal was as a novelty. Their great disadvantages were the limited number of passengers they could carry, and also the small quantities of coal and water they could take, which forced them to make frequent stops for refuelling. Their failure was to some extent due to their designers not being able to free themselves from the tradition of the horse-coach, which they tried to adapt, instead of designing a completely new type of vehicle.

A few progressive spirits realized that the population of Brighton was now steadily diminishing, and that the town was in a decline because it had outgrown its transport system, but apart from these there were not many people in Brighton who felt that a railway was an urgent necessity. The ugly, black steam-engines pouring out clouds of filthy smoke over the countryside were felt to be quite alien to the traditions of the town, in which the gay, dashing coaches with their splendid horses had played so romantic a part. It was not until 1835 that the railway question began to be seriously considered, and a committee was then formed to discuss the merits of the six different lines which had been proposed for the town. These arguments chiefly revolved around the rival merits of Sir John Rennie's 'Direct Line', which would pass through Clayton, Haywards Heath, Merstham and Croydon, and the 'Natural Line' proposed by Robert Stephenson, son of the famous George Stephenson. This was planned to avoid steep gradients and tunnels, and was to pass through Shoreham, Horsham and Dorking. Endless meetings were held, and at length a Parliamentary Enquiry took place, which cost the various promoting companies nearly £200,000. It lasted eighty days, during the whole of seven of which Sir John Rennie was in the witness-box. The Government then stepped in and appointed Captain Robert Alderson of the Royal Engineers to report on the problem. He decided in favour of Rennie's Direct Line, considering that the expense of the five miles of tunnelling would be more than offset by the shorter length of the route, and by the absence of steep gradients. Also, Rennie's proposed termini were rightly thought to be more conveniently placed, the Brighton station for the 'Natural Line' being planned to go behind Brunswick Square, a proposal that aroused strong opposition from the residents. The Bill authorizing the construction of Rennie's Direct Line received the Royal Assent in July 1837. The route was then re-surveyed in detail and the construction of the line went ahead under the London and Brighton Railway Company's chief engineer. This individual was John Urpath Rastrick, who was far from being the least distinguished amongst the remarkable generation of early nineteenth-century engineers.

Rastrick was born in Northumberland in 1780. He patented a steam-engine as early as 1814, and a year later was building a cast-iron bridge over the Wye at Chepstow. He worked closely with George Stephenson, and was one of the judges who chose the 'Rocket'. He was a member of the Institution of Civil Engineers and a Fellow of the Royal Society, and throughout the whole of his career displayed remarkable boldness, resolution, shrewdness and coolness, qualities that he needed to overcome the immense difficulties that faced him in the construction of the Brighton line. Because of the very heavy work involved in making the Merstham, Balcombe and Clayton tunnels, Stephenson himself had said the line was quite impracticable. Rastrick is buried in the Extra-mural Cemetery at Brighton.

Quite early in the history of the establishment of the railway there arose a serious challenger to the steam-locomotive, in the form of atmospheric propulsion. In 1826-7 a Mr. Vallance made proposals for an atmospheric railway to Brighton, in which the carriages were to be drawn by being attached to a piston in a tube about a foot in diameter, which lay between the rails. The tube had a continuous slit in the top, through which the fastening to the piston passed, and the slit was sealed by a leather flap coated with soft composition.

At intervals of three miles along the track the pipe was connected to pumping machinery driven by steam-engines, which extracted the air in the pipe before the piston, and the train was drawn along with great speed and force by the resulting vacuum. It was claimed that speeds of over 100 miles an hour could be reached and that collisions would be impossible. However, the inventor could not overcome the scepticism of his Brighton clients and the project failed. An atmospheric line was eventually built in 1845 between Forest Hill and West Croydon, and ran with some success, speeds of forty miles an hour being usual, and seventy miles an hour achieved occasionally, but the railway failed because of the unreliability of the sealing system, which was evidently susceptible to changes of weather and temperature, while the tallow composition proved irresistibly attractive to rats.

The first ground for the Brighton steam railway was broken at the great cutting north of Merstham Tunnel on 12th July 1838. The promoters of the Direct Line had realized the importance of linking Brighton with the harbour at Shoreham, and a branch railway to this place was constructed at the same time as the main line. The work involved the driving of a tunnel under the Dyke Road, the making of several cuttings beyond Hove and the building of a viaduct over the New England road. The work was pursued with feverish activity night and day by large teams of Irish navigators, or 'navvies', who although rough, uncouth and addicted to drinking and fighting at the week-ends, were nevertheless fiercely dedicated to their work of building the railroads, and took pride in their ability to work harder than two or three ordinary labourers.

The Shoreham Branch was, in fact, the first Brighton railway to be completed, and it was opened in May 1840 by the Directors, in the presence of Sir John Rennie. The band of the 12th Lancers played popular airs while the intending passengers were entering the station. 'As the clock was on the strike of three, the music took up the strains of the popular air *Off, off said the stranger.* . . . Precisely at three the whistle was blown . . . the train moved slowly, the band playing the National Anthem. The spectators who lined the sides of the cutting now commenced a "hurrah"; but before the first strains of music could be completed the engine was seen to be making rapid revolutions without biting the rails.' The brakes of the carriages had apparently been left on. When the trouble was remedied it was possible to start, and 'as the train proceeded with great velocity through the cutting and tunnel, repeated "hurrahs" were heard from the spectators, who had assembled in multitudes along the side of the cutting, on the New England bridge, at the north of the tunnel and on the bridges beyond.'[2]

The first train with a select company of 230 passengers made the journey to Shoreham in twelve minutes: the return trip took fifteen and a half minutes. A thousand free tickets had been issued and the trains continued to carry passengers all through the afternoon. In the evening the Directors entertained a large party to a splendid dinner at the Old Ship Hotel. During the next day 1,750 passengers were carried, many of them visiting the Swiss Gardens at Shoreham, a favourite pleasure resort immortalized in the opening pages of George Moore's novel *Esther Waters*. From the first day a horse-omnibus ran between Kemp Town and Brighton in connection with the trains, and by this means the isolation of the great Estate was broken down. In May 1940 the ominous news of the French collapse and of the British retreat towards Dunkirk did not prevent a quiet recognition of the centenary of the opening of the railway, in the form of a small exhibition of contemporary pictures and documents held in the Royal Pavilion, and organized by the Southern Railway.

Meanwhile rapid progress was being made on the main line. In March 1841 the beautiful Ouse viaduct was completed, crossing one of the loveliest valleys in Sussex, near Ardingly. Designed by the Company's architect, David Mocatta, in conjunction with Rastrick, it is one of the most elegant examples of early railway architecture, with its thirty-seven tall arches and eight charming little Italianate pavilions, four at each end of the viaduct, and the delightful stone balustrades. The Merstham and Balcombe tunnels were finished about the same time and it then became possible to open the main line as far as Haywards Heath in July 1841. Passengers were then carried between there and Brighton by horse coaches, the entire journey taking four hours. The complete line was not finished until September 1841; it had taken three years to build at a total cost of over £2,000,000. The opening took place on 21st September, and the occasion was regarded as something of a holiday by most people in the town. The day began with the ringing of the bells of St. Nicholas's Church, and in spite of a heavy sea-mist, large crowds of people assembled on the green slopes around the terminus to watch the departure of the first up-train, which left at a quarter to seven and reached London soon after nine. During the morning the mist dispersed and by noon it was a beautiful sunny autumn day. Enormous crowds had now gathered to see the crowning event of the day, the arrival of the first train carrying the Directors and their official guests and friends. Almost the whole population of Brighton seemed to have assembled at the station or on the grassy slopes overlooking the railway. The *Brighton Herald* reported with enthusiasm:

'... the aspect of the whole terminus—the light wide-spreading sheds which receive the trains, the spacious colonnades around the station-house, and the numerous offices within this beautiful structure, was the general theme of admiration ... every field and meadow, from Preston to Withdean and Patcham, had its mass of human life.

'It was along these elevated points, which look down on the railroad, that the approach of the train was first perceived. . . .'

The first sign of its coming was the appearance of a cloud of steam from the mouth of Patcham tunnel, and the next moment the long black train of ten carriages was seen gliding along towards the terminus. On its arrival at the station the band of the Scots Greys played the National Anthem and the Directors and their friends alighted. Very soon afterwards a second train arrived which was said to have done the journey in an hour and three-quarters. Along the route, at Haywards Heath, Hassocks and Clayton, country people from miles around had gathered to see the trains go by.

Thousands of tickets for admission to the Brighton station-house were issued, and the visitors were amazed by the sight of the vast arching roof of glass upheld by daringly slender columns of cast iron. The architect of the station-house was David Mocatta, a talented pupil of Sir John Soane, who built most of the stations and bridges of the line, as well as the Ouse via-duct; and the façade was designed by him in the delightful Italian style that he adopted for most of the railway's buildings, even for the smallest but none the less charming signalmen's cottages. Unhappily the station front has for long been hidden behind later clumsy and ugly additions to the original building.

In the evening most of the houses were illuminated to celebrate the occasion, there was a firework display in Ireland's Royal Gardens north of the Level, and the Directors of the Company were invited by the Town Commissioners to a banquet at the Old Ship at which were served turtle soup, turbot, venison, game and joints with endless side-dishes, sweets and puddings. In the speeches that were made it was said that Brighton was now on the grand route between London and Paris, and would 'become the direct communication between the two great capitals of the greatest King-doms on the earth'. This prophecy was hardly fulfilled. The Company's chairman, John Harman, also expressed the belief that 'the traffic likely to come to Brighton would be very superior, and that as Brighton was one of the first watering-places in the Kingdom, the railway would be trans-porting the most respectable and the highest families in the Kingdom to the resort at certain seasons of the year.' The Directors had tried to pro-vide accommodation for this class of visitor to travel in the greatest com-fort by running certain trains for first-class passengers only. Although second-, third- and even fourth-class carriages were also provided, the two last were extremely primitive at first, hardly better than cattle-trucks. They were completely uncovered and some were even without seats. The passengers had to endure the smoke, fumes and sparks from the engine, and 'an almost constant descent of fine ashes'. These conditions were especially trying in strong wind or rain and while going through the tunnels.

The times taken by the different classes of trains for the journey in the first years were one hour and forty-five minutes for expresses, two hours for first-class trains and two hours and a half for mixed trains. These last stopped at every station. The fares were 14s 6d first class, 9s 6d second class and about 4s third class for the 'Parliamentary' trains, which were run once a day at a statutory charge of 1d a mile, and stopped at every station.

A line from Brighton to Lewes was opened in June 1846, and before the end of the same month a line was open eastwards as far as Hastings. The west coast line from Brighton to Shoreham was extended to Worthing in 1845, to Chichester in 1846, and Portsmouth in 1847. By that time as many as fifty-four passenger trains were starting from or arriving at Brighton every day, as well as many goods trains, and the station was always thronged with people.

The audacious and far-sighted planning which Rennie had devoted to the cuttings, tunnels and viaducts of the railway was evident also in his imaginative final choice of the site for the station. The easiest site presenting itself would have been on the Level or the Steine north of the Pavilion, but Rennie realized that this would have destroyed the character and amenities of the town's centre. No other suitable level place offered itself, so Rennie decided to create one by excavating a plateau from the side of the eastern slopes of the Dyke Road ridge, at a height of 130 feet above sea-level. The gigantic task of cutting into the chalk hillside and building the station employed 3,500 men and 570 horses. The siting of the station aroused a great deal of criticism at the time from those who regarded it as being too far from the town, but the growth of Brighton has proved the wisdom of Rennie's choice.

To carry the line to Lewes from this site across the London Road a viaduct was necessary, and this remarkable example of railway engineering was built in only ten months, the last arch being completed in March 1846. There were many objections to a viaduct in the beginning, but this was chosen because an embankment, although cheaper, would have obliterated a great many houses and blocked one of the principal approaches to the town. One of the chief objections to a viaduct was that it would be liable to be blown up by an enemy and this is, in fact, what happened, when the viaduct was bombed in a low-level daylight raid by German Focke-Wulf bombers in May 1943, and the central arch destroyed. However, within four hours the gap had been bridged with girders and trains were once more crossing again.

The viaduct was built on a bold curve, and was constructed chiefly of stone and yellow stock bricks. It is 400 yards long, 67 feet high where it crosses the London road, and consists of one central elliptical arch 50 feet in span and twenty-six other semicircular arches of 30 foot span. It was magnificently conceived and built, and we now regard it as among the finest achievements of early railway architecture, with a beauty that arises from its faultless lines and proportions and from its functional adequacy that survives today after a hundred and twenty years. Even at the time it was built it was considered an impressive sight, one visitor reporting 'that it gave quite a classical character to the scenery', appearing to him no doubt like a Roman aqueduct in a romantic landscape by Claude. Another writer said that it had 'a most magnificent appearance from whatever point it may be viewed'. Certainly when new, its brickwork not yet grimed by smoke and shining in the sunlight, and with its splendid curve unobscured by the buildings that have grown up around it since, it must have been a magnificent sight, the tall arches striding across the green tree-covered slopes of the Preston valley. It was thus that it was seen, framing the extreme northern edge of the town far beyond the main mass of Brighton's buildings, when a remarkable drawing of the town was made from a French balloon in August 1846, a lithograph from which is to be seen in the Royal Pavilion.

The line crossed the Lewes road by an immense skew-bridge of similar design and construction to the viaduct, and like it still much admired as a splendid example of early railway architecture.

The greatest engineering feat in the construction of the entire line from London to Brighton was the making of the Clayton Tunnel through the South Downs, at a depth of 270 feet and for a distance of 2,266 yards. The prevalent Italian style of the railway buildings was departed from in this instance for the tunnel entrances, for these were designed in the castellated style beloved of early Victorian devotees of the romantic. It is possible also that the castellated style was adopted in the hope that nervous passengers, especially those in open third-class carriages, would have their fears of the tunnel collapsing upon them allayed by the impression of massive strength, like that of a medieval castle, that would be given them by this style. A signalman's cottage was built into the northern entrance, and this was occupied until quite recent years. Although the occupants became oblivious in time to the noise of the trains, they never ceased to be startled when the penetrating screech of the whistle sounded through the house as a train entered the tunnel.

The coming of the railway truly marked the beginning of the modern age for Brighton. Apart from all the social and economic advantages it brought—the rapid movement of immense numbers of people for business and pleasure; and the transport of vast quantities of goods and merchandise making possible the expansion of a large and attractive residential resort away from London—the railway brought into the life of the south a new scale of existence. To the vision of a population not usually accustomed to human creations on a scale greater or more complicated than that of the horse-coach, was now presented the staggering ingenuity and audacity of the railway with its deep cuttings, long tunnels driven through the Downs; the immense Ouse Valley and Preston viaducts, and the steam-locomotives that drew their long burdens with almost unfailing certainty and precision. The astonishing thing about the railway was the suddenness with which it became firmly established as the principal means of transport, carrying enormous numbers of passengers and immense tonnages of goods with undreamed-of speed. The great virtue of the railway that brought this about was its phenomenal reliability. Unlike the early days of the motor-car and the aeroplane, in which their progress was delayed and frustrated by continual breakdowns and disasters, the early history of steam locomotion was generally marked by a very small proportion of failures and accidents. Even such tragedies as the Clayton Tunnel disaster of 1861, in which twenty-three people were killed and 175 injured through a signalling failure, seemed only to emphasize the normal dependability of the railway. The reason lay in the basic simplicity of the steam-locomotive and the almost complete dependability of the track, whereas the coaches were frail vehicles, subject to the fatigue and collapse of horses and to the impassability of the roads in bad weather. The immediate success of the railway where Brighton was concerned was due very largely to the fact that the town had lagged behind some other towns like Bath and Southampton in adopting this method of transport fifteen years after the opening of the first public railway in Yorkshire, by which time steam-locomotion had already amply proved itself. In any event, steam had been brought to a high stage of efficiency long before it was applied to public transport.

On the coming of the railway the coach traffic dwindled away immediately almost to nothing. A few months before the trains began running the coach proprietors saw that their traffic was doomed and made a last effort to reap a harvest by increasing their fares by about half, to 12s outside and 21s inside. Within a fortnight of the railway's opening they were reduced to 6s outside and 12s inside. Almost overnight splendid horses, for which at one time a price of from sixty to a hundred guineas would have to be paid, could be bought for ten or less. A diminishing number of old-fashioned and timorous people continued to travel by coach while they could, but by 1843 their journeys were run by only one firm in Brighton, the 'Red' coach office, owned by Mr. Capps, who kept a single coach, the 'Victoria', running until as late as November 1845. A few years later that most splendid of all the Brighton coaches 'The Age' began running again, in the summer only, not for serious travellers, but for the sake of a few romantic enthusiasts who looked back with nostalgia to the days of the coaches, smartly painted in scarlet, yellow, blue and black and drawn by glossy-coated half-blood horses; of the guard with his yard-long shining copper trumpet; of the ostlers at a posting-house unharnessing a team of smoking animals almost before they had come to a standstill and buckling in a fresh team of horses that immediately lunged their weight into the collars and were off again at full speed.

'The Age' was kept running in much the same spirit as in 1959, after steam-locomotives had been abolished, a private company of enthusiasts bought the famous 'Bluebell Line' branch of the Southern Railway in mid-Sussex and continued to run it as a holiday diversion with various celebrated types of engines and carriages.

But the passing of the coach was no bad thing in one respect, in that it brought to an end an enormous amount of suffering for horses. Those of the Royal Mail coaches, and of crack vehicles like 'The Age', were well cared for, humanely treated, and changed at reasonable intervals on the journey. Especially in the latter days of increasing competition over speed, too many of them on other coach lines were driven mercilessly fast and beyond proper stages, and forced to continue galloping up hills by means of a heavy, two-thonged whip called a 'flogger'. In 1816 a coach was started by a new company to run to Brighton with the undertaking that if the journey was not accomplished in six hours the passengers would have their fares refunded. This could be done only by forcing the horses to gallop all the way. On one journey the coachman broke three whips, and in one week fifteen horses died, after which the authorities stepped in, as they considered the great speed dangerous to the passengers and cruel to the horses.[3]

With the coming of the railway the decline in the population and prosperity of the town was immediately arrested. For some years the towns of Margate and Ramsgate had been attracting fashionable crowds in preference to Brighton, but with better transport to the South Coast these two other towns were almost completely forsaken by upper-class visitors. And despite the lack of encouragement given to the lower classes by the railway company's chairman at the opening dinner, this section of society persisted in coming to Brighton in such numbers that eventually their needs had to be properly recognized by the provision of cheap excursion trains.

The Brighton line has been famous throughout its history for fine locomotives. The earliest ones were from the firm of Sharp and Roberts, and were called 'Sharpies'. They were extremely reliable and helped to lay the foundations of the railway's success. Another famous series of engines were designed by the draughtsman of the E. B. Wilson Company, David Joy, in 1846, and known as 'Jenny Linds' after the first one, which was named after the Swedish singer who had lately taken Covent Garden by storm, and who sang at the Brighton Town Hall in 1847.

An extraordinary example of the way in which classical architectural notions invaded even the functional world of locomotive design was the shaping of the steam-domes of some early engines as a section of a fluted classical column on a square base and surmounted by a flattish brass or copper dome. They were even called 'Etruscan' domes. During the early years of the Brighton line the whole policy of engine design and ordering was anarchic. For a short period it was in the hands of a joint committee of the Brighton, Croydon, and Dover Railways, but this arrangement came to an end in little over a year. In 1847 the Brighton Company appointed a Locomotive Superintendent. The man chosen was John Chester Craven, a tough, ruthless and grim-faced engineer who had gained his experience in the famous Railway Foundry at Leeds, and with various early railways in the north.

To the mild-mannered farming and fisherfolk of the south, the fierce, rugged ways of the railwaymen who came to Brighton, who had built and worked with heavy machinery, were something to marvel at, but even amongst those men who were accustomed to the rougher side of life in the almost savage conditions of the Industrial Revolution, Craven had the reputation of being 'a terrible man', to such an extent that one engineman who had been reprimanded for an accident for which he was admittedly not to blame, twice attempted suicide rather than face him after another accident. The number of accidents on the Brighton line at one time was higher than the national average. Engines ran off the rails and boilers blew up. Many of these accidents were due to the fatigue and carelessness of the men who in those days worked appallingly long hours, but some were due to the state of nervous anxiety in which they existed through their fear of Craven. He came to Brighton brooding under a black cloud of tragedy. His elder son had run away from home after a ferocious flogging by his father, and was afterwards found dead in the snow.[4] Craven dominated the Brighton Railway in despotic fashion and created palatial quarters for himself on the front of Brighton station. As a designer he was something of a genius, but an uncoordinated and unsystematic one. At any one time he would be likely to be designing several locomotives, all fantastically different from each other and from anything that had been built before. The most successful locomotives produced under Craven, such as the superb express engines Nos. 162 and 163 with single 7 foot diameter driving wheels, were in fact designed by his son William, who was a more balanced personality, and left his father as soon as he could be independent. Craven resigned in 1869 from what had now become the London, Brighton and South Coast Railway. His departure was possibly not without some encouragement from the Board, for the chaotic state of the locomotive department had become something of a scandal. Nevertheless he had managed to acquire a fairly considerable fortune, and he continued to take an interest in Brighton, becoming an Alderman in 1881. That entertaining and informative authority on railway history, Mr. Hamilton Ellis, reminds us that in the east aisle of St. Peter's Church, where Craven 'worshipped the God of Wrath,' may be seen his memorial window, 'a vast, hideous and very expensive-looking Passion of Our Lord, something like a sacred strip cartoon with all its instalments presented together'.[5]

Craven's successor, appointed in 1869, was William Stroudley, a portly, energetic, dapperly dressed little man from the Highland Railway. Where Craven had been hated, Stroudley was worshipped. He was an autocrat, but a kindly, benevolent one, and his reputation for honesty and fairness caused him to be regarded as something of a god by the railwaymen. He rooted out the abuses and corruption that had developed during the interval between Craven's resignation and his own appointment, many of them of earlier origin, and brought a breath of sanity into the organization of the Brighton railway works. He introduced a considerable degree of standardization in engine types, which brought about improved efficiency and economy. One of his inspired ideas was that every driver should have his name painted in the cab of his engine, with the mileage run underneath. This was but one of many ways by which he encouraged a feeling of personal trust among his men and a sense of pride in the engines in their charge.

Stroudley's locomotives, like their designer, became a legend. One of the most famous types were the 'Terriers', little tank engines with six coupled driving wheels, ('o-6-o' in railway terms). They were small, but remarkably powerful. Fifty of them were built in eight years, and fifteen of them were still in use after nearly eighty years. One of them, originally called 'Morden' but renamed 'Brighton Works', was a familiar sight at the station, where it was used for shunting duties up to 1960. Another of this type was 'Brighton', which was sent to the Paris Exhibition in 1878 and so astonished the French with her fantastic acceleration that she was awarded a gold medal. She was working again at Brighton as late as 1955.

Stroudley's most famous engines, however, were those of the 'Gladstone' class, which, despite their diminutive size, were among the most celebrated English express locomotives of their day. Based on one of Stroudley's earliest types (the B 2's and G 3's) they were tender engines with the unusual arrangement of four driving wheels in front (o-4-2). The first, which gave its name to the class, was built in 1882, and the 'Littlehampton' built in 1891 remained in service until as late as 1933. The 'Gladstone' itself has survived, being preserved in the York Railway Museum, but something of what these engines were like may be seen from a superb model of a Class B2 prototype 'Como', made by the late Dr. Bradbury Winter, which is in the Brighton Museum. The blunt front aspect of these pugnacious but at the same time jolly-looking engines gave the impression of a bull charging headlong, and their powers of speed and acceleration were remarkable. Just after the First World War the present author travelled many times behind the Gladstone class engine 'Arthur

Otway', and would hurry frantically, or dawdle endlessly, rather than go in a train behind any different locomotive.

Stroudley aroused enormous public interest in his locomotives by the original colour schemes in which they were painted, based on his so-called 'Improved Engine Green', which was really a deep golden ochre. This also is to be seen on Dr. Winter's model. Stroudley devoted careful thought as well to the design of the lettering on the company's engines. It was by encouraging pride in the company's engines in ways like these, and by the fact that during the twenty years of Stroudley's career with the Brighton line there was no major accident, that he built up much of the high repute and even *mystique* which arose around the name of the London, Brighton and South Coast Railway. Stroudley died at the untimely age of fifty-six in Paris, in December 1889, from bronchitis caused by a chill that he caught while attending some comparative trials in France with his Gladstone locomotive 'Edward Blount'. Stroudley's best memorial is his legendary reputation, and in the fact that his engines continued to give wonderful service for many years after he was gone.

From the earliest days of the railways first-class passengers travelled in great comfort. For years many of them rode in their own carriages fastened on to flat trucks. But the first-class railway coaches were no less comfortably equipped than their own vehicles, for they were designed in exact imitation, a railway coach of early days looking as though made up of three or four ordinary coach-bodies placed end to end. A remarkable example of the persistence of the carriage-building tradition was given by the fact that the curved shape of the lower part of horse-carriages was perpetuated in curved mouldings or in curved painted lines on the exterior of the railway coaches. As in the road-coaches, the seats were upholstered with padded backs and sides extending up to the cloth-quilted ceiling. Second-class passengers had to be content with much more spartan conditions, with hard, bare seats and unpadded sides. Passengers belonging to what were unblushingly referred to as 'the very lowest orders' were treated with frankly cynical harshness, the deliberate policy of the railway companies being to force the poorer passengers into the better carriages. The third- and fourth-class coaches had open sides, the latter being without a roof. It has not been established definitely whether the hundreds of holes that were drilled in the floors of the fourth-class carriages were a humanitarian concession to enable rain-water to drain away or a sadistic device to add further to the discomfort of the travellers by causing fierce and bitter draughts to blow up their skirts and trousers.

In the 1840s the companies were compelled by law to run at least one train per day for third-class passengers at a fare of a penny a mile, in carriages provided with seats and fully protected from the weather 'as far as consistent with the necessary admission of light and air'. On the Brighton line in 1845 the 'parliamentary trains' were equipped with third-class coaches which were roofed in and had sliding shutters in the sides which could be opened to admit light when weather conditions permitted, while fixed louvre ventilators ensured a continuous supply of necessary air regardless of the wishes of the passengers. But the penny-a-mile trains with even these rudimentary comforts usually ran only once a day, often at some unearthly hour of the morning, and fourth-class carriages with completely unprotected open sides were still being built for excursion traffic as late as 1864. They were later converted to third-class working by covering in the sides with glass windows, and continued in use until the 1880s.

It was during Stroudley's time, in the 1880s, that Pullman cars were introduced on the Brighton line. They were entirely American in their design and decoration, which was of the excessively ornate kind popular at the time. Stroudley's own first-class saloon coaches were also extremely luxurious and elaborately decorated, even the gutter-rail being finished with scalloped ornament, the windows engraved with fancy patterns round the borders, and the lavatory windows embellished with the company's coat of arms. The second-class carriages were also very comfortable, but the old policy of not pampering the third-class passengers persisted, not only in the 1880s but as late as the 1920s, in some surviving rolling-stock which, as the present author recalls, had a hard, narrow stuffed seat with only a stuffed strip along the very upright back.

It was the excursion train and the day-tripper that brought about the downfall of Brighton as an exclusive resort of wealthy and fashionable society, and its rebirth as the truly democratic pleasure resort of modern times. The day-tripper and the middle-class holiday-maker were now regarded as such remarkable phenomena that they were thought worthy of being immortalized in three brilliantly drawn colour lithographs by 'Alfred Crowquill', published in 1848 at Mr. Mason's Repository of Arts at 80 King's Road. The first of these, entitled 'The Beach Hotel', shows a somewhat plebeian couple, the man dressed in a neck-scarf, short jacket, check trousers and light top-hat. His wife wears an obviously imitation ermine tippet and a feathered hat. Seated on one of the wooden groynes, they are about to enjoy the meal they have brought in a basket, including a large bottle of beer. This may have had some allusion to the practice so often complained about by hotel- and restaurant-keepers in Brighton from that day to this, that the day-trippers so often brought their own food and drink, buying nothing during their stay and leaving behind their empty bottles and rubbish. The next lithograph depicts a rather more genteel couple, the man wearing a glossy silk hat and carrying a stick with an ivory handle which he thoughtfully sucks as he watches his wife, charmingly dressed in a ribboned bonnet, velvet bodice and taffeta skirt, who is sitting beside him 'Sketching from Nature'. At the edge of the sea are bathing-machines and we remember that even in Victorian times an interest in the forms of bathers, with or without costumes, was often as much a matter of interest to women spectators as to men. The third picture represents a pair of young girls bathing, dressed in long dark smocks. The old Chain Pier is in the background. One of the girls is apparently alarmed by something just out of the picture, but she is reassured by her friend, who cries, 'Don't be frightened, dear! it is only a little swell from the Pier!'

6 Harbours and the Lifeboat

At the time of writing this chronicle, when the building of a Marina or yachting-harbour at Brighton is about to begin, it is interesting to recall earlier efforts to provide something of a haven for this harsh, bare and storm-swept coast. As early as 1806 a plan for a harbour was considered at a meeting held at the Old Ship Hotel. Two stone piers were to be built out opposite East Street and West Street, and their extremities joined to enclose a harbour space of about fourteen acres, with a wharf and graving docks. Fifty warehouses were to be built between the East and West Piers. It is hardly necessary to add that this scheme, which would have destroyed completely Brighton's character as a pleasure resort, came to nothing through the lack of financial support. A more reasonable proposal was made in 1830 when Captain Brown concurred in a suggestion that was made to turn the Chain Pier into a breakwater by filling up with chalk and stone the space between the clumps of piles that supported the towers. The proposal met with strong approval, but the project had to be abandoned, again because of the enormous cost.

Another early scheme for a Brighton Marina is shown in a lithograph of 1842 illustrating 'A Proposed Harbour on the Recoil Principle'. What this principle consisted of in relation to the harbour was not explained by the inventor of the scheme, Mr. George Adolphus Wigney, in various descriptions of the proposal which he contributed to the *Mechanic's Magazine* that year. Mr. Wigney was a well-known brewer of Brighton, and also a man of vision, who believed that the importance of Brighton would be greatly enhanced by the possession of a harbour. 'We are sadly deficient in marine scenery' he wrote 'and the means of gratifying a very large proportion of our visitors who are habitually partial to scenes of naval and mercantile activity'. Furthermore he realized that Brighton was lacking in facilities for harbouring the larger steam-vessels that were now being built. By 1842 Southampton had taken away from Brighton the important cross-channel steampacket trade. Mr. Wigney's scheme was for a gigantic breakwater encircling the Chain Pier, extending from West Street to Royal Crescent. The western arm was to be 1,500 feet long and the sea-ward section 3,000 feet long. The cost of the harbour was estimated at £150,000. The breakwater wall was to be constructed of solid concrete encased in iron plates. In addition to the harbour, there were to be tunnels underneath the promenade leading northwards beneath West Street to the railway yards, so that goods could be transported direct to and from the harbour and the railway. In effect Mr. Wigney's aim was to create a commercial port at Brighton. An end would have been put to bathing and to many other delights of the beaches, there would have been pollution of the water and fouling of the shore. The Palace Pier and West Pier would never have been built. The only blessing would have been the preservation of the Chain Pier, which would have been protected within the encircling harbour walls from the storms which eventually destroyed it. Understandably, little public support was forthcoming for the scheme, which would have destroyed a great deal of Brighton's character and beauty.[1]

In 1845 an ingenious proposal was made by a Captain Tyler for a floating breakwater, to be constructed in sections which would be anchored in the sea in staggered formation. An experimental portion of three sections was actually built and moored off Brighton.[2] Each section was of open timber construction, which it was believed would absorb the force of the waves by rising and falling with them instead of resisting them, which would rapidly destroy a rigid structure. The breakwater attracted a great deal of interest and it was inspected by officials of the French Government. After being moored off Brighton for some twelve months, during which time the breakwater was put to no very severe test, the sections were being towed away to Shoreham Harbour when one of them broke loose and was washed up on the Brighton beach, where it remained for a considerable time until it was eventually broken up and sold for firewood.

The long, straight, inhospitable coastline of Brighton caused it to be the scene of a number of shipwrecks during the centuries, and a lifeboat of some kind was installed there at least by 1855, when John Wright, 'a much-respected owner of many pleasure-boats and bathing-machines', provided 'a sturdy boat' for the express purpose of rescuing shipwrecked mariners. Indeed, as early as 1796 the Prince of Wales had subscribed a thousand guineas to Lionel Lukin,[3] the inventor of the first practicable lifeboat, which was stationed at Bamburgh on the Northumberland coast, in order to assist him in his experiments, in which he was not strongly encouraged by the marine authorities of the day and which had brought him to the point of acute financial distress. Lukin was a fashionable coach-builder in Long Acre, and a close friend of the Prince, having been introduced to him by William Windham, Secretary of State for War and Colonies.

The wreck of the brig *Pilgrim* at Brighton during a tremendous gale in December 1857 focused fresh attention upon the problem of saving life at sea. A branch of the Royal National Lifeboat Institution was founded in Brighton, and at the same time the pennies of Sunday School children all over the poorer parts of London were collected and devoted to the purchase of a new lifeboat for the town, called the *Robert Raikes* after that pioneer of the Sunday School movement. A tablet recording these events was to be seen on the sea-wall near the West Pier until recent years. Again there was a connection with the Prince of Wales, for later, as King George IV, he had contributed a thousand guineas towards the foundation of the Sunday School movement, against the advice of the then Archbishop of Canterbury, who believed that any improvement in the education of the lower classes 'would lead to revolution'.[4] The King, moreover, gave the land in Trafalgar Square upon which the headquarters of the National Sunday Schools Association was built, as an inscription upon the frieze of that building reminds us to this day.

The people of Brighton had hardly become accustomed to the innovation of the railway when a fresh scientific novelty was presented to their attention, this time devoted to the science of warfare, in the course of what became known as 'Captain Warner's Experiment'. In describing this event the *Illustrated London News* quoted the words of Burke on 'improving the mystery of murder, from the first rude essay in clubs and stones to the present perfection of gunnery, cannoneering and bombarding, mining'.

Captain Warner announced in June 1844 his intention to demonstrate at Brighton 'how no ship could chase a vessel furnished with his implements of warfare, without being perfectly destroyed'. A barque of 300 tons, the *John o' Gaunt*, was chosen for the experiment, and after some delays the vessel arrived at Brighton, where on 19th July a huge concourse of people assembled on the beach and sea-front to witness the demonstration of Captain Warner's 'Invisible Shell'. There was 'an attractive attendance of ladies whose generally fashionable attire, as they were seated at the windows and in the coaches, coupled with the elegant equipages interspersed, greatly enlivened the scene'. An impressive number of titled people were present, as well as many Members of Parliament and representatives of the Army and the Navy and some directors of the East India Company. Several hours passed without any activity until the crowd became restless and people suspected they had been made the victims of a hoax. In particular Lord Brougham, who regarded himself as presiding over the proceedings, and who had been manifestly chafing for some time, gave loud utterance to his expression of displeasure, 'and watching through his telescope the slow process of getting the barque under way with a small body of men', commented on the tardy movements of the *John o' Gaunt*'s crew 'in a manner which intimated that if he himself had been on board, matters would have gone much more smoothly and swiftly'. The commentator went on to say that 'His learned and mercurial lordship lying prone on the battery parapet, with a huge telescope resting on his white hat, was not one of the least lenitives of the tedium of delay.'

At length, just before six o'clock, the vessel had been brought into position and Captain Warner in a steamboat near by hoisted a flag to show he was ready. Two men who had been manoeuvring the barque into place now hurried out of her and rowed away with remarkable haste. The signal had already been given from the West Battery for Captain Warner to fire his device, when consternation was caused by the appearance of some curious persons in a small boat who sailed close up to the doomed ship to see what was going on, despite the efforts of two armed revenue cutters that were there to keep off intruders. At last these were got out of the way, and the Captain indicated his intention to fire by hauling down his flag. 'The grand crisis had now arrived . . . the suspense of all was painful, the silence was deep and unbroken. At six o'clock precisely, the devoted vessel appeared to be struck midships, at which point shot up a huge column of water. . . . Then a loud booming and gurgling noise, indicating a submarine explosion, but not approaching a loud report. "The vessel is struck," was uttered by a thousand voices. . . . In less than a minute the vessel was riven almost from stem to stem. "She is filling!" "She is sinking," the spectators exclaimed, and in less than two minutes and a half the vessel literally tumbled to pieces as if by magic.' By sunset nothing appeared above the sea but the top of the foremast. There was intense speculation as to how the vessel had been destroyed, but the exact method used remained a secret. It seems most likely, however, that some form of floating mine was allowed to drift from the supposed victim to its 'pursuer' and to explode against its side. Captain Warner was congratulated by Lord Brougham and others at a dinner held in the evening, and Brighton rejoiced in an exciting event that had brought many thousands of visitors to the town from London and from many places around.

7 Victorian Churches

It is perhaps not surprising that the great era of church-building in Brighton was not during the Regency age, with its atmosphere of raffishness, worldliness and at times somewhat crude gaiety, but the Victorian period, and that its characteristic ecclesiastical style was not the classical, with its implications of rationalism and intellectualism, but the Gothic, which inspired a sense of mystery. This was a style that recalled the splendour and devotion of the Church in medieval times and which was declared by both its great champions, Charles Welby Pugin and John Ruskin, to be the only truly moral architecture. None the less the Gothic style had some of its roots in the age of George IV, in the romanticism of the Regency; in the cult of the Picturesque; in such aspirations towards the mysterious and the sublime as the building of William Beckford's stupendous Fonthill Abbey; and in the re-creation of medieval splendour at Windsor and Belvoir. The new parish church of St. Peter at Brighton, built to the order of the Town Commissioners in the time of George IV, from 1824 to 1828, was not only one of the first manifestations of the new movement of religious fervour in this country, and one of the very first early nineteenth-century churches to be built in Gothic style, but also one of the most beautiful. This was to be expected of a design by Charles Barry, who was later to become architect of the new Houses of Parliament, and to be knighted by Queen Victoria after their completion. Barry had little sympathy with the more antiquarian curiosities of medieval architecture like high rood-screens, deep chancels and dim chapels. He used Gothic with the serenity and purity of the classical spirit in which he had been trained, and his tower of St. Peter's, built of dazzling white Portland stone, soars out of the valley of the Steine at the junction of the London and the Lewes roads, offering its beauty to the visitor from either direction, its unorthodox but exciting proportions narrowing sharply from its broad base into elegant slenderness, the graceful curves of its ogival tower-window, and its finely tapering crocketed pinnacles, breathing a spirit that combines the aspiration of Gothic heaven-seeking height with the spare dignity of the classical outlook. It is deeply regrettable that when a chancel was added and the nave lengthened by Somers Clarke in 1906, although a very beautiful 'Perpendicular' window was added by him, most unfortunately a different kind of stone from the original Portland was used, probably on the grounds of expense. Criticisms expressed at the time were swept aside with many assurances of that unconvincing kind to which we have in these days of modern makeshifts become only too accustomed, that in time the new material would 'merge into the original stone', but with the passing of years the Portland stone has become whiter, and the substitute more and more dingy and sordid.

St. Peter's marked a contrast to the existing churches of the town like the Chapel Royal and St. James's no less in the character of its religious activity than in its architecture. Although the days of an entirely free and open church had not yet come, a much larger proportion of free seats were set aside than ever before for those who could not afford to rent pews. The Vicar was the Rev. Henry Michell Wagner, who held the incumbency for over forty years, and was the father of an even more famous Brighton priest, the Rev. Arthur Douglas Wagner, who eventually carried the remarkable revival of the Church in Brighton to its richest fruition.

The elder Wagner was a High Churchman of the old school. As a young man he had been tutor to the sons of the Duke of Wellington, in whose honour he named his own son Arthur. His father, Melchior, hatter to George II, had married Anne, the daughter of the Rev. Henry Michell, Vicar of St. Nicholas, Brighton. Henry Wagner was a zealous, devoted clergyman, possessing a very large personal fortune which he used unsparingly for the good of his people, and which at the same time gave him great influence and independence in the affairs of a parish that was so large, numbering 80,000 souls at the time of his death, and so far from the administrative centre of the See that it was described somewhat ruefully by the Bishop of Chichester as 'a bishopric within a bishopric'. He was an example of the best kind of benevolent despot. There are many stories of his autocratic ways. When William IV was intending to visit Brighton on a Sunday, he asked for the church bells to be rung for him. Wagner answered that on such a day the bells were rung only for the King of Kings, for which remark Queen Adelaide commended him. When the town rates for the upkeep of the church had not been paid to him, Wagner stopped the tower clock, which caused some consternation, and much amusement. While Mr. Wagner was riding along one day a street-urchin called out 'Who stopped the clock?' whereupon the Vicar dismounted and 'administered personal correction'. Had he passed the matter off with a laugh he would have been an even greater man, and would not have been summoned as he was and fined for assault. Henry Wagner founded a spiritual kingdom and also a realm of worldly power was extended by his son Arthur by means of five other churches, all built with funds from the Wagners' immense fortune and also raised by private subscriptions and grants from public bodies.

The new movement of building began modestly with the erection of All Souls' Church in Eastern Road in 1834. Its rather grim brick and stucco exterior of Grecian form, designed by Mew, seemed to look back to the preceding age rather than to the future, but the interior was given a Gothic triforium and clerestory in a clever recasting of the building by Edmund Scott and his partner Hyde later in the nineteenth century. The chief beauties of the interior were the six fine stained-glass windows by a distinguished local artist, Charles Eamer Kempe, born in 1837, the son of Nathaniel Kemp, who was the uncle of Thomas Read Kemp. (Charles added the 'e' to his name.) When the church was demolished in 1968 the windows were removed and reinstalled in the south transept of Norwich Cathedral.

All Souls' was the first church in Brighton to have a surpliced choir. This was accompanied by a large barrel-organ which had a repertoire of twenty-four tunes, but which also had a regrettable tendency to produce the wrong tune.[1]

Christ Church, in Montpelier Road, followed in 1838, built in Gothic style of brick and stucco by George Cheesman of Brighton, again with a rather depressing exterior. Its tall spire, modelled upon that of Chichester Cathedral, is its most imposing feature. The church became famous through its incumbent, the Rev. James Vaughan, a notable preacher who remained in charge from the opening of the church until his death in 1889.

The architect of Christ Church also reverted to the classical style of the Regency age when he designed St. John's, Carlton Hill, in 1840, but he failed to capture the earlier purity of inspiration, for his Doric façade was extremely ponderous and badly proportioned. The front has probably been improved by the remodelling of recent years, the original neo-Greek pylon doorways being remodelled with pediments and fluted pilasters of more agreeable classical character.

The church was originally intended to serve not the wealthy and fashionable residents and visitors of Brighton, but the enormous population of poor people that was then growing in the streets of small houses round about Carlton Hill. The congregation has today largely vanished, together with the slums, but the church has become a special interest of Brighton College.

One of the most significant advances in the life of the Church in Brighton was made when the elder Wagner built St. Paul's Church in West Street, in 1848, at his own expense for £14,000. The beauty and richness of its interior marked a great step forward from the bare meanness of the earlier proprietary preaching halls. The structure was plain, built in un-pretentious Gothic style in Brighton flint with quoins of white Caen stone. The architect was Richard Cromwell Carpenter (1812–55), after Pugin the leader of the Gothic Revival, designer of St. Mary Magdalene's, Munster Square, London, and of Lancing College, Sussex. It is unusual in plan, the east end being built against the street with an entrance at the north side of the chancel, and has a plain tower, the intended spire for which was never built. Eventually, a delightful octagonal lantern was added, designed by R. H. Carpenter, the original architect's son. It is supported by four pinnacles, and crowned by a short spire of timber and lead construction in French Gothic style, making one of the most distinctive landmarks of Brighton, whether seen from the Downs or the sea, although now it is overshadowed by the modern skyscraper hotel blocks. Another entrance is by a long covered way or 'cloister' by the side of the church, leading to a narthex or lobby at the west end. The interior was, as William Beckford said of Fonthill, 'well calculated for mysteries', with its tall narrow nave and sharply pointed arches soaring into the darkness of the timbered roof; but the chancel bursts into splendour and glory with a magnificent roodloft in gilding and colour by H. Ingram on Carpenter's fine original screen, and with the beautiful decorative patterning of sky and stars in the ceiling, which was the last work to be designed by G. F. Bodley. Burne-Jones painted the triptych of the high altar. R. C. Carpenter designed the splendid seven-light eastern window, and the glass here and in the other window is by Hardman, mostly from Pugin's cartoons. Those in the narthex are by Kempe. The building of this church, with its features of stalled chancel, rood-screen, sedilia and piscina that had hardly been seen in any church erected since the Middle Ages, all intended to be used in the ritual service of the church, was hailed as a victory by a writer in *The Ecclesiologist* for 1849, who declared 'our principles have triumphed'.

The services in the early proprietary chapels and churches had been of the simplest order, making no strong demands either upon the credulity of the worshippers or upon the need for them to lead lives of penitence and spiritual devotion. The fashionable crowds were lured by the eloquence and personal attraction of a spellbinding preacher. The churches were mostly open only from Sunday to Sunday, offered little by way of the sacraments or spiritual consolation, in the visitation of the sick and the old, or in active work amongst the poor. The new churches were to have their fine preachers as well, if anything of an even more persuasive eloquence and social elegance, and imbued with compelling spiritual ardour. But to their appeal was added the powerful attraction of dramatic and moving liturgy, of rich and colourful vestments, of sensuous music and singing. Those who felt a bleakness in the simple evangelical services were drawn by the changing colours and moods of the liturgical year, by sonorous rituals reviving the splendour and depth of medieval piety, and by the emotional satisfaction of sacramental rites. These manifestations were brought back into the English Church after centuries of spiritual apathy and aridity through the influence of the Tractarian Movement—the 'Oxford Movement' of the 1830s, led by John Keble, John Henry Newman, Hurrell Froude and Edward Pusey, who aimed to make the Church live again in the minds of men as it had done in the great ages of faith. Their liturgical observances were paralleled by a hitherto almost unheard-of religious dedication on the part of the clergy, a new ascetism in their personal life, and intense selfless activity in giving consolation to the sick and aged, in taking help to the poor and in conducting missions amongst the most wretched classes of society.

Henry Wagner's son, Arthur Douglas Wagner (1824-1902), was placed in charge of St. Paul's, and soon began to introduce the liturgical practices of the High Church school, whose leaders he had met while at Trinity College, Oxford. Archdeacon Manning, who like many others in the Oxford Movement was later to secede to Rome, delivered the opening sermon at St. Paul's, and John Keble, the great poet of the Oxford band, author of *The Christian Year*, also preached from its pulpit. At first there was not even a surpliced choir, but soon there was a fully choral service, and an elaborate ritual that filled the critics of the church with consternation. In those days the majority of church-people were not only convinced that the intrusion of any form of beauty in their services was displeasing to the Almighty but that ritualistic public worship had sinister associations with popery. As the different seasons of the liturgical year took their course the clergy at St. Paul's wore vestments of the appropriate colour laid down by the ancient Church in England. The priest appeared in maniple, chasuble and stole of white, red, purple or black, and the altar was dressed with a frontal of one of these colours accordingly. Arthur Wagner's church was for some time the only centre of ritualistic worship on Tractarian principles in the south of England, and for a time he was supposed by some people actually to be in collusion with the Jesuits on account of the 'Romish practices' conducted in his church, but these were introduced only gradually, as the influence of the Tractarian Movement generally increased throughout the country. Henry Wagner was sadly perturbed by the idolatrous nature of the services now being conducted at the church he had himself built, and when invited by his son to preach a sermon at St. Paul's chose for his text from Matthew 17:15, 'Lord, have mercy on my son, for he is lunatick, and sore vex'd'! The wealthy society of Brighton, and many of the very poor, who had been reached through the mission work that was carried out by Arthur Wagner and his friends in the most wretched streets of the town, flocked to the church for every service, on weekdays as well as on Sundays. Matins on Sunday mornings were so magnificent that a pamphlet which was published on the subject of 'Puseyism in Brighton' referred to 'The Sunday Opera at St. Paul's'.[2]

The success of St. Paul's was quickly followed up by the building of All Saints' in Compton Avenue, by R. C. Carpenter in 1847. Although intended for ritualistic observance, because of lack of money the interior displayed a pleasant simplicity rather than rich grandeur. The church was demolished about 1956, and the site is now covered with a block of modern flats.

Although created out of a later eighteenth-century building, St. Stephen's Church in Montpelier Place must rank as a Victorian church, since it was not dedicated as such until July 1851. It had begun its existence as the elegant ballroom, designed in Adamesque classical style by John Crunden, and built adjoining the Castle Hotel in 1767. While the Royal Pavilion was being finally transformed by John Nash for George IV, the Castle Ballroom was bought by him and converted for use as a private chapel, being consecrated in January 1822. When the Royal Pavilion Estate was bought by the Town Commissioners in 1850 the Bishop of the Diocese claimed the materials of the Chapel, on the grounds that a building once consecrated belongs to the Church. It was not regarded as being desecrated in any way by being demolished stone by stone, and being rebuilt in Montpelier Road as a new church. It was said that 'only a slight alteration of form and detail was made in the re-erected church.' The shallow vaulted ceiling, the columns with their delightful foliated capitals, and the decorated cornice remained, but the decorative paintings of Dawn and Night, of episodes in the story of Cupid and Psyche, and of the Aldobrandini marriage which added so much to the charm of the original building were not preserved, no doubt because of their pagan character. The result was an impression spoken of as one of 'remarkable neatness'. The first incumbent, the Rev. George Wagner, nephew of the Vicar of Brighton, regarded the church as 'pre-eminently ugly in an architectural point of view', so deeply had the prejudice against the classical style grown under the pro-Gothic Tractarians. Unlike St. Peter's and St. Paul's, the congregation numbered few fashionable patrons. Most of the parishioners were of the poorer sort, and a coal-club and blanket-lending society were among the many good works carried out by the church. No doubt for this reason, and because of the slender resources of the parish, no great advances in ritualistic worship were attempted. During the 1930s the church had a reputation for its services of spiritual healing, which became famous throughout the country. The building is now used as a Deaf and Dumb Institute, and it is usually possible to look inside during the day-time, and to try to imagine the scenes of brilliant gaiety that took place within those walls during the early days of the Prince of Wales in Brighton.

One of the greatest monuments of the Victorian church-building movement, St. Michael's, is not one of the Wagner churches, but was provided by two devout ladies, the Misses Windle, with the encouragement of Charles Beaulands, its first curate-in-charge, who had been assistant priest at St. Paul's. St. Michael's is, in fact, two churches, the first begun by G. F. Bodley in 1858, a graceful little building built in the primitive simplicity of the North Italian Gothic style that was advocated by Ruskin and

Street. Bodley's adoption of red brick, following Butterfield's use of it at All Saints', Margaret Street, London, and elsewhere, marked an innovation in Brighton in breaking away from the flint walling, dreary stucco, or drab Kentish rag stone of earlier churches. The stained glass of the western windows, of superb design and colour, was the first large-scale work in this medium of the Pre-Raphaelites, William Morris, Edward Burne-Jones, Ford Madox Brown and Rossetti. A fine medieval Flemish triptych was placed above the altar, and in a little *flèche* was hung a Russian bell from a church at Sevastopol, given by a hero of the Crimea. By the time the church was opened, in 1862, it was obvious the building was too small, and almost immediately plans were made for its enlargement.

Bodley's ideas had by now moved so far away from his earlier conceptions that he allowed the new work to be designed by William Burges, but this was not carried out until 1893, long after the architect's death, by his friend John Chapple. The northern aisle of the old church became the southern aisle of the new church, with a grand cathedral-like nave for which Burges had sought inspiration in the elegant Gothic of Northern France. The new church is not only one of the finest of the few works left us by Burges, but among the grandest achievements in Victorian Gothic church-building in this country. The elaborate carved, painted and gilded reredos by Romaine Walker with its statues in canopied niches; the very elegant parclose screens of wrought iron at the back of the choir, the choir-stalls to the design of Burges, carved in the true medieval manner; the marble-work of the sanctuary and altar, and some excellent glass in the nave and chancel windows, are all worthy adornments of this splendid church.

It is a testimony to the zeal and religious dedication of Arthur Wagner in carrying Christianity into the slums of Brighton that the two first churches built at his own expense should have been, not great masterpieces of grandeur and beauty like his own first church of St. Paul, or his later churches St. Bartholomews and St. Martin's but two humble mission-churches, St. Mary and St. Mary Magdalene's, opened in 1862, and the church of the Annunciation, built some two years later. St. Mary's was a simple work of G. F. Bodley, and was spoken of as a sort of 'holy shed' with plain white-washed walls and simple timber roofs, but it possessed on a cheerful, homely and spacious atmosphere. It is recorded that Arthur Wagner himself summoned the people living near by to the services at St. Mary's by walking round the neighbouring streets ringing a handbell. The building fell into disuse in modern times, and is now the property of the Electricity Board. The church of the Annunciation followed the design of its predecessor and at first was almost as unpretentious, but it was partly rebuilt in 1881 by the Brighton architect Edmund Scott, and was enriched with a small tower, an east window by Carpenter from St. Nicholas's Church, glass by Burne-Jones and Rossetti, and painted panels in the wooden roof.

After these unpretentious beginnings, Arthur Wagner's aspirations in church-building developed in some five years into the stupendous conception of a church that would be grander than almost any other in Britain. This was St. Bartholomews, Ann Street, west of the London Road near Preston Circus. Its beginnings were humble enough, as a little rubble and brick mission church started in 1868, which survived as a church hall until recent years. The name of the mission, later to be taken over by the new church, derived from the ancient priory of St. Bartholomew in Brighton, in a surviving part of which Arthur Wagner's father had once lived. Although the church is the very remarkable work of a little-known Brighton architect, Edmund Scott, there is no doubt that the gigantic conception owed much to Wagner himself.

The stupendous building, of purplish-brown bricks outside, with long, steeply pointed roof and immensely high walls relieved only by shallow brick buttresses and a line of narrow pointed windows, rose up above the surrounding sea of slum-dwellings west of the London road like an immense Noah's Ark. Indeed, that is precisely what it was called by its detractors. Over 180 feet long and 140 feet high at the top of its gilt metal cross, it is 4 feet higher than Westminster Abbey. Built from 1872–4 at a cost of probably £18,000, the project aroused vehement opposition as soon as its details became known. The founder had always been suspected of dark and sinister popish designs. It was hardly to be imagined that such a vast building was to be used simply as a church. A writer in the *Brighton Herald* for 12th July 1874, who signed himself 'A true Protestant and no sham', expressed the deepest disquiet over such features as a certain 'dark spiral staircase apparently shut out from observation on various landings, off which little and almost dark rooms, or cells, as they might be called, are built. The question naturally arises, to what are these little cells to be appropriated? There can be only one answer, nunneries!' It was also suggested that these mysterious chambers were intended as 'anchorites' cells'. They were, in fact, part of the structure of the double triforium.

The flood of abuse in the Press preceded an acrimonious Council debate in October 1893, in which the building was described as a 'cheese warehouse', a 'Noah's Ark in brick', a 'monster excrescence', a 'brick parallelogram', a 'huge barn', 'uselessly large, painfully ugly, and sadly out of place', and finally as 'the Wagner folly'. Not since the building of the Royal Pavilion had a building been the subject of such abuse, nor its creator so vilified, although both buildings and patrons stood at such opposite poles of nature and purpose. The debate only petered out when it was realized that although the height of the building exceeded by a few feet the amount stated in the plans, the statutory fine of forty shillings which could be imposed would be hardly likely to embarrass someone who was paying £18,000 for the building. There were more practical objections to the new erection. The inhabitants of the small, poor dwellings at the side of the church complained that the immense height of the new building caused a down draught which made their chimneys smoke intolerably. With characteristic large-minded autocratic decisiveness Arthur Wagner bought up as many of the properties as he could, and stilled all further objections by drastically reducing the rents.

In the finished church Edmund Scott combined great size with severe beauty of design so as to create an effect seldom attained other than in one of the great cathedrals. St. Bartholomews is indeed one of the great churches not only of Britain but of Europe. Inside, an overwhelming sense of awe is created in the visitor by the immense hall of the nave, without aisles or chancels, and by the vast walls of variegated brickwork, their colours now softened by age, the great length of the interior relieved only by nine bays formed by internal buttresses of brickwork. Built into the northern wall (liturgically the east end) and dominating the whole length of the church is a towering cross formed of hard chalk, a traditional Sussex material used for chimney-pieces in many country houses in the south. The great dignity of this wall has been spoiled by the feeble mosaics that were introduced early in the present century, but the austerely magnificent marble baldacchino, the green and white marble pulpit, and the baptistery with green marble font and walls lined with green marble, set within the recess of one of the bays, are wonderful features in a splendid scheme of decoration designed by H. Wilson that was never completely realized. The Lady Altar with a frontal of *repoussé* silver-work is another feature that excites wonder, and is a remarkable example of *Art Nouveau* decoration.

All the 1,500 seats of St. Bartholomews were free to all comers, rich and poor. Much of the opposition to Wagner from his Protestant colleagues arose not so much from antagonism to his ritualistic opinions but through his breaking of the price-ring of pew rents, from which many of the clergy derived comfortable incomes. As the most spectacular church of Anglo-Catholicism in the south of England, St. Bartholomews became the centre of what was called the L.B. and S.C.R. (London, Brighton and South Coast, not Railway, but Religion).[3] Although its congregation has dwindled, it remains today one of Brighton's most magnificent possessions, equal in its very different way in splendour to the Pavilion. Unlike many other of the town's architectural treasures, it has not been overshadowed by the vast increase in scale of surrounding buildings. With its immense height and bulk it comes into its own amidst the new skyscraper flat and office blocks around, still proclaiming the purpose of splendour in the worship of God and humbleness in the service of the poor, to further which it was built.

Hardly had St. Bartholomews been opened when Arthur Wagner was once more at work on new plans, this time for a great church to serve as a memorial to his father's forty-six years' work as Vicar of Brighton. Designed by Somers Clark, St. Martin's is regarded by many people as being the most beautiful church in Brighton; it is certainly one of that architect's most successful achievements, and the interior furnishings, mostly given by the founder's brother, Mr. Henry Wagner, are of the richest and most elaborate kind. Externally the simple early Gothic design is impressive and satisfying, with its walls of deep red brickwork, pinnacle-capped buttresses at the west and east ends and tall lancet windows. On entering one is struck by the spaciousness and beauty of proportion of the interior, and by the sumptuous harmony of the decorations and appointments. The stained glass is all excellent for its period; the baptistery, with its font of Sussex and Sienna marbles, stands impressively on a wide platform at the west end; and the high altar and reredos, also designed by Somers Clark, is one of the finest of its date in the country, with richly carved and gilded canopies and pinnacles, sculptured shafts with statues in the niches and painted panels. The building, which was opened in 1875, is a fitting memorial to the priest who endowed Brighton with a group of remarkable churches that are hardly equalled in any other part of the country.

No such sumptuous beauty of decoration is to be found in the next of the great Victorian churches to be described. The church of St. Mary, built in 1876 to the design of Sir William Emerson, is remarkable, however, for the wonderful grace and strength of the interior. An exciting sense of space is created by the immense arches spanning the nave, and the illusion of extreme depth is given to the vista by the arches of the transepts being set at an angle at the crossing, so that they dramatically heighten the perspective as they lead the eye into the beautifully formed and vaulted apse beyond. Other great beauties of the church are in the exquisitely crisp and lively carving of the stone capitals of the columns. The exterior is impressive with the noble curve of the baptistery apse and the fine proportions of the tall gabled portal, but the red stone has weathered badly where exposed and the building has not been improved by the police box and public lavatories which have been added at the side.

For some years after it was built St. Paul's Church in West Street was usually so crowded with fashionable people that there was no room for the poorer folk who lived in the congeries of small dwellings to the west of the church. Mr. Wagner decided to build another church as a chapel-of-ease to St. Paul's, for the poor people and children of the district. Imbued with ardent missionary zeal, he placed his church in the heart of the enemy's country, next to the brewery in Russell Street.

In this last church-building enterprise of his, Mr. Wagner intended once again to attempt the heaven-scaling heights to which he had aspired with the lofty walls of St. Bartholomews. He was, however, eventually compelled by force of circumstances to abandon this soaring ambition, for although the design of the architect, R. H. Carpenter, was not at all changed, in execution it became more symbolic of a descent into limbo, for when building was about to begin the owner of the brewery obtained an injunction in Chancery against the great height to which the walls were to be carried, on the grounds that they were obstructing his lights. Rather than sacrifice the original design, Wagner decided to lower his church below the ground, and therefore excavated to a depth of between 30 and 40 feet in order to bring his building below the set limit. The change that was made in the name of the church, from The Transfiguration to The Resurrection, appropriately expressed the somewhat tomblike character of the subterranean building and, it was to be hoped, of the new spiritual life that was to rise out of its depths. The entrance to the building was at street level, and from a vestibule decorated with paintings a flight of stone steps led down to the nave some 16 feet below, creating a rather startling effect. Because of the absence of lower windows the church was extremely gloomy, but was spoken of as being 'not without a certain kind of sombre grandeur'. The interior was adorned with a number of paintings, including a copy of Raphael's Sistine Madonna and two Flemish primitives, but the altar and other appointments were less elaborate than at St. Paul's. When completed in 1879 the church was found to be so 'damp and earthy' that it was almost impossible to use, so a narrow trench was dug entirely round the walls to create an air-space which resulted in a complete cure. Alas, by 1908 the congregations of both St. Paul's and of its chapel-of-ease had dwindled sadly, and now that Mr. Wagner was dead the enormous costs of upkeep which were very largely met out of his own pocket could no longer be paid. Three years later the Charity Commissioners authorized the sale of the Church of the Resurrection, which had cost some £14,000 to build, for the sum of £3,500. It was intended to apply the money to the provision of a mission-hall which would not be so expensive to run. At the public inquiry one of the church representatives indignantly observed that if his opponents thought that 'St. Paul's was going to appropriate the money for candles and incense' they were very much mistaken. A few years later it became a meat-store, a use for which the coldness of the semi-underground building no doubt made it unexpectedly suitable, though the shade of Mr. Wagner would have been aghast at the spectacle that was presented of great sides of beef hanging among the timbers of the 'waggon-headed' roof and lit by windows in the stonework tracery of Gothic arches. The building continued to be used in this way until late in 1965, when the enemy which Wagner had challenged on first choosing his site achieved an ironic triumph at last by taking over the building as a store for beer-barrels, but no doubt it will not be long before it is completely swept away with the completion of the immense modern development of the West Street area.

Although summoned to the Jerusalem Chamber at Westminster Abbey in 1867 to give evidence to a Royal Commission on the principles and practices of the Ritualists, and made the subject of fierce personal abuse, Arthur Wagner was protected from the worst consequences of his policy by his own great strength of character, by his wealth and his by no means negligible public influence. Other ritualistic churchmen at the time, however, like the Rev. James Purchas at St. James' Church and the Rev. James Vaughan at Christ Church, suffered intensely from persecution by the more rabid and disreputable of their opponents, and Purchas was driven to an early death by their persecutions.

For six years between 1847 and 1853 the congregations at the Church of the Holy Trinity, Ship Street, were electrified by the sermons of their very remarkable minister, the Rev. F. W. Robertson. It was said of him that 'he employed the highest eloquence that has ever been listened to in this town; not the rounded and flowing phrases of oratory, but the burning words and flashing thoughts that are struck out by the heart and intellect when they are both struggling to give a visible form to the great convictions and desires that fill the speaker'.[4] The fervent intensity of his thought seems to have been too great for his delicate frame, for he died at the age of only thirty-seven. Fifteen hundred people attended his funeral, including the members of the Brighton Mechanics' Institute and the Brighton Athenaeum, two institutions to which he had given special support. He is buried in the Extra-Mural Cemetery.

Lady Byron, widow of the poet, who lived for a time in a house near the Pavilion (long ago demolished) was a great friend of Robertson's. She followed his body to the grave and left some verses in memory of him. He had accompanied her to Reigate in April 1852 to meet the poet's sister, Augusta Leigh, in an attempt to reconcile them, but failed. Robertson said of Brighton, 'Even round this Brighton of ours, treeless, and prosaic as people call it, there are materials for poetry.'

One of the most important of Brighton's late-Victorian nonconformist churches is the Congregational Church at the Seven Dials, built by Thomas Simpson in 1870, in what has been called 'a farrago of Rhenish, Cornish, and Franco-Venetian'.[5] The circular interior is remarkable, and the firm and bold detail of the building is powerful and impressive, although it is spoiled, as were so many of Brighton's churches, by being faced in stucco or Roman cement of the dreariest colour and texture.

8 The Piers, Aquarium and Clock-tower

With the building of Brunswick Town and its surrounding streets of new houses, with its own church and the newly built Grand and Norfolk Hotels, the western end of Brighton was almost a completely self-contained town, practically independent of the ancient Brighthelmstone with its smelly beach and fish-market and warren of narrow lanes, and was regarded as being very much more select than the old town. It was soon felt that the west end of Brighton should have its own pier where the delights of a promenade over the water could be enjoyed and the steamboats from places along the coast and from the Isle of Wight could call. The West Pier was opened in October 1866, having taken three years to build at a cost of £30,000. The structure was designed by the engineer Eusebius Birch, who also built the Aquarium some years later. However much one may like the idea of having some new public amenity in the town, whether it is to be a pier or a yachting harbour, there are few people as a rule who want to have it right on their own door-step, and the people of Regency Square protested vociferously against the West Pier, which was built opposite their homes, because of the square toll-houses which they considered to be unsightly, and were so large that they obstructed their view of the sea. Nevertheless the pier became immensely popular, and frequently on Sundays more than 10,000 people paid for admission. In the year 1875 more than 600,000 people passed through the turnstile.[1]

In 1894 the pier was nearly doubled in size by an almost complete reconstruction that included new landing-stages for steamboats, and a handsome concert-hall holding 1,500 people. The West Pier was always celebrated for its sideshows, which included in June 1890 a display of performing fleas. These miserable creatures gave by their frantic leaps an impression of moving the various devices to which they were attached by means of silver wires fastened to their necks, and their spasmodic evolutions were described as 'Drawing water', 'Driving and drawing a Hansom Cab', 'Flea turning windmill', 'Cannon fired by a flea', 'A morning drive with carriage drawn by fleas with fleas inside', and 'A duel with steel swords'. It was all described as 'Highly amusing and instructive'.

One of the pier's attractions was a small cannon that was fired precisely at noon every day (when sunny) by the sun's rays directed on to the touch-hole by a burning-glass.

For some years before the storm of November 1896 which destroyed the Chain Pier its doom had been pronounced, not only because it had become unsafe, but because it was too small for the large cross-Channel and pleasure steamers that were now coming into use, so in 1891 it was sold to a company which in that year began building the new pier that was to take its place. The Palace Pier was not completed until three years later, and during this time it was screened from the sea-front by a wooden hoarding, which gave the centre of Brighton a derelict appearance that was emphasized by the dilapidated state of the Royal Albion Hotel. Even before the Pier was completed the promoters of the scheme were faced with liquidation. As owners of the old Chain Pier, a claim of £6,000 was made against them for damage caused to the West Pier by the timbers of the Chain Pier which were hurled about in the gigantic waves when it was wrecked and cut the West Pier in two. The Palace Pier company also suffered damage to their own pier amounting to £2,000, and a further claim of £1,500 was made by Volk's Electric Railway for damage caused to their property, all from the same cause. The Board of Trade demanded the removal of the old Chain Pier, and the only way the Palace Pier company could see to meet their obligations was to sell the ironwork of that part of the new pier that had been constructed, but they then found the revenue from this source would be entirely swallowed up by the cost of the removal of the iron. At length a new company was formed under Sir John Howard, who was the donor of the Howard Convalescent Home at Kemp Town, and also of a wing in the Sussex County Hospital. Sir John's company obtained possession of the half-finished pier and in 1889 the main section of the deck was open to the public. When open at last it was an immediate success. It was perfectly sited at the foot of the Steine, so that the crowds pouring headlong into Brighton at holiday times almost instinctively continued on to the pier without hesitating. It was, moreover, a highly attractive creation, with its golden oriental domes and delicate filigree ironwork arches, outlined at night in electric lights, that were inspired by the Pavilion's fretted stone lattices. The Pavilion thus from now on became a model for the architecture of pleasure and with this miracle of genius as its exemplar the Palace Pier has set the standard of gaiety and elegance for piers and other holiday buildings all over the world, not least for some of the amusing constructions at the Festival of Britain in 1951. In 1901 a theatre was added at the end of the pier, and nine years later a pavilion for concerts and dances was built near the shore end. A bandstand (now a restaurant) and a winter garden (now the Palace of Fun) were erected, the theatre was remodelled, and over its entrance was built one of the first film-making studios in this country. The present entrance canopy and clock-tower were erected when the roadway was widened and the Aquarium was rebuilt in 1930.

The Palace Pier from the beginning seemed to possess an atmosphere of slightly raffish gaiety that was quite different from that of the West Pier, which was frequented by the visitors to the Grand and other smart hotels at the far end of the front, and was regarded as more 'select'. The penny-in-the-slot machines on the Palace Pier especially helped to create this impression. Machines like those which displayed a series of antiquated saucy photographs in something resembling cinematographic motion by turning a handle were to be found in almost every seaside resort. 'What the Butler Saw' and 'Her Saturday Night', which revealed a young lady about to disrobe for her weekly bath, but which plunged into darkness with a loud click at the crucial moment, are fairly common all round our coasts. These machines, of which there are still fourteen in service on the pier, were made by the International Mutoscope Reel Co., U.S.A. Most of the photographs are dated 1927, and have such titles as 'Bedroom Secrets', 'Artist and Model', and 'Parisian Can-Can', but three of the subjects have an appeal to violence—the Paterson-Monaghan Fight, 'Flirting with Death' (a stunt air crash), and 'Mechanical maniacs' (stunt car crashes). But the Palace Pier is more widely celebrated for a highly individual and intriguing type of machine, that might more properly be called animated models. These are hardly to be found in any other resort than Brighton but Blackpool, where they were made apparently during the decade before 1914 by Mr. Leonard Lee. The machines are quite unlike the usual commercial machines mass-produced in cast iron or sheet metal, and are individually made of wood and other homely materials, and driven by clockwork motors, which at the height of the summer season have to be wound up four times a day. The subjects are all somewhat gruesome and horrific, but the scenery, especially the stonework of castles and prison-cells, is cleverly rendered, and the modelling of the faces of the various characters is skilfully done. 'The Guillotine' is the maker's last work. In a French prison a door first reveals the seated prisoner and a chaplain. Next another door opens to show the prisoner escorted by guards. The double central doors now disclose the condemned man prone on the guillotine. As the clock chimes the chaplain raises his crucifix, the flag dips, the blade falls and the head rolls into a basket. In 'The Mysterious House' clocks and cupboards open to reveal ghosts and devils, pictures tilt on the walls and a portrait bust of Beethoven turns its head. 'The House of Mystery' and 'The Haunted Chamber' display a similar theme. 'The Haunted Church-yard' is another particularly fine model, again with very convincingly executed stonework, while the reclining drunkard is modelled with charac-ter. As the church clock tolls midnight the tombs open to give up ghosts and skeletons, while in one a devil is revealed with the slogans 'I've got my eye on you' and 'He's drawn his old-age pension.' The daily takings in the summer season prove 'The Guillotine' to be by far the most popular of all the machines.

An interest in the marvels of science had been aroused in the minds of many people for the first time in 1851 by the exhibits at the Great Exhibition of 1851 in Hyde Park, and when Paxton's remarkable iron and glass structure was transported near Dulwich and became the Crystal Palace, many Brightonians were enthralled by the wonders of the deep displayed in the aquarium that was established in that building.

Further interest in the beauties of the seashore had been awakened about the middle of the century by the writings of the naturalist Philip Gosse, which described the life of the rock-pools and shallow waters of the coast. The time was ripe for Brighton to have its own Aquarium, and in 1866 plans were being made. As so often was the case where Brighton enterprises were concerned in the early days, the scheme was conceived on a grand and audacious scale. A new road was to be made along the sea-front from the Steine to Black Rock, on land to be reclaimed from the sea; the Marine Parade was to be widened, with a new wall along its outer side, and the Aquarium was to be built on the space in between. The designer was again the engineer Eusebius Birch, and his original scheme showed a skyline broken here and there by turrets which were intended as lodges for the gate-keepers and similar purposes, but the Town Council very wisely insisted that no part of the building should be allowed to rise above the level of the Marine Parade, so as not to obstruct the view of the sea. The buildings extended for a distance of about a third of a mile from their western end, and were sunk deep into the ground. A broad flight of granite steps led down into a large open court surrounded by red-brick arches with terracotta columns and ornaments presenting, it was said, 'the appearance of a Pompeian court'.[2]

Inside were a large entrance hall, two corridors, one of them 224 feet long, both lined with large tanks, a central hall, having a tank 100 feet long, a conservatory, a reading-room and a restaurant. The main halls had a Gothic roof of variegated bricks supported on alternating round and octagonal columns of Bath stone, polished green serpentine marble and red Edinburgh granite, and the capitals were carved with foliage and 'appropriate marine subjects (by Mr. Purkiss)'.

The place seemed like a vast Victorian cathedral that had been engulfed by the waves, with its windows set in the arches of the walls, instead of being filled with stained glass, looking out into dimly luminous depths of the sea peopled by strange denizens of the deep whose grotesque faces and trailing tentacles appeared spectrally against the glass and then vanished; and indeed all through the years of its existence there has been a feeling of the suspension of time inside the halls of the Aquarium, and the demeanour of the visitors has always had in it something a little hushed and unhurried. Those twilit aisles have always been favoured by lovers and newly wedded couples, sitting before the tanks or walking slowly between the columns hand in hand, rapt and spellbound with each other if not by the 'finny marvels', so that it seems that all who were in the cathedral when it was overwhelmed have become immortal and are spending a blissful eternity in these marine halls remote from the ordinary world.

The opening of the Aquarium on 10th August 1872 was planned to coincide with one of the annual meetings of the British Association for the Advancement of Science and it was in this way that Brighton recognized the growing preoccupation with science during the nineteenth century, particularly with the natural sciences and the light they shed in those days of religious misgivings upon the origins and evolution of the earth and of life. Among the distinguished visitors who were present at the opening three Eastern gentlemen in magnificent oriental robes attracted great attention. Like magi they appeared as a portent, no one seemed to know from whence. In the course of his address the Mayor expressed the belief that natural history was one of the most attractive and elevating studies known to science, and found material for profound thought in the fact that fish could be taught to come to the water's edge to be fed at regular times. In the afternoon a 'most elegant and *recherché déjeuner*' was given at the Royal Pavilion. In response to the Mayor's toast of the Aquarium Company, the Vice-Chairman of that body, Mr. Stevens, created a sensation by enlarging upon the fact that the building of the Aquarium had gone on satisfactorily day by day, until the roof was fairly on, when 'a posse of jackdaws began to attack the building and pull down in all directions everything that gave uniformity and grandeur to the structure [hear, hear, and a cry of 'Shame']. One fine morning, a little jackdaw was seen hopping about on the roof, with straight edge and tape, measuring out destruction by the yard [laughter and applause]. When this little bird was questioned as to his commission, he said he was trying to ascertain how far in height they had exceeded their limits [O! Oh! and laughter] as the old birds in the nest were going to make them keep strictly within their Act of Parliament. . . . The end was that they had to pull portions of the building down again. Those wicked old birds were stone blind to beauty, and they would listen to no remonstrances. Then it was proposed to build a splendid clock-tower at the entrance, with four illuminated dials, but they would not have it, they knew the time of day without that [laughter] . . . whatever there was in the building that was out of keeping with the original design, and offensive to the eye, was not due to the engineer, nor to the architect, nor to the directors, but to the jackdaws of Brighton [great applause].' One of the aldermen immediately rose to protest against these 'unseemly and indecent remarks', but when he found he could not be heard because of the uproar, 'mingled with those felicitous sounds known as "catcalls" ', he mounted on a chair but was pulled down by his coat-tails. Eventually the Mayor restored order, but even then the climax of the occasion had not been reached, until at the end of a speech Mr. Frank Buckland, a celebrated naturalist who worked enthusiastically for the Aquarium for a number of years, produced 'apparently from his pocket' a couple of 'juvenile alligators' which were henceforth to be added to the Aquarium.[3] There was another uproar at the Council meeting following this event, but eventually Mr. Stevens apologized to the Mayor, and the permission of the Council was given for the erection of the clock-tower with a gateway, toll-houses and turnstiles, and these, all combining to look something like the Albert Memorial on a smaller scale, were added by October 1874. This had not been achieved, however, without a fierce struggle between the more progressive members of the Council, led by Sir Cordy Burrows, and the Works Committee, who he said were so obstructive that were the country to be invaded by the French 'it would only be necessary to put the Works Committee to the front, and in them the invaders would find sufficient obstruction'!

The Aquarium was but modestly stocked at first, although it soon acquired an octopus, which became one of the most famous exhibits, and a sturgeon which had been caught in Rye Harbour. This was such a novelty that a poem about it appeared in the *Brighton Herald*.[4] The building had been planned, however, on such ambitious lines, with one tank 100 feet long and another of 55 feet, that no difficulty was found in accommodating very large specimens of this kind.

All through the Victorian age the Aquarium was one of the most popular resorts of the town. The terrace gardens which were formed on the roof, with their pleasant stone balustrades and broad walks uncluttered by buildings of any kind, were regarded as one of the most delightful marine promenades in the kingdom. The directors were strongly criticized for pandering to the new craze for roller-skating by providing a rink in the building for this pastime, but one of the speakers at the opening delivered the excruciating remark that it was appropriate to look for 'skate' at an Aquarium.

The recitals and orchestral concerts held at the Aquarium under the musical direction of Mr. Kuhe soon became an established feature of the musical life of Brighton. Indeed, for some thirty years after the opening of the place they rivalled in importance those held at the Dome, many of the most famous orchestras and soloists appearing at the Aquarium. The Corporation even maintained a municipal orchestra at the Aquarium from 1908 right through the Great War until 1918, when the following slump caused it to be disbanded.

Queen Victoria's Diamond Jubilee of 1887 was commemorated in Brighton a year later by the erection of a clock-tower in the centre of the town, at the junction of West Street, Queen's Road, North Street and Western Road, on the site of 'an old and ill-formed shelter'. The tower may be regarded as Brighton's Albert Memorial, in the sense that it serves as the principal focus in the town of anti-Victorian feeling, and indeed even hatred, just as the Prince Consort's monument in Hyde Park did at one time for London and the nation as a whole. It was designed by the architect John Johnson, not in the spiky Gothic of many Victorian buildings, but in a rather pleasing baroque classical style, and consists of a square tower of white stone with a red granite base, on the four sides of which are porticoes with Corinthian columns and pediments, which enshrine medallion portraits in coloured mosaic of Queen Victoria, the Prince Consort, the Prince of Wales and the Princess Royal. At the top of the tower, which is 75 feet high altogether, are a bold cornice, four corner-turrets and a gilded dome carrying a mast with a gilt time-ball and a weather-vane. At one time the clock was controlled 'by direct electrical communication' from Greenwich Observatory, and the time-ball rose (by hydraulic power) and fell precisely upon every hour. This ceased to work many years ago. The clock-tower cost £2,000 and was the gift to the town of John Willing, a wealthy local advertising contractor. It was inaugurated upon his seventieth birthday, on 20th January 1888.

Over and over again in modern times proposals have been made for its demolition or removal, and the feeling directed against it has on occasion been so intense as to seem out of all proportion to any aesthetic shortcomings which the clock-tower might have. In truth, the monument is extremely charming and delightful, and it is hoped that it will for long be allowed to remain. So far the high cost of its demolition has been the greatest factor in its preservation.

One of the most delightful features of the sea-front at its western end is the King's Road Bandstand, more usually called the 'Birdcage Bandstand'; it was built in 1884 with delicate tracery in cast iron and a shallow bulbous dome to its roof, all in the highly individual and pleasing tradition of pleasure architecture established by the Brighton Corporation in the latter part of the last century. Efforts have repeatedly been made from time to time to have this charming structure removed, but so far the expense of demolishing it and replacing it with some other feature again has effectively prevented these efforts from succeeding.

9 Victorian Hotels

The boom years of the 1860s saw the building of a great new hotel on the sea-front at the western end of Brighton. Opened in 1864, the Grand Hotel was described by Cuthbert Bede[1] as a 'cyclopaean pile with its nine tiers of rooms, with their elaborate ornamentations and bronzed and gilded balconies, from which visitors could luxuriate in the lovely panorama of sea and land that was spread to the view'.

The hotel was designed by the architect J. H. Whichcord and built at a cost of £160,000, on the site of the old West Battery House and ammunition ground. With nine floors and 150 bedrooms it was far larger than any other Brighton hotel of the time, and was one of the first three hotels in the country to be provided with lifts, the lift for guests being described as an 'ascending omnibus'. It was also remarkably advanced in being equipped with electric light and with external fire-escapes, a feature not possessed even in recent times by the Bedford Hotel where three people were burned to death in 1964, or by the King's Hotel which was badly damaged by fire in 1967.

The Grand Hotel was designed in the revived Italian renaissance fashion which had been introduced by Sir James Barry into London with the Traveller's Club in 1829 and into Brighton by the same architect (who also designed St. Peter's Church here) with the Queen's Park Villa in 1830. The style then became established in this country as one of the most pervasive and agreeable modes of design in the mid-Victorian period, and the Grand Hotel owes much of its charm to the Italianate features of its balconies, round-arched windows and bowed fronts surmounted by roof-pavilions. Nevertheless its unusual height caused it to be criticized by some people, while the author of *Moorecroft's Guide* considered it not quite 'in harmony with our climate and still less with the Anglican character'. Already the doctrine proclaimed by Welby Pugin and John Ruskin that Gothic was the only style morally justifiable for buildings in this country was finding acceptance. But it is hard to reconcile Moorecroft's opinion of the Grand with his praise of the Norfolk Hotel, which was built only a year later with five storeys and sixty-five bedrooms in a slightly more florid version of the same style as the Grand. Moorecroft regarded it as more beautiful than any other building in Brighton. For a long time the ugliest building in Brighton was considered to be the Metropole Hotel, which was built of red brick and terracotta in 1890 between the two other hotels. The architect was Alfred Waterhouse, who had designed the town halls of Hove, Manchester and Reading, as well as the Natural History Museum, South Kensington, and it is typical of his heavy-handed treatment and choice of materials of harshly aggressive colour. The building was one of a number in Victorian times that broke away from the elegant and gracious Regency and Early Victorian tradition of building in the white stucco or light yellow bricks which accord so well with the seaside atmosphere, but because of its conspicuous position on the sea-front it gave greater offence than the other red-brick buildings of its time, for example some of the Victorian churches, that were mostly built in areas away from the sea-front, and were surrounded by other buildings of their own day.

The brashness of the Metropole's architecture became associated in the minds of many people with the smartness and vulgarity of some of its patrons. C. B. Cochran, the famous musical-comedy showman, who was born in Brighton in 1872, was employed in the office of a surveyor near the site of the hotel and some of the plans were drawn in that office.[2] Cochran remarked that the Metropole was considered 'somewhat flash' and that when it opened 'the ladies of the Gaiety with their cavaliers were much in evidence on Sundays'.[3] Gabrielle Ray, Julia James, Lily Elsie (the original Merry Widow), Phyllis and Vera Dare, and that queen of Edwardian beauties Lily Langtry—the 'Jersey Lily'—were some of the idols of the stage who were brought down by their gallants to Brighton in gay 'four-in-hand' coaches, or in the new motor-cars.

In more recent years we have come to enjoy Victorian architecture, and many lovers of Brighton felt a pang of regret when the charming little spire on the top of the Metropole was removed in modern times to make room for extra storeys designed in modern style.

10 Volk's Railway

The astounding engineering achievements of the Victorian age whetted people's appetites for further mechanical marvels, and they were especially fascinated by novel forms of mechanical transport. Brighton was to see a number of intriguing experiments of this kind, and although the town had been slow to adopt the steam railway, it was here that history was made by the establishment of the first electric railway to provide a regular public service in Britain. It was indeed one of the first electric railway lines in the world. This was Volk's Electric Railway, running along the sea-front from the Palace Pier to Black Rock, which for over eighty years has been one of the most delightful features of Brighton's amusements. Its originator was a Brightonian, Magnus Volk, who was born of a German clock-maker at 40 Western Road on 19th October 1851. As a boy he developed a genius for mechanical and electrical things, and made windmills and steamships for himself from odd parts in his father's workshop. He was only fourteen when his father died, leaving his mother and five sisters to carry on the business, but the boy was already an expert in clock-making and by working early and late he managed to keep the family business going, producing not only clocks but scientific toys like electric shocking-coils and model telegraphs. These were in such demand from all over the world that by the time he was twenty he was employing a score of men and girls in his workshops. In 1881 he was awarded a gold medal for a street fire-alarm system. In the following year he equipped his house with the first domestic electric light and telephone systems in Brighton. (The first public use of electric light had been four years earlier at the Gaiety Theatre in Park Crescent.) Volk was then employed by the Corporation to install electric light in the Royal Pavilion, and this was completed in 1883. Much of his original wiring there, which ran in highly dangerous wooden mouldings, survived until 1947, when the building was re-wired.

At this time he had in his works an electric motor he had made, a Siemens electric dynamo and a small Crossley gas-engine, and he conceived the idea of using them to drive an electric railway car. He obtained from the Corporation a six months' licence to experiment with a line on the sea-front, and moved his equipment to one of the arches under the promenade near the Aquarium. A Brighton man, J. T. Chappell, laid for him a light two-foot-wide track for a distance of about a quarter of a mile from the Aquarium to the Old Chain Pier. Another Brighton man named Pollard built a small double-ended four-wheeled car with ten seats, small end-platforms for the driver, and a canvas canopy. To this Volk fitted his electric motor which drove the wheels through a belt-drive, the electric current being drawn from one rail and after driving the motor returning to the other rail. In front of the wheels were fixed small brushes to sweep away seaweed and any small pebbles that might accumulate on the track.

The railway was opened at twelve noon on Saturday, 4th August 1883, by the Mayor, who rode in the first car with other dignitaries, driven by Magnus Volk wearing a peaked cap. The railway was an immediate success, and on the following Monday, the Bank Holiday, the little car drove incessantly up and down the track at six miles an hour for eleven hours, carrying thousands of passengers. With the encouragement of this success, Volk was given permission in the following year to extend his railway with a wider track to the Banjo Groyne, a distance of about three-quarters of a mile, at the bottom of Paston Place in Kemp Town. There was a loop for passing and a stopping-place half-way. Two new four-wheeled double-ended cars were provided each with a 10 h.p. electric motor placed under the floor, and with the controller above the driver's head. Each car could carry thirty passengers, and was luxuriously equipped with engraved plate-glass windows, a panelled ceiling decorated with hand-painted flowers and gilt mouldings. There were as well blue silk curtains looped with blue and white silk tassels, cloth cushions, small mirrors, a clock and a barometer. New and more powerful generating equipment was installed in an arch near the eastern terminus.

At the opening of the rebuilt line on 4th April 1884, the first car was so laden with overweight aldermen that the springs were forced down and the car grounded on the sleepers of a level crossing. From this day onwards a regular five-to six-minute service was operated winter and summer until 1940, apart from interruptions caused by gale damage and the last war. Setbacks took place fairly frequently for a time not only from storms but because of sabotage to the line by disgruntled cab-men who thought the railway took trade away from their carriages that plied along the Madeira Drive, and from fishermen who imagined that the line cut visitors off from the beach, and discouraged them from taking trips in their boats. However, Volk's Railway was believed by most of the residents and visitors to be such an attraction that public subscriptions were raised to help Magnus Volk to repair the damage to his line. Medical opinion was rapidly forthcoming in support of the new mechanical wonder, in the best traditions of Doctors Russell, Awsiter and Relhan. Dr. Hawkesley of Lewes Crescent wrote:

'As a physician I can conceive of no more advantageous mode of administering the reviving and purifying influence of sea-air than by the action of these smoothly gliding cars, conducted almost on the sea itself.'

From the beginning Magnus Volk had visualized his electric railway extending as far as Rottingdean, but this would have involved either an impossible climb for the railway to the top of the cliffs, or an expensive viaduct or embankment along the shore beneath the cliffs, which were then not protected or strengthened by the present sea-wall. There were no limits to Volk's fertile inventiveness. With a tremendous leap of the imagination, he decided that in order to travel along the coast at high tide the wheels of his cars would have to move through the sea, along a track laid on the rocky shore with the cars themselves raised above the wheels on stilts. The rails ran some sixty to a hundred yards away from the shore from the Banjo Groyne to Rottingdean, two and three-quarter miles to the east, where a light steel pier a hundred yards long was built out to meet it. At Ovingdean Gap there was a small landing-stage; the rails were set in concrete blocks dovetailed into the chalk bedrock of the shore. The cars were raised above the wheels on four legs, each 23 feet long, and the current was drawn from an overhead wire. The wheels were housed in casings and were driven by two 25 h.p. electric motors by means of gearing and shafts which ran down two of the legs. The other two legs contained shafts that operated the brakes. The electricity came from a small steam-driven power station under the Rottingdean pier. The cars looked like a combination of a seaside pier, an old-fashioned pleasure yacht and a tram-car. The tubular legs and diagonal bracing rods of the cars resembled a section of a pier, while the main platform was like the upper deck of a pleasure steamer, with lifebelts hanging on the railings and even a small lifeboat suspended in davits.

On the platform stood an open-topped saloon like a tram-car. The luxury of the interior furnishings almost equalled that of an ocean liner. In the centre was an upholstered seat, with plants and flowers set in troughs between the two backs. There were heavy curtains at the windows on the seaward side, possibly to shut out on a rough day the terrifying sight of approaching foam-topped breakers. There were also a carpet and a pretty electrolier. The strange appearance of the car on its long stilts immediately gained for the seashore railway the name of 'Daddy-long-legs'. Magnus Volk can hardly have realized the brilliance of his creation. An Emett railway years before that celebrated caricaturist of railways was born, the 'Daddy-long-legs' possessed all the ingredients of dottiness combined with practicability, of fantasy and functionalism, that appealed to holiday-makers and trippers.

The seashore railway was officially opened on Saturday, 28th November 1896, when the first car, the 36-ton 'Pioneer', made its inaugural run to Rottingdean, laden with the Mayor and Mayoress of Brighton and other local celebrities. The tide was out and the journey was accomplished in thirty-four minutes at a speed of about six miles an hour. The line was a terriffic success, but only one week after it had been opened the same storm that destroyed the old Chain Pier, on the night of 4th–5th December, overturned the car standing at Rottingdean pier and almost completely destroyed it. The landing-stages at Ovingdean Gap—the half-way halt—and at Black Rock were also wrecked. Undaunted, Magnus Volk repaired the cars and the stations, with financial help from the public, and by the following May the line was working again. The summit of the railway's fame was reached in February 1897, when King Edward VII, then Prince of Wales, travelled by the 'Daddy-long-legs' to Rottingdean and back, accompanied by his daughter the Duchess of Fife, and her husband, whom the Prince was visiting at the time for the Duchess's birthday at her home in Lewes Crescent.

The railway continued running for two or three years and was enormously popular with the holiday crowds, although when the first novelty had worn off the return trip to Brighton at high tide, when the car was slowed down by the sea to a mere walking pace, could be rather tedious. However, the line ceased not for any defect of its own, but because the Corporation had found it necessary to build out long concrete groynes from the cliffs into the sea, to prevent erosion of the cliffs, and there was no means of carrying the line over the groynes. In 1900 the railway closed, but the wreck of the car remained standing at the Ovingdean jetty for another ten years, until it was removed, together with the remains of the other landing-stages, by a German firm of scrap-metal merchants. The principal relic of the Seashore Electric Tramroad surviving today is the long curving double line of massive concrete blocks that once carried the rails, which are still to be seen at low tide along the shore to Rottingdean.

In 1901, in compensation to Magnus Volk for the loss of the Rottingdean seashore railway, he was allowed to extend his original sea-front railway from Paston Place to a new terminus near the Borough boundary at Black Rock. From the former station the line was carried for some distance on a wooden viaduct from 15 to 20 feet above the beach, and to travel in one of the cars while rough seas were breaking on the beach beneath was a thrilling and spectacular experience. In course of time, however, the beach became built up with shingle by the action of the waves, until the viaduct became completely buried, and the rails now run at the level of the beach.

Magnus Volk made his last public appearance on 7th May 1937, when a new station was opened at Black Rock. The Corporation had built a swimming pool here and shortened the line a little. On the 20th of the same month Volk died, in his eighty-second year. On 1st April 1940 the Corporation entirely took over the line, which they had previously leased to Volk's company. They found themselves the possessors of ten four-wheeled cars, including the two original ones of 1884, but they were not allowed much time in which to play with their new toy. After the fall of France in June 1940, the beaches were closed. The two terminal stations were demolished and the cars were trapped in their sheds by the barbed wire entanglements. By the end of the war military occupation, salt-water corrosion and neglect had all but wrecked the railway, but it was restored and rebuilt by the Corporation, with a redundant tram-shelter serving as a station at the Aquarium and a new one at Black Rock. The line was again overhauled in 1960, and despite a suggestion that the railway should be brought up to date with modern streamlined cars, it was wisely decided to continue with the old cars, which were reconditioned by some aged engineers whose service went back almost to the beginning of the railway. The cars were now painted in an early-Victorian colour scheme of yellow and dark brown with large initials V.R. on the front and sides, which stood both for Volk's Railway and Victoria Regina. It will be a sad day for Brighton if ever the gaily painted toy-like cars cease to run along the sea-front of the town.

11 The Devil's Dyke

One of the favourite haunts of excursionists and day-trippers was the Devil's Dyke, a deep abrupt gash in the smooth slope of the Downs five miles north-west of Brighton. Legend has it that the Dyke was dug in the chalk by the Devil so as to allow the sea to rush in to submerge the churches of the Weald. The reality presents no less puzzling mysteries. The deep ravine with its steeply sloping sides, cut with machine-like precision and covered with smooth turf, is obviously water-worn, yet unlike other Downland watercourses it is not open to the sea but closed at each end. The Dyke was a favourite object for an excursion to King William IV and Queen Adelaide. Queen Victoria paid it a visit, and the Prince Consort, intrigued by wonders of all kinds, went by horse to look at it *incognito*. The high point of the Downs above it is crowned by an ancient hill-camp, and near by was an inn, which eventually became an hotel with amusement park attached. For years the Dyke was only reached on foot, or horseback, or by carriage. A railway was an obvious necessity, and the Brighton and Dyke Railway Company opened its line in 1887. By means of zigzag plotting the gradient was kept as low as 1 in 40, and the station was 200 feet below the hotel. The return fare was tenpence.

The new railway brought trippers to the Dyke in many thousands. The enterprising proprietor of the hotel, Mr. J. H. Hubbard, estimated the number in one year as about a million. One Whit-Monday alone he had over 30,000 visitors. He provided a fun-fair with tea-gardens, roundabouts, side-shows and souvenir stalls, and even published a newspaper, the *Devil's Dyke Times*. At length Mr. Hubbard's enterprise literally soared to enormous heights when he promoted two serious engineering works. One was an aerial cableway across the 1,000-foot-wide ravine, strung from two latticework steel towers. It was opened in 1894. It was of some value in saving trippers the long walk from one side of the Dyke to the other, but was mostly patronized for the terrific thrill of gazing down from the little car suspended from a thin wire to the depths of the valley below.

The Dyke Steep Grade Railway was of greater value, since it gave access to the hotel from the foot of the Dyke, and so to the roads from Brighton. There were two steep tracks and the cars were hauled up by cables wound by oil engines. It was opened in 1897, and was estimated to to have carried over 275,000 passengers a year, as well as great quantities of farm produce and other supplies for the hotel. Eventually the aerial cableway and the funicular railway became the chief objects of an excursion to the Dyke for many thousands of trippers, and their money was diverted from the hotel and restaurant, which suffered instead of benefiting by the additional attractions. Both the funicular railway and the aerial line were out of use by 1908 or 1909.[1] Nothing remains today but the scars of the track up the side of the Dyke, and the foundations of the cable-towers and the engine-house, and the Devil's Dyke has reverted to its primeval majesty, uncluttered by the works of man.

At one time it was firmly believed by certain persons that the Indian Mutiny was 'planned' at the Devil's Dyke Hotel.[2] It is true that Azimuth Khan, Prime Minister to the Indian rebel Nana Sahib, was sent by his master to England in 1856. During part of this time he stayed at the Dyke Hotel and the enormous volume of his correspondence with India apparently gave rise to the supposition that he had been sent as a political spy.

With the coming of the motor-car and the motor-coach, the little steam railway to the Dyke lost a great deal of its popularity, and at last, in January 1939, the trains ceased running. The track was later taken up and the station at the Dyke demolished.

For several years after the last war, Mr. Leslie Kramer, a Brighton entertainments promoter, endeavoured to make the Devil's Dyke and the hotel more attractive to visitors by installing a number of popular attractions.

Early in 1964 Mr. Kramer made a number of ambitious proposals for improvements estimated to cost a quarter of a million pounds, including a full-sized replica of a Sussex windmill to be built on top of the Dyke to disguise the water-tanks of the hotel, and, most remarkable of all, a one-fifth scale replica of the Temple of Abu Simbel in Egypt, which was to be built into the side of the Dyke itself.[3] Mercifully these proposals were rejected, and at last Mr. Kramer, discouraged by continual frustrations, gave up the property.

In 1967 the hotel was taken over by new owners and most pleasingly rebuilt as a restaurant with cafeteria and bars, in traditional Sussex materials of stone, brick, hung tiles and natural timber, but of modern design, and in admirable conformity with the surroundings.

12 The Theatres

The owner of the Duke Street Theatre in the early years of the nineteenth century, Hewitt Cobb, had little interest in a theatre except as a financial venture, and no doubt perceived the benefits that would result from a larger and more up-to-date theatre in a more fashionable part of the town. The site he chose in New Road, on Crown land overlooking the Prince of Wales's Pavilion, could not have been better, and the moment for the change also was well timed, when the Prince was spending so much time in Brighton over the building of the Royal Stables and the improvements to the Pavilion. The Theatre Royal was established by Cobb in partnership with John Brunton, the last lessee of the Duke Street Theatre, and it was Brunton who laid the foundation-stone in September 1806. The theatre opened in June the following year with Charles Kemble's performance of Hamlet, with Mrs. Kemble as Ophelia.

Together with the new scenery and equipment, the building cost the partners £12,000, but by the end of the second season Brunton had to sell his half-share in the theatre in order to pay his way as manager. Cobb had brought about the downfall of one lessee after another at Duke Street by forcing the rent up year by year, and now in New Road Brunton found himself again in the difficulty of having to pay a high rent and at the same time to hire expensive productions with the best stars of the day in order to attract the sophisticated Brighton audiences. From its earliest days the Theatre Royal enjoyed a special position in the world of the stage. Few other theatres in the provinces, if any, could command such a fashionable clientele, and the metropolitan character of Brighton made it the ideal theatre even then, as now, at which to try out new plays before opening in London. During the theatre's earlier years there was no shortage of managers who were attracted by the possibilities of the Theatre Royal. A few were successful, many struggled along maintaining a precarious balance between success and failure, while for others the experiment would end with flight from the bailiffs or by absconding with the takings. Despite the fluctuating fortunes of the management, the standard of the productions was extremely high, and the Theatre Royal became noted for the appearances of the greatest performers. Mrs. Siddons, the 'great Sarah' and 'Queen of Tragedy', appeared there no less than nine times, on two of which occasions she performed Lady Macbeth. Mrs. Jordan, Joseph Grimaldi, Edmund and Charles Kean, William Macready and Madam Vestris are among the many great names that appeared frequently upon the Theatre Royal's playbills, and cause its annals to parallel those of the British theatre itself. By the mid-nineteenth century the theatre had its own company, which presented plays regularly.[1] Occasionally they were reinforced by famous actors and actresses from London, but the nucleus of every cast was always drawn from local talent.

In 1854 the succession of changing (and sometimes vanishing) managers came to an end, when a new era of forty years' constant and successful management was inaugurated by the leasing of the building to Henry Nye Chart. After a few years he bought the theatre from the owners, and in 1866 had the upper storey demolished and a new auditorium erected on the walls of the old. The original portico of 1806, with its colonnade of square columns, together with the charming bow-windows at the southern end of the frontage, had survived up till then and was retained, as a drawing dated 1860 in the Brighton Reference Library shows, but a round-arched colonnade was built out on the first floor over the lower colonnade to screen the windows of a conservatory that was made within. The architect was C. J. Phipps, F.S.A., of London, who had designed the new theatres at Bath, Nottingham and South Shields, and the building was re-opened on 15th October 1866. The altered frontage, but still with the colonnade of square columns of the original building, survived at least until 1885, when it was shown in an engraving.[2]

It probably remained until 1894, when the *Brighton Herald* reported: 'The Theatre Royal was re-opened after re-modellings of so extensive a character as to amount almost to an entire reconstruction. The flat-fronted, ugly old frontage was replaced by the present frontage of red bricks and terracotta; the main entrance in the centre of the building was converted into an entrance to the pit, while the lumber yard enclosed by folding wooden doors gave place to the present vestibule and entrance to the stalls and circle; the dangerous old wooden staircases were replaced by widened stairways and corridors of concrete; the roof over the stage was greatly raised; electric light was substituted for gas; and the entire building was reseated, upholstered and redecorated.'[3]

It was undoubtedly at this time that the present colonnade of round, bulbous terracotta columns with Ionic capitals replaced the original colonnade. The colonnade of plain round columns in front of Weston's, the gunsmith's shop adjoining the theatre on the left, is all that remains of a long colonnade which stretched down New Road and round the corner in front of 'Wright's Royal Colonnade Library, Music Saloon and Reading Rooms', now occupied by Clark's Restaurant, and for some distance along North Street. The corner portion was removed in September 1912, and the remainder, apart from the part outside Weston's, was finally demolished in 1922.

Nye Chart himself played most of the leading roles in his productions at the Royal, and in July 1865 the company was joined by a young, attractive and clever actress, Ellen Elizabeth Rollason, who made her début as Pauline in *The Lady of Lyons*. She also scored triumphs in other plays— *Lady Audley's Secret* and *The School for Scandal*—and was one of the most popular actresses of the theatre. Two years later she married Mr. Chart.

When, in 1875, Nye Chart died, his widow assumed control, and during her almost legendary reign the theatre achieved a reputation of remarkable brilliance. More and more the local casts were supplanted by first-class touring companies from London, often bringing with them plays that had achieved success in London. On Thursday afternoons the entire company of a West End play would travel to Brighton for a 'flying matinée'. At Christmas-time the pantomimes became a forcing-ground for future London musical-comedy stars. By the Edwardian era audiences were composed more than ever before of Londoners visiting Brighton on holiday, and it became the theatre's policy to present light, amusing holiday programmes of musical comedies, farces and burlesques as well as more serious plays, including occasional Shakespeare. In 1906 Mr. Brandon Thomas brought the fourteen-year-old farce *Charley's Aunt* to Brighton with his own company, and received a tremendous ovation. To the Theatre Royal's roll of great performers of the past were now added such names as Ellen Terry, Mrs. Patrick Campbell, Sarah Bernhardt, Martin Harvey, Henry Irving, the Kendals, Seymour Hicks, Weedon Grossmith, Julia Neilson, Fred Terry, George Giddens and Matheson Lang.

The coming of the talking pictures in 1926 dealt a severe blow to theatres everywhere, and for some years the Royal was in a sorry plight, until in 1937 the management was taken over by J. Baxter Somerville, the manager of the Lyric Theatre, Hammersmith, and several other successful theatres. Under 'J.B.', from 1937 until his death in 1963, the theatre enjoyed a period of success that equalled, and even probably surpassed, anything that it knew in the palmiest days of Mr. and Mrs. Nye Chart. Indefatigably he investigated the activities of little-known experimental theatre companies as well as the programmes of provincial repertory theatres, seeking for interesting productions to put on at Brighton. Almost every great London success during the last twenty years had a previous showing at Brighton, and at one time as many as twenty-five successful London plays running at a time had their première at the Theatre Royal. Even during the difficult times of the last war the theatre was kept going by 'J.B.'s' tireless enthusiasm, backed financially by Lewis Cohen (later Lord Cohen) and his colleagues of the board of directors. For long periods the theatre ran at a loss, but it was kept going long after less dedicated managers and directors would have given up in despair. With its unbroken tradition since Georgian days, the Theatre Royal is one of the great provincial theatres of this country, and its closure would be a disaster to the whole world of the British stage.

Only a few yards away from the Theatre Royal in New Road was Wright's Music Hall, opened in 1854, which in its day was the most popular variety theatre in Brighton. It was later known as the Oxford Theatre of Varieties, and presented 'the first artists in Europe in dancing, negro, comic and buffo singing'. The best seats in the house, the orchestra stalls, which were carpeted, were only 1s 6d. The Oxford was burnt down in 1867 and was rebuilt as the New Oxford, where a boy was killed by a cannon during one of the performances. It was one of the last of the old-time music halls to retain the institution of the chairman, who announced the turns with a rap of his hammer and a facetious quip, often at the expense of any member of the audience who caught his eye, and cried out at intervals, 'Give your orders, gentlemen, the waiter's in the room.'[4] That great showman the late Sir Charles Cochran made his first stage appearance at the New Oxford. The theatre was again burnt down in 1892 and rebuilt in Louis-Seize style as the Empire.

In 1905 it became the Coliseum Theatre of Varieties, and two years later was renamed the Court Theatre. In the late 1930s it became a cinema, but was reopened after the last war for plays as the Dolphin Theatre. In 1952 it was renamed Her Majesty's Theatre, and two years later was again converted as a cinema, but this time for Continental films and called the Paris. It was finally closed in 1963 and its florid Edwardian Louis-Seize fabric demolished, to be replaced by an undistinguished, flat-fronted office building in red brick.

In the last quarter of the nineteenth century one of the most popular places of entertainment was the Royal Hippodrome, or, as it later became, the Gaiety Theatre, in Park Crescent Place, off Lewes Road. During the twenty-five years of its existence it offered successively the thrills of the circus, the boisterous humour of the music hall, and the spine-chilling horror of melodrama.

A hundred years before it opened as a permanent circus in 1876, travelling circuses had visited Brighton from time to time and set up their tents on the Level, and by 1808 a Mr. Saunders had established a permanent circus building in Grand Parade, but the venture was doomed to failure, and after some four years it closed from lack of support and was finally demolished. One of the most famous circus proprietors, William Batty, who rebuilt Astley's Circus in London after one of its many fires, made his home in Mighell Street, Brighton, and from 1840 made regular visits to the town with his company. The greatest circus proprietors in Brighton, however, were the Ginnetts. Jean-Pierre Ginnett and his brothers left their home near Marseilles during the Franco-Prussian war. They came at first to Southend and bought a pony with which they travelled performing various acts, acquiring another pony, a monkey, and eventually other animals until they had created a circus. Jean-Pierre was the clown of the company and his brothers the riders. It was under Jean-Pierre's son Fred that Ginnetts' circus became one of the largest in the country, and it was he who decided to give it a permanent home at Brighton in Park Crescent Place. The design of the building was based on the Grand Cirque in Paris, with a ring 50 feet in diameter and seats for 1,500 to 1,700 patrons. It was opened as Ginnett's Royal Hippodrome on 31st October 1876, with prices from 3s to 6d, with the added inducement that Tilling's Lewes Road omnibuses would convey visitors to the circus free of charge, returning after the performance. This was made possible by the stables for the horse-buses being immediately opposite the circus entrance. Ginnett's circus became one of the most popular features of the Brighton season. In the opening weeks, as well as an 'equestrian pantomime', there was 'Ohmy! the glittering Star of the Air and Falling Comet in his weird gyration and outstanding fall from the Roof to the Ground'. In the following winter season 'Ethardo' made an ascent to the roof up a spiral ramp while balancing on a large ball. There were also at various times such ingenuous entertainments as pony and goat shows, prizes for the best conundrum, and baby shows with 'a charming new bonnet' offered to the prettiest mother.

In November 1878 Fred Ginnett, no doubt with the aid of Magnus Volk, made history by introducing electric lighting at the Hippodrome four years before it was adopted in London theatres. His arc lamps, which gave 4,000 candlepower, were probably of a similar type to those installed at the Paris Hippodrome earlier in the same year. But the new lighting was in a sense too successful. In circus performances the horses were frightened by the strong shadows, and for this reason the lights could only be used occasionally, so they were removed and reinstalled in a local skating-rink. Ginnett was full of ideas for more elaborate entertainments. By 1877 he had built at the rear of the Hippodrome another hall, boldly called 'the new Grand Olympia', where he ran a riding school and planned various elaborate spectacles, but his chief ambition was to stage full theatrical performances, and in 1882 he made a very reasonable plea to the magistrates for a licence, for the sake of the '20,000 people in the north of the town who could only afford 6d for a stage play'. But his efforts to obtain a full dramatic licence were thwarted for years by Mrs. Nye Chart, the enterprising proprietress of the Theatre Royal, and Ginnett was forced to continue with circus performances and military spectacles such as the 'Battle of Ulundi' with 'real Zulus and (by permission) real soldiers'. However, by 1889 Ginnett had come to terms with Mrs Chart and in the following July the Hippodrome reopened with a full dramatic licence under the new name of 'the Gaiety' and with 'Tommy' Phillips of the Theatre

Royal as manager and stage-manager. After opening with an ordinary play, and a brief period as a music hall, the Gaiety Theatre became the local home of melodrama. With the gallery the most fully supported part of the theatre, at 6d, the general standard of the productions was never very high, and there were complaints about the dilapidated scenery—'The way in which a worn-out scene with Gothic tracery is made to do duty for all kinds of purposes is not creditable to the resources of the establishment.' The clients, however, received full value for their money in blood-curdling thrills and suspense. In *The Fast Mail* two trains thundered past each other on the stage, and in *The Slums of London* the hero was tied to a stake near a box of dynamite timed to explode in five minutes. His wife rushes in, hurls the box into the river, where it explodes, and then cuts the wires by which the villains plan to destroy three London bridges!

The Gaiety was doomed, however, by its own creator, for within a year after its management was taken over by the Charts, Ginnett had built a new Hippodrome in Brighton, in North Road, which after a few years brought about the downfall of his earlier theatre. Its opening marked the jubilee of the Ginnetts as a circus family and it was here that they enjoyed their greatest prosperity. Louis-Pierre's daughter, Mrs. Adelaide Austin, celebrated her eighty-seventh birthday in Brighton, and could look back on almost eighty years as a circus performer.

In 1894 Ginnett renamed his second Hippodrome the Eden Theatre. It was larger and far better equipped than the Gaiety and now presented every kind of tragedy, comedy, farce and pantomime, with melodrama of a much higher standard of production than at the rival theatre. Indeed, the reputation of the Theatre Royal itself was challenged for a time by the Eden Theatre, where many of the best actors of the day were to be seen. The Eden was later renamed the Grand, and was devoted to variety performances, which continued without interruption throughout the last war. In 1955 the theatre was closed and converted to a factory for the making of reproduction period furniture. One night in 1961 it was burnt down, and it was later demolished to make way for a new office building.

In an attempt to compete with the Eden Theatre, the Gaiety reduced its prices to 6d for stalls, 4d pit and gallery 3d. Eventually it was taken over by Messrs. Evans and Dunkin, who by now controlled the Empire and Eden Theatres in Brighton. They improved both the buildings and the productions, but they had overstepped themselves and went bankrupt. Various managers and lessees tried to make a success of the Gaiety, but eventually, in March 1900, it closed. In February 1901 it was bought by the Fryco Mineral Water Company for £6,000. In his entertaining account of the theatre Mr. Gunnell[5] describes how when the doors were once more unlocked 'it seemed as though time had stood still within those walls. Everything was just as it had been left. The stage was set for a production with a carpet on the floor, scenery and furniture in position. Down in the orchestra pit the kettle-drums, bearing a coat of arms, stood ready for the overture. In the pay-boxes were rolls of tickets. In the "Olympia" a Cinderella coach rested up to its axles in mud in the middle of what had once been a sawdust ring. . . .' There was every appearance of one of those rapid departures that were not unheard of at one time in theatrical circles. After serving as a mineral-water factory for many years the building was demolished in 1930. The firm had built a special concrete floor for their heavy plant within the old structure, and on this was built the block of flats that stands on the spot today. The Gaiety Theatre is now only part of the legend of the full-blooded glittering and boisterous world of entertainment in the last quarter of Brighton's Victorian age.

The Hippodrome Theatre in Middle Street was first opened in 1897 as an ice-skating rink, but it did not receive its name until 1901, when it was greatly enlarged and converted to a theatre. For over half a century it was the principal variety theatre in Brighton, and a number of important plays were presented there, including *The Doctor's Dilemma* with a memorable performance by Vivien Leigh as Jennifer Dubedat. Unfortunately in recent years the theatre was run at an increasing loss, chiefly because the entertainments presented were booked by a London organization, and consisted mostly of shows that were being sent on routine tours round the provinces, and were not selected with any knowledge of or regard for the special preferences or dislikes of Brighton audiences. The theatre was closed in 1965, and in spite of several commendable efforts to have it used as a film and television studio, it succumbed to the fate that has overtaken so many local theatres and cinemas, and became a bingo hall.[6]

From 1901, when the new pavilion on the Palace Pier was opened, until quite recently, the Palace Pier Repertory Theatre presented theatrical performances of remarkably high and consistent quality, often in the face of difficulties caused by the reluctance of the public to venture out on the half-mile walk along the pier in a fierce gale on a winter's night. During the years after the last war the company struggled along gallantly, presenting an agreeable series of comedies, crime plays and other entertaining fare. Many famous actors and actresses of today played in their early days on the Palace Pier, particularly Ralph Lynn, Barry Sinclair, Hermione Gingold, Sybil Wise, Judy Cornwall, John Parry, Julie Christie, Francis Cuka and Nigel Green. Through lack of support the Palace Pier Repertory Company was disbanded in 1964.

13 Early Social Movements

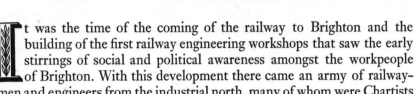

It was the time of the coming of the railway to Brighton and the building of the first railway engineering workshops that saw the early stirrings of social and political awareness amongst the workpeople of Brighton. With this development there came an army of railwaymen and engineers from the industrial north, many of whom were Chartists and followers of the social reformer Robert Owen, and who had already served an apprenticeship as labour leaders in various parts of the country.

Chief amongst them was George Henderson, an East Lothian engineer, a keen trade unionist and a disciple of Robert Owen. With his workmates he became a virile political influence in the town, and established the Brighton branch of the Mechanics' Institutes, which with their libraries and reading-rooms were among the chief influences in the education of the workers of those days.

The co-operative trading and political movement in the town had been active even before the first co-operative shops were opened at 10 Queen's Place, Upper North Street, and at 31 West Street, in 1828. This early movement had its own four-page monthly journal called '*The Co-operator*'. Another early working-class organization was the Working Men's Institute that was founded in Brighton in 1848 and attracted no less than 1,000 members at its beginning. With the aid of institutions like these Henderson and his friends began to organize and unite the workpeople; they brought the leadership which the people needed, and they supplied the knowledge, the experience and the technique of action in the working-class struggle for which they had been waiting. Above all they inspired their followers with a sense of purpose and unity. Furthermore it was with the coming of the railway that a new order came into being with regard to the relationship of worker to employer. Hitherto almost all employment in a town like Brighton had been on the basis of an individual serving a private employer. The railway employees were working for a public service, although it was privately owned. In this sense railways were national from the beginning, long before they were nationalized. In 1891 the railway employees numbered no less than 2,651 workers, including 215 engineers.[1]

Fresh impetus was given to the advance of the working-class movement in Brighton with the boom in building that followed the opening of the railway. To the engineers and railwaymen were now added hordes of building workers whose wages and conditions gave rise to extreme discontent and agitation. The building in 1890 of the gigantic Hotel Metropole in particular provoked continual serious disputes, and among the workers on this project were men who had already been prominent in big labour conflicts in London a year or two earlier. At the same time new political ideals were fermenting, resulting in Brighton in the formation in 1889 of a branch of the Social Democratic Federation.

One of the chief early reformist pioneers was George Jacob Holyoake, to whose memory a plaque has been attached to the house in Camelford Street, off Marine Parade, where he lived for many years. He was an indefatigable speaker and pamphleteer on socialism, he invented the form of religious disbelief known as 'Secularism' and in 1841 was the last person in this country to be imprisoned for atheism. His principal work is an autobiography, *Sixty Years of an Agitator's Life*, published in 1897. It was chiefly through the grievances of the building workers that the Brighton Trades Council came into being in 1890, on the lines of those that were being formed in all the main industrial cities of Britain at that time. The inspiration came from Will Evans, an engineer, a shy and studious person who was usually seen deeply immersed in a book or pamphlet when walking along the street, but who in public became a fiery champion of the rights of labour against the employing class, and, although self-educated, used his tongue and pen especially in the Town Council with scarifying effect.[2] The labour movement at this time developed in a national atmosphere of industrial unrest and of common purpose amongst the workers. The Dockers' Strike and the dramatically successful strike of the London match-girls were serving as an inspiration to workers all over the country.

At the meetings of the Trades Council, and at the great May Day demonstration that was held every year on the Level, crowds of workers were addressed by many speakers who later became well-known figures in the national labour movement, such as Will Thorne, Ben Tillett, Tom Mann, and Margaret Bondfield, who eventually became Minister of Labour in the Labour Government of 1929–32, and was the first woman Cabinet Minister. She had, in fact, begun her working life in 1887 as an assistant in a draper's emporium in the Western Road, Brighton, where the girls worked until nine o'clock every night and later on Saturdays; they slept in bare dormitories and had few opportunities for leisure, recreation or education. These experiences were the background of her later successful campaigns to ameliorate the conditions of shop-assistants.

From those early days onwards the labour movement in Brighton developed in size and influence, indeed to such an extent that when the General Strike descended upon the country in 1926 the working classes of Brighton, which were expected to give it little support, achieved almost complete unity in bringing local industries and services to a standstill. The stoppage in Brighton was, in fact, the most complete of any town in the south of England, and the Brighton workers were incredulous and overcome with a sense of betrayal when the strike was called off by their national leaders.

14 Late Victorian Social Life

The coming of the railway was attended not only by many benefits to the town but also by certain evils, in the shape of the criminal and disreputable types who flocked down to Brighton at the time in much greater numbers than ever in the past. The races were held then only on the first three days of August immediately after the Bank Holiday. It was believed that most of the more serious crimes in the town were committed by persons who came for the races,[1] and these events were no longer patronized by the aristocracy to the same extent as formerly. The Duke of Richmond transferred his patronage entirely to Goodwood; royalty no longer entered horses at Brighton, and the Queen's Cup was withdrawn in 1849. Partly because of this blow to Brighton's pride a new race committee, the Race Stand Trustees, was formed and purchased the old stand. A new stand was erected in 1851 at a cost of £6,000, and the railway supported the committee's reforming activities with a contribution towards the stand and an annual grant to the race fund. With the new stand and improvements to the course and with more stringent regulations of the conduct of the races, these events were placed on a more reputable footing, while the large attendances that the railway made possible ensured their financial success. By 1884 the races had attained a new pitch of prosperity, and in that year the Brighton Corporation acquired the rights vested in the Race Stand Trustees. They made further improvements to the course, and extended the racing to two days in the spring as well as the three days in August. The racing brought in so much money that in 1890 the Trustees were able to make a purchase that was of immense benefit to the town, when they bought for £13,500 the Queen's Park Estate and made a free gift of it to the Corporation.

The purchase consisted of 16½ acres of ground, the German Spa, the lodges, and the 'pepper box', an ornamental tower which had originally been a water-tower, later called 'The Observatory', in the grounds of Mr. Attree's Italian Villa. The robes of the Mayor and Corporation were also conveniently provided by the Trustees out of the profits of the races, for such an expenditure if made directly out of the rates would undoubtedly have given rise to strong criticism.

J. Ashley Sterry, a writer in the *Pictorial World*, gave a lively picture of Brighton as it was in 1880, when he took an afternoon stroll in the town. He thought a sunny day in December as good as August, indeed even more

315

pleasant. In the Steine he conjured up memories of the Regency, then walked down East Street, where he saw a wonderful shop for French chocolate and *bon-bons*, where two young schoolgirl friends made him spend more in a few minutes than he had bargained for in one day. There was a toy-shop that was 'toy-dom *in excelsis*', but he was horrified to see displayed in the window amongst the beautiful toys a selection of birch-rods for punishing children, and the sight struck him even at that time as an instance of the harshness underlying the hypocritical Victorian senti-mentality about children. He saw 'ancient dowagers in marvellous sealskin jackets going critically up one side of East Street down the other, and peer-ing through their double eye-glasses as though they were doing the pictures at the Royal Academy'. At Streeter's, the old Bun Shop in Pool Valley, kept by 'some quaint little ladies', he once more bought some square buns, the like of which were unobtainable anywhere else in Britain, which were precisely the same then as they were when he was a boy. Near by a troop of schoolboys were dashing into Brill's Baths for a swim, and not far away on the front was a 'wonderful lace-shop' owned by a firm with the truly Dickensian name of Chillmaid and Tinkler. There was Lewis's antique shop, full of bric-à-brac, silver and superb china; and Trufitt's the barbers, who made wigs for King George IV. In West Street there were more antique shops; Chippendale furniture at Colling's and old English pottery at Acton's.

On the sea-front were to be seen several well-known Brighton char-acters; the man who sold religious tracts at the bottom of Regency Square, and 'Dizzy' the seller of brandy-balls, so-called because of some facial resemblance to Lord Disraeli, and who was said to have brought out a new sweetmeat when his model published his new novel *Endymion*, and called it 'Endymion Rock' in compliment. Some of the more amusing eccentrics Sterry once knew had disappeared. He saw no longer the 'Star-Gazer', who walked about with his face turned to the sky, and who carefully shut every gate he saw open.

Another odd character, who had been christened 'the Hardened Sinner', used every morning to have two dozen oysters and a pot of stout brought to his bath-chair on the Esplanade and devoured his luncheon in full view of all the passers-by. But Sterry regretted there were no more great characters of the stature of Martha Gunn, Smoaker Miles, Mr. Tupper the Librarian, and the M.C.s, Mr. Wade, Mr. Eld and Colonel Eld. He never wearied of what he called the 'Kaleidoscope of the Cliff' where along the King's Road there passed an endless stream of people, invalids in bath-chairs, children in goat-chaises—'There is a magnificent equipage just gone by, drawn by a fierce black goat, with green eyes and portentous horns. . . . Look at the portly mammas in sable, the winsome maidens in otter, the beauties in bearskin. Observe the variety of coats, the tailor-made dresses, the hussar-like scarlet-faced costumes, the Tam-o-Shanter caps, the granny bonnets, and the sailor-boy hats.' He noticed some four of five authors of some of the most popular novels of the day. Among them was one of the earliest writers of Wild West stories, Bret Harte, author of *The Luck of Roaring Camp*.

With them, too, was Mary Elizabeth Braddon, one of the most famous best-selling lady novelists of the Victorian era. Her early literary efforts appeared in the *Brighton Herald* in 1858 and 1859, and in August 1859 she was appearing as an actress at the Theatre Royal. At that time she was lodging at 34 New Road. She first became famous with a lurid story, *The Trail of the Serpent*, published in serial form in 1860, and in 1862 she produced *Lady Audley's Secret*, of which over a million copies were sold, and which made the fortunes both for herself and her publisher. Oscar Wilde made several visits to Brighton, usually staying at the Royal Albion Hotel. One day in February 1894 while driving along the Hove sea-front in a carriage his horse bolted and did not stop until the carriage crashed into the railings of Regency Square. A local writer suggested that Mr. Wilde displayed such courage that he must have regarded the incident as 'an accident of no importance'.[2]

Another figure often seen in the fashionable parade was the great Victorian journalist, George Augustus Sala, who produced two entertaining little books about Brighton, *Things I have Seen and People I have Known* in 1894, and *Brighton as I Knew It* in 1898. Sala's mother was a widowed music-teacher, and he described how when he was young his mother organized a grand benefit concert every year to help the family finances. It was always a matter of agonized suspense as to whether the celebrated principal artistes would forgo their fees, in view of the declared object of the concert.

In order to make a silent, but eloquent appeal, little Sala was 'duly washed, waxed and polished', and taken by his mother when she went to settle with the artists after the concert. Several of them declined their fees, but Madame Malibran, the famous operatic contralto, swept up her thirty guineas without compunction, merely patting the little boy benignly on the head as she put them into her reticule. Mrs. Sala then called upon Paganini in his room at the Old Ship Hotel. Sala wrote: 'I can see Paganini now—a lean, wan, gaunt man in black. He looked at me long and earnestly; and somehow, although he was about as weird a looking creature as could well be imagined, I did not feel afraid of him. In a few broken words my mother explained her mission, and put the fifty guineas down on the table. When I say that he washed his hands in the gold—that he scrabbled at it, as David of old did at the gate—and grasped it and built it up tiny little heaps, panting the while, I am not in any way exaggerating. He bundled it up at last in a blue cotton pocket-handkerchief with white spots and darted from the room. And we—my poor mother convulsively clasping my hand—went out on to the landing and were about descending the stairs when the mighty violinist bolted again from his bedroom door. "Take that, little boy," he said, "take that", and he thrust a piece of paper, rolled up almost into a ball, into my hand. It was a bank-note for fifty pounds!'[3]

Another familiar figure was Mr. Kuhe, who came to Brighton from Prague in 1847 and brought Jenny Lind here in that year, when she was paid £500 for singing at the Town Hall. He organized not only many of the most important concerts in the town at the Aquarium and the Dome, but inaugurated the annual Brighton Music Festivals which have continued in one form or another ever since.

On the sea-front, at the eastern corner of West Street, stood Mutton's, the famous restaurant, where one could drop in at odd times for a plate of turtle soup and a glass of sherry. Unlike many establishments of this kind, Mutton's was by no means patronized exclusively by men. It consisted also of a pastrycook's shop, and during his sea-front walk Sterry observed inside several 'big babies, spoiling their dinners and covering their seal-skin jackets with flakes of pastry.'

Cuthbert Bede, in the novel of Brighton's life which he wrote in 1866, described how one of his characters, Helen Merredew, 'striving to subdue the surging of her petticoats' in the fresh wind of the sea-front, was gazing at the display of French novels in the windows of Jeff's bookshop near St. Paul's Church, when she encountered a 'pretty, merry-looking girl, whose long brown hair, damp and glistening with the sea-water in which she had been bathing, was hung out in the sun to dry, by being permitted to fall to its natural length over her shoulders. '"Are you going to Mattins?", enquired the first. "No, I am going to Mutton's," laughed the other. Mutton's and Mattins, what a difference!'

'Cuthbert Bede' was the pseudonym of a clergyman named Edward Bradley, perhaps more widely known as the author of *The Adventures of Mr. Verdant Green*, a classic novel of Oxford life.

To continue the episode in Bede's Brighton story, Helen decided at length to go in search of her friend—'Here is Mutton's', said Edgar, her escort, as they came to a shop-door whose dark green painted doorway bore the announcement 'Real turtle-soup always ready'. Having been 'blown into the shop' through its double glass door, Helen found herself in the famous inner room of the restaurant, lit by a domed skylight from which hung a glass chandelier. On one wall was a large mirror standing over a buhl cabinet, on which were figures and ornamental flowers under tall glass shades, other figures being upon a stand in front of the long window. Altogether, Mutton's was, as Edgar had reported it to be, 'an institution of Brighton', and the truth was that the two worlds, of fashion and faith, intermingled no less freely in the 1860s in the plush-seated mirror-lined saloons of the famous Brighton restaurant than they did in the incense-perfumed, choir-resounding aisles of St. Paul's where, as we have already remarked, the services were so 'high' that they were referred to in a local pamphlet as 'the Sunday Opera'.

Richard Jefferies, the author of several works of passionately poetical nature mysticism, who lived at No. 5 (now No. 87) Lorna Road, Hove, for several years, surveyed the throngs of fashionable people and their inane ways of passing the time with a cynical and ironic eye.[4]

'It is a Piccadilly crowd by the sea—exactly the same style of people you meet in Piccadilly, but freer in dress and particularly in hats. All fashionable Brighton parades the King's Road twice a day, morning and afternoon, always on the side of the shops. The route is up and down the King's Road as far as Preston Street, back again and up East Street. Riding and driving Brighton extends its Rotten Row sometimes to Third Avenue, Hove. These well-dressed and leading people never look at the sea. Watching by the gold-plate shop you will not observe a single glance in the direction of the sea, beautiful as it is, gleaming under the sunlight. They do not take the slightest interest in sea, or sun, or sky, or the fresh breeze calling white horses from the deep. Their pursuits are purely "social", and neither ladies nor gentlemen ever go on to the beach or lie where the surge comes to the feet. The beach is ignored; it is almost, perhaps quite vulgar; or rather it is entirely outside the pale. No one rows, very few sail; the sea is not "the thing" in Brighton, which is the least nautical of seaside places. There is more talk of horses.'

There was a less brilliant side to life in Brighton. Because of severe unemployment in winter, when most of the hotels, restaurants, boarding-houses and lodging-houses were either closed or had so few visitors that few workers were required, there was a great deal of appalling poverty in Brighton. However, as a result of the work of many charitable institutions of the town, and of the social welfare measures introduced by the Town Council, actual pauperism decreased considerably between the passing of the Corn Law Amendment Act of 1834 and the 1860s. The immense Workhouse and Infirmary built on the Race Hill in 1865–7 and the Industrial Schools founded at Warren Road, Woodingdean, at the same time were large, well equipped and in advance of similar institutions in other parts of the country at the time. The effects of poverty were aggravated by the shocking state of housing for the poorer classes, and by drink. A guide-book, *Brighton As It Is*, written by 'a Graduate of the University of London' and published in 1860, included a 'short account of the social and inner life of its inhabitants which was, in fact, one of the first social surveys ever to be made of an English town, conducted in accordance with the principles of 'a new Science . . . not unaptly termed Social Science—'. The author called attention to the houses of the poor 'which are situated in narrow streets and courts, are for the most part ill-ventilated, badly drained, if at all . . . the numbers which are huddled together in them render decency and decorum next to impossible. Many of them being built with inferior bricks and mortar made of sea-sand are wretchedly damp so that even the walls are covered with lichens, and their miserable tenants, unable to endure the depression of spirits which is the necessary result, try to drown their uneasy sensations in the neighbouring beer shops!' Before very long the first slum clearances were being made by the Council. Pimlico and Orange Row were the first to go, in the 70s; Little St. James's Street, Cumberland Place and Spa Street followed in the late 80s and 90s. The new houses were erected by private builders in all these areas except the last.[5]

Drunkenness, assaults on women and children, 'juvenile depravity' and many other crimes were, in the opinion of the clergy and of the judges and magistrates, almost always 'the fruits of intemperance' and in fact they considered that 'the greater proportion of crimes committed in Great Britain' was then 'attributable to the drinking customs'. Because of the heavy demand created by the enormous influx of visitors in the summer season the number of public houses and beer-shops in Brighton was very great, but even so the number was disproportionately large, totalling, in 1860, 479 liquor-shops compared with 541 provision-shops in the whole of the town.

Beyond all question the drink-shops contributed enormously to the poverty, degradation and misery upon which they flourished. It was 'well known to the police' that there were at least seven public houses and ten beer-shops which were 'notorious resorts for thieves and prostitutes of the lowest grade', and in the Government returns 'twenty more are described as suspected houses'.

The glamour which has been cast in recent years over the music halls of the 'Good Old Days' by emasculated reconstructions on radio and television existed in reality in the case of comparatively few of the better houses. Even Sickert's evocation of the light, the colour, the brilliance, gaiety and excitement of the London music halls did not penetrate below the surface. The author of *Brighton As It Is* described the scene at the Canterbury Music Hall, which he 'felt bound to state was a considerable improvement upon the other dirty public-houses with which this portion of the town is infested'. As well as the 'small tradesmen with their wives and families', and a few citizens, clerks and shop-assistants, and an occasional footman in plush from a titled family, he observed in the pit the 'old women, toothless, with grimy faces and slatternly garments, foul mouths and wickedly old lustful eyes', and the 'young mothers, with bare-headed, bare-footed, ill-clad children on their knees, who had much better be at home in bed'. Yet he admitted that the Canterbury Hall was far more

THE BEDFORD HOTEL,
by Thomas Cooper, 1829, destroyed by fire, 1964

CANNON OF THE WEST BATTERY
at the time of its demolition, 1858

THE BEDFORD HOTEL:
the Grecian Hall, by Thomas Cooper, 1828

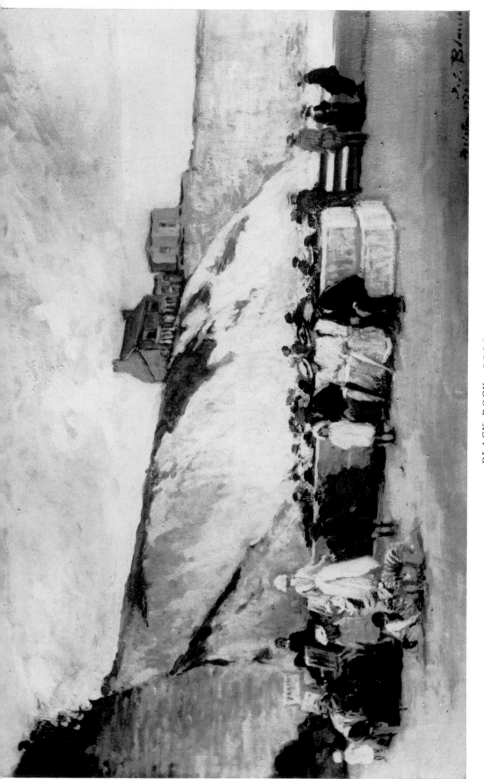

BLACK ROCK, 1922
Painting by Jacques-Emile Blanche

MARLBOROUGH HOUSE, THE STEINE
Designed by Robert Adam, 1787

ANDREW'S FISHING TACKLE SHOP, BARTHOLOMEWS,
built *c*. 1790–1800, as in 1935

THE CHURCH OF THE HOLY RESURRECTION,
built 1874, in use as a meat store, 1965

ST. STEPHEN'S CHURCH, MONTPELIER PLACE, *c.* 1935;
originally built as the Castle Hotel Ballroom

THE CHURCH OF THE HOLY
RESURRECTION,
Little Russell Street, in 1906

THE AQUARIUM ENTRANCE
AND CLOCK-TOWER
as originally built in 1871, *c.* 1908

FLINT-COBBLE BUILDING OF *c.* 1790, and slum-children of *c.* 1922, in the Carlton Hill area

'THE DRUID'S HEAD', Brighton Place, *c.* 1950

THE RAILWAY VIADUCT AT LEWES ROAD,
being repaired after bombing in 1943
Drawing by Muirhead Bone

respectable than the 'penny gaffs' which used to flourish in many parts of the town. The dancing assembly rooms in different parts of the town were regarded as of a much lower grade—'the social evils engendered by places of this description can hardly be exaggerated'. Crime had been on the decrease, like extreme poverty, in recent years. The more serious offences were mostly committed 'by strangers from London and elsewhere, and particularly at the time of the races, when criminals of all classes flock to the town'. In Brighton, however, it was found that prostitution was an especially prevalent evil. The number of prostitutes was recorded in the Judicial Statistics for 1859 at 325, but there were 'good grounds for believing that double that number would be nearer the truth'. Twenty-five of them were under sixteen years of age. No allowance had been made for the large annual importation of 'gay women from London'. The number of public brothels was stated to be ninety-seven, but these were far from being the only places where prostitution was carried on. At night the scenes on the beach in front of the King's Road, on the Level, and 'opposite the Theatre Royal', presumably in the Pavilion grounds, were said to beggar all description. The colonnade of the Theatre Royal after eleven o'clock presented a 'very animated appearance being then used principally as a promenade of the women of the town'. The lowest prostitutes infested the neighbourhood of Church Street and Edward Street, and in one of the lanes leading from the former there was 'a whole block of houses, too notorious to be required to be named, entirely garrisoned by females of the most depraved and abandoned class'. Many of them existed in conditions of apalling servitude and wretchedness, not even being allowed by their exploiters to possess their own clothing.

It was to help such miserable creatures that the Rev. George Wagner founded St. Mary's Home for Female Penitents in 1855. A remarkable work of reclamation and help was carried on at the Home, to which women and girls were often sent by the police, by doctors and from the hospitals, and by the Wagners and their clergy who carried out mission work amongst the poor 'and often degraded' occupants of the wretched streets round about their churches. It was claimed that Mr. George Wagner himself persuaded five women to give up keeping brothels and to turn to a better way of life.[6] After his death the Home came under the control of the Rev. Arthur Wagner. Originally established in two small houses capable of receiving twelve penitents, the institution came eventually to consist of the 'home for fallen women' and a lying-in hospital, housing about forty occupants, and in addition a Nursery for Orphan Children; an Industrial School in which young girls were trained for domestic service; an Infirmary for aged and disabled women; and a Dispensary for the poor of the district. There were also blanket-lending societies, coal clubs and other provident institutions carried on by the district visitors connected with the place. The Home occupied almost the whole of the western side of Queen's Square and also all the houses except four in Wykeham Terrace, a row of pleasant Victorian Gothic houses on the eastern side of Dyke Road, just below the Church of St. Nicholas. This terrace was built between 1822 and 1830.*

It was said that the buildings of Wykeham Terrace and the houses of St. Mary's Home in Queen's Square were connected by 'an underground tunnel'. In fact, they backed on to each other. The sinister light in which so many of Mr. Wagner's activities seemed to appear because of his addiction to idolatrous 'Romish' practices must have caused this convenient feature to assume an alarming significance in the minds of some persons.

The various institutions were administered by St. Mary's Sisterhood and the rule of the place was extremely strict. Humility, obedience and silence were enforced upon everyone; the penitent girls, who did the heavy work of the institution, being punished for offences such as using bad language, insubordination, or trying to escape, by the deprivation of food or by solitary confinement. The inmates were expected to submit to 'constant surveillance . . . as a perpetual act of penitence'.[7] Their unfortunate state was harshly emphasized by their humble dress and by the unequivocal name given to them. When called for an interview with the Superintendent Sister, Miss Caroline Graeme, not only the penitent women but even the staff were compelled to remain kneeling before her throughout. The place came under severe public criticism in 1863 because of the part played by Mr. Arthur Wagner and Miss Graeme in the affair of Constance Kent, a probationer-nurse in the hospital, who, following a 'confession' extracted from her while at the Home, underwent trial for the brutal murder of her four-year-old stepbrother and eventually served a term of twenty years' imprisonment. A penetrating and illuminating account of the affair is given by Yseult Bridges in her book *Saint—— with red hands?* Several years before coming to Brighton Constance Kent had, together with the child's nurse, Elizabeth Gough, been charged at Salisbury Assizes with the murder of the boy, but they had been acquitted through lack of evidence. After spending some years at a convent school in France, she took a post in St. Mary's Home. After the terrible ordeal of her trial she ardently longed for religious consolation and wished to take part in the long programme of services and exercises of penitence at the Home that culminated in the spiritual rebirth of Easter, but her history had become known and she was refused confirmation and communion on the grounds of her unexpiated 'sin'. On three successive days she was summoned to the dreaded ordeal of an interview with the Superior and, kneeling, forced to answer questions on the crime in which she had become involved, and on the subject of 'the sin which could aggravate a sin in God's sight'. A written 'confession' was extracted from her, but it was couched in such formal language that it seems unlikely it could have been written by herself, but was drawn up instead by a trained legalistic mind. The Home Secretary himself was doubtful of its authenticity and was loath to accept it, but Constance Kent insisted, and once more she came to trial. No witnesses for the defence were called, and it was believed that the so-called confession could have been demolished by a clever counsel. Indeed, it was widely held that Constance could not possibly have committed the murder as she described it, but that she confessed to the crime in order to shield her father. He was said to have killed the child, who was a witness to his illicit affair with the nurse, in order to silence him. On a direct instruction from the judge to the jury, Constance was declared guilty and sentenced to death, but this was afterwards commuted to imprisonment. In the cold, harsh, dreary limbo of a nineteenth-century prison her only fulfilment was in the execution of beautiful mosaic work for the Bishop's private chapel at Chichester, for East Grinstead Church and St. Paul's Cathedral. After serving a term of twenty years she went to Canada to work among the children of poor immigrants. Of her later history nothing is known. The storm of public criticism that arose over her condemnation without a full trial was intensified by the refusal of the Rev. Arthur Wagner to divulge as a witness at the trial what had been told him by Constance Kent under the seal of sacramental confession. Canon Hutchinson, later Vicar of St. Bartholomew's wrote: 'He stood his ground, and a great—a really great victory was won. One might almost say that from that time the Confessional in the Church of England remained unchallenged.' There are few who would wish this to be otherwise, nevertheless the greatest disquiet still persists in the mind over Miss Kent's written 'confession' and regarding the influence that seems undoubtedly to have been brought to bear on her. The Rev. E. Paston Hood of the Queen's Square Congregational Chapel, a poet and one of the best-known Free Church ministers of the time, gravely doubted the truth of the confession extracted from Constance Kent. 'Long before she surrendered herself to justice she had lost her freedom; her life was in those coils and snares which is in the power of those institutions, with their vast police of reserve and scrutiny, to create,' he declared in one of his sermons.[8] Today it seems clear that in the condemnation of Constance Kent a crime was committed no less horrible than the murder of her little step-brother. After Constance Kent was sentenced the sisters of the Home were mobbed and insulted in the street, and Mr. Wagner himself was assaulted on several occasions, once by a man who fired a pistol at him, and who was sent to prison for twelve months.

Opposite Wykeham Terrace at No. 91 North Street (now No. 13 Dyke Road) is a pleasant little building of fifteenth-century French Gothic design, with a charming oriel window and finely carved foliated capitals to the columns flanking the entrance door. The cornerstone was laid by the

Rev. H. M. Wagner in June 1867, as a partly obliterated inscription records. Up to about 1939 the building was used as the school for poor girls founded in 1819 by a Dr. Swan Downer. In 1939 it became the Refuge Church, but since then it has been occupied by a succession of business firms. Swan Downer was a Brighton man who is said to have made a large fortune from trade in London. He left £7,100 for the endowment of the charity school for poor girls and £5,000 to provide clothes for forty-eight poor men and women. The schoolgirls wore a uniform of blue frocks with white collars and cuffs. The women were provided with two complete sets of clothing a year, of a very antiquated sort, consisting of a mob cap, coal-scuttle bonnet, sleeve mittens, a black woollen shawl and scarlet flannel petticoats. The beneficiaries, clad in this quaint and distinctive garb of a century earlier, were a familiar sight about the streets of Brighton until fairly recent times, but in the passage of years Swan Downer's funds have diminished in value, the school has become unnecessary, and the poor folk are now allowed to choose their own clothing. In 1969 the building became 'Sloopy's Nite-Spot and Discotheque', decorated inside in deep midnight blue and violet. Could he but know of its fate, Wagner would turn in his grave, but one is at least thankful that the charming building has been preserved.

In 1795 a row of tiny almshouses, of charming Gothic design with pointed windows, had been built in Lewes Road near the bottom of Elm Grove. They were endowed by a Mrs. Margaret Marriott at the request of the then late Philadelphia and Dorothy Percy, daughters of the Duke of Northumberland. They were known as the Percy Almshouses, and intended 'for the reception of six poor widows of the Church of England who have received no parochial relief'. During the 1850s the Rev. H. M. Wagner and his sister extended the terrace by adding to the original portion, which is now numbered 4 to 9, the houses at either end which are numbered 1 to 3 and 10 to 12. These were dedicated in memory of the Marquess of Bristol.

Difficulties have arisen in recent years because of the lack of modern amenities in the old houses, and the trustees are faced with the prospect of rebuilding on the same site, or selling the site for redevelopment and building elsewhere, either of which courses would involve demolition of these charming buildings, and the trustees are reluctant to agree to this.

Less well known were Howell's Almshouses, an undistinguished row of little stucco-fronted houses behind the shops in George Street, Brighton. They were erected in 1859 'for the benefit of reduced inhabitants of Brighton and Hove' by Mr. Charles Howell, who lived for many years at the Dial House in Hove Terrace. His father, Mr. Thomas Howell, had the distinction of being Brighton's largest lodging-house keeper, owning seven of these establishments. He was also the proprietor of a stage-coach which ran between Brighton and London. By 1965 Howell's Almshouses were becoming ruinous, but four old ladies continued to live on in them, without gas, electricity or any modern cooking arrangements, until they were at last rehoused by the Corporation in modern homes for the aged.

By the middle of the nineteenth century the circulating libraries had ceased to serve, as they had done for nearly a century, as centres for social amusement, presenting musical evenings and opportunities for 'illegal loo'. With the Victorian era social intercourse moved more into the private sphere, and into the large cosmopolitan hotels. The bookshops reverted more strictly to their basic business of bookselling and the sale of stationery.

One of the best amongst the bookshops and subscription libraries in Brighton was Treacher's, which occupied a bow-fronted building at the corner of North Street and East Street. The shop was taken over and rebuilt by Hannington's, the adjoining draper's and department store, in 1924. If the visitor was not attended to by the manager, Mr. Clifford, himself, he might have been served by a rather studious young man who in 1888 at the age of about twenty was serving as the bookseller's apprentice. The son of a Hove architect, this was Edward Verrall Lucas, who eventually became famous as an essayist, novelist, travel-writer, and above all as an authority on Charles Lamb. After a few years he left Treacher's and worked as a reporter on the *Sussex Daily News*.[9] One of his friends in Brighton in those days was the present writer's father, for whom 'E.V.L.', amongst other writings which included a number of parodies of the music-hall songs of the day, wrote a lengthy and somewhat sententious atheistic poem on 'Futurity':

> *When we die is there nothing but space,*
> *Or is there a Something beyond?*
> *Is Heaven but a figure of speech*
> *Of which cushion-thumpers are fond?*
> *Or is it a solid reward?*
> *John describes how they opened the Seal—*
> *But t'was probably only a dream—*
> *Is it palpable, actual, real?*

Some years later Lucas was commissioned to write the volume on *Sussex* in the 'Highways and Byways' Series, which became a classic of English topographical writing that is still popular today.

During the year 1881 the most poignant alarm was aroused in the country districts around Brighton, as indeed it was throughout the whole of rural England, by the suggestion that the end of the world in that year had been foretold in the prophecies of Mother Shipton, the reputed witch and prophetess who is supposed to have lived in early Tudor times. Her alleged prophecies had an extraordinary effect on the popular imagination, especially among the poorly educated and more credulous people all over the countryside, many of whom through the course of that year deserted their homes and spent the nights in praying in the fields, churches and chapels. This particular prophecy gained an especially strong hold amongst the people living in the country round about Brighton, for a new version of *The Life and Death of Mother Shipton*, by Richard Head, which was first published in 1684, had been issued in 1862 by Richard Hindley, a Brighton bookseller with a shop in North Street, and a great many copies were circulating in the district; but as the year of the supposed ending of the world wore on, and especially as the nights became colder, and the stores of food began to diminish because of the neglected crops, the country people became less and less strongly convinced of the truth of the prophecies and gradually returned to their homes. Towards the end of his life Hindley confessed that he had himself invented the prophecy which he attributed to Mother Shipton in the garbled version of her *Life* that he had printed, and which was the cause of the disruption of life in the rural districts of England for many weeks in the year 1881. Hindley died at 12 Prince Albert Street at the age of seventy-three in 1893.

From the great days of cycling in the 1880s, and for many years afterwards, Brighton and the Brighton Road became specially associated with this pastime. The distance of the town from London, almost exactly fifty miles, made the journey something of a challenge, the return run being something that could be accomplished in one fairly strenuous day, or the single trip down to the sea in a comfortable half-day's journey.

The ancestor of the bicycle, the dandy-horse or hobby-horse, was introduced into England as early as 1819, having been invented by the Baron Charles de Drais, Master of Woods and Forests to the Grand Duke of Baden, and the Duke of York was caricatured at the time as saving £10,000 a year on travelling expenses by using one of the machines for visiting his old father the King at Windsor. The dandy-horse was so called because the word dandy as applied to an excessively fashionable man had only just been coined. The machine consisted of two heavy wooden wheels joined by a wooden rail upon which the rider sat, holding on to a bar by which he steered the front wheel, and he propelled the machine by striking at the ground with his feet. Dandy-horses, which weighed fifty pounds each, could be bought at Johnson's Repository in Long Acre for about eight pounds each, and it was reckoned that a man could travel at a speed of eight to ten miles an hour on one. Some extraordinary feats were performed with these machines. On several occasions riders competed with the coaches, and one trip to Brighton is recorded to have been done in nine hours. Dandy-horses were popular for a short time only. The feminine version, called 'The Ladies' Accelerator', never caught the fashion at all.

The police were opposed to dandy-horses and forbade the use of them in the Metropolis, on the grounds that the crowded streets made them dangerous. They came into vogue again many years later in the 1860s, when they were more lightly constructed of iron, and with the wheels driven by pedals or by oscillating cranks, and they were now known as velocipedes. These gave place in the 1870s to the 'ordinary bicycle', or 'penny-farthing' as it was more often called, with its large wheel driven by rotating cranks, and a small tail-wheel. It was with these light and speedy machines that cycling first came into its own, although they were extremely dangerous because of their tendency to tip over forwards when the brake was applied, especially when going downhill. Cycling clubs came into existence, the men dressed in brass-buttoned pea-jackets, breeches and pill-box caps, and led by a bugler. The 'safety bicycle', with two wheels of equal size, was invented in 1876 by a Brighton clockmaker, H. J. Lawson, who demonstrated it in a race from Brighton to Shoreham. The bicycle now entered upon its golden age of the 1880s, and from then onwards the Brighton road was crowded at week-ends with swooping flights of cyclists of both sexes mounted not only on safety bicycles but on tricycles and other machines of strange design that were brought out in enormous numbers by ingenious inventors. An interesting collection of early bicycles, including an original dandy-horse, is to be seen in the Brighton Museum. It was not until the enormous increase in the numbers and speed of motor-cars upon the roads after the Second World War that cycling became impossible as a pastime for pleasure.

One of the greatest tragedies of the political history of these islands occurred in 1892, when the Irish Home Rule movement received a setback by which the accomplishment of its aims was deferred for thirty years. This reverse was the result of the scandal caused by the divorce case in which the great Irish Nationalist leader, Charles Stewart Parnell, became involved on the very threshold of his party's triumph.

The lady in the case was Katherine Wood, whose mother had been a lady-in-waiting to the Princess Caroline, and a friend of the artist Constable. Katherine first met her husband, Captain O'Shea, while staying with her family at Brighton, where he was stationed with the 18th Hussars, but it was not until 1867, several years after their first meeting, that she at length gave in to his persistent urgings that she should marry him, and then only with great reluctance and misgiving. At first they lived on Marine Parade, but they later took a house at Patcham. Katherine first met Parnell at the House of Commons, where she had gone to invite him to one of the political dinners in support of the Irish Party which Captain O'Shea had asked her to give. The two fell in love at first sight. Because of O'Shea's long absences from home on military and political business the marriage was already proving unsatisfactory. Parnell was frequently invited to their house by O'Shea, but when the Captain returned home unexpectedly on one occasion to find Parnell's portmanteau in one of the rooms, he challenged Parnell to a duel in France. Mrs. O'Shea and her sister succeeded, however, in smoothing over the quarrel. For several years Parnell and Katherine refrained from taking steps for her to obtain a divorce from her husband, for fear of imperilling the Irish cause by the scandal, and Captain O'Shea took no action against them, although for long he had known of the situation. Early in 1882 a daughter was born to Katherine by Parnell, but it died only two months later. In 1887 Parnell and Katherine came to live at 10 Walsingham Terrace, Hove, then called West Brighton. Although he had had no scientific training, Parnell was interested in mining and mineralogy and was convinced that gold was to be discovered in Ireland. He set up in the basement of the house a furnace and laboratory in which he burnt and tested mineral ores, and indeed discovered small quantities of gold in mineral ores from quarries in Co. Wicklow. Brighton station was then being rebuilt, and Parnell made drawings of the great iron roof with the object of building a large iron cattle-shed on the same principle for his own estate at Avondale.

In those days there was nothing beyond the western side of the house but open cornfields stretching away to Shoreham with the great rampart of Cissbury Camp in the far distance, and from their windows they watched the sunsets that seemed to them, as they do to all who come to Brighton, to be more wonderful than anywhere else in England. In the spring they would often drive out to the Downs and walk there where the salt-tanged sea-air mingled with the pungency of wild thyme in the downland turf. Once as they walked for miles along the crest of the Downs they watched for over an hour the motionless figure in the distance of a shepherd standing clear against the skyline, his dog a tumbled heap at his feet, his flock showing grey against the green distance. It was a scene like one of Constable's downland sketches. A favourite haunt of theirs was the little shop which still exists in Pool Valley, that was devoted to the sale of crystal, onyx, jet and other stones, and Parnell had a necklace and a locket made for Katherine, of crystal, onyx and gold. At that time he was trying to invent a vessel that would cut through the water without being affected by the motion of the waves, and made a number of ingenious models which he tested off the underdeck of the Chain Pier. One day when they walked on the Pier the weather was tempestuous, and they were unable to test the model because of the heavy waves. Katherine described in her biography of Parnell how they wondered if the difficulties that prevented their being always together were not beyond their endurance.[10] The whole pier-head shuddered under the impact of the waves, and Parnell remarked that the old structure could not last much longer. Katherine could not stand against the wind and as she turned to cling to him he picked her up and held her clear over the raging water and threatened to jump into the sea with her so they would be free for ever, but with amazing courage she calmed him with a few common-sense words; and he turned and carried her to the upper deck away from the horrible roll and sucking of the sea beneath their feet.

In 1889 Parnell was cleared of charges which had been made in *The Times* of his having been personally responsible for organizing outrages in Ireland, when letters in which the charges were made were proved to be forgeries. *The Times* settled an action he brought against them by a payment of £5,000 damages out of court. But despite this triumph Parnell's hold upon his followers was weakening because of his increasingly frequent absences from Parliament while visiting Mrs. O'Shea. The divorce proceedings of 1890, with costs against Parnell, especially alienated the large body of his Catholic supporters, and at the General Election two years later his party collapsed. Parnell and Katherine were married at Steyning in 1891, a year after the divorce, and spent the evening of their wedding-day on the beach near their house, talking for hours of all they had gone through to be together, but the agonies of the public scandal and his frantic endeavours to regain his lost political influence proved too much for him. It was truly said that Parnell sacrificed both his cause and himself to his private life, for only five months after his marriage to Katherine, on 6th October 1891, he died in her arms at Brighton.

15 Apostolic Amorists

he present writer once discovered a friend, who was making a visit to his rooms at the Pavilion, on his hands and knees examining with extreme care the long stretch of painted Chinese wallpaper which adorned the walls of the corridor. The wallpaper had been installed for King George IV in 1823 at a cost of £43, and the friend had been told that this decoration which depicted a continuous landscape with groups of Chinese figures engaged in various pursuits, belonged to a well-known class of paintings representing 'The Pleasures of the Chinese', other common subjects being 'The Cultivation of Tea' and 'The Making of Silk'. When the friend was asked what he was seeking so assiduously, he replied that he was looking for 'a certain pleasure'. The quest and enjoyment of 'a certain pleasure' has not only been a major factor in the life and attractions of Brighton, it has also played no small part in the activities of various unconventional religious sects from time to time through the centuries. In Brighton during Elizabethan days a curate of the Church of St. Nicholas was suspended from his office on suspicion of being a member of a sect known as 'The Family of Love'. At this distance of time we may perhaps charitably conjecture that he was, in fact, a member of one of those many circles of 'Brothers and Sisters of the Free Spirit', sometimes known as *Homines Intelligentiae*, that existed throughout Europe, but especially in the Netherlands and Germany, during the sixteenth century. They believed that they were inheritors of the Holy Ghost, and that through its power they could be exalted to a condition of spiritual perfection in which they would be immune from the guilt of sin, even of the sins of the flesh, so that while still on earth both sexes could live at times in a state of nakedness, unashamed, with a frankness like that of modern nudists, and enjoy love-making without a sense of sin. Scenes of spiritualized eroticism of this kind are depicted symbolically in the painting in the Prado Museum at Madrid called 'The Millennium', by Hieronymus Bosch, who is believed himself to have been a member of such a sect.

This idyllic, primeval innocence was hardly achieved by the Rev. Henry James Prince, who established himself in Brighton around 1840 as Minister of Adullam Chapel, Windsor Street, Brighton, and as the leader of a sect holding the belief that 'spiritual marriages' with 'soul mates' were possible regardless of whether or not the persons concerned were already married or not.[1] Born in 1811, he had been ordained in 1840, and became curate of the little town of Charlinch in North Somerset. Here Prince exercised his magnetic gifts as a preacher to such effect, particularly amongst the ladies, that he was inhibited from preaching by the Bishop of Bath and Wells, and later in more distant pastures by the Bishop of Salisbury, the Bishop of Ely and the Archbishop of Canterbury. A book which he wrote entitled *Strength in Jesus* was sold by booksellers in Brighton and other towns in the south of England, and in it he described himself as 'minister' of Adullam Chapel, Windsor Street, Brighton. His own address was given as 2 Windsor Terrace, Brighton, which was in Queen's Road, near the chapel, which was demolished in the 1920s to make room for the Regent Cinema.

Prince must have wielded a compulsive power over his hearers. His vitality and personal charm were probably enormous. Also the years of Prince's stay in Brighton were the beginning of the most fashionable era in the history of the town, far exceeding the Regency days in the display of wealth and the pursuit of pleasure. The number of splendid carriages and coaches, always a symbol of affluence in Victorian days as much as motor-cars are in our own, was greatly increased, and the carriage processions along the sea-front were an important feature of the social programme. If there is any social activity that can rival the attraction to the fashionable world of a new medical treatment, it is a new religion or a popular preacher, and so in Brighton for a time the appeal of sea-bathing was challenged by an interest in the doctrines of Brother Prince.

In wealthy circles the vague sense of guilt aroused in certain minds, especially in the female sex, by the pursuit of vapid fashionable pleasures could be assuaged by reading religious books and pamphlets of a suitable kind. Prince's successful book, *Strength in Jesus*, was followed by a pamphlet entitled *How You May Know Whether You Do or Do Not Believe in Jesus Christ*, of which it was said over 19,000 copies were sold. It was priced at threepence, and cheaper editions were sold at three-halfpence, including a Welsh edition at the same price. A booklet called *The Charlinch Revival*, priced at a shilling, told of his early successes as a curate in Somerset. *Letters to his Christian Brethren at College* is a work in which he scarified his former colleagues, and *Scarcely Saved, or the Account of a Soul that was Taken to Heaven out of the Very Mouth of Hell,* sold at twopence, must have excited feelings of tension, danger and subsequent release only paralleled in our own day by the exploits of James Bond. It was, however, in *The Great Declaration* that Prince announced that God had chosen him above all men to be the perfect man in whom sin could not exist. He was immortal and those who believed in him likewise would never die. Time alone would bring the fruition of this promise. Of more immediate significance was the assurance that for all true believers, the act of love between the sexes could be carried out in a freedom transcending the bonds of marriage, and in complete innocence of sin. The fleshly pleasures could thus be invested with an aura of spiritual holiness, especially if enjoyed with Brother Prince.

Prince collected some £30,000 mostly from his disciples in Brighton, but it was fortunate for the town that it was in the seclusion of the country, at Spaxton back in the Somersetshire of his beginnings, that Prince eventually set up his *Agapomene* or Abode of Love, where he took as 'brides' not only members of the community that gathered round him but young girls brought from Bristol and elsewhere, and the religious observances degenerated into complete licentiousness.

However reprehensible sexual licence may be, it never seems quite so deplorable as a *folie de grandeur* carried to ridiculous extremes. The latter was the case with another religious eccentric, an evangelical preacher named John William Wood who, in 1887, set up a chapel in a disused riding school in Edward Street.[2] He styled himself 'King Solomon', and called his adherents 'The Army of the Lord'. The chapel was draped with red curtains and 'King Solomon', dressed in flowing robes, sat on a dais side by side with his 'Queen Esther'. With him was a 'King David', a 'King Saul', and a 'Queen of Sheba'. In front of the dais, marked off by a heavy gilded railing, was a circular space in which the younger female members of the flock performed ritual dances until they reached a state of intense emotional hysteria, and finally collapsed in the ring in a more or less prostrate condition. It was then that under the influence of the 'Power of the Spirit' they broke into prophecy and exhortation, which sometimes took the form of demanding the ejection from the select circle of persons said to be possessed by the devil, but who were most probably individuals who had aroused jealousy through attracting an undue share of 'Solomon's' favours.

It was known that the chapel building had been provided for 'King Solomon' by a wealthy lady of his flock, and it was openly declared that under the influence of the 'Power of the Spirit' others were induced to contribute money and to give up jewellery, which was speedily sent to the pawnshop. These happenings became a public scandal, and inevitably aroused the anger of other religious enthusiasts in the town, as well as providing a source of amusement for the rowdier elements of the population. More and more frequently when meetings were held there were scenes of disorder outside the chapel, and eventually 'Solomon' was compelled to forsake all his glory for the prosaic banalities of the bankruptcy court.

With his funds greatly reduced he moved his court to 'The Ark of the Living God' at Portslade, where, with a few faithful subjects, he ruled 'The Kingdom of Amon-God and Solomon-David-Jesus'. His commands were sent forth on paper with strange gold lettering, the central device consisting of the word 'God Jehowoodvah Jesus-God'.

Like his biblical namesake, 'King Solomon' felt himself entitled to enjoy a plurality of wives and concubines, though perhaps not aspiring to the traditional number of a thousand mentioned in the Old Testament. However, there seems to have been no reluctance on the part of the ladies of his gathering to join the circle of 'Queens', and they lived together in the community in apparent amity. One of the ladies was the wife of a sea-captain, who on returning from a voyage went to the house to take his wife away. She refused to leave and Wood supported her. The police were called and the captain's wife was removed to a lunatic asylum. It was obviously so much more satisfactory, everyone thought, that she should spend the rest of her life amongst the insane than that she should continue to enjoy 'a certain pleasure' with a religious fanatic, even though the opportunities for 'sin' might be considerably diminished by the demands of her fellow 'Queens'. The local populace stoned the windows of the 'Ark' and the landlord gave Wood notice to quit. He refused and the landlord had the windows removed. At last Wood was evicted, together with 'Queen Bathsheba' and her three children. He was pelted with stones by the crowd, whom he anathematized in colourful biblical language: 'To hell with ye who persecute me. Devils await ye, generations of vipers.'

In the deserted, wrecked rooms of the 'Ark' were found hymn-sheets printed in gold with the signature 'King Solomon, Jesus, Coreadeapeah, Ahmed, Son Bedige-Cashigah, King of Israel and of All Nations, New-shallah, Ishallamah, Oshalladah, the Signet of Jehovah God-Amon'. After being away for a while Wood returned to Portslade, where he spent the rest of his day sending out extraordinary messages and manifestoes, in which he declared he had been commanded from on high to change the name of Brighton to Yathakah, and that he was to take over the Royal Pavilion for his work and rename it 'The Sanctuary of Jehovah'. Wood died in 1916 at the age of eighty-five, at a house at No. 35 Carlton Terrace, Portslade, which he called 'Arregosabach'. The house was demolished in 1955. A remarkable circumstance was the existence in recent times amongst Portslade children of a story regarding a 'Golden Calf' which was said to have been set up and worshipped in the neighbourhood some years ago. Was this legend, which seems to have amounted to something resembling 'folk-memory', inspired perhaps by tales of strange rites and ceremonies that were carried on at the 'Ark'? It was a curious turn of fate that caused the riding school which had been the headquarters of Solomon's 'Army of the Lord' to be acquired in 1891 by that no less dynamic and colourful, but infinitely more worthy and respectable organization, the Salvation Army, and used by them in their admirable work in fighting poverty, vice and degradation in the surrounding slums.

16 Late Victorian Writers, Artists and Art-collectors

What with the opening of the Aquarium, the visit of the British Association for the Advancement of Science, the great exhibitions of science, industry and the arts in the Dome and Corn Exchange, the newly opened public library and museum, and the exhibitions of pictures held in the art gallery, to say nothing of the flourishing concerts and theatres, cultural life in Brighton in the latter half of the nineteenth century was of a richness and intensity that has hardly been surpassed at any other time.

Many of the wealthier residents were collectors of pictures, such as William Percival Boxall, who possessed paintings by Lely, Morland, Opie, Vandevelde and Greuze, and Sir Cordy Burrows, who had works by Wynants and the Sussex marine painter R. H. Nibbs in his collection, and presented a work by Van Balen to the Art Gallery. J. H. Trist collected the Pre-Raphaelites, and Henry Willett possessed a very distinguished collection of Italian, Flemish, Dutch and French paintings, a large portion of which he presented to the art gallery when it was rebuilt in 1901, after they had been on loan in the building for some years. C. A. Ionides had a group of old masters and some works by the Pre-Raphaelites, and by Watts and Legros, but also showed more adventurous taste in acquiring works by the French realist painters Delacroix, Courbet, Daumier, Rousseau and Millet. Even more advanced in his tastes was Captain Henry Hill, who lived at No. 53 Marine Parade, Brighton, and was at one time Quartermaster of the 1st Sussex Rifle Volunteers. The greater part of his collection was formed in the 1870s when he was approaching his sixtieth year. His earlier purchases were conventional enough, consisting of watercolours by David Cox, paintings by Morland, Leslie and Crome, but before long he was actively collecting paintings by living British artists such as Frank Hole, Fred Walker, W. Luker, Val Prinsep, George Mason, W. L. Wyllie and F. R. Lee. He had no taste for the Pre-Raphaelites, or for the late Victorian grand masters like Leighton, Poynter and Frith, but was intrigued by the works of the Barbizon School and other pre-Impressionist painters long before they were generally popular in England. He possessed fine examples of Corot, Daubigny, Millet, Rousseau, Dupré, Israëls, Fantin-Latour, Durez, and William McTaggart the Scottish Impressionist, and works by Jean Cazin and his wife Marie. It was said that her dark, almost monochromatic landscapes dominated Hill's collection. He also bought J. M. Whistler's 'Nocturne, blue and gold; Valparaiso' which is now in the Freer Art Gallery at Washington.

There were remarkable opportunities in London during the early 1870s for a collector of advanced tastes, because of the large number of French artists who had come to England as refugees from the Franco-Prussian War, including painters like Camille Pissarro, Daubigny, Bonvin and Ricard, followed later on by the fugitive communards Tissot and the sculptor Dalou. There were also the important exhibitions held in London between 1870 and 1875 by Paul Durand-Ruel, in which works by Courbet, Manet, Fantin-Latour and the Impressionists were shown, many of them for the first time in England.

At a time when fashionable collectors were buying the works of Bougereau, Rosa Bonheur and Carolus Duran, Captain Hill bought Manet's 'Garden and Orchard' canvas, which was the artist's first work to be seen in this country before 1897. He also bought 'La Classe de Danse' by Degas, which is now in the Louvre, and 'La Répétition d'un Ballet sur la scène', which is now in the Metropolitan Museum, New York. 'L'Absinthe', also now in the Louvre, Hill purchased directly from Degas himself, who was visiting Brighton at that time, most probably as Hill's guest. Hill died in his seventieth year, and his collection was dispersed in two sales held in 1889. The first sale included six ballet scenes by Degas. The largest sum that any of them fetched was £66 paid for one by Sickert. In the second sale he also bought 'L'Absinthe' for £180. It was hissed by the assembled buyers when it was placed on the easel. Ronald Pickvance[1] said of Hill that he was 'an untypical Victorian collector' and 'alone of his age and generation in coming to terms with some of the most *avant-garde* French painting of the period'.

Another Brighton art-collector whose taste was in advance of the fashion of the time was Walter Taylor, who in 1911 was the first connoisseur in England to have works by Matisse, Dufy and Marie Laurencin in his collection. He also bought the works of the Camden Town Group, including Spencer Gore, Harold Gilman and, of course, Sickert himself.

A distinguished water-colour artist, whose work has been much sought after in recent years, was Douglas Fox-Pitt, born in 1864, the son of General Pitt-Rivers. He lived in Brighton at 25 Russell Square from 1913 until his death in 1922. His water-colours of the beach, the sea-front and the old Chain Pier, one of which is in Brighton's Art Gallery, are full of the sense of dazzling sunshine, of the broad expanses of the sea and shore and of the liveliness of the people he depicted in them.

A frequent visitor to Brighton in Victorian and Edwardian days, although not a permanent resident, was Charles Edward Conder (1868–

1909), whose lithographs and fan-paintings on silk have a frothy, decorative charm highly evocative of the period. Several of his works are in the Brighton Art Gallery, including a large oil-painting of the sea-front in which, for the sake of improving the composition, the artist has shown the chalk cliffs of Rottingdean as lying to the west, instead of to the east, a circumstance which causes much distress to certain old residents of Brighton who frequent the Gallery.

Another water-colourist whose handling of light and space in this medium approached even closer to Cézanne's mastery of the technique was Claude Flight, a painter, decorator, engraver and writer who was born in 1881 and died in 1955. He worked a great deal in Brighton and a 'Beach Scene' of his is also in the Art Gallery.

A writer who was particularly sensitive to the unique spirit of Brighton, and especially to certain sexual overtones and undertones which form part of the complex emotional tone-colour of the place, was John Cowper Powys, the oldest member of that famous family of writers which also included Llewelyn the essayist and atheistic philosopher, and Theodore Francis, the novelist and short-story writer. A story-teller in the tradition of Dickens and Dostoevsky, John Cowper Powys's novels *Wolf Solent*, *A Glastonbury Romance*, *Weymouth Sands* and *Porius* are part of his gigantic achievement in the realm of the novel, and are only now beginning to receive generally the recognition they deserve. Soon after coming down from Cambridge, about 1892, like innumerable young men in search of his first job he had turned his 'conscientious but reluctant steps to the famous offices of Gabbitas and Thring' (what Dickensian names!) and learned from those celebrated scholastic agents of a post as a teacher of German in a girls' school at West Brighton.[2] 'This was something I had never heard of. Girls' school? *School* of girls! I saw them like gleaming porpoises; shoals and shoals of them, waiting for their new professor at West Brighton . . . flocks and flurries of girls . . . what an incomprehensible thing for my destiny to evoke! The very word "girl" . . . thrilled me at that time of my life in a manner impossible to describe. It conveyed to my mind a sort of fleeting, floating, fluttering fantasy of femininity, a kind of Platonic essence of sylph-hood . . . Thus the word "girl" almost ceased for me to have the least connexion with the living personalities of real girls.' Taking a hansom-cab to London Bridge he caught the next train to Brighton, and on arriving was struck by 'the shrill voices of the newspaper boys selling Brighton papers, voices that had a distinct Cockney flavour, for the Sussex dialect has some ancient affiliation, which I am not enough of a philologist to analyse, with the manner of speech of England's Metropolis'. He went on: 'Brighton, itself, as I soon discovered, has many old-fashioned alleys and time-mellowed retreats, snugly protected and sequestered, and quite as redolent of the regency and of the whole Georgian era as its more fantastically rococo Pavilion. Blustering, free-blowing winds, smelling of the salt sea, and in summer-time whirling up the thick dust [he is writing of 1892] in raw, scorching, sun-warmed clouds, give to the dingiest and most squalid quarters of the great sprawling town a certain curiously invigorating character. These heady Brighton winds seem to play the part of a sort of *aerial ale*, of a nature so profoundly English that they cause satisfaction rather than perturbation to the crowds of London visitors who contemplate from the wet pebbles and asphalt parades the redoubtable excursion-boats and excursion-yachts—in my day the latter seemed all called *Skylark*—which vociferating "captains", often in dripping tarpaulin, were for ever pushing out and dragging in. White dust, white glare, white houses, white sea-foam alternated with the rolling bottle-green breakers and with the motley crowds of jostling, lively, good-humoured people, moving from pier-head to pier-head and from brass-band to brass-band. . . . Eventually I came to be familiar with every portion of this vast pebbled beach, up which the Channel waves roll with a large, primeval heave of deep-sea waters, unbroken by any obstruction, for Brighton, as Londoners know so well, has a more elemental exposure than any other seaside resort. I came to know its pier-piles, its stone groins, its shelters, its sea-walls. I came to know each spot along its colossal front, where between beach and parade, the sweet-sellers, the cockles-, mussels- and winkle-sellers, the minstrels with blackened faces, the Punch-and-Judy shows, the comic singers, the preachers, the toy-vendors, the fish-dealers, the photographers, the fruits-and-nuts pedlars, the toy-balloon men, the "captains" of the yachts *Skylark*, the fishermen, the pleasure-boat men, were all wont to be found.' He goes on to speak, with all the frankness of a Rousseau or a Restif de la Bretonne, of his own eccentric mania for contemplating the 'ethereal loveliness' of 'imaginary sylphs' and of his discovery of 'that curious pack of creatures who are to be found almost everywhere, but who particularly infest the Brighton sea-front,' attracted by the aura of sexual provocativeness with which the image of Brighton has become surrounded—'In and out of these motley scenes I would follow my maniacal quest for provocative feminine forms basking in that blazing sunshine and amid the smells of sea-weed and fish and tar and sweat and sandwiches and rope and paint and cheap perfumes and foam-drenched petticoats and bilge-water and beer. I ultimately became aware of certain other men—and their eyes, eyes that had almost lost all human expression, shocked me and terrified me—who had evidently reached a point of obsession far beyond my own. No heartless seducer of women, no neurotic perverts, that I have ever encountered have had such a look of being hopelessly *damned* as these elderly gentlemen betrayed in their curiously high-coloured faces, as if they lived on the hearts' blood of women, as they hunted and stared and eternally stared and hunted !

337

It was at this time, in 1899, that Powys published his first book of poems, and made his discovery of the poems of W. B. Yeats in North's bookshop in the Western Road. He also began collecting volumes of the classics, which he 'especially delighted to purchase when they took the shape of leather-bound quartos and worm-eaten folios. Such bookish treasures were unbelievably cheap at the end of the last century.' These he bought at 'an amazing second-hand shop . . . in the very heart of Brighton, within a few hundred yards of the Regent's famous Pavilion. It was kept by a dignified little man called "Mr. Smith" whose chief assistant was a huge, black-bearded fellow, resembling the ogres in fairy-tales but with one of the mildest and most Early-Christian countenances I have ever seen.'

One of his chief friends during these years while he was staying in Brighton, and for several years afterwards at Court Farm, Offham, near Lewes, was a Brighton poet, Alfred de Kantzow, whose simple unaffected verses, of a somewhat Wordsworthian cast, were published from time to time in the *Brighton Herald*. Some of them appeared in two small volumes, the first of which was entitled *Ultima Verba* (Last Words). For the second volume it was difficult to think of a title that would go beyond this, but with the aid of a Latin dictionary the poet and his friend Powys eventually concocted the title *Noctis Susurri* (Sighs of the Night).

Also lecturing in Brighton in those days was a young man named Roger Fry, of King's College, Cambridge, who in January 1896 came to give a course of University Extension lectures on 'Italian Painting from Giotto to Leonardo da Vinci' at the headquarters of the Y.M.C.A. in Mrs. Fitzherbert's old house. It is not difficult to imagine the consternation of the great art critic of later years, who called attention to the then unaccustomed beauties of African art in his work *Vision and Design* of 1928, could he have seen the Brighton souvenir shops of the 1960s with their windows offering to the hordes of holiday trippers modern African masks and elongated figures of African natives and animals carved in wood.

Another novelist who visited Brighton was the American Henry James, who came in December 1906, to spend Christmas with some friends at 16 Lewes Crescent, Kemp Town. He wrote to W. E. Norris from Brighton on 23rd December 1906, describing the horrors of the train-journey from London. He spoke of being 'still a little ruffled by a sense of the break-down of things (the "public services") that compelled me yesterday, coming down here from Victoria, to be shoved into (as the only place in the train) the small connecting-space between two Pullmans, where I stuck, all the way, in a tight bunch of five or six other men and three portmanteaux and boxes: quite the sort of treatment (One's nose half in the W.C. included) that the English traveller writes from Italy infuriated letters to the *Times* about.'[3]

By 26th December he had recovered, as this letter to his friend Thomas Sergeant Perry reveals: 'I am spending the so equivocal period with some very quiet old friends at this place, and I write this in presence of a shining silvery shimmery sea, on one of the prettiest possible south-coast mornings. It's like the old Brighton that you may read about (Miss Honeyman's) in the early chapters of the "Newcomes".'[4]

The name of D. H. Lawrence is certainly one that would have escaped the columns of 'Fashionable Visitors' in the local newspapers when he came in 1909, and several times after, but his effect on the English novel and indeed on the outlook of several generations of young people after him was to be revolutionary. He wrote of his first visit to Brighton in a letter to Blanche Jennings on 8th May 1909,[5] when he stayed in lodgings in the High Street, Rottingdean, having ridden down from Croydon on a bicycle over the North and South Downs.

'I have lain an hour', he wrote, 'on the sharp, shelving shingle on Brighton beach, and the sun has soaked through my shut eyelids into my eyes, and I'm giddy still with it. Brighton is splendid—big, stately, magnificent, with a sea like pale green jewels—is lapis lazuli green?—and all wavering, shimmering, intermingling with purple-lovely-inexpressible. But Brighton is stately, and I am not, so I pushed my way through the wind, and here I am at Rottingdean.

'. . . I was terrified to see the swimming sun sink so quickly and deliberately behind the round hill where the windmill stands up, stately but a bit ridiculous. Then Brighton in the red fusing light looked like a wonderful imagined place. . . . I went down on the wide beach, where nobody was because the stretches of sand are wet and chalky, and the rocks are rough and pooly—only three shrimpers waded along the wonderful, outspreading ruffling water, pushing their great nets before them, picking out the little objects, and moving on again through the marvellous green light overflushed with muddy gleams. The sand was wet, and aswim with yellow and red fires—then the lights of Brighton came out like night flowers opening, and I came home to write to you.'

Helen Corke, a poet and also the author of some widely adopted textbooks and economic histories, who was a powerful influence in Lawrence's development, and to whom he addressed many of his most fervent verses, remembered how 'On 1st October 1910 he and I walked from Brighton over the cliffs, a nine-mile walk to Newhaven'.[6] In the same year Lawrence and his sister Ada were visiting Brighton at Christmas, and were invited to spend Christmas Day with Philip F. T. Smith at the hotel where he was staying. Smith was the enlightened and humane headmaster of Davidson Road School, Croydon, where Lawrence was then teaching. He wrote:[7] 'There was a whist party during the evening attended by the usual boarding house company comprising many unattached ladies of uncertain age.

The proceedings were somewhat languid and should be accelerated. This he proceeded to do to such an extent that threatened the old ladies to join in "hunting the slipper" and other boisterous round games. I heard then, for the first time, Lawrence's peculiar laugh which was in after years quoted (see Huxley) as a characteristic exhibition of his exuberance. The following day I walked with Lawrence for a day's tramp over the Downs. During the day he talked more freely than formerly of his literary ambitions. . . . He discussed the publication of a recent book by a well-known author. He described the work as salacious and remarked, "If I cannot write without dipping my finger in it I will not write at all." '

Five years later, in May 1915, Lawrence again visited Brighton, this time spending two days with Lady Cynthia Asquith, who was staying down there with her children at the time. Lawrence was then living in a cottage at Greatham, Pulborough, Sussex, which had been lent to him by Viola Meynell. Lawrence wrote to Lady Cynthia:

'When we talked in Brighton, lying on the cliff, I did not take much notice of what I said, because my subconsciousness was pre-occupied with the idea of how pleasant it would be to walk over the edge of the cliff. There seemed another, brighter sort of world away below, and this world on top is all torture and a flounder of stupidity.'[8]

Lawrence was at this time suffering in the early stages of his lifelong illness, exasperated by having been declared a bankrupt, and agonized by the war with Germany, which he regarded as marking the height of criminal stupidity and folly.

Although it cannot be regarded as imperative that Brighton should have produced, amongst a host of highly gifted painters, one really great artist, yet once this capricious gift of fortune has been bestowed, does it not seem inevitable that such an artist should be found to possess qualities of genius that are curiously appropriate to the spirit of the place?

Aubrey Beardsley is now recognized as a master, indeed one of the very greatest masters of black-and-white art, in which medium he achieved miracles of design, conveying on the flatness of a page by means of his sensitive but assured line, and by the masterly manipulation of the masses of light and dark, a compelling sense of space, form, weight and volume. To the conventional late-Victorian world of the 1890s the drawings of the unknown boy in his early twenties that appeared in the pages of *The Studio* and *The Yellow Book* seemed unhealthy, perverse and even bordering upon the pornographic.

Aubrey Beardsley was born in Brighton, at 12 Buckingham Road, on 21st August 1872. There were London jewellers amongst his father's forebears, but the father himself never succeeded in holding any employment for long. The family was kept by the mother, who worked in London as a governess teaching French and the piano. From the first she was the encouraging influence in her son's life, so that he could read and play Chopin before he was five, and he was only nine when he and his ten-year-old sister Mabel appeared in the drawing-rooms of wealthy patrons, or at public entertainments, including concerts in the Royal Pavilion, when the two children played piano duets and some nocturnes that Aubrey had composed. At the age of ten he was making menus and dinner cards for his mother's friends, in order to help the family budget, and earned £30 in six weeks by drawing the guest-cards for a fashionable wedding. These are amongst his earliest surviving drawings. In 1884 Aubrey went to Brighton Grammar School, becoming a boarder a year later. It was through the perceptiveness of two intelligent masters, H. A. Payne and A. W. King, that despite his complete incompetence in mathematics he was encouraged to the uttermost in less formal studies, in reading, writing, drawing, acting, designing the costumes and scenery for the school plays and even illustrating the programmes. A companion of his at the school was Charles B. Cochran, who later became the famous showman and theatrical producer, and they collaborated in presenting an elaborate school entertainment staged to celebrate Queen Victoria's Diamond Jubilee. Beardsley is to this day at once the most distinguished and the most embarrassing of their past scholars. At the age of sixteen he became a clerk in the London office of the Guardian Fire and Life Assurance Society, but already he was known to be suffering from tuberculosis. He met Burne-Jones, who told him, 'You will become a great artist', and soon afterwards he was chosen by the publisher John Dent to illustrate a new edition of Malory's *Morte d'Arthur*, a commission he came to find extremely boring, although some of the illustrations are amongst his best work. Another important commission followed—the illustrations for Oscar Wilde's play *Salome*—and he was only twenty-one when he became the principal artist of *The Yellow Book*, a periodical which achieved an undeserved reputation for decadence, perversity and naughtiness chiefly on account of his drawings, despite the innocuous nature of the text which included stories by Henry James, Arnold Bennett and its editor Henry Harland; some charming tales by Baron Corvo, and poems by the eminently respectable Poet Laureate William Watson, who incidentally spent the last years of his life at a house on the sea-front at Rottingdean. Beardsley's reputation suffered severely because of his artistic association with Oscar Wilde, with whom it was widely imagined Beardsley had had an improper relationship. In fact, the young artist quickly lost his early admiration for Wilde. He resented the older man's arrogantly patronizing attitude with its implication that Beardsley had only been carried to fame on the wings of his own soaring genius. In the panic that attended Wilde's trial and imprisonment, Beardsley was dismissed from *The Yellow Book*. For a time he supported himself with commissions given him by Alfred Smithers, a minor publisher with a side-line in mild pornography. It was for him that Beardsley executed the illustrations to the works of Aristophanes and Juvenal, which embody some of his finest and most mature work, although some of it is indecent even by our most permissive modern standards. With his illustrations to another new periodical, *The Savoy*, and with other remarkable work of his last phase, he began to rise again in public estimation. Despite the waywardness of his pictorial imagination, Beardsley possessed deep religious feelings, as may be judged from his beautiful drawing of the Virgin and Child that was published in the first number of *The Savoy* in January 1896. He was received into the Roman Catholic Church in 1897. His health improved for a while following his move to France, where he lived in Paris and later at Dieppe, that favourite haunt of artists and writers in the 1890s, but eventually, at Menton, after a spell of severe weather, he collapsed and died at the age of only twenty-five years, on 25th March 1898. A commemorative plaque today marks the house in Brighton where he lived as a boy.

Beardsley's work contains elements far more significant than the late pre-Raphaelitism of Burne-Jones, or the sinuous lines and the handling of black masses deriving from Japanese art, or the flowing shapes of the *Art Nouveau* movement. Beardsley's miraculous line and his command of form owe much to his study of Mantegna and other Italian artists of the *quattrocento*, and have an affinity also with Greek vase-painting and even the drawings of medieval artists. Sir Kenneth Clark has suggested[9] that Beardsley's influence on some of the great figures of the modern movement such as Kandinsky, Paul Klee and even Picasso has been enormous, and he has reminded us that writing as early as 1908 Julius Meier-Graefe, the pioneer historian of modern art, regarded Beardsley as one of the essential men of genius of his time. The original drawing by Beardsley intended as a cover-design for the issue of *The Yellow Book* for April 1895 was given to the Brighton Art Gallery by the publisher and collector Mr. John Lane, who lived in Brighton, in 1926. Again because of the scandal that arose over the trial of Oscar Wilde, he was dismissed from his post of Art Editor of *The Yellow Book*, and on account of Beardsley's association with Wilde the drawing was not used. It represents a faun reading to a girl seated in a flowery meadow, the volume of her billowing skirt marvellously suggested by the artist's space-creating line.

Is it altogether too extravagant a notion to imagine that in the sophistication, the incisive elegance, the brilliance, the clear-cut vision and, not least, in the provocative eroticism of Beardsley's work we may perceive qualities that are implicit in the atmosphere and spirit of Brighton itself?

Another memorial tablet commemorates the birthplace of Eric Gill, the stone-carver, wood-engraver, typographer and religious polemicist, at No. 32 Hamilton Road, Brighton, where he was born on 22nd February

1882, eldest son and second child of his parents' family of eleven. His father was the Rev. Arthur Tidman Gill, Assistant Minister at the Chapel of the Countess of Huntingdon's Connexion in North Street. The family moved to Cliftonville Road, and afterwards to Preston View, Highcroft Villas, in Dyke Road Drive. The back garden of the house overlooked the sidings of the railway station and it was here that he began to acquire that intense interest in steam-locomotives which played so strong a part in his artistic development. With his sisters Eric went to the kindergarten school near by which was kept by the Misses Browne, who were the daughters of 'Phiz' the illustrator of Dickens. The boy had a passion for drawing, and by the age of ten he was producing a 'monthly magazine of Fun and Frolic', priced at 1d, and liberally illustrated with pictures of the objects he had seen around Brighton that fascinated him—locomotives, windmills, railway carriages, goods trains, bridges, tunnels, houses, horses and cabs and the Brighton paddle-steamer.[10] As a young man he received an early inspiration in the idea of the beauty and simplicity that is attained in perfect fitness for purpose, in looking at the steam-locomotives that passed to and fro before the house, their sleek shining bodies combining elegance and power, and he himself has described how years later, when designing the series of sans-serif type-faces that bear his name and were adopted by the London Transport Board in the 1920s, he gained much help from studying at Brighton station the noble lettering on the locomotives which had been designed in the drawing-office of William Stroudley.[11]

17 Preston Park and Manor

reston Park, a large and pleasant expanse of 67 acres on the western side of the London Road, some two miles out of Brighton, was bought by the Corporation in 1883 for £50,000 from Mr. and Mrs. Bennett-Stanford. The purchase money came from a bequest of £70,000 made to the Corporation in 1879 by William Edmund Davies, a Brighton bookmaker, as the inscription on a plinth in Preston Park records. Billie Davies was a legendary figure in racing circles, and known as 'The Leviathan of the Turf', chiefly because he never refused the heaviest bets, and paid out his clients' winnings immediately. On the Cesarewitch of 1848 he accepted a bet of £1,000 to £12,000 on the winner, paying up on the following day. Three years earlier a proposal had been made to buy for £30,000 a large expanse of meadow-land near the village of Preston, but the idea was turned down because of the great cost, and with the excuse that the sea-front and the Downs provided all the open space that was needed. With Billy Davies's bequest there was a change of heart and the land was bought, although the price had by then increased by another £20,000, and Brighton acquired its magnificent park adjoining the London Road at Preston.

At the northern end of the Park stands Preston Manor, a house probably originally of early date, which was given its present Georgian form in 1738 by Thomas Western, Lord of the Manor of Preston, which at one time, as 'Preston Episcopi', consisted not only of the Parish of Preston but also most of the eastern half of Hove, including the greater part of the Hove foreshore. Eventually the house became the property of Sir Charles and Lady Thomas-Stanford and soon after taking up residence at the Manor, in 1905, they employed a young architect named Charles Reilly, who was later to become Principal of the Liverpool School of Architecture, and to be knighted, to carry out alterations, which consisted of adding a new wing at the west end, building verandas on the north side, and widening the entrance hall. In March 1932 Sir Charles Thomas-Stanford, who had been Mayor of Brighton from 1910 to 1913, died, having in 1925 bequeathed the house and surrounding grounds to the Corporation, to be preserved as a building of historic interest and to be used 'exclusively as a Museum and Reference Library' especially devoted to Brighton and Sussex.[1]

Lady Thomas-Stanford, who in her will had left the pictures, clocks, furniture and other contents of the house to the Corporation, died in

November 1932, and in January 1933 the Manor was taken over by the Corporation and subsequently opened to the public. With its remarkable collections of English seventeenth-, eighteenth- and early-nineteenth-century furniture, silver and porcelain, this agreeable Georgian house richly represents the setting of the domestic life of a wealthy Brighton family as it was lived over a period of more than two centuries in Brighton, and as such complements the picture of life at the Royal Court in the Pavilion.

18 Libraries and Museums

I t is perhaps natural that a town as sensitive as Brighton to new modes of thought and activity in so many fields, in fashion, dress, medicine, religion, politics, engineering, architecture, art and literature, should come to possess libraries and museums somewhat exceeding in scope and richness those of more ordinary provincial towns of a similar size.

The first important library in Brighton was that belonging to the Brighton Literary Society, which was established by Mr. George Wagner, brother of the Vicar of St. Peter's Church, and others about the year 1812. Later there was a Mechanics' Institute on the pattern of those that were then being established in many towns throughout the country. After some years the Mechanics' Institute passed into oblivion and a new Literary Society arose in its place, with headquarters in St. James's Street at the back of Gillman's feather-shop, the only evidence of the existence there of a temple of the muses being Doric columns that flanked the doorway. Its activities were confined to running a library and reading-room which performed a useful service for some years, but with the expansion of the town there was a demand for more advanced activities. About 1835 two lively young men settled themselves in Brighton at the beginning of their careers, one as a medical practitioner, the other as headmaster of a private school for boys. The first of the individuals was John Cordy Burrows, who later became a distinguished surgeon and was one of the most progressive members of the Town Council. Eventually he was three times Mayor, and a Freeman of the Borough, and was knighted. The other was Dr. Henry S. Turrell, whose Proprietary School in Ship Street became a famous institution of the town. These two joined the old Literary Society and strove to infuse fresh vigour and life into its comatose body by organizing a number of lectures, the first by Dr. Turrell himself on 'The Fortifications of Paris'. Another was given in the Town Hall by the famous Brighton architect, Charles Busby, on astronomy, illustrated by means of an orrery, or planetary model, set in motion by water power. A few years earlier, in 1833, Dr. Gideon Mantell, the celebrated geologist, had come from Lewes and settled in Brighton at No. 20 The Steine. He founded the Mantellian Institution, under whose auspices occasional evening meetings and lectures were held at the house. The Institution received influential support for a time, but it was too exclusive for a town like Brighton, and it came to an end when Dr. Mantell removed to London in 1838, following the disappointment of his hopes of setting up a successful medical practice. Meanwhile, all attempts to rejuvenate the Old Literary Society having failed, Mr. Cordy Burrows and Dr. Turrell became honorary secretaries of a new body which was eventually known as the Brighton Royal Literary and Scientific Institution, with Prince Albert as its patron, and which had its headquarters in the Albion Rooms, adjoining the Royal Albion Hotel.

The old society quietly passed out of existence and its books were sold, but in 1842 the Mantellian Institution presented most of its books to its successor. The new Institution organized lectures, mostly given by local celebrities, collected objects of scientific and historical interest, and built up a library collection with funds raised by holding soirées in the Royal Pavilion, in the course of which members and their friends peered with wonder through microscopes or watched with amazement streams of vivid, crackling sparks emitted by whirling electrical machines. At length other societies competed by giving soirées at lower and lower fees, and eventually for nothing, and the Institution was compelled to discontinue them. At last, in 1869, the Institution closed its career after a useful existence of twenty-eight years. The members gave up their shares, raised subscriptions to pay off their debts, and finally presented the whole of their very fine collection of books, together with their museum, to the Corporation for 'the free use and enjoyment of the public'. It was from these collections that the public libraries and museums of Brighton were to evolve.

The people of Brighton had always been in the forefront of modern movements, but an attempt to establish a public library under the first Public Libraries Act of 1850 was premature and met with a disastrous defeat. However, even the opponents of the scheme now felt somewhat shamefaced, and in 1869 a public library was established under the general powers granted by the Pavilion Purchase Act of 1850,* in upper rooms at the Royal Pavilion, where the various museum collections which had become the property of the town had been housed since 1862 under the same powers. It was obvious that new quarters must be provided for both the library and the museum, and it was decided in 1871 to make use of the old stabling and coach houses fronting on to Church Street, which had been part of the Royal Stables built by the Prince of Wales. The new Public Library, Museums and Picture Gallery were formed in the space east of the present entrance corridor, and consisted of the present museum galleries centring upon the large picture gallery. This part of the building had originally been intended for an indoor open stable court. The buildings were remodelled by the Borough Surveyor, Mr. P. C. Lockwood, all the principal architectural features being carried out 'in Moorish style', but the exterior fronting on to Church Street seems to have retained the appearance it had in the days of King George IV, as shown in one of the small aquatints of John Nash's *Views of the Royal Pavilion*.

347

A number of local worthies had already given or bequeathed their libraries to the town, and now, no doubt because of the splendid quarters that were being provided, some further important collections of books were presented, even while the new building was being prepared. Amongst them was a collection of some three hundred important pamphlets and books, some of them extremely rare, which had belonged to Richard Cobden, the famous political writer and economist of the Manchester School, who had lived at Mayfield in Sussex up to his death. These were given through Mr. Henry Willett, who was later to make even more splendid gifts to the Institution. The museum collections from the Pavilion were now sorted out, classified and rearranged, and were augmented by several important additions, including a large series of chalk fossils given by Mr. Henry Willett, and his famous collection of British Pottery and Porcelain, then only on loan. There were ivories and armour given by Sir Charles Dick, and a large collection of British Birds was bought 'at a very small outlay'[1] from the Norwich Museum.

The Picture Gallery was the first part of the remodelled building to be completed. Brighton's first public art gallery, like its museum and library, had been at the Royal Pavilion, where in the years following the acquisition of the building by the townspeople, the Brighton and Sussex Society of Fine Arts held exhibitions of pictures in some small upper rooms. Although they worked with great enthusiasm, showing pictures lent by well-known London artists, the dark, low rooms were unsuitable for this purpose. In 1860 the Society gave place to a committee of local artists, who were given permission to exhibit in the Great Kitchen, which had the advantage of a good top light and large walls. The committee, calling itself the Brighton Arts Society, included amongst its members several highly competent local painters, whose works exist today in the Art Gallery's collections, including F. W. Woledge, R. H. Nibbs the marine painter, W. H. S. Scott, George de Paris, H. Earp and F. Earp. A descendant of these last two artists, St. John Earp, is an artist living in Brighton today.

The committee of artists continued their work until 1865. Apart from an exhibition of modern paintings, chiefly by foreign artists, held in the following year, there were no more exhibitions until 1873, when the new Picture Gallery was opened in January with a loan exhibition which included paintings chiefly lent by Mr. Henry Willett and by Captain Hill.

The opening proceedings were rounded off by a grand soirée in the evening, when the whole of the buildings were 'brilliantly lighted up' and opened 'to a rapid influx of company'. Microscopes, spectroscopes, galvanic batteries, an electric telegraph 'with facilities for despatching messages to the most distant quarters of the globe' were in evidence, together with a number of working models from the Railway Works. Sir Cordy Burrows gave a talk on 'The Brain', the Vicar of Brighton, the

Rev. Dr. Hannah (later Bishop of Chichester), sounded a warning note in a lecture on 'The Use and Abuse of Free Libraries and Museums', and Mr. T. W. Wonfer, a member of the Museum Committee, described 'The Means by which some animals escape notice'. The proceedings were only marred by the refusal of Mr. George Scott, Curator of the Museum, to give to the *Herald* reporter a list of members of the Library and Museum Sub-Committee, inquiring at the same time, 'Who wants to know anything about *them* ?'[2]

Almost as soon as the new building was opened it was realized that the accommodation was still very inadequate, especially for the library, which was confined to two rooms on the upper floor, and eventually, in 1894, fresh plans for the enlargement of the building were drawn up. Some open stable and carriage courts immediately north of the Dome, and west of the existing museum premises, were adapted to provide a Lending Library and two reading-rooms on the ground floor, with a new entrance corridor between them and the Museum. The original George IV façade was now very considerably altered. It was given greater height so as to allow for the provision of three large new exhibition galleries on the first floor of the Museum portion, and for a fine Reference Library room above the new Lending Library. The original graceful Saracenic arches of the Museum façade were slightly altered, chiefly to enable new entrances to be made, but the Library portion of the façade was very drastically changed, becoming now encrusted with ponderous Indian ornament around the windows and with minaret-like pinnacles above the parapet. Although very different from John Nash's original façade, the new frontage had very vigorous character, and is a remarkable example of Victorian design in the difficult idiom of orientalism. When, in 1966, the minarets, copings and other portions of this façade became decayed, it was fortunately decided by the Corporation to restore the work as closely as possible to the Victorian original. The greatly enlarged and transformed buildings were opened in November 1901. To signalize the event Mr. Willett presented his magnificent collection of pottery and porcelain, which had hitherto been on loan, together with a splendid selection of paintings by Flemish, Dutch and Italian masters. He was one of the outstanding art-collectors of his day, and his name appeared frequently in the earlier editions of Berenson's catalogues of Italian paintings.

In 1916 a no less remarkable addition to the collections was received in the form of the bequest of the collection of the late L. M. Bloomfield, of Withdean, Brighton, who left his library of 13,000 volumes and some 2,000 pictures and prints to the town. Before coming to Brighton Mr. Bloomfield owned Woodhall Towers, a fantastic imitation Belgian château near Pinner, Middlesex. He had been the head of a famous firm of makers of military caps and helmets which is still in existence. His interests chiefly concerned the game of bowls, horses and dogs, and his collection of books, which included many early manuscripts, some of them beautifully illuminated, and about thirty early printed books, including works by Caxton and Wynkyn de Worde as well as many volumes from the early Nuremberg and Venetian printers.[3] In addition to these remarkable book-treasures, the Bloomfield Collection is extremely rich in original works of literature and history, and on the arts and architecture of the seventeenth, eighteenth and early nineteenth centuries.

Five years later James George Lewis left his large library of foreign books, and in 1928 the Corporation received nearly £6,000 from the residue of his estate, to be invested and applied to the purchase of books in French, German, Italian, Spanish and Russian. The investment has grown with the years, and the product of it has been devoted to building up a representative collection of standard editions of important authors, and definitive works in foreign languages upon various subjects. The Lewis Collection is now especially rich in modern foreign works on art and architecture. In 1930 William Done, a schoolmaster of Brighton, also left a large sum, the interest of which was to be used for buying works 'of special character' for the Reference Library, and this has been used in recent years to purchase important works of a kind rarely found in any but the largest libraries.

The initial collections of the Brighton Library were of extremely fine and varied quality, but with the addition of the gifts and bequests made by many distinguished scholars, men of science and letters and collectors of Brighton, the Reference Library became one of the richest collections in the whole country, surpassed only by those of the great universities and the larger cities. It possesses many works that are not to be found even in the British Museum.

In 1896 some concern was expressed over a decline in the number of books that were being issued from the Library. This falling-off was attributed by the local paper to the increase of cycling amongst young ladies, who were, it was said, 'to be seen in large numbers careering along morning, noon and night . . . in fact, novel reading', it was suggested, had 'succumbed to wheeling'.[4]

From 1906 to 1935 the institution flourished under the direction of Mr. Henry D. Roberts, M.B.E., whose outstanding contribution to its work was the organization of a series of important international exhibitions of modern art, beginning with an exhibition of Modern French Art which opened on 10th June 1910. This exhibition was to be of some historical importance, for in it were shown, for the first time in England, paintings by those French artists who were later to be known as the 'Post-Impressionists'. This showing actually pre-dated the first Post-Impressionist Exhibition which was held at the Grafton Galleries, London, in August 1910.[5] The Brighton show was organized by Bernheim Jeune and a

London Committee that included Robert Dell, editor of the *Burlington Magazine*, Boris Ansep the Russian mosaic artist, Roger Fry and Clive Bell. There were works by all the Impressionists and also by Cézanne, Gauguin, Signac, Odilon, Redon, Maurice, Denis, Bonnard, Vuillard, Matisse, Rouault, Friesz, Vlaminck and Derain. Had this remarkable event been celebrated by the purchase which could then have been made of a canvas by Bonnard or Vuillard for £100, or of a Gauguin for £200, three noughts at least could have been added to the value of the picture today and the Gallery would have been enriched by a treasure of great importance. The local Fine Arts Committee purchased instead for £100 a large canvas by Gaston La Touche entitled 'Swans at play'.

In the course of the next twenty-five years Mr. Roberts organized exhibitions of modern art from Belgium, Spain, Denmark, Sweden, Norway and other countries. In the hope of arranging an exhibition of modern Italian art during the days of Mussolini, Mr. Roberts waited in the dictator's ante-room for several days until noticed by him, when Mr. Roberts obtained his blessing for the project, with the promise that all expenses would be paid by the Italian Government.

BATTLE-SCENE AND TRANSFORMATION

1900 to 1969

1 Edwardian Days: 1900 to 1914

At the beginning of the new century Brighton was passing through a period of depression. For some years the place had ceased to attract wealthy fashionable visitors in great numbers. The few who did come patronized the newly built Metropole Hotel, and the Royal York Hotel, once so much favoured by the Royal family, was derelict and ruinous. In 1901 Harry Preston, who had been successfully running hotels at Bournemouth, came to Brighton and took over the Royal York. Preston put all the money he possessed as he tells us[1] and a great deal more into the place, rebuilding it from top to bottom, and before long distinguished names were appearing again in the guest book.

This was the beginning of a new era in the social life of Brighton, in which Harry Preston's genial personality and enthusiasm for yachting, motoring, flying, boxing and the theatre helped to bring about a renewal of the town's importance as a mecca of the sporting and theatrical world. Undoubtedly the greatest single influence in the renewal of Brighton's success was the rapidly growing popularity of the motor-car, and Brighton was fortunate enough to have become established at the beginning as a motoring centre when the town was chosen as the objective for the run on Motor-car Day, 14th November 1896, when motorists celebrated their emancipation from the old-fashioned laws governing steam road-locomotives under which motor-cars had been ruled hitherto, and which had compelled a man with a red flag to walk in front to give warning of their approach. The Veteran Car Run, which takes place from London to Brighton every year in commemoration of the original event, is now a gay and exciting occasion in which over two hundred early motor-cars take part, and is watched by thousands of spectators both along the route and at Brighton, but the first run was a dismal and not altogether triumphant affair. At the breakfast held before the run at the Hotel Metropole in London the Earl of Winchelsea ceremonially tore a red flag in two. The intended procession of cars never materialized. Fifty-four cars were listed to start, but only thirty set off from Hyde Park at the appointed hour of 8.0 in the morning. Heavy rain and wind discouraged many of the entrants even if it did not actually interfere with the engines. The cars and their drivers were to have been welcomed by the Mayor of Brighton at Preston Park, but the cars straggled in only one at a time, with long intervals in between. The first to arrive was a Bollee steam-car, which made the journey in 2 hours 30 minutes and 25 seconds. The next did not appear for another two and a half hours, having taken 4 hours 53 minutes and 15 seconds. Out of the thirty cars that started only seventeen arrived safely. The famous veteran driver Newman Savory, who started in the first run, did not reach Brighton until fifty years later, when he came driving a 1901 Wolseley car in the first Veteran Car Run to be held after the war, in 1946, accompanied by J. Eason Gibson, the famous motoring writer. The joys, tribulations and excitements of early motor-car runs have been immortalized in the famous film *Genevieve* in which Kenneth More, Dinah Sheridan, John Gregson and Kay Kendall played the principal parts. The actual car that gave its name to the film, a 1901 Renault, is appropriately preserved in the Montagu Motor Museum at Beaulieu Abbey.

From 1901 onwards the motor-car rapidly improved in speed, reliability, comfort and appearance, although at first the industry forfeited a great deal of public confidence because of the large number of speculators who entered this field expecting to make fortunes quickly, and who failed financially. Especially scandalous were the dubious ramifications of the Great Horseless Carriage Company, later the Motor Manufacturing Company, a 'blatantly dishonest organization'[2] which lasted from 1895 until its collapse in 1903.

Nevertheless, every year saw greater numbers of motor-cars on the road. Brighton was the ideal distance for a day's run from London, and offered a multitude of distractions at the journey's end. Soon the Brighton Road began to emerge from the obscurity and neglect into which it had fallen since the end of the great days of coaching. Harry Preston was the promoter in 1905 of a scheme to have a tarmac surface laid on the Madeira Drive, from the Palace Pier to Kemp Town, a distance of nearly a mile, to enable it to serve from time to time as a motor-racing track. There was heavy opposition in the Town Council to this proposal, which was quite revolutionary.

The roads of Brighton then were still the macadam kind of crushed stone, and many of the streets were laid with wood-blocks and even with brick, but however ideal these may have been for horse traffic they were quite unsuitable for motors because of the dust that was raised by a fast-moving vehicle and also because of the danger of tyre-bursts caused by sharp stones. At length Harry Preston's supporters won the day, and Brighton's first Motor Race Week was held in July. Many of the names of owners, drivers and mechanics that took part are now famous in the annals of motoring—The Hon. C. S. Rolls, Clifford Earp, S. F. Edge, J. T. C. Brabazon (later Lord Brabazon of Tara), Sir Ralph St. George Gore, A. Lee Guinness, and Theodore Schneider, founder of the Schneider Trophy races of the 1920s which played a part in the development of the Spitfire. S. F. Edge's six-cylinder 90 h.p. Napier was 'acknowledged to be the most perfect motor in view'. Although the motor-car was now a fairly familiar sight, many people had never seen the immense 100 h.p. racing-machines, and were frightened to go near them when they started with a noise like a 'terrific cannonading . . . the cars throbbing, belching forth petrol fumes, and appearing to be on the point of bursting into a thousand fragments'. 'But it is quite refreshing', the *Gazette* reported,[3] 'to see Mr. Schneider start. No oil-stained, dirty grimed overall for him. A dapper, pleasant figure in blue serge, with a white carnation in his button-hole, a cigarette between his lips, and a smile on his face on the famous rush along the Madeira Road with none of the worried, anxious looks which other competitors wear.' But the most popular of all the entrants were the lady drivers. On the first day Miss Victoria Godwin won several heats in a 30–35 h.p. Ariel.

The second day of the meeting was Ladies' Day, for which the men dressed in frock coats and Panama hats. The ladies' dresses were a feast of colour, tailor-made costumes in light material being especially favoured. Blouses were 'in every shade of silk', and 'parasols were immense'. The chief race of the day was a duel between Mrs. Herbert Lloyd and Mrs. Bennett-Stanford, who lived at Preston Manor—'the latter popular lady, who bears a name long honoured in Brighton, was attired in a muslin dress with blue spots and her large biscuit coloured hat was secured by a motor veil. Mrs. Lloyd wore a light dust coat, no hat and her eyes were shaded by goggles presenting a rather curious appearance.' 'The Gallant Struggle' ended in favour of Mrs. Lloyd, in her slightly more practical garb.[4]

The principal event of the meeting was the Flying Race for the *Autocar* Challenge Cup, in which all the largest cars took part. Clifford Earp entered a 90 h.p. Napier driven by the famous pioneer motorist S. F. Edge; J. T. C. Brabazon drove a 90 h.p. Mors; Sir Ralph St. George Gore was in a huge 100 h.p. Mercedes; A. Lee Guiness had a 100 h.p. Darracq; C. S. Rolls was driving a 150 h.p. Dufaux; and Theodore Schneider was at the wheel of a 100 h.p. Rochet-Schneider. The race was won, and a new English record set up for the flying kilometre, by Clifford Earp, at 97.20 miles an hour, and immense delight was caused when 'plucky Miss Levitt' came in fourth, with a 90 h.p. Napier that covered the track at 77.62 miles an hour. 'The huge racing monsters literally hurled themselves along the track at a speed touching close on 100 miles an hour, the roar of engines likening to the sound of an artillery volley.'[5]

Deliberating afterwards upon the lessons of the Motor Race Week, the *Gazette* considered that the motor-car had 'definitely come to stay' and that it was hoped the meeting would become an annual event. The price it was believed one should pay to obtain a reliable motor-car was said to be not less than £800, an amount very close to the price today of a popular car. One could, however, buy an Orient 'buck-board automobile', consisting of little more than a tiny engine on an open wooden frame with wheels, for as little as eighty-five guineas.

The fashionable Press greeted the advent of the motor-car with enthusiasm. 'King Petrol, with a rush and a roar, is advancing on his all-conquering career', commented a writer in the *Brighton Season*,[6] and added: 'It is King Petrol who will help his Bride by the Sea to retain her supremacy. And so—long life to King Petrol!'

The idea of the motor-track was a stroke of genius, for the Madeira Terrace, the elevated walk that is carried on elegant cast-iron latticed arches, formed as it does today a superb grandstand, while the Marine Parade above provided room for thousands of additional spectators. Ever since that time the Madeira Drive has been the scene not only of the Veteran Car Run, but also of other motoring events such as the Vintage Car Rally and the International Motor Speed Trials that are held every September. On 30th August 1905 the first motor-omnibus service between London and Brighton was inaugurated with the 'Vanguard', an open-topped two-decker omnibus with solid rubber tyres. In summer it left the Hotel Victoria in London at 9.30 a.m. and arrived in Brighton at 2.0 p.m.; returning from Brighton at 4 p.m. and reaching London again at 9.0 p.m. From then onwards trips to Brighton by motor char-à-bancs became more and more numerous, especially at weekends and holiday times. The fares were lower than by the railway, and the trippers discovered fresh incentives to spend a day at the seaside and to enjoy a novel experience in making the journey through the countryside of Surrey and Sussex.

The Grand Hotel was offering 'full boarding terms at 10s 6d per client', while the boarding houses offered rooms for as little as 3s 6d a night. P. and A. Campbell's two paddle pleasure-steamers, the *Glen Rosa* and the *Brighton Queen*, made trips to neighbouring seaside resorts and the Isle of Wight. Trams had been replacing the old horse-drawn buses since 1901, and by 1905 were running on most of the main routes of the town.

There were donkey rides for children along the beach and lower promenade near the Palace Pier, and nigger-minstrels playing banjos, with blackened faces and wearing straw boaters, striped blazers and white flannel trousers. On the lawns below the promenade near the Metropole Hotel a concert party called 'The White Coons' gave performances during the summer of 1906. The men, who included the comedian Will Pepper, dressed in white suits, white Homburg hats, and three-inch-high stiff double collars. Miss Folly, who wore a white dress and a white balloon-hat, sang a song about a shy girl who married a rich suitor:

> *The snail was pale and fearfully young and shy ;*
> *Such a frail female, you'd think she was going to die,*
> *But when she found he'd five thousand as well,*
> *Well then, my word! The snail came out of her shell!*

At the Palace Pier Theatre popular concerts were given by Mr. Bernhardt, and the Hippodrome, ten years old in 1907, was packed to the doors at Whitsun when the comedian Fred Karno presented his 'screaming sketch' called *Saturday to Monday*. Playing a very small role in the cast was a young comedian named Charlie Chaplin. The manager of the Theatre Royal, Cecil Beryl, presented the musical comedy *The White Chrysanthemum*, and the West Pier Theatre was besieged by crowds eager to see Lewis Waller's romantic costume play *Monsieur Beaucaire*. For a time the Grand Theatre in North Road was the most popular theatre in the town, chiefly because it was lit by electricity and smoking was permitted.

Harry Preston's efforts to restore Brighton to its former brilliance and reputation had not yet borne their greatest fruit when in 1906 the *Daily Mail* published a front-page article on the town in which Brighton was condemned as an unenterprising, unattractive and outdated holiday resort. Bursting with indignation, Preston went to London and interviewed Kennedy Jones, the editor, telling him about the new sea-front parade and the tarmac motor-road, and pointing out that although he professed to cry 'Britain for the British', by decrying English resorts he would drive our own people to spend their money at inferior places across the Channel. Next day Kennedy Jones published on the main page a second article giving a more favourable impression of Brighton, and this did much to improve the reputation of the town. Two years later King Edward VII began a series of visits, staying three times in twelve months. On the first occasion, in February 1908, he travelled down from Buckingham Palace by car and stayed for a week with his daughter the Duchess of Fife and her husband at their house at 1 Lewes Crescent. Every day during his visit he lunched and dined daily wih his friend Arthur Sassoon, who lived at 8 King's Gardens, Hove, in a state of extreme splendour attended by forty servants. His half-brother, Reuben Sassoon, was living near by at 7 Queen's Gardens, Hove, while another half-brother, Sir Albert Sassoon, had lived at 1 Eastern Terrace, Brighton, for twenty years after taking the house in 1876. Charles Cochran, the Brighton-born musical comedy impresario, reported Henry Labouchere to have described Brighton as 'four miles long, and one mile in depth, with a Sassoon at each end and another in the middle'.[7] King Edward's friendship with this wealthy family of bankers, as well as his desire to visit his daughter, were strong encouragement for him to make a stay in Brighton, and were undoubtedly an important influence upon the renewal of the social prestige of the town.

The King had expressed a wish to be allowed to enjoy his stay in quiet and privacy, and it was therefore regrettable that in the words of the *Brighton Herald*[8] 'fifty so-called unemployed led by a misguided person named Hardy, must needs choose the very hour of the King's arrival to make a demonstration in front of his mansion.' Hardy was arrested, the banners were confiscated by the police, and the crowds dispersed. The newspaper remarked on the incident: 'The Chief Constable rendered the working classes and the other classes a wide service. It is well known that people have not been slow to proclaim from the housetops that the glories of Brighton have departed. . . . Had King Edward been driven from Brighton by his quietude being invaded by ranting demagogues and their following demonstrating beneath his windows, Brighton would have received a blow from which it would be many a long day in recovering. As it is the King is declared to be deriving both health and enjoyment from his holiday; and this fact, and the fact that he has been rejoicing in floods of sunshine is being chronicled in the press all the country over. Nothing could exert a finer influence on the fortunes of Brighton. Nothing could be more calculated to bring about an influx of rank and fashion to the town. . . . The success of the King's visit will do more to aid employment than would be effected by any number of socialistic demonstrations. The man who will militate against the success of the visit is an enemy of his town.'

The King quite clearly had not been annoyed by the demonstration, for he came again in the following year, and could be seen in the early mornings strolling along the terrace of the private gardens of Lewes Crescent overlooking the front and the sea. After a few days the seats at the end of the Marine Parade in front of the King's house began to be crowded with inquisitive people waiting for the King to appear. The Chief Constable, Sir William Gentle, solved the difficulty of ensuring the King's quiet and privacy in inspired and unobtrusive fashion. He had a quiet word with the Borough Surveyor, and all the seats where the curious spectators had been accustomed to wait were found to have been given a fresh, wet coat of bright green paint every morning.

In December 1908 the King stayed for six days at Hove with Arthur Sassoon while recovering from a cold. He returned there for a long weekend in the following February, and came again in January 1910. On these occasions the King frequently sat enjoying the sunshine in one of the shelters of the Hove sea-front, and with commendable good taste the local residents and visitors made no attempt to invade his privacy at these times.

In January 1911 the *Gazette* reported with gratification that the visits of the King in the years past had 'created goodly influences'.[9] During one of his visits the King attended at the police gynasium in two of the arches on the lower promenade, where a number of the very poorest children were being fitted out with boots and winter clothing provided out of the fund established by Sir William Gentle. The King sat amongst the children, who were being entertained by the police with cocoa, buns and oranges, and afterwards gave Sir William a substantial donation towards his fund. Many of the waiting mothers burst into tears of happiness when they saw

360

their children warmly clad, but there were a few who could hardly wait until the children had reached home before stripping the new clothes off their backs and taking away their new boots to raise a few shillings on them at the pawnshop.[10] In 1911 Sir William Gentle reported that only one case of a child's boots having been pawned had occurred in that year, and the practice was completely stopped by having all the garments and boots stamped with his name.

An extraordinary aspect of Brighton life in those days was the activities of the bird-catchers. A number of families specialized in this traffic. Every morning in the season some twenty to thirty men went out from Brighton on to the Downs, where they set nets to catch birds of all kinds. Larks and wheatears were sold as delicacies to the big hotels. Singing birds were kept alive and sold in cages. Sparrows and starlings were plucked and sold by the plateful, as they are still today on the Continent, but the most profitable catches were the examples of rare varieties or species of birds that were occasionally caught, and for which ten shillings or a sovereign would be given by wealthy collectors for their private museums.[11]

Once more Royal patronage had restored the fortunes of Brighton. In honour of the Royal visits the eastern end of the Marine Parade at Brighton was named King's Cliff, while Hove responded by giving its sea-front the name of King's Way. In 1908 the increase in the number of the wealthier visitors to Brighton encouraged the railway company to start running the luxury train, the 'Southern Belle'. By this time the one-hour train service between London and Brighton had been inaugurated.[12] During the summer of 1908 Mr. A. G. Vanderbilt was running a daily coach drawn by five American horses, and for the poorer classes there were excursion trains arranged by the National Sunday League for 2s 6d return. One could lunch at Sam Izaacs's restaurant in West Street on sausages, mashed potatoes and onions for 4½d, and in the afternoon go to Eastbourne and back on the excursion steamer for 9d. Tea with bread and butter, jam and a slice of fruit cake cost 6d.

A famous institution during Edwardian days was 'Cheeseman's Oyster Bar', a shop now occupied by English's Restaurant, but then run by the two redoutable and autocratic Cheeseman sisters. In no circumstances would they allow smoking in their bar, so as not to spoil the flavour of the oysters. King Edward entered smoking a cigar and called for oysters, but the sisters refused to serve him until he had extinguished his cigar, which he did without a murmur. The only person who is supposed to have got the better of the sisters, according to Sir Harry Preston, was the writer Maurice Baring, who entered and asked for a single oyster. This was solemnly served up to him without comment.

In the depressed state of the town during the early years of the twentieth century the future of the Aquarium was in the balance, but in 1901 the

Corporation wisely stepped in and bought the building for £30,000, and made a number of alterations and improvements, including the building of a Winter Garden at the eastern end. For a number of years the building remained open as it had done in the past with fair success, and by 1909 Brighton Aquarium possessed one of the finest marine collections in Europe, having more different species in its tanks than did any of the aquaria of Berlin, Naples, Blackpool or Hamburg. From this time onwards until the end of the First World War the Aquarium knew some of its most successful years.

In the early years of the new century the popularity of the music halls began to be threatened by the advent of the cinema. In 1951 a stone tablet was placed at No. 20b Middle Street commemorating the work of William Frieze-Green, one of the great pioneers of the cinema, who lived there for a time. It is true that he experimented at this house with colour photography, but most of his important early cinema experiments took place in London, and his patent on the first motion-picture camera was taken out in 1898, before he came to Brighton. There were other pioneers of the cinema who carried out important early experiments in Brighton, and who became known as 'the Brighton School'. The foremost of these was George Albert Smith, who later became famous as the inventor of the first practicable colour-film system—Kinemacolor. His first cinema studio at St. Ann's Well Gardens, Hove, is reputed to have been the earliest of its kind in the world. A later studio of his, in Wilbury Road, Hove, still bears the name 'Kinemacolor' on its outside walls. As a lecturer in astronomy, Smith thoroughly understood the science of optical projection as applied to still lantern slides, and after seeing an exhibition of early films by the French brothers Lumière at the Empire Theatre, Leicester Square in 1896 he resolved to develop the possibilities of the invention. He employed Alfred Darling, who lived at Ditchling Rise, Brighton, to make his first cinematograph camera, and before long Darling's cameras had become the standard machine of the new industry. It was a Darling camera that the first news-camera-man took with him to South Africa for the filming of the Boer War. After a few years Smith was exporting as many as 400 films a week to the United States. They were extremely short, running for only a minute or two, and consisting only of a single incident or comic item. Trick films were especially popular: it was not for some time that the idea of a long screen-play developed. Towards the end of his life Smith received many honours from the film industry for his pioneer work. One of his agents was James Williamson, a chemist of Church Road, Hove, who began making films in a back-garden studio, but later built the studio in Wilbury Road that was taken over by Smith when Williamson moved to London. A number of other early film-makers came to Brighton from London to shoot their films. They were attracted to the town by the clear air and bright sunshine of the coast at a time when London was subject to cloudy weather, smoke and fog, and artificial light was not very efficient.[13] Numerous small cinema-halls sprang up in Brighton—the Congress Hall, Union Road; the Gem Electric, London Road; the Tillney, Edward Street; the Coronation, North Street; the Princes and the Byron, North Road; and the Imperial, St. James's Street. Prices ranged from ½d on a Monday night to 1d, 3d, 6d and 1s. A programme of the Court Theatre, New Road, when in use as a cinema in the early 1900s included such titles as 'A Tour through North Wales', 'Tulips', 'The Cabin Boy', 'The Last Cartridge', and 'From Earth to Moon', a remarkable fantasy by the famous French film-maker Meliés.

One of the most intriguing Brighton personalities of the period between the two world wars was Lady Marguerite Abinger. Noted for her lavish entertaining, famous for her spicy conversation and for her generous gifts to charities, she was the widow of the sixth Baron Abinger, and lived at West Cliff House at the foot of Montpelier Road.

Much of her fascination for Brighton residents and visitors arose from the fact that she had been the 'tragic widow' in a sensational French double-murder case. Her first husband was Alphonse Steinheil, a French portrait painter. One morning in the summer of 1908 her husband and her mother, Madame Japy, were found gagged, bound and strangled in her house. Marguerite herself was tied to her bed with a cord round her neck. Marguerite stated that the outrages had been carried out by two masked men and a woman who broke into the house and forced her to give them her jewels. Some time later she was arrested and after being kept in prison for thirteen months was charged together with her groom with complicity in the murders. Her innocence was eventually proved conclusively and her acquittal was hailed with acclamation. A young Englishman, heir to the Abinger barony, who had been present in the court throughout the trial, told Marguerite that he had fallen in love with her and wished to marry her. She refused him at that time, however. Being ten years older than her admirer, she may have feared that his feeling was only a passing infatuation, but several years later when he succeeded to the title they met again. He renewed his proposal and she became Lady Abinger.[14] Lord Abinger died in 1927 and afterwards his widow presented to the town the handsome black and yellow baronial coach of the Abingers which was to be seen for many years in the Art Gallery.* Built in 1830, it is a splendid example of the coach-builder's art, with its luxurious appointments that include door-handles, plaques of the family arms and other mounts all in solid silver.

Lady Abinger lived on for many years in a flat in Adelaide Crescent until her death in 1954. The family mansion on the sea-front had been demolished several years earlier and was rebuilt lavishly in Regency style as a restaurant and hotel which was given the name of Abinger House. In the 1890s it was the residence of Mr. Gerald Loder, Liberal M.P. for Brighton, and afterwards Lord Wakehurst. He was one of the leaders of Brighton society in late Victorian and Edwardian days.

Another highly picturesque figure in Brighton life was the American millionaire Walter Winans, who made long visits to the town in Edwardian days. Born in St. Petersburg (Leningrad), he was famous as a crack shot with a revolver, especially on horseback, and as a champion driver of trotting horses. To see him flashing along the sea-front in his light, rubber-tyred carriage behind a pair of smart American horses was one of the sights of the Brighton season.

During the early years of the new century the people of Brighton were treated to scenes of hitherto undreamed-of novelty and excitement. Soon after coming from Bournemouth to the town Harry Preston acquired *My Lady Ada*, the first and only motor-yacht on this stretch of coast to be seen for some time. When a torpedo-boat flotilla made a visit to Brighton in 1906, Preston lent the yacht to the Mayor to serve as his official flagship. About 1907 Preston changed the boat for a new and more powerful craft, *My Lady Molly*, which was built at Shoreham by a famous yacht-builder named Sam Saunders, who bore a remarkable resemblance to King Edward VII himself. The boat was 60 feet long with a 75 h.p. engine. The Sussex Motor Yacht Club came into existence and before long motor-yacht races were adding a new thrill to the attractions of Brighton. A more ominous portent was the appearance of a 'great army airship' over the town towards the end of 1910, and the beach was the scene of another wonder when André Beaumont, the French pioneer aviator, had his Blériot monoplane brought over in pieces from France *via* Newhaven and put it together on the beach at Black Rock. With Preston as passenger the machine skimmed over the water, then soared into the air and flew for three-quarters of an hour.

The first machine to fly to Brighton was a Blériot piloted by Oscar Morrison, who came the forty miles from Brooklands Aerodrome in sixty minutes on 15th February 1911. He would have taken less time if he had not mistaken Worthing for Brighton until he remembered that the latter place had two piers and flew along the coast until he found them. He landed on the beach at Paston Place, breaking his propeller on the pebbles in the process. It hung for years as a souvenir at the Royal York Hotel, where he was fêted after the flight by Harry Preston and the Deputy Mayor at a grand luncheon. On the 12th April another air pioneer, Gustav Hamel, landed on the Brunswick Lawns, also in a Blériot, and was met by Harry Preston and his brother. Hamel won the first prize of £80 in the Grand Brighton Aerial Race, which was organized by the Preston brothers and Mr. Rosenthal of the Palace Pier Company, and which took place from Brooklands to Brighton on 6th May. Graham Gilmour in a rear-engined

Bristol biplane came second and in the course of the flight 'repeatedly waved both his hands at the same time—a daring achievement', as the *Brighton Gazette* remarked. Gilmour was a particularly handsome and dashing aviator, and a great favourite with the public. When he landed on the Hove Lawns on the following Sunday the crowds climbed over the railings and swarmed round his plane. The *Gazette*[15] recorded that 'Ladies in tight hobble-skirts performed the most extraordinary aerobatic feats in getting over the barrier, and gentlemen who gallantly endeavoured to assist their movements had to perform a rather delicate task.'

The Easter season at Brighton in 1911 was more crowded and successful than ever before, chiefly because the town was thronged with soldiers. In 1862 about 12,000 soldiers of volunteer regiments had been brought to Brighton for an Easter holiday field-day, as a military operation to show how easily large numbers of troops could be brought by railway to a threatened point in the event of invasion. Ever since that date the Easter Volunteer Reviews that were held on the Downs had become increasingly popular public spectacles, but in 1911 the town was made more gay and colourful than ever before, with the sea-front crowded with volunteers in every imaginable kind of uniform, and with the military bands of the different regiments playing outside all the chief hotels throughout the day. Brighton now seemed completely to have recovered from the period of stagnation through which it had been passing. The Town Council was now laying a tarmac surface on the London Road at Preston, and a 'magnificently reconstructed' theatre was opened together with a Winter Garden on the Palace Pier.

A guest who stayed at the Royal York Hotel about this time was Arnold Bennett, who had been a journalist, an editor of a women's magazine, and a writer of short stories and some novels. He was then writing *Clayhanger*, and described in that novel the life of Harry Preston's hotel, which he called the 'Royal Sussex'. The housekeeper in the story, whom he described as making an eagle-eyed inspection of the rooms after they had been dusted by the page-boy, was based upon Miss Beatrice Collings, sister of Mr. Preston's wife, and the page-boy himself was Hardy, Mr. Preston's valet, who later was placed in charge of his wine cellar.

The Baroness Angela Burdett-Coutts, granddaughter of the famous actress of the time of King George IV, was accustomed in the last years of her life to spend several months of each year at the Royal York Hotel, engaging the whole of the first floor for herself and her suite. Although over ninety, she retained her clarity of brain and sharpness of wit, and Harry Preston describes how every night she enjoyed a specially prepared four-course dinner. 'It was an Epicurean repast. With the fish she would take a half-bottle of Berncasteler, a very choice old wine, and with the roast a small bottle of excellent old vintage champagne. Later on she would take a pot of strong black tea, and then retire for the night and sleep like a baby.'[16]

Ever since Claude Graham-White took Harry Preston for a flight over Brighton and swooped so low over the town that the plane nearly crashed into the chimneys of the Royal Albion Hotel, Preston had dreamed of owning that building as well as the Royal York, and in 1913 he bought the hotel for £13,500. Arnold Bennett was a visitor here also, and *Hilda Lessways*, the sequel to *Clayhanger*, which he published in 1911, contained like the earlier novel some graphic descriptions of Brighton in the late Edwardian era. One of Bennett's characters from 'Bursley' remarks in the earlier novel on 'the steep streets of houses that sprawled on the hilly mounds of the great town like ladders; reminiscent of certain streets of her native district in the Potteries'. To Bennett's characters from the Five Towns Brighton seemed a town of wealth and luxury that contrasted strongly with 'the pleasure cities of the poor and the middling such as Blackpool and Llandudno'.

The year 1912 was one of great activity. The proposal made a year earlier for a University College to be established at Brighton was carried a stage further at a meeting in the Royal Pavilion early in the year. Queen Alexandra came to Brighton and visited the Danish Art Exhibition at the Art Gallery in May, and the Corporation far-sightedly bought 1,000 acres of land at Ovingdean from Mr. Steyning Beard for the sum of £35,000, in order to keep control over possible future developments. Paderewski, Melba, Clara Butt, Backhaus and Mischa Elman performed at the Dome, and in July Lieutenant Salmson brought the first hydroplane to the town. He stayed for several days, 'delighting the inhabitants with masterly exhibitions', of which the climax was a race between the hydroplane and Harry Preston's motor-yacht *My Lady Molly*. A further sensation was caused when Mr. Hicks 'looped the loop' in an aeroplane at Shoreham.

Another notable event in the art world took place in the public Art Gallery when in December 1913 the painter Walter Sickert, who was a frequent visitor to Brighton and who later had a studio in Sussex Square, opened the first exhibition of the Camden Town Group of painters, entitled 'An Exhibition of the work of English Post-Impressionists, Cubists and others'. It included works by such distinguished figures as Ethel Sands, Sylvia Gosse, Walter Bayes, Charles Ginner, Harold Gilman, J. B. Manson, Spencer F. Gore, Lucien Pissarro, and Sickert himself. Another artist represented was Walter Bevan, who lived in Hove, and who is now recognized as one of the leading English Impressionists. The Art Gallery were more perspicacious on this occasion, buying his picture 'Cab-yard at Night' for £40. It is now regarded as probably the best of all his works.

Writing to his friend the painter Jules Lessore at the time, Sickert described the setting of the exhibition he had opened:

J'ai la tête romanesque
Et j'adore le pittoresque

Giroflé-Girofla

I was sitting, Federico mio, today in the beautiful Great Gallery by the Pavilion at Brighton, dominated by the magnificent portrait of the magnificent George IV. ('Is he a gentleman?' 'Has he any Greek?') The gallery which is still *the* example of proper picture-hanging. Pictures, considered as a permanent factor in the architecture of a room, and not as items in a lending library. The life-sized or larger than life portraits or drama-pictures, hang on the friese above the picture-rail. Below are perhaps a couple of lines of cabinet pictures up to perhaps 30 × 25 inches.

This, the traditional grand style of hanging, that nothing can ever replace, is a reminder that three or more centuries of temporary exhibitions have not been without the deleterious effect that has arisen from the usual competitive, I might almost say combative nature of temporary exhibitions of works by living painters.

The consequence of line and centre hanging, apotheosis hanging, has tended to tempt, say six generations to ignore the stance of the figure and its whole ambient. It has also kept, say, six generations in a blue funk about what is called the face, and what the patron, if any, will say when he comes to 'look into' the face. I had the exquisite joy of seeing a surgical friend of mine whip a lens out of his pocket. He was not clear as to whether it would have been wise to operate or not.

Rd. Sickert Ll.D.

Two years later Sickert painted his famous picture 'Pierrots', now in the Tate Gallery, showing entertainers on the pier at Brighton, a work glowing with the brilliant colours of the costumes, the light of fairy lanterns and of the purple night sky.

In the summer of 1914 Brighton was congratulating herself upon her still mounting prosperity resulting from the visitors who crowded the hotels and from day-trippers, both of whom were coming to Brighton increasingly by road. The *Brighton Gazette* observed 'not only has the private automobile taken possession of the road, but the public motor conveyance, of which there are many striking developments this season, has captured the crowd'.[17] Many of the visitors had come for the traditional Sussex Fortnight of horse-racing at Goodwood, Plumpton, Lewes and Brighton. The *Brighton Gazette* remarked:

'The motor vehicle has completely altered the situation where people travelled to Goodwood, Lewes and Brighton by train from London for the Sussex Fortnight, and now they prefer to make their headquarters in Brighton where the hotels are perfect, the entertainments of first-class merit, the piers are unique. . . .' The paper went on to suggest that

'Partly owing to the facilities provided by the motor-car for trips in the neighbourhood, and partly to the conveniences afforded for outdoor entertainments, the opportunities for gambling dens have been minimized.' Some twenty years earlier a 'horde of sharks' had descended upon Brighton for the Sussex Fortnight, but now, although gambling was not entirely abolished, 'modern conditions had provided such powerful counter attractions that the ranks of the "adventurers" have been thinned out. . . .' At the height of the summer's gaieties the minds of visitors and residents were brought back once more to the threatening happenings in Europe, when in July a French aeroplane flying the *tricolor* landed on the beach at Brighton. The disquiet aroused three years earlier when the French aviator Blériot made the first crossing of the Channel by air and showed that Britain was no longer an inviolable island had receded into the background, but it was now renewed with greater force. The French had landed on the shores of Brighton once before in her history with terrible results, and if a French plane could land, 'why not a German?' asked the *Gazette*. The news from Austria, Russia, Germany and the Balkans now became more and more menacing, but the pleasures of that glorious golden summer were undiminished.

2 The First World War

Even if the worst should happen, it was envisaged that Brighton would not inevitably be a loser by a European war. It was believed that 'Restrictions on Continental travel should increase the rush to English pleasure resorts' and it was even anticipated that many foreign families 'might find a refuge on these shores'. It was not long before these predictions were being fulfilled. People poured into Brighton for that fateful August Bank Holiday week-end of 1914. The trains from London were so crowded that people stood all the way in the guards' vans. Volk's Railway, the tramways, the motor-coaches and the hotel char-à-bancs flourished exceedingly. The second week of the Sussex Fortnight had opened 'oppressed by the prevalence of turf ruffians, but a courageous effort was made to lift the gathering to its proper level of importance.'[1] The *Brighton Gazette* considered[2] there was 'little sign of the War Cloud' that week-end, and afterwards remarked that 'the complete serenity of the holiday crowds was regarded as expressing their quiet determination to do their duty, and it was a patriotic manifestation'. A few days later the *Gazette* concluded that 'Brighton had resolved to keep smiling'. At a meeting at the Dome Dr. Haden Guest was protesting against the forcible feeding of suffragettes on hunger strike in prison, by which, he stated amid cheers, 'every principle of medical etiquette was outraged'. The capitulation of the Government to women's demands for the vote in order to ensure their participation in the war effort was foreshadowed in the resolution then unanimously passed. 'That in view of the disaster of war now facing the nation we demand that the Government shall without delay make peace with the women of the nation and as a first step grant an amnesty to all prisoners connected with the suffrage movement.'

By 19th August the *Gazette* was convinced that 'things were looking a lot brighter all round', and in the issue for 22nd August the paper reported that Brussels had fallen, and that 'Brighton is itself again'. The hotels were making a recovery, the shops reviving, traffic on the railways, trams and buses was normal, and the depression of a fortnight before had vanished. In the first days of the war large numbers of Germans, many of them waiters, tailors, hairdressers and musicians, and their families left the town, which was now invaded by hundreds of French and Belgian refugees who had lost their homes in the German advance, while the offices of the French Consul in the town were besieged by people anxiously trying to

369

get news of their relatives still in France, and by men wishing to take up military duty. A 'stern, steely demeanour' was now apparent, and comparisons were made with the days of Napoleon's threat to the Sussex coast just over a hundred years earlier. Houses were commandeered by the Army, many bookings for holidays were now being cancelled on the grounds that 'the beach was no longer safe for children'. Brighton was full of absurd rumours, and a number of timid women refused to open their doors to anyone in the belief that Germans had already landed 'and were marauding the town'.[3]

An unfortunate German named Paul Buckwaldt was arrested on suspicion of being a spy, but was soon discharged. The paper noted there was a 'Slump in Socialism', and socialist speakers on the sea-front were so forcibly threatened at a meeting at the fishmarket that it was broken up by the police.[4]

The Southdown Hunt refused to recognize the war as a serious threat, and decided at a meeting that they 'considered it absolutely necessary that they should hunt if they possibly could'.[5]

In September the first batch of 300 wounded men arrived in Brighton, to be taken to the 2nd Eastern General Hospital at the Grammar School building in Dyke Road. Those who saw them arrive were shocked by the terrible wounds caused by modern shells, and by the fact that many of the victims were hardly more than boys. Almost for the first time the British people began to relize that a modern war was different from any kind of conflict known before. Looking back on the events at the beginning of the war, the *Brighton Gazette* spoke of a 'confused impression of wreck, disaster, labour troubles and political disputes', and recalled that at the beginning of 1914 Brighton 'was being electrified, dazzled, cajoled and almost whipped into a craze for Germanizing the town',[6] and that we had been 'within an ace of being dominated by the group who wanted to Germanize local institutions'. During the previous year a number of influential personalities had made visits to Wiesbaden, Düsseldorf and other towns in Germany to study revolutionary new methods that were then being applied in German business and local government, and which had aroused interest throughout Europe, particularly in the fields of municipal trading, education and town management. The 'Wiesbaden pilgrims' had expressed their enthusiasm for the new methods so successfully that the Town Council was said to be 'thoroughly impregnated with the German views'. Proposals made at a public meeting held at the Dome, for the reorganization of Brighton's municipal life on German lines, were only defeated by a hostile demonstration being made by a group of local businessmen headed by Harry Preston and some friends.[7]

Easter Monday following the outbreak of the war was marked by an almost complete 'absence of the tripper'. Just before Easter a remarkable succession of brilliantly moonlit nights brought out thousands of people upon the sea-front to gaze upon the astonishing spectacle of moonlight almost as bright as day upon the sea, the piers and the sea-front buildings; a scene that was heightened by the absence of light from public street-lamps because of the wartime lighting restrictions. At the suggestion of King George V, the Royal Pavilion had been converted into a hospital for wounded Indian soldiers, and was remarked upon as 'the most delightfully picturesque hospital in the world'. The *chinoiserie* wall decorations were boarded over and the State Apartments became hospital wards. For two years the Pavilion housed wounded soldiers of many different castes and religions, who lived amicably together with the aid of nine separate kitchens, duplicate water taps in every ward, and multilingual notices. More than one account has survived of wounded Indian soldiers being brought in unconscious, waking up amid the fantastic oriental decorations of the ceiling in the Music Room or Banqueting Room, and imagining they had died and were waking in Paradise. In this way the Royal Pavilion achieved a romantic fulfilment beyond the wildest imaginings of its original creators. There was also a less poetical side to this episode. A high wooden fence had been built round the Pavilion grounds to ensure privacy, and it was considered 'worth a penny to take a ride on the trams along the Steyne to get a glimpse of the Indians in the grounds'.[8] Before long as the wounded soldiers began to recover the livelier ones climbed over the fence at night and roamed about in the slum area of Edward Street and Carlton Hill opposite the Steine, in search of female companionship, the swarthy faces and tall turbans of Sikh and Pathan warriors arousing terror amongst some of the girls and women of the neighbourhood, and delighted fascination amongst others. Two memorials of the Indian occupation of the Pavilion exist today. One is the *Chattri*, a small domed monument on the Downs near Patcham dedicated to the memory of the Indians who died at the Pavilion, and built on the site of the burning *ghat* where their bodies were cremated. Pilgrimages continue to be made to this day and commemorative services to be held there by visiting Indians. The Chattri was designed by an Indian architect, E. C. Henriques. The other memorial is the South Gate, designed by Thomas Tyrwhitt, F.R.I.B.A., which was the gift of the people of India made in commemoration of those who were tended in the Pavilion in 1914 and 1915. It was dedicated to the inhabitants of Brighton by the Maharajah of Patiala on 20th October 1921. It is unfortunate that the South Gate was designed in the very ponderous Gujerati style of Indian architecture, for it accords very imperfectly with the delicate fantasy of the Pavilion itself. There were many gateways and temples shown in the Daniells' *Views of Oriental Scenery* that would have provided more suitable models.

The news of the first Zeppelin raid on London in May 1915, when ninety bombs were dropped, many of them incendiary, brought thousands of people flocking to Brighton, while the bombardment of Scarborough and West Hartlepool by a German battleship about the same time caused many people to take their holidays on the South Coast instead of in the north. Once more in Brighton the ancient awareness of a possible attack from the sea was revived, and in order to serve as a protection against bombardment from the sea, boxes three feet high and a foot thick were built in a continuous line behind the railings of the sea-front and filled with shingle, a device that might have proved more of a danger than a protection, for the explosion of a shell would have converted the pebbles into shrapnel with deadly effect. Many of the larger houses in the town had been converted into hospitals, and the town was crowded with wounded soldiers in their shapeless hospital uniforms of bright blue flannel. Ex-King Manuel of Portugal established a convalescent home for wounded officers in Eastern Terrace, and took a continual interest in the place. The 1st Battle Squadron of the British Fleet paid a visit of three days to Brighton, and the officers of the ships were entertained by the Mayor at a grand ball at the Pavilion. Rudyard Kipling spoke at several meetings in the town to encourage recruiting, and in July 1915 Lord Kitchener visited the Indian Hospital. King George and Queen Mary had paid their first visit to the Hospital in January. In August they came again and presented a Victoria Cross to Jemadar Mir Dast for conspicuous bravery on the battle-field. The King also bestowed one Military Cross, one Order of British India, four Indian Orders of Merit and four Indian Distinguished Service Orders. That summer and autumn there was 'a remarkable influx of visitors'. The *Brighton Gazette* observed that 'Throughout the war Brighton had fulfilled an important mission . . . it had an important role to play in providing a haven of refuge', and the scenes on the sea-front at week-ends 'recalled the palmiest days of October and November thirty years ago'.[9] Queen Alexandra, the Princess Royal and Princess Maud visited Brighton, and the Municipal Orchestra at the Aquarium was playing to such crowded audiences that its performances were continued throughout the winter.

The lists of fashionable visitors at the hotels and boarding-houses that appeared in the local newspapers were now only rivalled in length and distinction by the lists of killed and wounded. The only Victoria Cross to be won by a Brighton man was awarded posthumously to Lieutenant E. F. Beal, of the Yorkshire Regiment, who was killed in action in March 1918. He was a member of a well-known family in the town which still owns an important and long-established bookselling and stationery business in East Street.

In the later stages of the war restrictions and shortages began to become more keenly felt. Tram services were more restricted and Pullman cars were reduced in number. The Dyke Road and Kemp Town branches of the railway were closed. There was now greater stringency in municipal spending. Especial alarm was caused by demands for increases in the salaries of corporation officials. Everywhere in the town women were replacing men in almost every sphere of work, especially as tram conductors, as canteen and hospital workers, for delivering milk and bread, and for work on the farms in the surrounding countryside. Although enough elderly men were left to run the lifeboat, there was a shortage of men to launch it, so the fishermen's wives, 'a hefty, healthy, strong-limbed body of helpers', turned out to haul the lifeboat down the beach into the sea. The girls and women in the upper ranks of Brighton's society worked in the hospitals, drove ambulances in England or in France, or served in the Women's Army Corps or the Women's Air Force. As late as 1916 naturalized Germans living in the town were still being rounded up for internment, and in that year also great indignation was felt in the town by the removal and destruction by the military of many of the town's bathing-machines which had been stored in the Madeira Drive arches after the previous season.[10] Alderman Carden, who was to become a far-seeing benefactor of Brighton after the war, led the protests with a passionate speech in the Council chamber on the destruction of these monuments of the town's rise to fame.

The darkening of the streets at night was also strongly objected to as discouraging visitors, and was spoken of as a 'not altogether scientific way of queering the pitch for the enemy'.[11] A little later on some improvement was brought about by the introduction of daylight-saving, which caused long light evenings.

Entertainments were now on a very restricted scale. Such concert parties as there were consisted of rather elderly artists, the younger men having gone into the army and the girls taking up nursing or some other kind of war work, so when a pierrette troupe was formed with a number of 'talented juveniles' with the name of 'The Chocolate Creams' they were a tremendous success and had to give repeat performances when they appeared for war charities. Their most popular number was 'Daddy's learning French'.[12]

There was 'an unexpected concentration of Society upon Brighton'.[13] The town was a favourite place for a week-end of relaxation for Mr. Lloyd George, the Prime Minister, Mr. Asquith and other members of the war-time Coalition Government, and Horatio Bottomley, editor of *John Bull*, who was eventually to be imprisoned for fraud, spoke in January 1917 at the Hippodrome Theatre on 'Truth and Justice'.

The year 1917 was 'a year of phenomenal prosperity' for Brighton. The town had 'escaped the terrors existing only a few miles away, and its comparative peace and security were the secret of the remarkable influx of people'.[14] The town was filled with members of the royal families and aristocracy of Britain and Europe, the wives of wealthy industrialists and financiers, with actors, actresses and popular journalists. The fashionable Sunday-morning parades on the sea-front continued, and the weekly feature 'Fashion on the Front' filled an entire closely printed column. 'Lady S——, who had her soldier son with her, wore a dress of a lovely shade of violet panne beneath a long rich coat of silver musquash decorated with collar and cuffs of skunk fur. Mrs. A—— du C——, a London Australian, was wrapped in beautiful furs, a long full coat of glossy dyed musquash bordered with a deep flounce of sable fitch, a deep sailor collar of this fur and a muff to match. The Hon. Mrs. —— wore a lovely wrap of leopard-skin flounced and lined with cub-bear, and a toque of black velvet with gold embroidered veil.'[15]

There were plays at the Palace Pier Theatre, the Theatre Royal, and the Hippodrome; concerts at the Aquarium and on the two piers. In December 1917 the Government gave permission for some single-day race meetings at Lewes, the first time that horse-racing had been allowed anywhere in Britain since the outbreak of the war. The *Brighton Gazette* reported that 'the tripper element was eliminated', and their commentator confessed he was 'almost inclined to ask, "Is there a War on?"' In fact, the name of Brighton became something of a byword in the popular Press as a resort especially frequented by 'profiteers', munitions-millionaires and other vulgar *noveaux riches*, who rubbed shoulders with the aristocracy in the grand hotels of the town. In this atmosphere the news of the Russian Revolution of 1917 was received with a particular spasm of horror, for it seemed not only to threaten the very foundations of the established order of wealth and privilege throughout the world, but brought with it the more immediate fear that the Germans, now relieved from Russian pressure in the east, would be able to concentrate fresh new forces in the west. To one man in Brighton the news brought not revulsion and terror, but victory and hope. This was Prince Peter Kropotkin, now aged seventy-five, who as a young man had been imprisoned in Russia for his very moderate revolutionary activities. He escaped to France and eventually to England where he lived in exile for over forty years; most of that time in Brighton, where he was a well-known figure. He lived from 1912 to 1917 at No. 9 Chesham Street, near Kemp Town, and wrote several of his works there. Later he lived at Rottingdean, where at his fireside he used to entertain the socialists and trade union workers of the town by recounting his experiences under the Tsarist régime, and expounding his social theories. On leaving Brighton to return to Russia, he was presented with an illuminated address 'by the Trade Unionists of Brighton' recording the help he had given to English workers and recognizing his 'heroic dedication to freeing humanity throughout the world'. He lived for five years in the new Russia, where he was honoured as a pioneer revolutionary. The Brighton and Hove Trades Council had been founded in 1890, and from that time onwards had made steady progress in establishing and strengthening the trade-union movement in the town. During the Great War the Council was concerned with a host of problems arising directly out of war conditions, such as allowances for soldiers' wives, food control, exemption from the fighting services, and the protection of active trade unionists, who were often victimized not only by private employers but by official and public organizations. There were strong protests against the Munitions Act, which on one hand demanded the sacrifice of the workers' hard-won social rights, while permitting uncontrolled inefficiency and profit-making on the part of employers. But in those days even radical thought in Brighton was not advanced enough for the Trades Council to support on principle, rather than from personal affection, their Vice-President, R. Penifold, who was sent to prison as a conscientious objector. The National Service Tribunals in Brighton were no less harsh and intolerant than those elsewhere in the country.

Towards the end of the war there were angry demonstrations by the poorer and working classes of Brighton against the gambling in food scarcities, the obvious corruption and inequality in food distribution and the enormous profits that were being made out of the people's deprivations. The popular agitation against these abuses was strongly supported and well organized. A huge demonstration in January 1918 marched under the banner 'The wives and children of our fighters shall not want for food' to the Brighton Food Committee Offices, and a few days later a deputation was received by Lord Rhondda, who had some remedies put into effect.[16]

At last, in November 1918, the long, criminally mismanaged and useless war was over. The event was not greeted in Brighton by any large-scale rejoicings. The *Brighton Gazette* observed that on receipt of the news 'in the twinkling of an eye there burst out in every district a galaxy of flags', but remarked that there were no 'wild demonstrations of joy', but rather 'a calm and dignified observance'. The memories of the past four years had chastened public sentiment. Also the *Gazette* recalled that after the Franco-Prussian War of 1870-2 the Emperor Napoleon III had written to the French ladies of Brighton to say he was 'convinced the Germans would eventually be defeated.'[17]

Brighton had good cause to be grateful for the 'amazing prosperity' it had enjoyed, with its 'complete freedom from war risks'. It was estimated that the normal population had increased during the war by 30,000 newcomers who established themselves permanently in the town. There was a boom in property and household investments during and immediately after the war, lodgings were at a premium, and the trains became so crowded with London commuters that the issue of season tickets was restricted. On the other hand, the war bonuses and increased salaries of public officials 'had become the major factor in a rise of 1/- in the pound in the rates, with the prospect of more to come'.[18]

3 The Twenties

———————✐

The early 1920s were hardly the most brilliant period of Brighton's existence. The town was still suffering from the depressive reaction that set in after the war, and even visually the place was not in its most exciting phase. Although the houses of Kemp Town and Brunswick Town were mostly smartly painted in white or pale cream, their appearance was by no means uniform. Some of the Georgian buildings in the principal streets were in a bad state of repair, while the prevailing colour of many of them was a dreary leaden blue-green. East Street, now one of the gayest and brightest of Brighton's fashionable shopping streets, was a depressing place, the Victorian Gothic red-brick façade of Brill's Baths near the sea being dingy and sordid, and disfigured with large notice-boards. The sea-front was said to exhibit a state of 'stagnation and miasma',[1] the Aquarium was labouring under a debt of £23,000, and the Municipal Orchestra which had been established there was finally abolished.[2]

There were vague feelings in the town that 'Brighton needed bucking up' and suggestions were made for the electrification of the railway, for through trains from the north and Midlands, and for wholesale street widening and the tidying-up of the sea-front.[3]

The increase in population, which had been fairly steady since 1890, was now slowing down. From a figure of 131,237 in 1911 the population ten years later had only increased by some 3,500 persons, to 134,790. Nevertheless the Brighton Council was already tackling the problem of the slums, and in 1922 built the astonishing number of 500 new houses.

By 1925 Brighton was beginning to emerge from the depression of a few years earlier. The town began to become more popular as a Christmas resort, especially for family parties at the hotels of visitors from London and other parts of the country.[4]

The building, therefore, in 1921 of Brighton's first super-cinema, the Regent in Queen's Road, was very remarkable as an audacious enterprise in attracting holiday visitors that was in advance of its time, more characteristic of the trends in entertainment of ten years later. Some of the giant picture theatres of the 1920s and 1930s, such as the Granada Cinema at Tooting, are now beginning to attract the attention of art historians and connoisseurs as buildings no less revealing of the taste and artistic attitudes of their times than are those of the Georgian and Victorian ages. Brighton's first super film palace was one of the very earliest of its kind in the country, and is fully worthy to rank amongst the best of the others as a monument of its time.

The Regent marked a great advance in cinema design, in providing not only an auditorium for 1,700 persons, but also unusually spacious foyers and galleries, and a large restaurant and a café for its patrons. Much of the success of the design and planning of the building was due to the skill and taste of the architect, Mr. Robert Atkinson, F.R.I.B.A., a specialist in the design of theatres, who some fourteen years later was to carry out the very successful conversion of the Victorian Moorish interior of the Dome into a fine modern concert hall. At the Regent Cinema Mr. Atkinson wisely avoided the tawdry cubistic modernism of the early 1920s and carried out the interior design in a robust Adamesque adaptation of Roman classical motifs that has not become dated or lost its attractiveness with the passage of the years. Part of the auditorium, however, has been modernized fairly recently. Two years after the opening of the cinema the now famous Regent dance hall was formed in a superstructure on the roof that was originally intended as a winter garden. When first opened the cinema was referred to as a 'gorgeous Temple of the Silent Drama', and as 'the largest, finest, most artistic kinematograph establishment in the country, if not in the world'.[5]

Towards the end of 1925 there were still many complaints about the dingy and unattractive appearance of certain parts of the sea-front, especially of Regency Square and Bedford Square,[6] but by the New Year some improvements had been carried out under the direction of a brilliant new Superintendent of Parks and Gardens, Mr. B. H. MacLaren. Picturesque in appearance and profane in his speech, Mr. MacLaren achieved worldwide fame for breaking away from the unimaginative dreariness then typical of municipal gardens. Paved walks, flower-beds, lawns and a children's paddling pool were laid out on the lower promenade near the West Pier, the unsightly high iron railings were removed from the gardens of the Steine, and Preston Park was changed 'from railings and gloom to openness and light . . . dark masses of the dismal eunonymus have been swept away; hedges have been thrown down; vistas have been opened out and something altogether new has been set up in the way of tennis courts, bowling greens and sports pavilions. Preston Park seems to be a new place',[7] the local paper recorded.

Mr. MacLaren's pioneering work has been admirably continued by his no less imaginative successor, Mr. J. R. B. Evison, whose remarkable flower displays still keep Brighton in the forefront of municipal gardening. The Western Lawn of the Royal Pavilion was also improved by the removal of the unsightly high fence which had surrounded it for years, and the lawns and flower-beds were laid out afresh. The Aquarium was passing through one of its most successful phases, having more visitors than it had known at any time since the building was acquired by the Corporation, and the increasing popularity of Brighton was reflected in an increase of 16 per cent in rail traffic to and from the town during 1925.[8]

Concerts and recitals by visiting orchestras and soloists at the Aquarium and the Dome flourished, but the lack of a municipal orchestra in Brighton was widely deplored. The Corporation signalized their growing regard for Brighton's historical and literary associations by attaching memorial tablets to the houses where distinguished persons had lived in the town. A start was made with a tablet to Dr. Russell, on the Royal Albion Hotel, built on the site of the house he had occupied. Other tablets were erected at the same time to Charles Dickens, on the Bedford Hotel; to Herbert Spencer on his house in Percival Terrace; and to Mrs. Fitzherbert on her house on the Steine. This admirable practice has been continued in later years, more recently in conjunction with the Regency Society. In April 1926 the Royal Pavilion was painted pale grey instead of the dreary 'workhouse yellow' it had been for several years, but the suggestion (a very good one) of the School of Art that the doors of the building should be painted carmine was not accepted by the authorities.[9]

Twice daily in those years a note of excitement was struck as a fanfare of trumpets was sounded from the roof of Needham's Drapery Emporium at opening-time and closing-time. This establishment was in a group of fine bow-fronted late Regency houses that stood at the north-eastern corner of Castle Square on the site of the old Castle Hotel, where the Electricity building now stands.

For half a century or so after the completion of Kemp Town in the 1850s there were few buildings on the coast beyond Arundel Terrace, and east of the Slopes the cliffs were still in their natural state. In the early years of the present century the Abergavenny Inn and two or three residences in a single block stood near the cliff edge at Black Rock, a projecting corner of the shore which is said to have taken its name from a large black rock which was at one time visible at low tide.* A landslide left the two buildings in a precarious position on the very edge of the cliff, and the usual way to gain access to the shore was by entering a little creamery and sweetshop in the building adjoining the Inn, when one was able to reach a path leading from the back of the house to the beach. If one bought nothing in the shop one was asked to pay a penny for the privilege of passing through it.

By 1921 a square 'terrace garden' had been laid out at Black Rock, on the site of the present bathing-pool, with large white blocks of stone used for building the sea-wall set out in lines to form seats.

The celebrated French portrait painter Jacques-Emile Blanche, who came to Brighton several times to visit his friend Sickert, painted in 1922

379

the fine view of Black Rock which now hangs in the Art Gallery, and which shows the terrace with the cliffs, the Inn and houses and the landslide beyond. The Inn and houses were demolished in 1935, when the building of the new sea-wall and promenade, stretching three miles eastwards along the coast to Rottingdean and Saltdean, was begun. Sickert was then living in Sussex Square, and while there painted his great portrait 'The Admiral'. Often he would drive down to Brighton in a taxi-cab which he left outside the house, with the meter ticking up enormous sums of money for an hour or two until he was ready to return to London again.

Although enormous advances had been made in social improvements, especially in slum clearance, there was a very great deal of poverty and unemployment in Brighton in the 1920s. Harry Cowley—'The Guv'nor'— a chimney-sweep and champion of the poor, worked devotedly at the Brighton Unemployed Men's Club in Tichborne Street and was praised by the Brighton Member of Parliament, Sir Cooper Rawson, for the success of his efforts in collecting and distributing food to people in need.

Various church organizations and charities did valuable work in ameliorating the lot of the poor. There was the Brighton, Hove and Preston Blanket Lending Society, which was in existence up to as late as 1940, when the beginnings of the Welfare State made its work appear to be superfluous. Blankets were lent to poor people for the winter months for a deposit of tenpence, repayable if the blankets were returned properly washed. They were only lent to persons bringing subscribers' recommendations. For every five shillings subscribed, tickets were given enabling three blankets to be lent.

A great many unemployed miners from the Midlands, the North and South Wales had come to the south of England in the hope of finding work, only too often to be disappointed. A remarkable woman Labour supporter and social worker, Jane Lloyd, set up a welfare committee to help the wives and children of these unemployed men who had come to Brighton. Conditions of work and rates of wages in heavy industry, apart from the severe unemployment amongst the miners, in those days were appallingly bad, and generally the workers had many real grievances.

Amongst the workers and the unemployed of Brighton there existed a feeling of strong sympathy with the mood of industrial unrest that existed in various other parts of the country. This was very largely due to the hundreds of railway workers employed in Brighton. When the General Strike was declared on 1st May 1926 the solidarity of the Brighton workers with the strikers elsewhere was virtually complete. By Tuesday the 4th all services were at a standstill. There were 'no trains, no trams, no buses, no newspapers'.[10] A procession of about 2,000 strikers headed by a brass band marched on the Town Hall during a meeting of the Transport Committee, with the object of persuading that body not to allow the trams to be run by volunteers. A large body of police was drawn up in front of the Town Hall and the procession was diverted away from the building without any deputation having been received.[11]

It is difficult for us to imagine nowadays the bitter hatred that was felt by many people for the strikers. While the procession was still marching along near the Town Hall the column of men headed by their band found themselves confronted by an approaching car driven by a woman. The *Herald*[12] described the incident:

'Seeing the strikers the woman must have stamped on the accelerator. At a bound the car leapt forward at tremendous speed. It literally ploughed its way through the body of strikers. Several were flung to the ground, others had to leap for their lives. Some dashed for the car and some of them mounted the footboard. The police drew their truncheons and flung themselves on these men. The woman continued to drive on at speed.'

Harry Preston was invited to join the corps of mounted special police that was being raised by the Chief Constable, Mr. Charles Griffin, and helped also to recruit several of his friends. He describes how he and his friends took the oath '. . . administered by a charming lady J.P., Miss (Blanche) Fair, well known in Sussex for her good works—and collected peaked caps, tunics somewhere around our respective sizes, and clubs'.[13] The men were recruited from amongst local farmers, sportsmen, hunting men and retired cavalry officers. They were a highly disciplined force, and were called the 'Black and Tans'[14] by the strikers, in allusion to the special constables who achieved a terrible reputation for savage violence during the Irish troubles of 1920. They went into action on 11th May, when they were called upon to assist the regular police in escorting the volunteers who proposed to bring out the trams in order to get public transport going.[15] The driving platforms of the trams were festooned with barbed wire to protect the volunteer drivers from possible attack, but many of the windows had been smashed by the strikers, and the sides of trams had facetious slogans chalked on them such as 'I have no pane, dear Mother now . . .'

A crowd of strikers and the general public, estimated at some 4,000 people, had assembled outside the Lewes Road tramway depot, and it was clear that the strikers had no intention of allowing the trams to be taken out. The crowd was called upon by the Chief Constable to disperse, but without result, and the police advanced in a wedge formation, led by Mr. Griffin on foot, and supported by '50 mounted men carrying ugly looking shillelaghs, obviously ex-cavalrymen, yeomanry and artillerymen'. In a few moments 'The Battle of Lewes Road' was in full swing. There was 'a fierce and determined fight . . . blows were struck and stones and bottles thrown . . .'[16] After a savage struggle the strikers were driven back and dispersed. Many men on both sides were injured and twenty-two arrests were made by the police. Later several of the strikers were sent to prison, while others were fined. Leaving aside the rights and wrongs of the affair, deep resentment against the police, lasting even up to the present day,[17] was felt by many of the people present who saw the strikers and others struck down by the mounted men. Amidst the heat of the fray the *Herald* reporter was impressed by the very peculiar circumstance that 'at least one of the mounted police constables wore plus fours'.

Although Harry Preston mentioned rumours of 'ugly doings at the Tram Depot', it does not appear that he was actually present himself at 'The Battle of Lewes Road'. During the strike his two hotels, the Royal Albion and the Royal York, had become in his own words 'two mausoleums',[18] but Brighton quickly recovered from this episode, and the following summer season was one of the most successful the town had experienced. At Christmas in 1926 Harry Preston raised the sum of £3,500 for the local hospitals by means of one of his annual boxing tournaments that were held at the Dome for various charities. Jack Dempsey, Georges Carpentier, Bombardier Billy Wells, Tommy Burns, 'Boy' McCormick and Jimmy Wilde were among the world-famous boxers who took part in fights there.

4 The Thirties

ith the opening years of the 1930s Brighton embarked upon one of the most prosperous and successful periods of its history, not only as a holiday resort, but as a residential town. It was an era that was marked by the building of several great monuments to pleasure—three super-cinemas; the Sports Stadium, 'S.S. Brighton', in West Street; the building by the Corporation of the two open-air swimming-pools, at Black Rock and Rottingdean; the rebuilding of the Aquarium and the widening of the London Road, North Street and Western Road, which up till then had been narrow and lined with seedy, dark, old-fashioned shops. It was, moreover, a decade that saw an enormous expansion of the town of Brighton, and remarkable advances in social welfare.

As the focal point of Brighton's world of gaiety and amusement there was Sir Harry Preston at the Royal Albion Hotel, welcoming actors and actresses, artists, authors, boxers, film stars, journalists, musicians and writers, members of the nobility and of the Royal Family. Among his visitors at the hotel were Hilaire Belloc, G. K. Chesterton, Arnold Bennett, James Agate, Signor Marconi, Tallulah Bankhead, Frances Day, Hannen Swaffer, Tom Driberg and Lord Rosse. It was the customary ritual of Maurice Baring, the novelist and poet who had a house at Rottingdean, after the dinner he gave at the Royal Albion to celebrate his birthday every year, to wade into the sea attired still in full evening dress, balancing a glass of champagne on his head.

When Sir Harry Preston was asked on one occasion who were the two most interesting men he had ever met he replied, 'The Prince of Wales (Edward VIII) and the Rev. R. J. Campbell.' The latter person was the incumbent of Holy Trinity Church in Ship Street, who for the six years from 1924 to 1930 preached there with a fervour that recalled the days of his predecessor, the Rev. F. W. Robertson. Although Campbell's love of horse-riding, motoring and the theatre would have been an immediate recommendation for him to Preston, the admiration that the *hôtelier* expressed for the priest was a measure of the spell that Campbell cast over all who met him.

When Campbell first came to Brighton he had already become famous as the author of a work, *The New Theology*, which shocked the orthodox and foreshadowed his break with the nonconformist faith of his early life.

In the following six years Campbell filled the empty seats of Holy Trinity Church and made it famous all over the country. His voice was not strong, and he read his sermons from a typewritten script, but his personal magnetism was intense and there was a mysterious haunting quality about the quiet sympathetic tones in which he spoke that deeply affected his hearers, and was said to have recalled the impression made on his audience by J. H. Newman.[1]

The Great War had put a stop to various schemes that were proposed for the improvement of the Aquarium, but encouraged by the prosperity of the town during the late 1920s, the Corporation in 1929 began a vast scheme of reconstruction that was completed two years later at a cost of £117,000. The exterior of the Aquarium was then reconstructed in the fashion we see today, with white stonework in place of the Victorian terracotta. The Gothic clock-tower and archway were removed from the entrance and replaced by bronze gates and two square stone kiosks with pagoda-like roofs. The clock itself was then transferred to the entrance of the Palace Pier, but the statues of the Four Seasons that supported it were rescued by Mr. B. H. MacLaren and placed in the charming little public gardens at Patcham, but they have long since disappeared. He also designed the new pavilions and entrance at Preston Park, during the middle 1930s, and replaced the iron railings and unsightly fence which for many years had disfigured the Royal Pavilion with the elegant stone balustrade that encircles the eastern lawn today.

To the roof-terrace of the Aquarium were also added in 1929 a restaurant and bandstand, with some other small buildings discreetly sited below the level of the Marine Parade above. The interior was changed very little, except for the Winter Garden, which was transformed into a modern concert hall. The original tanks were retained, with improved equipment for pumping and aeration of the water. The large tank in the main hall, 100 feet long and holding 110,000 gallons, was still at that time the largest in existence, and enabled the large sea-creatures like dolphins and even small whales to be kept in reasonable conditions. The whole scheme, designed by the Borough Surveyor, David Edwards, and his staff, was admirably conceived and formed a great improvement to the sea-front of the town.

During the Second World War the building was in military occupation and suffered damage and neglect. After the war the Corporation leased the Aquarium to a private company, with many restrictions upon the character of the attractions to be provided, but considerations of taste are notoriously difficult to enforce and the Aquarium today is a depressing spectacle. The roof-terrace is cluttered with an amusement arcade and a miniature electric railway. The interior is inexpressibly dreary. In an attempt to improve the decoration large areas of the walls have been covered with

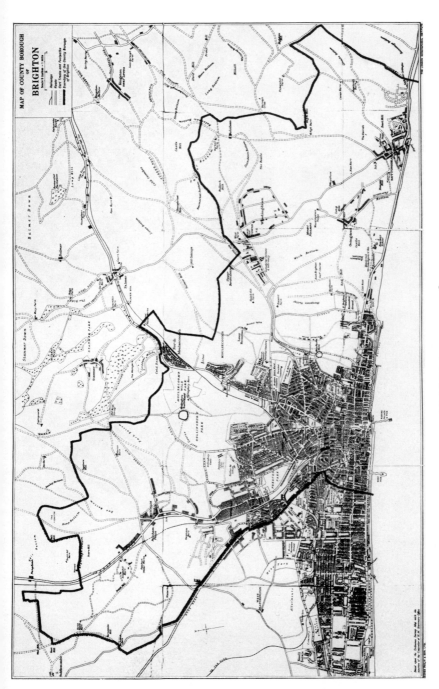

BRIGHTON IN 1928,
published by George Philip and Son

THE ROYAL PAVILION, 1877:
the Entrance Hall, with the statue of Lt.-Col. Pechell, V.C.

THE ROYAL PAVILION:
the North Drawing Room, *c.* 1930, before restoration

THE ROYAL PAVILION:
the North Drawing Room, 1966, after restoration

THE ROYAL PAVILION:
Queen Victoria's Bedroom, after restoration, 1968

ST. BARTHOLOMEW'S
CHURCH, 1872

ST. BARTHOLOMEW'S
CHURCH, 1872: the interior

ST. GEORGE'S CHURCH,
KEMP TOWN, 1824

BRIGHTON VERNACULAR
ARCHITECTURE:
house in Grenville Place,
built *c.* 1790, demolished
1966

LEWES CRESCENT, KEMP TOWN,
designed by Charles Busby, 1824

THE ROYAL CRESCENT,
built 1797–1806

BRUNSWICK SQUARE, HOVE:
the east side

THE SASSOON MAUSOLEUM,
built *c.* 1880; now 'The Bombay Bar'

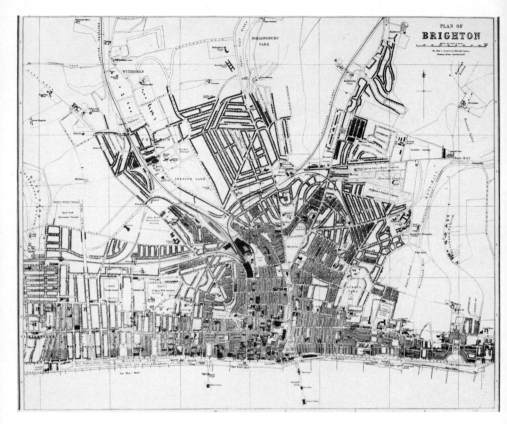

BRIGHTON IN 1939,
published by John Bartholomew and Sons

sheet boarding and painted, and the Victorian Gothic columns of once-polished serpentine marble and red granite have been painted grey, the capitals with their carved 'marine emblems' gilded with bronze paint, and the vaulting of variegated brickwork painted over. The original part of the building is obviously out of date and possibly beyond improvement, although it is a fascinating piece of Victorian architecture. In the course of a century damp seems to have penetrated the whole fabric, so that it seems that the sea is threatening completely to inundate the building and will before long take complete possession, the 'finny denizens of the deep' at last roaming in the sea-filled aisles and corridors themselves, no longer confined to their tanks. The cost of a major reconstruction would probably be immense, and the outlook of modern people encourages them to prefer the open sunlight to twilit caverns, but it is difficult to believe that Brighton would not be a suitable place for an up-to-date aquarium, not in underground darkness, but consisting perhaps of large open tanks under a glass roof, surrounded by smaller tanks in the shade of arcades, the whole of these activities linked up with the work of a marine biological laboratory connected with the University of Sussex.

However, in 1967 two dolphins were brought to the Aquarium, and these intelligent and playful creatures were such a great success with the public that the ballroom, built in 1931 and more recently used as the Montagu Motor Museum, was remodelled with an immense tank to form a 'dolphinarium' on the lines of those which are so popular on the Californian coast and elsewhere.

Almost ten years after the opening of the Regent Cinema, Brighton's second giant picture palace, the Savoy, was built in 1930, its enormous façade of pale cream ceramic tiling replacing Sir Gilbert Scott's Victorian Venetian-Gothic exterior of Brill's Baths that had been erected in 1876. The interior was no less spacious than that of the Regent, with seating for 2,300 persons, two restaurants, two cafés, and a large garage in the basement. Possibly under the influence of the Royal Pavilion, the architect, Mr. William R. Glen, F.R.I.A.S., gave the building a truly magnificent Chinese interior, though perhaps in the manner of Peking rather than of the Prince Regent's legendary Cathay. This remarkable scheme of decoration, however, has been completely replaced in recent times by a modern interior. The exterior survives, though, as a typical example of an entertainment building of the 1930s in a commendably restrained and innocuous version of the architectural design of that era.

From the middle of the nineteenth century onwards, when Louis-Philippe, later Emperor of the French, visited Brighton, Brighton has felt a keen affinity with France. This was celebrated in October 1930 with a 'Fête de France'—a Grand Historical Pageant held at the Dome, including *tableaux* of Joan of Arc, a sixteenth-century Minuet, Napoleon and

Josephine, and the Marseillaise. There were also a French café, and a French band in the Corn Exchange, the Royal Pavilion and the grounds, and the grand programme ended with the exhortation 'Beware of Pickpockets'! The members of Brighton's residential society threw themselves with enthusiasm into organizing fêtes of this kind. Another was a Fête and Market called 'The Hive of Industry' held in aid of the Royal Sussex County Hospital at the Dome in November 1930, organized by the Busy Bee Club. Every day a kind of pageant was held with local girls performing the *tableaux* of 'The Dragon-fly Dragoons', 'The Grasshopper Guards', 'The Caterpillar Corps', and 'The Bee Brigade'.

During the 1930s the old houses in the lower part of the Sussex Street and Carlton Hill area—steep streets leading eastwards up from the Steine and Grand Parade—came under a slum clearance order and were demolished. Robert Hayward, who was born, brought up and educated in this area, has graphically described the teeming life of this maze of narrow streets, alleys and courts, which was Brighton's foreign quarter.[2] It was here that the Italians came, many of them from districts around Monte Cassino, and settled down as vendors of ice-cream and 'hokey-pokey' in the summer and roast chestnuts in the winter. Hard-working and frugal, they settled down peaceably amongst the Brighton natives, who accepted them without question as neighbours and friends. In their season came the men from Brittany, who hired a disused stable in Sun Street where 'Johnny Roscoff' and his compatriots braided up their golden, rustling onions into strings which they carried hanging from wooden poles on their shoulders and sold to housewives and lodging-house keepers.

Despite the appalling poverty and bad conditions in which most of the people lived there was amongst them in those days a remarkable freedom from viciousness and violence. For children their great release was found on the beach, with the sun, the sea, the sand and the boats. Two abandoned fishing-boats left opposite the fish-market, the *Cyril Stephens* and the *Ellen Maud*, over which the children scrambled playing at pirates, or revenue men versus smugglers, provided a natural adventure playground, of a kind which it has been found difficult to establish since in any part of the town.

The cheapness of fish at Brighton, where herrings were sold for sixteen a shilling, and scraps could be had for the asking at the fishmarket, was the great safeguard against malnutrition. The local fishing industry was still flourishing and profitable in the 1920s, with a sizeable fleet of luggers and 'dandies' lying offshore. In Carlton Hill were the 'herring dees', a dark and mysterious place where fish lay steeping in great vats of brine, while in the smoke-room hung hundreds of bloaters strung on rods, curing over smouldering oak sawdust. 'At times the savoury odours from this place would hang in the air and an aromatic and appetizing pall would envelop the entire neighbourhood, kippering both fish and residents alike.'

Drunkenness was prevalent in the quarter, usually as an escape from the harshness of life. There were vendettas amongst the foreign elements, but on the whole standards of morality were high, although every evening two ladies of uncertain age and dubious virtue and 'with faces like Irish navvies' made their way down Carlton Hill to ply their trade in the town.

Eventually the slums were demolished and the inhabitants moved to new Corporation housing estates at Whitehawk and elsewhere. Although there was something vital and picturesque about life in the Carlton Hill quarter, and indeed there were many who were sad at leaving the little houses where most of their lives had been spent, there were few who would look back on those days of poverty and struggle with regret.

In the late 1920s and early 1930s Brighton suffered a great deal from the unfortunate reputation it had gained as a resort of the toughs and gangsters who infested the race-course and the low quarters of the town, making war on each other and exacting tribute for 'protection' from bookmakers, publicans, café proprietors, and from the people engaged in the more shady activities of the town. They aroused a feeling of special horror throughout the country by their ferocious practice of slashing their victims and rival gangsters with razors. Many of these undesirable folk had stayed on in Brighton after the 1914-18 War, when they had come down from London not only to avoid the air-raids but also following the wealthy classes upon whom they flourished, just as a horde of thieves, sharks, tricksters, panders and harlots had swarmed down to Brighton in the wake of the Prince of Wales and his pleasure-loving followers in the late eighteenth and early nineteenth centuries.

Graham Greene's famous novel *Brighton Rock*, published in 1938, was believed to give an authentic impression of the life of the Brighton gangsters, and despite the fact that it expressed in a remarkable way the sense of enchantment created by the heat, the dazzling light, the sea and the air of Brighton on a summer's day, the book, and later on the film that was made from it, were roundly condemned by loyal Brightonians as giving a false impression of life in the town, and creating harmful publicity.

In London and many other large cities criminals such as these formed a far larger proportion than they did in Brighton, but their existence in a town where every activity, whether good or bad, always took on a special intensity of interest, inevitably became spotlighted by the sensational Press. But in truth these sordid undercurrents of life in Brighton were very largely confined to the race-course and to a few public houses, dance halls, amusement arcades and cafés in a very restricted quarter of the town, and the majority of residents and visitors were quite unaware of these disturbances below the surface.

The unfortunate impression that was current at this time of Brighton as a haunt of crime and violence was heightened by a succession of four murders which took place in the town during the space of a few years. Three of them, including the two notorious and grisly Brighton 'trunk murders', occurred during a single year, and the town came to be referred to somewhat cruelly as 'The Queen of Slaughtering Places'.

The first of these crimes was committed in April 1928. One evening Mr. Ernest Friend Smith, a retired wholesale druggist of sixty-seven, was walking quietly along the Madeira Drive when he was attacked by three men and forcibly thrown into a car. He was taken to the Downs, cruelly battered, and robbed of fourteen pounds and a gold watch. He returned home in a terrible condition and died a few weeks later. As a result of police investigations, two men, Taylor and Weaver, were arrested and brought before the Brighton magistrates on a charge of murder. Later strong doubts were thrown on the evidence produced at the trial and, almost at the last hour, the death sentences which had been passed were commuted to long terms of imprisonment.[3]

In June 1934 the torso of a woman was found in a trunk left unclaimed at Brighton station. The legs were discovered later in another trunk at King's Cross luggage office. A few weeks later the body of another woman was found in a trunk left in a house in Kemp Street, Brighton. At first the police believed that the two cases were connected, but this theory was quickly abandoned. Who the victim of 'Brighton Trunk Murder No. 1' was, and who was the murderer, were never established. The victim of the second crime was Violette Kaye, a prostitute, and a man calling himself Tony Mancini, who had been living with her in a house at Park Crescent, was accused of her murder. After wheeling a trolley with her body in a trunk from Park Crescent to Kemp Street, Mancini had continued to live in the latter house with the corpse in a cupboard of his room for over a month after the woman's death, and the weight of circumstantial evidence against him seemed overwhelming. Nevertheless he was acquitted through the astonishing skill of the defence counsel, Norman Birkett (later Lord Birkett) in demolishing the case for the prosecution in the course of one of the most sensational and dramatic murder trials for many years. Mancini's defence was that he was afraid to inform the police when he had found Violette Kaye's murdered body because he had previous criminal convictions and was afraid he would be thought guilty of the crime. It appeared that Kaye was possibly being blackmailed, and could have been murdered by another man. After the trial Mancini disappeared, and the houses in Kemp Street were renumbered in order to make difficult any attempt to identify the house where the body had been found.

These two trunk murders were not the first of their kind in Brighton. An earlier crime of this sort had been committed in the town in 1831, when John William Holloway, who was employed as a painter on the Chain

Pier, murdered his wife and placed her dismembered body in a trunk, which he then wheeled on a barrow to a little wood in Lover's Walk at Preston, where he buried the remains. Holloway was executed in public at Lewes, after exhorting the spectators in an impassioned speech to repent of their sins.

The magistrates adopted stern measures in dealing with crimes of violence. In December 1925 a man was sentenced to receive twenty-five lashes of the cat-o'-nine-tails and five years' imprisonment for armed robbery in Brighton,[4] but the reign of terror of the race-gangs was not finally broken until June 1936, when sixteen men were arrested at Lewes Races after a mêlée in which a gang of thirty men, known as 'the Hoxton Mob' and armed with iron bars, coshes and other weapons, attacked a bookmaker and his clerk. The Brighton police were there in strength, having learned that some trouble was brewing chiefly from information gained by Detective Sergeant Walter Collyer, who was noted in the C.I.D. for his knowledge of race-ground crooks. Sentences totalling 432 years' penal servitude were imposed on the men, and these heavy penalties effectively repressed gang violence on race-courses not only at Brighton but throughout the country from then onwards. Many of the breeding-places of crime were now being eradicated as some of the worst slums of the town were swept away in the course of the remarkable municipal improvements that were an outstanding feature of its history between the two wars. The density of housing in the centre of Brighton was the highest of any county borough in England and Wales, with the exception of West Ham.[5]

Between 1920 and 1931 the Corporation cleared large areas of slum property, specially in the Carlton Hill district, and resettled the inhabitants in great new housing estates at Moulsecoomb, Whitehawk and Manor Farm, all on the east side of Brighton. There was also at this time an enormous amount of commercial building development, especially at Patcham, Ovingdean, Woodingdean and Rottingdean, all on the outskirts of the Borough, but the standard of design and layout of these houses was in general far below that of the municipally planned estates. In some areas of private speculative development not one house appeared to have been designed by an architect. On the other hand, the Corporation's housing estates at North and South Moulsecoomb were among the most imaginatively laid-out housing schemes in the country, ranking almost equal with the famous garden cities of Letchworth and Welwyn. Planned to consist of some 900 houses, they were begun in 1927 and not completed until a few years after the last war. Over many years they have been studied as admirable examples of housing design and layout by town planners who have come from all over the world. At this time also the Corporation bought up or obtained control over huge areas of land surrounding Brighton, not only to preserve the beauties of the downland but for recreation and to protect the water-supply. All these effects culminated in the great extension of Brighton's boundaries in 1928, when the county borough was increased in size by more than four times, from 2,714 to 12,565 acres. It was then that the entire villages of Patcham, Falmer, West Blatchington, Ovingdean and Rottingdean were brought within the borough, as well as huge tracts of open downland, including the beautiful valleys between the Falmer Road and the Lewes Road, as well as the great expanse of Hollingbury Park, crowned by the earthworks of an impressive Iron Age camp.

The northern slopes of Hollingbury, 90 acres in extent, described at the time as 'a glorious stretch of wild, almost rugged downland with deep valleys and furze-clad heights', became Moulsecoomb Wild Park, a remarkable feature to be found existing only two miles from the centre of a densely populated modern town.

Much of the initiative for these enterprises came from Alderman Sir Herbert Carden. Born in 1867 of an old Brighton family, he became a well-known solicitor and served on the Council from 1895 until his death in 1941. He was Mayor during three years of the Great War. It was mainly due to the energy and foresight of Sir Herbert that Brighton was a pioneer in such municipal enterprises as corporation trams, telephones, electricity, road-widening and housing, as well as in the purchase of downland. Carden himself stated that between 1895 and 1936 Brighton bought over 12,000 acres at a cost of about £800,000. This could not have been achieved through the normal processes of municipal purchase, as the price would have been increased enormously were it known that the Corporation was the buyer. Instead Carden bought the land himself and transferred it to the Council for the same price. He himself told how he went to London to buy a few acres at Hollingbury, 'and when I got there I bought the lot'. The whole of the Devil's Dyke he bought with his own money and resold to the town at the same price, in order to preserve its beauties and amenities. In many of his later operations he had the advice of his friend the late Sir Charles Reilly, the famous architect and town planner, who had rebuilt part of Preston Manor in 1905, and lived in Brighton for long periods after his retirement from the post of Principal of the Liverpool School of Architecture. Carden's part in the preservation of Brighton's green belt of downland and in the creation of 'Greater Brighton' was recognized in 1926 by his being knighted and being elected a Freeman of the Borough. He has been called the 'Father of Modern Brighton'.

The extension of the Borough in 1928 was marked by the erection of the two massive stone pylons that marked the gateway to Brighton at the new boundary of the town on the London Road near Pyecombe. The foundation-stones of the pylons were laid by the late King George VI and the present Queen Mother (then Duke and Duchess of York) in May of that year. The two pylons cost £2,000, of which £1,000 was contributed by Sir Herbert Carden.

After the collapse of the General Strike there was little improvement in labour conditions, and unemployment continued to rise until it reached the total of over two million men out of work when the great depression of the early 1930s descended upon the country. A constructive attempt to relieve unemployment and at the same time to create urgently needed coastal defences as well as to provide new attractive amenities was made by the Corporation when a new coastal road to Rottingdean, the Marine Drive, was made at a cost of £180,000 between 1929 and 1932, together with the construction of new concrete groynes and a sea-wall with an undercliff promenade stretching over three miles from Black Rock to Rottingdean and Saltdean, at a cost of £400,000. A large proportion of the cost was met by the Government's Unemployment Grant Committee, and in the final stages of the work as many as 500 men were employed, some of them consisting of Brighton unemployed, and at least half coming from the depressed areas of the north of England and South Wales.[6] The miners proved especially skilful at the work of cutting back the face of the chalk cliffs to a safe angle, and in constructing the new sea-defences. The Undercliff Walk now provides an agreeable promenade not only in summer but in winter, when one can enjoy the sunshine while sheltered from the cold north and east winds.

The electrification of the main London to Brighton railway line in 1933 also created much-needed employment for a great many Brighton men, and again provided an improved amenity in the form of a clean and efficient railway service.

Brighton's middle-class pleasure-loving society and visitors flocked to Sherry's Dance Hall in West Street, which had been converted from the old West Street Concert Hall in 1919, and also to the café above Boot's chemists' shop in Western Road, where a small orchestra played until early in the last war. At the end of 1935 Alig's Swiss Café in East Street closed, after being in existence since 1870, when Signor Alig came from Switzerland and established in Brighton 'the atmosphere of the foreign café as found in the Italian speaking parts of Switzerland . . . he brought with him the light meal, the light pastry, the numerous makes of Swiss chocolate, and the long thin cigars that are smoked in Italy.'[7] Alig's café was a favourite haunt of journalists, and of the French, Italian and German residents of Brighton. There were continued pleas for the re-establishment of a municipal orchestra, and the public neglect of music was deplored by the Vicar of Hove, Canon F. J. Meyrick, who considered that 'people preferred to dabble in excitements and revel in sex'.[8]

Although there was no great religious movement in Brighton during the 1930's to compare with that inspired by the Wagners in Victorian times, this period saw the building in 1933 of one fine church, St. Wilfred's in Elm Grove. Designed by H. S. Goodhart-Rendel in a plain 'high-shouldered' modern Gothic idiom in red brick, the building has a lofty, sparely ornamented interior, which was greatly enriched in 1940 when the Lady Chapel was decorated with a magnificent large mural painting, stretching round the three walls of the chapel. This exceedingly beautiful work was painted by the German refugee artist Hans Feibusch, who later became famous for his mural paintings in Chichester Cathedral, St. Elizabeth's, Eastbourne, and many other churches. It was the first work carried out by the artist in this country, and was one of the many works of art commissioned or inspired by the then Bishop of Chichester, the late Dr. G. K. Bell.

The leader of Brighton's literary circle during the late 1930's was the historical novelist, David L. Murray, who came from Lewes in 1938 and lived at Chichester House, Chichester Terrace, Kemp Town until 1944, when he moved to Hove. After living there for several years, Murray moved to live in London, where he died in 1962. From 1938 to 1945 he was editor of *The Times Literary Supplement*. He achieved a measure of popular success with his first four novels, but it was his novel *Regency* published in 1936 that established him pre-eminently as the novelist of Brighton. In the fashion-able mode of the 1930s it was presented as a 'cavalcade' of characters and events in the four great periods of Brighton's history, which Murray dubbed 'Moresque' (Regency), 'Gothic' (Victorian religion), 'Babylonian' (Edwardian) and 'Ferro-Concrete' (Modern). Described as a quadruple portrait, Murray depicted in his book the four incarnations of a fatal woman, the first as 'Regency', a mistress of the Prince Regent, each of them expressing in her life and character the essential spirit of her time.

The fourth of Brighton's great ages into which Murray had divided his romantic novel of Brighton, *Regency*,—'Ferro-Concrete', was symbolized by S. S. Brighton, the Swimming Stadium in West Street, which was opened in June 1934. The building was a rectangular block faced with cream-glazed tiles, and contained what was then said to be the largest covered sea-water swimming pool in the world—'bigger and deeper than the famous baths of Berlin, and better than anything in America'—measuring 165 feet in length and 60 feet in width. The sea water was filtered, warmed and subjected to ultra-violet ray treatment, regardless of the fact that this process had already taken place under natural conditions. The interior was ornamented with 'as many devices of a giant liner as was possible', and the bath was open to swimmers for eighteen hours a day. A great many swimming championships of different kinds were held there, and it was the centre for bathing-beauty contests. But the heyday of indoor swimming was soon over. Only fifteen months after its opening the bath was covered with a floor supported on tubular steel scaffolding, and converted to an ice-rink with the aid of fifteen miles of refrigerator piping, and the Swimming Stadium became the Sports Stadium. Ice skating became a craze that continued in popularity for another thirty years, and the Brighton Tigers were a world-famous team for ice hockey, the fastest game on earth.

On New Year's Eve 1936 a new type of spectacle was created when fourteen young ladies in absurd costumes performed an ice-ballet called 'Viennese Memories' to the music of Johann Strauss. Despite the ridiculous dresses a new element of charm and grace entered the entertainment world. The following summer an ice show called 'Marina' created a sensation, and was followed by a succession of ice ballets, ice carnivals and ice pantomimes that were continued after the war with mounting success. Everything went on ice.

To many visitors an essential element in the attractions of Brighton was the delights of one of the town's most famous temples of pleasure, Sherry's Dance Hall in West Street, which throughout the 1920s and 1930s, and even during the Second World War, was 'the glamorous, glittering mecca of dancing' of the South Coast. Immortalized by Graham Greene in his novel *Brighton Rock*, its atmosphere of somewhat strident gaiety was heightened for many of its patrons by its associations with Brighton's underworld of crime and gangsterism. It was originally built in 1867 for a Mr. William Child in the same agreeable Italianate style as the Grand and Norfolk Hotels, with a four-storey white stucco façade and round-headed windows, and was intended at first as an arcade of shops with a glass roof, but this project never materialized and it became instead the West Street Concert Hall. In 1872 the British Association hired the building for a meeting of their geographical section, at which the explorer and missionary H. M. Stanley, who found Dr. Livingstone in Africa, read a paper on his discoveries in Northern Tanganyika. The hall became a roller-skating rink in 1877, but in 1882 it was seriously damaged by a disastrous fire, one of four that occurred in the history of the building. It was reopened again as a skating rink in 1892, and later, with the coming of the cinema, it became a 'picture palace'. In 1911 it was transformed into a restaurant, but in 1918 it reverted to films, becoming the Coliseum Picture Theatre. A year later the hall took the legendary name of Sherry's, then beginning its long career as a 'palais de danse'. In latter years the place has been a skating rink again, and more recently as amusement hall known as the Ritz Palace of Varieties. In February 1969 the Italianate façade was demolished, to be remodelled in modern style at a cost of £150,000 as a luxurious entertainment centre, the interior decorated in a style intended to create a 'Southern Mississippi' atmosphere, with a restaurant, bars, a nightly cabaret, bands and dancing.[9]

In the 1930s the Royal Pavilion continued to serve, as it had done for

393

over eighty years, as the public assembly rooms of the town, and was used not only for grand civic receptions, balls and banquets but for private entertainment, and for concerts, lectures and meetings. Long years of such use had sadly damaged such original decorations as remained and in the 1880s the Corridor was repainted in sombre Victorian colours and the walls and ceilings of two drawing-rooms covered with dark brown and gold Victorian *lin-crusta*. In 1933 under the direction of Mr. Roberts some Victorian overpainting of additional garments which had been applied to the figures in the wall-decorations of the Banqueting-room were removed and in 1937 the *lin-crusta* was stripped from the South Drawing-room and, a charming *chinoiserie* colour scheme of 1854 revealed and restored by Mr. Wilfred Frost, then the Pavilion's staff decorative artist. Mr. Frost also discovered in the cellars some original painted Chinese wall-papers which had been returned eighty years earlier by Queen Victoria, and hung them in the wall-panels of the Saloon, thus restoring the room to the appearance it possessed in 1818. The original northern pair of doors of the Saloon had been retained by Queen Victoria, but Mr. Frost executed the remarkable reproductions of them, in ivory and gold lacquer, which exist there today.

At this time also the by now very dingy Victorian Moorish interior of the Dome was demolished and remodelled as a modern concert and conference hall by Mr. Robert Atkinson, F.R.I.B.A., the architect of the Regent Cinema and Ballroom, who gave the Dome a new interior that conveys some undertones of the oriental spirit of the Royal Stables, but nevertheless has not dated as have so many interiors of that period.

One evening in September 1935 a Mrs. Maude Philipps, widow of a sometime Secretary to the India Office, was sitting in the sunshine on a seat outside the Dome when she was startled by a series of crashes above her head, and a shower of broken glass came falling around. It was not until the following day that the mystery was solved for her. That evening a gala concert was being held to celebrate the reopening of the Dome after the alterations. On taking his stand at the rostrum the guest conductor, Sir Thomas Beecham, took the opportunity of expressing his opinion regarding certain defects in the hall and especially in the manner of his reception by the Town Council. With characteristic vigour Sir Thomas complained: 'I had to walk up three flights of stairs to my room. I am waiting for some celebrated prima-donna to visit this building. Then there will be an atmosphere in these walls compared with which a tempest outside will be insignificant. We are rather warm here. I must inform you that the windows are hermetically sealed. There are windows which no one else can open. I have put my stick through three or four. Before I go home tonight I am going to put it through all of them. That is not the worst. You will not believe this in Brighton. There was no refreshment in my room. Brighton of all places.

Some years ago I went to Aberdeen. You know what to expect when you go there. But I found the town illuminated, carpet on the floor . . . cigars and champagne in the artists' room for everybody. . . . Here there was nothing, not even water. In Brighton if you please—this home of rich, and some say mysterious entertainment . . . I don't mind, but I know that if those grand warhorses of song, Melba and Tetrazzini, were to get up those stairs they wouldn't come down again!'[10]

The first major challenge to the supremacy of the late-Georgian architecture on the sea-front came with the building of a new block of flats, Embassy Court, on a corner site at the eastern end of Brunswick Terrace in 1935. This immense block, 110 feet and twelve storeys in height and some 75 feet wide, designed by Wells Coates, and built of white concrete, with continuous cantilevered balconies forming broad white horizontal bands across the façade and along the side of the building in Lansdowne Place, represented an affront not only of scale but of character to the adjoining five-storey Regency buildings, which happened to consist of a portion of Brunswick Terrace notable for its varied and picturesque classical detail, in which bowed fronts combined with columns, porticoes and pavilions in a particularly individual way. Quite clearly the building of a block of flats of this character was intended as an assertion of the spirit of modern design that would eventually come entirely to supplant the Georgian architecture of the sea-front. Naturally the building aroused bitter criticism not only amongst lovers of traditional architecture, but also amongst many persons who would not have been antagonistic to the erection of such a building in a suitable position, but who considered its introduction there to be a brash and vulgar intrusion. Others considered that Embassy Court was at least 'better than the heavily academized post-Regency houses and the shabbily vulgar Victorian hotels'. Sir Herbert Carden greeted its appearance with enthusiasm, and advocated the pulling down of the whole of the sea-front from Kemp Town to Hove and rebuilding with hotels and flats of the same character. 'Even Sussex Square will have to go,' he declared. In this he did at least foresee the inescapable destiny of Brighton's Georgian sea-front, however much one may hope that its realization will be long delayed. Sir Herbert even advocated the demolition of the Royal Pavilion in favour of the building of a modern conference and amusement centre on the model of the Bournemouth Pavilion, or the Bexhill Pavilion, one of the finest achievements in modern architecture, which had been designed by Erich Mendelssohn. Of the Royal Pavilion, 'It is a complete anachronism n the modern age,' he declared. This was the one blind spot in his otherwise remarkable vision of Brighton's future. He did not live to see the Prince Regent's Pavilion become the envy of every other resort not only in Britain but throughout the world.

The erection in 1939 of Marine Gate, an immense building designed by

Maurice Bloom, the owner of Courtnay Gate, Hove, did not provoke such intense criticism, for although no less modern in style than Embassy Court, it was far removed from any Georgian surroundings, and was placed in isolation on the cliff-top beyond Black Rock, surrounded by green grass against which the white concrete masses of the the buildings contrasted effectively.

Among the lesser surviving monarchs of Europe, one of the most engaging was King Boris of Bulgaria, who was eventually to be assassinated by Hitler's orders during the Second World War. Two of his chief interests, of a sort that at one time or another occupy the minds of most youthful males, were butterflies and railways. The King was able to indulge both of these passions in one visit to Brighton, in September 1938, by means of a trip on the Brighton Belle electric train, and by inspecting the remarkable collections of lepidoptera in the Booth Museum of British Birds in the Dyke Road.

The King arrived at Brighton having travelled part of the way in the driving-cab of the train. At the station he was met by the Mayor and the late Alderman H. W. Aldrich, then Chairman of the Museum Committee, and taken by them to a private luncheon that was held in the Royal Pavilion. The building had not then been restored and furnished. The meal was laid out in the central Saloon, and in the middle of the proceedings a plumber who had been engaged on some repairs in the building blundered in. He was well into the room before becoming aware of the rather impressive assembly of people present, and pulling off his cap, tiptoed heavily on his hobnailed boots across the floor, clutching his bag of clanking tools and blushing furiously with embarrassment. Two members of the King's suite pulled automatic pistols from their pockets and flung themselves in front of their master, fully resolved to intercept an assassin's bullet. The plumber passed on and out of the farther door. The guards sank back into their seats mopping their foreheads. King Boris, who had obviously enjoyed the episode immensely, beamed at his hosts and observed, 'That is the sort of thing that could only happen in England!'

5 The Second World War

After the ignominious Munich settlement of September 1938 there were few people who could give themselves to the delights of Brighton with an easy mind. The general sense of depression was increased by a rise in unemployment, and there were demonstrations of out-of-work men in Brighton in January 1939. In the following month the Council expressed the mounting anti-German feeling by refusing to allow the purchase of a German fire-escape for the town, and Sylvia Pankhurst spoke at the Dome on the menace of dictatorships. The Hove justices were less preoccupied with international affairs than with a new threat to public morals, and when granting a licence for a bar at the King Alfred Swimming Pool refused to allow people to drink while wearing bathing-costumes. Brighton formed an Emergency Committee to take control of the town in the event of war, and decided to spend only £600 on a new mayoral car instead of the £1,600 proposed.

In August with the invasion of Poland the black-out was imposed over southern England, and air-raid shelter trenches were dug in school playgrounds and in the parks. The 70th Sussex Searchlight Regiment was mobilized and left for their stations in the countryside, and the 159th Heavy Coastal Defence Battery was set up at its war station at the bottom of Lewes Crescent. The Council approved a scheme costing £25,000 for strengthening the cellars of the Royal Pavilion, the underground passage to the Dome, and the storage basement of the Public Library, Art Gallery and Museum, in order that they should serve as air-raid shelters. Orders were given that the work must begin at once, and the basements had to be cleared overnight. Rubbish, old equipment, broken furniture and nameless junk that had accumulated since the middle of the previous century were loaded into Corporation rubbish vans and lorries and taken to the refuse destructor. Thousands of books from the Library were taken up to the Booth Museum of Birds and stacked on the floor, where they remained for the duration of the war. The storage basement of the Museum and Art Gallery presented a bizzare spectacle as dozens of glass cases containing ancient stuffed birds and animals were demolished by the staff and swiftly carried away to the waiting rubbish vans. The more valuable museum and art gallery specimens were also removed to the Booth Museum.

On 1st September Brighton was declared to be on a war footing. All cinemas and theatres were closed, but the Sussex County Cricket Club held its customary end-of-season dinner. The last electric tram to run in Brighton left the Aquarium at two o'clock in the morning, without ceremony, for its final run to the depot.

On Sunday, 3rd September 1939, at 11.17 in the morning, as the people of Brighton listened to the voice on the radio of the Prime Minister, Mr. Neville Chamberlain, announcing the fact that we were at war with Germany, the air-raid sirens wailed out their dismal warning over the town, and the inhabitants, with the knowledge in their minds of Hitler's bombing of the cities in Poland, waited for the cloudless blue sky to become blackened by the immense German air armada with which we had been threatened. The sky and sea remained unviolated. The approach of only a single unidentified aircraft, later found to be British, had caused the alarm foolishly to be given over the whole of southern England. The streets of Brighton and the sea-front on that glorious Sunday morning were almost entirely deserted, except for some policemen, air-raid wardens and other officials hurrying to their posts. There was a sense of anti-climax when the all-clear signal was given and people came out into the open again. The 'phoney war' of the first year had begun.

In anticipation of intense air-raids upon London, Brighton had been appointed an evacuation area for children and patients in hospitals. On 4th September the evacuation began: 21,500 children arrived in Brighton and another 9,000 in Hove, and were billeted in private homes. The difficulties that were created by the coming of children from unspeakable London slums into pleasant homes, and even worse miseries caused to many of the children through their being deprived of the presence and affection of their parents, became a major national problem. As schools were shared with the newcomers, school hours were halved, and the residents and visitors became accustomed to seeing groups of children being taken on to the beach and the piers and into the Museum and Art Gallery in a desperate attempt to keep them amused and occupied.

After a few days the cinemas and theatres were allowed to reopen for restricted hours. A meeting of the Allied Supreme War Council was held at Hove Town Hall, at which were present in addition to the Prime Minister, General Gamelin (the French Army chief), Admiral Darlan (the French Naval chief), Lord Chatfield (Minister for the Co-ordination of Defence), Viscount Halifax (Foreign Minister) and the French Prime Minister M. Daladier. Almost a year went by in Brighton and Hove without any other remarkable event, and many of the evacuees returned to their homes.

The Corporation took over Volk's Railway in April 1941, but were not allowed to use their acquisition for very long before it was closed by the military. About the same time a new theatre, the Imperial, was opened in North Street. After staging plays and variety shows for a time it became the

Essoldo Cinema and is now a bingo hall. In May the opening of the first railway into Brighton a hundred years earlier, the Brighton and Shoreham line, was commemorated by a small exhibition of prints and relics held in the King's Apartments at the Royal Pavilion. The building, then almost entirely unrestored and without any of the furniture that fills the rooms today, was used exclusively as assembly rooms, but the number of social functions being held at that time was very small. With the worsening news from France all people of German and Austrian nationality in the town were rounded up by the police and herded into the grandstand on the Race Hill before being sent into internment. A number of quite harmless Germans and Austrians who had in fact come to this country to escape Nazi persecution suffered great hardship at this time, but were afterwards released. Among them was the Rev. W. Oelsner, the Curate of Preston Church, who had himself been a victim of the Nazis. After the appeal on the radio by Mr. Anthony Eden for men not in the forces to defend their homes against the expected invasion, hundreds of men rushed to join the local Defence Volunteers, which afterwards became the Home Guard. At first without weapons, except perhaps for shot-guns and improvised pikes, they guarded key-points on the sea-front, the Downs and the railway. On 10th May, the first day of the Nazi invasion of the Netherlands, a Dutch seaplane alighted near the West Pier, bringing Dr. E. N. Van der Kleffens, the Dutch Foreign Minister, and his wife, and Mr. M. Welter, the Dutch Colonial minister. The Chief Constable gave them lunch in his office, and afterwards the Mayor, Alderman J. Talbot Nansen, accompanied them by train to Victoria. Other Dutch refugees who came to Brighton about this time were members of the firm of Moninckendam, diamond merchants of Amsterdam, who brought with them quantities of industrial diamonds. The firm set up a temporary factory in a disused school building in Wellington Road, Brighton, and later moved to more permanent headquarters at Southwick, where they remained for some years after the war. The industrial diamonds that were produced by the firm were of immense importance to war industries. It was said that one small box of diamonds sent to America would pay for two shiploads of other goods.

In the midst of these excitements a party of American visitors who appeared to be singularly unconcerned about the warlike goings-on round about arrived at Rottingdean for the amiable purpose of taking measurements and details of the parish church in the churchyard of which Sir Edward Burne-Jones the painter is buried, with the object of erecting a replica of the church in a town in California. Towards the end of May holiday visitors to Brighton sitting in their deck chairs on the piers heard the news of the fall of France on the loudspeakers. The halcyon weather of that idyllically beautiful summer seemed to mock at the idea of danger coming from over the water, but the pitifully inadequate measures which remained left to us after the fall of France were put into action. The piers were closed, and people walking on the sea-front were startled by loud explosions as the military blew gaps half-way along the piers, no doubt in the hope that the German troops who had overrun France in the blitzkrieg would be discouraged by these obstacles. The sea-front was barricaded with sandbags and barbed wire, machine-gun posts were erected at strategic points, and a battery of heavy six-inch naval coast-defence guns was established on the front below Lewes Crescent. The beaches also were closed to the public, and on the beach promenade the windows of a public house were being filled with sandbags, to turn it into a defence point, the sign still swinging outside proclaiming its name with melancholy resignation—'The Fortune of War'. On the beach a fun-fair in an arch under the promenade was also being fortified, and over the window from which the barrel of a machine-gun protruded there remained an archway surrounded by coloured electric lights forming the word 'Fairyland'. The big hotels were closed, and nearly all the visitors to Brighton had returned to their homes. The town and sea-front of Brighton were overlaid with a deceptive somnolence that was broken only by a loud explosion as another gap was blown in one of the piers, or by the roaring of squadrons of Spitfires and Hurricanes in formation only a few feet above the house-tops. On the doors of the Hotel Metropole was the notice 'Closed' and upon the litter-strewn steps where more than one Prince of Wales had trod, as well as South African gold and diamond millionaires, the leading actresses, sportsmen and demi-mondaines of the day and the most famous members of cosmopolitan society, there now lay sprawling the ragged figure of the tramp 'Feathers', asleep.

One evening the appeal was made by radio for all owners of boats over 30 feet in length to report to the naval authorities, and later it became known that at least twenty-three vessels from Brighton had taken part in the great evacuation of the British army from Dunkirk. Two of the famous Brighton pleasure steamers of the P. and O. Campbell fleet were sunk by bombs while serving at Dunkirk, the *Brighton Queen* and the *Brighton Belle*, the latter being mercilessly bombed with 300 French and Algerian soldiers on board, but most of them were saved. Two of the three *Skylarks* owned by Captain Collins were lost, as well as several of the small fishing-craft that ferried backwards and forwards again and again to the bomb-blasted beaches. The names of these boats—*Our Doris, Mary Joyce, Royal Rose, Seaflower, Cornsack, Four Winds, Flower of the Fleet*—and many others which took part in that great adventure are like talismans that conjure up memories of blissful untroubled holidays in Brighton in the past.

Some bombs were dropped harmlessly on Hove towards the end of June, but in July the first air raid on Brighton occurred when bombs were dropped early in the morning at Kemp Town. On 1st July King George VI inspected the defences against invasion at Brighton, and the following day Mr. Winston Churchill, who had been appointed Prime Minister only a short time before, also made a tour of inspection and lunched at the Royal Albion Hotel. There were several small raids on Kemp Town, Whitehawk and Hove in July, and people in Brighton saw the first German bomber shot down off the coast by an English fighter plane. The temporary lull in activity enabled the military to open parts of the beaches for the August Bank Holiday, but they were closed again afterwards. Brighton was not yet a restricted area, and the Council made some attempt to compensate for the loss of the beaches by encouraging sun-bathing in Preston Park. The Aquarium was occupied by troops, and such members of the Orchestra as were not serving in the forces, as well as others from the West Pier Orchestra, were brought together by a Brighton alderman, Mr. J. Horton-Stephens, and formed into the Royal Pavilion Orchestra under Jan Hurst, who had been leader of the Aquarium Orchestra. The new orchestra played on the lawns of the Pavilion, and on wet days in the rooms, giving pleasure and keeping up the spirits of thousands of elderly people, war-workers and members of various services in their leisure moments, all through the war and for several years afterwards. Some outdoor ballet and theatrical productions were also presented, mostly with amateur performers and children, such as the Donna Roma Ballet and Doris Isaac's Dancing Juveniles.

In August the aerial activity became intensified as the day-time raids were stepped up. The sun would glint upon silvery specks incredibly high in the sky, as the Heinkel and Dornier bombers crossed the coast on their way inland, while a pattern of white vapour trails was traced around them by the British fighters, and there came down from the air the harsh tearing sound of machine-gun fire as though the silken canopy of the sky were being rent. People watched from their homes in Brighton or from the streets and the sea-front as the most decisive battle of history was fought out overhead. As the Spitfires and Hurricanes broke up the formations of enemy bombers and protecting fighters, watchers would see as many as half a dozen separate fights develop, and after the raiders had been dispersed the British fighters flew back low over the roof-tops of the town performing crazy 'Victory-rolls' of jubilation. A National Savings fund to raise enough money to buy a Brighton Spitfire fighter was started with a Spitfire Ball at the Regent Cinema, and in two weeks 10,000 people visited the exhibition in the Corn Exchange of wrecked German aircraft that had been brought down on the Downs and in the fields around Brighton. As the miraculous summer of 1940 wore on people at last began to wonder if the invasion, once watched for hourly, was after all perhaps to be delayed, and welcomed with relief the gales and rough seas of early autumn, but the opening of a new phase of the war was marked for Brightonians when on 7th September 1940, in the middle of a speech by Sir Kenneth Clark at the opening of an exhibition of modern pictures in the Art Gallery, the sirens sounded, and the wavering drone of hundreds of German aircraft overhead was heard as they made towards London for the opening attack of the 'blitz'. Bombs had been dropped on Brighton in minor raids from time to time all through the summer, but on Saturday afternoon, 14th September, one of the worst raids on Brighton in the whole of the war took place, when twenty high-explosive bombs were dropped in Kemp Town, one of them a direct hit on the Odeon Cinema, which was crowded with children at the time. Four of the children and two adults were killed, and twenty injured. Other bombs fell on a large block of flats. After another raid a policeman found in a street a copy of Erich Remarque's book *All Quiet on the Western Front* which had been blown out of a house several streets away. Once the town was dive-bombed, and at another time people were machine-gunned in the streets by a low flying raider. One night in September thousands of incendiary bombs were dropped, and the streets were filled with innumerable blazing points of bright red, green, blue, yellow and orange fire. Some of the fire bombs were explosive, and burst, injuring the Civil Defence workers who were trying to extinguish them. Later one learned to leave them alone while they were burning harmlessly in the streets. High-explosive bombs followed the fire bombs and the railway works were hit and a gas main was set on fire in the London Road at Preston. From now on until the end of the war, with some intermissions of a few weeks at a time, few days passed without bombs being dropped on Brighton. People tried to carry on life as normally as possible in the town. The Theatre Royal carried on its performances throughout the war, as did the Hippodrome and Grand theatres with their variety shows, something they were not able to do afterwards. Max Miller, a resident of Brighton, was the most popular comedian at the Hippodrome. At the Dome the Brighton Symphonic Players presented orchestral concerts with Herbert Menges as their conductor, and sometimes with the London Philharmonic Orchestra under their own conductor Malcolm Sargent. Chamber concerts were held in the Art Gallery and the Royal Pavilion, with the principal string quartets and solo artists of the day. Often these performances were punctuated by the explosion of bombs, and on one occasion when bombs fell near the Pavilion the chandeliers of the Banqueting-room swung wildly with the blast, but miraculously were not damaged. Most of the removable parts of the chandeliers had been removed and stored for safety, and the wall-paintings had been boarded over. The town was full of soldiers, at one time many of them Canadians. The swimming baths at Hove became the naval shore establishment H.M.S. *King Alfred*, a name it retained after the war. Roedean School also became a naval establishment, H.M.S. *Vernon*, and a young naval officer who later was to become H.R.H. Prince Philip, Duke of Edinburgh, took part in torpedo training at Moore's Garage in Russell

Square. The great hotels and many houses round about were taken over by the R.A.F., and the Royal Albion Hotel was used by bomber pilots recuperating after carrying out long series of bombing raids over Germany. Their well-deserved rest was rudely disturbed when bombs were dropped on the Palace Pier opposite. With so many soldiers, sailors and airmen stationed in the town some special measures had to be taken for their entertainment. Denis Mitchell, who had been at one time manager of the S.S. Brighton, organized nightly dancing for their benefit at the Dome, and a banner appeared over the entrance to the building bearing the message 'Dance away your Dumps at the Dome'. One night when the building was crowded with service people of every kind a large bomb fell in the Pavilion grounds, only a few feet away from the south wall of the building. With the dance band going full blast, accompanied by the Dome organ played by Douglas Reeve, the explosion was hardly noticed, but the south wall of the Dome may be seen today to be slightly out of the vertical as a result of the blast.

With Hitler's invasion of Soviet Russia, the likelihood of any attempt by Germans at a landing on our shores now seemed remote, and Brighton people threw themselves enthusiastically into raising money for Mrs. Churchill's Fund for Medical Aid to Russia. A bunch of 100 bananas, grown in a Brighton man's hothouse, was sold for 300 guineas towards the Fund. Throughout the war one National Savings campaign followed rapidly upon another. The Fighter Fund was so successful that two Spitfires were paid for instead of the one aimed at. A campaign held in Brighton to recruit women for the A.T.S. secured the highest number of recruits of any drive throughout the country. In a campaign held in October 1942, £760,000 was raised in National Savings for the adoption by Brighton of a destroyer, H.M.S. *Kipling*, and when this vessel was sunk in the Mediterranean, another £730,000 was raised to buy another to replace her. A plaque commemorating these efforts was presented to the Mayor by a young R.N.V.R. officer, Lieutenant Laurence Olivier (later Sir Laurence), who was then serving in the Fleet Air Arm. Towards the end of the war, in 1944, he was released to enable him to take part in the direction of the Old Vic Theatre Company, together with Ralph Richardson and John Burrell.

The raids went on, and bombs fell in the sea just off the beach while a German refugee, Frau Irmgard Litten, was giving a lecture in the Dome in connexion with one of the savings campaigns entitled 'If Hitler Came'. Bofors anti-aircraft guns had been set up all along the sea-front, and by 1942 they had scored a remarkable number of hits. Two enemy raiders were once brought down by a single salvo. A more regrettable achievement of theirs was scoring a direct hit at twenty yards' range on the top of one of the delightful cast-iron lamp standards on Marine Parade during the excitement of an attack. One morning in August 1942 the sea and air off Brighton were filled with action and noise. Hundreds of planes flew out across the coast and aerial battles broke out in all directions. Destroyers were seen steaming towards the French coast, and a convoy of motor-barges travelling down-Channel was bombed, but the raiders were driven off by R.A.F. fighters while anti-aircraft shore batteries put up an intense barrage against the German raiders. It was the morning of the ill-fated raid on Dieppe, and the following day there were to be seen in the streets of Rottingdean and Brighton little groups of haggard Canadian soldiers who had been landed at Newhaven after the raid. In the autumn four German fighter-bombers attacked Brighton at a low level with bombs and cannon fire. Eight people were killed and many injured. Marine Gate, the block of modern flats at Black Rock which had been opened only a year or so before, was heavily bombed, and the destruction revealed in one of the flats an immense hoard of scarce food, whisky and clothing which had been secreted there by a local black-marketeer.

The people remaining in Brighton strove resolutely to keep up civilian morale with the best kind of entertainment, and the Brighton Symphonic Players had the enterprise and courage to organize a one-week Music Festival, during which the Bournemouth Philharmonic Orchestra appeared, as well as soloists including Moura Lympany, Eda Kersey, Albert Sammons, Eileen Joyce, Moiseiwitch, Pouishnoff and Maurice Cole. A 'Religion and Life Week' was held at the Dome, with the Archbishop of Canterbury, the late Dr. William Temple, and the Bishop of Chichester, the late Dr. Bell, among the speakers. At the Diocesan Conference held at the same time Dr. Bell declared that 'the old world as we knew it before the war with its privileged and leisured classes was doomed, and a belief in its return was sheer delusion'.

At that time Dr. Bell spoke out vehemently against our heavy bombing of open German cities, and especially against such raids as the one carried out on Dresden, when over 100,000 people, many of them refugees from eastern Europe, died.

Years afterwards Dr. Bell was portrayed as a principal figure in the highly controversial play by Rolf Hochhuth, *Die Soldaten*, which was performed in Berlin in 1967 and in London two years later. During the course of a bitter argument in the play the Bishop face to face with Winston Churchill makes a passionate speech condemning the bombing of cities. Although he would have been astonished at the idea of being represented in a play as an heroic world-figure, Dr. Bell was not lacking in the moral fervour and courage and deep Christian convictions that caused him to express opinions that were regarded during the war as traitorous, but concerning which he would have found many more supporters nowadays than he did then.

Air raids, many of them severe. continued throughout 1942 and 1943.

A stick of bombs fell across the village of Rottingdean, damaging a block of flats on the sea-front and destroying the Vicarage, where the housekeeper was found alive kneeling in prayer under the stairs, the only part to remain intact. Kemp Town was frequently attacked, probably because of the prominent target of the great gasholders near by. In one raid a direct hit was scored on one of the gasholders, and an immense orange flame, some 300 feet high, flared out in the sky above it. On one occasion in May 1943 twenty-five raiders attacked the town, destroying many houses and other buildings, but four of the bombers were destroyed, one by a fighter and three by anti-aircraft fire. In the same month six Focke-Wulf fighter-bombers flew in at low level over the town and scored a direct hit on the great railway viaduct at Preston, a little to the west of the London Road. One of the arches was destroyed, but the rails and sleepers were left hanging across the gap. In one of the most remarkable repair operations of the war, steel girders were thrown across the gap and within twenty-four hours the vital goods traffic was passing across the viaduct again.

As Hitler met with great reverses in Russia, the faint hope that we might not after all be conquered strengthened into the conviction of eventual victory, and people began to turn their minds to the time to come after the war. The invasion strong-points on the roads around Brighton were cleared away, and the municipalities of Brighton and Hove began to prepare plans for the postwar development of their towns. Alderman B. Dutton-Briant made a plea in a speech to the Chamber of Commerce that old Brighton should not be pulled down to make way for the new, but Brighton's first planning report, published in April 1944, was described by one critic as 'a miserable mouse'.

The expectation for the opening of a second front in Europe was now building up to a new height of intensity. In tree-sheltered by-roads along the coast and in the downland valleys around Brighton fresh concentrations of army vehicles were being built up every day. For some days the Corn Exchange was closely guarded by armed sentries while officers from different sections of the Army were engaged on an instruction course centred upon a large contour model in sand of the long-conjectured secret coastline.

One morning it was seen that the concentrations of tanks and lorries had disappeared and the houses where troops had been quartered were empty. A few days later, at 2.30 in the morning of 6th June 1944, Brighton-ians were awakened by a loud continuous roar overhead far surpassing the noise of any of our earlier 1,000-bomber raids, and watchers from windows, from the sea-front and the streets saw the dark shapes of the immense fleet of bombers, fighters, transport-planes and gliders silhouetted against the moonlit sky as they passed over the coast towards France. Many of them, bombers and fighters, passed and repassed again and again as the morning wore on, and across the water was heard the dull rumble of gunfire and bombing. It was D-Day; the invasion of Europe had begun. A day or so later a grim indication was given of the drama that was being enacted on the opposite coast when an empty landing-barge, blasted by explosions, was washed ashore at Brighton. Soon the first batch of wounded arrived at Brighton hospitals, followed in a little while by the first German prisoners, who were put to work filling air-raid shelter-trenches in the parks, or sent to neighbouring farms to help with the harvest.

The next few weeks were the quietest Brighton had known during the whole of the war until then. The municipality turned its attention to the campaign for 'Holidays at Home', and the Royal Pavilion Orchestra played at performances of a local ballet company on the Royal Pavilion lawns. In August 1944 the Southern Railway made a commemorative gesture to a handful of people by holding an exhibition in the Art Gallery celebrating the opening of the first railway between Brighton and London a century earlier. For the Bank Holiday week-end the ban on visitors to Brighton was lifted and the night-time curfew ended. In a little while the promenades were cleared of the high jungle-growth of rusty barbed wire.

Serving as a lieutenant in the Welsh Guards, who were stationed in houses in Preston Park Avenue, was Rex Whistler, the brilliant young decorative artist whose remarkable mural paintings at the Tate Gallery, at Plas Newydd and many other great houses, together with his ballet and theatre designs had struck a new note of decorative beauty and nostalgic charm.

A little before D-Day the Welsh Guards left Brighton and were stationed near Southampton before crossing the Channel for the invasion of France. A few days after their departure the present writer was told by Mrs. Alec Holden, who had been a Lady-in-Waiting to the Princess Louise, that in the house near her own in Preston Park Avenue, where the Welsh Guards had been stationed, Rex Whistler had painted some remarkable mural decorations on the walls of a room used as the officers' mess. The house was deserted, but a window had been left open, and one found oneself confronted by a great painting occupying most of an entire wall, depicting the figure of the Prince Regent, naked except for the blue ribbon of the Garter, with the badge of the order resting on his buttock, kneeling before the reclining figure of a sleeping girl, who wore round her waist a blue girdle bearing the name Brighthelmstone. Below was the title of the picture written in a cartouche 'Allegory: H.R.H. the Prince Regent awakening the Spirit of Brighton'. In one corner was written 'Rex Whistler, June 5-7, 1944'. The impact of this picture, painted with great mastery in rich tones of crimson and cerulean blue, was intense. Looking around one saw on the opposite wall a *chinoiserie* decoration of bamboo plants, peonies and other flowering shrubs and trees with a Chinese bird-cage hung in the branches and birds and butterflies flying around. In the centre of this was a huge oval medallion containing a silhouette portrait of George IV surrounded by an inscription containing a reference to the artist's own name, 'Georgius IV Rex'. On the end wall of the room was a large crest of the Welsh Guards, painted with such realism that it seemed at the distance of only a few feet to be modelled in white plaster with the Welsh leek in gold relief. It was felt that these paintings, which perfectly expressed so much of the spirit of Brighton, should be preserved, and a letter was sent to the artist to obtain his permission to remove them, but almost immediately came the tragic news of Rex Whistler's death in Normandy. He was the first officer of the Welsh Guards to be killed in action after D-Day. The Colonel-in-Chief of the Welsh Guards, Sir Alexander Stanier, Bt., D.S.O., and Rex Whistler's mother, Mrs. Turner, were both anxious that the paintings should be preserved for the town, and it was agreed by the Corporation that the owner of the house should be compensated for the damage that might be caused by their removal. Through Alderman Dutton-Briant, who happened to be serving as an Army Welfare Officer for Sussex, arrangements were made with the Army authorities for the paintings to be removed. The famous picture-restoring firm of Drown and Son of Doughty House, Richmond, removed the principal painting, cutting it away from the wall with plaster adhering to the back of the wallpaper, and winding it on to a great wooden drum about 8 feet high. The plaster was removed and the painting fastened to canvas, mounted on a stretcher and framed. The medallion portrait and the crest were also removed and mounted, but the difficulties of detaching the *chinoiserie* decoration from the wall were found to be too great and it remains to this day where it was painted. The arrangements which had been made for removing the paintings were apparently not known to a fresh army unit which came to occupy the houses in Preston Park Avenue. When the present writer went with a van to remove the paintings from the house, he was placed under military arrest and taken off to a guard room by a captain and a sergeant armed with revolvers, past grinning groups of soldiers. When the news of the arrest of the civilian who had been removing army property was telephoned to Sub-District Headquarters, a few crackling words from the Brigadier-General in command which seemed almost to detonate the telephone instrument brought about one's speedy release.

The acquisition of 'The Spirit of Brighton' was celebrated at a ceremony in the Art Gallery on 15th April 1946, when at the same time the painted crest was presented to the Welsh Guards by Sir Osbert Sitwell on behalf of the Corporation. Rex Whistler had been one of Sir Osbert's closest friends, and had designed the wrapper of the book *Brighton* which he had written in conjunction with Miss Margaret Barton in 1935. The 'Allegory' now hangs in one of the upper rooms of the Royal Pavilion, together with the silhouette portrait of King George IV.

The facts of Brighton's experiences under air raids were now disclosed. There had been 1,058 siren warnings and 685 local alarms. There were 56 air raids on the town, the first on 15th July 1940, and the last on 22nd March 1944. A total of 381 high-explosive bombs was dropped and incendiary bombs were too numerous to be recorded. Civilian casualties numbered 988, of whom 198 were killed, 357 seriously injured and 433 slightly injured. Over 5,000 houses were damaged, and 200 completely destroyed. Kemp Town, south Whitehawk, and the area between these parts and the Steine were the mostly badly hit. But the danger to Brighton was by no means past. In November 1944 the warning of attack by unpiloted flying-bombs was given, and before long these obscene missiles began flying in over the town from the sea, at a height of about 200 feet, belching orange flames from their tails and accompanied by a harsh vibratory roar. People on the Downs and sea-front cheered as they saw one of the first of the bombs to be destroyed when it was pursued by a British fighter and shot down over the sea. However, most of the flying-bombs passed on towards London, and as the launching sites were overrun by the Allied armies on the Continent the stream of attacking missiles shifted farther east over Kent.

At length the German resistance collapsed, and Victory in Europe— VE-Day—was celebrated on 8th May 1945. The church bells rang for the first time since the outbreak of war. Bonfires were lit on the Downs and on the beaches, American soldiers in the town kissed all the girls in sight, and the streets were filled with crowds of jubilant people. With the instinct of the ordinary British people for spontaneous celebrations, tea-parties were arranged in many of the poorer streets, the children and old people sitting down at trestle tables to eat the food that miraculously appeared for the occasion after years of privation. Brighton's famous street-musicians, Marc Antonio the harpist and his colleague Alexander the violinist, played all day long in West Street and in a few hours collected a sum of money that almost compensated for the lean war years. The town was thronged with visitors for the Whitsun week-end, but the beaches were not cleared of mines until July, after bulldozers had raked deeply up and down along the stretches of shingle.

In spite of the atmosphere of relief and jubilation, the typical social problems of the postwar period were soon to raise their heads. Returning servicemen found an acute housing shortage, and immense indignation was aroused by the existence of many empty houses in the town. Harry Cowley, a chimney-sweep known as 'The Guv-nor', organized a band of Vigilantes to commandeer empty houses for the families of servicemen who needed homes. After the war of 1914-18 Harry Cowley and his friends had seized sixty-four houses for this purpose, and several people who were put in them at that time were still tenants in 1945. The Viligantes held processions and meetings of protest on the fishmarket, and were solemnly warned by the various authorities not to take the law into their own hands. One or two families were placed by them in empty houses, and the activities of the Vigilantes eventually resulted in the Corporation officially requisitioning suitable empty properties for housing those in need. The fall of Japan was celebrated on V-J Day, 15th August 1945. There was dancing on the Pavilion lawns, on the Aquarium terraces and in the streets, and mammoth bonfires were lit on the beaches. Hundreds of deck-chairs and beach-huts which had survived the war were smashed into pieces and thrown on the flames. The National Fire Service was called out twenty-four times in the course of the day to deal with fires which had got out of control. A few days later there were big crowds at the first race meeting to be held in Brighton since the beginning of the war. Some details of Brighton's industrial war efforts were now published, and were seen to be remarkable for a pleasure town. Mr. Alan A. Saunders, managing director of a firm of builders' merchants in the town, had been made Co-ordinator of Radio Production for the whole country, and was responsible for the production of radar sets and other detection equipment. Early in the war he was told 400 submarine detector sets were needed. On his own initiative he ordered 4,000, which were quickly found of vital value. Thousands of radar sets and much other electrical equipment were made by the firm of Allen West, who also built sections of the 'Mulberry Harbour' on to which troops and supplies were unloaded off the French coast at the time of the invasion. The strange shapes of these sections which had been seen being towed along to their destination had caused great puzzlement to Brightonians. Hundreds of steam locomotives had been made at the Brighton Railways works, which was bombed on several occasions. Towards the end of the war thirty large 2-8-0 locomotives were made for the L.N.E.R. at the rate of one engine in 3½ days. Now that the war was over plans were made to start turning out locomotives of the Merchant Navy class, which gave splendid service in the Southern Region until the abolition of steam, and by June 1947 the works celebrated the completion of the 1000th loco-motive to be made there.

With the discovery of the Nazi state archives, Hitler's plans for the invasion of England in 1940 were now revealed. One invasion force was to have landed on the coast between Brighton and Portsmouth, and another on the Downs behind Brighton to clear the communications between that town and London. The English traitor Joyce, who as the Nazi radio com-mentator 'Lord Haw-Haw' incurred such detestation and caused much bitter amusement amongst his English listeners, had announced that the Royal Pavilion was not to be touched, as Hitler intended to use it as his personal headquarters, but it is certain that even if the invaders had been hurled back into the sea Brighton would have been destroyed in the process.

6 Recovery and Re-planning: 1945 to 1960

_____

As soon as the war was over everyone was anxious to see the town re-established as a pleasure resort as quickly as possible, and before long many of the town's familiar holiday attractions were set going again. Early in the summer of 1945 a new *Skylark*, replacing one which had given five years' service in the Navy during the war, returned to Brighton beach; the Hotel Metropole was reopened; the gaps in the two piers were filled in, and they were reopened during the summer of 1946. The Aquarium was leased to a private company, and opened again, but with a ban on fun-fairs, automatic machines, and wrestling or boxing matches, and the first Veteran Car Run since the war began was held in November 1947. The Brighton Philharmonic Society, which had been active all through the war, now put forward an ambitious scheme for its future development which was eventually approved by the Council, and an impressive series of concerts was organized for following seasons. The orchestra, directed by Herbert Menges, now became fully professional, and gave concerts not only in Brighton but at Hastings, Eastbourne, Folkestone, Swindon, Croydon, Portsmouth and Southampton. In December 1945, H.R.H. the Princess Elizabeth, who had opened a new wing at the Children's Hospital, attended a concert at the Dome. The Brighton Corporation gave valuable help to the Society at this time by making a £3,000 guarantee against loss, and although this was eventually cut to £1,000, the Race Ground Lessees contributed another £1,000 out of their funds, and other help came from the Arts Council.

Almost immediately after the war the Council was confronted once more with the vexing 'problem of the tripper', which had perplexed the townspeople ever since the coming of the railway, and which was to exercise their minds perpetually in the years to come. In some quarters it was believed that the wealthier visitors, whether of our own country or from abroad, were deterred from coming to Brighton because of its popularity among the day-trippers, who it was said had been encouraged by a mistaken policy on the part of the Council in the past. There was intense rivalry between those who would have Brighton develop as another Blackpool, and those who would rather aim at the respectable dignity of Eastbourne and Worthing.

In February 1946 a proposal was brought forward in the Council for a 'Coney Island' type of fun-fair with scenic railways, roundabouts, and every kind of popular amusement, to be established in Sheepcote Valley near Roedean, but this was defeated. It is hardly likely, even if this project had been thought desirable, that trippers in search of such amusement would have made the journey to this rather remote part of the borough. Again, in 1950 another proposal to set up a fun-fair on the sea-front was also rejected, and the Council's decision supported by the Government.[1] The problem seemed especially difficult of solution, if only because however little might be done expressly to encourage day-trippers, they could not be expected to be insensible to the charm and attractions of Brighton, and it was not possible for them to be driven away completely, and however distasteful they might be in some quarters, they made an important contribution to the livelihood of many others, especially of the small shop-keepers and café proprietors.

There were many difficulties in the way of those who were trying to re-establish Brighton's hotel, catering and entertainment industries. There were shortages of building materials, of coal, of newsprint and of food, even bread, which was now rationed although it had not been restricted during the war. The number of visitors to Brighton in the summer of 1947 was only 60 per cent of those in the previous year, in which many people had celebrated the return to peacetime by taking a seaside holiday. The slump was not, however, peculiar to Brighton; it affected most seaside resorts. Many people were now beginning to go abroad for their holidays, and the wealthy American and other overseas visitors had not yet begun to visit Brighton.

A carefully considered scheme which was put forward by the owner of one of the hotels summed up the wisest and most practicable ideas for the improvement of Brighton that were being considered at the time. His suggestions included the prohibition of parking of cars and coaches on the sea-front; the closing of most of the cafés, fish-stalls and small shops in the arches under the sea-front; the removal of the 'dodge-'em' car-track from the beach opposite the Aquarium; the improvement of the lower promenade around the old fishmarket; and the creation of a Continental atmosphere on the front by the provision of colour, flowers and music.[2]

Certain other developments were not popular amongst the people they concerned. Amongst the fishermen of Brighton intense bitterness was aroused by the Council's decision in January 1946 not to allow thenceforth the holding of the fishmarket on the beach, up-to-date and hygienic new market-buildings having been provided inland. There was not a little regret amongst the residents and visitors over the disappearance of this highly picturesque, if odiferous, traditional feature of Brighton's life. To one small boy taken there by his father very early on a summer's morning the scene at the beach fishmarket in its heyday fifty years ago was a fascinating one, with the shouting of the fishermen, the boats being hauled up on to the beach by men at the old wooden capstans, the cries of the fish auctioneers; the groups of people standing around, some of them smart visitors from the hotels, others the more sombrely dressed but sharp-eyed landladies of the Brighton boarding-houses; the little boys many of them barelegged and barefooted running in and out amongst the onlookers, and pelting each other with pieces of fish; the strange sea-creatures which had sometimes been brought ashore—a pathetic looking lump-fish or a spiky parrot-fish—the beautiful sleek shapes of the porpoises, so regrettably captured and to be cut up revealing white flesh inside the black skin—'Just like pork, mum,' cried the auctioneer to the surrounding lodging-house keepers—and, most vivid memory of all, the nectar-like coffee, of a flavour never recaptured since, served by a man with a barrow, from a square, polished copper urn with little pointed battlements round the top, looking rather like a model of the Pavilion. The fishermen were not easily to be dispossessed of their ancient market, however, although after the last war little more than two hundredweight of fish was sold there each week from boats landing on the beach. It was not until 1964 that the fishermen were finally reconciled to using the new fishmarket in the town.

Even before the end of the war the Hove Corporation had been planning a vast and revolutionary scheme for the development of that borough, which would involve the clearance of the Regency buildings of Brunswick Square and the adjoining Terraces, and their replacement with skyscraper blocks of flats. The Corporation met the storm of protest that arose by giving an assurance, which carried no conviction at all, that the destruction of the Regency buildings would in no way alter the character of Hove. The storm burst in January 1946, when the Hove Council announced their intention of clearing the centre gardens of Brunswick Square to form a car-park, and in March the Council turned down an appeal against their decision. This was reversed, however, by the East Sussex Appeals Committee at Lewes Quarter Sessions soon after, as a result of petitions by the residents. The affair provided an interesting instance of the way in which a local authority's decision could be nullified. The plea of Alderman Dutton-Briant a year or so earlier for the preservation of old Brighton was only one of many expressions of disquiet regarding the future of Brighton's Georgian heritage, and the formation of a preservation society was to a great extent precipitated by the Hove Council's intentions over Brunswick Square. The Regency Society of Brighton and Hove was formed in December 1945, at a meeting in the Royal Pavilion, which was addressed by the Duke of Wellington. The first principal officers of the Society were William Teeling, M.P. (now Sir William), Chairman; D. L. Murray, J. L. Denman, F.R.I.B.A., and Eric Gillett, M.A., Vice-Chairmen; Clifford Musgrave, Honorary Secretary; and Antony Dale, Honorary Treasurer. This fresh awakening to the aesthetic beauty and historical associations of Brighton and Hove caused new attention to be turned to the Royal Pavilion, which had been placed in the charge of the present writer in 1940. Professor Sir Charles Reilly, the one-time Principal of the Liverpool School of Architecture, and a member of the Brighton Fine Arts Committee at that time had suggested to members of the Council that important developments might eventually be possible in the direction of making it a centre of historical and aesthetic interest for the late Georgian period. The idea of seeing the original furniture of the building once more in its rooms was one that many people had wished to see realized, and in July 1946 the first Regency Exhibition was held under the inspiration of Lady Birley in aid of charities. A private committee with the title of 'The Regency Festival' was formed to organize the Exhibition in conjunction with Brighton Corporation, and with the help of many lenders the principal rooms were now filled with furniture of the Regency period. King George VI and Queen Elizabeth lent from Buckingham Palace some important articles of furniture originally belonging to the Pavilion, and the building appeared appropriately adorned for the first time for a hundred years, although the decoration of the rooms, much of it Victorian, had not then been replaced or restored, and was in a sad state through the enforced neglect of the war years. The visit of two Queens, when Queen Elizabeth, now Queen Elizabeth the Queen Mother, and Queen Mary together attended the Private View, was a unique event even among the many Royal occasions in the history of Brighton.

In July there was some dispute in the Council over a request from a film company to stage various scenes of a film version of Graham Greene's novel *Brighton Rock* at the Brighton race-course. There were some persons who felt the project should not be allowed at all, because of the unfortunate impression of Brighton as a centre of gang violence that would be revived, but eventually the company were allowed to use part of the course. A month later parts of a film version of Norman Ginsbury's play about the Prince Regent, *The First Gentlemen*, were filmed in the Royal Pavilion itself. The restoration of the building had then hardly begun, and the rooms contained no furniture at all. The stores of most of the antique-dealers of London were ransacked for *chinoiserie* to furnish the rooms with lacquer cabinets, porcelain vases and Chinese hangings, so that an oriental scene was created almost surpassing in lavish splendour anything that had been known in the days of the Prince himself.

During the war, and for several years immediately following, a number of chamber concerts and recitals given by some of the leading soloists and instrumental combinations of the day were held in the Royal Pavilion under the auspices of the Public Library and Art Gallery departments. Some of the concerts were presented by the Frank Bridge Society as a memorial to the gifted composer who had been born in Brighton in 1879 and died in

413

1941. Some of the most distinguished writers gave literary lectures, and the notion that the writing and reading of poetry were activities remote from the life of ordinary men and women was dispelled by the sight of the huge audiences that crowded to hear Cecil Day Lewis, Sir Osbert and Edith Sitwell, Walter de la Mare, Richard Church, Louis MacNeice, John Pudney and Dylan Thomas reading their own poems.

In October 1947 the Corporation performed the most far-reaching and imaginative act since their purchase of the Royal Pavilion Estate in 1850, when they decided to buy the Stanmer Estate for £224,000 from the Trustees of the Chichester family, who had been compelled to realize their assets by the incidence of three levies of estate duty within a few years. The estate consisted of nearly 5,000 acres of land, including most of the villages of Falmer and Stanmer, and parts of the parishes of Ditchling, Plumpton and St. Ann Without, Lewes. There was also the handsome Georgian mansion, built in 1722, and set in a beautiful downland park. Some 3,245 acres were set aside as a perpetual open space and as well as providing invaluable opportunities for recreation and pleasure the estate has furnished the people of Brighton with sites for new schools, a new municipal College of Education, and the new University of Sussex.

The most notable event of 1947, however, was the conferring in October of the Freedom of the Borough upon Mr. Winston Churchill. The event coincided with the holding of the Conference of the Conservative Party at Brighton in that year. After a triumphal drive along the Madeira Drive and back along Marine Parade, the ceremony took place in the Dome, and was followed by a luncheon in the Corn Exchange. After receiving the Freedom Mr. Churchill launched upon a humorous recital of his early recollections of Brighton and Hove, where in one or the other—'the boundaries were not then defined with such scrupulous precision as now,' he remarked— 'I learned to ride, to swim and to dance, and began to learn by heart many of those passages of poetry which have been such a pleasure and comfort to me during my life—heroic poetry and famous tales and literature of the past'. Mr. Churchill described the visit he made to Brighton after the fall of France and the Dunkirk withdrawal, when he came to inspect our very exiguous coast defences: 'We dined—four or five of us—in the Royal Albion Hotel, which was otherwise almost deserted. Looking out of the window I saw where the old Chain Pier used to stand and saw the Grenadier Guards sandbagging the kiosks to repel a landing. One of the kiosks I had always known in my young days as being devoted to the performing flea. The particular performing flea we were concerned with at that time is not now performing and for that fact we are entitled to rejoice in a great deliverance.'

During the war the Sports Stadium at Withdean had been used by the military, and early in 1948 ambitious proposals were made by Mr. Denis

Mitchell, who during the war had organized dancing at the Dome for the forces, to establish a permanent Circus, Rodeo and Zoo at the Stadium. The Zoo was the only part of the scheme that was realized except that a number of international tennis tournaments were held there from time to time. By June the Zoo was in full swing, with apes, baboons, bison, sloth-bears, dingoes, lions and lionesses with their cubs, peacocks and cranes, wallabies, and Peruvian llamas on which children were given rides round the grounds, and a porcupine which wandered about the grounds and on several occasions frightened some timid tennis players from the courts. There was also a small railway track with a fantastic Emett-type locomotive called the 'Withdean Flyer'. In recent years the Stadium has reverted to its original purpose as a municipal sports ground for cricket, football, tennis and occasional athletic meetings, horse-shows and displays.

Certain sections of the Council again incurred criticism when in June 1948 an attempt was made to impose a ban on political meetings on the sea-front at the old fishmarket during the holiday season from May to October. The Labour Party fiercely challenged this proposal, which they regarded as a ban on free speech, and certainly it would have been a pity to abolish one of the traditional features of the life of Brighton's sea-front. The proposal was rejected, and the Council were mercifully unaware of the peculiar happenings on the sea-front that would be causing them deep anxiety in some twenty years' time, when the beatniks and the Flower People were to make it their headquarters. Another traditional feature of the Brighton scene disappeared about the same time, when the last of Brighton's bath-chair men, Mr. Charles Dolding, retired. He recalled that at one time there had been over twenty bath-chairs plying for hire on the sea-front, but for many years his had been the only one remaining. In the summer of 1948 a second Regency Exhibition was held, and it was then that the famous Dolphin furniture, which had been presented to Green-which Hospital in 1813 in memory of Lord Nelson, was first shown at the Pavilion. It is now a permanent feature of the display.

Towards the end of 1949 two well-known Brighton characters who had occupied pitches close to each other over many years died within a few weeks of each other. Harriet Gunn, a flower-seller who had sat outside Hannington's shop in East Street with her basket, was taken ill and died in her sleep in November 1949 at the age of seventy-six. As she lay in her last illness the East Street musicians Marc Antonio the harpist and Alexander the violinist played her favourite tunes beneath the bedroom window of her home at Whitehawk. During the war when warned by a policeman to take cover while the bombs were falling she replied: 'That little old Hitler won't shift me.'[3] Mrs. Emily Gardner, the newspaper seller whose pitch was outside the Westminster Bank in Castle Square, died in February

1950 at her home at the age of sixty-eight. She had a phenomenal knowledge of her regular customers, and never needed to ask them which paper they wanted. After being away from Brighton in the Army for over four years, one of her customers was given his paper as though he had never missed a day.[4]

With the opening of the new decade the *Herald* looked back over the past ten years and considered 'the curious fact that the forties have always been bad for Britain. The 1840s have an evil reputation as the "Hungry Forties"; the 1740s saw the last battles between England and Scotland; in the 1640s civil war; and so we may go back. None of these decades in previous centuries can, however, equal the evil reputation of the 1940s, with the misery of the World War, and the disillusion which came after. . . .' It was with a sense of relief that the *Herald* turned its back on this dark period and looked forward to 1950 as 'a year of destiny'.[5]

The immediate prospects for the town in the new year of 1950 were not auspicious. Unemployment was very high[6] and the Aquarium lessees had incurred a loss of £20,000 in two years' working. The Corporation accordingly reduced their rent from £14,000 a year to £10,000. Nevertheless, the town had already begun to look forward to exciting events two years ahead, when Brighton was, in June 1949, chosen as an official festival town for the 1951 Festival of Britain, that was intended to mark the beginning of a new era of prosperity for the country.[7] A certain amount of alarm was expressed when Brighton's plans for taking part in the Festival of Britain were made known, especially over the cost that would be involved, estimated at £25,000. The principal events suggested were a Regency Festival and Exhibition, a six-day pageant followed by military displays, and the setting up of an open-air theatre on the Royal Pavilion lawns. The one feature of the programme that was believed 'would command unanimous approval' was the Regency Festival, which, it was realized, would cost the town nothing and provide revenue.[8] The programme of military displays, however, estimated to cost over £15,000, was regarded as 'pathetic', and the proposal to create an open-air theatre on the Pavilion Lawns was looked upon as downright vandalism. As for the permanent amenities to be provided to commemorate the Festival, a bathing-station was considered to be superfluous now that everyone undressed on the beach, and the idea of a bandstand was thought to be completely divorced from the Festival.[9] A week later 'grim tidings of the international situation and of the sacrifices that will be necessary to secure an adequate defence programme' caused the *Herald* to express the hope that the local festival celebrations, which were only too likely to prove a 'fiasco', would have to be postponed, if not entirely abandoned.[10] Before the national festival took place, however, Brighton held an important event of its own, the Centenary Festival which in June 1950 commemorated the purchase of the Royal Pavilion by the town a hundred years earlier. Powers had been obtained from the Council in the previous October to develop the Pavilion as a Royal palace, restored and furnished, and as an exhibition centre for the arts and life of the Regency period. The State apartments, which had to some extent already been restored to their original condition, were now arranged with furniture and works of art of the Georgian period and opened to the public for three months from July to September. By the standards that were to be achieved in later years it was a very modest display, yet over 80,000 persons visited the Centenary Exhibition, which was opened by the tenth Duke of Devonshire.

A great many plans for the improvement of the town and its attractions were put forward during the next few years, almost all of them from the Council rather than from private enterprise, but very few of them were realised. The successive 'credit squeezes' and 'economic blizzards' of the late 1940s and 1950s prevented any expenditure on civic schemes, and private speculators had not yet come forward with imaginative proposals.

Although Brighton's magnificent sea-front had been restored, many of the inland areas of the town were rendered empty and derelict, by slum-clearance if not by enemy bombing. It was to be years before these areas were built upon, new building often being delayed, even when building restrictions had eventually been abolished, through property changing hands several times amongst different speculators without any development being carried out. The Council's resources were already stretched to the uttermost in meeting the cost of vitally necessary new housing, new schools, and improvements in social welfare services. There seemed little money to spare for the illuminations of the sea-front and for military-band concerts on the sea-front and in the parks that were so freely suggested, still less for the 'Edinburgh-type' festival of the arts that was being recommended even then as an attraction for the better type of visitor.[11]

As early as October 1947 an ambitious scheme was put forward for the creation of a gigantic pleasure beach three quarters of a mile long and stretching 500 yards out to sea, between the Aquarium and the Banjo Groyne at Kemp Town. The whole project, which was estimated to cost at least £1,000,000, was to be built on 'Mulberry Harbour' floating sections, which would carry 'promenades, boulevards, a Continental terrace and a motor-boat harbour'.[12] Another major proposal for the improvement of the sea-front was an ambitious scheme put forward in December 1949 by Councillor Lewis Cohen (later Lord Cohen) for the building of a large music and entertainment pavilion between West Street and Little Russell Street, on the lines of a scheme suggested before the war. As well as a concert hall for 3,000 persons, there were to be conference halls, restaurants, a ballroom, a popular dance hall, play-rooms for children, a library and reading-room and garages.[13] The scheme was, however, foredoomed to failure, because of financial stringency and the impossibility of obtaining building licences at that time.[14] Nevertheless the scheme approached more closely in scope than any other project put forward during the post-war years to the great development that was to be carried out beyond West Street by private enterprise in the 1960s.

The Council continued to make plans for sweeping away the sordid and ruinous shops along the sea-front beyond West Street, and while rejecting a scheme of the Ideas Committee to build a new £20,000 band-stand beyond the West Pier, approved a suggestion, that proved to be abortive, for a bandstand near the foot of West Street. This was the first of many proposals for a new bandstand on the sea-front that threatened to involve the destruction of the charming Victorian bandstand like an oriental birdcage in cast-iron filigree, that stood beyond the West Pier. This bandstand had been much criticized because public lavatories had been built beneath it, and the noise of continual flushings and gurglings of water was remarked upon as being a drawback to the enjoyment of the music.[15] Furthermore, the number of seats that could be arranged around it was very limited, amounting to only about 300, which caused the takings from the hire of deck-chairs by listeners to be small. The Entertainments Committee had spent £1,372 in 1950 on military bands on the sea-front, and proposed to spend another £1,000 the following year in the hope of attracting visitors. It was hoped that a new bandstand might be built as the 'much-needed improvement or amenity that would be of lasting value to the community'[16] that towns were being encouraged by the Government to provide as a permanent memorial to the Festival of Britain, which was to be held in the following year to mark Britain's recovery from the war and the beginning of a new era of peacetime prosperity. Curiously enough, however, this proposal was dropped in favour of a scheme to build a bath-ing-pavilion near the West Pier at a cost of £13,000. There had been little demand for such an amenity by comparison with the desires expressed for a bandstand, but the suggestion was made that the bathing-pavilion would be an attraction to foreign visitors, who, it was said, were shocked at the idea of undressing on the beach. This modest bathing-pavilion built at the western end of the beach, and of charming design with white columns, but most inappropriately for its situation of dark brown bricks, was, in fact, the only civic development carried out on the sea-front after the war. Opened in August 1952,[17] it was ignored by bathers, and by 1954 it was already being regarded as 'both an eyesore and a white elephant', and it was eventually, in 1957, leased to the Milk Marketing Board for use as a milk bar.

Mr. Cohen again pleaded for the building of a music pavilion, as well as for an open-air bathing-pool in the centre of the front,[18] and a year later made a revolutionary proposal to create a 'chain of gardens' right through the valley of the town from Preston to the sea. The old properties on the eastern side of the London Road from St. Peter's Church to Preston Park were to be swept away to form gardens, and the southern end of the Steine was to be opened up to the sea by the removal of Royal York Buildings and the Adelphi Hotel. The fantastic cost of buying up all the properties that were to be demolished, and the enormous loss of rateable value that would result, were insuperable obstacles to the scheme. Mr. Cohen himself hardly expected his scheme to be adopted and two years later was putting forward a proposal for a 'Continental Bathing Plage', with twenty-six tents on a timber decking laid on a concrete base 150 feet long and 25 feet wide, to be sited on the beach west of the West Pier. The estimated cost was about £4,750. If successful, the experiment could be extended to other beaches. Although the scheme offered an attractive means for bathers to avoid the agonizing experience of walking upon the large pebbles of the beach, it was strongly criticized, one objector suggesting that English men and women would object to being laid out in ordered rows, but preferred jolly and untidy family groups, with an occasional pram and a dog.[19]

The most acute controversy over building plans was probably that generated over the question of the site of the new Town Hall and Civic Centre that had long been needed. The departments of the Corporation had long outgrown the accommodation in Thomas Cooper's stately classical building in which more space was devoted to staircases and corridors than to offices. Of three sites originally suggested, one on Pavilion Parade, directly opposite the Royal Pavilion, was chosen by the Planning Committee. The other two sites were the existing Town Hall site and one between Church Street and North Road, directly north of the Public Library and Museum building.[20] The Council rejected the Planning Committee's suggestion and decided on the existing site. Nevertheless, two years later the Committee succeeded in persuading the Council to change their minds and to revert to the site on Pavilion Parade.[21] This decision aroused the fiercest opposition of the Regency Society and many other persons who believed that the immense façade of a vast new municipal building would overwhelm the small mass and delicate outlines of the Royal Pavilion opposite. The decision not to use the existing Town Hall site was determined by the realization that this site, which was so close to the sea-front, would be of such immense financial value that it should be devoted to the amenities of Brighton as a holiday town and pleasure resort instead of being used for the purposes of local government, which could be carried out on a less expensive site. Eventually, however, the Council were compelled by the Government to keep to their original decision to use the old Town Hall site, on the grounds that the Corporation were already the owners. The bandstand idea was revived in 1952 when it was decided to build a new one, not at the centre of the front, but near the West Pier, on the site of the existing Victorian bandstand, at a cost of £14,500,[22] but nothing was done, and in February 1954 the proposal to rebuild the Western Bandstand at a cost of £13,000 was once more revived.[23] But the high cost and practical difficulties of this purely temporary scheme caused the Council in October to abandon it yet again,[24] and instead to call for new plans for an ambitious entertainments centre including a bandstand, to be built out over the beach at the bottom of West Street, at a cost of some £160,000.[25]

It now seems extraordinary that the Corporation planners should have been so strongly preoccupied with the idea of bandstands as necessary features of a seaside resort. No doubt they persisted in the mind as part of a vision of Edwardian gaiety, or of the rather stilted formal delights of the Kursaals of once fashionable Continental spas like Wiesbaden and Marienbad. It did not then appear that the ideas of modern holiday-makers were in the 1960s to undergo radical changes, in which military bands and bandstands no longer formed a part. Eventually notions of providing bandstands came to be abandoned when it became obvious that the municipality could no longer afford the high cost of hiring the bands to play in them.

After the war the craze for ice-skating, ice-hockey and spectacular ice-shows at S.S. Brighton which had begun in 1934 revived with even greater vigour than before. The first big ice-show to be presented there after the war was a more fast-moving, streamlined and sophisticated production than any of its predecessors. It was called *Hot Ice*, and filled the Stadium day after day, night after night for the whole summer season of 1945. The judo championships and basketball championships of Great Britain were also held at the Stadium, and the famous American basketball team, the Harlem Globetrotters, with their legendary player Goose Tatum, took the place by storm.

Apart from Sir Harry Preston's boxing matches held at the Dome before the war for charity, boxing was never very successful in Brighton and was not popular at S.S. Brighton. On the other hand, wrestling was phenomenally successful and continued there with a weekly show for over eight years. But always it was the great spectacular ice-shows that drew the greatest crowds to the Stadium. With the corps of beautifully dressed skaters moving with aerial grace across the ice in perfectly planned and timed evolutions, and the star performers darting about with astonishing speed and elegance, these shows had a fascination that no other kind of performance could surpass. Year after year through the 1950s the summer ice-carnivals and the Christmas ice-pantomimes were given to packed audiences. A new venture that was begun in 1955, an ice-circus, was not so successful, but the Tennis Circus, in which many of the world's leading professional players appeared, drew enormous crowds. Then the proprietor, Mr. Tom Arnold, sold out to new promoters, Mr. Nicholas Van

Slochem and Mr. Fred Taylor, who changed the name of the Sports Stadium to the Brighton Palladium, and presented there a series of concerts, at which some of the most popular artists of those times appeared— Shirley Bassey, Ted Heath, Lonnie Donegan, Cliff Richard, Jayne Mansfield, and the late George Melachrino with his string orchestra. Nevertheless even such stars as these failed to fill the hall, so ice-hockey was staged again and the place boomed once more. The building was no less thronged for the great political party conferences of the 1960s that were held there, when members of the Conservative Party, the Labour Party and of the Trade Union Congress sat on chairs upon a wooden floor that covered the ice, which had not been allowed to melt for over fifteen years—a circumstance that prompted various jokes about politicians with cold feet. But before long television had undermined the success of every kind of entertainment presented at the stadium, even of the great ice-spectacles, and in 1967 S.S. Brighton was demolished to make room for the new Top Rank Entertainments Centre. For over thirty years the building had been the centre for a unique phase in the history of pleasure, a monument of the taste in entertainment of its age.

In the years following the war the Corporation-owned Dome concert-hall became increasingly important as a centre for entertainment, conferences and meetings, under the management of Mr. H. F. Brazenor and later of Mr. Douglas Reeve. By the attainment of their fortieth anniversary in 1965 the Brighton Philharmonic Orchestra had successfully weathered a succession of financial crises with the aid of grants from Brighton Corporation and the Arts Council of Great Britain, and more recently with substantial help from Southern Television, Ltd. The Orchestra organized comprehensive programmes of concerts and recitals given by themselves and the principal other British and international orchestras and soloists. Where once the horses of the Prince Regent had been housed in palatial splendour was now heard the music also of the Vienna Boys' Choir, the Red Army Choir, the Dutch Air Force Band, and of the jazz orchestras of the 1950s and 1960s.

During these years the Council considered a large number of grand schemes for conference and entertainment centres, but far from being discouraged by the failure of them to be realized, they now turned their attention again to a grand scheme, first put forward in May 1954, for the improvement of the derelict sea-front site between West Street and the Grand Hotel by the erection of a mammoth conference and entertainment centre to cost no less than £1 million.[26] They now also reaffirmed their decision which they had made as long before as 1946, that this area should be developed by private enterprise.[27] The Council proposed that the buildings to be erected by private developers should provide not only music and entertainment of many different kinds for the pleasure of visitors, but all the facilities which the Council believed were so essential for visiting conferences, including large halls for meetings and exhibitions that could be converted to use for dances, concerts, receptions and banquets.[28]

The Council themselves were now becoming acutely aware of their financial difficulties. Brighton's annual municipal expenditure had doubled in the last nine years,[29] and Mr. Cohen had pointed out earlier that plans that were being prepared in the Borough Surveyor's office for various non-profit-making schemes already passed by various committees would, if carried out, involve an expenditure of over £2 million.[30] The cost of preparing the plans alone was enormous. The Council's ambitious new scheme for the West Street entertainment and conference centre was destined never to be achieved. Important developments under private enterprise that were already being contemplated at the Hotel Metropole were to make the Council's various schemes superfluous. During 1957 various proposals had been put forward that the Government should be persuaded to amend the betting and gaming laws in order that Brighton might become another Monte Carlo by the establishment of a casino, which it was believed would be a powerful attraction to foreign visitors.[31] Some three years earlier a great deal of amusing controversy had been wagered over a similar proposal to set up a casino in the Royal Pavilion, but the Council then rejected out of hand any idea of allowing roulette and baccarat in the Prince Regent's oriental palace.[32] However, the desire to have a casino at Brighton was achieved when, after the Government's revision of the gaming laws, gambling was permitted and in 1962 a casino was set up by private enterprise at the Hotel Metropole. At the same time the hotel was greatly enlarged and in a towering block behind was created a large conference centre with exhibition halls, and flats above.

In the fifteen years that followed the ending of the war the Corporation had exercised great imagination and foresight in the planning of much-needed amenities upon the sea-front for the pleasure of visitors and residents. Of all the many schemes submitted and discussed, many of them over and over again, only one project, a minor one, and that a failure—the Western Bathing Pavilion/Milk Bar—was achieved. Over and over again the Council were defeated by financial stringency, sometimes internal and domestic, sometimes imposed by the Government. Large sums of money could be made available only for vitally necessary (and always drastically scaled-down) developments in housing, education and social welfare. The Council were faced with one of the fundamental anomalies of civic planning in our time: that while massive developments were possible in the field of private enterprise—big new office buildings and blocks of flats were rising up everywhere—large sums of money could rarely be found for public developments in the realm of recreation and cultural activities. Perhaps it was as well that some of the ideas put forward were not put into effect;

perhaps some serious mistakes were avoided, but possibly also some valuable opportunities were lost in those years. Nevertheless with the approval by the Government of Brighton's Development Plan in June 1958 the *Herald* declared that Brighton had made a significant advance towards 'The City Beautiful of which visionaries like the late Sir Herbert Carden had dreamed'.[33] As part of the general approval given to the plan, official blessing was given to the building of the new Civic Centre and Town Hall, of a new regional College of Art, a new College of Technology, new Police Headquarters, Law Courts and other local government buildings. The years from the ending of the war had been a time of recovery, of imaginative speculation over the shaping of a new Brighton. The following decade of the 1960s was to see the realization of many new projects that would determine the appearance and character of the town for a century to come.

7 The Pavilion Restored

H.M. the Queen, then H.R.H. the Princess Elizabeth, visited the Pavilion in April 1951, and inspected the beginnings of the process of restoring the decorations of the King's Private Apartment. While passing through the unrestored rooms, then lacking any furniture, Princess Elizabeth inquired about the circumstances in which the original furniture of the rooms had been removed to Buckingham Palace and Windsor Castle. The return in 1956 and after of much of the original furniture to the building for which it had been designed would thus seem to have been the result of thoughts that passed through the mind of the Princess during this visit to the Pavilion.

The Third Regency Exhibition was held in 1951, the year of the Festival of Britain. The principal feature of the display in that year was the showing in the Banqueting Room of the magnificent silver-gilt dessert-service made by the goldsmith Paul Storr and other Regency craftsmen for Edward Lascelles, Earl of Harewood. It was lent by the Princess Royal and the present Lord Harewood. The King's Private Apartment, which had lost its original decoration and had only plain distempered walls and dark varnished woodwork, was now restored to its former state, with an exact reproduction of the original decoration painted by Roy Bradley, the gifted decorative artist of the Pavilion, with a Chinese design of dragons, stars, phoenixes and waves in white outline on a green background. The dark varnish of the doors, skirtings and mouldings was removed, revealing the original decoration in silvery grey-green, 'grained in imitation pollarded elm-wood', as the original accounts stated. During the course of the twenty years from 1948 onwards almost the whole of the Pavilion interior was restored by Mr. Roy Bradley, assisted by Mr. Derek Smith. Original decorations, such as those of the Music Room, were dramatically revealed in their former brilliance by the removal of heavy layers of dirt and time-darkened varnish. Where the originals had not survived, as in the Corridor, sombre Victorian replacements were removed and new decorations created in the spirit and exact colour of the originals. In certain rooms the sky-ceilings were re-created by Mr. Derek Rogers, Assistant Curator and himself a talented landscape painter. The Regency Exhibition of 1951 was the last of its kind organized in conjunction with the private committee known as 'The Regency Festival'. Henceforth the exhibitions were organized by the Royal Pavilion Committee of Brighton Corporation.

By 1949 public interest in the Royal Pavilion had developed to such an extent through the influence of Queen Mary and of writers on the period such as Osbert Sitwell, D. L. Murray, author of the novel *Regency*, Sir Roger Fulford, the biographer of George IV, and many others, and also because of the interest aroused by the Regency Exhibitions, that the time seemed appropriate to consider the future use of the building, and whether the priceless original decorations should continue to be damaged by functions of a kind that had too often been held in the building in the past. In October 1949 the Council had approved by a large majority a scheme submitted by the Royal Pavilion Committee by which the use of the State Apartments would be restricted to functions of an appropriate character, such as concerts, lectures, meetings, dinners, dances and receptions, in order to reduce the risk of future damage, and that for four months of the summer, June to September, the State and Private Apartments should not be available for ordinary lettings, but should be arranged with period furniture and works of art so as to present the building as a past Royal residence, restored as closely as possible to its appearance at the time of King George IV. There was in certain quarters considerable opposition to this scheme when put into practice, especially from those who had been accustomed to use the building for grossly inappropriate functions, and who had been accustomed to setting up bars in the State Apartments often at the cost of causing damage to the decorations and fittings by allowing barrels of beer and trestle tables to be rolled and carried through the rooms. In practice also conferences had an overriding claim on the use of all the rooms, and it was found difficult to make considered plans in advance for an extended period for the furnishing of the rooms during the summer. Nevertheless under these new powers that were granted by the Council the State and Private Apartments were furnished from June to September 1950, to celebrate the centenary of the purchase of the Royal Pavilion by the town, and in the summer of 1952 the first full-scale Regency Exhibition to be entirely organized by the Royal Pavilion Committee of Brighton Corporation was held, with H.R.H. the Princess Royal as Patron.

With this exhibition the augmented furnishing of the Royal Pavilion during the whole of July, August and September became an annual event, and for the rest of the year henceforth all the rooms of the building were to remain fully furnished, except for the Banqueting Room and Music Room, which continued, as they do still, to be used other than in the summer for civic entertaining and for important local social and cultural events.

The exhibition staged in 1954, opened by the Earl Spencer, was the grandest Regency Exhibition held up till then, and the seal of Royal approval was set upon the Committee's new policy by the loan from Buckingham Palace by H.M. the Queen, of a magnificent silver-gilt banqueting display consisting of articles by Regency craftsmen which had been bought by King George IV, and which had probably been used at the Pavilion in his time. There were also large groups of silver and gold plate lent by the Earl Spencer and the Marquess of Londonderry.

Before very long, however, the new policy was being fiercely attacked by those persons who had been accustomed to hold social functions of every sort to be held without restriction in the building, and assertions were also made that conferences were being kept out of the Pavilion.[1] Despite the enormous numbers of visitors who came to see the State Apartments restored and furnished, amounting then to some 200,000 persons a year, it was said that the Pavilion had been 'closed to the public' and the building was referred to in a derogatory fashion as having become 'a dead museum'. These ill-informed and inaccurate criticisms reached a climax early in 1955, when the policy of developing the Pavilion as a Regency exhibition again came before the Council.[2] With a certain absence of logic, the *Herald* announced the news that the exhibition period had been cut down from four to three months with the somewhat inconsequential headline 'Pavilion for the people', a question which had not arisen in the debate, and despite the fact that the number of persons who would use it as a conference hall would be much smaller than those who would have visited the building as an exhibition.

Nevertheless it was now clearly laid down that the State and Private Apartments should be used for a Regency Exhibition every year during July, August and September, and not be available for conferences at that time, and that during the rest of the year the Music Room and Banqueting Rooms only should be available for approved social and cultural events and conferences, the smaller State and Private Apartments remaining fully furnished throughout the year. The Royal Pavilion Committee now had a charter by means of which it became possible to embark upon a series of annual Regency exhibitions that has continued without interruption ever since, and for most of the Pavilion to remain fully furnished throughout the year. The following summer the Committee's exhibition policy received even greater approval and encouragement by an act of Royal generosity that was in fact the most significant event in the later history of the Pavilion. This was the return on permanent loan by H.M. the Queen of a large collection, numbering over a hundred articles, of the original furniture which had been removed to Buckingham Palace by Queen Victoria over a hundred years before.

Since 1945 a fairly large collection of Regency furniture had been built up, for the purpose of furnishing the rooms and enabling them to serve as a museum of furniture and works of art of the Regency period, but this magnificent addition enabled the interior of the Pavilion to be restored more accurately to its appearance in the days of Royal occupation than could otherwise be possible, and heightened immeasurably the significance of the building as a past Royal residence, as an embodiment of the taste and arts of the Regency period, and as a memorial of Royal greatness in the patronage of the arts. During several following years the Queen sent back many further pieces of original furniture, culminating in 1960 in the return from Windsor of the superb set of four pedestal candelabra which were made for the North Drawing Room in 1818. Each 7 feet high, the shafts are formed of hexagonal vases of Chinese porcelain and are crowned with branching candelabra of ormolu. After 112 years they were restored to their original places in the window-bay.

In July 1968 the summer Exhibition was officially opened by H.R.H. the Princess Margaret. It was the first occasion on which a Royal personage had performed this function and it was in this year that the Coronation robes of King George IV lent by Madame Tussaud's were exhibited for the first time since 1934. It was believed that the robes had been destroyed in the bombing of Madame Tussaud's establishment in London during the war, but they were dramatically rediscovered there in 1966 and lent to the Royal Pavilion. Up to the end of the Second World War the largest sum ever received from the admission of visitors was less than £300, and to cover the expenses of the building a large amount of money had to be provided from the town rates. By 1968 over £30,000 was being received from visitors, and the Pavilion was making a contribution of several thousands of pounds towards the rates.

Of all the varied occurrences that had taken place in the history of the Pavilion, up to recent times there was one type of incident that had never been experienced. This was a hoax, but the deficiency was remedied with complete success in the autumn of 1963. One morning in October the Director received a letter giving the address of a well-known London hotel from a person purporting to be the private secretary to an Arabian prince, stating that he wished to visit Brighton and would appreciate being shown over the Royal Pavilion. The Mayor had received a similar intimation, and the Director was requested by him to make the visitor welcome. The following morning at the appointed hour a large black Cadillac drew up at the portico of the Pavilion, and out of it stepped a tall lean figure in a black Arabian robe with white head-dress, who was introduced as Prince Emir Khalid ibn Abdul Asir ibn Saud, fourth son of King Saud of Arabia, by an African gentleman who was said to be the Prince's private secretary. A young Englishman introduced himself as representative of a travel agency which was arranging the Prince's visit. At an early stage of the tour of the rooms the Director had an uneasy suspicion that the 'Prince' was a student, and the affair a hoax, and he confided this belief to Professor Asa Briggs of the University of Sussex, who was also visiting the Pavilion together with Professor Hugh Trevor-Roper, who had been giving a lecture at the University. These suspicions aroused in the minds of everyone delighted recollections of the time when Duncan Grant, while an undergraduate at Oxford, had impersonated the Sultan of Zanzibar, and had reviewed the Home Fleet! The Director also confided his suspicions to one of the Pavilion attendants, who had served in the Middle East during the War, but this individual mentioned that he had given an Arabic greeting to the 'Prince', and had received without hesitation the correct reply in Arabic. Nevertheless, the Director's suspicions were not allayed; indeed, they were strangely confused by a remarkable circumstance. He noticed that the Prince's head-dress, of fine white cotton, had the words 'Made in England 30 yards' stamped faintly on the cloth, and yet the head-dress was made with the most exquisite drawn-thread hem-stitching. Quite clearly no one who could read English would have expended such delicate labour on the end of a roll of cloth. After dismissing the notion of inveigling the visitors on to the Pavilion roof and leaving them there for a while with the doors locked, the Director decided to take no more positive action than to refrain from presenting the usual volume of the history of the Royal Pavilion that was customarily given to important visitors. The tour of the rooms was hastened and tea was served in the Committee Room, where Professor Briggs and Professor Trevor-Roper were also present. The proceedings passed off in the slightly strained atmosphere that would have prevailed in the most genuine circumstances, and at length farewells were made and the party departed in their Cadillac. Later in the day the hoax was announced in the evening papers. The 'Prince' was Patrick Cook, a nineteen-year-old building-diploma student from the Brighton College of Technology. He had, in fact, spent three months in the Middle East studying buildings, and there had bought his robe and head-dress. His companions were two other building students. What might well have aroused the most serious suspicions of all was the fact that the 'Prince's' bearing was if anything too regal, having rather more dignified reserve than is usually affected by visiting foreign royalties. The Director's son did point out that one should not have been taken in by an Arabian prince who arrived in a Cadillac that was at least three years old.

However, it would have been a pity to have spoiled the perpetrators' fun when they had gone to such great trouble, and the history of the Royal Pavilion would not have been complete without an event of this kind once in a while. The Brighton *Evening Argus* felt that 'though Paddy's prank might aptly be named "Mr. Musgrave's Dance" one cannot help feeling discretion was the better part of valour in this case. . . . No, Mr. Musgrave did well to keep his dark thoughts to himself. To have acted might have been to risk a serious breach in diplomatic relations with Saudi Arabia. But 'ware the next foreign potentate who shows his nose inside the Royal Pavilion.'

As it happened, a genuine Middle Eastern personage with his *entourage* did visit the Pavilion a week or two later, but the Director found singular difficulty in arousing in himself any enthusiasm for the visit, and discovered he had a long-standing engagement in London on that day. He entrusted the duties of conducting the visitors to his deputy and learned afterwards that valuable presents had been given by the Royal personage to all who had rendered services to himself and his party.

8 Teddy-boys, Beatniks, Mods, Rockers and the Flower-Folk

An amusing minor phenomenon of life in Brighton during the early 1950s was the appearance of the 'Edwardians', or 'Teddy-boys', on the sea-front—groups of young men sporting their interpretation of the male costume of the days of Edward VII—black knee-length jackets with fobbed pockets and velvet collars, 'bootlace' ties, thin drainpipe trousers, fancy waistcoats and long hair curling over their ears and necks. Their dress was an exaggeration of trends that had already been observed in the clothes of men of the wealthier classes, in which there was a break-away from the wide trousers and short jackets of the previous two decades. Unfortunately there was a tendency for violence to occur when the Teddy-boys were attacked by youths who did not approve of their style of dress, or who resented their girl-friends being invited to dance with a courtly bow. There were several struggles and fights at local dance halls. A coach load of Edwardians from Southsea arrived in Brighton intent upon avenging a previous defeat, but they were encountered by a solid phalanx of police who prevented their admission to the dance hall and escorted them back to the railway station for the next train home.[1]

Some months later there was another outbreak of violence when a gang of Teddy-boys from London, armed with hooked cobblers' knives sharpened to a razor-edge, attacked local Edwardians who were sitting quietly drinking in a dance hall. In the resulting mêlée, in which chairs were thrown and tables knocked over, several bystanders were slashed with knives.[2] After this disturbance all youths wearing exaggerated forms of Edwardian dress were barred from the local dance halls,[3] and the outbreaks of violence ceased.

In the midst of the general anxieties over continuing inflation and the 'credit squeezes' of 1955 to 1957, Brighton people found some relief in the wild controversies that raged over the new frenzies that had descended upon the haunts of the young with the advent of 'Rock 'n' Roll' dancing, although the Archdeacon of Lewes, the Ven. J. M. L. Morrell, urged the Moral Welfare Association not to be too intolerant of these new manifestations, nor too easily shocked by the sins of the flesh, and he deplored the fact that young delinquents found a warmer welcome in the cinemas and dance halls than they did in the churches,[4] while Miss Helen Prior, the dedicated warden of Brighton Girls' Club over many years, urged a large audience at the Hotel Metropole not to condemn 'Rock 'n' Roll', which she declared was 'most infectious and attractive'.[5]

During the late 1950s the brash vulgar smartness of the 'Edwardians' gave place to a cultivated wretchedness of appearance among young people when there appeared on the beach and on the lower promenade between the piers groups of outlandish-looking folk dressed in ragged and dirty clothes, the men as well as the girls with long unkempt, unwashed hair, the two sexes often indistinguishable from each other. They sat aimlessly about on the beach in groups, seeming hardly to move all day long, occasionally listening to a guitar played by one of them, sometimes embracing, or talking in desultory fashion. At night they bedded down in sleeping-bags, still in groups, on the shingle when fine, but in wet weather taking shelter under the piers.

These were the beatniks, or as they quickly came to be called in Brighton, 'beachniks', disciples, usually at a very considerable remove, of the American 'beat' poets, Jack Kerouac and Allen Ginsberg of San Francisco, who had gained an enormous following for their ideas not only in America but in this country also. With its sunshine and beach and its nearness to London, Brighton seemed the only city in Britain able to offer delights comparable with those of the Californian coast. Although few of them had ever heard of their masters, those who had any awareness of the underlying philosophy of their cult would have said that they had contracted out of ordinary civilized life, believing that they owed no obligation to the community. They were in revolt against the materialistic values of the 'affluent society' of their day, against the ruthless commercial rat-race, and the conventions of bourgeois society. Their most admirable characteristic was their detestation of war and fear of destruction by the hydrogen bomb, towards which they believed we were rushing because of the stupidity and wickedness of the older generation. Many of the beatniks were supporters of 'C.N.D.', and brought discredit upon the majority of earnest and worthy young members of that admirable movement by their dirty appearance and questionable behaviour. Most of the accepted social values were rejected by them. They shared their money, their food and often sex in common. When money became necessary to buy food some of them would find employment of the lowest menial kind, such as washing-up in hotels. A few of them were artists of a sort, and offered their pictures for sale to passers-by on the sea-front. Despite their rejection of convention in any form, they usually dressed, men and girls alike, in what had been arrived at as the lowest form of dress—dirty and ragged blue jeans and the cheapest kind of drab ex-army coats. They were almost invariably dirty and verminous, and prone to catch and spread not only the once-common skin infections due to dirt which had almost been stamped out in modern society, but also the more loathsome contagious diseases, facts which caused the medical authorities the greatest anxiety. Many of them went barefoot, and they gloried in their dirt as a badge of their protest against society. They did not scorn the delights of sea-bathing, but when they indulged in this refreshment they rarely undressed, but went into the water fully clothed so as not to disturb the precious layer of sacred filth. Some were frankly good-for-nothing layabouts, but others were genuinely poor, ill-educated or psychologically maladjusted persons, ill fitted to take any ordinary job, and others were sons and daughters of comfortably-off or even wealthy parents, and had been to some of the best schools in the land, or had been to university, but had not completed their courses. Often their rebellion was merely the age-old passing intransigence of youth. They were especially prone to break away from families where a too formal or rigid code of social and moral behaviour had been insisted upon. Some of them were not whole-hearted devotees of the beatnik's philosophy, but joined up with them for a week or week-end or so for the fun of it, and for a new experience. But there were some whose lives seemed likely to be turned into tragedy by this way of life. In California it had been common for beatniks to get 'high', to rise out of the dreary monotony of ordinary life by taking drugs, especially mescalin and later 'L.S.D.' A number of the beatniks had their lives ruined through drug-taking, or by contracting venereal disease. The not uncommon spectacle of a young girl, ragged, dirty and barefoot, with tangled, lice-infested hair, who could have been beautiful, and whose pleasant voice proclaimed her gentle upbringing, but in whose face one seemed to detect a deep unhappiness, was a disturbing experience. Most of the more simple-minded beatniks were pitifully ill-educated and inarticulate, and would listen for hours entranced to the talk of the religious and political cranks and charlatans of every conceivable kind that infest the sea-front.

There was a distinction to be drawn between the true beatniks and the lazy young layabouts who came down to Brighton for a cheap Bank Holiday week-end, and especially between the former and the many decent young people without much money who wanted a holiday, and who hitch-hiked or biked their way down to Brighton with sleeping-bags and were prepared to sleep on pebbles under the pier.

The beachniks were for two or three seasons a source of some interest and amusement to certain visitors to Brighton, but they caused much annoyance to some of the residents and shopkeepers, especially those near the sea-front, and eventually the Corporation began to discourage the vagrants of whatever kind sheltering at night on the beach, by smoothing out the pebbles with a bulldozer or washing them down with hoses during the middle of the night. As the winter approached the temporary vaga-bonds, whether from the East End, Hampstead or Kensington, returned to their normal haunts, and most of the true hard-core beatniks joined an international corps of their fellows who settled at Tangier, or travelled to Nepal, a country that was not only close to the Himalayan heart of their philosophy but provided a society which permitted the use of drugs.

The next mass irruption of young people into the Brighton scene was accompanied by the screaming of scooters and the fierce roar of powerful motor-bikes, as the Mods and the Rockers, the two factions into which the kingdom of youth had now divided itself, descended upon Brighton at Whitsun 1964, and became involved in clashes amongst themselves and the police, the news of which was avidly seized upon by the sensational Press and by anti-youth moralizers of every kind. This first Brighton invasion followed a violent descent by Mods and Rockers upon Clacton-on-Sea at Easter 1964, when there were serious clashes of young people with the police following battles between the two factions, and much damage and destruction of property.

Who were the Mods and Rockers? The true Mods, like the genuine beatniks, formed only a small proportion of their later following. They began about 1960 as a small movement strictly confined to boys, with strong homosexual tendencies, worshipping clothes, which they changed several times a day, and were meticulously clean and smart in their appearance. To some extent they were a result of the 'affluent society' of 1957–62. The Mods had known nothing of wartime and postwar austerity, and made the first big challenge to girls as fashion-spenders and trend-setters. They rarely worked hard at steady jobs, but relied on the dole, on liberal allowances from indulgent parents, or on petty larceny and questionable dealing.[6]

The new moderate Mods, or mod-Mods as they might have been called, brought something of a breath of fresh air into the world of youth, especially with the introduction of the scooter, which quickly became one of the chief badges of membership. The motor-scooter had for some years been particularly favoured by young people generally for the independence it gave them, enabling them to stay out late at night when buses and trains had stopped, and to travel about at their own will not only in this country but in the nearer countries of Europe. Unlike the motor-bikes, the scooter was mechanically simple, its working parts covered in and therefore not likely to spoil the Mods' elegant clothing. Other aspects of the new Mod life, prompted by revolt against authority, especially that of parents, were the habit of sitting about in disc clubs and coffee bars, and staying up at 'All-night Raves'. The necessity for keeping awake at proceedings like these, and the desire for more exciting experiences, tempted some of the more foolish ones to take pep-pills. A minority of what might be called False Mods, who, unlike most of the others, belonged to the lower strata of young hooligans, became especially addicted, and under the influence of pills and drugs committed a number of acts of violence and crime, but the majority of the Mods were peace-loving and harmless, addicted only to their clothes, pop-music, dancing and to the liberty given them by the scooter. At best Mod culture was a decorative veneer on the ordinary life of young people.

The Rockers were a completely different faction, who came into being partly as a result of the activities of the false Mods, or criminal fringe of the movement. Rockers were young men strongly prone to violence, suffering feelings of inferiority over their masculinity, the descendants of the Teddy-boys of the 1950s who had carried flick-knives and who rioted in cinemas. They rode huge and powerful motor-bikes and wore high black ex-Air Force boots, and black leather jackets ornamented with brass studs forming their owner's names, and phrases like 'Hell's Angels', or symbols like a skull and crossbones. Unlike the Mods, the Rockers rarely used their vastly more powerful machines for long journeys, or for travel abroad, but chiefly for short high-speed trips on arterial roads, their ambition being to 'do the ton', or 100 miles an hour.

The Rockers were mostly neurotic, crude and violent, less intelligent than the Mods and had benefited less from education. Consequently they hated the Mods, whom they regarded as cissies, and attacked them whenever they met, which was usually on Bank Holiday week-ends at seaside resorts.

After battles at Easter in 1964 between Mods and Rockers at Clacton and Hastings, the Brighton police organized measures to deal with such occurences that might take place at Brighton.[7] On Whit Sunday the Rockers arrived first at Brighton and were in possession of the sea-front when the Mods descended on the town riding their scooters in swarms, like lemmings on their insane migratory rush to the sea. 'Down with the Rockers,' shouted the Mods, and battles began between small groups of youths. Stones and various missiles were thrown, but the police moved in quickly, made a number of arrests, and broke up the crowds of young people. Minor disturbances went on all day, and at one time a gang of six Rockers marched down North Street crying, 'We want blood.' The following day fighting broke out again round the Aquarium, where the Mods, who greatly outnumbered the Rockers, drove them off the promenade under a shower of deck-chairs and litter baskets. More arrests were made and the groups of young people were moved on by the police and shepherded away from the front. It was reported that a crowd of some 3,000 watched the battles,[8] and the police appealed in vain with their loud-speakers for the spectators to go away.[9]

Several hundred pounds' worth of damage was done on the sea-front and a number of people were injured. On the other hand, it was stated by some persons that the number of serious incidents was extremely small in relation to the huge influx of young people, that the police were in an extremely apprehensive state and needlessly rigorous in moving on those who were doing no harm, and even that a certain press photographer paid some Mods and Rockers to stage a struggle to provide the picture of teen-age violence that he was otherwise unable to obtain. At the end of the day hundreds of scooters and motor-bikes swarmed out of Brighton, and crowds of hitch-hikers stretched along the roads to London for a distance of twenty miles out of Brighton, many of them causing danger to motorists and themselves by ambling about over the roadway.[10]

Of the young people who had been arrested, twenty-six came before the courts the following morning, and some stern sentences were passed on the offenders. Two youths, of eighteen and nineteen, were sent to prison for three months. Most of the charges were for carrying offensive weapons such as chains, lengths of piping, bottles, knives and stones; for assaulting the police, and for obstruction and insulting behaviour. Nine youths were sentenced to three months in a detention centre, one of them having 'admitted to insulting behaviour, but who was not proved guilty of even the mildest violence'.[11]

The incidents provoked indignant reactions from older people against the teenagers, who were referred to by one prominent townsman rather incomprehensibly as 'sawdust caesars'. Questions were asked in Parliament; the inevitable suggestion that the cat-o'-nine-tails should be used was made, together with another proposal, which was very properly rejected, that a corps of vigilantes should be formed to deal with any future trouble. The police were congratulated on having dealt admirably with the situation, and indeed their handling of the problem had been so skilful that no further attempts were made by Mods and Rockers to choose Brighton as a battle-ground. In fact, the Brighton riots were the death-knell of the Mod movement. The nucleus of true Mods were bewildered by the explosion of their world, and the mod-Mods felt somewhat shamefaced. After that episode everything seemed an anticlimax. The Mod outlook and Mod fashions, dancing, music and records had by now become part of the accepted pattern of teenage life. A practical and imaginative solution to the problem of those decent and inoffensive but non-affluent teenagers who would once have spent the night in sleeping-bags under the piers or on the beach was provided by a young student at the Municipal College of Education, Dan Elwyn Jones, who arranged for some church and school halls to be used as shelters for young holiday-makers at week-ends, where they could spend the night on camp-beds in their own sleeping-bags and cook their own meals. This type of accommodation and the element of organized community life provided by this scheme were highly approved by the teenagers, who disliked sleeping rough on the beach and at the same time would have regarded a room in a boarding-house or hotel as stuffy, conventional and beyond their means. Naturally there were opponents to the scheme amongst the less tolerant older people of the town, who imagined that an undesirable type of visitor was being attracted to Brighton, and there were inevitably a few hooligans who created a little trouble, and one or two drug pedlars who tried to make money out of the clientèle that was so conveniently presented to them, but these undesirable individuals were quickly dealt with.

For the August Bank Holiday week-end of 1967 six church halls were open as shelters, and the scheme provided a successful and constructive solution to the non-affluent teenage week-ender. Also associated with the scheme was the Brighton Archway Venture, organized by Dr. Josephine Klein, a lecturer in sociology at the University of Sussex. In one of the sea-front arches, No. 167, which had been leased to the organization by the Corporation, Dr. Klein and some volunteers ran a social and information centre where young people would rest, meet and drink coffee, but these activities created objections from the sea-front traders who claimed that their customers were driven away by the undesirable youngsters. A local newspaper's account of these difficulties was headed 'Arch-angel Jo under fire'.[12]

The spring of 1967 brought more than the usual lavish display of wall-flowers, daffodils, tulips and crocuses to the parks and gardens of Brighton. The beach and sea-front also burst into blossom, with the gay dresses of the Flower Children, or 'Hippies', members of the latest youth cult, who like others before them had gravitated to Brighton as a lotus-eaters' paradise.

Although scorning the dirt and squalor of the beatniks, as the Mods had done earlier, the Flower Children developed from a movement in San Francisco in which the by now middle-aged Allen Ginsberg, who had been high priest of the beatniks, was again a leader. By a curious dialectical process of the emergence of opposites, the beatnik dirt and squalor were now transformed into an exotic beauty and gaiety of dress, for the design and colouring of which inspiration was sought in oriental dress styles, and especially in the colour and design of Tibetan art, which was supposed to have been produced on a higher level of consciousness than ordinary design. Men as well as girls wore long hair and long necklaces, while an essential article of equipment, proclaiming their esoteric philosophy, was a little brass bell worn round the neck. One Brighton jeweller sold 4,000 of these brass bells to the Hippies in one week, and flew to Bombay to obtain more.

The most astonishing reversal of values was the Flower Children's complete rejection of violence. 'Make Love, Not War' was one of their slogans, and 'If anyone attacks you, give him a flower' was another. 'Love and Beauty' were the keynotes of their philosophy, filled out with some bogus oriental mysticism. Apart from their hysterical protestations over the innocuousness of the soft drugs to which some of their members were addicted the Flower Children did little harm; they added a decorative brightness of colour to the scene, their pacifist philosophy was commendable, and they possessed a sense of the enjoyment of life and a determination not to be diverted from it by the pursuit of social and financial values. Like the Mods and many other sections of youth, however, they were vulnerable to commercial exploitation by drug-pushers, and by the promoters of dubious journalistic, film and theatrical enterprises. Completely lacking in intellectual fibre, they were incapable of taking a positive part in shaping the world that they were to inherit.

Towards the end of 1967 the Archway Venture was causing fresh anxiety to the authorities. The comforts offered at the reception centre in one of the sea-front arches, and the facilities for sleeping provided in church halls and school buildings seemed now to be exploited by hooligans, 'drop-outs' and wasters of the worst kind, and bitter protests were made to the Council by the owners of the small shops on the lower promenade. Archway 167 was described as a 'cesspool of iniquity' and a correspondent to the local paper stated that persons frequenting the arch even engaged in public in the act of making love.[13]

The Archway Venture was undoubtedly an extremely admirable and valuable enterprise, not only in providing cheap accommodation for poor young people visiting Brighton, but also in giving opportunities for the group of sociologists of the University of Sussex under Professor Klein to study the motivation and behaviour of those young people who appear to drift into becoming beatniks or Flower People and who generally wish to opt out of conventional society, and to carry out reclamation work amongst those who had lost all will and ability to lead a happy and useful life. The importance of this work was indicated by the fact that the Department of Education and Science was contributing £15,000 a year towards Professor Klein's activities. Many correspondents to the local papers declared that reports about the inhabitants of the archway were greatly exaggerated and that Arch 167 was 'bright, clean and cheerful'.[14]

The Corporation eventually refused to renew the lease of the arch, although as the Chairman of the Beach Committee admitted, there had been no complaints about the centre for some time, and the centre was closed down at the end of 1968.[15] The traditional haunts of fried fish and chips, of whelks, cockles and mussels, were invaded by culture when another arch, No. 185, became in 1968 a centre of the arts, where recitals were given by the poets John Pudney, John Ward, Lee Harwood, Elaine Fenston and Gerald Gardner, and concerts of Asiatic music were given by the David Pendlebury Ensemble.

9 The University of Sussex and Student Life

Despite Brighton's admirable record in pioneering many different movements in the arts, education, religion, medicine, engineering and other fields, the notion of Brighton as a powerhouse of intellectual force was at one time hardly one that occurred immediately to the imagination. Nevertheless the extreme beauty of Brighton's buildings, seashore and countryside; its intoxicating air and the changing lights of sea and sky; its glorious days of spring, autumn and even of winter weather, can stimulate more than the sense of pleasure. They can create an atmosphere of mental excitement favourable to new developments of thought and knowledge. The domination of the town by mere wealth and fashion was over with the coming of the railway. Increasingly from then onwards the town became open to fresh advances in mind and culture.

It must have been clear even in the earlier years of this century when the idea of a University of Sussex was first put forward that the town of Brighton with its libraries and museums, its art gallery and exhibitions, its historic theatre, and its independent symphony orchestra, was not unfitted to be the centre for a great university, and that with the development of its work important new spheres of human advancement would be created in the town. The spirit of intellectual excitement which it is believed is an important element in the chemistry of Brighton must therefore have reached a highly volatile point in the mind of Mr. William Stone, Brighton's Director of Education, when in 1956 he conceived the idea of reviving earlier proposals to establish a university in the town.

The idea of founding a university college in the town had first been put forward at a meeting in the Royal Pavilion on 12th December 1911, and nearly £3,000 was then raised towards this object, but the Great War and the depression of the 1930s caused the scheme to be abandoned, the accumulated funds being applied to the purchase of books for the Brighton Technical College, which was then providing courses for degrees in the arts and sciences. The idea that the Technical College should become a college of London University was again put forward in 1944 by Mr. E. J. Hutchins, Headmaster of Varndean School, in an address to the Fabian Society, and when Stanmer Park was acquired by the town in 1947 it was contemplated that the land would provide an admirable site for a university. From 1953 onwards[1] the idea was being freely discussed, and although at the end of 1954, because of the financial stringency existing at the time, the prospect of the establishment of a new university institution in Sussex or indeed elsewhere in the country within the next twenty-five years 'seemed extremely remote',[2] some six months later Mr. Stone declared that his personal hopes of a University of Sussex had never been dimmed.[3]

Mr. Stone organized a series of lectures which were held in the Royal Pavilion under the auspices of the Brighton Education Committee, and given by a number of the most distinguished persons in the academic world, on the theme inspired by J. H. Newman's famous volume *The Idea of a University*. It must be admitted that the prospects for the success of the proposal at first were not wholly propitious. Two schemes for some developments of an entirely different kind in Brighton were very prominently before the townspeople at this time, one for a casino to be established in the Royal Pavilion, another for a gigantic amusement park to be set up in a valley near Roedean School. Margaret Musgrave remarked: 'It is obviously only necessary to have a fun-fair on the Downs and a casino in the Pavilion for Brighton to become the ideal university city!' Fortunately the fun-fair came to nothing, and when a casino was eventually established it was at the Hotel Metropole, a place more obviously appropriate for such a purpose, with its traditions of slightly raffish high life. Curiously enough, the Royal Pavilion would not have been as suitable for a casino as its disreputable associations might have suggested, for King George IV in his own words was 'not a gambling man'.

In February 1956 Mr. Stone submitted to the Education Committee a memorandum on the proposal to establish a university in Brighton. This was adopted by the Council as the basis for a scheme to be presented to the Government, whose approval was given in June 1958.[4] A 'gesture of faith' in the university project had been made in 1958 when Mrs. Helena Normanton—who had already brought distinction to her native town of Brighton by becoming the first woman lawyer to be called to the Bar, and one of the first two women barristers to take silk—gave £20 towards the university funds. At her death in October 1957 it was revealed that Mrs. Normanton had left the sum of over £20,000 towards the establishment of the proposed university. A year later, in 1959, the University College of Sussex came into being, with Mr. John Scott Fulton, one-time Fellow of Balliol, Principal of the University College of Swansea and Vice-Chancellor of the University of Wales, as the first Principal. In 1963 the Royal Charter was granted by which the university college was advanced to the status of the University of Sussex, and the first Congregation for the Installation of the Chancellor took place in June of that year at the Dome, when the Viscount Monckton of Brenchley was installed. The representative of Universities throughout the world dressed in their colourful academic dress formed an impressive spectacle, as they marched in procession, and symbolized the union of the University of Sussex with the ancient traditions of learning that had been established in Europe in the Middle Ages. The new University of Sussex was fortunate in being the first of the seven new institutions of this kind that were established in this country in recent times, for it thus became possible to secure the services of some of the most brilliant academic personalities in Britain to form the nucleus of the tutorial staff. Professors Asa Briggs, David Daiches, J. P. Corbett and Martin Wright formed a group who established the highly individual character which the University of Sussex possessed from its beginnings, and which captured the imagination of the Press and other writers and thinkers, and of those concerned with these new institutions that were to shape the world of the future. A new approach was developed to the planning of courses with the object of creating amongst the undergraduates a broad cultural awareness as a necessary basis for their subsequent specialization, and by means of the different schools of international studies—European, American and Afro-Asian—to promote a universality of outlook. Fresh thought was given as well to the breaking-down of the barriers between the arts and sciences and to increasing the emphasis upon liberal values in the study of science.

The University began its work with fifty undergraduates working in three early Victorian houses at Preston, but new university buildings were already being erected in Stanmer Park, to the design of Sir Basil Spence, and in October 1962 the first building came into use. Falmer House, which remains the central and principal building of the completed University complex, is square in plan, constructed round a large central courtyard, and built of pinkish-red bricks; prefabricated concrete arches forming the roof and the vaulted ceilings of all the upper rooms. An important feature of the building is the staircase tower, its walls not only faced but also lined internally with squared flints in traditional Sussex fashion. At night the building becomes especially delightful, the lights in the different rooms as seen across the quadrangle bringing to life the brilliant colours of the window hangings and seat cushions against the background of light pine woodwork of interior walls and staircases. The dining-hall is a vast room, rising up through two storeys to an immense barrel-vaulted roof lined with wood. A great abstract mural painting by the Sussex artist Ivon Hitchens decorates one of the huge expanses of brick walling.

The beautiful surroundings of the park, which had been picturesquely landscaped in the eighteenth century, if not by 'Capability' Brown himself, then by some pupil, disciple or rival, caused Sussex to be one of the most fortunately sited universities on the whole country, and every possible advantage was taken of the opportunities for enjoying the beautiful views and vistas that were presented by the landscape of the park with its natural and informal but none the less carefully contrived grouping of trees and sculpturing of the gentle grassy downland slopes. In arranging the great complex of buildings that grew up around Falmer House hardly a tree was disturbed. Even the physical location of the University seemed to symbolize its individual character. Unlike some other universities, free of the domination of a cathedral city, and midway between the medieval country town of Lewes and the glittering, sophisticated modern resort of Brighton, the setting of the University of Sussex seemed to favour independence of thought. Its only visible link with the past is Stanmer House itself, from which it is separated by a fold of the Downs, half a mile of distance and two centuries of time, but which the University leased from Brighton Corporation to serve for a time as administrative headquarters and as a social centre. The fabric had been preserved by the Corporation when the building was purchased together with the rest of the estate from the Chichester family, and now with the aid of the Corporation and of the Pilgrim Trust the University restored the principal rooms as closely as possible to the style of the different periods of the eighteenth century in which they were formed.

The seal of royal approval was set on all these endeavours by the visit of the Queen in the following year, and of Prince Philip, Duke of Edinburgh, in the next. The Principal was knighted in 1964, and was awarded a Life Peerage as Lord Fulton of Stanmer two years later. At an early stage the University began to equip itself with the outward trappings of tradition, by obtaining a grant of arms from the College of Heralds, and by commissioning the talented modern silversmith Gerald Benney to make a ceremonial mace of silver-gilt. The undergraduates, however, were more scornful of traditional values, and refused to wear gowns on ordinary occasions. On his retirement in 1967 Lord Fulton was succeeded as Vice-Chancellor by Professor Asa Briggs.

At an early stage in the development of the University, the first Chairman of the University Council, Alderman S. M. Caffyn, C.B.E., of Eastbourne, had most generously offered to present a new Church of England chapel building to the University, but this proposal was vehemently rejected by a number of the undergraduates and academic staff, on the grounds that the existence of such a sectarian building would be an affront to the independent outlook of the University. The prospect also arose of chapels for Roman Catholics, the Free Churches and other faiths being erected around the University buildings. The vexing problem was solved by a happy inspiration on the part of Lady Fulton, who suggested that the chapel should not be a sectarian building, but a meeting house which could be used for services of all denominations, and even for a non-religious meeting or concerts. The meeting-house project was by no means yet assured of an easy passage. Sir Basil Spence produced a design for a circular building, with a semicircular tower and a conical roof with a ventilating hood of a design inspired by the roofs of Kentish oast-houses. On being submitted to the Brighton Corporation for approval, the scheme was rejected by the Planning Committee on the grounds of the unsuitability of the design, especially of the roof, which was described by one member as 'a cut-down oast-house'. This decision, one of the very few ever made by the Planning Committee involving the rejection of a major scheme by a reputable architect, aroused intense anger, not only in University circles, but amongst many other people, as coming ill from a Committee which had passed many highly objectionable designs without quibble, particularly for several prominent modern buildings in Brighton. The design was modified chiefly in order to simplify the character of the roof, and was eventually approved. As finally built, the Meeting House is of great charm, sited in a glade of trees between Falmer House and the Physics Building. It is circular in plan, with pink brick walls honeycombed with openings to give an exciting cellular construction. The shallow conical roof with its lop-sided 'oast-house' capping is still regarded by some critics as an unhappily whimsical feature, contrary to the values of intellectual honesty for which it is believed a university should stand, especially as in any event oast-houses are not characteristic of that part of Sussex around Brighton. If not strictly functional, however, the asymmetrical capping supplies a note of informality to the exterior. Some little while later a design by Sir Basil Spence for a new Sports Pavilion costing £71,500 was submitted to the Planning Committee, and this was again rejected because of the appearance of the building. It was discovered, however, later in the day that the Planning Committee had already given full planning permission for this scheme eight months earlier.

One of the most exciting and imaginative of all the University buildings is the Arts Centre, upon which work began in October 1967. Financed by the Gulbenkian Foundation and by the late Dr. Lytton Gardner, after whom the centre has been named, the centre was designed by Sir Basil Spence's firm of Spence, Bonnington and Collins, as a complex of circular elements. A large circular theatre, seating 600 people, is surrounded by smaller circular units housing a foyer, studios and workshops for rehearsals, for the visual arts and for music. These different sections are connected with each other by catwalks, so that no one aspect of art shall be cut off from another. The Director of the Arts Centre, Dr. Walter Eysselinck, a drama producer and playwright, had already organized an enterprising series of dramatic presentations and exhibitions in connection with the University, and intended to develop the University's policy of encouraging young and progressive painters, sculptors, potters, musicians and other artists to make residental visits to the University so that the undergraduates and staff might watch them at their work and discuss it fully with them.

The impact of the new intellectual power-house upon the life of the gay and frivolous town of Brighton was complex and interesting. The boarding-houses and smaller hotels of the town were filled with students in term-time, which conveniently coincided with the off season, and the rooms of Brighton landladies resounded to arguments on existentialism, Trotskyism, racial problems, the theology of Teilhard de Chardin and the taking of L.S.D. The University was a godsend to the less serious sections of the Press. Every manifestation in the district of an interest in sexual freedom, religious disbelief, political intransigence and drug-taking was attributed to the influence of the University. The compilation of a survey by a member of the academic staff, of ideas of sex, morals and beliefs amongst modern young people, was immediately seized upon by one of the national weekly papers as evidence that the University of Sussex was a 'den of iniquity—a place of drugs and debauchery, sin and sensuality'. Intense anger was aroused in some quarters by the use of the phrase 'the wise non-virgins' of Sussex University, in relation to those girl students who obtained advice on contraception. The Minister of Education was urged by several M.P.s to set up an official inquiry into alleged 'moral laxity' at Sussex, but this demand was most sensibly rejected, and the charges were indignantly refuted by the new Chancellor of the University, Lord Shaw-cross. In some quarters it was firmly believed that it was chiefly due to the carefully planned political activities of the left-wing University students and staff that in the General Election of 1964 a Conservative majority of 5,746 at the previous election in the Kemp Town division was converted into a victory for the Labour candidate, Mr. Dennis Hobden, by seven votes after four recounts, and that in the election of 1966 the same candidate was returned with a majority of 831 over his Conservative opponent. To entertain this suggestion, however, would be to do less than justice to the activities at that time of the Brighton Labour Party and their supporters as a whole.

The sound academic work performed by the students in the early years of the University was shown by the fact that in 1967, 393 students graduated and of those who sat only three failed to get their degrees. A number of highly commendable non-academic activities of the students received little or no attention from the national Press, owing no doubt to their unsensational nature. It was left to the local Press to describe the admirable work carried out by undergraduates in their voluntary decorating scheme by which the homes of old-age pensioners and needy families were decorated for them, and in their work for the Moulsecoomb Adventure Playground in which the undergraduates joined with students of the Municipal College of Education, the Technical College and other local colleges. This came into being from the discovery that the children of that district had nowhere to play. In the laying-out during the 1930s of what was then regarded as one of the finest municipal housing estates in the country little attention had been given to the recreational and cultural needs of the community. The Adventure Playground was a piece of waste land where large concrete water-pipes, tree-trunks and other objects were placed for children to scramble over, and they were encouraged to build their own climbing frames and play-huts with timber given by well-wishers. The playground was naturally condemned by many adults of the neighbourhood as a hotbed of juvenile delinquency, and some local householders did not scruple to tear down the play-huts and to steal the timber to build their own potting-sheds and chicken-houses. The Corporation eventually took an interest in the scheme, and a permanent warden was appointed. The playground became important as a place where students could meet and talk with the children and offer them positive friendship, leadership and happiness. Play-groups meeting in local halls to stimulate creative activities such as painting and woodwork among the children developed out of the scheme, and eventually a group was formed to include the children's mothers and to draw them into various schemes to benefit the children, by means of which some of them were given holidays at the Burwash Place Children's Pursuits Centre. It was the first holiday that many of them had ever had.

After the last war there were remarkable advances in all fields of education in Brighton, not only through the establishment of the University, but with important developments in other institutions. The Municipal Teacher's Training College, which enjoyed a reputation for excellence all over Britain, evolved into a College of Education in a vast new building set amidst the woods and green slopes of Falmer, on the outskirts of Brighton. It was designed by the Borough Architect, Mr. Percy Billington, the designer of Brighton's large postwar schools and other public buildings. Confronting the University in a somewhat challenging manner across the Lewes Road, the new College is able to offer mind-enlivening contacts between two important groups of students.

The Brighton School of Art and Crafts became a regional College of Art, and its original Victorian building in Grand Parade was demolished and replaced between 1965 and 1968 by an immense modern building. When the question of who should design the new College was being considered the name of the great French architect Le Corbusier was suggested by the Dean of Chichester, the Very Rev. Walter Hussey, who believed that the creator of the famous 'Unité de l'habitation' at Marseilles, and of the revolutionary new church at Ronchamp, probably the most original as well as the most controversial figure in world architecture, was the man to produce a unique and imaginative design that would place Brighton in the forefront of modern architecture and bring visitors to the town from all over the world. The suggestion was, however, turned down by the authorities, and the final designs were prepared by Mr. Billington with the firm of Messrs. R. H. Matthew and S. A. W. Johnson-Marshall as consultants.

The main portion of the new College was opened in June 1967. It is one of the most attractive modern buildings in Brighton, the main façade on Grand Parade taking the gentle concave curve of the street, while the fenestration has been carefully planned to form an agreeable transition from the Georgian bow-fronted houses adjoining.

The Brighton Technical College, again one of the most famous institutions of its kind in the country, expanded and split into two, the section for more advanced studies becoming the College of Technology, housed in a gigantic long, high and narrow modern building, set end-on to the line of the Lewes Road at Moulsecoomb in order to reduce the amount of traffic-noise reaching the study-rooms and laboratories. Again the designs were prepared by Mr. Billington, with the firm of Matthew and Johnson-Marshall as consultant architects.

In the light of these developments, the idea of a Brighton whose significance is primarily that of a pleasure city, even though heightened by historical associations and a rich architectural setting, and enriched by fine cultural institutions, is one that needs to be brought into line with new conceptions of Brighton as a city combining the qualities of a pleasure resort with aesthetic and intellectual values—a new Geneva, perhaps. Apart from official institutions, a very great number of private tutorial establishments had also grown up in the town, many of them providing for foreign students from all parts of the world, especially from the Near and Middle East, Africa, India, Pakistan and the Far East. By 1967 the student population of Brighton had grown to be the largest in England apart from the large university towns of Oxford, Cambridge, Manchester and Birmingham, with some 7,000 students in the town undergoing higher educational studies, of whom over 3,000 were attending the University, and nearly 4,000 the two Technical Colleges, the College of Art, the College of Education and other municipal institutions.

10 Brighton Transformed

From time to time in the development of cities comes the need for a change of scale in the buildings, to meet the needs of increasing populations. When John Nash's 'Metropolitan Improvements' of 1812–30 were completed in London, Carlton House was overshadowed by the new buildings of Carlton House Terrace and Pall Mall, but in their turn Nash's Regent Street gave place in 1922 to buildings on a vast new scale, although incomparably poorer in aesthetic merit. Could we see Nash's Regent Street today it would appear to our modern eyes to be ludicrously small in scale. One may still see a sample of its size and character in the domed corner buildings of Victoria Square, London. Now, in its turn, the new Regent Street is to give place to a development of even greater scale, and no doubt of even less pleasing character.

Brighton's first change in scale took place in the great building boom of 1815–26, when the early traditional houses of 1770–1805 gave place to the imposing new houses, streets, squares, terraces and crescents of Busby and the Wilds. For nearly 150 years the centre of Brighton has been spared any vast new development. Expansion in Victorian and modern times was mostly effected by building on the outer fringes of the town, where land was cheaper than in the centre. The growth of population and of business and other activities since the last war have been forcing upon Brighton the need for another great change of scale. Sites occupied by small private houses in the centre of the town, although possibly used for offices for many years, now have immense commercial value. How is the challenge of these modern demands to be met by the lovers and custodians of Brighton's heritage of late Georgian architecture, to which the town owes so much of its fame and its appeal for visitors from all over the world?

The first challenge to the Georgian architecture of Brighton was made in 1935 with the erection of the Embassy Court apartment building in the brutal, monolithic concrete manner of the time. Marine Gate at Black Rock, another white concrete block of flats, was built in a slightly more elegant modern style that conflicted in no way with the Georgian architecture, for it was built beyond Kemp Town on the cliffs towards Rottingdean. During the 1930s also most of the large new buildings, such as the Alliance Building Society's offices in North Street, the Odeon Cinema and some large office blocks in West Street, were not near enough to any of the Georgian buildings to overwhelm them with their greater height and bulk.

446

After the war new building was not possible for several years, because of scarce supplies, but when restrictions were removed widespread demolition of old buildings began, especially in parts of the town that had been scarred by wartime bombing. In the Edward Street and Carlton Hill district the Corporation continued its admirable programme of slum-clearance begun before the war, and some excellent blocks of flats and offices, a new Police Station, Law Courts and an intriguing Spiritualist Church have been built in this area where they do not conflict with the character of Georgian Brighton. The dark masses of certain towering blocks of flats and offices built east of the Steine, however, appear as an ugly backdrop to the view of the Royal Pavilion looking eastward from the Pavilion's western lawn, to some extent mutilating its enchanting oriental skyline.

With the sweeping away of old property beyond West Street, the nature of the threat to the harmony of Brighton's sea-front architecture began to be apparent. As many as sixteen different schemes for building on a colossal scale in this part of Brighton were suggested, especially for the building of an immense group of conference and entertainment buildings on the western side of West Street down to the sea-front.

For years in the late 1950s and early 1960s the enormous area beyond West Street, between Western Road and the sea-front, in which many buildings had been removed by bombing and demolition, lay waste, empty and derelict. Rebuilding on these sites was long delayed because of the many changes of ownership that took place amongst different developers.

It was widely feared that the Georgian buildings of Brighton would in a few years' time be completely overwhelmed by enormous new buildings. In order to allay public anxiety over future building, Sir Hugh Casson was called in by the Corporation in 1960 to advise them on the future planning of the centre of Brighton and the sea-front, and to recommend a choice amongst the many schemes put forward. The Borough Surveyor had already laid down certain planning principles which should be followed, providing amongst other things that there should be no major disturbance to the Regency façade from Black Rock to the Aquarium; high buildings should be permitted between the Palace Pier and West Pier, but the height should diminish westwards to merge with Brunswick Terrace, and any high buildings should not be sited immediately upon the sea-front.

Sir Hugh considered that the 'subtopian mess of lamp-standards and road signs' at the Aquarium roundabout, where the visitor receives his first dramatic glimpse of the sea, should be cleaned up and the site re-planned to make 'a setting—strong, clean and simple—worthy of the occasion'. The Lanes area he regarded as 'Brighton's Kasbah', where the heart of the old town was preserved and was still bursting with vitality. Vehicles should be kept away, and arcades and pedestrian shopping lanes

447

should be developed. Sir Hugh also recommended that sea-front buildings should not exceed 160 feet in height, that taller blocks, where possible placed in groups, could be permitted behind the sea-front buildings and climbing up the steep slopes north of the front. Sir Hugh emphasized the point that many of the existing buildings in the western part of Brighton were 'of considerable charm and quality' and he went on specifically to say: 'The area round Russell Square and Grenville Place needs particularly sensitive handling, and St. Paul's Church—one of the finest of its period in the country—should not be ignored, but be properly integrated into the new plan.' It was not long before Grenville Place had been completely demolished, although some of the charming black and white cobble-fronted houses were in good condition, having been lovingly repaired and maintained by their modern tenants. Also swept away at the same time were the equally delightful but more decayed houses with columnar porches north of Clarence Square, to make space for the enormous development between Cannon Place and West Street.

Two buildings that were erected at the western end of the sea-front aroused the strongest criticism, including a protest from the Regency Society in their Annual Report for 1966. The first of these was Cavendish House, a fifteen-storey block of flats which was built on the site of the Union Club in King's Road, a bow-fronted Regency building. The Society objected to the use of black bricks for the walls, which they regarded as 'a lamentable development in the case of large modern buildings'. Similar bricks were used in the new block of flats on the sea-front at Rottingdean, and it was felt that the Planning Committee should not allow large new buildings 'to be faced with this ugly material'. The use of unsuitable materials indeed constitutes almost as great a threat to the beauty and harmony of new buildings in Brighton as bad design. White cement, stucco or light yellow stock-bricks have shown themselves in the past to be the ideal materials for the most pleasing effect on a sunlit sea-front, and even to give the most telling impression in cloudy weather. The dull black bricks complained of are quite unlike the black glazed bricks or 'mathematical tiles' used in Regency Brighton, for these give brilliant reflections of the light of the sky. The modern bricks seem to give a particularly sordid impression, especially when, as often happens, they become discoloured by the efflorescence of salts drying out from the bricks, or deposited by the sea-winds. Variegated rustic bricks, which unfortunately have been used on several modern buildings in Brighton, are as out of place in this sophisticated town as are the blatant red bricks and terracotta of Victorian times, and will, with dull black bricks, be regarded with as much disfavour in years to come as are the former today. Another deplorable effect is due to the rusting of iron window frames and the corrosion of bronze fittings, causing the staining of concrete walls, as may be seen at Embassy Court,

THE ROYAL PAVILION:
the east front

THE ROYAL PAVILION:
the Banqueting Room, 1866

THE ROYAL PAVILION:
the Music Room, 1966

THE ROYAL PAVILION:
the Saloon, with the Dolphin furniture

PARK CRESCENT,
designed by A. H. Wilds, 1829

MONTPELIER VILLAS, BUILT *c*. 1845

OLD AND NEW ARCHITECTURE:
the portico of the Royal Newburgh Assembly Rooms, built 1826,
and the Hotel Metropole conference block and 'Sussex Heights',
1968

TRIPPERS' FARE ON THE LOWER PROMENADE, 1960

BRIGHTON'S NEW SKYLINE, 1966

THE 'SKYLARK' SETTING OUT, 1890

Brighton, and even on more recent buildings. The essential character of Brighton is of a white city—white stucco, white-painted woodwork, even white concrete, echoing the white of the foam-capped waves and the white clouds in the deep blue skies of Brighton. The use of materials such as red or brown bricks which conflict with this impression is likely to be disastrous.

The second object of the Regency Society's attack was the Top Rank Entertainment Centre at the corner of King's Road and West Street. The design of this building seemed especially unfortunate. A long low block of white concrete on a fortress-like sloping base of black bricks, the walls are windowless, and are crowned by a 'faceted fascia' of anodized aluminium of a pale gold colour. This feature was intended to glitter in the sun, and at night to appear to float above the building as a band of reflected light. It was, however, variously described by critics as a 'ruff', a 'ham-frill' and a 'barbaric crown', and seemed overwhelmingly ponderous for its position. Furthermore, the low bulk of the building itself is out of scale not only with the other new developments beyond West Street but even with the existing Victorian buildings on the opposite corner. In the words of the Regency Society, 'the blind façade turned towards the sea seems the height of perversity and a shocking waste of the site . . .'

One early threat to the familiar Brighton never materialized. The Hotel Metropole and some surrounding properties had been bought by Mr. A. V. Poster, and it was believed there was an intention to demolish the building and redevelop the site. Although the Metropole had for a century been criticized for its brash vulgarity, after this lapse of time it had come to symbolize the gaiety of fashionable Brighton in late Victorian and Edwardian days, and consequently held a warm place in the hearts of many Brightonians. The hotel was not after all demolished, but an audacious rebuilding scheme was embarked upon. This provided for the addition of two further storeys to the building, necessitating the insertion of bridging beams at the fifth storey. The question of making modern additions to a structure of red brick and terracotta designed in High Victorian style by Alfred Waterhouse, architect of Manchester Town Hall, the Prudential London headquarters, and Hove Town Hall (now destroyed by fire), was a challenging one. The timbers of the pinnacles, turrets and cupolas of the original roof were found to be unsound, and some change of character was bound to result, especially by the loss of the amusing little pointed green bronze spire which had made the hotel such a landmark of the seafront. The familiar skyline now gave place to a central boldly overhanging concrete roof of very low pitch with its ridge projecting forward, making a structure reminiscent of a ship's bridge. This form is repeated in two new terminals which were added to the original buttress-like window-bays that rise up the face of the building. Similar roofs appear over the projecting

449

bays at each end of the building. The architects were R. Seifert and Partners.

The interior was very considerably remodelled at the same time, providing once more a combination of Victorian grandeur in the original marbled arches, barrel-vaulted ceilings and panelled walls, with the strong colour contrasts of modern decoration. A remarkable period piece that has been retained is the charming marble fireplace in the Residents' Lounge. This was described at the time as 'the work of the chisel of Prince Victor Hohenlohe', whose sculptures were frequently exhibited at the Royal Academy, and whose mother was Countess Gleichen, half-sister to Queen Victoria.

In the new upper floors fifty new flats and 192 new bedrooms have been provided, and the new restaurant in the roof, the Starlit Room, quickly became famous for the magnificent view of the coast, extending from Selsey to Seaford, that can be seen from it.

The rebuilding of the Metropole was but a part of a gigantic scheme of development associated with it, consisting of an immense 300-foot-high, thirty-storey tower block of over a hundred flats at some distance behind the Hotel, together with five new conference and exhibition halls on three floor levels at the base. Although sited far back from the sea-front, the tall tower provoked strong criticism from the Regency Society and others, because of the way in which it dominates the skyline of almost every view of Brighton, especially from along the coast in either direction, completely overwhelming the delicate Gothic tower of St. Paul's Church near by.

Profound relief was also experienced by the lovers of Victorian Brighton when it became known in 1965 that the Government would not give approval to the demolition of the Grand Hotel, which had been bought by Mr. Poster for £130,000.

Seifert and Partners were the architects also of the new seventeen-storey Bedford Hotel, which rose on the site of Thomas Cooper's late Georgian building that was burned down in April 1964.

Brighton Square, completed in 1966, is one of the most imaginative and delightful improvements carried out in Brighton in the whole of its history. Apart from two ancient flint-walled cottages adjoining the Druid's Head in Brighton Place that were pulled down before any question of a preservation order could be raised, the new Square, with twenty-four shops, fifteen maisonettes and flats above, and garaging space at a lower level, was created without any violence being done to the maze of alleyways known as The Lanes. The site, between Meeting House Lane and Brighton Place, the centre of old Brighton, had been occupied previously only by a nest of yards and derelict sheds. The little shops of the new Square, with their bow-windowed flats above, are all in the scale of the old buildings of The Lanes, and are built in similar traditional materials, with flint-cobbled walls, hung tiles and white-painted weatherboarding. Rising above the

Square to one side is a pretty little four-sided spire, and below it a restaurant has a terrace overlooking the Square, where there are tubs for plants and café tables where people can sit in the open air. The various entrances to the Square have been cleverly designed to lead naturally to and from the old parts of The Lanes, the vista of one alleyway being splendidly filled by a round-headed window in the fine old flint wall of the Elim Chapel, Brighton's first dissenting Church. This pretty little development, at the same time traditional and sophisticated, is especially admirable because it has taken nothing from the essential Brighton, but given the town something more in its own unique kind. Away from the traffic of the main streets, a place where one can walk about in peace, it is rather like one of the little squares off the beaten track in Venice, away from the Piazza, and its designers, Fitzroy Robinson and Partners, thoroughly merited the premier award of the Civic Trust that was made to them in 1966. The owners, who were a consortium consisting of a local store—Hannington's—and the Church Commissioners, are to be congratulated on their enterprise, and the Corporation deserve the highest praise for the helpful way in which they set aside the usual building regulations, which if insisted upon would have made the project impossible.

The Churchill Square development, on the other hand, makes no concessions to tradition either in design or in the choice of building materials. It is executed uncompromisingly in concrete, steel and glass. First conceived by Brighton Corporation in 1935, it consists of an immense shopping area set well back from the Western Road, two huge super-markets, a large department store, three tall office blocks and a multi-storey car-park. Extending over the whole of the area between West Street, the sea-front, Cannon Place and Western Road, it covers a space of about sixteen acres that included few buildings of any beauty or character except the early cobble-fronted houses of Grenville Place and a charming but ruinous terrace of houses with columnar porches of about 1815. Much of the area had been destroyed by wartime bombing and was derelict.

All the new buildings are linked by a series of open piazzas leading down from Western Road to the sea-front, and in this way the development embodies some of the best aspects of modern planning, in providing open spaces and features of human scale, removed from motor-traffic, between the vast blocks of buildings.

The central part of the scheme, Churchill Square, itself consists of a shopping precinct built round a paved court, and the immensely long glass-fronted buildings might have had a monotonous and claustrophobic effect had they not been relieved by the spacious paved areas and by two isolated medium-sized buildings, one cubical in shape, another circular, that stand on the upper side of the Square, adjoining Western Road.

In the centre of the Square rises a tall piece of abstract sculpture of dark concrete, 30 feet high, by William Mitchell, called 'the Spirit of Brighton'. Standing like a jagged remnant of a ruin, it may seem to symbolize the wartime destruction that overcame that part of the town, or perhaps, with its rough surfaces that recall the textures of pebble and flint, of boarding and brick, it may be felt also to express something of the ancient character of Brighton, and to point the contrast between the poverty and hardship of the fishermens' town with the spacious ease and affluence of the modern life that has taken its place.

At several different times after the war various proposals were made for the construction of a harbour of one sort or another at Brighton. One project we have mentioned which was put forward in October 1947, was for a £1,000,000 pleasure beach three-quarters of a mile long, and stretching 500 yards out to sea, enclosed within 'Mulberry Harbour' sections of the kind that had been used so successfully for the artificial harbour established off the French coast at the time of our invasion of Europe.[1] The project was intended to include a pleasure garden, a casino, 'boulevards', a 'Continental terrace', harbour for boats and fishing, and a car-park for 1,000 cars. A giant scenic railway was to encircle the area, on a sea-wall built up from the sea-bed. The proposed site was between the Aquarium and the Banjo Groyne at Kemp Town. The promoters were Mr. Kenneth Moorhouse and Mr. C. B. Taylor, the lessees of the Aquarium, but nothing came of the proposal. Again in July 1960 the Borough Surveyor put forward a more modest scheme for a yachting and boating harbour to be built at the Banjo Groyne at Kemp Town, at a cost of £300,000, but this was again defeated by the financial difficulties of the time.

The most elaborate and costly scheme for a sea-front harbour at Brighton ever conceived was put forward in October 1963 by Mr. Derek Head of the architectural firm of Overton and Partners, on behalf of the developers, Mr. Henry Cohen and his Associates. Mr. Cohen was the proprietor of a group of local garages, and a keen yachtsman, who realized the need for a sheltered boat-haven on the stark, inhospitable Brighton coastline. Stated to be 'the most revolutionary scheme of its kind in the world',[2] and then estimated to cost £9 million, it was intended to provide berths for 3,000 boats, and there were to be as well helicopter and hovercraft stations, blocks of flats, a hotel, restaurant, shops, clubs, a conference hall, swimming-pools, a bowling-alley, theatres, and cinemas, a casino and car-parks. The project promised to be the greatest single development ever created in Brighton, apart from the West Street–Western Road rebuilding project. It was to be known as the Brighton Marina, and Mr. Head, the architect, declared that 'he himself had to go to the public library to look up the word after agreeing to take on the job'.[3] The site, covering thirty-three acres altogether, twenty-three on shore and ten over the sea, was to be on the eastern shore below the Madeira Drive, between Duke's Mount and the Madeira lift with its clock-tower. In November 1963 the scheme was approved by the Borough Council in principle, for they were assured that the cost would be entirely borne by private developers, and they foresaw recovering an immense income, possibly of a quarter of a million pounds a year from rates on the Marina properties.

Before very long the plans had developed far in advance of the original project for a yachting harbour. The proposals for helicopter and hover-craft stations were dropped, because of the problem of noise that would have been created, but instead a cross-Channel motor-ferry station was included. Apart from the boating harbour there were now to be a sports drome and ice stadium, tennis and squash courts, a 'teenage area' with coffee bar and dance floor, a curling rink, a golf range, an 'oceanarium' with shark and dolphin pools and other marine tanks; a nylon-covered ski slope, a night club, dance floor, restaurants, a casino with bars, lounges and foyers, three hotels and a motel, a shopping piazza, cafés, a public house and 179 luxury flats and houses. In the Marina itself, almost entirely encircled by two piers, were to be deep-water moorings for 1,700 yachts and a three-storey boat-park for smaller craft. Also to be provided were a dinghy beach, boat-showrooms, a boatyard, a yacht club with bars, restaurant and dance floor and a 'boatel' with two restaurants.

It was stated in the Council chamber that the Marina would now extend over 100 acres of water for two-fifths of a mile westwards of the Palace Pier and that it would be the finest yachting marina in Europe, and possibly in the world. It was described by the Chairman of the Planning Committee, Mr. Ivan Dudeney, as 'the greatest and most exciting scheme that had ever come before the Council',[4] and as something that would 'put Brighton ahead of Blackpool'.[5] One councillor declared, however, that 'You will have a conglomeration of hotels and a shanty town. . . . You have a vista of the sea today. You will not have it afterwards. You talk of yachts on the sea. There will be petrol stations, petrol fumes, tar and litter.'[6] As the scheme came to be more widely discussed there were found to be many more opponents to it, particularly amongst those who believed that the Marina would destroy the beauty and amenities of Brighton's eastern sea-front, above all of the Kemp Town crescents, terraces and squares.

Never since the proposal for the purchase of the Royal Pavilion in 1850 had the residents and lovers of Brighton been divided by bitter controversy as they now were. Lord Holford of Kemp Town (then Sir William Holford), the distinguished architect and town planner, protested strongly against the choice of the site for the Marina in a letter to *The Times*,[7] in which he suggested that the new marine centre would be better sited immediately east of Black Rock, where it would not affect existing amenities, and where there would be better access for traffic by existing roads from various directions.

The letter summed up the feelings of many people who did not object to the making of a yachting harbour in a suitable place, but who were disturbed by the thoughts of its destroying the beauty of the sea-front, and who feared the consequences of building a complete pleasure town of no small size immediately before the eastern part of Brighton.

The letter was 'very seriously considered' by the promoters of the Marina,[8] and by January 1965 the Brighton Marina Company were already negotiating with the Council for a site east of the town and were making new investigations into sea and shore conditions there. By June a new site on the beaches immediately east of Black Rock had been agreed upon by the promoters, and revised plans were approved by the Council in September 1965.

The entire project was now estimated to cost £11 million. After a public inquiry planning permission was given by the Minister of Local Government and Housing, in September 1966. The Marina Bill was the subject of acrimonious debates in the Commons. At the Third Reading of the Bill its opponents said that the proposed Marina would do great damage to Brighton and might be used as a precedent for other seaside resorts. Nevertheless the Bill was passed without a division, and went to the House of Lords. The *Guardian* newspaper now published a leading article violently attacking the scheme.[9]

The writer declared there was nothing wrong with a Marina, but Brighton's project would contain 'a theatre, cinemas, what might be called a citadel of entertainment—including a supermarket, a night club, a curling rink, and various other fancies including 500 "residential units" (i.e. flats) and garaging for 3,500 cars, all this high-grade fun-fair being comprehended under the title of the Brighton Marina. There are places on the coastline where a development of this kind would not come amiss, if only because they have no particular character to wreck. The white cliffs of Sussex are not among those places.'

In moving the Second Reading in the House of Lords Lord Teynham, the distinguished wartime destroyer captain, and a director of Southdown Services, the local omnibus and coach company, explained why the scheme for a yachting harbour alone was not practicable. He said: 'Several marinas have been built, with no other revenue-producing elements attached, with the result that the cost of berthing the small ships is prohibitive, as the return on the capital investment has to be obtained solely on the harbour works. Both the promoters and Brighton Corporation were anxious not to make this mistake.' Lord Goodman, a solicitor and Chairman of the Arts Council of Great Britain, had previously tabled a motion calling for the Bill to be referred to a Select Committee of the Lords, 'to consider how far the works proposed to be authorized by the Bill, or other provisions of the Bill, go beyond what is necessary to provide a harbour for pleasure craft, and whether they are desirable or not, having particular regard to the unique character of Brighton and its environs'.[10] Lord Goodman said further that the issue was 'not about yachting either, but a question of enclosing beach land for private purposes',[11] and the Bill was given its Second Reading with the understanding that Lord Goodman's motion would be accepted as an instruction to the Select Committee.

The next move in the Battle of the Beaches was a thunderous broadside fired by *The Times* on 25th October 1967, with an article headed 'The truth about Brighton Marina: story of a watchdog with neither bark nor bite', in which the news team of the paper claimed to have 'established that at crucial stages the public was misled by an untruth told at a press conference' especially concerning the nature and extent of the financial backing for the project. The impression had been given by the Brighton Marina Company that the project was backed by Sir Robert McAlpine and Sons, the civil engineering concern, and also by Shell-Mex and B.P. Ltd. Both these assumptions were later proved to be incorrect. However, a substantial backer had eventually been found, in the Allied Land and Investment Company, a big London property company. *The Times* compared the Brighton Council to 'a watchdog that did not bite or even bark. It just sat and wagged its tail. . . . Sherlock Holmes once spoke of a watchdog that did nothing in the night-time. What, then, was Brighton Council doing in the broad daylight? How did the press conference statement about McAlpine's and the later invocation of Shell go uncorrected?'[12]

The Council's main defence was that any misstatement or misunderstandings there were about backers were irrelevant, 'because Mr. Cohen had, in the summer of 1965, agreed to a special clause in the Parliamentary Bill. This laid down that work could not start on the Marina until the Council made sure enough money was there to finish the job'. Eventually the Bill passed through the Lords in March 1968, after a long and brilliant debate. The voting was sixty-seven in favour of the Bill and thirty-eight against.

The next move towards the realization of the Marina scheme was the promotion of the Parliamentary Bill required to provide for the construction of the access roads which the Government insisted were necessary before work on the Marina began. At a Town Meeting held at the Dome on 20th December 1968 the Council's resolution to proceed with the Bill was defeated by a small majority, but this decision was reversed by a large majority at a Town Poll that was later held by the Council. Public feeling obviously tended generally now to support the idea of a Marina, which was expected to add some £200,000 a year to the town's income from rates, as well as providing attractive amenities. The cost of constructing the Marina, originally estimated at £9 million, and later increased to £13 million, was now estimated at £14 million. Confidence in the future success of the scheme was increased by the announcement of three offers that were under consideration for taking over the financial promoters, the Allied Land and Investment Company, but a further set-back occurred when on 17th March 1969 the Roads Bill was rejected by the House of Commons at a second reading by a majority of six votes, but the promoters of the scheme declared that they were determined to overcome all obstacles and to go ahead with the project, even without the special roads. There were a number of people who felt that the history of the Marina scheme had been so entertaining that it should be kept alive indefinitely, but never actually realized—a goal for ever madly to be pursued, but never won, unless perhaps if ever it were achieved, it should be supplanted by a new controversial proposal, such as the scheme to erect a 'Skydeck'—a tall, slender tower similar to the London Post Office tower, on the Marine Drive near Black Rock, which was proposed in 1965.[13] Estimated to cost £1½ million, it was to consist of a 993-foot tower, 300 feet of which was to be an aerial mast, and it was to contain shops, cafés, a revolving restaurant and round about its base, a small marina. The project was shelved at the time because of the lack of financial support.

11 Fairs and Festivals

espite the transformation of Brighton sea-front that had taken
place with the rebuilding of the Hotel Metropole, and the
erection of the new Bedford Hotel, of Cavendish House and
the Top Rank Entertainments Centre, the 'off-beat' side of life
in Brighton continued as it had done for over two hundred years. One of
the derelict shops on the sea-front beyond West Street continued to bear on
its façade, right up to the time of its demolition in 1965, the painted signs
of Edwardian days—'The Never-Synk Safety Bathing Costume' and 'The
Safety Bathing Costume'. A tattooist's shop in Queen's Road displayed a
notice 'No persons under 16 will be tattooed'. A coffee bar in Upper North
Street was called 'Royalists' Roost'. It did not stay open for long. In
Middle Street a notice painted on the end of a building pointed two ways:
'Mesmer Berg and Madame Fay, Clairvoyants' to the right, 'Licensed
Betting Office' to the left. Near by another building which carried on its
front door the name-plates of the Ministry of Social Security, 'open to the
public Monday to Friday', and of the Inland Revenue Machine Centre,
also bore on its façade and adjoining windows signs with the words
'Amusements', 'American Bar', 'Lounge Bar', and 'Take Courage'. This
seemed to exemplify the Welfare State carried to excess. In September
1964 a woman was fined £15 by the magistrates for wearing a topless dress
in the Western Road. 'I was hoping to set a trend,' she stated. Madame
Margaret, a clairvoyant in Queen's Road, was reported as engaging not
only in human palmistry but in 'reading doggies' paws'. 'Dogs are part of
the Universe as much as human beings, and they all have their different
characteristics,' she declared.[1]

Clients consulting a certain clairvoyant on the Palace Pier would sometimes be startled by the faint trilling of a bell as the sybil gazed into the
crystal ball. 'Don't mind that, dear,' she would exclaim, 'it's only my
fishing-line', and would dive under the tablecloth and haul up a silver,
wriggling fish at the end of a line which had been let down through a hole
in the floor. An evangelist who had collapsed on a deck-chair with fatigue
and heat, fast asleep, had carefully arranged his banner so that it continued
to show its slogan 'Think on Eternity'.[2]

The spectacle of 'beachcombers' searching among the pebbles for lost
coins and other property is one of the familiar but rather puzzling sights of
the Brighton sea-shore, for one does not imagine that the results could

457

possibly justify the long hours spent by the searchers in their dreary occupation. Yet it appears that an average winter days' findings amount to as much as 4s in small coins. The most fruitful time for a search is after a rough sea has turned over the pebbles and brought to light coins lost long ago. In summer the amounts are greater, and wristwatches and other valuables mislaid by bathers are sometimes found then. The 'beachcombers' jealously guard the territories which they have marked out for themselves, and fiercely resent any intrusion by a stranger.

Since the ending of the Second World War a series of improvements to the Art Gallery and Museum were carried out, and some important new collections acquired, especially of English paintings, silver, Worcester porcelain, early musical instruments, French and English portrait miniatures, and of antique jewellery ranging over thirty centuries in date from the personal collection of the late Mosheh Oved, the famous London jeweller and poet. The Museum has been especially enriched by the addition of remarkable collections of Mr. Edward James of West Dean, Chichester. They include outstanding groups of French, Chippendale and Sheraton furniture, Chelsea porcelain figures, and—a rare feature of any European art gallery—a collection of Surrealist pictures.

From time to time the idea had been put forward of holding in Brighton a Festival of the Arts that would create for the town fresh renown of the kind that had resulted from the world-famous festivals of Edinburgh and Bath.[3] Festivals on a small scale and under semi-private auspices had been held in Brighton in 1946, 1948 and 1951, but apart from the Regency Exhibitions which were the main feature on each occasion, and Regency cricket matches held at Hove which cost nothing, they were not a success. The excellent concerts and recitals which had been organized were failures financially, no doubt because the month of July when they were held was not a time of year when people wanted to be indoors.

Many people believed that Brighton was not a suitable place in which to hold a Festival because the town was too near London, and it was unlikely that any better attractions could be organized than those to be found in the Metropolis. Many other people were aware of the heavy losses incurred over various provincial festivals, and were convinced that any money that might be available would be better spent in helping and improving the various permanent attractions of the town, such as the theatre, the symphony orchestra, the art galleries, the Royal Pavilion and the various entertainments, all of which justify Brighton being regarded as a perpetual festival town. Opinion on the subject was strongly divided, but eventually it became obvious that the only solution was to try the experiment of having a Festival.

There were good reasons for believing that something must be done to restore Brighton's one-time high place in the entertainment world. The year 1964 had seen a slump in popular entertainment. Ice shows were no longer held at the Sports Stadium. There were no more summer variety performances at the Essoldo Theatre, which had gone over to Bingo; the Hippodrome variety theatre had closed and the Repertory Theatre on the Palace Pier had given up through lack of support.[4]

Accordingly in June 1964 a Festival organizing committee was formed and Mr. Ian Hunter, who had been organizer of the Edinburgh Festival for several years, was appointed Artistic Director and given the task of arranging an International Festival of the Arts in Brighton in April 1966. The cost of mounting the Festival was estimated at £35,000. Brighton Council voted an annual grant of £10,000 towards the cost, and the remainder was provided by other public bodies and private subscribers. An important aim of the organizers was not merely to provide the conventional musical and dramatic events associated with such Festivals, but also to arrange a series of more lively activities that would point to contemporary and future developments in the arts. After a while, however, it was found there was not enough time to organize a successful festival for 1966 on the elaborate lines contemplated, and it was postponed until April 1967. In the meantime the Council went ahead with a scheme for *Son et Lumière* performances in the grounds of the Royal Pavilion, which was to be bathed in multicoloured lights while the voices of actors from loudspeakers told the story of the various personalities whose lives had been bound up with the building. Apart from a regrettable misconception of the character of Mrs. Fitzherbert, who gave the entirely false impression of being a blowzy Irish trollop, the performance was strangely moving, with the voices of the different characters seeming to proceed from different rooms in the building, which were lit up in turn as the plot demanded. The façade of the Pavilion was lit, now dimly, now brightly, in colours ranging from pale moonlight to pearly dawn, and from time to time plunged dramatically into darkness, so that the audience, who were seated in deck-chairs in a grandstand facing the Pavilion, and who were, if prudent, swathed in blankets, were able to forget the rain, the blustering wind and the cold of the miserable summer of 1965. Although an interesting experiment, the *Son et Lumière* performances, which were extremely expensive to produce because of the costly technical equipment necessary, were not a success financially, and it became clear that the Royal Pavilion was not a suitable subject for such treatment. Although fascinating and amusing in its way, the story, unlike those of the Tower of London, Hampton Court and Greenwich Hospital, was a comparatively slight one, and did not extend as those did over centuries of time, nor was it connected as were those buildings with the most momentous episodes of our national history. Consequently there did not exist the appeal to mass audiences that would, despite periods of bad weather, have ensured financial success. Even had the Pavilion possessed such a story, there was not the room on the small lawns around the building for any such huge audience as would have been necessary. The experiment was not repeated in the following years.

A Sussex-Normandy Fair held in Brighton in September 1966 was, on the other hand, a resounding success. The first plans for the Fair were announced by the *Herald* on 3rd December 1965 with the words 'Ooh-la-la in the Lanes', while the *Argus* for the same date promised 'A touch of French dressing' for Brighton. The Fair opened with motor speed-trials on the Madeira Drive; a trade fair was held during the week in the Metropole Exhibition Halls; and the Continental atmosphere invaded the lawns of the Royal Pavilion, with café tables and chairs set about between the rows of paintings in an open-air art exhibition. There were fashion shows, orchestral concerts in the Dome, and band concerts at the Aquarium. Wine was sold by the glass in the open in Regency Square, Brighton Square and the Pavilion grounds, there was dancing to relayed music in the squares and on the sea-front, and acrobats and jugglers gave performances in the streets. A French coastal minesweeper, the *Vega*, lay off the coast for people to visit her during several days, and an exhibition of the work of Dieppois painters and sculptors was held in the Art Gallery. The week ended in a blaze of light and sound when an Anglo-French firework display was staged on the beach at Madeira Drive, and 3,000 teenagers danced the night away in an 'all-night rave' with eight pop and folk-music groups on the sea-front. It was one of the most exciting and successful public events ever held in Brighton, and the glorious weather of September 1966 helped to emphasize the impression given by the Fair of Brighton as a town with more of a Continental atmosphere than any other resort in Britain.

The long-awaited Brighton Festival opened in April 1967. The nucleus of a rich programme of events was provided by some productions of the National Theatre at the Theatre Royal, and an impressive series of musical events at the Dome, the Royal Pavilion and in the new College of Art. Sir Laurence Olivier, Director of the National Theatre, brought to Brighton Strindberg's *Dance of Death*, with himself and Geraldine McEwan in the principal roles. Also from the Old Vic came the farce by Feydeau *A Flea in her Ear*, directed by the famous Comédie Française actor and producer Jacques Charon, with Robert Lang and Geraldine McEwan in the principal parts. During the second week at the Theatre Royal Robert Bolt's controversial play *Brother and Sister* was presented, starring Flora Robson. Each morning during the Festival a Children's Theatre Workshop production took place at the Palace Pier Theatre with Manchester University drama students and children from Brighton schools, under the direction of Miss Marjorie Sigley, who with Miss Naftali Yavin wrote a special play for children called *The Stoppers*, which was performed every afternoon for a week. The Brighton Youth Theatre put on performances of Dylan

Thomas's *Under Milk Wood* at the Dorothy Stringer School. A local amateur group, the Centre Players, produced *Fings Ain't Wot They Used T'Be* at the Union Hall, Air Street, and the Brighton and Hove Repertory Company presented the Regency comedy *The Man with a Load of Mischief* in conjunction with another amateur company, the New Venture Theatre.

After many years of festivals all over Britain and Europe, it would appear to be difficult to achieve originality in a musical programme, yet for the Brighton Festival a remarkably exciting and satisfying series of concerts was drawn up. The Warsaw Philharmonic Orchestra under Witold Rowicki provided the opening concert at the Dome, and other concerts were held in the Dome by the Brighton Philharmonic Orchestra, the Bournemouth Symphony Orchestra, the English Chamber Orchestra, the Trinity College Orchestra and the London Philharmonic Orchestra. A number of Chamber Concerts and recitals were held at the College of Art and in the Royal Pavilion, including at the latter a concert of 'Music for George IV' presented by the B.B.C., consisting of works of the kind that would have been played for the monarch in the building. Several exhibitions were held in the Brighton Art Gallery, including paintings by Marjorie Brooks, the Edward James Collection of Surrealist pictures, contemporary British drawings, and most intriguing of all, a display of 'Rude Seaside Postcards' by Donald McGill, the famous practitioner of this classic form of popular art that was so singularly appropriate to Brighton. Never had an exhibition in the Art Gallery been so rapturously received. For days the visitors stood four deep in front of the display screens, able for once in a lifetime to examine these fascinating aspects of life at the seaside without a sense of guilt.

Other items in the Festival programme that aroused enormous interest and amusement amongst the public and in the newspapers, even if they were the least successful financially, were the Fringe Events. The most elaborate of these was the exhibition of Kinetic Art on the West Pier, which aimed at providing an 'Audio Visual Environment' in which endlessly changing image patterns of light and colour were projected on to screens accompanied by sound effects. An experimental exhibition of 'environmental sculpture' on the Regency Square lawn seemed to consist of little more than a series of cylindrical steel sentry-boxes and hollow steel spheres through which one was expected to wander, reminding one of those 'Haunted Houses' on the pier or in the fun-fairs. One walked through passages past mural decorations lit by spotlights, crossed over a pond by means of stepping-stones and pushed one's way through curtains of clinging muslin fabric. The fringe event that aroused the greatest derision and puzzlement was the display of 'concrete poetry', in which words, lines and phrases of abstract poetry appeared at different places in the town in tangible form. On a board near the Pavilion the word 'seas'

461

appeared repeated twice at each of the four extremities of a cross-shaped layout, with the word 'ease' in the middle. This 'poem' was entitled 'Sailor's Cross'. The feeble inanity of it was exceeded by a poem called 'Amber Sands', which consisted of twenty-three large ampersands (the printers' & sign) cut out of wood, painted yellow and mounted horizontally on short legs on the Western Lawn of the Pavilion. This pretentious and witless punning was supposed to represent a 'visual experiment' based on Brighton, although the town has no sand to speak of, and if there is any it is not amber; moreover, the signs were painted bright yellow, not even the amber of traffic lights, and certainly not the deep amber of the Bronze Age cup in the Museum. Other examples of concrete poetry were three transparent perspex cylinders about 6 feet high, standing on end, and covered with thousands of letters in small adhesive lettering, which were installed in Brighton Square. Another device, a box-like structure in deep blue and purple transparent plastic, was covered with the five vowels endlessly repeated. The printed poem fifty-four words long that appeared broken up into three-word groups at various places in the town was more amusing. The whole poem was revealed on posters displayed at one or two central points, one of them behind the Royal Albion Hotel. Called 'Permutation Poem' and written by Edwin Morgan, it ran 'gay tasty loud blowy red gold hopping tingling jellied sand boat pier bunting candyfloss fish bucket sport cats transistor crash guitar birds kite dance roundabout eels scene huge new mellow happy lazy high blue green cool spring sun sea music cloud orchestra pavilion terrace theatre cake art symphony diver steak show dogs poetry happening'. This succession of words seemed to have a vaguely evocative seaside quality, although it lacked the richly sensuous word-imagery and associative magic of the writings of James Joyce and Dylan Thomas. It was a disconcerting experience to see in a bus serving the sleepy outlying village of Ovingdean a notice bearing the Festival sign, and the three words 'Hopping Art Dogs'. It occurred irresistibly to one that the phrase might well have been applied to the Festival Committee, especially after they had discovered that the £4,000 loss sustained by Brighton Corporation over the Festival (in addition to their initial contribution of £10,000) represented almost exactly the cost of the Kinetic Art Exhibition on the West Pier which took only some £200 in admission fees.

Another manifestation of concrete poetry was a raft moored offshore a quarter of a mile out between the two piers, carrying three pylons bearing the words 'LOVE', 'PASSION' and 'BEAUTY' in large letters set vertically. These words swayed with appropriate tempestuousness in the wild seas, and after a few days of buffeting in the waves 'LOVE' seemed distinctly unstable, 'BEAUTY' much bedraggled and 'PASSION' at the point of collapse. 'All passion bent', as one observer remarked.

The Festival provided what might prove to be the classic example of

Brighton's off-beat attitude to life. In what other place would the attempt have been made to improve the sea by dyeing it with different colours? This exploit, worthy of the inhabitants of the legendary city of Gotham, was a failure, large quantities of red, blue and yellow pigment which were poured into the sea from boats immediately vanishing without affecting the immemorial colour of the water.

The concluding minor fringe event was again an almost predictable fiasco. This was a bonfire of ugly things on the beach. People were encouraged to bring out ugly furniture, pictures, works of art and other horrors from their attics and basements to be burned on a modern 'Bonfire of Vanities' like the works of Botticelli in the days of Savonarola. Local wits facetiously suggested that the Pavilion should form the nucleus of the holocaust. As it happened, hardly any horrors were found to feed the flames, and the event literally 'fizzled out'. All the attics and cellars of Brighton had already been thoroughly combed through over and over again by the innumerable antique dealers of Brighton, to their great profit, for the monstrosities of Victorian and Edwardian days, and of the 1920s and 1930s had begun to be sought after as gems of popular art and gimmickry.

Brighton's first International Festival of the Arts was regarded by its promoters as having turned out to be a tremendous success, despite the heavy financial losses. Even though some of the fringe events were failures, they had undoubtedly caused immense amusement and produced more publicity than many of the more important features of the programme. The theatrical and musical sections of the Festival were undoubtedly magnificent. The Council decided that they would back three further festivals, and committed themselves to annual contributions of £15,000 which would give opportunities for greater success by permitting better advance planning of events. For the second Festival to be held in May 1969 one of the two main themes was to be the part played by Czechoslovakia in world culture—in music, in drama and the cinema. Another theme, to be expressed in art exhibitions and various entertainments was to be 'The Roaring Twenties and the Jazz Age'—'an age that had not lost the secret of luxury, an age that rediscovered "style", and invented the cocktail'.[5]

The townspeople's appetite for fairs and festivals was now thoroughly whetted. The Brighton and Hove Hotels, Guest Houses and Restaurants Association organized a nine days' Gastronomic Festival, which took place in July 1967, with the object of 'giving extra colour and atmosphere' to the two resorts. The main events were seven evenings in different hotels devoted to the gastronomic pleasures of seven nations or regions. Unaccountably the Swiss dinner at the Salisbury Hotel had to be cancelled through lack of support, but the Normandy dinner at the Beach Hotel was a great success, as were also the Old Vienna Night at the Kingsway Court and the Polish Night at the Queen's hotel. The Eaton Restaurant was fully booked for the Burgundy Night, and the Italian Night at the King Alfred and the Gala Provençale at the Hotel Metropole were no less outstanding occasions. One man, and one man only, was bold enough to take a £15 Roving Ticket for the whole of the Festival, and ate his way without mishap through all six of the memorable meals. In addition to these momentous feasts there were a number of lesser events—music playing, and open-air cafés selling wine on the Pavilion lawns, in Regency Square and in New Steine Gardens, and a race between waiters and waitresses holding trays carrying champagne and glasses on the Fishmarket Hard.

From now on it seemed that fairs and festivals would follow one upon another so fast that the vision of Brighton as a town perpetually *en fête* was not unlikely to be realized.

Even in the permissive 1960s, certain sections of the Brighton Council resolutely struggled against the continuance of the air of sexual tolerance to which the town owed so much of its appeal. With the handing over of police authority to the County Council, the Watch Committee ceased to exist, and its function as guardians of morality passed, rather incongruously, to the Fire Brigade Committee, who were regarded as having 'the necessary expertise'. Accordingly in 1967 it fell to the lot of four councillors to decide whether a certificate of approval should be given for the showing in Brighton of the film version of James Joyce's *Ulysses*, at the Continentale Cinema, which specialized in films other than the ordinary popular successes. After seeing the film at a special session, the committee discussed the matter in the street outside the cinema and decided to refuse a certificate. The authorities at Burgess Hill, however, were more tolerant, and it was possible to see the film there, or in London, where it was shown for a long period. Later on, however, the ban on the film in Brighton was lifted.

In July 1968, when a Scandinavian film called *I—a woman*, which had been refused a certificate for general showing by the British Board of Film Censors, was submitted for showing in Brighton, only one member of the Fire Brigade Committee, the Chairman, attended the private session, and refused the certificate. Later he admitted he had no right to ban the film without a quorum of the Committee. 'I was wrong, says Councillor who banned sex film', ran the headline in a local paper.[6] The matter was again debated by the full Fire Brigade Committee, who gave their approval to the film. As a result of the great publicity which had been given, the film was shown to crowded houses for a season of several weeks. The suggestion was then made that in future the full Town Council should deliberate upon such questions, but this was not agreed, and the Fire Brigade Committee continued to act as arbiters of morals in the realm of the cinema.

12　The Future of Brighton

Despite grevious losses in recent years of fine Regency buildings from the Bedford Hotel downwards, indeed of whole streets and terraces of Georgian houses, the town of Brighton to-day, though certainly not more beautiful as a whole than it was in the days of King George IV, is undoubtedly more bright, gay and elegant than it was from the last days of Queen Victoria until the 1950s, when so many of the buildings were drab, unpainted and in disrepair. Now, even if some of the Regency buildings have been swept away, so too have many nondescript Victorian and later erections; the Regency buildings are now generally in good repair, brightly painted, and some of them with missing original features such as bow-windows and window-canopies restored. And the newer buildings, although they may be ponderous, even brutalistic in design, are mostly, unless built in black or red brick, bright and smart, and the newly created areas of Brighton Square and Churchill Square provide gay and pleasant spaces for shopping and refreshment away from the din and danger of motor-traffic, on land chiefly occupied previously by slum-dwellings, mean streets, and derelict shops or workshops.

What is to become of Brighton? We must hope that the two principal architectural groups, the monumental compositions of Kemp Town and Royal Crescent and of Brunswick Town will be preserved for as many years as possible. With careful conservation and maintenance and even if necessary a certain amount of rebuilding they could be made to last another hundred or two hundred years. Their attraction as prestige residences for the wealthy would justify the very high rents that would be necessary, as has been proved possible in the case of Cumberland Terrace in Regent's Park. The Royal Pavilion, that unique monument of its era, should be preserved 'for ever', even if necessary to the extent of completely rebuilding the fabric in a hundred or two hundred years' time.

On the sea-front from the New Steine eastwards to Kemp Town, the preservation of the surviving blocks and terraces of Georgian houses, including Eastern Terrace, Percival Terrace and Clarendon Terrace should be regarded as of an importance equal to Kemp Town. Almost more vital than the question of preservation is that of the character of the modern architecture that is to arise in Brighton. It is unthinkable that in the Old Steine, in Pavilion Parade opposite the Pavilion itself, on the sea-front and in the smaller squares, streets and terraces, the design of new buildings should continue to be at the whim of the different owners of the various properties and their architects, resulting possibly in a white concrete block being flanked on one side by a featureless façade of glass, and on the other by a frontage of red or dull black brick, with other buildings in neo-Georgian or neo-baroque style near by. It could be only too easy for the new architecture of Brighton's sea-front and principal streets to become in thirty years as dated and distasteful as are today the tawdry, trumpery and vulgar façades of the buildings erected in the 1930s on the north side of Western Road and in West Street. Already in recent years we have seen the erection of an important new bank building in North Street in a clumsy and insensitive imitation Georgian style. The gay and delightful Victorian façade of the Paris Cinema was replaced by a dreary flat frontage of red brick, and some charming bow-fronted Regency houses in Richmond Place gave place to a flat-fronted red-brick office building with small windows in a depressing version of a Georgian style half a century earlier than the Regency. The unique character of Brighton's architecture was very largely due to the fact that like the great terraces and villas around Regent's Park and nearly all the other buildings of the London improvements of the 1820s which were designed by John Nash, it was infused with a unity of spirit. Almost the whole of Brighton's massive building development in the same year was designed chiefly by one remarkable architect, Charles Busby, and by his partners the two Wilds who were in close accord with him.

Since its foundation in 1945, the Regency Society of Brighton and Hove has, with Antony Dale as Honorary Secretary, achieved remarkable success in securing the preservation of Brighton's buildings, in giving advice on the restoration of special features such as wall-surfaces, balconies and windows, and in giving support to various other organizations in their efforts towards the preservation of particular buildings and areas.

The rebuilding of Brighton during the next thirty years will determine its appearance and character, and consequently its appeal and value for another century or more to come. An opportunity now presents itself that will not occur again for another century or so, to ensure in the rebuilding of Brighton the creation of a sea-front, and of squares, terraces, crescents and streets of a beauty and a harmony that could be not only equal to that which they possessed at the end of the Georgian age but possibly even more enchanting, exciting and magnificent.

Certain salient features of Brighton cry out for special treatment. The whole area between North Street, the Old Steine and Ship Street—the greater part of the ancient Brighthelmstone—could be closed to wheeled traffic and be developed as a large 'pedestrian precinct' on the lines of the admirable Brighton Square development of the Lanes. The decaying cement-walls, tunnel-entrance and shelter-pavilions of the Kemp Town slopes should be repaired, the massive sloping walls preferably

466

dealt with by completing the refacing in brick that was begun years ago at the western end. Eventually, too, the decaying wall of the magnificent Madeira Terrace should be re-faced. The comprehensive traffic plan prepared for Brighton by the firm of Hugh Wilson and Lewis Womersley provides for many of these improvements, especially for the isolation from traffic of the central 'Brighthelmstone' area. One of the most interesting suggestions made by these consultants, who have been called in by Brighton Corporation, is for the creation of a large open piazza in front of St. Bartholomew's Church off the London Road near Preston Circus. Such a development would enable the impressive frontage of this remarkable church to be seen to better advantage than is now possible, with a huddle of mean little houses crowding right up to its walls. Furthermore, new dignity and beauty would be given to a decaying and sordid area of Brighton, and a pleasant place of relaxation and rest provided for the thousands of people who frequent this popular shopping area.

Perhaps the greatest danger that threatens Brighton is the possible loss of the charm and beauty of its sea-front, with the gigantic scale and ponderousness of its new buildings, but Brighton may still perhaps be saved by its natural advantages, and on calm summer evenings, when the pearly glowing sky seems to merge with the placid expanses of the still sea, the faint mistiness in the air may soften the harsh outlines and overwhelming height of the tall new buildings and give even them a touch of the magic that surrounded the terraces of the Georgian age.

But whatever Brighton's architectural fate may be, there will always be the exhilarating air, the dazzling sunshine, the ever-changing sea and sky—all those elements that go to make up 'the brilliancy of Brighton'; something that creates a wonderful sense of well-being and gives the promise of delight—that stimulates the mind to fresh thoughts and ideas; something that has created the idea of Brighton as a pleasure city that is unique on the face of the earth.

Notes

p. 20. These later finds are preserved in the Museum of the Sussex Archaeological Society, Barbican House, Lewes.

p. 22. It is not mentioned in the deed confirming the gift of the church of Brighthelmston by Henry I in 1120, so it was probably not founded until after that date. The first record of the chapel is *c.* 1185.

p. 26. The name of the French admiral who is supposed to have led the attack on Brighton in 1514 was actually Primauget, a Knight of Rhodes. This was presumably Hervé de Primauget or Portsmoguer, a Breton, who commanded the French naval forces at Brest when Sir Edward Howard made his ill-fated attempt to destroy the harbour.

p. 27. An interesting point arises here over the question of the 'grete Shippes' shown in the drawing. It has been supposed by some historians that only galleys and foists were used in the raid of 1514, yet there were 'basiliskes and othe greate artilerie', which indeed would have been necessary to bombard 'hill-valleys' and the town to prevent rescue operations. Basilisks were brass cannon 12 feet long and weighing 4 tons each and 'grete Shippes' would have been needed to carry them, not galleys and foists.

Various commentators have followed each other in describing the parties of soldiers that are shown on the roads leading down from Poynings and Lewes into Brighton as being bands of troops coming to the rescue of the townspeople, but the flags they carry bear large crosses like those flying on the French ships, and the men stand in waiting attitudes rather than as though they were hurrying along. It seems more likely that these men are French soldiers, posted on the main roads into the town to intercept any relieving forces.

p. 27. Dr. Gairdner based his theory on the belief that the detailed inscriptions on the drawing were in a style of handwriting typical of 1514, but that the date 1545 was more characteristic of the end of Henry's reign. But this argument is inconclusive. It has been pointed out by Mr. Carr-Laughton that the inscription could have been written in 1545, and the date, which is admittedly of a later style, could have been inserted at any time up to the early part of the seventeenth century. The date of a person's handwriting style is largely a matter of the person's age. One usually continues to write in later life more or less as one did in early maturity, when one's handwriting became formed.

Dr. Gairdner's theory has in turn been questioned more recently by a naval historian (L. G. Carr-Laughton in *Royal Hist. Soc. Trans.*, 3rd ser., Vol. X, 1916), who asserts that certain of the 'grete Shippes' in the drawing, particularly the high stern-castles, had not come into general use as early as 1514, and furthermore, the earlier attack was supposed to have been carried out only by galleys and foists.

p. 34. See note for p. 68.

p. 41. For many years it was supposed that a Bible which had belonged to the Carver family must have been the martyr's own, but as it is a 'Breeches' bible, not published before 1560, it could not have belonged to Derek Carver. However, it may well have been the possession of his son, and the names of many later members of the family are inscribed in it. The volume is now preserved by the Sussex Martyrs Commemoration Council.

p. 53. It has been suggested recently that this particular symptom may have been caused by the Royal malady porphyria, a complaint mistakenly confused with insanity, from which King George III and some of his descendants suffered.

p. 56. The artist was believed for many years to have been Johann Zoffany, R.A., but this cannot be confirmed, for this artist did not set foot in England until about 1761. He was then only twenty-seven or twenty-eight years of age, and employed in painting clock-faces until he entered the studio of Benjamin Wilson, as a painter of backgrounds and draperies at a salary of £40 a year. Possibly Zoffany had a hand in the painting of Russell's portrait, and may even have brought it down to Brighton, which might have given rise to the legend it was painted by him. The attribution to Wilson is amply supported by the style of painting, which is typical of Wilson, and unlike that of Zoffany.

p. 68. A drawing dated '9 Nov. 1799' shows the west bottom end of West Street with the King's Head Inn, on which is inscribed 'at that time (14 Octbr 1651) the George Inn kept by one Smith. The house in which King Charles 2nd was concealed till the boat was got ready to carry him to the continent after his escape from the Battle of Worcester. Nicholas Tettersell, the fisherman navigated the boat.'

p. 94. It has often been conjectured as to whether Holland made use of the existing farmhouse as part of the new villa, perhaps forming the south wing, but an extract from a document dated 22nd November 1787 (Bishop, *The Brighton Pavilion*, p. 10) expressly states that 'all the buildings had been pulled down, and a messuage erected and built for the residence of His said Royal Highness . . .'

p. 123. The Church afterwards took careful steps to ensure that such a situation should not so easily arise again, with the Pope being compelled to make a ruling fraught with so many political and dynastic implications. None the less in recent times the Church has recognized even a registry office marriage as a binding ceremony in the eyes of Heaven, after the reconciliation of one party, a Catholic, with the Church and the admittance into it of the other.

p. 154. The late Sir Eardley Holland, P.P.R.C.O.G., F.R.C.S., F.R.C.P., made an exhaustive study of the accouchement of the Princess Charlotte over many years, after being called to attend a lady patient at Claremont House, Esher, where the Princess died. He delivered the William Meredith Shaw Memorial Lecture on the subject in 1951.

p. 167. This question of when the Prince first met Lady Conyngham is of particular interest in connection with the subject of the descent of the Denison family, which is discussed in detail in the first volume of the memoirs of Sir Osbert Sitwell, *Left-hand, Right-hand*.

p. 167. It would more probably have been the North Gate, which adjoined Lady Conyngham's house.

p. 169. Information supplied by Sir Owen Morshead, formerly Royal Librarian.

p. 185. The Marine Hotel was seriously damaged by fire in 1968, and may eventually be demolished.

p. 193. The building is unusual in having below it extensive vaults, probably intended originally for burial purposes, but for many years during the nineteenth century and after they were leased as wine vaults. For a time after the last war they were used for storing the stock of a second-hand bookseller, and they are now again serving as wine and beer cellars.

p. 236. NOTE. The principal works written by Count Guiseppi Pecchio while at Brighton were:

Storia della economia pubblica in Italia, 1829.
Vita di golo Foscolo, 1830.
Saggio storico sull' amministrazione finanziarie dell'ex-regno d'Italia, 1830.
Storia critica della poesia inglese, 1833-5.

p. 237. The letter, dated 'Jan. 15th, 1834', was presented to the Pavilion by Miss Cleeve, whose family were connected by marriage to Lord James O'Bryen, a distinguished Admiral, who had become a friend of the King in the latter's naval days when Duke of Clarence. O'Bryen was appointed Lord of the Bedchamber on the accession of William IV. He succeeded his brother as third Marquess of Thomond in 1846.

p. 322. The Terrace appears on a plan of Brighton for 1830 which is in the Borough Surveyor's office, but not on a similar plan for 1822.

p. 347. The holding in Brighton of the Annual Meeting of the British Association for the Advancement of Science in 1872 opened the eyes of local members to the poor accommodation which had been found for the library, and especially to the squalid condition of the museum collections and the unsatisfactory personality of the curator— 'The whole thing odiferous of mould, damp, dust and neglect, presided over by as much conceit and pomposity as can be crammed into one brainless head, a fit emblem of the worthless unclassified rubbish, which form the staple article of most provincial museums, and render them the laughing stock of men of science.'

p. 363. This coach is now on loan to the Museum of Carriages, Maidstone.

p. 379. The name Black Rock has also been said to derive from the discoloration of the rocks on the shore by the coal that was landed there for the gas works a little way inland.

References in the Text

Abbreviated titles only are given for works which are fully described in the Bibliography. Full titles are given only for works to which isolated references are made, and which are not included in the Bibliography.

PART I

FISHERMEN AND FARMERS

The beginnings to 1770

Chapter 1. EARLY BRIGHTON
1. Curwen. *Archaeology of Sussex*. 1954. p. 76.
2. Harrison and North. *Old Brighton, Old Preston, Old Hove*. 1937. p. 7.
3. Martin. *History of Brighton*. p. 3.
4. *Sussex Place Names*. p. 291.
5. P.R.O. Mins. Accts. Hen. VIII. No. 1474. A.D. 497.
6. *Sussex Place Names*. 1929-30. p. 29.
7. Public Record Office.
8. P. Dunvan. *Lewes and Brighthelmstone*. p. 52.

Chapter 2. A TOWN IN FLAMES
1. B.M. Cotton MS. Aug. I.i. 18.
2. Sitwell and Barton. *Brighton*. 1935. p. 29.
3. Edward Hall. *Chronicle*. Ed. Ellis. 1809.
4. Holinshed. *Chronicles*. An. Reg. 5.
5. Ibid.
6. J. Gairdner. *R. Hist. Soc. Trans*. 3rd ser. Vol. I. 1907. pp. 19-31.
7. B.M. Add. MSS 5683. Fol. 57.
8. Erredge. p. 64.

Chapter 3. FISHERMEN AND TOWNSMEN
1. C. Webb and A. E. Wilson. *Elizabethan Brighton: the ancient customs of Brighthelmston, 1580*. 1952.

Chapter 4. THE ROYAL ESCAPE
1. F. E. Sawyer. Sussex Arch. Coll. 1883. Vol. 32. p. 87.
2. Harrison and North. *Old Brighton, Old Preston, Old Hove*. 1937. p. 57.
3. Sussex Arch. Coll. 1882. Vol. 32. p. 89.
4. Idem. p. 102.
5. Idem. p. 96.
6. Goodwin's *Rentall of the Manor of Brighthelmstone*.

Chapter 5. FAITH AND FANATICISM
1. Erredge. p. 134 et seq.

471

Chapter 6. TERRORS AND JOYS OF THE SEA
1. Harrison and North. p. 34.
2. Erredge. p. 73.
3. Erredge. p. 74.
4. Erredge. p. 67.
5. Erredge. p. 77.
6. Erredge. p. 68.
7. Erredge. p. 69.
8. Camden. *Magna Britannia*. 1737.
9. Gilbert. *Brighton : Old Ocean's Bauble*. 1954. p. 53.
10. Erredge. p. 219.
11. R. Manning-Sanders. *Seaside England*. 1951. p. 24.
12. A. M. Lower. *Worthies of Sussex*. 1865. p. 214.
13. A. Pasquin. *New Brighton Guide*. 1796. p. 6.
14. R. Manning-Sanders. p. 22.

Chapter 7. DR. RUSSELL AND THE SEA-WATER CURE
1. Gilbert. p. 57.
2. F. Burney. *Diary and Letters*. Ed. Austin Dobson. 1904–5. Vol. 1. p. 440.
3. Gilbert. p. 60.
4. R. Sickelmore. *History of Brighton*. p. 121.
5. Bishop. *Brighton*. p. 226.

Chapter 8. FASHIONABLE VISITORS
1. Relhan. *Brighthelmstone*. 1761.
2. B.M. Lansdowne MSS 91, 983.
3. Jesse. *George Selwyn and his Contemporaries*. Vol. 1. p. 264.
4. Erredge. p. 223n.
5. P. Phillips. *Diary*.
6. Bishop. *Brighton*. p. 161.
7. Ibid.
8. F. Burney. *Diary and Letters*.
9. Bishop. *Brighton*. p. 161.
10. Idem. p. 113.
11. *F. Burney. Diary and Letters*, quoted by Bishop. *Brighton*. p. 120.

PART II

PRINCES AND PALACES

1770 to 1820

Chapter 1. BALLS AND ASSEMBLIES
1. Bishop. *Brighton*. p. 27.
2. Bishop. *Brighton*. p. 30.
3. Bishop. *Brighton*. p. 118.
4. Bishop. *Brighton*. p. 102.

Chapter 2. THE COMING OF THE PRINCE OF WALES
1. Fulford. *George the Fourth*.
2. Genest. *History of the Stage*.
3. Sitwell and Barton. p. 98.
4. *Sussex Weekly Advertiser*. 2 August 1784.
5. *Morning Post*. 13 July 1786.

6. Wilkins. *Mrs. Fitzherbert and George IV*. 1905. p. 169.
7. *Sussex Weekly Advertiser*. 17 July 1786.
8. Bishop. *Pavilion*. 1903. p. 8.
9. *Sussex Weekly Advertiser*. 6 November 1786.

Chapter 3. THE MARINE PAVILION
1. Horace Walpole. *Letters*.
2. D. Stroud. *Henry Holland*. 1966. p. 73.
3. C. Langdale. *Memoirs of Mrs. Fitzherbert*. 1856.

Chapter 4. EARLY THEATRES
1. Bishop. *Peeps into the Past*. p. 47.

Chapter 5. FASHION, FUGITIVES AND THE BRIGHTON CAMP
1. Bishop. *Pavilion*. p. 14.
2. C. J. Apperley. *The Chase, the Rod and the Turf*. 1927.
3. Sitwell and Barton. p. 145.
4. Bishop. *Pavilion*. p. 20.
5. *Gazette*. 17 October 1796.
6. *Gazette*. 24 October 1796.
7. *Herald*. 4 July 1794.
8. *Herald*. 10 April 1794.
9. *Herald*. 17 October 1794.
10. *Herald*. 6 January 1795.
11. Ibid.
12. *Herald*. 10 February 1795.
13. *Herald*. 25 April 1796.
14. *Herald*. 30 May 1796.
15. *Herald*. 5 September 1796.
16. *Herald*. 3 October 1796.
17. Ibid.
18. *Herald*. 10 October 1796.
19. *Herald*. 12 December 1796.

Chapter 6. THE LUCKLESS MARRIAGE
1. A. Aspinall. *Correspondence of George, Prince of Wales*. Vol. II. 1789–94. p. 453.
2. *Herald*. 19 October 1795.
3. Jerningham. *Letters*. 2 July 1796.

Chapter 7. ORIENTAL EXPERIMENTS
1. Unidentified newspaper cutting.
2. Brayley. *His Majesty's Palace at Brighton*. p. 2.
3. Musgrave. *Regency Furniture*. pp. 30, 31 and 145.
4. Honour. *Chinoiserie*. p. 225.
5. Musgrave. *Royal Pavilion*. p. 36.
6. Moore. *Life of Byron*. 1860. p. 70.
7. Idem and Gronow. *Reminiscences and Recollections*. 1862. p. 211.
8. Mrs. Calvert. *An Irish Beauty of the Regency*.
9. Grant. *English Landscape Painters*.
10. J. C. Loudon. *The Landscape Gardening of Humphrey Repton*. 1840.
11. Royal Archives.

473

Chapter 8. THE REGENCY
1. *British Medical Journal.* 8 January 1818.
2. Pavilion archives.
3. Anecdotes of the Princess Charlotte. MS in collection of Stephen Musgrave.
4. Idem.
5. *Sussex Weekly Advertiser.* 16 March 1818.
6. Pückler-Muskau. *Letters on England.* 10 February 1827. p. 165.

Chapter 9. THE PAVILION TRANSFORMED
1. *Sussex Weekly Advertiser.* 10 February 1817.
2. Quoted in Musgrave. *Royal Pavilion.* p. 69.
3. J. G. Loudon. *The Landscape Gardening of Humphrey Repton.* 1840.
4. Royal archives.
5. Reproduced in Musgrave. *Royal Pavilion.* Plate 50.
6. Royal archives.
7. Bishop. *Pavilion.* p. 76.
8. Raikes. *Journal.* 1858.
9. *Herald.* 18 May 1826.
10. C. S. Parker. *Sir Robert Peel.* 1899. p. 317.

PART III
LATE GEORGIAN
1820 to 1840

Chapter 1. BUILDINGS OF THE 1820s
1. C. A. Busby. *Designs for Villas and Country Houses.* 1808.
2. A. Dale. *Fashionable Brighton.* 1967.
3. J. Sawyer. *Churches of Brighton.* c. 1880.
4. *Herald.* 28 December 1844.
5. Dale. *Fashionable Brighton.* p. 134.
6. Information from Lady Monnington.
7. Dale. *Fashionable Brighton.* p. 83.

Chapter 2. GEORGIAN CHURCHES
1. A. Pasquin (John Williams). *New Brighton Guide.* 1796. p. 5.
2. *Herald.* 18 January 1958.
3. Idem. 13 June 1959.

Chapter 3. THE BATHS
1. Erredge. p. 229.
2. A. B. Granville. *Spas of England.* Vol. II. p. 562.
3. Manning-Sanders. p. 36.
4. Page's *Handbook to Brighton.* p. 100.
5. Idem.
6. Idem. p. 104.
7. *Gazette.* 5 August 1869.
8. Ibid.
9. Andrew Kidd in *Argus.* 18 September 1969.
10. Granville. Vol. II. p. 563.
11. Gilbert. p. 72.

12. Page. *Handbook*. p. 105.
13. Granville. Vol. III. p. 562.
14. Merrifield. *Brighton, past and present*. 1857.
15. Gilbert. p. 69.

Chapter 4. COACHING DAYS
1. S. Margetson. 'The Mail Coach revolution'; in *History Today*. January 1967.
2. Bishop. *Brighton*. p. 251.
3. *Gazette*. 18 October 1823.
4. *Herald*. 6 November 1830.
5. Idem. 6 October 1830.
6. Idem. 14 September 1957.

Chapter 5. GEORGIAN INNS AND HOTELS
1. Bishop. *Brighton*. p. 194.
2. Idem. p. 213.
3. *Herald*. 19 July 1822.
4. Bede. *Mattins and Muttons*. Vol. I. p. 56.

Chapter 6. THE WINDMILLS
1. Bramwell. 'The Windmills of Brighton'.

Chapter 7. PLEASURE GARDENS AND THE GERMAN SPA
1. Erredge. p. 299.
2. Gilbert. p. 74.
3. Ibid.

Chapter 8. THE CHAIN PIER
1. Bishop. *The Brighton Chain Pier*. 1896.
2. L. T. C. Rolt. *Thomas Telford*. 1958. p. 118.
3. Bishop. *The Brighton Chain Pier*. 1896. p. 18.

Chapter 9. KING WILLIAM IV
1. Croly, George. *George the Fourth*. 1830.
2. *Herald*. 24 July 1830.

PART IV

VICTORIAN MARVELS AND MYSTERIES

1840 to 1900

Chapter 1. QUEEN VICTORIA
1. E. Longford. *Victoria, R.I.* 1964. pp. 76–7.

Chapter 2. EARLY VICTORIAN BUILDINGS: 1830 to 1850
1. Dale, *Fashionable Brighton*. 1967. p. 154.
2. Porter. *History of Hove*. 1897. p. 18.
3. *Herald*. 25 July 1857.
4. R. Kerr. *The Gentleman's House*. 1865. p. 55.
5. Dale. *Fashionable Brighton*. p. 164.
6. Idem. pp. 72 and 169–70.

7. *Herald.* 12 December 1931.
8. Dale. *Fashionable Brighton.* p. 170.
9. Granville. Vol. III. p. 568.
10. Altwick, *Brighton since the Grant of the Charter.* 1929. p. 27.
11. Merrifield, Mrs. *Brighton Past and Present.* 1857.

Chapter 3. PURCHASE OF THE ROYAL PAVILION
1. H. D. Roberts. *The Royal Pavilion.* Chap. XVIII.

Chapter 4. EARLY VICTORIAN WRITERS AND ARTISTS
1. F. Harrison. *Historical and Literary Association of Brighton and Hove.*
2. Idem.
3. C. R. Leslie. *Life of John Constable.* 1843.

Chapter 5. THE RAILWAY, 1820 to 1860
1. Gilbert. p. 132.
2. *Gazette.* 14 May 1840.
3. J. Ashton. *Social England.* p. 354.
4. H. Ellis. *The L.B. and S.C. Railway.* p. 46.
5. Idem.

Chapter 6. HARBOURS AND THE LIFEBOAT
1. *Herald.* 19 September 1969. *Pictorial Times.* May 1845.
2. *Illustrated London News.* 3 May 1845.
3. Royal archives.
4. Royal archives.

Chapter 7. VICTORIAN CHURCHES
1. H. S. Goodhart-Rendel. 'The Churches of Brighton and Hove'; in *Architectural Review.* Vol. XLIV.
2. 'Adam Bede.' *The Natural History of Puseyism with a short account of the Sunday Opera at St. Paul's, Brighton.* G. Smart. 1860.
3. Nicholas Taylor in *Architectural Review.* July 1967.
4. Bishop. *Pavilion.* p. 174.
5. Nicholas Taylor. Loc. cit.

Chapter 8. THE PIERS, AQUARIUM AND CLOCK-TOWER
1. Gilbert. p. 154.
2. *The Times.* 12 August 1872.
3. *Gazette.* 15 August 1872.
4. *Herald.* 9 May 1874.

Chapter 9. VICTORIAN HOTELS
1. C. Bede. *Mattins and Muttons.* Vol. II. p. 169.
2. C. B. Cochran. *Secrets of a Showman.* 1925.
3. C. B. Cochran. *A Showman Looks On.* 1945. pp. 26–7.

Chapter 11. THE DEVIL'S DYKE
1. O. J. Morris. 'By Rail to the Devil's Dyke Hotel'; in *The Locomotive.* 15 August 1944.
2. *Herald.* 7 July 1934.

3. Idem. 1 and 11 February 1964.

Chapter 12. THE THEATRES
1. *The Times*. 20 March 1956.
2. W. E. Nash. *Guide to Brighton*. 1885. p. 111.
3. *Herald*. 6 September 1894.
4. H. M. Walbrook. *Robertson's Brighton*. *c*. 1891. p. 22.
5. R. Gunnell. 'The Brighton Gaiety Theatre'; in *Sussex County Magazine*. September 1954.
6. *Evening Argus*. 8 December 1967.

Chapter 13. EARLY SOCIAL MOVEMENTS
1. R. Blackwood in *Herald*. 8 July 1966.
2. Brighton Trades Council. *History of Fifty Years*. 1958.

Chapter 14. LATE VICTORIAN SOCIAL LIFE
1. Gilbert. p. 194.
2. *Herald*. 3 February 1894.
3. Harrison. *Historical and Literary Associations*.
4. R. Jefferies. *The Open Air*. 1885.
5. Gilbert. p. 157.
6. J. N. Simpkinson. *Memoir of the Rev. George Wagner*.
7. Idem.
8. G. H. Giddins. *Edward Paston Hood, Poet and Preacher*. 1886.
9. E. V. Lucas. *Reading, Writing and Remembering*. 1932.
10. K. O'Shea. *Charles Stewart Parnell*. 1914.

Chapter 15. APOSTOLIC AMORISTS
1. J. Montgomery. *Abodes of Love*. 1962.
2. W. H. Attwick. *Brighton since the Grant of the Charter*. 1854–1929.

Chapter 16. LATE VICTORIAN WRITERS, ARTISTS AND ART-COLLECTORS
1. *Apollo*. December 1962.
2. J. C. Powys. *Autobiography*. 1934.
3. Information from Professor N. Cunliffe.
4. *Letters of Henry James*. Ed. by P. Lubbock. pp. 59–61.
5. *Collected Letters of D. H. Lawrence*. 1962. Vol. I. pp. 53–4.
6. H. T. Moore. *Poste Restante*. p. 28.
7. H. T. Moore. *The Intelligent Heart*. 1954. p. 145.
8. Idem. p. 238.
9. Sir K. Clark in *Sunday Times Magazine*. 8 May 1966.
10. R. Speaight. *Life of Eric Gill*. 1966.
11. Eric Gill. *Autobiography*. 1940.

Chapter 17. PRESTON PARK AND MANOR
1. H. D. Roberts. *Preston Manor* (official handbook). 1959.

Chapter 18. LIBRARIES AND MUSEUMS
1. *Herald*. 19 September 1893.
2. Idem. 13 September 1873.

3. Brighton Public Libraries. Catalogue of Early Printed Books in the Bloomfield Collection.
4. *Gazette.* 14 July 1896.
5. R. H. Wilenski. *Modern French Painters.* 1940. p. 229n.

PART V
BATTLE-SCENE AND TRANSFORMATION
1900 to 1969

Chapter 1. EDWARDIAN DAYS, 1900 to 1914
1. H. Preston. *Memories.* 1928.
2. *Country Life.* 8 February 1905.
3. *Gazette.* 21 July 1905.
4. Idem. 22 July 1905.
5. Idem. 27 July 1905.
6. *The Brighton Season.* 1905–6.
7. C. B. Cochran. *A Showman Looks On.* 1945. p. 7.
8. *Herald.* 15 February 1908.
9. *Gazette.* 4 January 1911.
10. Recollections of Mr. W. E. Lower. (MS in Brighton Reference Library.)
11. Information from Mr. H. F. Brazenor, and recollections of Mr. W. W. F. Peacock. (MS in Brighton Reference Library.)
12. *The Brighton Season.* 1908.
13. Veronica King in *Gazette.* 2 February 1968.
14. *Sunday Express.* 10 July 1967.
15. *Gazette.* 10 May 1911.
16. H. Preston. *Memories.* p. 82.
17. *Gazette.* 29 July 1914.

Chapter 2. THE FIRST WORLD WAR
1. *Gazette.* 5 August 1914.
2. Ibid.
3. Idem. 15 August 1914.
4. Idem. 20 August 1914.
5. Idem. 29 August 1914.
6. Ibid.
7. Idem. 2 January 1915.
8. Idem. 19 July 1915.
9. Idem. 15 September 1915.
10. Idem. 22 January 1916.
11. Ibid. 22 January 1916.
12. Idem. 16 February 1916.
13. Idem. 25 October 1916.
14. Idem. 29 December 1917.
15. 14 January 1917.
16. Brighton Trades Council. *History of fifty years.* 1958.
17. *Gazette.* 18 November 1918.
18. Idem. 28 December 1918.

Chapter 3. THE TWENTIES
1. *Gazette.* 12 February 1924.

2. *Gazette.* 23 February 1924.
3. *Gazette.* 26 March 1924.
4. *Gazette.* 19 December 1925.
5. *Herald.* 30 July 1921.
6. *Herald.* 13 November 1925.
7. *Herald.* 14 April 1926.
8. *Herald.* 2 January 1926.
9. *Herald.* 1 April 1926.
10. *Herald.* 8 May 1926.
11. Ibid.
12. Ibid.
13. H. Preston. *Leaves from my Unwritten Diary.* p. 245.
14. *Herald.* 15 May 1926.
15. *Sussex Weekly News.* 15 May 1926.
16. *Herald.* 15 May 1926.
17. *Evening Argus.* 1 December 1926.
18. H. Preston. *Memories.* 1928. p. 263.

Chapter 4.   THE THIRTIES
1. *Sussex County Magazine.* Vol. 9. 1935. p. 693.
2. *Evening Argus.* 23 August 1963.
3. L. Knowles. *Court of Drama.* 1966.
4. *Gazette.* 19 December 1925.
5. Gilbert. pp. 214–15.
6. *Municipal Review.* August 1933.
7. *Herald.* 28 December 1935.
8. *Gazette.* 15 June 1934.
9. *Evening Argus.* 9 January 1969.
10. *Herald.* 21 September 1935.

Chapter 6.   RECOVERY AND RE-PLANNING, 1945 to 1960
1. *Herald.* 4 March 1950.
2. *Herald.* 4 November 1949.
3. *Herald.* 26 November 1949.
4. *Herald.* 11 February 1950.
5. *Herald.* 31 December 1949.
6. *Herald.* 28 January 1950.
7. *Herald.* 11 June 1949.
8. *Herald.* 24 June 1950.
9. *Herald.* 24 June 1950.
10. *Herald.* 5 August 1950.
11. *Herald.* 25 October 1947.
12. *Herald.* 25 October 1947.
13. *Herald.* 5 November 1950.
14. *Herald.* 5 November 1950.
15. *Herald.* 8 April 1956.
16. *Herald.* 18 November 1950.
17. *Herald.* 8 August 1952.
18. Ibid.
19. *Herald.* 3 January 1953.
20. *Herald.* 22 April 1950.
21. *Herald.* 8 and 15 March 1952.

22. *Herald.* 22 November 1952.
23. *Herald.* 27 February 1954.
24. *Herald.* 23 October 1954.
25. *Herald.* 30 October 1954.
26. *Herald.* 22 and 29 May 1954.
27. *Herald.* 27 November 1954.
28. *Herald.* 22 October 1955.
29. *Herald.* 20 February 1955.
30. *Herald.* 30 October 1954.
31. *Herald.* 2 and 22 March 1957.
32. *Herald.* 5 November 1955.
33. *Herald.* 28 June 1958.

Chapter 7.   THE PAVILION RESTORED
1. *Herald.* 26 January 1952.
2. *Herald.* 12 February 1955.

Chapter 8.   TEDDY-BOYS, BEATNIKS, MODS, ROCKERS AND THE FLOWER-FOLK
1. *Herald.* 8 May 1954.
2. *Herald.* 20 November 1954.
3. *Herald.* 4 December 1954.
4. *Herald.* 23 March 1957.
5. *Herald.* 18 May 1957.
6. *Observer* supplement. 27 August 1967.
7. *Herald.* 16 May 1964.
8. *Gazette.* 23 May 1964.
9. *Herald.* 23 May 1964.
10. *Gazette.* 23 May 1964.
11. *Herald.* 23 May 1964.
12. *Gazette.* 8 September 1967.
13. *Gazette.* 24 November 1967.
14. *Evening Argus.* 28 November 1967.
15. *Herald.* 31 January 1968.

Chapter 9.   THE UNIVERSITY OF SUSSEX AND STUDENT LIFE
1. *Herald.* 15 August 1953.
2. *Herald.* 18 December 1954.
3. *Herald.* 11 June 1955.
4. *Herald.* 5 July 1958.

Chapter 10.   BRIGHTON TRANSFORMED
1. *Herald.* 25 October 1947.
2. *Herald.* 12 October 1963.
3. *The Times.* 25 October 1967.
4. *Daily Telegraph.* 25 September 1964.
5. *Gazette.* 15 September 1964.
6. *Daily Telegraph.* 25 September 1964.
7. *The Times.* 17 September 1964.
8. *Gazette.* 15 January 1965.
9. *Guardian.* 11 July 1967.
10. *Gazette.* 14 July 1967.
11. Idem. 21 July 1967.

12. *Times.* 25 October 1967.
13. *Gazette.* 30 May 1965.

Chapter 11. FAIRS AND FESTIVALS
 1. *Evening Argus.* 2 May 1966.
 2. Idem. 15 February 1956.
 3. *Herald.* 7 and 14 September 1957.
 4. *Herald.* 11 December 1964.
 5. *Herald.* 7 February 1969.
 6. *Herald.* 26 July 1968.

Bibliography

Aitchison, George. *Unknown Brighton.* 1926.
Aldington, Richard. *Four English Portraits.* 1948.
Ashton, John. *Social England under the Regency.* 1899.
    Florizel's Folly. 1899.
Aspinall, A. *The Correspondence of George, Prince of Wales, 1770 to 1812.* 5 vols. 1963–8.
    The Letters of King George IV, 1812 to 1830. 3 vols. 1938.
Attree's *Topography of Brighton.* 1809.
Attwick, W. H. *Brighton since the Grant of the Charter, 1854–1929.* 1929.
Awsiter, John. *Thoughts on Brighthelmston.* 1788.
Barlow, George. *Daughters of Minerva.* 1896.
Barron-Wilson, Cornwell. *Memoirs of Miss Mellon, afterwards Duchess of St. Albans.* 1886.
Bede, Cuthbert. *See* Bradley, Edward.
Bew, J. *See* Phillips, Peregrine.
Bishop, J. G. *A Peep into the Past: Brighton in the Olden Time.* 1892.
    A Peep into the Past, 1746–61. 1895.
    Brighton Chain Pier. 1897.
    The Brighton Pavilion and its Royal Associations. 1903.
Blew, William C. A. *Brighton and its Coaches.* 1894.
Boigne, Comtesse de. *Memoirs of the Comtesse de Boigne.* 1907.
Bradley, Edward (Cuthbert Bede). *Mattins and Muttons.* 1866.
Bramwell, F. G. S. 'The Windmills of Brighton': in *Herald.* 6 and 13 August 1938.
Brayley, E. W. *Her Majesty's Palace at Brighton.* 1838.
Bridges, Yseult. *Saint with Red Hands?* 1954.
Brighton and Hove Gazette. *Brighton and Hove at War.* 1945.
Brighton and Hove Herald. *Brighton and Hove in Battledress.* 1945.
    Brighton as it is, its pleasures, practices, and pastimes, etc., by a graduate of the University of London. 1860.
    The Brighton Season. 1904–14.
Burney, Frances. *The Diary and Letters of Madame d'Arblay.* Edited by Charlotte Barrett. 1904.
    The Early Diary of Frances Burney. Edited by A. R. Ellis. 1889.
Calvert, Mrs. *An Irish Beauty of the Regency.* 1911.
Carey, G. S. *The Balnea.* 1801.
Carter, Ernest. 'Sea Voyage': in *Model Engineer.* Vol. 113. 1955.
Clark, Kenneth. *The Gothic Revival.* 1928.
Clunn, H. P. *The Capital by the Sea.* 1953.
Cobbett, William. *Rural Rides.* 1853.
Creevey, Thomas. *The Creevey Papers.* Edited by Sir Henry Maxwell. 1903.
Croker, J. Papers. 1884.
Croley, George. *The Life and Times of His Late Majesty, George the Fourth.* 1830.
Cunliffe, Mitzi. 'Changing Brighton, for better, for worse': in *Town Planning Institute Journal.* November 1967.

Dale, Antony. *Fashionable Brighton*. 1967.
Daniell, Thomas. *Oriental Scenery*. 1801.
Defoe, Daniel. *Tour through the Island of Great Britain*. 1724.
Dunvan, Paul. *Ancient and Modern History of Lewes and Brighthelmston* ('*Lee's History*'). 1795.
Ellis, Hamilton. *The London, Brighton and South Coast Railway*. 1960.
Erredge, J. A. *History of Brighthelmstone*. 1862.
Fen, Allan. *After Worcester Fight*. 1904.
The Flight of the King. 1908.
Frampton, Mary. *Journal, 1779–1846*. 1885.
Fulford, Roger. *George the Fourth*. 1949.
Gibbon, Edward. *Private Letters*. Edited by R. E. Prothero. 1896.
Gilbert, E. W. *Brighton: Old Ocean's Bauble*. 1954.
Gill, Eric. *Autobiography*. 1940.
Goodheart-Rendel, H. S. 'The Churches of Brighton and Hove': in *Architectural Review*. Vol. XLIV. 1918.
Gower, H. E. *Letters of Harriet, Countess Granville 1810–1845*. 1894.
Granville, A. B. *The Spas of England*. 3 Vols. 1841.
Greville, Charles. *Memoirs*. 1888.
Gronow, R. H. *Reminiscences and Recollections, 1810–1860*. 1892.
Gunnell, Robert. 'The Brighton Gaiety Theatre': in *Sussex County Magazine*, September, 1954.
Harper, C. G. *The Brighton Road*. 1906.
Harrison, Frederick. *Historical and Literary Associations of Brighton and Hove*. 1906.
Harrison, Frederick, and North, J. S. *Old Brighton, Old Preston, Old Hove*. 1937.
Herbert, Charles. 'A struggle with the Sea (Volk's Railways)': in *Magazine of Commerce*. Nov. 1909.
Hussey, Christopher. *The Picturesque*. 1927.
Jackson, Alan A. *Volk's Railway, Brighton, 1883–1964*. Light Railways Transport League.
Jefferies, Richard. *The Open Air*. 1885.
Jerningham, Lady. *Letters*. Edited by Egerton Castle. 1896.
Jesse, J. H. *George Selwyn and his contemporaries*. 1843.
Jesse, William. *Beau Brummell*. 1927.
Jones, Mrs. Herbert. *The Princess Charlotte of Wales*. 1885.
Knowles, Leonard. *Court of Drama*. 1966.
Lee, Charles E. 'Volk's Electric Railways': in *Tillings Staff Magazine*. Vol. 5. 1930.
Lee, William. *See* Dunvan, Paul.
Leslie, Anita. *Mrs. Fitzherbert*. 1960.
Leslie, Doris. *The Great Corinthian*. 1952.
Leslie, Shane. *Mrs. Fitzherbert*. 1939.
The Letters of Mrs. Fitzherbert, 1940.
Lindsay, Philip. *The Loves of Florizel*. 1951.
Manning-Sanders, Ruth. *Seaside England*. 1951.
Marsden, Christopher. *The English at the Seaside*. 1947.
Martin, Henry. *History of Brighton*. 1871.
Maskelyne, J. S. *The Locomotives of the London, Brighton and South Coast Railway. 1903–1923*. 1928.
Maughan, H. H. *Some Brighton Churches*. 1922.
Maugras, Gaston, *The Duc de Lauzan and the Court of Marie-Antoinette*. 1896.
Melville, Lewis. *The First Gentleman in Europe*. 1906.
Brighton. 1909.

Melville, Lewis. *Beaux of the Regency*. 1908.
Merrifield, Mrs. *Brighton, Past and Present*. 1857.
Moore, H. T. *The Intelligent Heart*. 1954.
Moore, Thomas. *Life and Letters of Lord Byron*. 1831.
Moorecroft, Frederick. *Brighton Guide*. 1866.
Morris, O. J. 'By Rail to the Devil's Dyke Hotel': in *The Locomotive*, 15 August 1944.
Musgrave, Clifford. *Royal Pavilion: an episode in the Romantic*. 1959.
    Regency Furniture. 1961.
Nash, John. *Views of the Royal Pavilion*. 1825.
Nash, W. E. *Guide to Brighton*. 1885.
Page, Thomas. *Handbook to Brighton*. 1871.
Page, William (editor). *Victoria County History of the County of Sussex*. Vols. I and II,
    1905–7.
Pasquin, Anthony (John Williams). *The New Brighton Guide*. 1796.
Phillips, Peregrine. *A Diary kept in an Excursion to Littlehampton near Arundel, and
    Brighthelmston in Sussex*. ('Bew's Diary'). 1780.
Pimlott, J. A. R. *The Englishman's Holiday*. 1947.
    Place-names of Sussex. 1929–30.
Porter, H. C. *The Theatres of Brighton*. 1886.
Preston, Harry J. *Memories*. 1928.
    Leaves from my Unwritten Diary. 1936.
Raikes, Thomas. A Portion of the Journal of Thomas Raikes. 1858.
Relhan, Anthony. *A Short History of Brighthelmston*. 1761.
    Reissued 1829.
Repton, Humphrey. *Designs for the Pavilion at Brighton*. 1808.
Richardson, Joanna. *George IV*. 1966.
Roberts, Henry D. *The Royal Pavilion*. 1931.
Robinson, L. J. *The Lanes of Brighton*. 1966.
Ross, C. H. *The Book of Brighton: as it was and as it is*. 1881.
Roth, Cecil. *The Sassoon Dynasty*. 1941.
Sala, G. A. *Things I have seen and people I have known*. 1894.
    Brighton as I knew it. 1898.
Sawyer, F. E. Captain Nicholas Tettersell and the Escape of Charles II. (Sussex Arch.
    Coll., Vol. XXXII.)
Sawyer, J. *Churches of Brighton. c.* 1880.
Scott, Walter. *Journal of Sir Walter Scott*. Edited by D. Douglas. 1890.
Sicklemore, R. *History of Brighton*. 1821.
    Descriptive Views of Brighton. 1824.
Simpkinson, J. N. *Memoir of the Rev. George Wagner*. 1862.
Sitwell, Osbert, and Barton, Margaret. *Brighton*. 1935.
Spencer, Colin. *Anarchists in Love*. 1963.
Stuart, D. M. *Portrait of the Prince Regent*. 1953.
Taylor, Nicholas. 'St. Bartholomew's, Brighton': in *Architectural Review*. July 1967.
Temperley, Harold. *The Unpublished Diary of Princess Lieven*. 1925
Thackeray, W. M. *The Four Georges*. 1875.
Thrale, Mrs. *Anecdotes of Dr. Johnson*. Edited by S. C. Roberts. 1925.
Treacher, H. and C. *The Brighton Almanack for 1863*.
Wagner, Anthony R. The Wagners of Brighton and their connexions: in Sussex Arch.
    Coll. Vol. XCVII.
Walbrook, H. M. *Robertson's Brighton*. 1896.
Wallis, James. *Wallis's Royal Edition: Brighton as it is*, 1842.
Walpole, Horace. *Letters*. Edited by P. Toynbee. 1903.

Webb, C., and Wilson, A. E. *Elizabethan Brighton : the ancient customs of Brighthelmston, 1580.* 1952.

Wheeler, Sheila. 'From Brighthelmstone to London-by-the-sea': in *The Architects Journal.* 12 July 1967.

Wigan, A. L. *Brighton, and its three climates.* 1845.

Wilkins, W. H. *Mrs. Fitzherbert and George IV.* 1905.

Wilson, Harriet. *Memoirs.* 1929.

Wright, C. *The Brighton Ambulator.* 1818.

Index